Nations
AND States

M000200662

Nations AND States

A Geographic Background to World Affairs

Thomas M. Poulsen

Portland State University

Dimitry Sharkov
Cartographer

PRENTICE HALL

Library of Congress Cataloging-in-Publication Data

POULSEN, THOMAS M.
    Nations and states: a geographic background to world affairs/
Thomas M. Poulsen
    p. cm.
    Includes bibliographical references.
    ISBN 0-13-678913-7
    1. Geography.   I. Title.
G116.P68   1995
910—dc20   94-13925

Acquisitions editor: *Ray Henderson*
Assistant editor: *Wendy Rivers*
Project manager: *Joanne Riker*
Interior design: *Andy Zutis*
Cover design: *Bruce Kenselaar*
Production coordinator: *Trudy Pisciotti*
Editorial assistant: *Pamela Holland-Moritz*

©1995 by Prentice-Hall, Inc.
A Pearson Education Company
Upper Saddle River, NJ 07458

All rights reserved. No part of this book may be
reproduced, in any form or by any means,
without permission in writing from the publisher.

Printed in the United States of America

10 9   8   7   6   5   4   3   2

ISBN   0-13-678913-7

Prentice-Hall International (UK) Limited,London
Prentice-Hall of Australia Pty. Limited, Sydney
Prentice-Hall Canada Inc., Toronto
Prentice-Hall Hispanoamericana, S.A., Mexico
Prentice-Hall of India Private Limited, New Delhi
Prentice-Hall of Japan, Inc., Tokyo
Pearson Education Asia Pte. Ltd., Singapore
Editora Prentice-Hall do Brasil, Ltda., Rio de Janeiro

This book is dedicated to

Richard Hartshorne

a mentor whose vision of the field of geography and whose
common-sense approach to understanding spatial aspects of
world politics remain an inspiration to his students,

and

George Hoffman

a collaborator who directed his untiring energy and
organizational skills to maintaining the vitality of regional
geography.

CONTENTS

2   An Introduction to Europe 22

3   Western Europe 38

4   The Middle Belt of Europe 84

5   The States of East-Central Europe 100

6 Southeastern Europe 112

7 Russia and the Commonwealth of Independent States 136

8 The Middle East and North Africa 160

9 Africa South of the Sahara 212

10 South Asia 236

11 Southeast Asia 254

12 East Asia 282

13 Australasia and Oceania 312

14 Latin America 322

15 Anglo-America 364

Index 386

PREFACE

International conflicts and civil wars are not simply products of failed diplomacy or policies of aggression. Virtually all have roots in endemic cultural features of the
earth's landscape that tend to be as permanent as the configurations of rivers and mountains. Patterns of languages, religious beliefs, and legal institutions form as
much a part of the environment enveloping territories as
do climates and vegetation. So also do collective perceptions of historical events and group stereotypes of other
peoples. It is within this overreaching context of ideas
and values that governmental goals are set and policies
established, sometimes with disastrous consequences.

The overall quest of geographers is to comprehend
the nature of the total environment of the earth's surface
as it varies from place to place. Because the field of
geography is so broad, individual scholars concentrate
upon limited aspects of that environment—physical features, economic relations, cultural phenomena, and like
categories. The focus of geographers upon linkages of
their studied topics to the land differentiates their
endeavors from those of scholars in the related systematic sciences, who tend to analyze the same phenomena
within the context of more abstract forms and

processes. In general, most studies by geographers
involve a mappable dimension.

Political geography is concerned with the role of
political ideas and processes as they affect territory and
are affected by it. Like political scientists, political geographers examine governmental institutions, voting behavior, diplomacy, conflicts and related topics. The focus of
political geographic endeavors tends to be much more
upon the regional manifestations and territorial linkages
of these phenomena, however, than is characteristic of the
work of political scientists. Ideally, the products of political geographic study enrich comprehension of aspects of
the world studied by all other branches of geography,
including economic development, cultural diversity, and
environmental degradation.

Like other disciplines, political geography has
evolved its own distinctive concepts, approaches, and
techniques. A particularly useful concept is that of the
nation, which is seen as a spatially expressed phenomenon having imposing functional linkages to a region's
economics, culture, politics, and other social processes.
The nation is best viewed as a collective state of mind
of a region's inhabitants that is derived from shared

experiences, oral traditions, formalized education, and mass media. The concept of nation is related to—but significantly apart from—the phenomenon of *nationalism*, which can be viewed as a demagogic appeal to national identity for political aims that often may be ulterior. The near-universal phenomenon of the nation tends to be undervalued by many Americans, perhaps because national identity within our vast country is so little subject to challenge by foreign groups, in contrast to general situations in Europe, Southeast Asia, and elsewhere. The title of this book, *Nations and States*, relates to the major tensions that result when boundaries of nations—regions characterized by shared national identities—are at variance with borders of politically organized states.

For many years I have taught an applied political geography course entitled Geography of World Affairs. I have conceived it as an exposition of those semipermanent human features of the landscape that account for the recurring incidents of tension and conflict besetting the earth. My lectures and discussions generally have sought to provide answers to the perennial geographic questions of "what?," "where?," "why?," and "so what?" as they apply to the political structuring of territory.

In organizing the course, a constant problem has been to provide suitable supplementary reading materials. I have found that most available textbooks in political geography are inadequate in providing answers to basic questions. Some appear to have been written more for professors than for students. Such works often tend to assume a background of basic information about locations and events in the world that few undergraduate or even graduate students have managed to acquire. Some texts emphasize techniques of measurement and analysis but offer few answers to substantive questions. Many lack historical depth, focusing upon contemporary manifestations of problems but tending to ignore deep roots. To my mind, geography requires appreciation of the time dimension just as much as history demands a sense of space.

A particular concern of mine has been that most available textbooks are topical in organization, introducing numerous themes in which political geographers busy themselves but not always successfully linking the topics together into a comprehensible whole. The case studies in such works provide useful glimpses of challenging political geographic endeavors, but they rarely develop topics fully or set them within a meaningful common perspective. The problem of coherence in some topical textbooks is magnified by co-authors who have differing views on approaches to the field and the nature of causation. A topical approach also tends to imply a greater universality of political geographic features among states and local political areas than can be demonstrated to exist. One simply cannot assume identical forms and processes of a political, economic, and cultural nature among such diverse parts of the world as Poland and Nigeria or Canada and Laos.

Another misgiving of mine concerning available texts is that often interesting theoretical viewpoints are advanced without adequate substantiation by a factual background. I believe that an individual desiring to be informed on world affairs requires a minimum of essential information about historic and political processes pertinent to a given problem before being able properly to understand its current political manifestations or to evaluate analyses by others. Too often in the social sciences there is a tendency to jam facts into procrustean beds of current theory rather than to let theoretical insights emerge from comprehension of total environments of problems.

These concerns led me to embark upon writing this book. The text employs a regional geographic perspective with the goal of presenting a comprehensive view of the political world. It seeks to provide key information about the processes that shape and reshape the world map. Each major world region is approached in common fashion, sketching the significant elements of political and historical features that have a bearing upon current world affairs. The focus is at the level of independent states because countries are the principal players in world affairs.

I cannot claim a high degree of originality in the presentation. In assessing the political geography of different world regions I can profess personal expertise for only a modest area—chiefly Eastern Europe, the former Soviet Union, and my own United States. Even for these territories I necessarily have to rely for facts and insights upon findings by other scholars from geography and related disciplines. For areas outside my own direct experience in the field I have been dependent upon a variety of published sources. Many studies by political geographers and other scholars are cited in the separate chapter bibliographies. In identifying specific events and processes I am particularly indebted to the series of area handbooks on virtually all states of the world that has been published in recent decades by the United States government. (A nearly complete collection is available on a CD-ROM, which was produced in 1991 by Bureau Development, Inc., under the title *Countries of the World*.) Specific volumes from this series are not cited in chapter bibliographies because there are so many of them.

In preparing this book I am indebted to a number of colleagues at Portland State University who have read portions of the manuscript and offered ideas and suggestions. Particular appreciation goes to Charles White of the P.S.U. History Department, who carefully read the initial draft of the text and afforded me the benefit of his great wealth of personal information and insights. Others who were generous with assistance are Clarke Brooke, Teresa Bulman, Martha Works, Louis Elteto, Victor Dahl, and Fred Nunn.

Reviewers who made helpful suggestions were: Edward F. Bergman, CUNY Lehman College; Dr. John Agnew, Syracuse University; Dr. Lewis M. Alexander, University of Rhode Island; Dr. Vernon Domingo, Bridgewater State College; Dr. Stanley Brunn, University of Kentucky; and Dr. Anthony V. Williams, Pennsylvania State University.

It should be stressed that I alone bear responsibility for the information and conclusions set forth. I express particular gratitude to my dear wife, Gladys, who has been both supportive and forbearing in the involved process of seeing this book into print.

T.M.P
Portland, Oregon

Nations

AND States

Introduction

I N August 1991, a bungled coup d'etat initiated the swift demise of the Union of Soviet Socialist Republics. In barely four months a fundamental player in international politics collapsed and disappeared. In its place appeared an independent Russia and fourteen other states.

Americans found the swift fragmentation of the Soviet Union to be astounding. For most of their lifetimes the USSR had been a constantly threatening competitor and rival. Although many people were aware that it contained Ukrainians, Latvians, and other non-Russian peoples, popular wisdom tended to assume that the Soviet Union, for all its inefficiencies, had found a solution to the kinds of ethnic problems that so long had bedeviled Europe and other areas, with perhaps, the notable exception of anti-Semitism.

The drastic changes that occurred in the former USSR were soon followed by other dismemberments of the former Yugoslavia and Czechoslovakia. People grew aware that similar fragmentations are quite possible in other seemingly permanent political entities, including India, China, Spain, and Canada. Indeed, only a few of the world's 170 states appear likely to survive the twenty-first century with present borders intact.

Explaining Changes of the Political Map

The nature and causes of change in the political map have challenged scholars since ancient times. Hippocrates, writing in the fifth century B.C., considered that spatial forms of states, their governments, and their relative power derived from elements of their physical environments. Aristotle expounded similar views in the next century.

In the revival of learning that followed the long period of the Dark Ages, Montesquieu in his *Spirit of the Laws* (1748) cited special challenges to peoples who came from cold climates or mountainous terrain and noted such matters as distinctive institutions emerging among peoples living on islands.

In the modern era, social scientists from a variety of disciplines have sought to comprehend the constantly changing political organization of territory. Political geographers, in particular, have addressed the problem for more than a century.

Political geographic contributions have been both *idiographic* ("specific problem oriented") and *nomothetic* ("theoretical" or "lawgiving"). The products of both approaches are complementary. Investigations of individual cases yield data and insights that reinforce or challenge general theories, and theoretical constructs have provided frameworks for understanding the interaction of elements impinging upon a given problem.

In recent decades both research and teaching in political geography, as in other social sciences, have tended to focus upon development of theory, although no single unified theory of state formation and functioning has become generally accepted in the field. Whatever theoretical consensus may emerge in the future, a vast accumulated store of information on individual states and their regional groupings has been compiled by political geographers that has utility for answering major questions confronting society today.

Although development of a valid theory of political geography promises much in the way of insight into causal factors in past events and the ability to predict future developments, generalizations based on induction from accumulated idiographic studies permit identification of numerous recurring regularities in the political geography of the world. Among them is the inherent meaninglessness of the term "natural boundaries" and the role of a common national identity for smoothing the flow of social and economic transactions. Despite their variance in theoretical underpinnings, specific studies have demonstrated predictive qualities. Thus, virtually all analyses of Yugoslavia identified the significance of political instability among Serbs, Croats, and Muslims long before civil war erupted in that territory.

Some Approaches to Theory

As noted above, theoretical conjectures about political aspects of geography were advanced as far back as the classical period of Greece and Rome. Although the principal focus of geographers through time has been an idiographic description of regional differences from place to place, many have offered explanatory generalizations of the factors and processes presumed to cause such differences.

Early theories generally assigned a determining role to influences of terrain, climate, and relative location in explaining observed political phenomena. Such *environmentally deterministic* views have maintained a vitality up to the present, although relatively few geographers now subscribe to them. Many writers in the fields of history and political science, however, attach particular significance to the environment, and a significant proportion of the general public tends to look first to physical geography to account for observed differences in societies and political organization.

Although political geographers have investigated territorial organization at all scales from local to supranational, most have given particular attention to the phenomenon of *states*. These constitute the highest order of sovereign political decision making, however much their governments may delegate authority to international bodies or regional alliances.

Comprehension of factors underlying the relative power of states has long been a focus of interest in political geography. As early as seventeenth-century France, scholars were compiling elaborate arrays of data on populations, resources, and economic activities as presumed determinants of the ability of governments to project their wills upon neighbors. Like environmental determinism, *power inventories* remain a staple feature of political geographic endeavor.

By the middle of the nineteenth century, geography had emerged in Europe as a vigorous scientific discipline, usually viewing itself as a holistic field with closest relationships to history. Geographers sought to make the complexity of regional differences from place to place comprehensible through careful observation and generalization.

The revolution in scientific thought brought about by publication of Darwin's *On the Origin of Species* had deep influences among early modern geographers, as it had upon students in other disciplines. Particularly influenced by Darwin's work was Karl Ritter, a German scholar who, with Alexander von Humboldt, is considered to be a founding father of modern geography.

In line with Darwin's reasoning, Ritter came to see human cultures as organic entities that had their own life cycles of birth, maturity, and death. He personally believed that humanity must live in unity with nature, and he advocated application of greater knowledge of the laws of nature to achieve better guidance of governments. His views went substantially beyond prevailing environmentalist outlooks on the functioning of states by ascribing a key role to the evolution of cultures.

Friedrich Ratzel (1844–1904) adopted and elaborated upon Ritter's concept of societies as organisms. Well aware of the constantly changing map of Europe, particularly amalgamations then occurring among the numerous, tiny German-speaking units, Ratzel advanced a series of generalizations about the growth and competition of states. At the heart of his views was a belief in the necessity of states to struggle with each other to achieve sufficient space (*Lebensraum*). The American political geographer Lewis Alexander has summarized Ratzel's seven "scientific laws" concerning the changing patterns of states (Alexander, p. 18):

1. The space of states grows with the growth of culture.
2. The growth of states follows other aspects of development, such as commerce, ideas, and missionary activity.
3. States grow through the amalgamation and absorption of smaller units.
4. The frontier is the peripheral organ of the state and reflects the growth, the strength, and the changes in the state.
5. In the process of growth the state seeks to include politically valuable areas, such as coast lines, river valleys, plains, and regions that are rich in resources.
6. The first impetus for territorial growth comes to a primitive state from beyond its borders, from a higher civilization.
7. The general trend toward amalgamation transmits the tendency for expansion from state to state and increases the tendency in the process of transmission (in other words, the process of amalgamation whets the appetite for greater expansion).

Ritter's and Ratzel's *organic views* on cultures had significant continuing influence upon scholars because of the simplicity of the biological analogy and the compatibility of their models of society with nationalist and imperialist ideologies and goals prevailing in Europe at the time. Their speculations and generalizations later became part of the core of ideas in the doctrine of "geopolitics" that emerged in Central Europe during the first half of the twentieth century.

Geopolitics

The Swedish scholar Rudolf Kjellén (1864–1922) first coined the term "geopolitics." In Kjellén's view, states were but one product of the appearance of national groups that constantly engaged in struggles for power with each other. His ideas particularly were adopted and enlarged upon by Karl Haushofer (1869–1946), who founded a journal devoted to geopolitics and created an Institute for Geopolitics in Munich during the 1920s. Under Haushofer's direction, the institute pursued geopolitics as an applied discipline with a goal of identifying discrepancies between existing patterns of territorial organization and an ideal political configuration.

The field of geopolitics caught the imagination of politicians and the general public in post–World War I Europe, particularly in Germany. However, most individuals working in Haushofer's Institute for Geopolitics were not trained geographers, but journalists and writers. Although employing terminology coined by Ratzel, Kjellén, and other scholars, much of the institute's published output appeared to be little more than propaganda exercises rationalizing Germany's expansionist activities in the period.

One feature of geopolitical doctrine was the assumption that configurations of land and sea had a determining influence upon international affairs. Such beliefs had been part of the environmental determinism of preceding centuries, when geographers and others had sought to decipher externalities that accounted for military strength. Among the most prominent North American advocates of this point of view was Admiral Alfred Thayer Mahan (1840–1914). In his book *The Influence of Sea Power Upon History, 1660–1783* and in other works, this American naval officer asserted the prime importance of control of the seas to achieve and maintain world power.

A British geographer, Sir Halford Mackinder (1861–1947), advanced a similar view of determinants of world power. Mackinder's paper, "The Geographical Pivot of History," delivered before members of the Royal Geographical Society in 1904, acknowledged Mahan's views on the importance of control of the seas but stressed the significance of the Eurasian landmass as an area impervious to sea power. A rapidly industrializing Russia then controlled much of inner Eurasia, but that region's space and resources were a tempting territorial power base for the recently unified Germany and/or an aggressive Japan or China.

In 1919 Mackinder elaborated upon his views in the work *Democratic Ideals and Reality*. As a new name for "pivot area" he borrowed the term "heartland," coined earlier by the British geographer Fairgrieve. Mackinder summarized his outlooks in this famous dictum:

Who rules East Europe commands the Heartland;
Who rules the Heartland commands the World-Island;
Who rules the World-Island commands the World.

The simplicity and seeming logic of Mackinder's vision of world power attracted many to his point of view. It is still an item of discussion among military strategists. Although modern political geographers generally reject contemporary significance of the heartland concept in an age of intercontinental missiles, most acknowledge Mackinder's contribution as a brilliant summary of existing power relationships at the turn of the twentieth century.

Mackinder's views served as a base for later theorists who took into account the changing technology of warfare. During World War II Nicholas Spykman advocated the importance to American national power of control of the "rimland," which he identified as those territories that surrounded the heartland as defined by Mackinder. Spykman argued that the states and colonial areas of Europe and the coastal lands of Asia contained the majority of the world's population and resources. If they fell under control of a single regime dominating the heartland, that entity would become unbeatable. He summarized his conclusions with the admonition that

who rules the Rimland rules Eurasia; who rules Eurasia controls the destinies of the world.

As the technology of warfare changed by mid-century, Major Alexander de Seversky saw control of the air as the principal determinant of state power. His influential work *Air Power: Key to Survival*, published in 1950, argued for American development of the ability to project such massive destruction from the air that the rival USSR and its allies would be deterred from aggression.

Viewpoints expounded by Mahan, Mackinder, Spykman, and others have been criticized by many scholars for unfounded assumptions and oversimplifications of history. Many geographers consider that because the ultimate goal of such studies was to assess global power, they belonged to a separate applied field of "power analysis" that properly lies outside the discipline of geography.

Whatever their evaluation among geographers, the views of American power analysts appear to have been influential in the adoption of a strategy of "containment" during nearly five decades of "cold war" between the United States and the Soviet Union following 1945.

Although most political geographers in Europe and America tend to reject use of the term "geopolitics" to describe their work because of its association with Nazi aggression during World War II, political scientists and others concerned with spatial power relationships have considered it a useful descriptor of their studies. These scholars constitute an active group in a number of countries.

Although environmental determinism, power analysis, and other theoretical pursuits drew adherents in the United States and the United Kingdom, most political geographers during the first several decades of the twentieth century involved themselves mainly in idiographic analysis. A landmark achievement was publication of *The New World* by Isaiah Bowman in 1919. Bowman was a leading American geographer called upon by President Woodrow Wilson to play a significant role in the treaty negotiations following World War I. His book drew in part from his European experience, but he provided a comprehensive political geography of the entire world. Bowman introduced a broad public to the geographic store of knowledge. The work was particularly valued for its thematic maps and discussions of world trouble spots.

A similar world survey was Derwent Whittlesey's *The Earth and the State*, published in 1939. Whittlesey saw international political problems principally to be responses to historical processes and environmental conditions. In the very first paragraph of his foreword, Whittlesey laments that while political geography "is perhaps the oldest kind of geography . . . there is even yet neither a universally accepted approach to the subject nor a consensus as to its content." This statement remains true today. Whittlesey's announced goal was to "lay hold of the areal differentiation of the world's principal states and legal codes."

The term "areal differentiation" had become current in discussions of the field of geography as a result of its use by Richard Hartshorne to describe the discipline's subject matter in his ground-breaking *The Nature of Geography*. In addition to being a leading theorist on the nature of geography, Hartshorne was a political geographer who published field studies of disputed boundary regions in Central Europe. In a major paper in 1935 he sought to set a course for political geography as the study of territorial forms of state units.

In 1950, in a presidential address to the Association of American Geographers, Hartshorne modified his views and called for an "areal functional approach" in political geography. In his revised model, states were seen as existing in constant internal tension derived from a variety of regional "centrifugal forces" of ethnicity, economic relations, and historical ties threatening territorial unity. Countervailing these were binding "centripetal forces," among which the most important was acceptance by inhabitants of all parts of an entity of a "state idea," or *raison d'etre* for the unit. In most cases such a state idea was acknowledgment by citizens that their government's actions were an embodiment of aspirations and goals of its preponderant *nation* of people.

Although Hartshorne's presidential address presented a theoretical model of a generic state, his prescription for political geographers was careful study of the problems of individual states. He argued that the total number of states constituted too limited a population to be able to develop meaningful scientific laws. He asserted that each state is a unique assemblage of elements with a distinctive pattern of evolution and development. Moreover, he noted that although state units formally are treated as co-equal in such international institutions as the United Nations General Assembly and the World Bank, it is evident that states are quite unequal: some are powerful, some are weak; some are rich, some are poor; some are stable, some are in flux. Save for their sovereign status, they share few other obvious common characteristics.

Hartshorne's model of state territorial functioning provided guidelines for many political geographers. Jean Gottmann contributed the useful concept of national "iconography" as part of the *raison d'etre* of a state. Stephen Jones offered a modular view of the geography of political decision making as a progression from a given idea to a formulation of policy to modification of territory.

Hartshorne's idiographic emphasis in geography was challenged in the 1950s by Fred Schaefer and others as being out-of-step with developments in other fields of science. Schaefer argued that focus on the specifics of places masked underlying systematic structural patterns that geographers could and should identify. Many political geographers saw the need for a more nomothetic approach, and eventually it became a dominant trend in the field.

At least four considerations motivated political geographers to emphasize development of theory:

1. Many sought the capability to relate specific political events to general processes of political development and change.
2. Some saw viable theory as essential for any ability to predict future actions.
3. More than a few were concerned to be able to interrelate the insights and conclusions of political geography with contemporary trends of inquiry in other social sciences.
4. A number wanted a theoretical platform to advance personal political and social goals within their societies.

The emerging discipline of systems science in the 1950s had a particular impact upon political geography. Armed with the possibility of manipulating vast amounts of data by computers, geographers began applying *systems theory* to the political organization of states. They visualized the state as a system of flows of ideas, demands, and transactions over which governments provide stabilizing actions. Such flows were subject to objective measurement. The resultant data, scholars assumed, would lead to causal explanations and the development of scientific laws.

Results of a systems approach to political geography generally tended to be disappointing. The studies

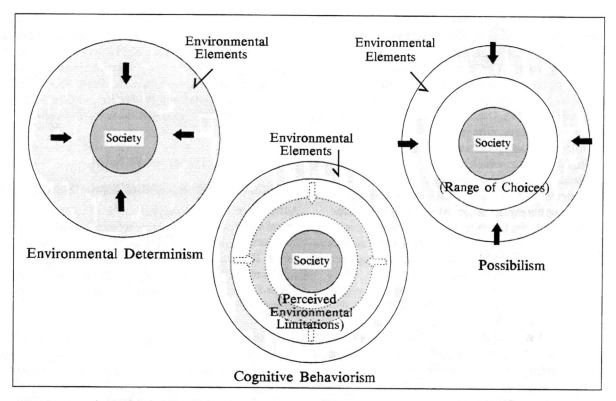

FIGURE A-1 MODELS OF HUMANITY

seldom achieved more than solemn elaboration of the obvious. In the quest for measurable elements, qualitative factors usually received little or no attention. Despite the power of quantification, the theory that emerged proved to have no better ability to predict events than did more subjective modes of analysis that preceded it.

A number of political geographers interested in theory registered disappointment at the systems science approach's idealistic assumptions, criticizing its model of society as being as "outmoded" as the one utilized in neoclassical economics. They assailed the method for the same lack of explanatory theory for which they had castigated the idiographic approach that preceded it.

Many geographers critical of the systems approach became interested in the *historical determinism* of Karl Marx, particularly for its avowed concern for *inequity* and *deprivation*. In part, their attraction was due to Marxism's consideration of "big" questions confronting humanity. Marxism sees societies resting upon essentially economic foundations. Social advancement requires economic change that can come about only as a result of tensions ("contradictions") developing within a society. For Marxists, the capitalist mode of organization and production dominating Western societies in recent centuries eventually must give way to new

forms, just as feudalism earlier lost out to capitalism. Conflict is the "motor" of history.

John Agnew explains the diversity of theories as a consequence of fundamentally different "presuppositions" of individuals concerning models of humanity, models of society, and models of knowing.

Agnew identifies a number of models of humanity that range from views of individuals being tightly determined by external forces to "voluntarist" positions that acknowledge few exterior limitations to human endeavor. Although for many theorists of a determinist bent the "external forces" tend to be primarily economic or cultural factors, the range of viewpoints parallels discussions of an earlier era over relations between individuals and their physical environment.

Figure A-1 presents three possible stances in a model of humanity. At one extreme, there is the notion that the course of a person's activities in society is tightly determined by "environmental externalities" (Model A). A second conception, dubbed "possibilism," maintains that ultimate external constraints are present, but that considerable room exists for choices within these limits (Model B). A third view (Model C) is that actual external constraints are few, if any, but societies act upon perceptions that such limitations exist. A "cloud factor" of collective and individual ideas obscures the full range of opportunities and alternatives that are present. Sometimes this last outlook is termed "cognitive behaviorism."

Differences in these presuppositions about models of humanity, according to Agnew, are related to similar contrasting views on models of society. He distinguishes between "holists," who view a society as greater than the sum of its parts, and "individualists," who believe that any general statements about a society ultimately must be reducible to the situations of the individuals who comprise the society. In some ways the two extreme positions are similar to an earlier geographic controversy about the nature of regions: Some saw them as distinct entities with a collective identity greater than their inhabitants; others viewed regions as rather arbitrary analytical tools for grouping together localities that ultimately are unique.

Agnew terms his third category of differences in presuppositions as "models of knowing." He distinguishes between "positivists" and "intuitionists." The former believe that the social sciences should use the "scientific method" of the natural sciences in their quest for generalizations or empirical laws. The latter reject that view, seeing explanation of individual human actions as the goal of social scientists over observation of external regularities of human behavior.

A key distinguishing factor between the two positions is acceptance or rejection of the notion that all things are *unique* in time and space. Positivists believe, for instance, that territorial problems of a given state can be understood as a particular consequence of the interaction of generally operating identifiable processes of an economic, political, and/or historical nature. Intuitionists are likely to ascribe the same event to a complex of influences, coupled with arbitrary decision making.

Despite the efforts in recent decades of a number of individuals to develop political geographic theory, no common framework of thought has surfaced comparable to the generally accepted theory in economics. Although many interesting and useful ideas have emerged, none of the theoretical positions advanced thus far by political geographers can reconcile all known facts about given situations in states nor predict future events.

Thus, one of the more useful theoretical concepts that have been developed in recent years is that of "core/periphery" relationships. In many states the capital city and its surrounding area dominate the economy, politics, and culture of a country. The American geographer Mark Jefferson observed this recurring regularity at the turn of the century and called it "The Law of the Primate City." In "core/periphery" theory, the metropolitan center exploits peripheral areas, a high proportion of which differ from the dominant area in ethnicity and standard of living. While the idea fits many states, it runs counter to the situation in many others. Thus, the peripheral areas of Catalonia and the Basque region have dominated Spain economically, and living standards in the borderland of Alsace-Lorraine are higher than in most of the rest of France.

The Approach of This Book

Although political geographers hold a variety of theoretical views, all are confronted by the necessity to take into account the observable political facts of the real world. This text is a survey of facts that the author considers critical to understanding contemporary problems. These facts may be summarized under the following categories:

I. The relative location of each state on the Earth's surface;
II. Actual areas of development (*ecumene*) within each state in comparison with gross area;
III. Areas of effective governmental control within each state and areas of neglect and/or insurrection outside such control;
IV. Patterns of national identity existing within each state's boundaries and across them;
V. The process of evolution of these features.

Some of the relationships among these facts are summarized in Figure A-2. In this example, two states share a hypothetical island. State B is a relatively homogeneous *nation-state* for National Group One. State A is a *multination-state*. Although National Group Two dominates State A, it coexists with two regional minority groups. One of these minorities is Group Three, which has no linkage to State B. The other minority consists of members of National Group One who live outside the borders of State B. Because this minority shares a common identity with National Group One, it can be termed an "irredentist" group. It has the latent potential to seek a change of borders between the states in order to be incorporated within State B, which is the avowed state for its nation.

This volume attempts to present these facts in a concise and logically organized manner. It views them as semipermanent features of the Earth's surface comparable to configurations of terrain, climate, and vegetation.

To use the example of the former Soviet Union cited at the beginning of this section, that entity occupied approximately one-sixth of the planet's land sur-

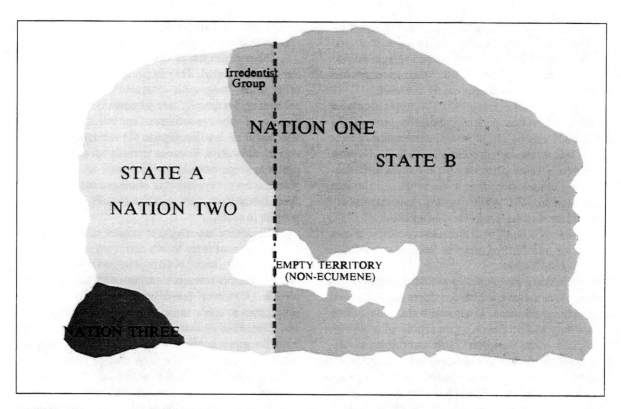

FIGURE A-2   IDEALIZED RELATIONS OF STATES AND NATIONS

face, but it lay at latitudes comparable to Canada's, with three-quarters of its area essentially unusable. The quarter that was settled was hardly larger than the developed part of the United States, or the territory of Europe west of the former Soviet border.

Although the regime of the USSR was more successful than many state governments in exerting effective control over all its nominal land space, it had to contend with the inherent geographic circumstance that half its population consisted of groups who saw the dominant Russians as foreign occupiers of their traditional homelands. Most Soviet minorities had been incorporated forcibly into a Russian-dominated state over the course of the preceding five centuries. For the Baltic peoples, Ruthenians, Moldovans, and others it had been a matter of only the preceding five decades. The Soviet Union was, in fact, a classic empire, although its colonial peoples did not live physically separated from the mother country of Russia in areas overseas.

A Russianized Communist party monopoly of power, an integrated military, a strong secret police organization, and economic interdependence tied non-Russians to Russians in the Soviet state. The weakening

of any of these binding forces was bound to create opportunities and encouragement for national separatism. All of these forces came apart in August 1991.

In analyzing and synthesizing political patterns, this text draws a fundamental distinction between *states* and *nations*. It sees the *state* is the basic unit of political organization of territory, with a government that functions as a sovereign unit. A quite different phenomenon is the *nation*, defined here as a spatially expressed collective group political identity. So defined, nations have emerged mainly during the past two centuries as products of economic modernization and mass popular education. *The lack of territorial coincidence of patterns of states with patterns of nations is a principal force driving world affairs.*

It should be stressed that spatial configurations of states and nations are not immutable. Thus, the German Democratic Republic recently disappeared from the world political map after more than four decades of functioning as a sovereign state. During those years the German nation remain intact, despite forced division between eastern and western Germanies. Germans again enjoy a single nation-state of their own. However, the spatial pattern of the German nation in Europe has changed substantially since 1945. Poland, Czechoslovakia, Hungary, and Yugoslavia, restored after several years of Third Reich occupation, expelled eight million German inhabitants from lands that their ancestors had inhabited since the sixteenth century or earlier.

The territorial extent of the German nation also shrank in the postwar period by the falling away of the Austrians to establish firmly a distinctive nation of their own. Their forebears had retained feelings of German identity for seventy years after the Prussians had intentionally excluded them from the first unified German nation-state in 1871. Although most Austrians openly had welcomed Hitler's *Anschluss* (annexation) of 1938, the debacle of World War II and subsequent four-power occupation transformed regional feelings to a distinctive national identity.

While this study focuses upon discordant patterns of states and nations, it also considers other political geographic phenomena. At a macro scale, these include the military and economic organizations of groups of states, such as the European Union, and cultural associations of groups of nations—for example, the Arabs. At lower levels, subdivisions of states often can be quite significant, particularly those based upon ethnic distinctions—for example, the Punjab. Subnation regionalisms similarly play roles in world affairs, among them the special role of Bavarians in the German nation and the significant cultural differences between northern and southern Vietnamese.

A criticism of the regional approach in political geographic study is that it describes many trees, but its idiographic facts get in the way of comprehending the forest. A counterargument is that the political organization of the world is not composed of an infinite number of trees, but of *a finite pattern of only 170 state units, each of which differs significantly in form, function, and ontology from its neighbors.* Such a configuration is not too complex to grasp by those seeking to master the essentials of political geography and world affairs.

Although every state is unique, groups of contiguous states tend to exhibit enough common political features to permit broader regional generalization. To amplify these similarities, this work is organized on the basis of a handful of major regions that display significant qualities of political homogeneity and coherence. The regions bear only partial resemblance to the conventional continents, which tend to be inadequate compartments for comprehending most geographic realities. "Anglo-America" and "Latin America" are more meaningful partitions of the Western Hemisphere than a division between "North America" and "South America." North Africa is much more closely tied to the states of the Middle East than it is to Sub-Saharan Africa. South Asia and East Asia each constitute parts of the Eurasian landmass that are as distinctive political and cultural entities as the peninsula of Europe.

The organization of discussions is essentially similar for each region. They begin with a broad overview of political-geographic characteristics and factors accounting for them. These particularly include spatial patterns of effective settlement and cultural differentiation and their relationships to the territorial organization of state units. Because virtually all contemporary problem areas have historic origins, an emphasis is placed upon the evolution of states and nations through time. Discussions then examine specific countries and peoples in detail.

The author has sought to present an ordered array of the pertinent facts with a minimum of value judgments. In many cases, state policies and prevailing popular sentiments contain elements of racism and xenophobia. However much such phenomena appear despicable to one's sense of propriety, they do exist, and understanding them is vital for comprehending the basis for group conflict. They cannot be wished away, and they are not likely to be changed any time soon. The author admits, however, that it is difficult to maintain neutrality in such matters as Franco's suppression of Basques and Catalonians, Stalin's massive deportations of entire nationalities in the USSR, and recent "ethnic cleansing" by Serbs in Bosnia.

Accompanying each chapter is a summary of the states under discussion. Totals of inhabitants and surface areas generally have been rounded to facilitate comparisons. It is the author's experience that most students have only limited awareness of the population size and territorial extent of the countries of the world, and he encourages readers to strive to develop a sense of magnitude and scale of political entities.

Bibliography

AGNEW, JOHN A., *Place and Politics: The Geographical Mediation of State and Society.* Boston: Allen & Unwin, 1987.

ALEXANDER, LEWIS M., *World Political Patterns,* 2nd ed. Chicago: Rand McNally, 1963.

ARCHER, J.C., and F.M. SHELLY, "Theory and Methodology in Political Geography," in *Progress in Political Geography,* ed. Michael Pacione. London: Croom Helm, 1985, pp. 11–40.

BRUNN, S.D., and K.A. MINGST, "Geopolitics," in *Progress in Political Geography,* ed. Michael Pacione. London: Croom Helm, 1985, pp. 41–76.

CLAVAL, PAUL, "The Coherence of Political Geography: Perspectives on Its Past Evolution and Its

Future Relevance," in *Political Geography: Recent Advances and Future Directions*, eds. Peter Taylor and John House. London: Croom Helm, 1984, pp. 8–24.

DERNKO, GEORGE, AND WILLIAM B. WOOD eds., *Reordering the World: Geopolitical Perspectives on the Twenty-First Century*. Boulder, CO: Westview Press, 1994.

DOUGLAS, J.N.H., "Conflict Between States," in *Progress in Political Geography*, ed. Michael Pacione. London: Croom Helm, 1985, pp. 41–76.

GOTTMAN, J., *La Politique des États et leur Géographie*. Paris: Hachette, 1952.

HARTSHORNE, RICHARD, "The Functional Approach in Political Geography," *Annals of the Association of American Geographers*, Vol. 49 (1950), pp. 95–130.

HARTSHORNE, RICHARD, "Political Geography," in *American Geography: Inventory and Prospect*. Syracuse, NY: Syracuse University Press and the Association of American Geographers, 1954, pp. 167–225.

KNIGHT, DAVID B., "Geographical Perspectives on Self-Determination," in *Political Geography: Recent Advances and Future Directions*, eds. Peter Taylor and John House. London: Croom Helm, 1984, pp. 168–190.

KOLOSOV, V. A., *Politicheskaya Geografiya: Problemy i Metodi*. Leningrad: Nauka, 1988.

MURPHY, A. B., "Evolving Regionalism in Linguistically Divided Belgium," in *Nationalism, Self-Determination, and Political Geography*, eds. R.J. Johnston, D. Knight, and E. Kofman. London: Croom Helm, 1988, pp. 135–150.

PACIONE, MICHAEL, "Introduction," in *Progress in Political Geography*, ed. Michael Pacione. London: Croom Helm, 1985, pp. 11–40.

SACK, ROBERT D., *Human Territoriality: Its Theory and History*. Cambridge Studies in Historical Geography No. 7. Cambridge: Cambridge University Press, 1986.

TREWARTHA, GLENN, "A Case for Population Geography," *Annals of the Association of American Geographers*, Vol. 43 (1953), pp. 71–97.

WILLIAMS, C.H., *Linguistic Minorities, Society, and Territory*. Multilingual Matters No. 78. Clevedon: Multilingual Matters Ltd., 1991.

1

The Misleading Political Map

HE traditional political map of the world is a notably misleading instrument for developing a background for understanding world affairs. Its compartmentalization of the earth into some 170 jigsaw-like pieces suggests a uniformity and equality among states that simply does not exist. While states are the basic building blocks of political organization and functioning, each is a unique assemblage of territory, people, and institutions.

The traditional map shows only legally recognized distinctions in the political control of territory, and then only as determined by the mapmaker. The shape, territorial extent, and locations of capital cities, which are the attributes of states depicted by traditional political maps, are actually among their least significant qualities. Indeed, it should be noted that traditional political maps of the world typically distort the size of states, since their customary projection creates great area disparities between tropical and polar regions. Although Greenland is about one-seventh the size of South America, it actually appears larger on the Mercator projection.

Among features of states critical to governmental functioning ignored by the conventional political map are the territory really under the effective control of a state government, the area of a state actually settled and productive, the degree of centralization of governmental decision making and authority within a state, the dependence of a given state upon another state, and whether a state is a nation-state or a multination state.

Patterns of Control and Development

In a number of states, governments do not exert effective control over the total areas nominally within their jurisdictions. These include outlying areas where authority is nonexistent or in the hands of rebellious groups. Governments may lack either the resources or the will to dominate the alienated parts. Among states with sizable areas beyond governmental control are Burma, Peru, Bosnia and Herzegovina, Afghanistan, and Indonesia.

Usually such disaffected regions lie in sparsely populated zones outside effectively settled areas. Few states are blessed with continuous occupation and economic development of all of their territories. Most have extensive areas that are essentially empty of population. Thus, only one-quarter of the lands of the former Soviet Union can be termed effectively settled, principally the compact area between Leningrad, Odessa, and Novosibirsk

known as the "Fertile Triangle," supplemented by small, outlying "islands" of population in the Transcaucasus, Central Asia, and spots along the Trans-Siberian railroad. Canada, which has a larger total territory than the United States, is really best viewed as a 3,000-mile-long "shoestring" of settlement that seldom extends more than 100 miles north of the U.S. border. Geographers have used the term *ecumene* to signify the settled and productive part of a state where humans dominate the landscape, as opposed to the *nonecumene* where the landscape dominates humans.

Sovereign and Dependent States

Although the majority of states have highly centralized governments, many function more as a collection of self-governing units than as unified entities. Such states are organized on a federal principle, with their central governments having direct responsibility for a limited number of activities—principally transportation, communications, and foreign affairs. Among notable federal states are Australia, Canada, and Brazil. The central government of the United States wields much greater authority than do its counterparts in those countries, although its role is still less than that of the governments of France and other more centralized states.

The process of decolonization that began following World War II has left only a handful of entities that are formal colonies or other types of dependencies. Britain retains odd islands and coastal foothold colonies, including St. Helena, in the South Atlantic, and Gibraltar; the French have a few so-called overseas territories in the West Indies and South Pacific; and the United States maintains the "commonwealth" of Puerto Rico and the "territory" of the Virgin Islands. However, many so-called sovereign states are in effect dependent areas. Their governments enjoy only a limited freedom of action in what they can do. The economic dependency of several Central American states upon the United States of America gives them less leeway in foreign and domestic policies affecting American interests than is enjoyed by states, say, in Sub-Saharan Africa or East Asia. Until the popular revolutions of 1989 in Eastern Europe, the states contiguous to the Soviet Union were very much constricted in both international relations and domestic programs. Currently, the member states of the European Union are in the process of voluntarily forfeiting their freedom to control their internal economic activities, a situation difficult to portray on future conventional political maps.

Nation-States and Multination States

The terms "state" and "nation" quite often are used interchangeably in popular American speech. However, it is useful for analyzing world political patterns to make a distinction between states as sovereign units of political organization and nations as socially cohesive groups of people with common political goals. Virtually all economically developed states of the world and many of the developing states are "nation-states" in the sense that a preponderant portion of their inhabitants identify with a single national group. However, nearly all such states have regions where a majority of the local inhabitants see themselves as members of a different nation. In a number of states these minorities are sufficiently significant to warrant identifying the units as "multination states."

Defining the concept of "nation" is an elusive task, because each national group exhibits unique qualities. In almost all cases but that of the multilingual Swiss, nations rest upon a common language. However, national identity goes far beyond linguistic uniformity. Latin America incorporates more than twenty nations that are Spanish-speaking; English-speaking Canadians and Americans constitute two quite different national groups.

Among elements shared in common by members of a nation are traditions, myths, group perceptions of history, religious beliefs, symbols, and even pastimes. Thus, foreign students may master the English language and live for extended periods in the United States, but they do not become "Americans" as long as references to "first-and-ten" (a term used in American football) or "George Washington's hatchet" (referring to a popular myth about the first president's essential honesty) remain incomprehensible allusions for them. Their children, socialized by public schools and peer groups, surmount the hurdles with ease. Karl Deutsch has labeled such shared elements "communications efficiency." The geographer Jean Gottman has applied the term "iconography" to such phenomena.

An important element in the iconography of most nations is a sense of "homeland." Often international disputes revolve around conflicting national claims to territories. Virtually all nations have a spatial dimension, a land seen as a nation's own. Usually the group constitutes at least a local majority of the population of that region. Groups that are distinctive in language and traditions but lack a territorial base do not easily fit the category of nation. Among these are the Gypsies, who are best seen as a caste or stratum within the societies where they live, in contrast to similar dispersed groups such as the Armenians and Lebanese whose national identity is ultimately related to a homeland base. Political leaders

of the black population of the United States have been frustrated in attempts to build a separate national consensus by the dispersal of blacks throughout America, without an areal concentration that could form a core area for national development.

The greatest share of individuals in the developed states of the world are members of national groups. This does not mean that they are necessarily "nationalists." "Nationalism" is a term used to designate political philosophies that emphasize the advancement of national interests as a primary goal in politics. In most nations, nationalists constitute only a small fraction of the populace. The majority of people tend to take their national identity as a matter of fact, at best distinguishing between people with whom they can easily communicate and those who are "foreigners." They may often see themselves as members of broader associations such as "Europeans" or "Pakistanis." However, when national identities are challenged by other groups, they can quickly transcend to nationalist viewpoints, passionately pressing for the defense of the interests of their nations. In times of stress in the Fertile Crescent of the Middle East, "Arabs" split into "Syrians" and "Iraqis." In this regard, it is interesting to observe that nationalist feelings often tend to be weaker in the cores of states than in the borderlands, where the constant presence of members of other nations forces an affirmation of identity.

In one sense, however, national groups are all nationalist, in that a hallmark of nations is the quest for political recognition of their distinctive identities. Almost always this is reflected in a pursuit of a nation-state of their own, although some nations, such as the Montenegrins of Yugoslavia, appear satisfied with local self-ruling autonomy within a broader state. Groups exist, of course, without such a common political agenda, although they are becoming fewer as the twentieth century approaches a close. In such cases, it seems appropriate to designate them as "peoples" rather than "nations." Included in this category would be such societies as the Balinese of Indonesia and most of the tribal groups of Africa. Indeed, the difficulties of building a common national identity in the profusion of languages and religions of most former colonies leads to consideration of the creation of a category that can be termed the "non-nation-state."

The Evolution of Nations

Nations are relatively recent historical phenomena that had their origins in Europe in the early industrial era. Although state organization can be traced back nearly to the dawn of history, nations are essentially a product of the past two centuries. Before the French Revolution of 1789, most states could be viewed as giant personal properties of their rulers. Their populations had little participation in governmental affairs, aside from paying taxes and providing military service. Horizons were extremely limited. The overwhelming majority of people were engaged in eking out a bare existence from the land, and time was measured by the calendar, rather than the clock.

Most affairs involved interaction only within a limited locality. Any broader associations of individuals were through a common religion determined by the ruler. Within a state one could often find quite different languages being spoken. It was principally the land-holding aristocracy and mercantile entrepreneurs who felt themselves and their fortunes bound up with events of the state. It was to such groups that William Shakespeare addressed the sentiment "this blessed plot, this earth, this realm, this England." For the overwhelming majority of the population on the island of Great Britain, the concept of "England" was a remote abstraction.

The progressive development of the commercial, agricultural, and industrial revolutions led to upheavals and dislocations throughout European societies. A habitual rural subsistence way of life was radically altered, as people drifted to the uncertainties of city living. Individuals from different locales were thrust together, sharing new ideas and perspectives. Larger numbers of them received formal educations. Spiritual support through traditional religions often could not meet the new challenges to life in an era of trade and manufacturing. New belief systems emerged, among them the class consciousness that became Marxism and the sense of territorial group identity that became nationalism.

The emergence of nations is usually dated specifically from the French Revolution. French philosophers had been notably influential during the eighteenth century in their propagation of the notion that a government's legitimacy stems from the will of the people rather than from divine providence. Their new "truths" were spread by organized believers, most notably the Jacobins in revolutionary France. They replaced traditional religion as the cement holding society together, although religious heritage, along with language, continued to play an important role in group identities. People who were different became "foreigners." French nationalists, who avowedly subscribed to the revolutionary ideals of "Liberty, Equality, and Brotherhood," soon pressed to expel from France the Alsatians who spoke a Germanic language. This was but the beginning of a sorry history of national excess.

Napoleon's conquering army served as a catalyst for the establishment of similar national identities throughout other parts of Europe. Contact with French soldiers opened exciting alternatives for tradition-bound societies dominated by feudal aristocracies and religion. Napoleon's reorganization of the political map also encouraged new ways of thinking. Thus, the concept of being "Italian" was planted by the gathering of city-states and papal lands into Napoleon's short-lived Kingdom of Italy. Despite sharing an elongated peninsula, a common religion, and a closely related set of Romance languages, the people of Italy had virtually no sense of communal association. Similarly, the separation by Napoleon of the South Slavic lands of Austria into the "Illyrian Provinces" marked the beginning of Slovenian and Croatian national consciousness. In the Slovene city of Ljubljana is found one of the few monuments to Napoleon outside of France, erected in appreciation of the role that he played in sparking the development of a Slovenian nation.

The establishment of national identities took divergent paths in different parts of Europe and, ultimately, in the rest of the world. Generally in Western Europe, rather large territorial states had been in existence for several centuries. The imposition of common governmental institutions and the associations with each other of merchants and administrators from all parts of the state territory had led to a degree of social homogeneity and coherence. National identities emerged more or less coincident with state boundaries, often with an active governmental role. In contrast, the German- and Italian-speaking lands of the middle belt of Europe remained fragmented into several hundred tiny independent units well into the nineteenth century, but, following contact with the French occupying legions, German and Italian national identities arose several decades before the actual establishment of amalgamated nation-states based upon the national principle. A still different process occurred in the ethnically diverse eastern belt of Europe, which remained apportioned among the Prussian, Russian, Austrian, and Ottoman empires throughout the nineteenth century. National movements grew to challenge imperial domination, ultimately shattering the empires and realizing new nation-based states by the end of World War I.

Among the oldest nations in the world are the national groups of the Western Hemisphere. The colonists on the Atlantic seaboard of North America were the first to create a state of their own based upon what was perceived as national interests. Although about a third of the population during the American Revolution had supported the old order of British governance and another third had been passive to the events, at least a third of the inhabitants of the thirteen colonies were active supporters of the Continental Congress and George Washington's army. They indeed constituted a nation, linked to each other by common language and, to an extent, religion, as well as by a shared homeland that their forebears had settled for more than two centuries. They also had a common political idea, a state of their own. Although the United States of America is ante-dated by numerous states in Europe and Asia, it is in fact the oldest of the nation-states, and its form of government has changed less over the past two centuries than that of any other state.

While stressing the early development of the nation-statehood of Americans, it is important to note that the old dynastic states of Western Europe were in the process of becoming nation-states at the same time. The articulation of national identity among the peoples of Europe and the Americas in fact occurred within the span of a few short decades at the end of the eighteenth and beginning of the nineteenth centuries. Americans have a self-image of being a younger nation in part because of their relatively brief occupation of North America. Their daily lives virtually never see historical relics earlier than the seventeenth century, and, in the western United States, history in the popular conception began scarcely a century and a half ago. European groups, on the other hand, perceive a far longer nation-hood than is warranted by their actual political histories. Virtually all Europeans come into contact daily with cathedrals, monuments, and other legacies dating back a thousand or more years. They confuse the evolution of their distinctive cultures with the evolution of their national political identities.

Elsewhere in North America, English-speaking Canadians, in large part defectors or expellees from the young United States, early coalesced into a distinctive nation before subsequently achieving their own self-governing "dominion" statehood in the mid-nineteenth century. Their unity came in part from a determination not to be part of the Americans of the "colossus to the south." Within their new state they had to contend with another nation, the French-speaking inhabitants of Quebec. Canada's domestic politics have revolved around that state's accommodation to dual nationhood ever since.

The process of nation-building was rather different in Latin America. Separation of the established colonies from Spain and Portugal was effected by small ruling oligarchies rather than by national movements. Within the bounds of the young states that emerged, however, distinctively different nations eventually evolved, despite an overall homogeneity in language and religion among the peoples of the former Spanish Empire.

States existed for millennia in East Asia, creating remarkable uniformities in cultures over broad areas. However, the evolution of their populations from peoples into nations came only after the diffusion of Euro-pean-spawned political ideas during the nineteenth and twentieth centuries. In other parts of Asia and Africa, European colonial control brought many individuals into contact with contemporary concepts of social orga-nization and governance. Notwithstanding the implanta-tion of common institutions and languages by the colo-nial powers, attempts to form national identities after political independence have been frustrated by extreme cultural diversities and tribal organizations in the former colonies.

The Role of Nations in the Functioning of States

Sovereignty is the ability of a government to make deci-sions in all facets of a society without purview by another authority. All 170 states of the world are nomi-nally sovereign, although, as noted above, many have governments that feel constrained by the possibility of adverse external economic and other consequences of decisions that they might make. Regimes also are lim-ited in formulating policies by the ethos of the nation or nations that they administer.

National iconographies embody group values and aspirations. Governments fly in the face of these only at political peril. They usually strive to convince their con-stituents that they are "of the people, by the people, and for the people." Even the most repressive regimes, backed by internal and/or external armed might, strive to present themselves in a favorable national light. It is instructive to examine the evolution of the East European regimes imposed by the Soviet Red Army after World War II. Although nominally national governments, they initially pursued policies that were essentially antination-alist, based upon an avowedly Marxist ideology of inter-national class solidarity as well as pressures to satisfy the needs of the Soviet state. Opposition was ruthlessly sup-pressed, including protests of a nationalist nature from within their own ranks. Purge trials of so-called Titoists in the late 1940s ended in executions of formerly promi-nent leaders, many of whom had sought to preserve aspects of the national heritage. With the passing of time and the relaxation of coercion, the regimes increasingly sought to elicit popular support by seeking to identify themselves more closely with national aims and values. Romania's communist leadership carried this the furthest by open criticism of the Soviet Union.

Territorial Aspects of States

Although national identity is the key dynamic force in the world's political geography, state organization is the medium in which it operates. To many persons, states are the basic building blocks of international affairs. They see the pattern of state organization as the one constant element in international politics, and believe efforts should be exerted to preserve the status quo. The potential fragmentation of Spain or Canada is seen inherently as a threat to the natural order of things.

The political map of the world, of course, is not a fixed entity. It has constantly changed over time. Some have seen its sequence of modifications as a type of animated drawing, and they have concluded that the states of the world are very much like organisms, with their own life processes of birth, development, and dissolution.

Thinking in terms of analogies can often lead to quite erroneous conclusions. Seeing states as living bodies can induce one to put them into such categories as "youthful," "mature," and "old age," or to accept territorial aggression as inevitable for survival. Karl Ritter, one of the nineteenth-century German founders of modern geography, allowed himself to speculate on the nature of states as seen in their changing boundaries. He was particularly aware of the rapid changes then occurring in his home area, as Prussia steadily absorbed its neighboring petty states and the European powers were scrambling for territories in Africa. His rather naive observations were later adopted as some of the axioms of the so-called doctrine of geopolitics that was used by the Nazi regime to justify its expansion against neighbors.

States, of course, are not some type of animal that must grow or die. The existence of stable external boundaries for five centuries in a state such as Spain does not mean that it is older and therefore inherently different from a state, such as Albania, which appeared only in the twentieth century. Like racial prejudice, classifications based upon observations of external phenomena are likely to be erroneous, if not pernicious. A holistic approach, involving all aspects of the functioning of states and taking into account the unique qualities of each, is necessary for analyzing the pattern of world affairs.

It is useful to visualize states as inherited institutional structures of territorial organization. They are directed and managed by a finite group of individuals who are subject to all the human vagaries. Their leaders can and often do pursue inherently irrational policies based upon faulty perceptions of problems confronting them.

Regimes in power face a variety of difficulties. Disorder and criminality are potential threats everywhere. Sustaining law and order must be a top priority for all governments. Economies also are beset by a multitude of pressures and perils. Regimes find it necessary to regulate domestic and foreign trade and the monetary system. They feel constrained to develop and maintain an infrastructure of transportation and communication.

A constant challenge for most states is the maintenance of their sovereignty. An implicit task is the preservation of the state's territory against covetous neighbors and discontented minorities. Virtually all states support military forces and develop protective alliances.

Although academically one can separate states from nations, the distinction becomes blurred when examining their actual functioning. In their tasks of maintaining law and order, promoting economic well-being, and contending with the governments of other states, regimes are both motivated and constrained by national values and institutions. If officials ignore national sentiments, they run the very real risk of losing power, a prospect no political figure wants to contemplate.

Recent events in the Persian Gulf serve to illustrate this point. Among the more traditional Arabic-speaking nations, the customary approach to resolving disputes is courtesy and protracted discussion. This places them at a disadvantage in responding to external threats from more militant societies. In 1990, traditionalist Saudi Arabia almost suffered the fate of overwhelmed Kuwait when its government delayed a response to the aggressiveness of the more secular Iraqi regime. Even when its extreme vulnerability to its militant neighbor was shockingly perceived, it found great difficulty in adopting the only viable defensive strategy available to it, namely, accepting on its soil the military support of the forces of a non-Islamic and non-Arab foreign power—the United States of America.

A similar example is seen in the former Soviet Union's attempt to establish a more efficient market-based economy with private property and differential rewards for entrepreneurship. President Mikhail Gorbachev had perceived that such a policy was limited by the traditional egalitarian values of the Russian nation. Peasant-grounded resentment against inequalities in wealth proved a much greater hurdle for reformation of the socialist command economy of the USSR than it was for the East Germans or Hungarians.

Although governments almost always find it expedient to recognize traditional national values in formulating and implementing policies, they also are prone to manipulate national iconographies for their own ends. Many of the world's conflicts among states derive from programs adopted to divert attention from a regime's mishandling of domestic responsibilities. For more than 150 years the people of Argentina have collectively believed that the British wrongfully deprived them of the Malvinas Islands, better known elsewhere as the Falklands. A corrupt and incompetent Argentine military regime found itself increasingly incapable of addressing problems of economic stagnation and runaway inflation. To distract its citizens from its record of failures, the Argentine military embarked upon an adventure to seize the Malvinas and thus identify with a traditional aspiration of the Argentine nation. Unfortunately for the ruling clique, the enterprise was a disaster. The British dislodged them from the islands, and popular revulsion drove the military rulers out of office. President Sukarno of Indonesia similarly created a specter of an evil "neocolonialism" in adjacent newly independent Malaysia to deflect attention from inflation and other problems plaguing his regime, but ultimately this was not sufficient to save him from losing his office.

Ties between the economy and the nation pose problems for governments in other ways. Regimes face constant pressures for the maintenance of an economic sovereignty that corresponds to political independence. Enterprises seek protection against lower-priced foreign competition. Such economic nationalism is inherently inefficient in all but the largest of states. In small countries it leads to the establishment of monopolies that not only lack competition to force savings in the production sphere, but also that cannot realize scale economies from mass production and from selection of sites that utilize the inherent comparative advantage of areas.

The period since World War II has seen the emergence of regional economic cooperation that holds the opportunity for small states to match the economic efficiencies of the large ones. Beginning with America's Marshall Plan for European recovery following World II, which required joint decisions by its recipients for priorities in investment, the states of Western Europe have increasingly integrated their economies. In doing so they have relinquished a degree of economic sovereignty in the process. Belgium, the Netherlands, and Luxemburg formed a customs union (Benelux) for the free flow of goods and services. Later, they joined West Germany, Italy, and France in a European Coal and Steel Community (ECSC), which allowed the movement among the members of raw materials, labor, and finished goods without the imposition of tariffs. In 1957 the same states signed the Treaty of Rome, which expanded economic cooperation to virtually all spheres of production and distribution within a new European Economic Community (EEC). A European Free Trade Association (EFTA), composed of most of the other Western European states, was formed at about the same time.

The EEC subsequently has doubled its membership. Now known simply as the European Union (EU), it has developed plans for complete free trade among its members. It should be noted that while the EU is a common market for its participants, it functions as a statelike entity in its economic relations with others. It has adopted a common system of protective tariffs, particularly for agricultural goods, that makes market access difficult for foreign producers.

One unanticipated consequence of the establishment of the European Union is the political threat that it holds out to its member states, many of which embrace more than one nation within their boundaries. If Belgium can function within the EU and assure its citizens a high standard of living, why not a separated sovereign state for the Flemings who live in its northern region? Nationalists who formerly were constrained by the unthinkability of attempting to maintain a viable economy in conditions of small area and population are currently thinking the unthinkable.

Problems of Multinational States

The prospects for minorities of economic well-being under political independence add to the problems of maintaining unity that are presented to governments when their states encompass more than one nation. As indicated above, regimes find it necessary to cater to the national aims and values of the dominant groups in their states. Pleasing one group usually results in antagonizing the other. Moreover, it is in the personal political interests of national minority leaders to seize upon any slights to their nation, intended or unintended, real or imaginary.

States have sought to accommodate minority nations within their borders in a variety of ways. Some have simply used suppression of political activities by would-be minority group activists. Often such stifling is accompanied by cosmetic concessions to national identities. The long-standing Soviet formula of "national in form, socialist in content" was one such approach. Although major national groups were granted formal self-government, including use of their native languages and even separate membership in the United Nations for the Ukrainians and Byelorussians, real power was concentrated in the administrative arm of the Communist Party of the Soviet Union, which operated on a highly centralized basis. The Ceausescu regime of Romania sought to denationalize its Hungarian minority by educational policies and propaganda that stressed the minority group's supposed differences in origins from members of the Hungarian nation and by minimization of contacts of its minority with Hungary, including even forbidding the importation of publications from that fellow communist state.

True federal systems that grant a maximum of local decision-making authority to national minorities have been employed with varying degrees of success in Canada and other states. They also have been used in nation-states that have contrasting regional interests such as Australia and the United States. Switzerland has been particularly effective in accommodating to the perceived needs of its diverse population by a federal system that devolves most government to the district canton level. In the process, the Swiss have become perhaps the world's only example of a multilingual nation.

There are political geographic problems peculiar to federal systems, however. One is establishment of an appropriate balance between federal- and regional-level governmental functioning. Demands by the French-speaking Québecois for even greater official recognition of their distinctiveness and expanded rights to promote their language have met increasing resistance from the rest of Canada. Unless Québec is willing to compromise, the future unity of Canada is in jeopardy.

Another problem is the prosaic question of location of the capital city. To avoid favoring economically and politically one component of the federation over the others by being the site of federal facilities, employment, and associated development, most federal states select neutral locations for their capitals. The District of Columbia was created on the border between the contrasting northern and southern states of the young United States. Ottawa and Canberra were similarly established for Canada and Australia, respectively. In Switzerland and the former Union (now Republic) of South Africa, different cities were selected as seats for legislative, executive, and judicial headquarters.

In contrast, in the postwar Yugoslav federation, Belgrade, the capital of Serbia, was also made the federal capital. Its enhanced development, particularly over the rival Croatian capital of Zagreb, contributed significantly to the strains between the two major constituent members of the former federation. A neutral site might well have dampened Croatian fears of Serbian hegemony. The British sought to weld their island colonies in the Caribbean into an independent Federation of the West Indies. Despite substantial investment of energies, the project foundered in the end over impossibility of agreement on which of the islands would be the new capital.

External Relations of States

The challenges of domestic problems to governments are matched by the difficulties of conducting international affairs. One of the disturbing constants in foreign relations is the generally negative image of neighbors that resides in the iconographies of most national groups. Stereotypes of insensitive or grasping or opportunistic adjacent peoples contribute to the generation of conflict when disputes arise. Problems become more acute when a portion of a nation is seen as being held hostage within the borders of another state.

Coincident with the flowering of national identity during the nineteenth century was a concern for members of the nation who did not live inside of the nation-state. After the unification of Italy in the 1860s it became that government's policy to bring into the young state those Italians who lived in Austria and France.

They were termed *irredenta* ("unredeemed"), and ever since this term has become a generic expression for fellow nationals living in a foreign land. Irredentist minorities are found in many parts of the world, and they usually represent potential threats to world peace. World War I began over a Serbian quest to bring into that state the Serbs of Austrian-annexed Bosnia. The alleged mistreatment of Germans in the Polish "Corridor" and the Czech Sudetenland was used as a rallying pretext in Germany for the inauguration of World War II.

Irredentism can also involve lesser nations within a state. The Indian government has been solicitous about the situation of the Hindu Tamil minority within the Buddhist nation-state of Sri Lanka. The former Soviet Union "redeemed" the Byelorussians and Ukrainians of Poland by annexing their lands at the onset of World War I.

Frontiers and Boundaries

The evolution of political boundaries was a contributing factor to the rise of irredentism. Although state boundaries have been depicted on maps since ancient times, their role in marking geographic discontinuities across the land is a relatively recent one. In the feudal period the territorial extent of empires and kingdoms was a matter of personal relations between rulers and vassals. It was not uncommon for local leaders at the margins of states to pay homage to more than one sovereign. States came together in frontier zones, rather than at boundary lines. The populations of such zones typically had more economic, religious, and social relationships with each other across the nominal dividing lines than they had with the peoples in the cores of their respective states. Although Flanders may have been partitioned between the Bourbon family ruling France and the Habsburg family of Spain and Austria, it functioned in many ways as a coherent entity of its own through the eighteenth century. Even in times of struggle, the battle lines of contending armies could usually be crossed with impunity by local noncombatants.

The frontiers of the world have virtually all been collapsed into boundaries over the past two centuries. The partitioning of Bosnia and Herzegovina is best viewed as reduction of a frontier zone to boundary lines. Political frontier situations remain only in remote areas, such as the "Golden Triangle" of Southeast Asia and the Amazonian borderlands of South America. This reduction of zones to lines is a product of the rise of economic nationalism that paralleled the rise of the nation-state. The development of protective tariffs in the nineteenth century led to an emphasis upon control of borders that has grown more intensive with time. The culmination was the "iron curtain" across central and southern Europe and the "Demilitarized Zone" separating North and South Korea.

The location of borders has become an increasingly critical element in relations among states over the past century. Existing lines that regimes have perceived to be disadvantageous have triggered wars. A major concern for the treaty makers after conflict has been to assure that their respective states acquire maximum benefits through redrafting boundaries. Incorporation within their states of as many members of their nations as possible has been a primary quest, as noted above. Much of the redrawing of boundaries in Europe during and after World Wars I and II reflected this motivation. Negotiators also have sought major areas of economic development and the inclusion of known or suspected concentrations of natural resources, particularly coal and petroleum. Polish acquisition of Lower Silesia and French moves to control the Saarland are examples of this desire. The general seaward extension of state boundaries and so-called economic zones above continental shelves also fall into this category. Other concerns have involved strategic sites for defense (or offense). Italy pressed for a "defensive border" along the crest of the Alps after World War I, and the Soviet Union secured the Japanese Kurile Islands in 1945 to protect the movements of its Pacific fleet.

The benefits of changing boundaries are often illusory. The economic gains of acquiring developed industry or resource complexes seldom match the costs of controlling a hostile population. The Netherlands and Belgium both rightly refused the offer by the victorious Allies after World War II to compensate them for wartime occupation by awarding them snippets of German territory. They could easily picture the long-term political costs of having unhappy Germans within their borders, coupled with constant irredentist pressures from a revived German state. France similarly has twice found it best to relinquish the Saar to Germany, after claiming it as war booty.

Although conventional wisdom runs to the contrary, the fact is that the acquisition of developed territories and their resources has its countervailing costs. Gaining new areas, however productive, at best has modest impact upon standards of living and economic functioning in the rest of a state. The impact of change in the status quo may have drastic effects on the newly acquired area itself by tearing it away from customary markets and suppliers, negating the benefits sought in its seizure.

Even claims to a greater portion of the ocean floor are not without their costs, since they engender potential conflict with neighbors due to the alternative ways that land borders may be projected into the sea and the lack of consensus concerning the seaward distance that a

state properly may declare as its own. Turkey and Greece have a long-running dispute in the eastern Mediterranean involving the seafloor extensions of their island holdings, and Argentina and Chile nearly came to blows over control of oceanic resources south of the tip of South America.

Also suspect is the supposed value of strategic gains. There is some truth in the saying that generals and admirals are always fighting a previous war. The constant change in military technology renders past security concerns obsolete. There are scarcely any strategic benefits to Russian retention of the Kurile Islands at the end of the twentieth century that are commensurate with the costs involved in Japanese refusal to support needed investment in Siberian development until the islands are returned. Italy's Alpine border has brought it grief for more than seven decades, as it has had to contend with militant actions of a German-speaking minority in the South Tyrol region. The state of Italy was not notably more secure, if only because it is easier to invade territory by advancing from higher ground. Its aims would have been better met had it demanded the far side of the Alpine crest such that its forces, if attacked, could retreat uphill. Even this military consideration, of course, had grown obsolete by the end of World War I.

This Italian quest also reflects a rather widespread sentiment that the best borders are "natural" ones that follow mountain ridgetops, rivers, or coastlines. These are seen as more-or-less neutral limits to state power that are dictated by the impartial forces of nature itself. French policy for decades was to secure *les limites naturelles* for the state.

To begin with, no borders are inherently "natural." All are the "artificial" results of treaty makers. The many borders that follow natural features are often less satisfactory than alternatives. Consider the western boundary between Canada and the United States. It is a straight line that follows the parallel of latitude 49°N. It cuts directly across the Cascade and Rocky mountains, as well as the North American Great Plains and Canadian Shield. Yet it is unmilitarized and less disputed than almost any other world boundary. In contrast, the Rio Grande riverine border between the United States and Mexico has seen substantial controversy and is likely to witness more. Its principal weakness is that the course of the river is subject to change through the natural processes of erosion and deposition. Territories on the Mexican side may suddenly find themselves separated from the rest of Mexico and contiguous with American land. The Chamizal district near El Paso was one such instance resulting from river change, and it required several decades before the United States reluctantly returned it to Mexico.

Another feature characteristic of rivers is that they are linking, rather than divisive, elements in the landscape. Until the development of rail transportation in the mid-nineteenth century, it was always easier to move by river and sea than it was to trek overland. As a result of the ease of interaction, populations of lowlands on both sides of a river have tended to be homogeneous. Examples include the Germanic-speaking populations of Baden-Würtemberg and Alsace-Lorraine along the Rhine and the Spanish-speaking majority along both sides of the Rio Grande.

High mountain crests tend to be better international boundaries, but the reason lies in their emptiness of population, not their inherent "naturalness." The same may be said for maritime limits to a state. By passing through vacant territory, there is not the problem of cutting across areas of mixed peoples with the inevitable leaving of members of a nation on the wrong side of the line. Many mountainous regions are, of course, populated, and such areas tend to have the same national groups on both sides of a water divide. Thus, the Basques occupy both sides of the Pyrenees, and the Ruthenians spill across the Carpathians.

Generally speaking, the best borders are laid out through empty tracts. This accounts for the stability and acceptance of the U.S.–Canadian boundary. It was *antecedent* to settlement. As people colonized the Great Plains and western areas of North America in the nineteenth century, they either stayed on "their" side of the international boundary, or, accepting the political status quo of the territory, adopted a new national identity.

Of course, most new borders are established across land that has long been settled. Such subsequent lines are bound to disrupt customary associations and linkages. Their harmfulness can be minimized by making them *consequent* upon the nationality patterns of a region, although, as noted earlier, it is impossible to separate groups completely in mixed cultural regions. All too often, a nonnationality criterion is used, with long-term disastrous results. Such *superimposed* borders are bound to be unsatisfactory to one party, if not both. A prime example was the 1920 decision in Ireland to allocate territory to the new Irish Free State and to the United Kingdom on the basis of the majority population of counties. The six northern counties of Ulster, which had Protestant pro-British majorities, also had substantial Catholic pro-Irish minorities. The latter have higher birth rates and have grown in proportion of population in subsequent decades. They have been fairly successful in making the political, social, and economic situation in Ulster intolerable. It seems likely that the selection of more consequent borders at the time of partition would have resulted in a far smaller discontented minority group and a less likely mass critical enough to support a rebellion.

Bibliography

ANDERSON, J., "Nationalist Ideology and Territory," in *Nationalism, Self-Determination and Political Geography*, eds. R.J. Johnston, D. Knight, and E. Kofman. London: Croom Helm, 1988, pp. 18–39.

BRUNN, S.D., "Future of the Nation State System," in *Political Geography: Recent Advances and Future Directions*, eds. Peter Taylor and John House. London: Croom Helm, 1984, pp. 149–167.

GLASSNER, MARTIN, and HARM DE BLIJ, *Systematic Political Geography*, 4th ed. New York: John Wiley, 1989.

HARTSHORNE, RICHARD, "Political Geography," in *American Geography: Inventory and Prospect*, eds. P.E. James and C. Jones. Syracuse, NY: Syracuse University Press, 1954.

HOOSON, DAVID (ed.) *Geography and National Identity*, Cambridge, MA: 1994.

JOHNSTON, R., *Geography and the State*. New York: St. Martin's Press, 1983.

JONES, STEVEN, "Boundary Concepts in the Setting of Place and Time," *Annals of the Association of American Geographers*, Vol. 49 (1959), pp. 241–255.

KNIGHT, DAVID B., "Identity and Territory: Geographical Perspectives on Nationalism and Regionalism," *Annals of the Association of American Geographers*, Vol. 72, No. 4 (1982), pp. 514–531.

KRISTOF, LADIS, "The Nature of Frontiers and Boundaries," *Annals of the Association of American Geographers*, Vol. 49 (1959), pp. 269–282.

KRISTOF, LADIS, "The Origins and Evolution of Geopolitics," *Journal of Conflict Resolution*, Vol. 4 (1960), pp. 15–51.

LAPONCE, J.A., *Languages and Their Territories*. Toronto: University of Toronto Press, 1987.

MACLAUGHLIN, J.G., "The Political Geography of 'Nation-Building' and Nationalism in Social Sciences: Structural vs. Dialectical Accounts," *Political Geography Quarterly*, Vol. 5, No. 4 (1986), pp. 299–399.

MELLOR, R.E.H., *Nation, State, and Territory: A Political Geography*. London: Routledge, 1989.

POUNDS, NORMAN, *Political Geography*, 2nd ed. New York: McGraw-Hill, 1972.

REYNOLDS, D., and D. KNIGHT, "Political Geography," in *Geography in America*, eds. G. Gaile and C. Willmott. Columbus, OH: Chas. E. Merrill, 1989.

DE SILVA, K.M., and R.J. MAY, *Internationalization of Ethnic Conflict*. New York: St. Martin's Press, 1991.

WILLIAMS, C.H., "Minority Groups in the Modern State," in *Progress in Political Geography*, ed. Michael Pacione. London: Croom Helm, 1985, pp. 111–151.

2

An Introduction to Europe

A SUSTAINING myth of Western civilization is the notion that there exists a physical "continent" named Europe. The perpetuation of this fiction results from a conventional partitioning of the world into landmasses advanced by the ancient Greeks. "Europe," "Asia," and "Africa" stood apart from each other in the eastern Mediterranean as distinctive areas with contrasting populations. They were separated by water bodies—the Mediterranean Sea, the Red Sea, and the Black Sea with the associated Straits and Sea of Marmara.

Later, the Greeks found that their "Europe" was, like southwestern Asia, an appendage of a broad Eurasian landmass. At different times they designated the Dniester, Dnieper, and Volga rivers to mark the presumed continent's eastern extremity. However, no water body served as a "natural break" in the vast plains area that extended continuously from what is now northern Germany to the low-lying Ural Mountains. Settlements of tribal groups spread across this broad region without interruption, in contrast to the fragmentation of communities in the eastern Mediterranean.

The problem of defining Europe's eastern margins remains to this day. The waters of the Mediterranean and Black seas have not isolated Europeans from their neighbors on other continents any more than the Red Sea separated "Asian" peoples from those of Africa. Water bodies link rather than divide adjacent lands. They are easy to cross, whether for trade or for conquest. The Greeks themselves established colonies throughout the shores of the Mediterranean, including their important African city of Alexandria in Egypt.

Water bodies do play an insulating role in cultural differentiation, however. Day-to-day flows in communication end abruptly at seacoasts. Observable differences among peoples result from the discontinuities of land and water. Europeans shared a culture that had evolved quite differently from that of the Iranians and other peoples of Asia. However, the belts of emptiness that insulated their development from innovations by Asians were not all water bodies, but included the barren high mountains of the Caucasus Mountains with the semiarid wastes that lay to the north and the Caspian Sea and the deserts of Central Asia that extended eastward well into China. (See Table 2-1.)

The Distinctiveness of Europe

Europe's distinctiveness both in Greek times and today is a cultural phenomenon, not a physical one. Europe is simply a land of the Europeans, a distinctive collection of peoples who have shared an interacting common history over several millennia. The present convention of using the Urals to mark the eastern limits of Europe is an absurdity. These exaggerated hills are rather continuously populated, and they separate nothing. If anything, the Siberian cities of Omsk and Novosibirsk assigned to "Asia" are more "European" than a number of ancient communities around Moscow that were long under the impress of the Mongols and Tatars.

Because of the distinctive historical experiences of the Russians and their subject peoples, geographers usually treat their vast land space as a continental entity in its own right, separate from both Europe and Asia. For this book, the western frontier of the Soviet Union is adopted as the eastern edge of Europe. The term "frontier" is used advisedly, for the Baltic peoples, the Byelorussians, the Ukrainians, and the Moldavians of the former western USSR occupy a transitional zone between what is clearly European and what is not.

The territory west of the former USSR's border is small in comparison with other continental units. Its area of some two million square miles makes it two-thirds the size of Australia. Unlike the land "down under," however, it is not a territorial monolith, but finds itself compartmentalized by a number of narrow seas. It often is described as a "peninsula of peninsulas." Seacoasts are everywhere. More than 80 percent of Europeans live within a hundred miles of an ocean or sea. One has to travel deep into the eastern recesses of Poland and Czechoslovakia to get as far as 300 miles from a coastline.

These penetrating bodies of water have both connected and fragmented Europe. Until the technological transformation of transportation that began in the nineteenth century, armies of soldiers and merchants found it far easier to travel great distances by water than by moving overland. The Greeks and Phoenicians early built commercial empires around the Mediterranean. The Romans held their vast conquests together much more by ships on seas and rivers than by caravans on roads. In the northern lands, the Baltic Sea was a highway along which the commercial towns of the medieval Hanseatic League gained their riches.

TABLE 2-1   EUROPE

Although commonly defined as a "continent," Europe is better visualized as a "culture area" with characteristics extending southward to the Sahara and eastward ultimately to the Pacific Ocean. Conventionally in the twentieth century its outer limits have been defined as the Mediterranean Sea and the western border of the former Soviet Union. With the collapse of the USSR in 1991, the Baltic states, Moldavia, and possibly the Ukraine and Belarus are again becoming parts of Europe. However, because of their continuing economic and cultural ties to Russia, they are treated later in this book with other parts of the former USSR. Many individuals have called for an economic and political unification of Europe and serious negotiations have taken place. Such an amalgamated unit would have two-thirds the territory of China and half its population. However, the division of the land among fifty nations inhabiting more than thirty states appears an insuperable handicap. The political diversity of the culture area is explained by its division into discrete linguistic, religious, and economic regions. The peoples of Europe speak more than forty languages divided among three major families (Germanic, Romance, and Slavic) and several smaller ones. Four religions (Roman Catholicism, Protestantism, Eastern Orthodoxy, and Islam) prevail in different areas. Major contrasts in standards of living characterize north and south. To understand this diversity it is useful to divide Europe into the following seven subregions:

Subregion	Total Population	Area (sq. miles)
Western Europe	120,000,000	332,000
Component States		
France, United Kingdom, Ireland (Éire)		
The Lotharingian States	34,000,000	45,000
Component States		
Netherlands, Belgium, Luxemburg, Switzerland		
Northern Europe	23,000,000	445,000
Component States		
Denmark, Norway, Sweden, Finland, Iceland		
Iberia	50,000,000	230,000
Component States and Territories		
Spain, Portugal, Andorra, Gibraltar		
Middle Europe	140,000,000	255,000
Component States		
Italy, San Marino, Germany		
East Central Europe	73,000,000	240,000
Component States		
Austria, Liechtenstein, Poland, the Czech Lands, Slovakia, Hungary		
Southeast Europe	70,000,000	300,000
Component States		
Yugoslavia (Serbia and Montenegro), Slovenia, Croatia, Bosnia and Herzegovina, Macedonia, Romania, Bulgaria, Albania, Greece		
Total	**510,000,000**	**1,850,000**

The seas did, of course, pose empty tracts that tended to shield peoples on opposite shores from innovations in language and culture. Despite a common ancestry of most Europeans, groups grew apart over the centuries because their interaction lacked the benefits of the territorial contiguity that marked the Russians or the Chinese. Like the seas, the emptiness of the mountains added further to fragmentation of cultures. More often than not, the few peoples who did live within them were refugees differing markedly from the invaders who had driven them from former homes in the adjacent lowlands.

The Varieties of Europeans

Europe is the most continuously settled of all the conventional continents. Only in the forest and tundra lands of northern Scandinavia and Finland, in the higher mountains, and in the dry core of Iberia does one find territories that can be termed "nonecumene." Virtually all of Europe's inhabitants see themselves as "Europeans." At the same time, virtually all sort themselves into "we" and "they"—"our" group and "foreigners." (See Figure 2-1.)

Although many groups sincerely believe that the differences between themselves and others is racial in origin, biology is not territorially compartmentalized in Europe. Folk migrations, marauding armies, and travelling merchants left a legacy of intermixture of physical types throughout the Continent. Some tendencies toward territorial concentrations of distinctive racial types do give weight to stereotyping, but a person needs to realize that not all Swedes are blond and blue-eyed, nor all Italians dark and dapper. Yugoslavia's Montenegro may be a source area of seven-foot-tall basketball players, but it is also an area where one may find people of much shorter stature.

Most Europeans are from the Caucasian branch of the human family. However, other racial strains are manifest on the Continent. Many are a legacy of an

FIGURE 2-1   THE STATES OF EUROPE

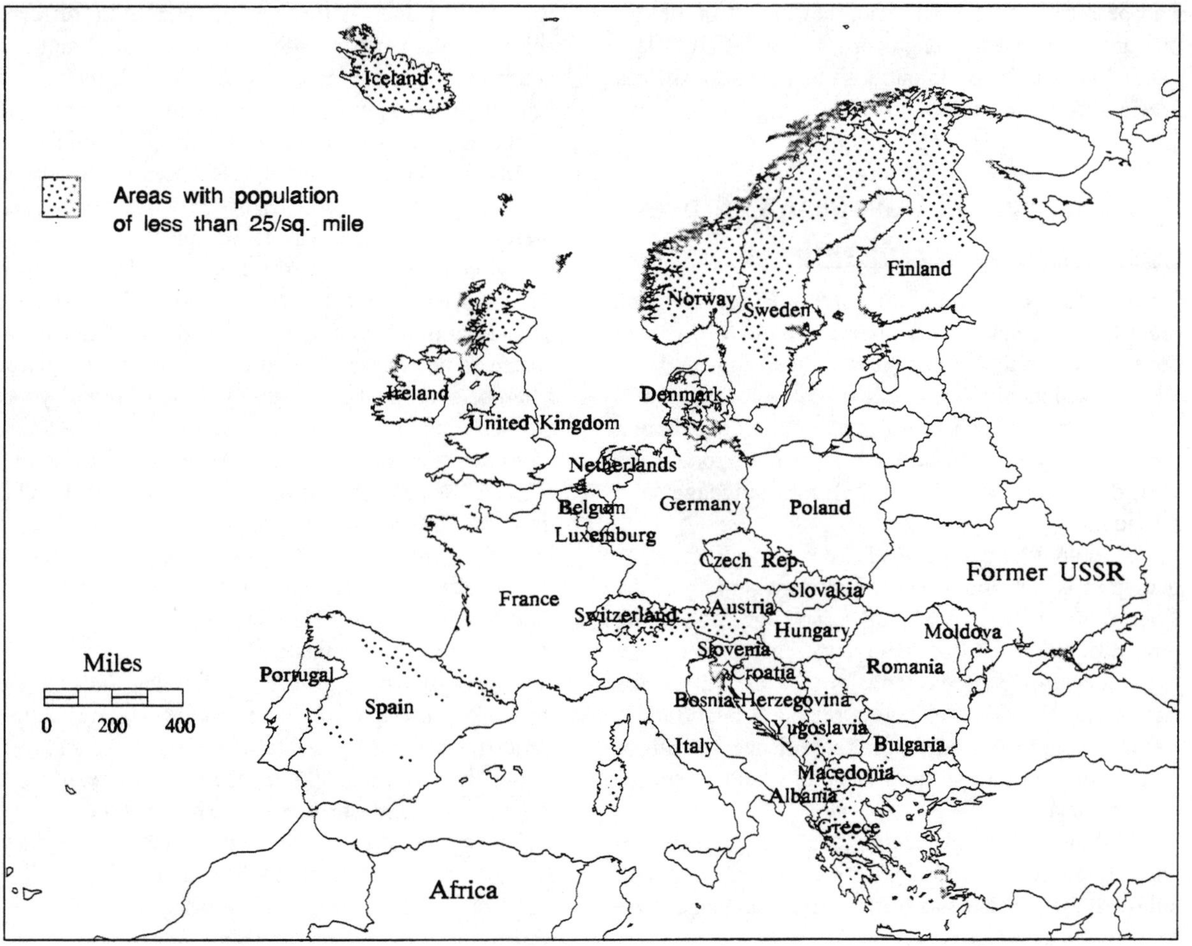

imperial era when Europeans dominated a good share of the peoples of the rest of the world and brought many of their subjects home to the motherland. Others are Asians and Africans working in the Continent's labor-hungry economic machine. Most non-Caucasians are concentrated in the cities. Frequently they have grievances over discrimination, including limitations on opportunities for employment. Their spatial fragmentation weakens their political influence, however, although occasionally they have a significant impact, as in protests by South Moluccans in the Netherlands in 1975 and 1977, and racial disturbances in Brixton and other districts of London in 1982.

The lack of major racial contrasts adds to the perception by Europeans that they have a common origin, together with a common history and a common destiny. The shared time dimension is real enough, since most European groups have had interactions with each other over the course of the past two millennia. The Roman Empire and an organized Christian religion played major roles in establishing this common European identity, and the European Union appears to be forging even greater linkages. Europeans are reminded every day of the existence of a European culture, with European architecture, European literature, European music, and European art. At the same time, they are aware of significant differences among peoples, most of all in language, but also in group outlooks and predispositions. The Europeans are a disparate lot.

The Diversity of European Cultures

To appreciate the cultural diversity of Europeans, one must have a sense of the differing paths of historic development of the various parts of the Continent. Each area has had a unique sequence of groups occupying it. Nearly every past occupant has had some impact upon the region's present culture. Particularly important are two distinctive strands of culture: language and religion.

Although human beings have been in Europe for perhaps a half million years, significant settling of the Continent began just 10,000 years ago, following retreat of the great continental ice sheets. With the gradual warming of the land, groups of individuals pushed into the newly emerging region of opportunity, leaving behind the overcrowding, pestilence, and struggles in their common cultural hearth land in south-western Asia.

Virtually all postglacial migrants spoke a variety of what is termed a "proto Indo-European" language, although the descendants of the parent language grew

further and further apart and became unintelligible to each other. The multiplicity of Indo-European languages in Europe is attributable to two principal factors. (1) Some of the linguistic variations are the result of differences in the time of out-migration from the common homeland, since any language continually changes over time. Later migrants brought with them a linguistic pattern significantly different from that of earlier groups. (2) A second factor was the differing evolution of languages in isolation from each other. Settlement in widely separated territories led to contrasts in patterns of linguistic development.

Differences in Language and Religion

The language map of Europe also reflects the assimilation of peoples into broader cultural uniformities through conquest and subsequent political organization (Figure 2-2). Particularly important was the role of the Romans, who came to control virtually all of western Europe. Their dialect from the hills of Latium became the common medium of communication throughout western Europe. Latin was spoken with differing accents in the various regions of the Roman Empire, of course, in much the same way that the pronunciation of English differs significantly among the former colonies of the United Kingdom. When the Roman Empire finally disintegrated, these differences, coupled with physical isolation, gradually magnified to result in the present distinctive Romance languages.

In central and eastern Europe, similar patterns of territorial expansion and assimilation led to the widespread domination of Germanic and Slavic languages. At the same time, it should be noted that conquerors could be overcome culturally by those whom they vanquished. The Franks, a Germanic tribe who seized Gaul as Rome declined, lost their German speech as their subjects assimilated into the Latin culture world. Only the name France is a reminder of their conquest. Similarly, the Central Asian Bulgars conquered the southern Balkan peninsula, only to be culturally overwhelmed by their Slavic subjects. They left only their name in the territory they had dominated.

The majority of peoples moving into Europe after the Ice Age brought with them similar religious beliefs. Groups worshipped assemblages of gods, many of whose attributes are still imbedded in folklore. Multiple divinities remain a feature of the south Asian lands to which ancestors of the early Europeans also migrated. However, the monotheistic Christian religion has long supplanted the ancient Indo-European deities.

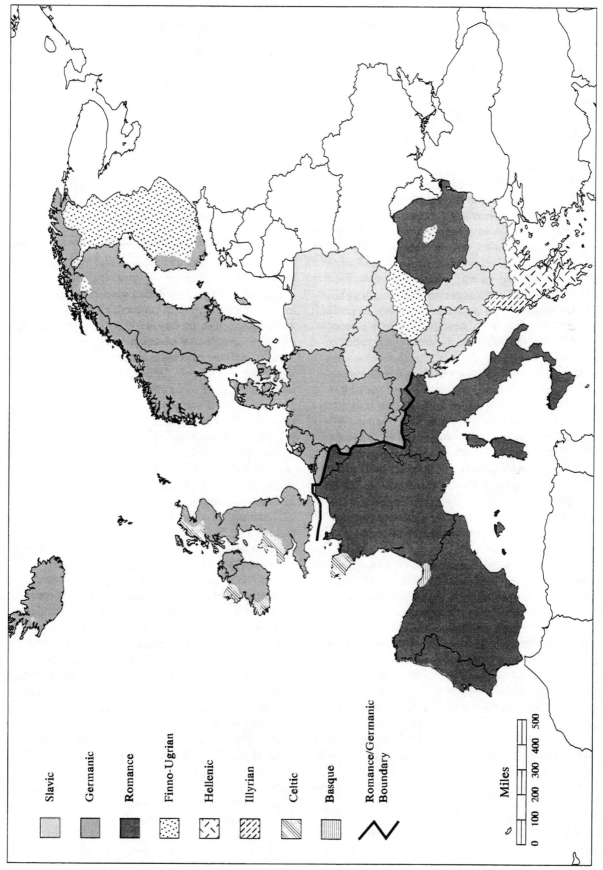

Slavic

Germanic

Romance

Finno-Ugrian

Hellenic

Illyrian

Celtic

Basque

Romance/Germanic Boundary

Miles

0 100 200 300 400 500

FIGURE 2-2 LANGUAGE FAMILIES OF EUROPE

A major reason for the success of Christianity, in addition to the inner qualities of its spiritual message, was its adoption by the Roman state. Originally one of several belief systems arising at the eastern end of the Mediterranean in competition with the pantheons of Greek and Roman gods, Christianity eventually gained acceptance at the highest levels of society. The growing failure of the Roman imperial system, like the recent collapse of communism in the Soviet Union and Eastern Europe, created fertile grounds for a new faith.

Christian beliefs have dominated Europe for nearly two millennia. The institutional organization of the Roman Catholic church has played a decisive role over the centuries in this continuing success of Christianity. However, the Christian religion has by no means remained a monolithic body. As in other great religions, it has seen its share of reforms and schisms. The Roman Empire, in its waning decades, sought to preserve itself by splitting into separate eastern and western parts. The Christian church, as an imperial institution, similarly became divided, never to reestablish effective unity. Christianity later spread from the competing centers of Rome and Constantinople into the Germanic- and Slavic-speaking lands of central and eastern Europe.

Subsequent religious fractures joined the continuing rivalry between eastern and western wings of Christianity. Heretical sects from time to time challenged the teachings and organizations of the established institutions. Particularly significant were early schisms of the Bogomils in the Balkan peninsula and of the Albigensians in France. Persecuted by both Roman Catholic and Eastern Orthodox Christians, the Bogomils adopted Islam after the Ottoman conquest, their descendants becoming the Muslim Bosnians of the former Yugoslavia.

The most profound European religious upheaval was the Protestant Reformation that took place in northern and central Europe in the fifteenth century. It sprang from resistance to the centralized control of Roman Catholicism by an Italian-based clergy, and it reflected other cultural divisions. After decades of warfare, Protestants and Catholics eventually agreed that the faith of hereditary heads of European states would be the required religion of their subjects. Contemporary contrasts between many peoples of Europe date back to this compromise, including the division between Dutch speakers in the Protestant Netherlands and in Catholic Belgium, and between French speakers in Protestant Geneva and Catholic eastern France. The current violence in Northern Ireland is a lingering echo of this old division (Figure 2-3).

A decentralized religious organization prevailed in the lands of Eastern Orthodox Christianity, perhaps defusing the potential for a schism comparable to the Protestant Reformation. In southeastern Europe each major linguistic group came to have its own self-governing church. As recently as the immediate post–World War II period, the Macedonians of Yugoslavia created an autocephalous Macedonian Orthodox church, separate from the national churches of the Bulgars, Serbs, and Greeks. In 1993 a similar autocephalous Montenegrin Orthodox church was formed. However, these religious entities are not recognized by neighboring Orthodox peoples.

The Emergence of National Languages

Patterns of language and religion thus had close relationships with patterns of political organization in the course of development of European culture over two millennia. The nineteenth century saw even closer ties, as nations began to flower. Languages particularly served as cornerstones of national identities.

The bonding of peoples into nations had reciprocal effects upon Europe's languages and religions. The modernizations of society that precipitated the development of national identity required ever larger proportions of the population to be educated. Literacy no longer remained a privilege for the few. Up through the Middle Ages, the educated wrote (and often spoke) classical languages that had been perpetuated by the religious organizations. These included Latin in the Roman Catholic world, and Greek and Old Church Slavonic in the lands of Eastern Orthodoxy. In northern Europe, the Reformation saw the appearance of the Bible in local tongues, fostering particularly the development of the Germanic languages.

In the larger states and empires, dominant languages assimilated ever-higher proportions of speakers of divergent vernaculars. In England, the Celtic-speaking areas steadily diminished: Gaelic preserved itself only in the highlands and offshore islands of Scotland, Welsh retreated to the northern uplands of Wales, speakers of Erse (Irish) became confined to Ireland's Atlantic fringe, and Cornish disappeared completely. Germanization similarly proceeded in Prussia, absorbing substantial numbers of former Polish speakers and all but obliterating the Slavic Sorbs of the Spree valley. In Austria, German replaced the Slavic dialect of the Slovenes who lived on the western margins of the Hungarian plain, leaving Slovenian speakers only in the valleys and basins of the Karawanken and Julian Alps.

The decline of many local languages was fostered by their lack of development of a written form. How-

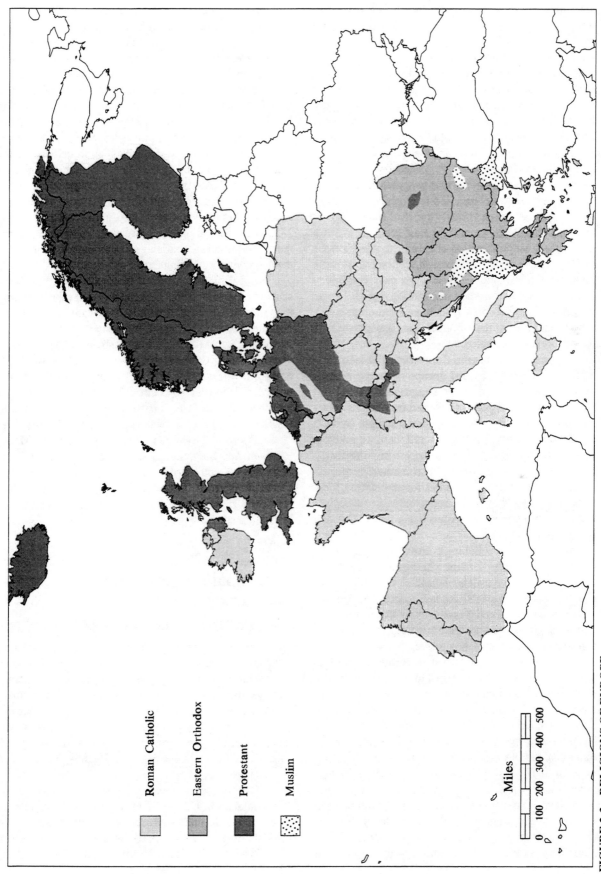

Roman Catholic

Eastern Orthodox

Protestant

Muslim

Miles

0   100 200 300 400 500

FIGURE 2-3   RELIGIONS OF EUROPE

ever, individuals emerged during the nineteenth century who took an interest in creating a literary language for most such groups. Thus, the Viennese-educated Vuk Karadzhich undertook the task of establishing a grammar and orthography for writing his native Serbian. His simple rules of "write as you speak and speak as you write" had counterparts in many areas. Numerous local vernaculars have managed to persist in Europe without literary forms, including Galician in northwestern Spain, Alsatian in eastern France, and Friulian in northeastern Italy. A Macedonian literary language appeared only in the mid-twentieth century.

National sentiments have led to attempts to resurrect some languages that virtually had died out, particularly in the United Kingdom. The most enduring effort has been the Irish preservation of Erse by making it the official language of Éire. Although 95 percent of the population of Ireland speak and write only English, Celtic Erse appears in road signs, official records, and occasional literary works. Children are exposed to it in school. The Gaelic of the highland Scots has seen similar attempts at perpetuation.

The last Celtic speaker in Cornwall died late in the eighteenth century, but local groups in recent years have sought to revive the Cornish language. Although it was not a written language, interested individuals collected information on vocabulary and grammar in the eighteenth century while it was still being spoken. Modern revival groups have had success in producing literary works, but they have been frustrated in questions of pronunciation. As a basis for re-creating the spoken language they have elected to utilize the distinctive English sound patterns spoken in the tiny Cornwall port of Mousehole.

Intellectuals in Edinburgh and Glasgow have endeavored to bring "Lallans (Lowlands) Scottish" back to life. Unlike the Celtic Gaelic of the highlands, Lallans was a version of Germanic Anglo-Saxon differing in vocabulary and pronunciation from the English of England. Its attempted revival has yet to gain significant popular appeal, however.

Similar politically motivated European intellectuals have successfully managed to distance their peoples from related dominant groups by creating new literary and even spoken languages. Norwegians adopted Landesmål, a rural dialect spoken west of Oslo, as the basis for a Norwegian language that differed from the traditional pure Danish Riksmål of the capital city. Slovaks similarly took pains to make their literary language quite different from Czech. In the former Yugoslavia, Croatians emphasized minor differences in vocabulary and pronunciation to assert the distinctiveness of their language from the virtually identical Serbian. Their assertiveness is reinforced by the contrast between the Latin alphabet that they have adopted with the Cyrillic alphabet used by the Serbians.

The increasing demands for general literacy saw standardizations of grammars, vocabularies, and spellings in most of Europe's written languages. In several cases such standardization bore a noticeably artificial character. Thus, the intellectuals in Romania who forged literary Romanian in the mid-nineteenth century took pains to purge from their dictionary the multitude of Slavic and Magyar words that flourished in the Latin-based popular language. Initially they employed Cyrillic to write the new literary language because it was the alphabet of the Old Church Slavonic traditionally used in Romanian Orthodox church services. In the 1850s, writers adopted the Latin alphabet to emphasize the "westernness" that played such an important part in the growing Romanian national iconography.

Local dialects continued to coexist with the new standardized written and spoken languages, particularly in rural areas. Educated people in many communities became in a sense bilingual, much as black children in America know the "king's English" of school and television while communicating with each other in the argot of the ghettoes. During a trip from the Italian border to the Black Sea through southeastern Europe, a trained ear will detect a steady change from village to village in the speech of the south Slavic peoples. The standardized Slovenian, Croatian, Serbian, Macedonian, and Bulgarian literary languages compartmentalize this spectrum of local languages into discrete segments, however, with administrative and state borders marking discontinuities of spellings, vocabularies, and even alphabets.

Principal Linguistic Divisions in Europe

As a result of this long set of evolutionary processes, the linguistic map of Europe is quite complex. Peoples speaking more than forty different languages occupy the Continent's two million square miles. In comparison, Anglo-America—the United States and Canada—is three times larger, yet has only the three major languages of English, French, and Spanish (although an additional fifteen languages are spoken by remnant aboriginal groups).

Each of the discrete languages of Europe tends to be dominant in a territory of its own, with the exceptions of Yiddish and Romany, which are spoken by the widely dispersed Ashkenazi Jews and Gypsies. Most languages are derived from the parent Indo-European,

TABLE 2-2 THE LANGUAGES OF EUROPE

I. Indo-European Family
  A. Romance Group (Derived from Latin)
    1. Catalan (Spain)
    2. Corsican (France)
    3. French
    4. Friulian (Italy)
    5. Galician (Spain)
    6. Italian
    7. Portuguese
    8. Romansch (Switzerland)
    9. Romanian
    10. Spanish
    11. Vlach (Yugoslavia)
    12. Walloon (Belgium)
  B. Germanic Group
    1. Alsatian (France)
    2. Danish
    3. Dutch
    4. English
    5. Faeroese (Denmark)
    6. Flemish (Belgium)
    7. Frisian (Netherlands, Germany)
    8. German
    9. Icelandic
    10. Norwegian
    11. Swedish
    12. Yiddish
  C. Slavic Group
    1. Bulgarian
    2. Czech
    3. Macedonian
    4. Polish
    5. Serbo-Croatian (Yugoslavia)
    6. Slovak
    7. Slovenian (Yugoslavia)
    8. Sorbian (Germany)
    9. Ukrainian
  D. Celtic Group
    1. Breton (France)
    2. Erse (Ireland)
    3. Gaelic (Scotland)
    4. Welsh
  E. Illyrian Group
    1. Albanian
  F. Hellenic Group
    1. Greek
  G. Indo-Aryan Group
    1. Romany (Gypsy)
II. Semitic-Hamitic Family
    1. Maltese
III. Uralian Family
  A. Finnic Group
    1. Finnish
    2. Lappish
  B. Ugrian Group
    1. Magyar (Hungarian)
IV. Altaic Family
  A. Turkic Group
    1. Gagauz (Romania)
    2. Turkish

but a half dozen have Uralo-Altaic origins, and Basque still confounds the linguists concerned with its origins. The Indo-European languages are conventionally divided into six groups, of which Romance, Germanic, and Slavic are major. Table 2-2 summarizes these linguistic relationships.

Patterns of States

Thirty-three states now occupy the territory of Europe. They range in size from Vatican City, with a minuscule 109 acres, to France, which has 211,000 square miles. Like the patterns of languages and religions, Europe's states are a legacy of a turbulent past.

For most of its history before establishment of the Roman Empire (and also in its immediate aftermath), political organization in Europe was localized, rather than expansive. Fortified trading communities devel-

oped in the Mediterranean basin, numbering as many as 600 by the fifth century B.C. They both contested with each other and formed alliances when threatened by outside forces. Phillip of Macedon and his son Alexander welded the Greek city states into large personal empires, adding territories as far away as India. However, these territories lacked institutions to extend their existence beyond the lifespans of their founders. Elsewhere in the Continent, tribal communities were general. These frequently shifted locations, reflecting an identity based upon group kinship rather than upon the shared territory that characterized the Mediterranean communities.

City-states and tribal organization have lingered in Europe up to modern times. Hamburg, Bremen, and Oldenburg flourished as independent entities until the unification of Germany in 1871. In the twentieth century, Danzig (Gdansk), Fiume (Rijeka), and Trieste functioned for several years as free entities between states that had conflicting claims to them. The mountains of Albania and Yugoslav Montenegro still harbor groups whose allegiance is more to tribe than to greater national identity.

The Roman Empire

The Roman Empire united the Mediterranean city-states with the tribal areas of western Europe. In the second century B.C. the empire stretched from southern Scotland to Egypt and Syria. Its growth was not the result of some grand design, but occurred principally as a result of preoccupation with security. Rome defeated adversaries and gained their territories, only to come into contact with new groups that became new adversaries. It maintained its territories with relatively few troops, relying upon general fear of its legions and its ability to transport soldiers quickly to any isolated trouble spots. Rome ruled indirectly through local leaders whose loyalty was maintained by subsidies and threats of legion attack. They were supervised by small contingents from Rome whose main task was to collect taxes and recruit soldiers for the legions.

Roman emperors imposed a common set of laws and practices within their realm. They established roads and fortified places that set the sites for subsequent overland routes and cities that have shaped Europe's geography to this day. The role of the Roman Empire in the establishment of Latin-based languages and the Christian religion has been noted above. Rome influenced groups outside of its clearly delimited boundaries, particularly the Germanic tribes east of the Rhine River.

The Roman Empire was a successful state for several centuries (see Figure 2-4). It provided conditions of law and order and it maintained an infrastructure of transportation and communication that facilitated the economic and cultural development of its far-flung peoples. Its patterns of regional specialization and exchange reinforced the coherence brought about by its military power and its effective administration.

Internal problems and external pressures eventually led to a dissolution of the empire, although a last remnant lingered until 1453, when it was terminated by the Ottoman Turks. A profound change occurred in A.D. 395, when the empire was split into two parts with capitals, respectively, in Rome and Byzantium (Constantinople). The ancient line of division can still be seen on the landscape of southeastern Europe, separating Roman Catholic Croats, Hungarians, and Slovaks from Eastern Orthodox Montenegrins, Serbs, and Romanians.

FIGURE 2-4   THE ROMAN EMPIRE IN THE FIRST CENTURY A.D.

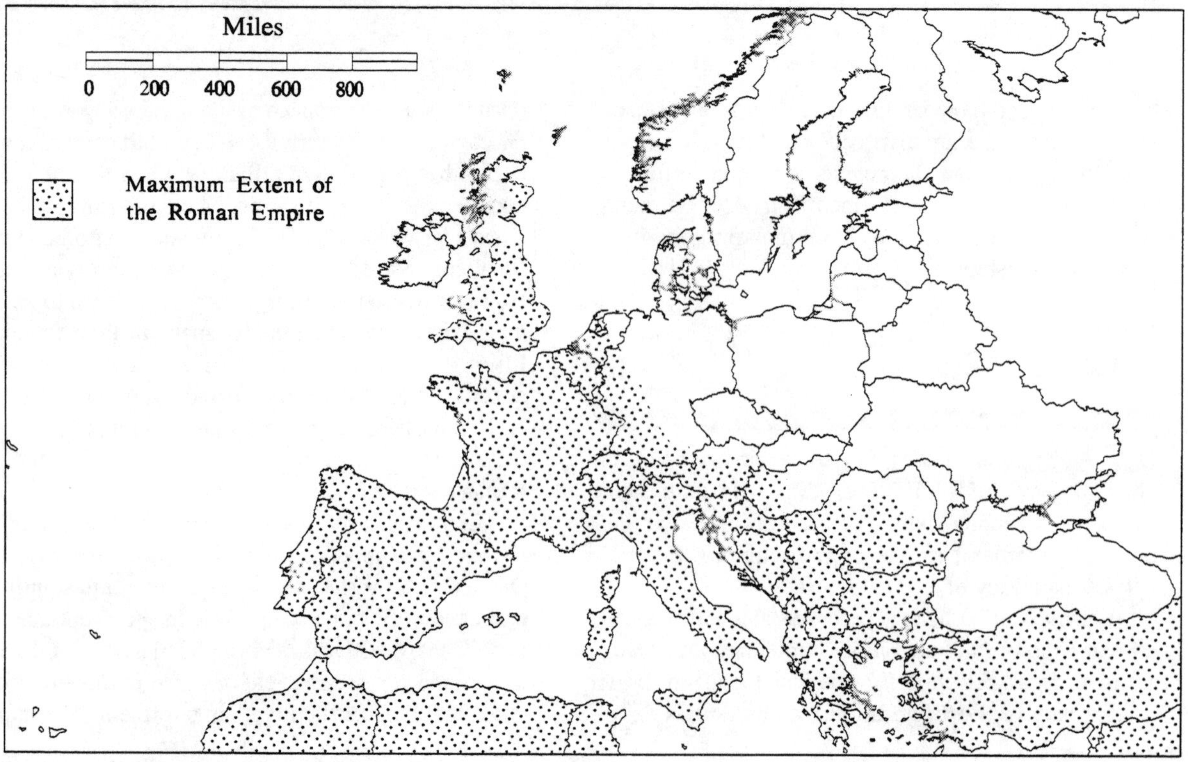

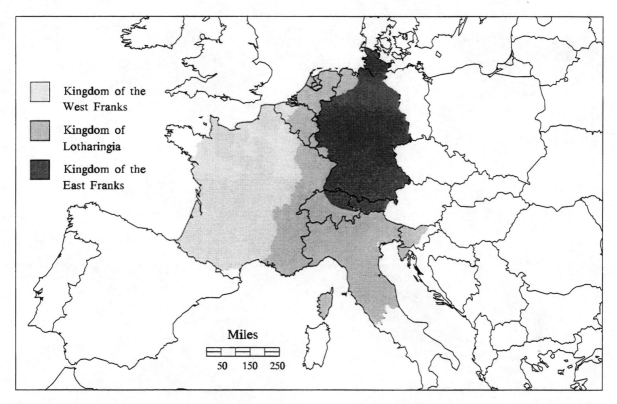

FIGURE 2-5 CHARLEMAGNE'S EMPIRE IN A.D. 843

The Roman Empires's failure led to the descent of Europe into the Dark Ages. Germanic and Slavic tribal groups, hitherto kept at bay by imperial legions, pressed into its developed lands as far as the Mediterranean and Atlantic. Anarchy made trade between contrasting regions impossible. The magnificent road system lost its reason for existence. Political organization again became a local affair.

The glories of the empire were remembered through the period of darkness, however. Christian monasteries perpetuated awareness of the benefits of a broad territorial state. Individuals from time to time sought to re-create the empire. The most successful was Charlemagne, who by A.D. 800 had welded together most of present-day France, Italy, and the German-speaking lands into a personal domain. His realm was apportioned among three grandsons in 843 (see Figure 2-5). The westernmost, the Kingdom of the West Franks, perpetuated itself as France. Eastward, the Kingdom of the East Franks evolved into the Holy Roman Empire, a successful defensive coalition of a multitude of tiny territorial units. Stretched along the Rhine and Po river valleys was a third kingdom, Lotharingia, which soon lost its

identity, becoming a frontier of contention between its neighbors. It remains today a zone of political-geographic instability between France and Germany.

Another example of the lingering role of the empire as a model for political organization was the adoption of the title "Tsar" ("Caesar") by the rulers of the Muscovite state of the sixteenth century. In similar vein, the head of the new German Empire of 1871 was designated "Kaiser." In the mid-twentieth century, Benito Mussolini sought to re-create a new Rome-controlled Mediterranean empire, and Adolf Hitler's aspirations for a "new order" in Europe had overtones of the old imperial domain, particularly in its symbolism.

Contrasts Among Western, Middle, and Eastern Europe

The evolution of Europe's political map after Charlemagne's empire took different paths in western, middle, and eastern Europe. In the west, relatively large territo-

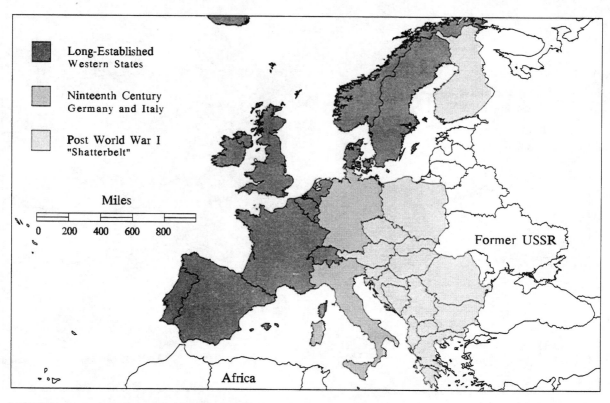

Long-Established
Western States

Ninteenth Century
Germany and Italy

Post World War I
"Shatterbelt"

Miles

0   200   400   600   800

Former USSR

Africa

FIGURE 2-6   EUROPEAN STATES GROUPED BY RELATIVE AGE

rial states had emerged by the sixteenth century. In addition to France, these included England, the Netherlands, Denmark, Sweden, Switzerland, Portugal, and Spain. A middle belt of Italian- and German-speaking territories remained fragmented into more than 300 feudal units until unification into new Italian and German nation-states in 1864 and 1871, respectively. In Europe's eastern belt, several large states emerged in the medieval period, including Poland, Bohemia, Hungary, Croatia, Serbia (Raska), and Bulgaria. However, all eventually came under the domination of four externally based empires: Ottoman, Habsburg, Prussian, and Russian. By the end of World War I, the empires had disintegrated, giving rise to a series of new states in a region that came to be known as the "shatterbelt" of Europe (see Figure 2-6).

The emergence of national identities during the nineteenth century affected state development in all three belts of Europe. These generally reinforced the territorial integrity of the long-established states in the west, although minority national political movements led to the twentieth-century separation of Norway from Sweden, Iceland from Denmark, and Ireland from the United Kingdom. The politically fragmented Italians

and Germans of the middle belt achieved national unities in the early decades of the nineteenth century that led eventually to statehoods not long after mid-century. In the east the old empires crumbled in part from the national disaffection of their subject peoples.

Economic distinctions. In addition to differences in language, religion, and political organization, Europeans also find themselves fragmented by disparities in economic development. Although virtually all European states have both developed areas and pockets of poverty, the Continent as a whole can be visualized as being divided between two contrasting regions whose outlines bear little direct relationship to political patterns. Northwestern and central Europe have emerged as one of the world's most developed and affluent regions. They have evolved commercialized and industrialized economies. A high proportion of their populations lives in cities. Southern and eastern Europe have lagged behind. They retain high rural populations, many of whom are barely above subsistence level. Their industry is confined mainly to capital cities and significant resource complexes.

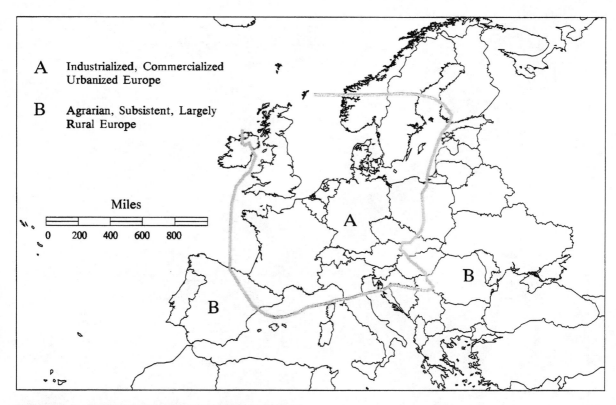

A   Industrialized, Commercialized Urbanized Europe

B   Agrarian, Subsistent, Largely Rural Europe

FIGURE 2-7   EUROPEAN DEVELOPMENT REGIONS

The line between the two areas can roughly be viewed as an arc swung about 750 miles from a pivot in London. As the map of European development patterns shows (Figure 2-7), the division cuts across Spain, France (Corsica), Italy, the former Yugoslavia, Hungary, Czechoslovakia, Poland, and the Norden countries. It also divides Ireland. Each of these states has internal political problems derived from contrasting regional economic development. In the former states of Yugoslavia and Czechoslovakia the economic division exacerbated profound differences in national identity that ultimately caused territorial separation. Spain faces a similar threat to its unity.

Reasons for the economic division are many. In contrast to a general poverty of natural resources in Europe's southern and eastern extremities, its center and northwest were generally blessed by an abundance of resources needed by nineteenth-century industry, most notably coking coal and iron ore. Suitable coal extends in a series of deposits from southern England through northeastern France, southern Belgium, the Ruhr valley of Germany, and on to Silesia in southwestern Poland. Iron ore is found in scattered deposits throughout the territory. In the early stages of industri-

alization much was taken from accumulations in swamps and bogs that were a legacy of the last glacial period. This was smelted by charcoal baked from trees in the Continent's shrinking forests. By the mid-nineteenth century, the baking of bituminous coal into gray, porous coke provided a more ample and desirable raw material for large-scale production of iron and steel. Substantial hard-rock deposits of iron ore occurred in England, northeastern Spain, and the Alsace-Lorraine region of France.

Europe's developed region also has some of the Continent's most fertile farmlands. They particularly lie in a belt roughly coincident with the coal deposits. Tremendous wind storms at the end of the Ice Age resulted in thick deposits of *loess* in areas where topography slowed the movement of air.

Developed Europe also can thank a social order that facilitated and encouraged the accumulation of wealth necessary for investment in productive facilities. Serfdom ended early, to be followed by revolution in agriculture. People flocked to cities—or were driven to them—providing an essential labor force as well as an increasingly affluent market. The southern and eastern fringes of Europe, in contrast, retained large medieval

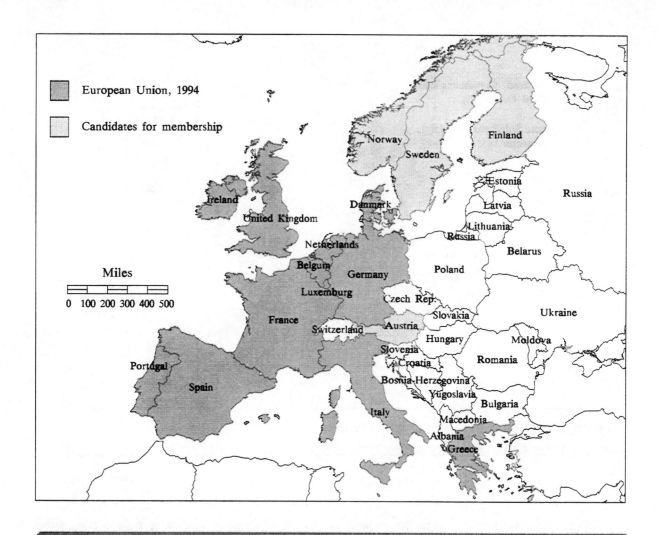

FIGURE 2-8 THE EUROPEAN UNION

estates, *latifundia*, well into the twentieth century. A high proportion of farm workers were without land of their own, working precariously as seasonal laborers. Those who had land were confined to so little that they could scarcely feed themselves. Neither they nor their governments could accumulate any capital wealth.

External domination also differentiated the two economic realms of Europe. Russian and Hungarian control brought little modernization to their sections of east central Europe, while adjacent Prussian and Austrian territories saw substantial progress. The Iberian and Balkan peninsulas long were frontier zones with the Islamic world and remained isolated from many of the processes of change that led to the emergence of developed Europe. They also were handicapped by the economic protectionism adopted by most European states during the nineteenth century. They were denied easy access for their wares in markets of their more affluent

neighbors and suffered from government support for inefficient producers within their states.

Many geographers also see a historical process of spatial diffusion contributing to growth for the north and west. The Industrial Revolution originated in the British Isles in a context of abundant raw materials, capital, and labor. Technological and organizational innovations taking place there spread first to outlying regions of the United Kingdom, and then across the English Channel to nearby coalfields of France and Belgium. As industry took hold in new areas, adjacent peoples became acculturated to the new way of living, paving the way for further development. Change over territory occurred slowly, however, and was slowed or stopped by wars and political barriers.

A primary rationale for the totalitarian movements after World War I in Europe was to accelerate economic development. The worldwide economic depression of the 1930s particularly hurt fledgling growth in southern and eastern Europe. Communists and Fascists competed for seizure of power from regimes that proved increasingly ineffectual in the face of internal and external stress. Economic disparities between regions contributed to popular demands for strong leadership. However, dictatorships in Italy and Spain did little to promote growth or redress territorial inequalities during the 1930s. Early developed regions in the north of these states continue to widen their lead over their more traditional southern territories.

Equalizing uneven development was a unifying theme of Communist leaderships installed in Eastern Europe after World War II. Regimes could point to substantial progress in establishing industrial plants in such past economically backward regions as Russian Poland, Slovakia, Serbia, Bosnia, and Macedonia. The traditionally agrarian states of Romania, Bulgaria, and Albania developed substantial manufacturing activity. However, full modernization throughout the region was not achieved by the time that their socialist systems collapsed in 1990. Continuing regional economic contrasts served to augment national differences and to cause the territorial fragmentation of Czechoslovakia and Yugoslavia. The newly found unity of the Germans similarly had to contend with an eastern region notably ill-equipped to compete with the affluent society of the west.

Europe's economic inequalities have been perpetuated by its division among numerous sovereign states as well as by its schism into contending political and military blocs. However, it has taken substantial strides to overcome the consequences of fragmentation. Beginning from a core involving France, West Germany, Italy, and the Benelux countries, Western Europe has gradually created a common market that facilitates economies of large-scale production and the utilization of regional comparative advantages. Internal borders have become steadily less frictional to the flow of raw materials, finished goods, and labor forces. A dozen states now belong to the European Union (EU), which achieved greater economic unity in 1992 by a variety of measures, including harmonization of regulatory statutes. Its goal of a common currency remains elusive, however.

This common market has provided a "have one's cake and eat it too" situation for its member states. The benefits of production efficiencies through removal of tariff barriers have complemented political satisfactions for nations by having states of their own. However, the success of the common market also has its potential politically destabilizing effects. Minority nations see possibilities of sovereignty for the small areas they inhabit without a sacrifice of economic well-being. If the citizens of Luxemburg can enjoy high living standards in their 1,000-square-mile territory, why not the Flemings of northern Belgium or the Bretons of northwestern France? As will be detailed in the following chapters, virtually all European states face separatist pressures from minority nations within them.

Similar association of the Communist states within the Council of Mutual Economic Assistance had fewer positive results due to structural problems of integrating their centrally managed economies. Since the revolutions of 1989/90, all these states harbor the goal of becoming part of the European Union. However, the legacy of more than four decades of socialist systems has left them unattractive candidates for economic absorption by the association of Western states, particularly as the latter reflect upon the problems Germany is experiencing in attempting to integrate the former German Democratic Republic.

Bibliography

BARZINI, L., *The Europeans*, New York: Simon & Schuster, 1983.

EAST, W.G., *An Historical Geography of Europe*, 5th ed. New York: Dutton, 1966.

HOFFMAN, G.W., ed., *Europe in the 1990s: A Geographic Analysis*. New York: John Wiley, 1989.

JORDAN, T.C., *The European Culture Area*, 2nd ed. New York: Harper & Row, 1988.

POUNDS, N.J.G., and S.S. Ball, "Core Areas and the Development of the European States System," *Annals of the Association of American Geographers*, Vol. 54 (March 1964), pp. 24–40.

3

Western Europe

WESTERN Europe is the hearth area of development of both the modern territorial state and the concept of nationhood. After millennia as a backward outer periphery of Western civilization, Western Europe in the sixteenth century came to dominate all of Europe and, indeed, the world. Its role as a center of production and innovation waned during the twentieth century, but steps taken in recent decades toward economic and political unification hold promise of revived leadership.

Europe's western fringe constitutes the Continent's most livable part. The area's 2,500 miles of latitudinal frontage along the Atlantic benefits from the ability of the ocean to serve as a climatic moderator. The oceanic water absorbs and holds much of the direct insolation (solar radiation) from the sun, releasing this stored energy in an even manner throughout the year. Because maritime air in these midlatitudes passes eastward over the lands, summer temperatures are more moderate than in continental areas to the east, where earth and vegetation immediately reradiate absorbed insolation to create higher air temperatures. Winter along the Atlantic Coast is warm for its northerly position because of the constant onshore movement of evenly released oceanic heat, in contrast to temperatures in continental areas, which drop precipitously as outgoing radiation from the earth exceeds incoming radiation from the sun.

Western Europe has long benefitted from more than a fair share of Europe's natural resources. These include arable soils on the lands, fishery wealth in the seas, and vital minerals underground. The region includes the western terminus of the belt of bituminous coal that extends from the fringes of the Pennine Mountains of England to the Donets Basin of the eastern Ukraine. Beds of iron ore and other minerals are located in many regions. Its livable climates, fertile soils, and rich minerals contributed to the early development of a dense concentration of population. Most of its territory is inhabited, aside from the climatically marginal lands of northern Scandinavia and the mountainous regions.

The pattern of West European states assumed much of its present outline by 1500. In contrast to the plethora of tiny feudal units contending with each other in German and Italian areas to the east, strong individuals and families on Europe's western margins were able to forge extensive domains that eventually evolved into the region's modern nation-states. The size of the units reflects both the area's physical geography and the status of transportation and communication during this period of political development. The presence of the English Channel, the North Sea, and the Baltic Sea, as well as the Alps and Pyrenees Mountains, resulted in an insulation of cultural developments, however easily the water bodies could be crossed by marauding armies. General difficulties of movement overland, particularly in areas of rough topography, set practical limits to effective control and administration from seats of power, with consequent confinements of areas in which governmentally induced homogenization took place.

Most of the region's boundaries have been fixed for 250 years. Their locations along shores and mountain crests also mark the edges of cultural groups, all of which have evolved into distinctive nations. The eastern border of France is an exception to this generalization, but its long duration has meant that French speakers to its east developed separate national identities within Belgium and Switzerland. The only major Western European irredentist group is in Northern Ireland, and it is the result of superimposition of a state border across that island in the early twentieth century.

Modern world economic development had its origins in Western Europe. The area saw the beginnings of commercialization of agriculture that led to the Industrial Revolution. Abetted by rich natural resources, Western Europe developed the world's first major industrial regions. Modernization did not take place uniformly within its small states, however. Each state evolved contrasts between affluent and depressed regions. In most cases thriving development occurred in core areas around capital cities, but peripheral zones lagged in advancement. A notable exception is in Spain, where the peripheral Basque and Catalonian areas of the northeast became modernized while the remainder of the state, including centrally located Madrid, languished.

The political geography of Western Europe is best viewed through consideration of the distinctive characteristics of the five major political geographic regions into which it falls. These are France, the United Kingdom, the Low Countries and Switzerland, the Norden states, and Iberia. (See Table 3-1.)

France

In many ways France is the pivotal state of Western Europe. It is the western apex of the main Eurasian peninsula upon which European civilization has developed. Iberia, the British Isles, and the Scandinavian

TABLE 3-1 WESTERN EUROPE

Two large, rival, long-established multinational states in addition to the twentieth-century nation-state of Ireland form the region of Western Europe. Each one of the large states has peripheral groups with economic and cultural grievances. Highly centralized and centralizing France contrasts with the governmentally devolved and accommodating United Kingdom.

State	Total Population	Area (sq. miles)	Distinctive Features of Group
France	58,000,000	210,000	
Dominant Nation and % Total			
French, 85%			Romance (French) language, Anticlerical Roman Catholic
Significant Regional Groups and % Total			
Corsicans, <1%			Romance (Corsican) language, Devout Roman Catholic
Occitanians, 3%			Romance (Languedoc) language, Devout Roman Catholic
Bretons, 3%			Celtic heritage and language (Breton, but most also speak French), Devout Roman Catholic
Alsatians, 2%			Germanic (Alsatian) language, Devout Roman Catholic
Basques, <1%			Unique Basque language, Roman Catholic
United Kingdom	58,000,000	95,000	
Dominant Nation and % Total			
English, 82%			Mixed Germanic/Romance (English) language, Anglican
Significant Regional Groups and % Total			
Scots, 10%			Mixed Germanic/Romance (English) language, Presbyterian
Ulstermen, 2%			Mixed Germanic/Romance (English) language, Anglican
Welsh, 2%			Celtic heritage and language (Welsh, but most speak English), Protestant
Potential Trouble Area and Possible Adversary			
Ulster (Ireland)	1,500,000	5,500	
Ireland (Éire)	3,500,000	27,000	
Dominant Nation and % Total			
Irish, 94%			Celtic heritage, mixed Germanic/Romance (English) language, Roman Catholic

states and Finland constitute peripheral realms lying beyond it. France is the only state that embraces both Mediterranean and north European cultures.

Its area of 210,000 square miles is the greatest in Europe outside the former Soviet Union. The majority of this territory has been associated within a single state of France for 1,200 years (Figure 3-1). The country has long benefitted from its large size, although it should be noted that it always has been smaller than the combined territories of the German-speaking area to its east, including the German Empire of 1871.

Like other segments of the Roman Empire, the territory of France fragmented into tiny political units during the Dark Ages. In the ninth century, Charlemagne united the quarreling entities into a personal empire that extended well across central Europe. The western third of his empire became the Kingdom of the West Franks in 843, when Charlemagne's domain was

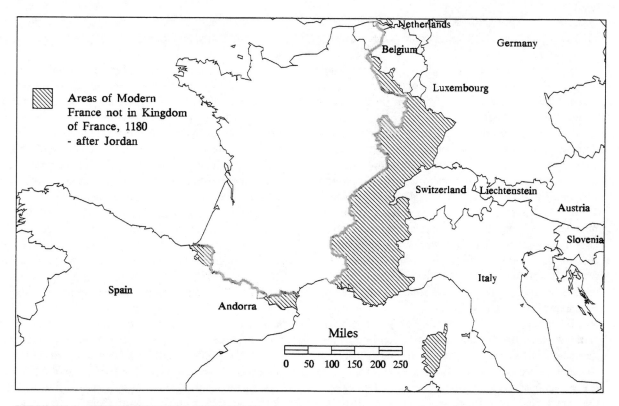

FIGURE 3-1   HISTORIC LANDS OF FRANCE

divided among his heirs into three parts. It then fell back into a period of feudal disunity until powerful kings again could forge a strong territorial unit. Paris became the center of this development, benefitting from the natural defensiveness of its marshy site and from its central position permitting easy communication with other regions.

Although France would seem to be a "natural" unit, its neighbors have long contested its peripheral territories. The Muslim Moors, who conquered and long controlled Iberia, moved for a time into France's southwestern corner. The Kingdom of the East Franks, which evolved into the Holy Roman Empire, challenged France's eastern margins, and the Norman kings of England struggled for centuries to retain their patrimony of Atlantic and Channel coastlands in Aquitane and Normandy. The Hundred Years' War of 1337–1453 finally resulted in the English being driven from most of the mainland. England held a bridgehead at Calais until 1553, but now only the Channel Islands remain as a token of the former vast British holdings in the French culture world.

France's border with Spain traversing the Pyrenees Mountains was settled in 1659. The principality of Andorra, jointly controlled by France and Spain, is a tiny reminder of the former independence of this thinly populated mountainous region. France's main frontage along the Mediterranean has not been challenged since the time of the Moors. The principality of Monaco is but another legacy of a feudal past. The Grimaldi family has dominated its 461 acres since 1297. It came under French control only in 1861.

France extended its borders into the Mediterranean to incorporate the island of Corsica in 1761. It also developed and maintained a foothold along the African shore in Algeria in the 1830s. This lasted for more than a century until the French were driven out in 1962. The boundary with the Italians and Swiss running through the Maritime Alps and Jura Mountains has been stable since the fifteenth century, with the exception of the 6,500 square miles of Savoy and Nice that became part of France only in 1860.

Its most contentious border has been in the northeast. Unlike the empty zones of seas and mountains that mark its other boundaries, the frontier with the Germanic culture world lies across a continuously populated region of plains and low mountains. Although German-speaking tribes have lived continuously on both sides of the Rhine River since Roman times, French governments have long considered that river to be a "natural boundary" of France comparable to its long-standing coastal and highland borders. Their eastern neighbor particularly has contested possession of some 5,600 square miles of Rhineland territory in the region known as Alsace and Lorraine.

For most of its recorded history this region was nominally part of the Holy Roman Empire, although it shared much in common with the similarly situated buffer territories of the Low Countries and Switzerland. The French acquired Alsace in 1648 and Lorraine in 1766. The provinces retained their Germanic culture, however, resisting the homogenization that strongly centralized governments had wrought in most of the rest of the kingdom. Radical nationalists after the French Revolution of 1789 saw these inhabitants as foreigners not capable of being assimilated and called for their expulsion across the Rhine.

Beginning in 1870, the territory of Alsace and Lorraine changed hands four times between France and Germany. The German victors of the Franco-Prussian War gained it as war booty. Their quest was for a more defensible border and the "redemption" of the region's Germanic inhabitants. However, the Germans also incidentally acquired one of Europe's richest deposits of iron ore, although technology for its utilization had not yet been developed. The territory was regained by France in 1919, seized by Germany in 1940, and taken over by France again in 1945.

The French have twice sought to incorporate the adjacent German-speaking territory of the Saarland. In addition to lying on the "French" side of the Rhine, the Luxemburg-sized area is a gateway to the ancient invasion route to France known as the "Lorraine Gate." It holds substantial reserves of coal. In 1919 the League of Nations established control over 730 square miles of the region for a period of fifteen years, the French receiving ownership of its coal mines as war reparations. A plebiscite in 1935 saw more than 90 percent of its inhabitants voting to join the territory with Germany, which then occurred. After World War II, the French again claimed the region for reparations. They withdrew troops in 1947, however, and a decade later permitted the region to be absorbed into the German Federal Republic.

The French nation. France rightly receives credit for taking the lead in the evolution of the body of ideas that coalesced to form the basis of the concept of national identity. Although the political and intellectual elite of France, as in other countries, had long identified with their state, the decade that followed the French Revolution of 1789 saw the instillation of a sense of commonality among virtually all its inhabitants. They became

Frenchmen, imbued with regime-propagated ideals of "liberty, equality, and fraternity" and pride in a glorious history.

An important element in French national iconography from its inception has been a notion of the inviolable unity of the state. The greatness of being French is viewed as related to its being the largest and most powerful country in Western Europe. A consequence of the state's shaping of national consciousness is the fact that neighboring peoples awakened politically with quite different outlooks and values. Their national evolutions in many cases were reactions to French unity.

The essence of being French includes an almost mystical reverence for French culture, particularly its language (Figure 3-2). Francien, the regional dialect of the Paris Basin, has become the standard for France. The French exhibit contempt for those who cannot speak it well. There is popular support to protect French from "contamination" by foreign words, particularly those originating in England and America. Although 90 percent of the inhabitants of France speak French, the notion of nationhood has long fallen short of the outer boundaries of the language. The 20 percent of the Swiss population speaking French have been drawn more closely to ideals shared with German and Italian speakers in Switzerland than to the slogans out of Paris. Similarly, the French-speaking Walloons of Belgium have shared only peripherally in the intellectual ferment that has taken place in France.

Part of the Swiss and Walloon abstention from enthusiasm for revolutionary France's proclaimed ideals was reaction to a pronounced anticlericalism that continues to play a role in the French value system. Although nearly the entire population of France has been Roman Catholic, particularly since the seventeenth-century expulsion of the Protestant Huguenots, the popular mood in Paris after the French Revolution has been to denigrate the established church. The assault on religion also has had repercussions upon peripheral regions within France, contributing to general resentments against central authorities.

Other centripetal forces. Although a common notion of nationhood is the principal binding element of modern France, the state benefits from other centripetal forces. Chief among these is the fact that most areas have been together within a single state for centuries. Only the fringe territories of Alsace and Lorraine, Savoy and Nice, and Corsica have traditions that developed under other governments. The significance of being part of a French state for so long relates to the centralizing role of regimes in Paris. They have created a homogeneity in cultural affairs and a coherence in economic activities.

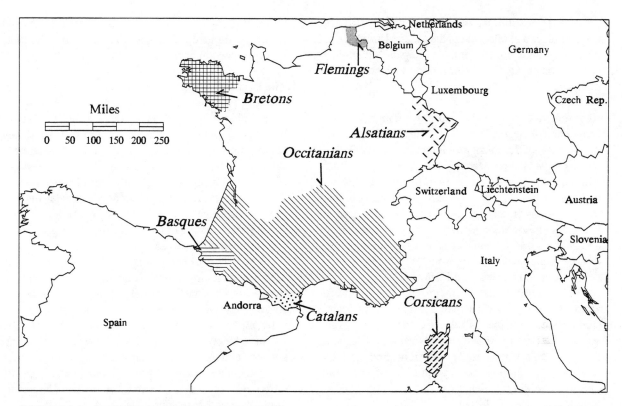

FIGURE 3-2 LANGUAGE GROUPS IN FRANCE

The French monarchy was conspicuous for its imposition of uniform institutions throughout its domain. Louis XIV gained particular note for his centralization policies in the 1600s. Local affairs increasingly became the province of central bureaucracies, as local privileges and traditions were usurped by the Crown. Noble families were severed from their regional power bases by being required to reside in Paris. Civil servants sent out from the center collected taxes and administered justice.

The process continued and accelerated after the French Revolution. The young republic dealt a major deathblow to regional loyalties by abolishing the historic provinces and substituting some ninety small *départements* to manage civil affairs. Like the county lines created in the American Midwest and West during the nineteenth century, the borders of *départements* were designed to be within a half day's horseback travel to their centers. The end result of royal and republican centralization was a state with fewer regional differences in ideals, outlooks, and ways of doing things than found in any of its neighbors. Major disagreements in France tend to be much more of a class than a regional nature.

The development of modern transportation and communication reinforced the institutional linkages of periphery to center. The French kings built post roads that radiated outward from Paris. In the nineteenth century, railroads similarly evolved with Paris as a focus, and much the same can be said for scheduled airlines in the twentieth century. Most long-distance travel from one peripheral part of France to another still tends to pass through Paris.

A second binding force is the network of commercial ties between firms throughout the state. For much of its history France has sought to protect its indigenous enterprises by protective tariffs. These have encouraged commercial associations of all parts of the state with each other and limited dependence upon markets and sources of supply abroad.

The dominance of Paris in all aspects of French civilization is a third element of the coherence of France. Paris is the archetype of a primate city, as the geographer Mark Jefferson defined that concept at the turn of the twentieth century. It contains more than one-sixth of France's population and an even higher proportion of its economic activity. Headquarters of major corporations are situated there, as are the state's most prestigious institutions in education and the arts. London plays a similar role in the United Kingdom, but in neighboring Germany, Italy, and Spain capital cities compete on an equal or lesser footing with one or more rival centers.

Regional problems. The cultural homogeneity and economic coherence of contemporary France have not left it without regional problems, however. Policymakers in Paris are concerned about increasing political and economic difficulties manifesting themselves throughout France's peripheral territories. Local consciousness has emerged to challenge the dominance of Paris. It is based upon distinctive regional languages and cultures and is reinforced by regional economies that are depressed in comparison with the boom qualities of Paris and northeastern France.

A half-dozen different groups are involved, although sentiments for actual separation from France tend to be far less than in other European states. They include the Bretons, Corsicans, Occitanians, Alsatians, Basques, and Catalans. In addition, France faces regional political movements within its few remaining overseas holdings, including the French Antilles, Reunion, and New Caledonia.

Some common elements of the dissident groups are involvement of local intellectuals in reviving languages and organizing movements, support from Roman Catholic clergy resisting two centuries of anticlericalism of the central government, and calls for reestablishment of the historic homeland provinces that were broken up at the time of the French Revolution. Most would seem satisfied with a greater autonomy within France, although nearly all have generated small terrorist movements modelled after the Basque terrorist ETA of Spain.

The French government is increasingly sensitive to the complaints of its peripheral peoples. No longer does it employ heavy-handed measures to repress local languages and cultures. In 1951 it passed a law permitting the use and teaching of local languages and dialects in the schools. Regions regained a degree of their historic identity in 1960 when France grouped the 96 *départements* into 22 "program regions" for economic planning and development. It addressed complaints of overcentralization by far-reaching legislation in 1982 that established locally elected councils in both program regions and *départements*. Presidents of these bodies have taken over the responsibilities of the former Paris-appointed *prefects*, whose duties have been reduced to maintenance of public order. The government has sought to redress the economic imbalance between center and periphery by planned deconcentration of industrial development, a move that has had mixed results. The following sections examine the four major

regional groups: Bretons, Corsicans, Occitanians, and Alsatians. France's Basques, Catalans, and Flemings will be treated in later sections.

The Bretons. The population of France's northwestern Brittany Peninsula constitutes one of its most disaffected minorities. The Bretons speak a Celtic language that has close affinities to Welsh and Cornish. They occupy an area of 10,000 square miles and number about 1,500,000. About half the adult population is now able to speak Breton, though only half of these use it in their daily lives. Among young persons under twenty-five years of age, only 6 or 7 percent employ it regularly. Three-quarters of the Breton-speaking population can neither read nor write their spoken language.

The Brittany Peninsula is mainly a hard crystalline rock plateau jutting into the Atlantic Ocean. Fishing is a significant industry, but its returns are low. The peninsula has few patches of fertile soils, and its maritime climate tends to be marginally cool for crops in the summer. Nevertheless, it produces a quarter of France's potatoes and more than 10 percent of its dairy products and vegetables. Despite government price supports, farm family income is low, and Brittany has a large out-migration to other regions.

Ancestors of the Bretons fled from Great Britain to Brittany in the fourth and fifth centuries A.D., seeking refuge from invading Angles, Saxons, and Jutes. Breton folklore shares much in common with that of the Welsh, including legends of King Arthur. Life was not easy for these settlers in their new homeland in Brittany, however. Beginning in the ninth century, Viking raids devastated their settlements. Their local clergy and aristocracy fled inland to other parts of France, where they acquired the language and culture of their hosts. There was much intermarriage, particularly with Normans. When noble families returned to reclaim their patrimonies, they differed markedly in language and culture from their subjects.

For four centuries Brittany existed as an independent duchy, resisting conquest by both France and England and playing them off against each other during the Hundred Years' War. In 1488 its army was defeated and Brittany was forced to accept union with France through royal marriage. In 1532 the kings of France became dukes of Brittany, signalling full incorporation of the duchy into the French state. The Bretons, however, retained responsibility for internal administration under their traditional representative assembly, whose approval was necessary for levying any taxes. Only Bretons could hold public office, and they could not be conscripted for military service outside their autonomous province.

Attempts by French kings in the seventeenth and eighteenth centuries to infringe upon Breton rights were met by resistance. The Bretons initially welcomed the new regime installed by the French Revolution. However, in 1793 the government decision to establish a French-only school in every community brought immediate resentment. This was followed by abolition of the local assembly and the division of the ancient duchy into five *départements*. Bretons rose in rebellion, but were soon suppressed. In the ensuing century France used a variety of means in an attempt to destroy the use of the Breton language. French republicans viewed the local language as a symbol and a tool of reaction against the Revolution. The language was prohibited in all official purposes, and children were punished for speaking it in school. Nonetheless, 90 percent of the inhabitants of Brittany knew the language as recently as World War I.

In the interwar years there was a cultural revival in Brittany that had strong anti-French overtones. An active terrorist organization derailed trains, destroyed French monuments, and engaged in other acts of violence. Its cause was helped by emanations from Paris, such as the 1925 statement by the French minister for education that "for the unity of France, the Breton language must die." The government repressed all Breton political activities in 1938. During the subsequent Nazi occupation of France, Breton nationalists collaborated with the German invaders with goals comparable to those of the Slovaks and Croats in central Europe. The Germans permitted a cultural flowering, including the teaching of Breton in schools. However, the Bretons did not gain separate statehood. They did stamp themselves as Fascists, however, to the Socialists and Communists who dominated the French Resistance movement. At the end of the war there were harsh reprisals. Language rights that had been gained during the German occupation were lost again.

For two decades after the war there was little overt political activity in Brittany. In 1966, however, the *Front de Libération de la Bretagne* was formed. It was a left-wing separatist group that modelled itself after Basque organizations in Spain. Although it gained headlines by such acts as setting off a bomb in the Palace of Versailles in 1978, it achieved little popular support.

The Bretons no longer face overt government threats to their language. However, radio and especially television have taken their toll, particularly among the young. The limited economic opportunities in Brittany have contributed to a continuing out-migration of Bretons, leaving a population of increasingly older people. Those who remain earn on the average only 70 percent of their counterparts in Paris. Low living costs have prompted many French citizens to come to Brittany to live in retirement homes along its coasts. These newcomers are perceived by the Bretons as condescending and demeaning. Economic hardship and the influx of strangers have kept alive resentments against the rest of France by Bretons, including those who have lost their linguistic heritage.

The Corsicans. The island of Corsica lies 100 miles south of the Mediterranean coastline of France, but only 50 miles west of the Italian Peninsula. Its 3,300 square miles contains a population of 230,000, only 155,000 of whom are native Corsicans. In 1880 the Corsicans numbered 300,000, but declined over ensuing decades by out-migration to metropolitan France and its colonies. Its cropped land decreased from 40 percent to less than 15 percent. In contrast, the Italian island of Sardinia, separated from Corsica by only eight miles of water, has more than doubled its population during the same time period.

Corsica has seen conquerors from all parts of the Mediterranean realm, including Phoenicians, Etruscans, Carthaginians, Romans, Vandals, and Saracens. In 1132 the Genoese first came to the island. They maintained a claim to Corsica until the eighteenth century, although their control was confined primarily to a half-dozen towns along the island coast. They were seldom able to exert effective control over the family clans which dominated the island's interior. The Corsicans declared independence in 1729 and fought the Genoese for the next forty years. Genoa proved unable to defeat them, and in 1768 they sold the island to France, which required an additional decade to finally subdue the inhabitants. It was in this historical context that Corsica's most notable son, Napoleon Bonaparte, was born in the town of Ajaccio in 1769.

The majority of Corsicans speak a language that is similar to the Tuscan dialect of Italian, although speech in the south is closer to the Sardinian dialect. As in other areas, the French have sought to replace Corsican with Parisian French. For many years they refused to acknowledge that the local language could be taught in schools, despite growing use in newspapers and literary magazines.

An autonomous movement gained momentum in the 1930s in reaction to French policies not only concerning the Corsican language but also toward other island traditions, including the leading role of the Catholic church, communal land usage, and the indigenous system of crude justice known as the *vendetta*. Italy tried to exploit such sentiments on the eve of World War II. However, after seizing control of the island in 1942, when Germany moved into unoccupied France, Italy found no mass support for its regime or policies.

Autonomist sentiments were rekindled after 1958 when more than 18,000 *pieds noirs*, former French settlers in Algeria, found new homes on the island. They purchased extensive tracts of agricultural land and established businesses that often were more successful than those of local entrepreneurs. The local population also reacted negatively to the establishment of a major training base for the French Foreign Legion. A general perception grew that Corsica was an exploited colony, despite a formal status as two *départements* of metropolitan France. Another source of discontent was a common belief that the French used the notorious family clans as an agency to control the mass of the population.

Terrorist activities grew during the 1970s. Bombings became a frequent occurrence, numbering 300 per year. Prime attention was given to disruptions in Paris, but violence was also directed against island newcomers, whose homes were frequently subject to arson. Such attacks prompted retaliation by the new settlers, many of whom had personal experience in combatting terrorism in Algeria. Their own underground organization declared war upon the nationalists, often bombing their dwellings.

Autonomous and often separatist sentiments have been abetted by the fact that Corsica is an island remote from the mainland with its own culture and a past history of hard-fought independence. It is also the most poverty-stricken part of France. In addition to the psychological aspects of group distinctiveness generally characteristic of islanders, there are practical problems of access. The island lacks a decent airport, and several major air tragedies have occurred. The large Corsican diaspora working in metropolitan France requires six hours travel by boat to reach the island from Marseilles. A major popular cause has been the demand that tickets for travel on ferries to the island be subsidized by the government to the same extent that train fares are reduced in mainland France.

The French sought to placate the Corsicans by offering cultural and economic concessions. They finally permitted use of the Corsican language in schools and on the radio, and they closed the Foreign Legion base in 1976. In 1960 the island's two *départements* had been made part of a broader developmental "program region" that included a segment of the southeastern mainland. In response to general complaints, the island was at length constituted as a single region and a locally elected president was installed in place of past centrally appointed prefects. In the economic sphere, transfer payments to the island grew to be five times greater than the amount of taxes collected.

Despite such concessions, violence continued during the 1980s. Machine-gun attacks against buildings flying the tricolor French flag were frequent. Assaults often were directed against the island's developing tourism industry. Despite their dramatic activi-

ties, however, separatist groups were not able to motivate more than perhaps 15 percent of the Corsicans to rally to their independence cause. The majority still saw a future with France, but wanted greater autonomy and, particularly, greater recognition of their distinctive language. Many felt the need for a French presence to contain the island's soaring crime rate. Already the island has one gendarme for every hundred citizens, in comparison to a mainland ratio of 1:300.

Playing upon such concerns, the French government offered more concessions to the islanders in late 1990. It sought further to isolate separatist groups by offering the island a greater self-rule and officially recognizing for the first time that Corsicans were a distinctive "people" within France, an action bringing protests from French conservative political groups. Its proposal did seek to strengthen central control over economic development, however, and this appeared to anger all Corsican factions. The most radical of the separatist organizations broke a two-year self-imposed truce and burned to the ground more than forty summer homes of mainland residents in a concerted attack in January 1991.

The Occitanians. The Occitanians constitute the largest minority in France and the most quiescent. Their area in the south of France occupies one-third of the state and contains one-quarter of its population. They are named for their distinctive Occitanian language, whose separate existence has been recognized since the eleventh century. It is a Romance language, with less Germanization than exhibited by Parisian French. It is usually termed *langue d'oc*, which means literally "the language where they use the word '*oc*' to mean 'yes'," as opposed to the northern *langue d'oïl*, which uses the word *oïl* or *oui* for "yes." There are several dialects of Occitanian, the most noted of which is Provençal. Although many works in Occitanian have been published, there is no standard literary form. In part this reflects regional rivalries associated with the different dialects. Occitania is sometimes identified as Languedoc, although northern French speakers usually term it *le Midi* and its people *les Meridionaux*.

For three centuries in the Middle Ages the Occitanians had one of Europe's most sophisticated civilizations. Their principal town of Toulouse became the center for a distinctive Manichean religious sect who called themselves the "Cathari." It had some parallels with the Bogomil religious movement of the Balkan Peninsula. Its leaders were often called Albigensians, since many had come from the town of Albi. Pope Innocent III declared an Albigensian Crusade in the thirteenth century to destroy the heretics. The result was complete defeat for the Cathari, followed by a fearful inquisition and atrocities. Modern Occitanians still harbor a widespread prejudice against Parisians, based in part upon the fate of their ancestors.

Despite its rich cultural heritage, the Occitanian language has been viewed in modern times, even by native speakers, as a vulgar, provincial *patois*. In recent decades, however, it has undergone a cultural revival similar to Breton and Corsican. This is a reflection of the development of a regional consciousness that reacts to the area's economic stagnation and also to images of affluent and haughty northerners who have built vacation and retirement homes in the region, or have come to it as tourists.

As elsewhere in France, local intellectuals have taken the lead in reviving the language and developing political movements for greater autonomy. In contrast to other regional activities, Occitania has witnessed little of the terrorism characteristic of radical regionalists elsewhere. Goals have been for greater autonomy within France, with virtually no calls for separatism.

The Alsatians. The German-speaking population of Alsace and Lorraine has been the most successful in preserving its culture against French pressures for homogenization. Ninety percent of the 1,600,000 people of the Alsace program region continue to speak one of several Alsatian dialects, although 80 to 90 percent also are fluent in French. This contrasts with the situation in the 1930s, when barely half were bilingual. The standard written and cultivated speech of Alsace is High German (*Hochdeutsch*).

Although the Alsatians politically have demonstrated their allegiance to France, their cultural ties remain with the Germanic Rhineland. They affirm the political-geographic truism that rivers unite, not divide, settlements on opposite banks. Many significant German developments had their origins in Alsace. It was the home of numerous German writers and poets. It published the first German-language Bible nearly seven decades before the appearance of Martin Luther's. The first German-language mass after the Reformation was conducted in Strasbourg.

After its acquisition by France in 1648, Alsace enjoyed the status of an occupied territory, retaining its old institutions while affairs in other parts of France underwent increasing centralization from Paris. Its autonomy abruptly ended with the French Revolution, when its territory was incorporated into France and was divided into *départements*. Some 30,000 of its nobility, clergy, and other prominent citizens fled across the Rhine to haven in the German area. Although a majority of Alsatians hailed the Revolution for ending feudalism and providing more economic opportunities, enthusiasm was chilled when it was announced in 1793

that all citizens unable to speak French were to be shot. The degree was happily not carried out, and Alsatians welcomed the statement of Napoleon, "Let them speak German as long as they use their swords in French." A number of Alsatians became generals in Napoleon's army.

During the nineteenth century Alsace faced increasing pressures upon its German language and culture. In 1852 schools were required to use French for instruction, although German was permitted for one lesson every day. Still, sentiments remained far more with France than with the German states. When Alsace was annexed to Germany in 1871, some 50,000 Alsatians fled to France. In 1914 more than 20,000 Alsatian men volunteered for the French army, although 250,000 Alsatians were conscripted into the German forces.

Alsace enjoyed considerable autonomy while part of Germany, gaining its own regional parliament in 1911. It also did well economically. After its return to France following World War I, Alsace lost this customary self-government. The French government attempted to end German teaching in the schools. In 1924 the regime sought to end the close relationship of local government with the Roman Catholic church. Both measures failed, but created local bitterness. Calls during the 1930s for a federal status within France were denounced by Paris as sedition.

Any nostalgia for past associations within Germany was destroyed when Alsace became part of the Third Reich in 1940. The Nazi government declared that German would be the only language in the region, and the names of all inhabitants were required to be Germanized. Speakers of the Alsatian dialect were given two years to master standard German. A half-million Alsatians migrated to France.

Despite their reinvigorated postwar enthusiasm for French ideals, the Alsatians received shabby treatment following reincorporation into France in 1945. The central government again banned German instruction in the schools, and it was only introduced for three hours each week in 1952. As a result, by the mid-1960s, less than 20 percent of the Alsatian population could read or write German, despite the fact that nearly all spoke a dialect of it.

Alsatians renewed demands for greater regional autonomy in the postwar era, although Alsace enjoyed some special dispensations not accorded other minority areas in France. The traditional system of religious control of schools had been allowed to continue. Ties of church to governmental affairs were maintained. Local self-government became more of a reality in 1960 when a program region was established for Alsace, and, after 1982, elected officials managed regional and local affairs. Although Alsatian groups have continued to press for greater autonomy, there have been no terrorist organizations comparable to those of the Bretons and Corsicans. Very little in the way of separatist sentiments exist, and certainly there are no irredentist feelings for Germany.

The region has benefitted from the growing unification of Europe. Establishment of the European Coal and Steel Community and the subsequent European Community have had direct impacts upon industrial development. Strasbourg, Alsace's principal city, became the seat of the European Parliament. Still, the region has remained one of the poorest parts of the Lotharingian Corridor between northern Italy and the Netherlands. A significant number of its citizens find it profitable to commute daily to work in Germany.

The British Isles

Although the region embracing the United Kingdom and the Republic of Ireland, like France, has had a long history of state organization, its development has taken a path quite different from that of its neighbor to the south (Figure 3-3). In contrast to the official centralization and homogenization characteristic of France both before and after its Revolution, governments of the British Isles have long permitted a variety of political relationships to evolve that have allowed a maximum of local control over local affairs. Regional identities have emerged comparable to the fractious nations on the European mainland, but only the Roman Catholic Irish adopted separate sovereignty as a goal and partially achieved it.

The major political entity of the British Isles is often termed "Great Britain." However, that appellation properly designates only the principal island, whose name arose in ancient times to distinguish it from "Little Britain," known now as the Brittany Peninsula of France. The Island of Great Britain covers 89,000 square miles. The adjacent island of Ireland has an area of 33,000 square miles.

The close proximity of the two islands and their separation by broad seas from the rest of Europe would seem to form an ideal basis for the emergence of a single political unit. For the greater part of their history, however, the islands have not been under a single government, and more often than not each has been divided into two or more political units. The two islands are far from being united today. Moreover, it should be noted that regimes based on Great Britain for long periods held extensive territories in what is now France, to say nothing of a worldwide empire upon which "the sun never set."

FIGURE 3-3   THE UNITED KINGDOM AND IRELAND

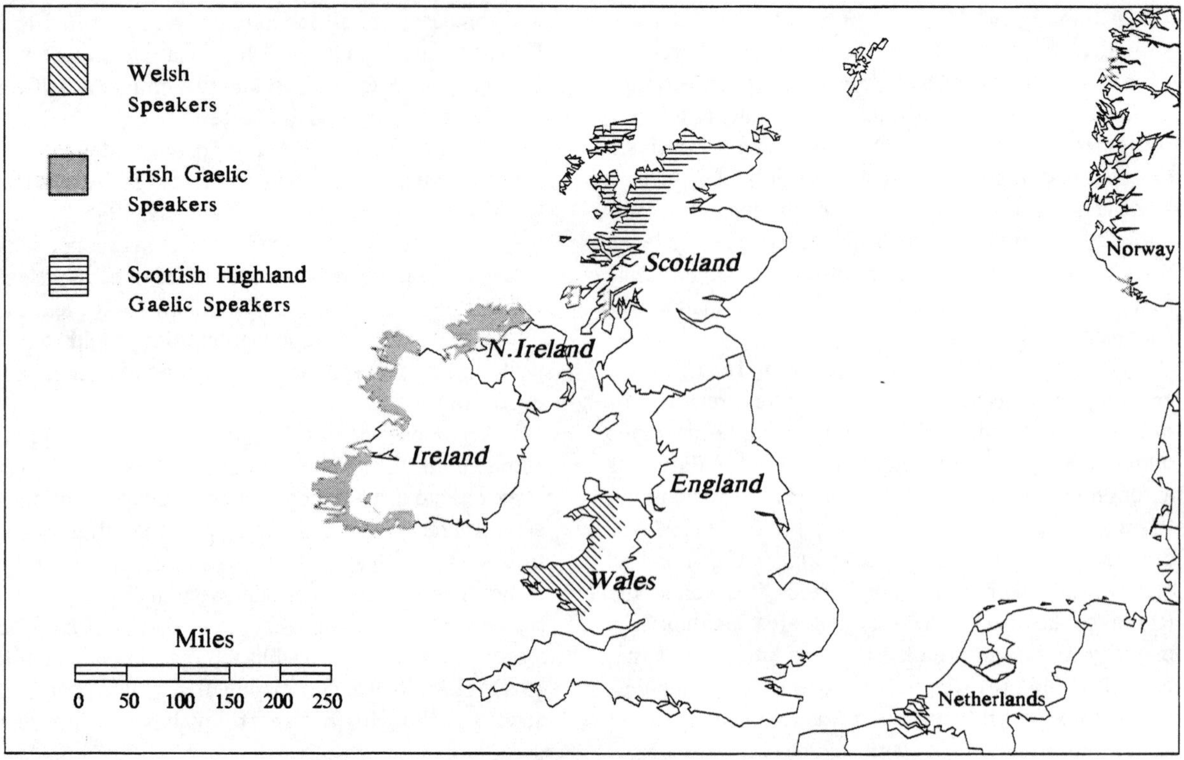

A major driving force in the guerrilla warfare in Northern Ireland is a belief that a united Ireland is "natural" and the present division between the Republic of Ireland and Northern Ireland is "artificial." In reality, of course, all political entities are "artificial" in the sense of being created by the arts of humankind. Other physical units with long histories of political fragmentation that have been seen as "natural" political entities are the "boot" of Italy and the Scandinavian peninsula. Such thinking derives from a conceptualization of territorial features through the agency of maps. Conventional maps tend to be quite misleading abstractions of political space because they usually fail to indicate such critical features as separation of areas of dense settlement by relatively empty zones and significant regional differences in language or other aspects of culture. They also imply a far greater significance to the impact of contrasts between land and water than is warranted by the traditional linking role of maritime travel.

The proper name of the dominant state of the British Isles is the United Kingdom of Great Britain and Northern Ireland, a designation dating from the separation of the Irish Free State in 1921. Prior to that it had been known since 1800 as the United Kingdom of Great Britain and Ireland. The Irish Free State has undergone its own name changes, becoming Éire in 1937 and the Republic of Ireland in 1949. Outside of Ireland and the United Kingdom are the Channel Islands and the Isle of Man, both of which are direct dependencies of the British Crown with their own legislative bodies and taxation systems.

The United Kingdom has a total area of about 95,000 square miles, making it slightly smaller than the American state of Oregon. Its population is 58,000,000. Within this area, England covers approximately 50,000 square miles and has 48,000,000 people; Scotland includes 30,000 square miles with 5,100,000 inhabitants; Wales has 8,000 square miles and 2,800,000 people; and Northern Ireland incorporates 5,400 square miles and 1,600,000 residents. Territory of the Republic of Ireland is 27,000 square miles with a population of 3,600,000. It is an interesting statistic that among states of the world, only Bangladesh, Taiwan, and the Netherlands have population densities per square mile that are higher than those of England and Wales.

For most of the past two centuries the United Kingdom has played a substantial, if not dominating, role within Europe. This has not always been the case, however. For much of their history the British Isles were on the outer periphery of European developments. Their prehistoric inhabitants had a rather primitive existence in comparison with the development of civilization in other parts of Europe. Romans found the northern Celtic Picts and Scots of Great Britain to be barbarians whom they finally gave up attempting to

conquer completely. They similarly saw no benefits from any invasion of Ireland. While continental Europe flourished during the Renaissance, the islands were most noted for their frequent civil wars. Yet they managed to produce the world's greatest literary figure in William Shakespeare, and after 1600 they came to dominate for a lengthy period a substantial portion of the world's peoples.

Political evolution. Despite their separation from the mainland of Europe by the English Channel and the North Sea, the British Isles have seen their fair share of human migrations from other areas. Prehistoric peoples found their way to Britain early in the postglacial period. The mainland Celts imposed a civilization upon the islands that lasted for a thousand years before limited conquest by the Romans at the beginning of the Christian era. The Romans established towns, built roads, and otherwise brought Mediterranean civilization to their British subjects for four centuries before withdrawing during the fourth and early fifth centuries. Subsequent invasions by tribes from Denmark and Germany placed new stamps upon the realm. Their own kingdoms suffered frequent incursions from Vikings, who had established bases along their coasts.

By the eighth century the Danes controlled most of eastern Britain, while Saxons had built the kingdom of Wessex in southwest England that eventually united most Saxon lands. Celts held out in the west, although Saxons were able to overrun the Cornish about the year 800. During this period many inhabitants of Cornwall and Wales fled south across the channel to reestablish a Celtic presence in Brittany. In 1066 Britain suffered its last successful invasion. The Normans, a Latinized group of Scandinavians based in northern France, defeated the Saxon king and extended their power throughout England.

All of these groups left legacies to British civilization, which sometimes is termed a "hybrid" society. An English language emerged that combined Anglo-Saxon and Latin-derived vocabularies, along with many Celtic terms, to establish the thickest dictionary in Europe. The presence of synonyms for virtually every word may well account for the popularity of crossword puzzles throughout the English-speaking world.

The Norman Conquest did not result in a unified state for the British Isles. Although the Normans were able to weld the Anglo-Saxons of England into a single kingdom, the Germanic settlers in the lowland waist of Scotland developed and maintained their own separate dynastic state. The Normans early subdued the Welsh, but Celts in Ireland and highland Scotland long defended their tribal territories. The Normans invaded Ireland in 1171, a century after conquest of England, but effective control was confined for centuries to a "pale" around Dublin. A movement of 100,000 troops from England against the lowland Anglo-Saxons of Scotland in 1314 saw massive defeat at the Battle of Bannockburn by 30,000 northerners.

Scotland and England were first formally united in 1407, but the Scottish kingdom continued to pursue a separate path for three more centuries. King James VI of Scotland became also King James I of England in 1603. However, only in 1707 were parliaments and administration combined to result in a single unified state. The Scots retained their distinctive legal system and church. Celtic-speaking highland Scots were not subdued until 1746. Despite recognition of English sovereignty, Wales also maintained a separate identity for several centuries. The heir to the English throne was first designated as Prince of Wales in 1284, but Wales became firmly united with England only in 1536.

The British identity. As in France, the existence of a single state for several centuries resulted in a rather homogeneous culture that emerged at the end of the eighteenth century as the British nation. Its characteristics differed markedly from its French counterpart, however. In contrast to traditional French intolerance for diversity, the British nation has been built upon acceptance of local distinctiveness. The Scots, Welsh, and northern Irish have retained separate identities while subscribing to the unifying ideals of British nationhood.

The iconography of the British nation includes the following elements: rule by people's representatives, accommodation to diversity, local self-government, and change by evolutionary rather than revolutionary means. It has developed in the context of a dominant English language and a Protestant religion. Its ideals and traditions have been transplanted to overseas regions of British settlement in the United States, Canada, Australia, New Zealand, and South Africa, and they also have been at least partially adopted by numerous other peoples who came under British control during its imperial period.

The unity of the British nation has seen frequent challenge. As elsewhere in Europe, separatist groups have sought to energize politically their surrounding populations by exploiting difficulties and reviving languages and traditions of a romanticized past. However, Scottish, Welsh, and even Cornish nationalists have been unable to achieve the successes of past counterparts in Austro-Hungary or tsarist Russia. Government policies of moderation, appeasement, conciliation, and accommodation have minimized the role of cultural differences. Grievances at best are of an economic nature and have proven insufficient to rupture the long-standing unity. There are increasing popular demands for greater devolution of authority, but these are in keeping with traditional British national values and fall far short of the sovereignty demands of minority nations elsewhere.

The Scots. The Scots are the largest minority in the United Kingdom, constituting about 9 percent of the total population. Most are concentrated in the lowlands between Glasgow and Edinburgh. Distinctions are still made between lowland Scots and highlanders, but most of the latter have given up their distinctive Celtic language in favor of English. In the 1981 census only 80,000 Scots, 1.3 percent of the total, could speak Gaelic. The majority are concentrated in northwest Scotland and on the offshore islands.

Although the main body of Scots gave up Gaelic for Anglo-Saxon speech by the sixteenth century, their language differed notably from the English developing in London. It was derived from the speech of seventh-century Anglian invaders and was closely related to Middle English. Often termed "Inglis" or "Lallans," its affiliation to standard English is perhaps best compared to relationships between Portuguese and Spanish, or Dutch and German. Many of the poems of Robert Burns are written in Lallans. The merger of the two kingdoms in the early eighteenth century led to the supplanting of Lallans by English. Some distinctive vocabulary remains, however, and pronunciation of English words by Scots includes a distinctive "burr." Groups of Scottish intellectuals have attempted to revive Lallans as a regional language and cultural medium, but they have gained little popular support.

A Scottish Nationalist Party has existed since 1928. It has long sought to capitalize upon a number of grievances, including Scotland's lower standard of living and its lack of control over local taxation, banking, employment, and licensing. Its program stresses Scotland's comparability in population size and problems with the independent Norden states, and it has sought full independence within the European Community. In recent years the party has denounced English appropriation of revenues from oil produced off the Scottish coast since 1973. The Nationalist Party gained eleven seats in the House of Commons in the 1974 elections. Scottish interests traditionally have been represented by the British Labour Party. It has promised greater devolution for Scotland when brought back to power in the British Parliament.

British government concessions to Scottish identity are numerous. It has allowed their distinctive legal and educational systems. Scottish banks are permitted to issue their own currency. In 1926 the government established a Secretary of State for Scotland, and this office was moved from London to Edinburgh in 1939.

While in power in 1979, the British Labour Party developed a plan for governmental devolution in the British Isles modelled after the federal institutions of the United States and the Federal Republic of Germany. It put the measure to a referendum in Scotland and Wales, setting a minimum of 40 percent affirmative local votes for adoption. Although the Welsh rejected the measure by a 4:1 majority, Scottish voters were more evenly balanced. Some 33 percent voted for adoption and 31 percent voted against. The 36 percent who abstained indicated, however, that the issue was not a particularly burning one. There was a frequently voiced concern about the added taxes that would be necessary for greater home rule.

Scotland faces its own minority regionalism. The Shetland islanders have been able to preserve their Gaelic identity in the face of Anglo-Saxon assimilation of Celts throughout the rest of Scotland. They number 23,000 in a territory of 900 square miles that lies 100 miles off the Scottish coast. They have had rather loose ties with Scotland for 500 years and generally they favor the English over the Scots. Increasing interest in Scotland for devolution has been matched by calls for more local autonomy in the Shetlands.

The Welsh. Although the Welsh have been closely associated with the English for seven centuries, many still see the latter as intruders. Others are firmly "Anglo-Welsh," loyal to the British Crown. Welsh identity rests much more upon a Celtic heritage than does that of the Scots. About 20 percent of the inhabitants of Wales can to speak the Welsh language, although less than 1 percent use it exclusively. Additional elements of Welsh identity include a folklore involving legends of sixth-century King Arthur and a regional symbol of the Red Dragon of Wales. There is also a fondness for group singing, perpetuated by the annual Welsh Eisteddfods, or song contests. Most Welsh speakers live in the north and west of Wales, beyond the belt stretching from Newport to Swansea that contains two-thirds of the population. Many of the inhabitants of this region are the descendants of coal miners from England and Ireland during the industrialization of South Wales in the nineteenth century.

Welsh grievances include the influx of such foreigners to their homeland and its despoliation by industrial development financed by English capital. Many residents resent a modern invasion by more affluent Englishmen who build vacation homes in its most picturesque areas. A dedicated terrorist group has burned down a number of such dwellings and attacked real estate agents engaged in the development and sale of such properties. This unhappiness is grounded in a perceived dilution of Welsh culture and a concern for

rising property values that makes home ownership unattainable for local inhabitants.

Welsh nationalists have had their own political party, Plaid Cymru, since 1925. It sees its principal goals as achieving a greater autonomy within a federated United Kingdom. Its name is derived from the Welsh identification of themselves as the *cymry* ("fellow countrymen"). The term "Welsh" derives from the Anglo-Saxon *wealas*, meaning "foreigners." Plaid Cymru's political significance has developed mainly since World War II. In 1970 it polled 11 percent of the vote. However, as noted above, the Welsh have voted strongly against devolution.

The British government has long placated Welsh feelings by local concessions. In 1964 it established a Secretary of State for Wales comparable to the one for Scotland, and much of the area's administration has been devolved from London to Cardiff. In recent times half the region's income has come from grants by the British treasury.

The Cornish. Tucked away in Great Britain's southwestern Cornwall Peninsula are 400,000 Brits who identify themselves as the Cornish. Their territory of 1,300 square miles is one of the most picturesque in England, receiving more than 3,500,000 tourists annually. Their ancestors spoke a Celtic language and had a developed literature. However, the Bible never was translated into Cornish, and this may have been the principal factor in the later demise of the language. Its last speaker died in 1777.

Like other peripheral areas of the United Kingdom, local incomes are 25 percent or more below the national average. Traditional sources of earnings in fishing and tin and copper mining declined precipitously during the nineteenth century, and the modern tourism industry is notorious for its low remuneration. Lack of opportunities resulted in substantial out-migration to England and other areas, including the United States. Like Wales, many English citizens have retired to Cornwall. It is estimated that only 45 percent of the present population was born of Cornish parents.

A local political movement emerged terming itself "Mebyon Kernow" ("Sons of Cornwall"). Its political agenda is directed against what is perceived as "internal colonization" by England and calls for Cornwall to be a separate unit within the European Community. It is part of a greater Cornish cultural reawakening that among other manifestations has seen the development of night classes in a revived Cornish language. Although much of the language's vocabulary, spelling, and pronunciation are not "genuine," the revival reflects general regional concerns for a lost heritage. Actually, the preserved elements of a decidedly dead language can be attributed to the diligent efforts of eighteenth-century English antiquarians, who collected linguistic details from small numbers of surviving Celtic speakers.

The Manx. The inhabitants of the Isle of Man constitute another Celtic group that has lost its language. About 65,000 of these people now live on the island's 227 square miles, only a third being able to trace themselves to Manx ancestors. In 1871 there were 12,000 speakers of the Manx language, but a century later only 160 were recorded, and these were almost entirely individuals who had adopted it as a hobby.

Unlike Cornwall, the Isle of Man is not a part of the United Kingdom, but only associated with it as a possession of the British Crown. As a nominally independent country it has its own parliament, currency, and, inevitably, its own postage stamps. Its ability to set its own relatively low rates of taxation has long induced individuals from England to settle within it, particularly in retirement. Local resentment has been manifested in some arson attacks on "foreign" homes. In 1975 a law was passed treating newcomers as residents of the United Kingdom and subject to British tax laws.

Channel Islanders. Another British territory associated with the United Kingdom but not a part of it is the Channel Islands. They represent the last British-held portion of the former Duchy of Normandy that embraced much of contemporary France. The islands have a combined area of only 75 square miles and a population of 140,000. Jersey is the largest, with 45 square miles and 80,000 inhabitants. Guernsey occupies 24 square miles and has a population of 55,000. Other islands include Alderney, Great Sark, Lesser Sark, and Herm.

They remained completely French in culture until the 1840s, when settlers from England first arrived. Norman French is still spoken by 10,000 rural inhabitants of Jersey and 4,000 on Guernsey. The islands benefit economically from their position as British territory off the coast of France, with tourism the principal industry. There is virtually no French irredentism present here. Indeed, Protestants on the islands exhibit a pronounced Francophobia.

Ireland. The conflict in Northern Ireland between Protestants and Catholics constitutes one of the most intractable internal state problems in the world. Continuing violence since 1967 has left more than 3,000 dead and shows no signs of abating. Its roots lie in the ancient history of the island, and British policies of flexibility and compromise so effective elsewhere among the diverse peoples of the United Kingdom have had virtually no success in finding a workable solution.

Ireland's history has known conflict since the island was first settled in the postglacial period. At the beginning of the Christian era its Celtic clans proved far more resistant to the Romans than their counterparts on the island of Great Britain. Later they successfully withstood incursions by Anglo-Saxons and Norsemen. The most long-lasting penetration in historic times was the peaceful one of St. Patrick, who converted the Irish to Christianity in the fifth century A.D. As a consequence, Ireland for centuries was the most progressive center of learning and development within the British Isles. Nevertheless, it remained torn by strife. Within the small island there were no less than five contending kingdoms by the beginning of the twelfth century.

It was then that the Normans, having imposed their will upon England, turned their attention to Ireland. With great hardship they established a presence on the island and apportioned its lands among their nobility. Over ensuing centuries the Irish peasantry gradually lost its Celtic language and adopted English. However, effective British control over the next five centuries was principally confined to a "pale" of settlement along the east coast around Dublin.

The Irish showed little enthusiasm for the English Reformation of the Christian church. The English, in turn, worried about the potential use of Ireland as a base by their religious enemies on the European continent. At the end of the sixteenth century the English set about complete pacification of the island. The last area to be subdued was the territory of the former northern Irish kingdom of Ulster in 1603. Traditionally this had been the region most resistant to English control and influence.

Exasperated by its long defiance, the English singled out Ulster for complete eradication of resistance. Its lands were apportioned among English landowners, who imported large numbers of land-hungry Scots to work them. The process was termed "the plantation" and permanently changed the cultural geography of the island. Group identities were principally of a religious nature in the seventeenth century. The relatively few English who controlled the land were Anglican, the Scottish immigrants to Ulster were mainly Presbyterian, and the native Irish remained Roman Catholic. Their numbers included many descendants of Norman landowners who became noted as Irish patriots.

The crusading zeal of Protestants against the "popery" of the Roman Catholics created lasting divisions. Particular antipathy was generated by Oliver Cromwell, who declared in 1654 that all Irish were to be banished "to Hell or Connacht." In 1690 the English completely defeated a joint Irish and French force at a battle along the Boyne River. To this day militant Protestants in Northern Ireland celebrate the victory by parades that pass through Roman Catholic sections of various towns.

Ireland languished as a colony of England during the eighteenth century. It was seen as peripheral, unruly, and otherwise uninviting to further English settlement. It lacked resources for industrial development and offered mainly cheap labor and cheap food. Its depressed economic situation was a source of continuing resentment by its inhabitants. In one of the ironies of history, the Scots Irish of Ulster spearheaded resistance to the status quo through their role in the formation of the United Irishmen. Imbued with the romantic nationalism unleashed by the American and French revolutions, this body sought an integrated unity of the three principal Irish religious groups against England. A rebellion in 1798 failed, however, and the Irish were again suppressed. A lasting consequence was an English decision in 1800 to incorporate Ireland fully into the United Kingdom.

Political unification did little to improve Ireland's economic situation. Only Ulster took part in the Industrial Revolution during the nineteenth century, providing ships and other manufactured goods for burgeoning British trade with the rest of the world. Formal integration with England also did not end the development of Irish national sentiments. As elsewhere in Europe, local groups emerged to celebrate the regional heritage. In Ireland the focus was upon Gaelic tradition.

Ulster remained aloof from these cultural-political developments. Its dominant Protestants were isolated from the rest of the Irish population and did not identify with a Gaelic past. They had genuine concern for the power of the Roman Catholic church, especially after Catholics at long last received the right to vote in 1884. They also had far fewer grievances than did the agricultural counties to the south as their industry flourished during the latter part of the nineteenth century.

Irish nationalism became an irresistible force by World War I. After suppressing a rebellion in 1916, the British government in the postwar period decided to allow the Irish to decide their future by plebiscite. In 1920, votes were held in the thirty-two counties, offering a choice between continuing union with the United Kingdom or independence in a dominion status similar to that of Canada and Australia. Six counties in the Protestant north voted for continuing union. The others opted for independence. The result was political partition of the island.

Determination of the boundary between the new Irish Free State and loyalist Northern Ireland was not an easy task. A proposal to establish a border based upon electoral returns proved difficult to achieve because of large enclaves of separatists in the industrial concentrations of the north and unionists in the Irish "pale" to the south. Finally, in 1925, negotiators representing sepa-

ratists, unionists, and the British government agreed to utilize the outer boundaries of the six unionist counties as the line of division. The Irish separatists agreed in part because they believed that the division was only an interim situation before the emergence of a fully sovereign united Ireland.

The new Irish Free State had 27,000 square miles and a population of 3,600,000. This amounted to 84 percent of the island's territory and two-thirds of its inhabitants. It was a true nation-state, based upon Celtic heritage and loyalty to Roman Catholicism. National feelings also involved reaction to British stereotypes of the Irish as intellectual and cultural inferiors. Irish-baiting has remained a staple of British humor.

Unlike the new nation-states that had emerged in east central and southeastern Europe, the Irish nation had all but lost its distinctive language. Earnest efforts were inaugurated to revive and modernize Gaelic as a national tongue, but they were never successful. The state incorporated a significant number of Protestants who had been in favor of continuing union with the United Kingdom. In contrast to the Roman Catholic minority remaining in Ulster, the southern Protestants were not perceived by the Irish nationalists as a threat. They were far fewer in proportion and were not segregated residentially as in the north.

The Ulster problem. The six loyalist counties found themselves with a 30 percent Catholic minority that clearly preferred union with the Irish Free State. The United Kingdom government accorded Ulster greater autonomy than enjoyed by either Scotland or Wales, including a parliament located in Stormont on the outskirts of Belfast. The Protestant unionists originally opposed this self-government, since they correctly perceived that it had been granted by the British in part to permit development of some type of workable accord with the southern Irish. Eventually they saw it as an opportunity to reinforce their domination of Northern Ireland through gerrymandering and other abuses.

In their subsequent history the two principal groups coexisted in a highly segregated fashion. Residence in cities tended to be in separate neighborhoods. Catholic children were educated in church schools, whereas Protestants dominated the public institutions. Although both school systems used a common syllabus, group values remained separate. Employers tended to hire members of their own faiths. Employment grew increasingly segregated, with Protestants finding jobs in manufacturing and government and Catholics becoming dockers and construction workers and also suffering a higher degree of unemployment.

The Irish Republican Army (IRA) that had been instrumental in forcing Britain to concede separation in the south maintained a shadowy existence among

Catholics in Northern Ireland in the years following division. It generated a reaction among Protestants, who gave increasing allegiance and militancy to the Order of the Orange, named for William of Orange, who won the Battle of the Boyne. Their concerns were amplified by the increasing numbers of Catholics in Northern Ireland, growing both by in-migration from the less affluent south and by higher birth rates. Catholics in Northern Ireland constituted 33 percent in 1937 and 38 percent of the population in 1981. Demographic projections indicate a Catholic majority by the year 2020.

In the 1960s the name of the Irish Republican Army was appropriated by a new generation of intense Irish nationalists imbued with socialist ideals. They designated themselves as the "provisional wing" of the IRA, and came to be known as the "Provos." Modelling themselves after the successful militant ETA organization of the Spanish Basques, they inaugurated a campaign of terror in 1969. They found ready external support from Irish communities in the United States and from the oil-rich regime in Libya, which readily provided weapons and funds to a number of dissident groups challenging governments throughout Europe. Provo activists found sanctuary and shelter among sympathizers on the republican side of the border, although Ireland has denounced their campaign of assassinations and destruction and has cooperated with the British in attempting to quell their activities. Protestants reacted with militancy of their own. Paramilitary groups sought retribution by attacks upon individuals associated with the IRA and other prominent Catholics. The United Kingdom found it necessary to impose direct rule upon the territory, suspending the Stormont parliament and stationing increasing numbers of troops to counteract terrorists from both sides.

The problems of Northern Ireland seem insurmountable. The two religious communities appear incapable of finding common ground. The issue is not a theological one, but a contest between two rival nations whose distinctiveness is based upon religious heritage. Protestants resist any possibility of being joined to the Republic of Ireland, where their status would be reduced from a three-fifths majority position to a one-fifth minority. The Catholics, in turn, see no hope in reforming Protestant attitudes. Although the majority of Catholics abhor the violence, many see their only chance at gaining equality in their homeland is by a wearying of British resolve to defend the northern Protestants. In this they may be right, as polls in the United Kingdom show increasing feelings of "a plague on both your houses." To the displeasure of the Ulster unionists, the British government did reach an accord with the Irish government for joint consultations on Northern Irish affairs.

The problem of Northern Ireland stems from the large minority of Catholics left in the north by the resort to county lines as a border in 1925. A possible future solution is to rectify the harm done by this superimposed boundary through a new repartition that would be consequent upon group divisions. The original problems of Catholic enclaves would remain, however, and it is difficult to see acceptance of such a resolution by either side. Too much time has elapsed and too many attitudes have been hardened.

The Lotharingian Corridor

The Rhine River forms the backbone of a distinctive political geographic region containing four states and several nations. This seam between the French and German culture worlds is sometimes termed the "Lotharingian Corridor" after Lothair, one of three heirs to Charlemagne's empire (Table 3-2). For a brief period between A.D. 844 and 867 this north-south belt constituted for its first and only time a unified state. Unlike the kingdoms of the East Franks and West Franks on either side, it did not hold together and was divided between its more powerful neighbors. Its parts were not easily absorbed, however, and through history this has been a region of small and independent-minded states. Lotharingia included a substantial part of northern Italy. Only the area from the Netherlands to Switzerland is considered in this section, however. The Italian area is treated in the following chapter.

In many ways, modern Lotharingia is a fossilized frontier (see Figure 3-4). Like other frontier zones between powerful cultural and political units, it shares characteristics of the cores on either side, but it also exhibits internal associations and features that give it a distinctive personality and coherence. The linking river still provides connectivity between its extremities. A person is virtually never out of sight of canal boats plying the Rhine, and the more modern transportation technologies of rail and automobile have tended to follow routes paralleling the waterway, tying together ancient towns that continue to serve as foci of spatial interaction.

Unlike the "shatterzone" of east central and southeastern Europe, this is not a region of hopeless cultural diversity. It partakes essentially of two traditions—German and French—with a dash of Italian civilization at its southern extremity. Its peoples, however, have resisted the processes of homogenization and integration that long ago welded into broader nations similar small groups that were located closer to cultural cores. Local dialects of German and French have become basic icons of national identity. However, aside from

TABLE 3-2 THE LOTHARINGIAN STATES

Four small states have emerged at different times and have served as buffers between France and the Germanic lands; they share aspects of the contrasting cultures of their stronger neighbors.

State	Total Population	Area (sq. miles)	Distinctive Features of Group
Netherlands	15,000,000	16,000	
Dominant Nation and % Total			
Dutch, 96%			Germanic (Dutch) language, Calvinist
Significant Regional Groups and % Total			
Frisians, 3%			Germanic (Frisian) language, Calvinist
Belgium	10,000,000	12,000	
Dominant Nations and % Total			
Flemings, 52%			Germanic (Dutch) language, devout Roman Catholic
Walloons, 42%			Romance (French) language, anticlerical Roman Catholic
Luxemburg	390,000	1,000	
Dominant Nation and % Total			
Luxemburgers			Mixed Germanic/Romance (Letzeburgesh and French) language, Roman Catholic
Switzerland	8,700,000	16,000	
Dominant Nations and % Total			
German Swiss, 67%			Germanic (German) language, mixed Roman Catholic/Protestant
French Swiss, 18%			Romance (French) language, mixed Roman Catholic/Calvinist
Italian Swiss, 4%			Romance (Italian) language, Roman Catholic
Significant Regional Groups and % Total			
Romansch, 1%			Romance (Romansch) language, mixed Roman Catholic/Protestant

the impressive literary evolution of Dutch as a written language for Dutchmen and Flemings, the local vernaculars remain basically oral traditions, with the written word either High German or Parisian French.

The long traditions of the Netherlands, Belgium, Luxemburg, and Switzerland as sovereign states fostered the development of modern notions of national unity much earlier than they appeared among Bretons or Catalonians, who were bound together with other peoples for centuries within dynastic states. Rivalry between the Lotharingian Corridor's more powerful neighbors also contributed to the preservation of local group distinctiveness. The small states survived to the modern era not only through patriotic efforts of their inhabitants but also because no adjoining unit would permit a rival to absorb them. Each of these states, then, is a political geographic buffer, a reflection of the region's frontier qualities.

Not all the peoples of the Lotharingian Corridor have managed to maintain independent states of their own through history. The position of the Alsatians within France has been discussed earlier. Across the Rhine they face the German-speakers of Baden and Pfalz, who in 1871 found their small states merged into newly unified Germany. Flanders and Friesland, Brabant and Burgundy long ago lost their identities.

Diversity besets the small states themselves. Only 999-square-mile Luxemburg lacks any regional minority groups. West Frisians form a significant people within the Netherlands; Flemings and Walloons vie in Belgium; and French-, Italian-, and Romansch-speakers coexist with a German-speaking majority in Switzerland. In contrast to the minorities of southeastern Europe, however, groups appear to have found a *modus vivendi* with other peoples within their states. Although the national identity of each group is strong, calls for

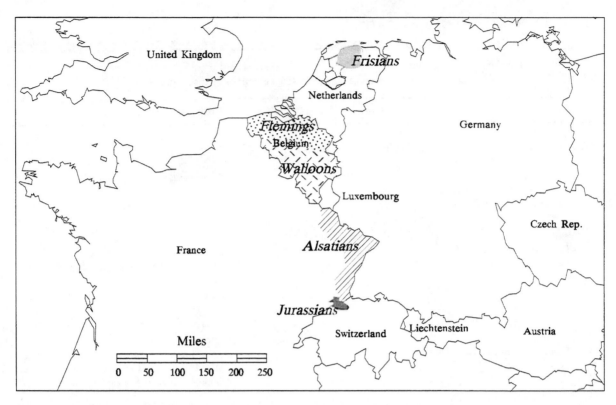

FIGURE 3-4 THE LOTHARINGIAN CORRIDOR

sovereignty tend to be limited to radical fringes. However, popular sentiments do include desires for local self-rule and the preservation of distinctive languages and traditions.

Although the Lotharingian Corridor lies at the peripheries of greater cultural and political agglomerations, it by no means has suffered the lag in economic development that characterizes the Celtic fringe of the British Isles or the southern margins of the Mediterranean states. It is endowed with a fair share of Europe's resources, including coal in Belgium, iron ore in Alsace-Lorraine, and the "white gold" of hydroelectric power of the Swiss Alps. The Rhineland embraces some of the best agricultural land in all of Europe. The region's natural riches have fostered one of Europe's heaviest belts of population. The Netherlands has a population density exceeded only by Bangladesh and Taiwan. In general, based upon all resources and economic development, the Corridor has less productive area than the United Kingdom or Germany, but more than Italy or Spain.

The most important single asset of the region is its central location. It long has profited as a bridge between the Germans and the French. Its producers are in a medial position to serve one of the world's most concentrated and affluent market regions. The industrial

agglomerations of southeastern England, northeastern France, and the German Ruhr are close at hand. The intensive efforts of the Dutch to reclaim farmland from the sea in their famous *polders* are understandable when one considers the superlative advantage of the drained territory for producing perishable vegetables and flowers to meet a surrounding demand that seems insatiable.

An important element in the success of the small states of the Lotharingian Corridor has been their readiness to cooperate economically with each other and with their neighbors. Luxemburg was part of a German customs union for eighty years before joining a similar arrangement with Belgium in 1921. Following World War II, in 1948, Belgium, the Netherlands, and Luxemburg formed the Benelux Economic Union. Later, they were among the founding members of the European Coal and Steel Community (ECSC) in 1952 and then the European Economic Community (EEC or Common Market) in 1957. Switzerland joined with six other states left outside the EEC to create the European Free Trade Association (EFTA) in 1960 and more recently entered into free-trade agreements with the enlarged European Union.

The Corridor's centrality has become increasingly important as Western Europe has moved toward economic, military, and political integration. Brussels in Belgium is the headquarters of both the North Atlantic Treaty Organization (NATO) and the European Union; Strasbourg in Alsace is the seat of the Council of Europe; and Luxemburg is the center of the European Parliament and the European Investment Bank. The main office of the European Free Trade Association is situated in Geneva, Switzerland.

The Netherlands

The northern anchor of the Lotharingian Corridor is the Netherlands. This 16,000-square-mile state is popularly termed "Holland." However, that name properly is applied only to the most prominent of seven historic parts of the United Provinces of the Netherlands, which became independent in the mid-seventeenth century. Holland embraces the sand dunes, alluvium, and marshes of the western margins of the deltas of the Rhine and Meuse (Maas) that make up virtually all of Dutch territory. Protected on its landward side by difficult access through the wetlands, and blessed by harbors opening to the North Sea and Atlantic, the province of Holland was in a favorable position to lead resistance by land and sea against Spanish domination.

The Romans had penetrated the southern edge of the deltas, but poor soils and waterlogged lands gave little incentive to advance further against German tribes that lived there. In the waning decades of Roman authority a group known as the Salian Franks came to dominate the area. Their language was a form of Low German that has evolved into modern Dutch and Flemish. The Salian Franks avoided the then-existing forest region farther south and west. There the local inhabitants were Romanized, speaking a form of Latin that became the Walloon dialect of French.

Charlemagne absorbed all of the Low Countries into his empire in the ninth century. Following his death, they were joined for less than three decades as part of the short-lived successor state of Lotharingia. In the dismemberment of that unit, the territory north of the Scheldt River went to the Kingdom of the East Franks and that to the south to the Kingdom of the West Franks. Then, as now, the Low Countries were peripheral to greater neighbors to east and west, split between them but benefitting by remoteness from centers of power.

During the feudal period the region fragmented into several fiefs that functioned independently with varying relationships either with France or with the Holy Roman Empire. The princes of Burgundy united them into a single state during the fourteenth century. In 1548 they became the "Circle" of Burgundy, an admin-

istrative unit within the Holy Roman Empire. It is from this period that the term "Netherlands" ("Low Countries") first came into general use. It should be noted that Burgundy included substantial lands farther south that were absorbed into France.

The system of territorial inheritance prevailing during the sixteenth century brought the Low Countries into union with Spain in 1516. In the following year Martin Luther issued his famous challenge in Wittenberg to Roman Catholic church authorities. Over subsequent years in the Low Countries adopted the Calvinist version of Protestantism. In 1555 the Spanish monarch Philip II set about to quash heresy in his realm, precipitating a war with the Calvinists of the Low Countries that ended only with a truce in 1609. At this point Spain had been successful in maintaining its hold only upon the southernmost provinces. The seven northern units successfully gained independence, a fact recognized formally in 1648. They had declared themselves a republic, the United Provinces of the Netherlands. As often happens, the temporary truce line with Spain became institutionalized as an international border.

The United Netherlands was virtually entirely Dutch-speaking. Although a high percentage of its population had remained Roman Catholic, its Protestants were a dominating minority that steadily grew into a majority. The remaining Spanish Netherlands, which eventually became modern Belgium and Luxemburg, was about evenly divided between Dutch and Walloon speakers. Its population similarly was split between Catholics and Protestants. The uncompromising attitude of the Spaniards toward the latter, however, led many Protestants to migrate to the United Netherlands, increasing the proportion of Catholics in the territory left behind and contributing to the growing Protestant majority in the north.

Over ensuing decades the two areas continued to drift apart economically, culturally, and politically. Before Dutch independence, Flanders had been the most productive part of the Low Countries. Its cloth makers and merchants in Bruges, Ghent, and Antwerp had grown prosperous in producing for European-wide markets. They slipped into decline after partition, however. To the Dutch fell control over the entrance to the Scheldt Estuary for a distance of forty miles, and they denied use of that waterway to towns in Flanders. The action promoted the Dutch ports of Amsterdam and Rotterdam but caused lasting harm to Antwerp. Flemings have remembered to the present day the disastrous consequences for their homeland of the Dutch action. (Perhaps in belated atonement, the Netherlands in 1963 agreed to assist Antwerp by permitting the digging of a new canal to the sea across Dutch territory.) Walloons in the Spanish Netherlands began to dominate commercial activities, and French became the language of preference among the middle and upper classes even in Dutch-speaking Flanders.

The independent Dutch state grew into a major seapower during the seventeenth century. It gained significant possessions overseas in India, the East Indies, the southern tip of Africa, the West Indies, and North America. Many of its gains were at the expense of Spain and also of Portugal, which Spain had ruined during the six decades between 1580 and 1640 when it had incorporated the Portuguese within the Spanish state. The Netherlands also became a major player within Europe, including investment in the development of iron and copper mines in Sweden and engaging in trade with the continental interior by sending horse-drawn barges up the Rhine and its tributaries as far as Frankfurt and Luxemburg.

The Netherlands had entered a bitter struggle with France during the sixteenth century. By allying itself with England, it managed to preserve its independence and to save its colonial empire. However, in the process it lost command of the seas to the British. During the Napoleonic Wars, French forces occupied the Netherlands. Defeat of the French led to its reestablishment as a kingdom, with the lost Spanish Netherlands (which had become the Austrian Netherlands) being joined to it by the Treaty of Vienna in 1815. This union was dissolved by a Belgian revolt in 1830.

The Netherlands has maintained itself essentially within its initial boundaries up to the present. One interesting quirk of its borders is the presence of a three-square-mile enclave of Belgian territory several miles inside the Netherlands. Baarle-Hertog, intermixed with the Dutch town of Baarle-Nassau, is a result of a decision while establishing the 1609 truce line to allow a respected Catholic loyalist to retain ownership of family property within the new state.

The Frisians. The Netherlands has one major minority group. Northeast of the Ijssel Meer, the former Zuider Zee, is a 1,300-square mile territory inhabited by the West Frisians. Related linguistic groups are found around Emden in Germany and in the southwestern Schleswig area of the Jutland Peninsula of Germany and Denmark. Their distinctive language is, like Dutch, of Low German origin and is the closest of the continental languages to English. This is understandable, since the Frisian homeland was the source area for the Angles, Saxons, and Jutes who invaded England.

The West Frisians number 700,000. All are bilingual in Dutch. They have been able to have their own language taught in their schools since 1937, and local road signs are now required to be in both Dutch and Frisian. In addition to their language, the iconography of the Frisians includes memories of historical opposition to Dutch incorporation. They have a group symbol of seven red water lily leaves against a white and blue background.

In many ways their position can be compared to that of the Welsh or Scots in the United Kingdom. They jealously preserve their cultural distinctiveness but appear content to participate as equals within the Dutch state. Popular support for separation or greater autonomy is notably weak. They have maintained some cultural linkages with the Frisians of Emden and Schleswig, but intergroup relations were harmed by support for the Nazis during World War II by the German Frisians.

Belgium

The evolution of Belgium was traced earlier. Belgium was formed from that territory of the Low Countries that remained with Spain after several decades of Dutch revolt. The Spanish later transferred the region to Austria. Occupied by Napoleon at the end of the eighteenth century, it was awarded to the Netherlands by the Treaty of Vienna, despite French objections that the former Spanish Netherlands should rightfully be part of France.

The union with the Dutch in 1815 proved to be short-lived, however. Two hundred years of separation had taken their toll, and differences between the two parts had grown substantially. The south had become almost entirely Roman Catholic and conservative in culture and politics. The United Netherlands had grown largely Protestant and more liberal. The Spanish Netherlands had developed close associations with France, and increasingly used the French language in commerce and administration. Bitterness was widespread over the closing of Antwerp's access to the sea. It should also be said that the Dutch did not exert much wisdom in their attempts to integrate the Belgians after the Treaty of Vienna. In 1830 the southerners revolted. They were supported by Austria, Russia, the United Kingdom, and Prussia, and their independence was formally recognized in 1839. The Belgians did not get all the territory that they desired, however. The Dutch retained a salient of mixed Flemish and Dutch territory in the southeastern province of Limburg, and much of eastern Luxemburg was given independent status as a grand duchy.

The young state of Belgium had the misfortune to be established at a time when group identity throughout Europe was shifting from a religious to a linguistic basis. Commonly shared Roman Catholicism no longer was a tie strong enough to bind its citizens together. Language-based division into two separate nations plagued the young state from its inception. French-speakers made up sixty percent of the population in the mid-nineteenth century. They tended to be better educated, more urbanized, and more affluent than the predominantly agricultural Dutch-speakers. Separating the two groups was a rather knife-edged line that had existed since the fifth century. It appears that most Walloons would have preferred to join France in 1839 rather than be linked permanently with the Flemings. Strong opposition by the British and Germans prevented realization of this goal, however.

A unified nationhood thus did not emerge among the inhabitants of Belgium, despite a century and a half of coexistence of Flemings and Walloons within an independent state and a preceding two centuries of separate status as the Spanish (and then Austrian) Netherlands. In contrast to the cultural-political amalgamation of four linguistic groups into the Swiss nation, the two Belgian peoples grew further apart. The reason quite likely lay in the initial adoption of a highly centralized form of government in Belgium that favored the Walloon majority, while Switzerland evolved a very loose federal framework. Another possible factor was that Belgium's independence did not occur as the result of a historic struggle with hallowed heroes, but was a consequence of historical accident and great-power rivalry. A geographic element in Belgium's divisiveness was the homogeneous character and compact territory of each group in comparison with the internal religious divisions and spatial fragmentation of the two principal Swiss linguistic groups.

As noted above, French culture pervaded Belgium during the nineteenth century. The majority spoke Walloon, a dialect of French, and written French was more or less the official language of government and commerce, and, indeed, had been adopted for business and administration by the Flemish middle classes. French-speaking activists were responsible for the 1830 separation from the Netherlands.

Flemish-speakers long suffered a sense of inferiority. They rejected their ancient Dutch heritage for religious reasons, but they found themselves a disadvantaged minority within Belgium. They had remained largely rural farmers while modern industrialization and urbanization developed in the Walloon region's coalfields. They experienced various kinds of discrimination, including the inability of many of their numbers to meet electoral qualifications of Belgium's suffrage laws.

Flemings reacted to their status by developing a separate national identity during the latter part of the nineteenth century. Waving their own flags, shouting their own slogans, singing their own patriotic songs, they internalized an anti-Walloon iconography. They also were able to identify with the glories of their medieval homeland province of Flanders, in contrast to the absence of a historic territory named "Wallonia" for the Walloon population. Beginning in the 1890s, the Walloon-dominated government started to yield grudging concessions to Fleming sensitivities. Official documents had to be in both French and Dutch, for instance. By 1914 Flemings could have their primary schools taught in the Dutch language.

Invading Germans sought to capitalize upon Belgium's internal divisions during World War I. They encouraged Flemish nationalism in various ways, including instituting an administrative division into separate Fleming and Walloon territories. They introduced Flemish as a language of instruction in the University of Ghent. In November 1917, during the German occupation, a "Council of Flanders" demanded full Flemish independence. Formal division terminated at the end of the war, but there remained enmities between the two groups that had been exacerbated during the German occupation.

Flemish nationalism continued to flourish during the interwar period. The Belgian army played a major role by bringing together farm boys from all parts of Flanders who jointly felt discrimination under a predominantly Walloon officer corps. They grew aware of common interests, and many joined the ranks of political nationalists. At length the regime felt impelled to divide the country administratively as had been done under the Germans, although there were few legal mechanisms to enforce Flemish political rights. The government confirmed the Flemish character of Ghent University.

A degree of cross-national common ground developed in the 1930s through the Belgian Fascist movement. Both linguistic groups had suffered during the world economic crisis, and elements of both reacted to antistate and antinational appeals by Belgian Communists. The success of Benito Mussolini in Italy presented them a model for resolving problems. Through skillful maneuvering, a Fascist leader brought both groups into a degree of cooperation against the traditional politicians. During World War II the Belgian Fascists actively collaborated with the occupying Germans. They provided volunteers for elite SS (*Schutzstaffel*) units of the German army, although, interestingly enough, they were organized into separate Walloon and Flemish brigades.

Flemings as a group tended to receive greater punishment after the war for collaboration, although Walloons resented Flemish pressures for Belgium's King Leopold to abdicate because of alleged wartime cooperation with the occupying Germans. The Walloons also found their political parties to have become a minority in the postwar parliament, since a higher birth rate among Flemings had meant that they now numbered more than half the population. Walloons also began to feel a decline in their customary economic superiority, as coal played out in the 1950s and industries grew obsolete. The Flemish port of Antwerp, in contrast, enjoyed a postwar boom.

The Walloons had originally evolved their national identity in close association with the overall Belgian state, which they treated as their own, viewing the Flemings merely as a backward and troublesome minority. Their attitudes changed, however, with the growth of Flemings in numbers and political power. Regional particularism began to replace a Belgian identity in Walloon iconography, which grew increasingly reactive to Flemish achievement. Many Walloon intellectuals contemplated once again advantages of becoming part of France. Their homeland, in their perspective, was a nonhistoric region that lacked the reminders of a grand independent past comparable to those found in Flanders.

Group antipathies reached a crisis stage in the 1960s in disputes over implications of a linguistic census. Open fighting between bodies of individuals flared on several occasions. In 1963 the government decided to institutionalize regional identities by creating an official division line between the two groups and establishing duplicate facilities for each area. The Brussels region was constituted as a separate administrative territory. Although it was predominantly Walloon-speaking, it lay well within the Flemish-speaking zone.

A major dispute developed over the five-century-old University of Louvain. It lay on the Flemish side of the border, with a student body about evenly divided between Flemings and Walloons. Flemish students demanded in 1968 that Walloon students and faculty be removed from Flanders and established in the Wallonian region. The government initially resisted their calls for change, but was then toppled from power. Its successor reluctantly decided to accede to Flemish demands, and the Walloons were installed in a new university in the town of Ottignies, near Brussels, at a very high cost.

The geographic division of the country was augmented by the establishment of greater regional autonomy for Flanders and Wallonia in 1980. Each received its own legislative assembly and executive. Brussels retained a separate status, although quarrels developed over Walloon insistence upon preserving a French identity for the capital city. Flemings reluctantly agreed, but resisted the spread of French linguistic identity to surrounding areas. A particular dispute focused upon a half dozen French-speaking suburbs of Brussels that were located in territory assigned to Flanders.

Autonomy within Belgium appeared to satisfy the Flemings, who had never shown any irredentist feelings for the Netherlands, despite formal establishment of Dutch as their official language. Walloons also appeared satisfied to be able to control their own affairs. However, they chafed at an increasing tendency to favor bilingual individuals for top positions in government and business. They saw this as unfairly favoring people from Flanders, since Flemings tended to know both Dutch and French, but Walloons had traditionally encouraged their children to learn German as a second language rather than Dutch. A surprising fact about Belgium is that some 30 percent of its marriages are of mixed language. In most cases the children speak French at home.

The Belgian Germans. Mention should be made of a hundred thousand German-speakers in Belgium. They live primarily in the eastern districts of Eupen, Malmédy, and St. Vith. They have found themselves variously over past centuries as parts of the Netherlands, Belgium, France, the Prussian Province of the Rhine, and Germany. In 1919 they were awarded once again to Belgium as war reparations. The dominant Walloons forbade local inhabitants to speak their native language during the interwar period. In 1940 the German areas happily rejoined Germany, but again they were returned to Belgium in 1945. In the postwar regionalist controversies they generally have made common cause with the Flemings, reflecting their minority status on the eastern edge of Wallonia.

Luxemburg

One of the more curious states of Europe is the Grand Duchy of Luxemburg, which occupies 999 square miles between Belgium, Germany, and France. Its total population is under 400,000. At one time its ruling family controlled a vast territory that extended to the North Sea and the Russian Empire. It provided four emperors to the Holy Roman Empire, four kings to Bohemia, and one king to Hungary. By the end of the eighteenth century, however, its lands had shrunk substantially, and the fortress of Luxemburg had been besieged and destroyed on at least twenty occasions by a variety of enemies.

Luxemburg was controlled at various times by Spain, France, Austria, and Prussia, and it had become one of the many tiny states of the Holy Roman Empire when the French captured it in 1795. The Treaty of Vienna in 1815 raised it from a duchy to a grand duchy and placed it under the personal rule of the king of the Netherlands, although substantial parts of the territory remaining to it were given to Prussia. Despite the fact that it had been part of the original Spanish Netherlands, only its western, Walloon-speaking region was given to Belgium when that state became sovereign in 1839. Remaining Luxemburg territory continued as a separate entity. Three years later it became a member of the nineteenth-century *Zollverein*, a customs union of the many small German states designed to provide the benefits of the type of common market then enjoyed within France, the United Kingdom, and other large European political entities. It became fully self-governing in 1868, and the link with the Dutch royal family was severed in 1890.

Luxemburg's small size has required the state to associate itself economically with one or another of its neighbors. Although it remained independent of the unified Germany that emerged in 1871, its economic linkages with the German area continued until the end of World War I. In 1919 it sought to enter a customs union with France. The French refused to agree to this, however, and in 1921 Luxemburg signed a treaty with Belgium to form a customs union for fifty years. After interruption during World War II, this agreement was reestablished and then superseded in 1948 when the Netherlands, Belgium, and Luxemburg established the Benelux Economic Union. With its neighbors it later became part of the European Coal and Steel Community and the European Economic Community.

The people of Luxemburg form a unified nation with a language of its own. *Letzeburgesch* is a dialect of Middle German that differs as much from standard High German as does Dutch. It is similar to German dialects spoken in small adjacent areas of Belgium, France, and Germany. It lacks the vocabulary and nuances necessary to become a written language. Many words are borrowed from French or German, which are studied in schools and employed as literary languages. Like the Alsatians of France, sentiments among educated people tend to favor being part of the French culture world, but there are also strong ties to the Germans.

Switzerland

Despite four major languages and two antagonistic religions, the population of Switzerland has developed one of the strongest national identities to be found in Europe. Like the Benelux states, its 16,000-square-mile territory lies between German and French culture worlds. It also forms a frontier zone between them and the Italian realm to the south.

The conventional view of Switzerland, nourished by novels and Hollywood motion pictures, is that of a land of mountaineers. Although it is true that in good weather mountains are always in view, the fact is that three-quarters of the population is to be found living on the flatlands of the Swiss Plateau. This region lies at an average elevation of 2,000 feet and stretches in an arc from Geneva in the southwest to the northern border with Germany. To the northwest are the low Jura Mountains, and to the south are the high ranges of the Alps with deep and flat-bottomed glaciated valleys.

Switzerland began as a confederation of four independent German-speaking cantons (districts) in 1291. They controlled the northern approaches to the famous St. Gotthard Pass, which was opened in the thirteenth century as the principal land route between Mediterranean and Central Europe. The cantons were appendages of the Holy Roman Empire but had received special exemptions from feudal obligations in return for preventing other powers from gaining the pass. The empire, headed by a Habsburg, sought greater control over the cantons, prompting their rebellion. The William Tell legend dates from this period. The new state took the name Schwyz from a canton that led the rebellion, and from this developed the English designation "Switzerland," the French *Suisse*, and the Italian *Svizzera*.

Later, the original cantons in the Alps united with the trading cities of Zurich, Geneva, and Berne on the plateau to form a larger state. It continued to expand by alliance and conquest. Switzerland benefitted initially by its remoteness from the major states of the time. France, Austria, and the larger German and Italian states were all far away from its borders. As time went on, none of its neighbors would tolerate its belonging to another state. Switzerland thus became a buffer that managed to avoid most of the wars surrounding it.

In the process of expansion many non-German speakers were brought into Swiss territory, although German was the only official language from 1291 to 1798. (See Figure 3-5.) The numerous German dialects spoken are collectively known as *Schwyzerdütsch* and derive from Middle High German. The dialects are nearly as different from High German as is the Dutch language; they are also very difficult to write, and they enjoy no special linguistic rights. The official language for the German section of Switzerland is standard High German, which is known as *Schriftdeutch*. About three-quarters of the population is identified as German-speaking. The German-speaking Swiss are divided between Roman Catholics and Protestants. (See Figure 3-6.)

The French-speaking Swiss number about 20 percent of the population. They too are divided between Roman Catholics and Protestants. They are concentrated along the western and southwestern fringes of the state. Although most German-Swiss learn to become bilingual in French during their school years, the French-speaking Swiss have developed a reputation for not learning German well. Slightly more than 4 percent

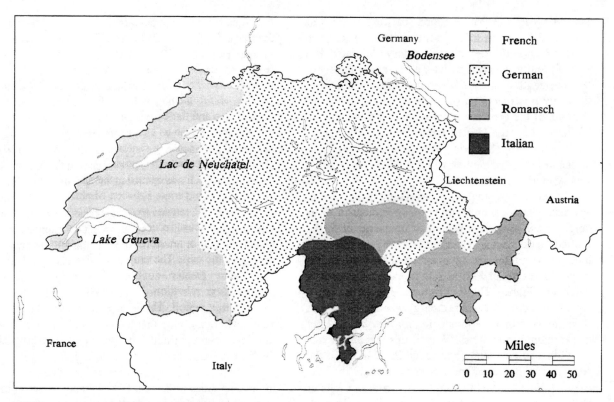

FIGURE 3-5   LANGUAGES IN SWITZERLAND

FIGURE 3-6   RELIGIONS IN SWITZERLAND

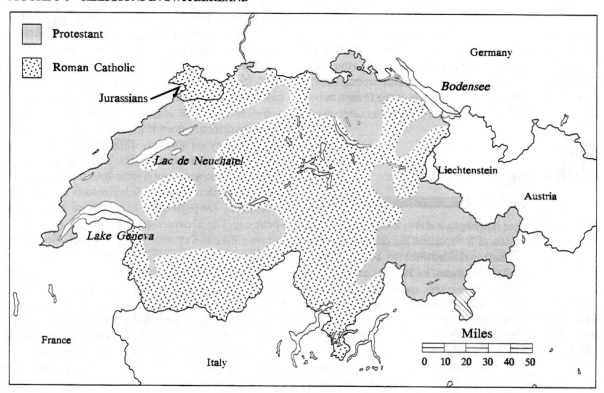

of the population speaks Italian and lives principally in the Ticino region south of the Alps.

In the mountain valleys of the southeast are the Romansch-speakers, who number about 50,000, which is less than 1 percent of the Swiss total. Their language is derived from Latin, but includes elements of Celtic, German, and Italian. At one time it was spoken throughout much of the Alps, but gave way to the spread of German over most of the mountain region. There are close ties to the isolated Ladin and Friulian languages of the Italian Alps. Romansch has a literature dating back to the fifteenth century, including a Bible that appeared in 1560. There are fourteen accepted variations in writing the language. In 1938 the Swiss recognized Romansch as a fourth national language, although it was not given the "official" status of the other three. That recognition came in part as a response to irredentist claims from Italy. The number of Romansch-speakers is declining, both from out-migration to other regions and from greater contacts with tourists.

The Swiss population constitutes the best, and perhaps only, example of a multilingual nation. Its unity has developed from coexistence within a single state for several centuries. A Swiss iconography has emerged based upon a strong pride in its long history, its democracy, and its freedom of religion. The William Tell legend is shared by all of its peoples, as is a sense of being mountaineers, however much this may be at variance with the operational reality of inhabiting a plateau. The different linguistic groups have tended to look inwardly at each other, rather than outwardly to the surrounding nation-states.

This is not to say that there exists no group exclusivity or cultural linkages abroad. During World War I the French-Swiss were pro-French and the German-Swiss pro-German, although sympathies of the latter decreased during the war. All groups opposed the German Nazi regime during World War II. In literary matters, French-Swiss writers have been part of the French cultural world, and German-Swiss writers of the German/Austrian tradition. The Italian-Swiss of Ticino have never expressed irredentist feelings toward Italy, but the presence of the empty alpine mountain region has created a general feeling of psychological isolation from other Swiss groups.

Part of the success of Switzerland in maintaining unity has been the devolution of government to the canton level. Each of the twenty-six cantons has tended to be rather homogeneous in language and religion. Nineteen cantons are predominantly German-speaking, six French-speaking, and one Italian-speaking. They manage local affairs in accord with prevailing sentiments and traditions of their inhabitants. Indeed, one canton stoutly resisted extension of the voting franchise to women until 1990. The federal government is responsible for such nationwide concerns as defense, foreign affairs, and operating the state's railways. Canton governments handle most other governmental functions. These include running local school systems. Most specify the language of instruction as the dominant language in the canton, although two languages are employed in schools in Berne, Fribourg, and Valais. Protestants form a clear majority in ten and Roman Catholics in twelve, with a balance of the two religions in four cantons.

The Jurassians. Switzerland was not completely immune to the waves of regional unrest that swept through much of Western Europe during the decades of the 1960s and 1970s. In the northwestern section of Berne Canton a group living in the Jura Mountain region successfully agitated for the establishment of a separate canton of its own. Although the goals of these Jurassians fell far short of sovereignty or irredentism, they displayed much in common with the struggles of Basques, Corsicans, and Northern Ireland Catholics.

The Jurassians are French-speaking Roman Catholics who found themselves after 1813 to be part of German Protestant Berne Canton, where they constituted 12 percent of the population and occupied 20 percent of the area (see Figure 3-6). During the Middle Ages their ancestors had lived in a feudal unit headed by the Roman Catholic Prince-Bishop of Basel. Following the Reformation, their territory became a political entity separated from Basel. In 1792, when European national identities began to develop rapidly as a consequence of the French Revolution, long-standing grievances against the German-speaking Swiss led three northern districts to proclaim their independence as the *République Rauracienne*. They then voted to unite with France and were constituted the *département* of Mont Terrible. After Napoleon overran Switzerland, he annexed four adjacent French-speaking districts to France.

To the dismay of local inhabitants, the 1815 Treaty of Paris returned all districts to Switzerland, where they were made part of Berne Canton. The residents chafed under what they perceived as pressures upon them for Germanization. In 1830, 1836, 1839, 1874, and 1915 there were outbursts of local separatist activity. It began again in 1947. Unhappiness was confined principally to Roman Catholic French-speaking districts. Protestant French-speakers in Berne Canton, who generally lived in the southern part of the Jura Mountains, opposed the actions of the separatists. By 1957 public opinion had become strongly polarized, and the Swiss decided to see whether a majority of inhabitants favored a referendum on Jurassian separatism. A positive vote on the question of holding a referendum occurred in 1959.

The ensuing decade of the 1960s saw increasing political activity and several acts of violence, including the bombings of barracks, a bank, a railroad, and buildings belonging to antiseparatists. Most of the actions were traced to a small group of three dedicated terrorists. A sharp economic decline in the region's economy contributed to tensions in the region. Its traditional cottage production of conventional watches suffered greatly from the development and widespread sale of electronic timepieces.

In 1974 the Swiss government conducted a referendum on separate cantonal status in the seven French-speaking districts of the Jura region. Voting was rather evenly split. However, there was a two-thirds majority for separation in the three northernmost districts and only a one-third minority in the three southernmost ones. The government decided in 1975 to recommend that the three northern Jura districts be formed into a separate canton, and the decision was ratified by 82 percent of Swiss voters in a nationwide referendum in 1978. Despite achieving their political goal, the Jurassian separatists have voiced unhappiness about the loss of the southern districts. Agitation has continued for the other districts to join the new Jurassian canton.

The Italian-Swiss. Although the population of the Ticino region has never wavered in its allegiance to the Swiss Confederation, the Italian-speaking Swiss have developed some grievances in recent years. These particularly are related to the migration of German-speakers into their region. German-Swiss now make up 10 percent of the area's population. Very few learn to speak Italian. They operate businesses or build vacation homes. They also have established separate German-language schools.

Unhappiness is also generated by substantial migration into Ticino from Italy. It is estimated that these newcomers now constitute 40 percent or more of the population. This local tension is part of a nationwide concern in Switzerland over foreigners who have come for menial jobs that native Swiss prefer not to take. Resentments derive from competition for higher-level employment and high social welfare costs for supporting the families of immigrants.

The Norden States

Northern Europe consists of five politically independent countries that sometimes are described as "states in happy disunity." They cover a territory three times that of the United Kingdom, yet share a collective population barely a third that of the British Isles. Despite a history of past conflicts, they maintain no ongoing claims against each other's territory, although two of them do have border questions with outside neighbors. Most often they are identified as the "Scandinavian countries." However, only Norway and Sweden actually are located on the Scandinavian Peninsula. Denmark long ago lost its share of that terrain unit, and Finland and Iceland also lie away from it. Their populations have adopted the term "Norden" as a joint designation for the region, and that term is used here. (See Table 3-3.)

Norden could well have emerged as a single nation-state in the modern era. Differences among its five states are no greater than regional differences within each one of them. They jointly share a higher degree of political-geographic homogeneity and coherence than found in many states functioning in other regions of Europe. Norden was the hearth area for the development of the Germanic languages. Danish, Swedish, Norwegian, Faeroese, and Icelandic remain mutually intelligible, although Finnish is a very different non-Indo-European tongue belonging to the Finno-Ugrian linguistic family.

Language is only part of the common culture of the region. All of the states, including Finland, became Lutheran after the Protestant Reformation. Their distinctive traditions in literature and art set them apart from other European areas. Scandinavian furniture design is sought after throughout the world. The countries share a common history of development in association with each other. Their past has involved shared control of extensive additional parts of Europe, including the British Isles, northern France, northern Germany, Poland, European Russia, and even substantial territories within the Mediterranean Basin. In the modern era they have adopted similar types of parliamentary democracies that lean toward democratic socialism.

Norden is also closely interlinked. With the exception of distant Iceland, the individual states are each other's closest neighbors and trading partners. The narrow waterways have long provided easier communication among their various settlements than was the case of such major powers as France or the Habsburg Empire. They early participated in the Hanseatic League that fostered and protected trade along the shores of the Baltic and North seas. In more modern times businesses have developed networks of production and distribution that ignore international boundaries. A common electricity grid began with the linking of Denmark and Norway by undersea cable in 1912 and now includes twenty interconnections.

In the twentieth century these countries have cooperated in a variety of ways. In 1952 they established the Nordic Council as a regional advisory and planning group composed of key officials from each state. They

TABLE 3-3 NORTHERN EUROPE

Five states live in "happy disunity" with a common history but past specific grievances against each other. They share cultural similarities in Germanic languages, Evangelical Lutheran religion, close economic linkages, high proportions of nonecumene (considering Greenland as part of Denmark; Estonia and Latvia also properly belong to this group, but are treated with other former parts of the USSR), the states have virtually no territorial disputes nor threats of secession.

State	Total Population	Area (sq. miles)	Distinctive Features of Group
Denmark	5,200,000	16,638 (+Greenland 840,000)	
Dominant Nation and % Total			
Danes, 97%			Germanic (Danish) language, Lutheran
Significant Regional Groups and % Total			
Faeroese, 1%			Islanders, Germanic (Faeroese) language, Lutheran
Greenlanders, 1%			Inuit (Eskimo) language, Lutheran or Animist
Norway	4,300,000	125,000	
Dominant Nation and % Total			
Norwegians, 97%			Germanic (Norwegian) language, Lutheran
Significant Regional Groups and % Total			
Lapps, <1%			Finnic (Saami) language, Lutheran
Sweden	8,750,000	174,000	
Dominant Nation and % Total			
Swedes, 90%			Germanic (Swedish) language, Lutheran
Significant Regional Groups and % Total			
Finns, 3.5%			Finnic (Finnish) language, Lutheran
Lapps, <1%			Finnic (Saami) language, Lutheran
Finland	5,000,000	130,000	
Dominant Nation and % Total			
Finns, 93%			Finnic (Finnish) language, Lutheran
Significant Regional Groups and % Total			
Swedes, 6%			Germanic (Swedish) language, Lutheran
Lapps, <1%			Finnic (Saami) language, Lutheran
Iceland	40,000	275,000	
Dominant Nation and % Total			
Icelanders, 94%			Germanic (Icelandic) language, Lutheran

abolished passport controls among their citizens. They collectively became parts of the European Free Trade Association. Although Denmark later elected to become a member of the rival European Community, agreements have resulted in virtually free movements of raw materials, goods, and labor throughout their territories. Scandinavian Airlines (SAS) is a joint venture facilitating commercial interchange with each other, as well as tying the region to the rest of the world. As a result of coordination of laws and regulations, workers and professional people move easily from one state to another.

Despite their large total territories, the Norden countries should be viewed as relatively small states best compared to those of the Lotharingian Corridor. They occupy Europe's northern fringe and include some of that Continent's most empty lands. The ecumenes of all are concentrated in their southern latitudes and are quite limited in extent (Figure 3-7). Indeed, aside from Iceland, their developed areas lie closer to each other than each does to its own outlying territory. The regions of Norway, Sweden, and Finland that lie beyond the Arctic Circle increasingly are seen as a common problem area requiring joint planning and development. The term *Nordkalotten* ("Northern cap") has become a common designation for their shared Arctic territory.

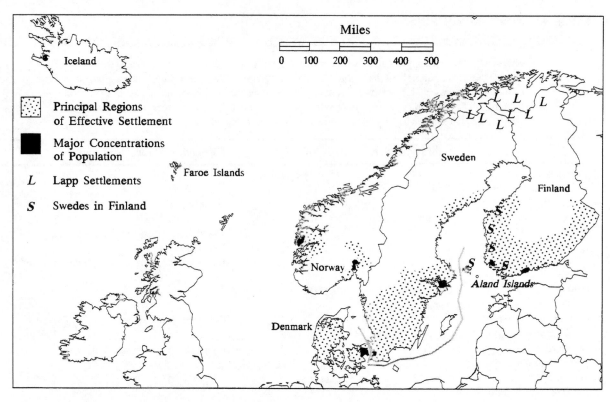

FIGURE 3-7   THE NORTH EUROPEAN ECUMENE

The Norden states have a number of other problems in common. Extensive offshore seabeds demand attention for fishery preservation and other resource management. The increasing pollution of the Baltic Sea has become a major concern for Denmark, Sweden, and Finland. As small states, they find that economic self-sufficiency is impossible, and they must develop exchange relationships with other productive regions. There are responsibilities for maintaining aboriginal peoples. They have to find ways of coexisting with states much larger and more powerful than themselves.

Like the Lotharingian countries, the Norden states jointly function as a frontier region, in this case between the former Soviet Union and the powers of Western Europe and Anglo-America. The interests of the western Norden states—Norway, Denmark, and Iceland—are closely linked to the West. Norway and Denmark joined the North Atlantic Treaty Organization (NATO). The Finns found that they had to maintain neutrality and close economic ties eastward with the USSR. Sweden, in deference to Finland's position, adopted a nonaligned posture in East–West rivalry. Both Sweden and Finland have established strong economic relations with Western Europe and Anglo-America, however.

Given their similar characteristics, interlinkages, and common problems, the question remains as to why the Norden peoples remain politically fragmented. It certainly is not the result of lack of attempts at union. King Canute the Great brought together Denmark, Norway, and England in the eleventh century, and his successors added the Baltic areas of Pomerania and Estonia. In the thirteenth century, Denmark, Norway, and Sweden joined together in what was called the Kalmar Union. Sweden soon broke away, but Norway remained under Danish control for four more centuries.

Sweden expanded eastward between the thirteenth and seventeenth centuries, incorporating Finland, southern Karelia, Estonia, and Latvia. It lost the last three territories to Peter the Great of Russia in the early eighteenth century, and its colony of Finland became part of the Russian Empire at the beginning of the nineteenth century following the Napoleonic Wars. It was compensated at the time by gaining Norway from Denmark, which had unluckily allied itself with Napoleonic France. Sweden's union with Norway lasted until 1905, although there was constant friction. Despite past failures at unity, intellectuals and politicians continue to debate the advantages of a future Norden amalgamation.

The principal reason for the present disunity of Norden is the emergence of separate national identities within each of its states. Although their limited areas of ecumene have been easily accessible to each other, they remain separated by empty mountains and bodies of water. Languages were differentiated, as pronunciations and vocabulary increasingly departed in different directions from the common tongue spoken in the thirteenth century and earlier. Danes thus think of Swedes as speaking "with marbles in their mouths." Past relationships have resulted in national iconographies embodying negative images of each other. Finns cannot forget the Swedish domination of two centuries ago; Norwegians and Icelanders preserve group memories of past Danish authoritarian control; Danes continue to regret the loss of Skåne to Sweden; and Swedes fret about Finland's post–World War I acquisition of the Åland Islands.

Complementing their separate national identities is the fact that no compelling reason exists to encourage unification. They "have their cake and eat it too," for they enjoy the psychological and operational benefits of national sovereignty, yet share a common market, easy movement across each other's territories, and assurance of defense of their homelands through formal and informal associations with NATO.

Norway

Long oriented to the Atlantic Ocean is the Kingdom of Norway. Its total area of 125,000 square miles is stretched across thirteen degrees of latitude in a convoluted coastline of more than 1,700 miles. The barren mountains and rocky headlands have offered little opportunity for agricultural settlement. The sea, however, has supported for millennia a fishing, trading, and, in the past, pillaging population. A quarter of Norway's 4,200,000 inhabitants occupy a string of tiny settlements along the edge of the sea all the way to the border with Russia. Half the population, however, is concentrated away from the Atlantic in the southeastern corner around Oslo Fjord, which was the base from which Harold the Fair Hair first unified the Norwegian state in 872. The name *Norvegr* ("Northern way") was used long before that period to designate the collection of numerous small tribal political units established in protected fjords along the coast.

Norsemen attacked European coastal regions as far away as the eastern Mediterranean. They particularly sought the accumulated wealth of the medieval Christian churches, and their plundering did not end with Christianization in A.D. 1000. Norwegians established control over extensive territories in the British Isles, Iceland, Greenland, and Anglo-America. They early subdued to the Lapps and Finns of the Arctic coast, competing with the Russians of Novgorod in collecting tribute from them.

Norway's early greatness ended by the fourteenth century. From their base in Bergen, German merchants of the Hanseatic League wrested control of Norwegian trade in fish and grain. The royal dynasty died out in 1319, and Norway, with its western lands, passed first to Sweden and then to Denmark. Up to half the population perished during the Black Death (bubonic plague) epidemic of 1349. Over ensuing centuries Norway retained the status of a separate kingdom, but steadily saw itself reduced to a Danish dependency.

It inevitably was involved in Denmark's long struggles with Sweden. These included few land battles with the Swedes, however. Despite their contiguity, the two kingdoms were well insulated from each other by the emptiness of the mountain region that lay between their respective areas of settlement. This frontier zone was reduced to a delimited boundary only in 1751, and even then the indigenous Lapps of the north were allowed freely to move reindeer herds across the arbitrary line.

The union with Denmark ended in 1814, following the unwise decision of the Danes to ally themselves with Napoleon. Norwegians had been caught up in Europe's wildfire spirit of nationalism of the time, and they proclaimed their independence as a nation-state. However, they were forced by the other European powers to accept the king of Sweden as monarch. Relations with Sweden were never happy. Norway was oriented westward, developing one of the world's largest merchant fleets. Sweden was concerned with Baltic lands to the east.

In 1905 Norway was able to break its tie to Sweden and to become independent. The issue precipitating separation was refusal of Sweden to permit establishment of Norwegian consular posts in the many world ports where their ships sailed. Following the break, the throne of Norway was offered to a Swedish prince, who refused it, and then to a Danish prince, who accepted.

The newly independent state could call upon a number of centripetal forces to support its unity. Through oral sagas and nineteenth-century universal education its population was aware of Norway's long history as a separate kingdom and the successes it had achieved. The population was homogeneous in language and religion as a consequence of social processes that had occurred during the past association with Denmark. It also shared a resolve not to come under Swedish or Danish domination again.

Norway also had some centrifugal problems of coherence, although these were never strong enough to threaten the integrity of the state. Its population was territorially fragmented among two major clusters around Oslo and Bergen and tiny communities along its extensive coastline. Linkage by sea was time-consuming, costly, and obsolete in an age of railroads and telecommunications. Its terrain demanded substantial investment to establish a modern infrastructure of railroads, roads, and telegraph lines. The first railroad between Oslo and Bergen was completed in 1909 at great expense because of the need to construct numerous tunnels and bridges. The southern coast city of Kristiansand was linked to the rest of the country by rail only in 1935, and the northern port of Stavanger only under German occupation in 1944. Rails were extended to the Arctic lands in 1962.

The Norwegian language dispute. A major concern for many intellectuals and politicians was the shakiness of Norwegian national identity. Despite a century of separation, Danish culture continued to dominate Norway's people. The Danish language had replaced indigenous Old Norse following the demographic losses caused by the bubonic plague. This was particularly through the agency of the Danish Lutheran Bible. All writing was in literary Danish, and the urbanized and educated population preferred spoken Danish to the dialects of Norway's rural inhabitants.

In the mid-nineteenth century a segment of Norwegian scholars had begun the so-called *Landsmål* ("land language") movement. It sought to institutionalize a local western dialect as an official Norwegian written and spoken language that would be independent of Danish and Swedish. A equivalent number of scholars supported as a literary standard the continued use of the Danish *Riksmål*, the "official" language, although modified in spelling and grammar to represent existing Norwegian pronunciation and usage. This rather arcane dispute reflected deeper conflicts between nationalist reformers and existing elite groups. It also had a basis in regionalist competition between eastern and western parts of the country. In 1885, while still under Swedish control, a left-wing opposition party gained control of the Norwegian parliament and recognized *Landsmål* as the official language of Norway. Growing popular opposition to Sweden gave it increasing stature, although it remained under constant attack from *Riksmål* supporters.

The dispute over language continued after independence and remains an active, if minor, issue today. The Norwegian parliament sought to establish a blended language, but in 1929 recognized the legitimacy of both languages under the names *Nynorsk* ("New Norse") and *Bokmål* ("book language"). School systems were given the right to adopt one or the other. Smaller communities in southern, western, and central Norway tended to adopt *Nynorsk*. Eastern and northern towns mainly

stayed with *Bokmål*. Currently less than 20 percent of the population supports the use of *Nynorsk* and less than 10 percent of the country's books are published in it. The geographic significance of the language conflict is its continued reflection of regional frictions, although these have none of the separatist overtones embodied by such literary language disputes as those between Serbians and Croatians or Castilians and Catalans. Norwegian scholars now tend to be more concerned by the intrusion into the vocabulary of numerous words borrowed from English.

Spitzbergen. Halfway between Norway and the North Pole lie the group of nine large islands and numerous small ones known as Spitzbergen, or Svalbard. They have a total area of 24,000 square miles and a population of under 4,000. For eight months of the year these lands are locked in Arctic ice. Norway's first recorded claim to the islands was in 1261, and it has challenged attempts by rival states to use the islands ever since. On different occasions during the seventeenth century Norway contested their use as a base by English, Dutch, French, and Swedish whalers. Their significance faded within a few decades when whaling ended. In the early twentieth century Norway established a meteorological station on the islands and also began mining coal there. A treaty drafted under League of Nations auspices recognized the Norwegian claim in 1920. It contained the proviso that any other state that had claimed the islands and had remained active in coal mining could continue. This applied only to Soviet Russia. The Russian government today continues to operate two of the three mines that it had established, and Norway also operates two of its own. Hopes of finding oil on the islands have not been rewarded, despite deep drilling of a half-dozen shafts.

Other regional problems. Norway's northernmost province of Finnmark remains one of the world's last frontiers of settlement. Its mixed population of Norwegians, Lapps, and Finnish-speaking *Kvens* requires continuing economic and social assistance. A dilemma is posed particularly in regard to appropriate governmental policy toward the region's 20,000 Lapps. It is a question of attempting to preserve their distinctive culture or giving greater opportunities to future generations through encouragement of assimilation into the Norwegian nation. Contact with the modern world has permanently altered their traditional way of life and brought problems of dependency and alcoholism. Only 20 percent continue to raise reindeer, and perhaps only half can now speak the Lapp language. Although Lapps are gaining group political awareness across the Norden states, their small numbers and local minority status pose few of the regional problems confronted by Canada in its Inuit community.

Sweden

The largest of the Norden states, with 173,000 square miles and 8,500,000 population, is Sweden. Much of its territory is unfavorable for agricultural settlement. Its northern areas lie in the latitudes of the Arctic Circle and beyond. Its southern reaches are dominated by the crystalline rocks of the ancient Kjoellen Mountains and the planed-off Fennoscandian Shield. As the center of Europe's last great continental ice sheet, Sweden lost its accumulated soils 20,000 years ago. Its exposed surfaces have only slowly weathered into new soils since that period. The moving ice also gouged great irregularities on the surface that are now filled with water as lakes and bogs. Only the central coastal area around Stockholm and the southern margins facing Denmark support large concentrations of people.

The "Old Finns." Sweden's internal and external political geographic problems are minor in comparison with other states of Europe. They chiefly involve its relations with Finland. Internally, some 200,000 Finns were recorded in its last census. Most were recent migrants taking advantage of Sweden's greater economic opportunities and higher living standards. However, a compact group of 20,000 living in the Tornio valley west of the Finnish border are "Old Finns," who remained in Sweden in 1809 when Russia acquired Finland and established the present international border. They tend to be bilingual in Swedish and evince virtually no irredentist sentiments. They have achieved what appears to be a satisfactory degree of local autonomy.

The Åland Islands. The Swedes have never completely accepted the loss of the Åland Islands to Finland. Their 25,000 inhabitants remain 96 percent Swedish-speaking. About 80 percent live on Fest-Åland Island, with the remainder scattered among eighty other units of the 6,500-island archipelago. Its dry land area amounts to 475 square miles and is continually expanding as the seabed of the Baltic Sea each century rebounds about forty inches after being depressed under the enormous weight of the glacier. The islands had been part of Sweden since the thirteenth century, but were taken by Russia in 1809 to protect the approaches to the Gulf of Finland and St. Petersburg.

Although inhabitants of the Åland Islands had overwhelmingly voted during an unofficial plebiscite in 1917 to be joined to Sweden, the newly independent Finnish state successfully pressed its claim to the islands through the League of Nations. A geographically interesting aspect of that organization's decision in favor of Finland was the weight it gave to the fact that the archipelago was tied directly to the Finnish mainland in winter by freezing of the shallow sea. Finland did accord the archipelago the status of an autonomous, Swedish-speaking region. It was demilitarized, which meant that young men have been exempt from service in the Finnish armed forces. The islands capitalize on their bridge position between Sweden and Finland for a developed tourism industry. Their young people are drawn to Sweden for education and employment.

The Lapps. Sweden's northern province of Norrbotten contains 10,000 Lapps, about one-fourth of their total numbers in Europe. Only 3,000 of these remain migratory reindeer herders, however. They continue to wander across the boundary with Norway in accord with a 1751 border treaty signed between Sweden and Denmark at a time when Norway was still merged with the latter kingdom. Other Lapps have assimilated to varying degrees into modern Swedish society, although those in the north often adopt the Finnish tongue over Swedish for modern communication. Most retain their distinctive Finno-Ugrian language and cultural traditions.

Baltic concerns. Sweden has national interests throughout the Baltic Sea region. It experiences directly the degradation of the sea and its bed, and has sought to develop regional cooperation for protection and restoration of the sea. Most of the lands around the Baltic were under Swedish control for extensive periods in the past. During the cold war period between the Western Alliance and the USSR, Sweden adopted a neutral stance, avoiding any provocations that might have led to the Soviet regime establishing direct authority over Finland. The Swedes felt similar sympathies for Estonia and Latvia, whose peoples have maintained their Evangelical Lutheran religion and other cultural features developed during long association with Sweden. Before Estonia and Latvia became independent, refugees from the Soviet Baltic states found Swedish havens, and the government of Sweden was in the forefront in pressing for their improved political status. Since their independence, Sweden has extended economic and technical support to its former colonial areas.

Finland

The easternmost of the Norden states is Finland, which occupies an area of 130,000 square miles and has a population of 5,000,000. Its history has been that of a frontier between Swedes and Russians. Much of its territory came under Swedish domination in 1155. Peter the Great seized its southeastern region of Karelia in 1721 and Russia added more territory in 1749. All of Finland became an autonomous grand duchy under the Russian tsar in 1809. Finland declared its independence in 1917, and, after a civil war and ensuing struggle with Red Army forces, it signed a peace treaty with Soviet Russia that recognized its separation in 1920.

The Russians encouraged the development of Finnish national feelings during most of their century of rule. This was done particularly to reduce Swedish influences. For much of the Russian period, though, Swedish-speaking administrators continued to manage local affairs. Although Finnish literature had begun in 1548 when Sweden reluctantly allowed translation of the New Testament, Finns could not use their own language in the court system until 1863. The privileged position of the Swedish language was not abolished until 1902. However, a hated process of Russianization had begun in the previous decade that served to further stimulate Finnish national feelings.

As elsewhere in Europe after the French Revolution, the emergence of popular national awareness began with interests in linguistic distinctiveness and traditional folklore. The most significant early event in the development of the Finnish national iconography was the compilation and publication in 1835 of the *Kalevala*, an epic poem of 23,000 lines that had been drawn from Karelian legends. Its author is famous for his statement that "We no longer are Swedes, we cannot become Russians, so let us then be Finns." Anti-Swedish and anti-Russian sentiments have since remained significant parts of Finnish identity.

The Karelians. When Finland became independent of Russia, it successfully acquired all of the territory of its predecessor Grand Duchy of Finland, including the Karelian Isthmus and the northern shore of Lake Ladoga. Peter the Great originally had annexed these to Russia to protect approaches to his transplanted capital of St. Petersburg. The new border came within a dozen miles of that city, which later was renamed Leningrad. Finland also gained access to the Arctic Ocean by being ceded a strip of territory, the Petsamo (or Pechenga) Corridor, which interposed Finnish territory between Soviet Russia and Norway.

As war clouds gathered in Europe in 1939, the Soviet Union requested that Finland transfer to it several small islands near Leningrad. Although Marshal Mannerheim, Finland's national hero of independence, recommended compliance, the Finnish government refused the Soviet request. The USSR responded with a greater demand, calling for a portion of the Karelian Isthmus and the lease of a military base on the Hanko Peninsula marking the beginning of the Gulf of Finland. It offered border adjustments in the north as compensation. Finland again refused, and the USSR commenced military operations. This "winter war" resulted in

Finnish defeat after six weeks of heroic resistance. The peace treaty was harsh. Finland lost the islands off Leningrad, all of the Karelian Isthmus, its third largest city of Viipuri (Vyborg), the northern shore of Lake Ladoga, and a small border district farther to the north.

More than 430,000 inhabitants of these regions fled to Finland rather than become Soviet subjects. They constituted a full 10 percent of the Finnish population, and their relocation placed great stress upon the Finnish economy and society. Homes and farmsteads were created for them in a process that involved assiduous efforts by every community. Karelian dialects tended to be noticeably different from standard Finnish, and a high proportion were Russian Orthodox in religion. Some Karelians returned to their former homes in 1941, after Finland had entered World War II as a German ally and within three months had regained the lost territories.

Finland lost them once again, following its capitulation in 1944. Finland was also forced to cede the Petsamo Corridor to the Soviet Union and to grant to the USSR a 50-year lease for a naval base on the Porkkala Peninsula, which lay less than twenty miles west of the Finnish capital of Helsinki. The Soviet regime dropped its earlier requirement of a similar lease on the Hanko Peninsula, but it demanded that Finland pay $300,000,000 in reparations over the following six years. More than 200,000 German troops were in Finland when Finland signed the armistice. The Germans reacted by destroying every structure in northern Finland during their retreat westward, towards Norway.

In the postwar period Finland found itself required to accommodate Soviet interests. It became a principal supplier of forest products and machinery to the USSR and abstained from joining alliances in the West. It steadily profited from this relationship, as the Soviet Union struggled to break its international isolation and modernize itself. Finland has pressed no formal claims to its lost territories, although the Soviet head of state was taunted with demands for the return of Viipuri (Vyborg) during a 1990 visit to Helsinki. The Finnish people showed particular concern for the fate of Soviet Estonia across the Gulf of Finland, with whose population it shared numerous similarities in language and culture. Like Sweden, Finland has extended aid to now independent Estonia.

The Swedes in Finland. In addition to the population of the Åland Islands noted above, more than 300,000 other Swedish-speakers live in Finland. These Finnish-Swedes are concentrated in three separated areas along the western and southern coasts and in the Helsinki region. They constitute about 6.5 percent of the total population, but their proportion is gradually decreasing because of a lower birth rate and intermarriage with

Finns. They are guaranteed cultural equality, and official documents and signs in Finland appear in both Swedish and Finnish. During the Karelian resettlement program, communes with Swedish majorities were not required to provide housing and farms for refugees, as these would alter local group balances. Instead, the Swedes in Finland were given the option of making financial contributions. Although they occupy compact areas, the Finnish-Swedes have not demonstrated any irredentist feelings. They exhibit a lively culture, with their own literary works and plays. They also maintain close contacts with Sweden.

Denmark

Another Norden country on the Baltic Sea is Denmark. Although its conventional image abroad is that of a peninsular extension of the European continent, it is really an insular state. Less than a third of Denmark's population of 5,200,000 inhabits the Jutland Peninsula, although it constitutes two-thirds of Danish territory in Europe. Its western margins are a particularly empty region of sand dunes and glacially deposited moraines. The other two-thirds of the population live compactly on a cluster of Baltic islands between Sweden and Germany. Denmark's capital of Copenhagen is located on the largest of these islands, Sjaelland, opposite the coast of Sweden.

The medieval Danish kingdom controlled substantial territories that have since been lost, including Pomerania, Skåne, Schleswig-Holstein, Norway, and Iceland (see Figure 3-8). Northern Estonia was once part of its domains, and the Estonian capital's present name Tallinn means literally "Dane town." Denmark had colonies in the West Indies and, in the nineteenth century, also on the west coast of Africa. All were eventually given up until only Greenland and the Faeroe Islands remain as Danish possessions, and both of these function in an increasingly independent fashion.

Skåne. Across a strait less than ten miles wide from the island of Sjaelland is the Swedish region of Skåne. Until 1657 it was part of Denmark, and its speech patterns still remain much closer to Danish than to Swedish. Its possession enabled Denmark in 1427 to begin collecting tolls on all ships entering and leaving the Baltic Sea. Its former herring fishery also contributed to Denmark's prosperity. Neighboring states supported Swedish conquest of Skåne in order to deny Danish control of both sides of the strait, although Denmark continued to exact tolls from passing ships until 1857, when pressure from the United States forced it to give up this source of revenue.

FIGURE 3-8 DENMARK'S TERRITORIAL CHANGES

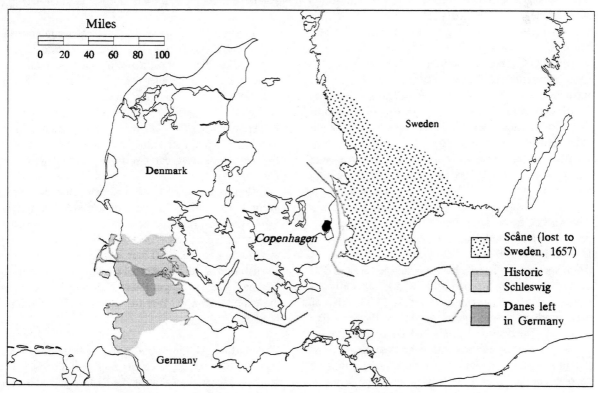

Schleswig-Holstein. In the modern era Denmark's most bitter losses have been those of the duchies of Schleswig and Holstein in 1864. It had long defended these approaches to the Jutland Peninsula against attacks by Swedish kings and German princes. Although Holstein was clearly German in language and culture, Schleswig was mainly Danish. Both enjoyed a distinctive status under the Danish monarch separate from the rest of Denmark. As part of a grand scheme for uniting the multitude of German states, Bismarck, the Prussian Minister of State, successfully contrived to force Denmark out of the two duchies with the aid of Austria. Despite heroically resisting the combined German forces for more than six weeks, the Danes ultimately were forced to give up a third of their state's territory and 40 percent of its population, including 200,000 Danish-speakers in northern Schleswig. The peace treaty provided that these Danes could be rejoined to Denmark if a plebiscite showed that they so desired. Following Prussia's annexation, strong efforts were made to Germanize all of the territory. Over the next three decades more than 50,000 Danes migrated northward. In 1878 Prussia unilaterally abrogated the plebiscite clause of the treaty.

Schleswig-Holstein became an issue again at the end of World War I. Following Germany's defeat, Denmark pressed a claim for return of Schleswig. It recognized that the Germans of Holstein and southern Schleswig would prefer to remain part of the German state. During the last decades of the nineteenth century many Germans had also settled in central parts of that duchy. A plebiscite in 1919 resulted in 80 percent of the inhabitants of northern Schleswig voting for return to Denmark. Central Schleswig had a majority electing to remain with Germany, however. After being rejoined to Denmark, northern Schleswig again was attached to Germany in 1940, following Denmark's complete capitulation less than three hours after a German invasion. It once more became Danish in 1945, when the post–World War I boundary was reestablished. A small number of German-speakers remain in northern Schleswig, and more than 30,000 Danes live across the border in German territory.

The Faeroe Islands. Denmark retains a vestige of its former extensive Atlantic territories in the Faeroe Islands. Lying 800 miles from Denmark and 350 miles from Norway, the islands have a combined area of 540 square miles and a population of 50,000. Only 35 square miles is cultivated, however, and 90 percent of their production for export consists of fish and fish products. The Faeroe Islands had become a part of Norway in the fourteenth century, and the language of the inhabitants remains perhaps the least modified descendant of the Old Norse language spoken throughout the Norden lands at that time. The language is closely related to modern Icelandic and to the *Landsmål* of rural Norway.

Denmark managed to retain the old Norwegian possessions of the Faeroe Islands, Greenland, and Iceland in 1814 when it was forced to cede the remainder of Norway to Sweden. Sweden had little direct interest in them, being primarily concerned in consolidating its control over the Scandinavian Peninsula. During the early nineteenth century, however, the Norwegians of Sweden pressed for recognition of the islands as a part of their territory. Denmark responded by abolishing the *Løgting*, the ancient Faeroese parliament that was perhaps the oldest in Europe, and formally incorporating the islands into Denmark as an ordinary county.

Danes considered the Faeroe Islands to be a rather poverty-stricken colony and had contempt for the local language. It was not until the twentieth century that the language was allowed in local schools, and it was not recognized as an official tongue until 1938. Denmark did permit the *Løgting* to be reestablished as a consultative body in 1852. At that time the total population of the Faeroe Islands numbered under 9,000.

The independence of Norway from Sweden in 1905 stimulated national passions among the Faeroese, who pressed for protection of their language and development of self-government within Denmark. They gained Danish recognition of a distinctive Faeroese flag designed in 1919, although it could not be flown officially until World War II, when it served to distinguish Faeroese fishing boats from those of German-occupied Denmark.

In 1945 the Faeroese sought greater autonomy for the islands. The Danes, in contrast, were in favor of even fuller incorporation within Denmark and presented the Faeroe people with the alternatives of either complete unity or complete independence. An island referendum showed an almost even split among the local population. Denmark responded by granting home rule in 1948 that met virtually all the objectives of the Faeroese seeking greater self-government within the Danish kingdom.

Denmark subsequently has protected the fishing grounds upon which the islands depend. The Faeroes were allowed to remain outside the regulations of the European Free Trade Association when Denmark joined that body in 1960. Later, in 1972, as a condition for its entering the European Economic Community, Denmark secured recognition of fishing limits around the islands from the other members of the Common Market.

Greenland. Although the island of Greenland occupies 840,000 square miles, its population of 54,000 is scarcely larger than that of the Faeroe Islands. Five-sixths of its territory is covered by an ice cap that in places is 10,000 feet deep. More than 90 percent of the population is located along Greenland's western shore. No more than 10 percent of its people are of unmixed European origin. The remainder are Eskimos and persons of mixed ancestry. Their local language, Greenlandic, is a mixed speech of many origins.

Eric the Red established a settlement of 3,000 Norsemen in Greenland in A.D. 960, and he gave the island its misleading name. In 1270 the Greenland colony recognized the authority of the king of Norway, but contact with the outside world was lost about the year 1500. Two centuries later a missionary sponsored by Denmark found that the Europeans had disappeared, although remains of their former farms were evident. Danes began trading with the approximately 7,000 natives, establishing a monopoly that was intended not only to benefit Danish commercial interests but also to protect and preserve the native culture. Ships exchanged coffee and sugar for local sealskins. Later the Danes introduced sheep as a source of meat, and encouraged offshore fishing for cod.

Denmark's government established a special administration for Greenland, whose authority was generally accepted by the local population. It was contested by the Norwegians, however, who maintained that Greenland had been part of Norway before that country's union with Denmark in 1380, and therefore should have remained with Norway when it was joined to Sweden in 1814. Norway particularly claimed part of Greenland's largely uninhabited east coast on the basis of continuous use by Norwegian seal hunters. An agreement with Norway gave Norwegians special rights in two areas, but in 1931 a group of Norwegian fishermen, supported by their government, landed in eastern Greenland and proclaimed it to be part of Norway. Denmark brought the matter before the International Court of Justice, which recognized Danish claims to the entire island. Norway accepted the decision, and officially ended all claims. Earlier, Denmark's claim to all of Greenland was subject to challenge by the United States, based upon the explorations of Robert Peary and Adolphus Greely. Any American rights were relinquished under the agreement by which the United States purchased the Virgin Islands from Denmark.

During World War II the United States established air bases in Greenland to provide refueling for planes bound for Europe. These have remained as part of Denmark's defensive contribution to the North Atlantic Treaty Organization. In 1953, in response to local requests, Denmark ended the colonial status of Greenland and made it an ordinary county (*amt*) of Denmark. However, Greenlanders found that they could not easily adapt to Danish patterns of economy and society. In 1979 the government of Denmark sponsored a referendum which showed that a majority of Greenlanders favored a special status with local self-government, which was then introduced. However, Greenland does retain the same rights as counties within Denmark, and it receives substantial subsidies from the Danish government.

Iceland

Although the island state of Iceland has an area of 40,000 square miles, less than one-sixth of its territory is actually settled. More than 5,000 square miles are covered by glaciers. Its population of 250,000 is concentrated in the southwest around the capital of Reykjavík. The first European settlement in Iceland occurred in A.D. 874 when a number of local Norwegian chieftains moved their clans there rather than accept the authority of Norway's first king, Harold the Fair-Haired. In A.D. 930 their descendants convened a parliament, known as the *Althing*. It met annually for several hundred years, until abolished by Denmark in 1801. The *Althing* voted in 1262 to swear allegiance to the king of Norway in return for receiving one shipload of lumber each year. A century later Iceland came under Danish control when the royal family of Norway died out and the crown passed to the king of Denmark.

Iceland was treated as a remote colony for most of its association with Denmark. Its population was exploited economically through a Danish monopoly on trade. Iceland maintained its separate language and cultural identity, however, owing largely to the publication of the Bible in Icelandic. Gradual governmental changes within Denmark had repercussions in its Atlantic possession. The ending of the Danish absolute monarchy in 1834 led to the establishment of a consultative assembly in Iceland that bore the ancient name *Althing*. Trade was made open to all in 1844, and Iceland received its own separate constitution thirty years later. In 1904 it gained home rule, and in 1918 Denmark acknowledged that Iceland was an independent state under the Danish king.

Britain occupied Iceland in 1940 after Denmark succumbed to the German army. A year later the United States assumed responsibility from the British for protecting the island, even though America had not yet entered World War II. The Americans established a major air base at Keflavík. It gave support to separatist parties by announcing that Iceland had the right to sever connections with Denmark at any time after 1943. A referendum in 1944 showed that 97 percent of the population was in favor of independence, and an Icelandic republic was duly implemented that year.

In 1949 Iceland joined NATO and the Keflavík air base was reactivated. Iceland's participation in NATO faced stiff internal opposition, however, particularly after a series of disputes with the United Kingdom over fishing rights on its offshore seabeds that began in 1952. The problem was complicated by the fact that Britain was the major market for Iceland's fish. In 1961 the matter was resolved. The United Kingdom recognized Icelandic authority over an area twelve miles from its coasts, and Iceland granted limited fishing rights to British trawlers inside that area for a period of three years.

The Iberian Peninsula

For many people contemplating the map of Europe it is bothersome that such a natural unit as the Iberian Peninsula is divided as it is. (See Table 3-4.) As noted above, the political partitionings of the Scandinavian Peninsula and the island of Ireland generate similar feelings. Observers of partitioned Iberia would be even more disturbed if they could perceive that the solid color marking Spain actually masks a half-dozen distinctive areas that have struggled with each other for centuries and even now threaten to separate. Although regional divisions do not threaten the unity of Portugal nearly as much, that country also has internal strains between its south and north.

The Iberian Peninsula's disunity, like that of southeastern Europe, derives from its long role as a frontier zone between European civilization and the Muslim world. It has been a peripheral area to both regions, intermingling their traditions in varying mixtures to give rise to contrasting social and cultural combinations in different parts. The physical character of the Iberian Peninsula has served to keep the different peoples isolated from each other. An arid tableland core, rent by deep canyons, is a sparsely populated zone insulating the distinctive groups clustered on the peninsula's periphery.

The inhabitants of Spain and Portugal have ancestors who moved into Iberia from both Europe and North Africa. The earliest were likely tribes of Berbers and Celts. Later, Carthaginians, Romans, Visigoths, Arabs, and Berbers added to the population mix. Each contributed elements of their languages, technologies, religious beliefs, legal systems, and values that today are reflected to varying degree among the population groups (see Figure 3-9).

Part of the distinctiveness of Iberia is its lack of continuous participation in the development of European civilization. It was well integrated with the rest of the Continent in Roman times, trading its products for goods from all parts of the empire and contributing some of Rome's most famous writers. The Germanic Visigoths seized control of the region during the period of folk wandering and involved Iberia in much the same political process that beset the rest of Europe.

Then, from 800 to 1500, most of the peninsula was the domain of the Moors, who linked it to the Muslim world south and east of the Mediterranean Sea. Iberia remained feudal in outlook, missing the creativity unleashed by the European Renaissance. These centuries were not the Dark Ages, however, for the Moors reestablished a tie to the learning of the Greeks and Persians that had been severed by the barbarian invasions of the Roman Empire. Iberia under the Moors experienced a period of greater tolerance for diversity in religion and culture than existed either before or after.

With defeat of the last Moorish kingdom in 1492, Spain became a unified Christian state. For the next three centuries it was deeply involved in European affairs as well as in developments in the Americas. Its new rulers immediately rejected the Moorish heritage, expelling, converting, or decimating its Muslim and Jewish inhabitants. Its Roman Catholic clergy became noted for intolerance of dissent. This was the home of the Spanish Inquisition. A Basque soldier and ecclesiastic, St. Ignatius de Loyola, founded the Jesuit order.

Spain's vast empire in the Americas continuously funneled treasure into the state. Almost as quickly it was dissipated, largely because of costly wars to maintain the European possessions acquired by its kings, which included for varying lengths of time the Holy Roman Empire, the Low Countries, Franche–Comté, and parts of Italy.

Beginning early in the nineteenth century, the peninsula, bogged down in defending its colonial empires, again drifted away from European developments. For the most part it missed the commercial, industrial, and political revolutions that transformed Europe into the workshop of the world. These events did touch its northeastern corner, which yet remains alienated from traditionalist regions to the west and south.

The Reconquest. The Moors had swept across most of Iberia and into southeastern France in a matter of months during the eighth century. However, they were never able to subjugate the Christian kingdoms of the peninsula's northern fringe. Leon, Castile, Navarre, and Aragón preserved their existence, often fighting with each other as much as with Muslim territories. For seven centuries Christian and Muslim states coexisted in various combinations of struggle and alliance. The Muslim Moors also had to contend with occasional invasions by militant co-religionists from Africa.

The tide began to turn in favor of Christian supremacy by the twelfth century. With the assistance of knights from Galicia and support from England, the

TABLE 3-4 IBERIA

The western peninsular terminus of the main peninsula of Europe consists of two moderately sized states, Spain and Portugal, which assumed their present form by the sixteenth century, plus the micro territories of Andorra and Gibraltar. Their histories and societies bear the marks of centuries of struggle with the North African Moors, whose last foothold in Iberia was ended in 1492. Spain contains several distinctive linguistic and cultural groups that have asserted national identities separate from the dominant Castillians. Catalonians and Basques are further distinguished by their more modern economies. Regional distinctions between north and south also are present in Portugal.

State	Total Population	Area (sq. miles)	Distinctive Features of Group
Spain	39,000,000	195,000	
Dominant Nation and % Total			
Castillians, 62%			Romance language, Roman Catholic
Significant Regional Groups and % Total			
Catalonians, 16%			Romance (Catalan) language, Roman Catholic, Advanced economic development
Andalucians, 12%			Romance (Andalucían) language, Roman Catholic, Moorish heritage
Galicians, 8%			Romance(Galego) language, Roman Catholic, Possible Celtic heritage
Basques, 2%			Unique Basque language, Roman Catholic, Advanced economic development
Portugal	10,000,000	36,000	
Dominant Nation and % Total			
Portuguese, 94% (including 15% living in Algarve)			Romance (Portuguese) language, Roman Catholic
Significant Regional Groups and % Total			
Azoreans, 2.5%, and Madeirans, 2.5%			Romance (Portuguese) language, Roman Catholic, Island dwellers
Andorra	55,000	181	
Dominant Nation and % Total			
Andorrans, 29%			Romance (Catalan) language, Roman Catholic
(No regional groups, but population 50% Spanish, 8% French)			
Gibraltar	30,000	2	
Dominant Nation and % Total			
Gibraltarians, 67%			Romance (Spanish) language (although most residents are bilingual in English), Roman Catholic
Potential Trouble Areas and Possible Adversaries			
Spain has continuously sought to annex Gibraltar ever since its capture by the British in 1704			

Portuguese succeeded in eliminating Muslim control over the western fringe of Iberia by 1249. The Christian states of the north and east eventually coalesced through marriage and intrigue into the dual core regions of Aragón and Castile. They pressed steadily southward for 250 more years, until finally eliminating the peninsula's last remaining Muslim kingdom of Granada at the end of the fifteenth century.

Regional Divisions in Spain. The marriage of Ferdinand of Aragón and Isabella of Castile that coincided with victory over the Moors symbolized achievement of unity in Spain. The reality was rather different, however. Not only did Portugal lie outside the combined kingdom, but also the old Christian states retained identities as separate units, jealously preserving their *fueros* (traditional rights and laws). Kings of Spain were obliged to seek confirmation from the regional assembly (*cortes*) of each territorial entity.

It was the Castilians, under Philip II, who successfully integrated the young state, playing a role similar to that of the Normans in England. They established a

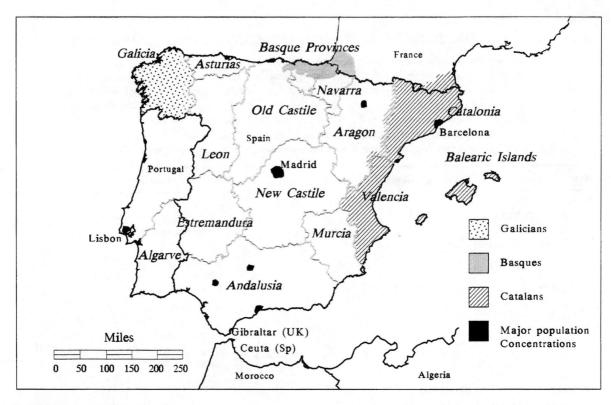

FIGURE 3-9   IBERIA

planned capital city (Madrid) around an old Moorish fortress in the desolate heart of the country. Favoring no particular region, Madrid immediately began playing a centralizing role comparable to that of Paris in France. The Basque and Catalonian areas of the northeast remained largely independent of the core, however. Inhabitants of the conquered Moorish states in the south, though entirely Spanish-speaking and Christian after the expulsions, were accorded an inferior status at which they chafed.

These elements of mistrust and disunity have persisted to the modern era, creating regional problems for the many kinds of government that Spain has witnessed over the past four centuries. Contact with the forces of Napoleon encouraged the development of peripheral national identities, which faced continuing domination by central authorities, however, until financial crises of the 1930s led to ending of the Spanish monarchy and establishment of a republic.

The new Spanish republic responded to increasing regional pressures by conceding autonomy to the Catalans, Basques, and Galicians. In reaction to these and other programs, part of the Spanish army rebelled in 1936. The ensuing civil war is most often viewed as a contest between leftist and rightist groups for supremacy. This is an incomplete perspective, however.

In many ways the war was primarily a confrontation between regions, with the forces of the Castilian core successfully vanquishing supporters of autonomy in the peripheral territories. The succeeding dictatorship by General Francisco Franco abolished all semblance of autonomy and forbade any usage of regional languages.

Franco died in 1975, and a new Spanish king, Juan Carlos, was sworn in as successor head of state. A revised constitution in 1978 established a semifederal system of governmental organization. Seventeen "autonomous communities" form the base of the system. Each has its own legislative and executive bodies and the right to declare its local language as official within the community. Each also has the right to fly its own traditional flag. Beginning in 1981, the first four regions to elect provincial councils were the traditionally disaffected Basque region, Catalonia, Galicia, and Andalusía. The others followed by 1983.

The Galicians. The northwestern corner of Spain throughout history has been the most difficult region to reach by ground transportation from other parts of the nation. It is blessed with a deeply embayed coastline and a humid climate that yields a greener landscape than occurs in much the rest of the peninsula. Its population retains a distinctiveness and self-awareness that sets it apart from the adjacent Castilians. The Galicians number nearly 3,000,000 in an area of 11,000 square miles.

Although they speak a Romance language, it is much closer to Portuguese than to Castilian Spanish. This is hardly surprising, given the region's relative isolation and its historic ties to Portugal. One element of regional consciousness that is surprising is the widespread belief by the population that it is of Celtic origin. Evidence for this is limited—a few Celtic words in the vocabulary, music and dance that resemble Welsh and Breton traditions, and traditional decoration similar to the circular and spiral designs of Irish motifs. The regional name, to be sure, like its counterpart Galicia in the Western Ukraine, is Celtic for "edge of the world."

It is likely, however, that the Galician population is primarily a blend of the autochthonous (native) Iberian peoples with the Germanic Visigoths, the Celtic influences being incidental. However, in most human affairs what people *believe* exists or happened is more important that what *actually* exists or happened. References to a presumed Celtic tradition abound in the daily life of modern Galicia.

In contrast to the strong spirit of rebellion in the Basque and Catalonian regions, Galicia long tended to accept its status and fate as part of Spain. During the nineteenth century, however, its people experienced a cultural revival. Like other budding European nationalisms, this initially centered upon concern for the local language, *Galego*, whose literary heritage was notably different from that of the rest of Spain. Instead of a focus upon heroic deeds of the *reconquista*, the language had developed in concert with the traditions of the troubadours of France. This came about as a result of close contacts established during pilgrimages from the rest of Europe to the Galician tomb of St. James, the patron saint of Spain.

The establishment of a political border with Portugal in the fifteenth century cut off the Galego language from the evolution of modern Portuguese, much as Flemish differentiated itself from Dutch following political separation. The Portuguese today value Galego as an archaic insight into their own cultural roots. After the sixteenth century, Galician authors wrote in Castilian, though the spoken language remained. New works in Galego began to appear only after Napoleon's 1808 invasion of Galicia, which touched off national feelings much as occurred in other parts of Europe. By that time, however, the language had been reduced to a peasant vernacular, with people in towns and cities having adopted standard Castilian.

During the twentieth century Galician national identity grew with the region's increasing economic problems. The small plots of its farmers became less and less economical. As in Brittany and Corsica, large numbers emigrated, many going to Latin America, especially to Argentina and Cuba. (Fidel Castro's father was born in Galicia.) Those remaining pressed for greater regional autonomy. Their overwhelming vote in favor of self-government in 1936 was voided by victory of the Franco forces, who had few supporters in Galicia despite it being the general's birthplace. Subsequently, Galician guerrillas continued harassing actions against the Spanish government as late as 1950.

Following implementation of the 1978 constitution, Galicians have appeared noticeably more satisfied with autonomy than have residents of Catalonia and the Basque region, perhaps because they lack the economic grievances against Madrid that have driven the eastern groups.

The Basques. For more than thirty years terrorists from the Basque region of Spain have gained international headlines. The organization *Euskadi ta Azkatasuna* (ETA, or "Basque Fatherland and Freedom") has used kidnappings, assassinations, and bombings to press its goal of complete separation of the Basque people from Spain and France. Founded in 1959 during a period of harsh repression of regional identities in Franco Spain, ETA militants have continued their operations during the more relaxed conditions of the present monarchy. Their activities, and the grudging support these receive from a significant segment of the populace, reflect a complex history and culture that is at odds with the rest of Spain.

The origin of the Basques is unknown. Their language has no commonalities with any other European tongues. Slight similarities to Georgian and other Caucasian languages have led some scholars to consider Basque to be a remnant of a pre-Indo-European vernacular likely spoken from Gibraltar to Tibet. Others have surmised that it may have West African origins, brought by groups seeking opportunities as Iberia warmed up from the subarctic conditions of the glacial age.

The preservation of *Eskerra*, the distinctive Basque language, is a tribute to the ability of their ancestors to resist acculturation by Romans, Visigoths, Moors, Spaniards, and the French. Their high mountain territory in the western Pyrenees was difficult to conquer, provided no particularly useful pass routes, and promised little reward for its subjugation. Even the unifying and centralizing Castilians concluded that it would be best to recognize the ancient Basque traditions of democracy and communal rights.

Conquest by Romans forced Christianity upon the Basques, and as a group they have remained among the most devout Roman Catholics in the world. Basques have played a major role in the propagation of religion in Spain and the Americas. The Society of Jesus was founded by a Basque, and Basques subsequently have contributed a number of leaders to the Jesuit order, including Pedro Arrupe of Bilbao, who headed the organization during the turbulent decades of the 1970s and 1980s. It also is no accident that members of the clergy have been among the most militant of Basque nationalists.

Although the Basque population by and large has retained its traditional piety and language, it has not remained an isolated European backwater comparable, say, to Albania. Contrary to their popular image as rural sheepherders, Basques have played distinguished roles in government and business throughout Spain and the Americas. They often have been called the "Yankees of Spain." Their entrepreneurs have made Bilbao, Spain's second port, famous for its commerce and shipbuilding. They have developed one of Europe's most important iron-mining regions. The per capita standard of living is the highest in the Iberian Peninsula.

Paradoxically, the modernization of the Basque region was a consequence of suppression of its traditions by central authorities in Madrid. When Castile absorbed the Basques during the reconquest, it was forced to recognize their ancient *fueros*, or rights that had been wrung from feudal lords centuries before the Magna Carta. These included democratic self-government and communal ownership of resources. In the periods 1833–40 and 1873–76, the Basques rebelled against centralizers from Madrid who sought to end such special rights. During these so-called Carlist Wars, the Basque slogan was "For God and the *fueros*."

Basque defeat in 1876 terminated the ancient rights, including community property and such local laws as Vizcaya Province's prohibition of the export of mineral ores. It also saw Spanish customs stations moved from the inland borders of the Basque provinces to their seacoasts. Urban entrepreneurs benefitted by this new access to the rest of Spain as a market for their goods and as a protection from outside competition. They garnered substantial capital and developed the region's huge iron deposits, which came to supply more than two-thirds of the ore imports of British industry.

Other Basques suffered. Many farmers were ruined by the influx of low-cost agricultural products from the rest of Spain and the higher prices of formerly duty-free consumer goods. Ending of the *fueros* meant that the population was subjected to a new tax burden, including high property rates on land and livestock and sales taxes on such staples as flour and salt. A major source of discontent was the influx of workers from the rest of Spain to take jobs in the region's burgeoning industry, diluting the region's distinctive Basque culture and language. Resentment grew against industrial pollution and despoliation of the countryside. Many Basques migrated to the Americas. More than a million went to the United States, chiefly to Oregon, Idaho, Nevada, and California.

Reaction to loss of traditional rights and the worsening economic situation of families stimulated intense national feelings during the 1890s. Basques were against whatever central authorities supported. Despite antipathy toward the "godless leftists" of the Spanish republican regime of the 1930s, they welcomed its offer of autonomy and sided with it against the perceived usurping centralizers of Franco.

For this they paid a heavy price. They suffered enormous losses during the Spanish Civil War. The dive-bombing of their regional capital of Guernica for symbolic purposes resulted in more than 1,500 casualties. The victorious Spanish nationalists completely suppressed the use of the Basque language from 1937 until the early 1950s, forbidding any public use of it, including publications. Franco declared it to be a language that was "fit only for dogs." Priests could not deliver church sermons in Basque. Even personal names on marriage and birth certificates had to be rendered in Castilian equivalents. The provinces of Vizcaya and Guipúzcoa were singled out as "traitor provinces" and subjected to confiscatory taxes. Navarre and Alava, in contrast, which had supported the nationalist forces, were allowed to retain their historic rights. The repression spawned an underground resistance movement that culminated in formation of the ETA.

The provinces of Alava, Vizcaya, and Guipúzcoa now form the Autonomous Community of the Basque Country. Navarre has long had a separate history and tradition, and constitutes a separate autonomous community within the present internal organization of Spain. The four provinces have a combined area of 6,500 square miles and population of 4,500,000.

Although up to 500,000 people have steadily spoken *Eskerra* over the centuries, they are becoming an ever smaller minority. Half the people of the region now are descended from Spanish migrants of the nineteenth and twentieth centuries. Of the remainder who identify themselves as Basques, no more than 20 percent actually speak *Eskerra*, mainly in small towns and villages. Eight modern dialects exist. The language has virtually died out in the southern plains region as a result of in-migration and Franco suppression. In the principal Basque cities of Bilbao and Pamplona it is seldom heard. It lacks the rich literary traditions of Catalan and Castilian, and saw little publication in the nineteenth and twentieth centuries until the few years of existence of the Spanish republic.

Although language may play a minor role in Basque daily life, no Basque wants to see its demise. It has, in fact, begun a revival since being given an official status. A multitude of publications have appeared.

In addition to preservation of the language, Basque iconography includes a romantic view of their role in history, a love of choral singing rivaling that of the Welsh, and proprietorship of their national game of *jai alai* and their energetic folk dance *la jota*. They have a national flag and an almost mystical concept of the Basque lands as *Euskadi*, although both are inventions of the Basque National Party at the end of the nineteenth century. Basques also have a general belief that other inhabitants of Spain are "tainted by Arab blood," and they cite the fact that the blood factor of Basques is nearly 100 percent Rh-negative while other Spaniards and Europeans exhibit about 60 percent Rh-positive and 40 percent Rh-negative.

A strong Basque national identity has not meant a unified Basque national movement. Although the ETA has been the most notable group in calling attention to Basque grievances through its terrorist activities, less than 15 percent of the Basques actually support it. Polls have shown that about half the population of the Basque region indicates an "understanding" of its aims. Its failure to mobilize a greater following reflects resentments toward its Marxist-Leninist ideology by a large segment of the traditionally religious Basque community, despite the fact that many younger monks and priests have played active roles in ETA activities. The ETA has also been plagued by several schisms that have resulted in internal strife.

A majority of Basques favor the program of the Basque National Party, which at one time cooperated with the ETA against Madrid, but more recently has strongly opposed ETA terrorism. It won the initial elections for a Basque parliament in 1980. A further split among the Basques involves the age-old rivalry between Navarre and the three other Basque provinces. Basque leaders in Navarre have strongly opposed the ETA, and a poll showed 57 percent of the population opposed union with the three northern Basque provinces.

A major goal of ETA is to establish a sovereign *Euskadi* state consisting of the four Spanish Basque provinces and the three adjacent *départements* in France that are home to 200,000 Basques. A common slogan painted on walls is "4+3=1." Separation of the French Basques occurred in 1529, when Spain and France reached a border agreement.

In contrast to the leading role of Spanish Basques in religion and economic development, Basques have played a minor role in France. They were passive to the French Revolution, although they had strong reaction to the anticlericalism of the Jacobins. The French Basques have remained largely rural. They have few grievances, never having felt exploited by an autocratic government. Many express pride in the fact that their traditional beret has become a symbol of Frenchness. Basque nationalist activities in Spain have contributed to their sense of being part of *Euskadi*, and they have played a role in giving haven to ETA members being sought by authorities in Spain.

The Catalans. Another group that has long resisted Castilian centralization and homogenization is the Catalan people, who live on both sides of the Pyrenees and also inhabit the Balearic Islands, the eastern fringe of Aragón, and much of Valencia. They are the most European of the Spanish groups. Like the Basques, they are also notably more economically advanced than the rest of Spain. Their Romance language is distinctive, being much closer to the Languedoc of France than to Castilian, and it has a rich literary heritage.

The ancient Romans established the Ebro River as their outer boundary with the territories held by Carthaginians from Tunisia. Charlemagne similarly used the river to mark the edge of African influence, maintaining Catalonia as a Christian bulwark against the Moors. By the Middle Ages, Catalonia had emerged as the heart of the Kingdom of Aragón. Catalans produced and exported textiles and iron to the rest of Europe from their principal port of Barcelona. Their merchant fleet outshone Venice and Genoa. The 1469 marriage of Aragón's King Ferdinand to Queen Isabella of Castile did not result in actual merger of the two kingdoms. Aragón continued as a separate entity with its own institutions for two centuries more until independence was dramatically terminated in 1714 by military defeat at the hands of Castilian Spain's Philip IV.

Despite their subjugation by Castile, Catalans continued to maintain economic and cultural connections with other European areas. Unlike the deeply religious Basques, they shared the enthusiasm of the French Revolution, including its anticlericalism. Napoleonic occupation gave birth to a sense of national identity, reinforcing general feelings of antipathy toward anything associated with the central government in Madrid. Catalans developed a range of political movements with the common aim of establishing self-government. Subsequent French currents of political thought, including socialism, syndicalism, and anarchism, also took root in Catalonia. In part these were due to the region's economic revival as a major producer of textiles and other manufactured goods.

Catalan national feelings were rewarded in 1932 when the new Spanish republican government voted into law a statute of autonomy. This provided for the reestablishment of a distinctive government, the *Generalitat*, that had jurisdiction over schools, local governments, taxation, and resource management. Autonomy encouraged a Catalonian cultural renaissance. The number of periodicals in the Catalan language grew to more than 400.

All was lost in Spain's civil war. Catalonians supported the losing side, providing the last bastion of the ill-fated republican government. Franco's Fascist government not only terminated the *Generalitat*, but prevented anyone associated with it from working for government again. Thousands of Catalonia's leading figures were jailed, and many were executed. More than 200,000 fled across the border to France. As in the Basque lands, all public use of the native language was forbidden. All business had to be conducted in Castilian. Place names, including even ancient names of streets, were transformed into Castilian orthography.

As has been the case in many other regions, oppression had the long-run effect of reinforcing local identity. The Franco regime eased controls in the postwar years as it sought to promote economic development and tourism. Fresh Catalonian political organization was an immediate result. After Franco's death, Catalonia regained its autonomous *Generalitat*, although with far fewer powers than it had enjoyed between 1932 and 1939. The new Catalonian Autonomous Community embraced 12,000 square miles with a population of 6,000,000. The many Catalan speakers of Valencia and Navarre were not included within its confines, however. (It should be noted that in Valencia the Catalan language is usually called "Valencian.")

The Catalan language received official status again. However, more than two generations had grown up reading and writing only Castilian, even though they spoke Catalan at home. Decline of the language was furthered by a massive influx of Castilian speakers during the Franco years. Some 40 percent of the population of Catalonia does not now speak Catalan. The Spanish centralists may well have triumphed in the end.

Andorra. A semi-independent Catalan entity exists between France and Spain. It has an area of 181 square miles and a population of 50,000. Of these, perhaps 20,000 are actually full citizens. An influx of Castilians has reduced the Catalan speakers to barely 30 percent. Only 6 percent speak French. The local government banned further immigration in 1976, although it took pains to permit an estimated million tourists to continue to visit the tiny principality each year.

Andorra is an anomalous territory that managed to elude incorporation into either France or Spain while regimes in those states were centralizing their power and ending internal feudal fragmentation. In the thirteenth century ownership of Andorra became the subject of a dispute between the Catholic church and the ruling nobility of the eastern Pyrenees. A compromise

in 1278 gave joint sovereignty to the Bishop of Urgel, whose seat was south of the mountains, and the Count of Foix, who resided on the northern flank. Following absorption of the County of Foix by France, the president of France has become the co-prince with the current Bishop of Urgel. Both France and Spain maintain official agencies in the territory, including separate post offices. The principal industries are mining, lumbering, and smuggling.

Another political-geographic anomaly of the Pyrenees is the Catalan community of Llivia, which lies two miles inside France. It was simply overlooked in the delimiting of this section of the border between France and Spain in 1659. It stayed Spanish territory at the time a village to its south was assigned to France, cutting Llivia off from connection to the main part of Spain. Its 2,000 inhabitants lack the highway connections of Andorra and cannot capitalize on their strategic position for trade in highly taxed goods.

Andalusía. Although Spain's southern region of Andalusía seldom experiences the terrorist activities of other alienated areas, its population also sees itself as different from the dominant Castilians and harbors feelings of oppression. Its citizens carried out their own mass demonstrations for home rule during the period of formulating a new constitution after Franco's death. Three days of rioting in the port city of Malaga saw twenty-eight injured and hundreds of thousands of dollars of property damage.

Andalusía has an area of 32,000 square miles and a population of nearly 7,000,000. Its name in Moorish times was Andalos, a corruption of the term "Vandals," a German tribe that had wandered into the region. The Andalusían dialect is distinctive, though not as distant from standard Spanish as Galician and Catalan. Its culture reflects its much longer period of Moorish control and the subsequent treatment by Madrid as conquered territory. To Europeans and Americans it is the embodiment of Spanish tradition in its traditions, its music, and its landscape. However, for Spaniards, it is an exotic region differing sharply from their home areas in the central Meseta or the Atlantic and north Mediterranean fringes.

Unlike the Basque country and Catalonia, it did not participate in the Industrial Revolution. Its economy is primarily agricultural, employing irrigation techniques developed in ancient times by the Arabs. In contrast to the small farms that characterize the old Christian kingdoms, land is held in large estates that were originally granted to officers after the fall of the Moorish state of Granada. Much of the rural population is landless, giving rise to severe economic and social problems that contribute to desires for autonomy.

Gibraltar. A long-standing irritation to Spain is the British possession of the Rock of Gibraltar. This is a peninsula of barely two-and-one-half square miles commanding the eight-mile-wide strait between the Atlantic Ocean and the Mediterranean Sea. The British acquired Gibraltar in 1704, and it has served as a major naval base since that time. Its native Spanish population left during the initial British occupation and were replaced mainly by immigrants from Genoa and Malta. The present population numbers 30,000.

Spain has repeatedly sought its return. In 1967 the United Nations passed a resolution calling for its decolonization. The British government responded by sponsoring a referendum on the colony's future. A total of 12,138 residents voted in favor of retaining the link with the United Kingdom, whereas only 44 voted for union with Spain. Two years later the Spanish government sealed off the border with Gibraltar, cutting off the colony from the 12,000 Spaniards who commuted to work daily from homes in the nearby town of La Línea. It reopened the border for pedestrians in 1982, and fully opened it only in 1985. The British had made it known that they could not support Spain's entry into the European Community until the Gibraltar problem was amicably resolved. The United Kingdom subsequently turned over air defense of the peninsula to Spain as part of its role in the North Atlantic Treaty Organization. In March 1991, after 287 years of unbroken defense of Gibraltar, the British withdrew their military forces and turned over responsibilities for defense to a local regiment.

Ceuta and Melilla. Although Spain gave up its Moroccan protectorate in 1956, it retained ownership of the two small enclaves of Ceuta and Melilla on the Mediterranean coast. It acquired Melilla in 1491, before the fall of Granada. The territories have a total area of 10 square miles and 125,000 inhabitants. They are not assigned to any Spanish province. Their continued possession has tended to weaken Spain's moral claims to Gibraltar.

Canary Islands. Lying 800 miles from Spain but only 80 miles from the African coast are the Canary Islands. They consist of seven volcanic islands with a total area of 2,800 square miles and a population of 1,700,000. Their name derives from the Latin word for dog, and was subsequently transferred to the singing yellow birds. Spain acquired the islands in the fifteenth century and long has treated them as an integral part of the Spanish state. They played an important role in Spanish navigation of the Atlantic during the Great Discoveries period. It was from the Canaries in 1936 that Francisco Franco launched his campaign against the republican government of Spain.

During Spain's ferment in the 1970s following the death of Franco, a shadowy "Movement for the Self-Determination and Independence of the Canary Archipelago" began broadcasting from Algeria. Its leader had earlier, in 1968, gained a statement from the Organization of African States (OAS) that the Canary Islands were an "unliberated" African territory held by "colonial" Spain. The OAS gave no recognition or support to the movement, however. Propaganda was directed against both foreign investment and the "Godos" ("Goths"), an unflattering Canary term for peninsular Spaniards. It was estimated that more than 60 percent of the tourism facilities in fact were owned by foreign investors, mainly Germans. Few residents of the Canaries rallied to the anticolonial call, however. Most saw that independence could do little to alleviate problems of inflation and unemployment. They did feel that local self-government would be more effective than the central bureaucracy in Madrid. As part of the general devolution of authority in Spain, the Canaries received the status of an Autonomous Community in 1978. Provision is made for each of the seven islands to have its own directly elected "corporation," the *Cabildo Insular*, to manage local interests.

Portugal

The west coast of Iberia is dominated by the Republic of Portugal, which embraces 35,000 square miles and has a population of 10,000,000. With the aid of Galicians from the north, the Moors were expelled from its central and northern areas in 1249. Up to that point Portugal had no particular identity separate from the other Christian kingdoms of Iberia. Such distinctiveness developed as a result of Portugal's subsequent different pattern of development. Rather than continue the reconquest on land, it sought to outflank the Moors by moving down the Atlantic coast and striking across Africa. These plans did not come to fruition, but Portugal did discover new territories and an oceanic route to India. It later attached to itself the western region of Andalusía as the separate Portuguese Kingdom of the Algarve.

The Portuguese developed trade and colonial holdings while the Spaniards were devoting their energies for 250 more years to expulsion of the Moors. They benefitted from an early alliance with the British, which remains one of the oldest international linkages still in operation. As a result, the Portuguese were better prepared to manage the colonial empire gained after the Treaty of Tordesillas than were the Spanish.

Portugal was isolated from the Spanish states by the emptiness of the mountains of western Iberia, which may account for its separate outlook and development. It was made a part of Spain in the period 1580 to 1640, which is usually referred to as "the sixty years' captivity." During this period its economy suffered and the rebellious Dutch seized much of its colonial holdings throughout the world. Following separation from Spain, Portugal never regained the advantages and momentum it once had enjoyed, although it retained authority over extensive territory in Africa and Brazil.

Portuguese national identity developed during the early nineteenth century in concert with the Napoleonic invasions. It did not suffer the disunity of Spain, although the southern Algarve region maintained particularist sentiments associated with its Moorish heritage. There have been no movements for separation or autonomy comparable to those of Spanish dissident groups.

Like Spain, Portugal did not participate in the major European economic and political developments of the nineteenth and twentieth centuries. Its population remained largely rural and self-subsistent. Nor did the country gain economically from its large overseas territories, but rather was obliged to expend substantial amounts to develop them and maintain law and order. Its standard of living was the lowest in Europe when a rebellion overthrew its monarchy in 1910.

Internal political problems led to the imposition of a dictatorship in 1926, which stifled economic development much as occurred later in Spain. Portugal was also faced with burgeoning costs to maintain its empire, including armed revolts in Mozambique and Angola. In 1974 a military junta reestablished constitutional government. The new regime proceeded to dismantle the last of its empire except for the tiny foothold of Macao in China and the Azores and Madeira Islands in the Atlantic.

The Azores and Madeira. Portugal retains ownership of two groups of islands off the coast of Africa. They lie 1,000 miles from the mother country and 3,000 miles from the United States. The Azores are divided into three groups with a combined area of 900 square miles and a population of 250,000. The island of San Miguel contains more than half the inhabitants. Madeira is somewhat closer to Africa, with 300 square miles and 270,000 residents. Up to a million islanders have migrated to the United States, particularly to New England, where 100,000 are located in the Boston area alone. The Azores, in turn, have seen many migrants from Portugal's former African territories.

Originally a colony, the islands were made an integral part of Portugal in 1931. The military coup of 1974 caused consternation in the Azores and Madeira because it brought Communist and Socialist political parties into power. This ran against political sentiments in the islands, whose population had family ties in the United States and also profited from an American military base. There was also a decline in traditional savings deposited by expatriates in America, who feared the money would go to wasteful leftist projects. Separatist movements appeared. The Portuguese government responded by granting the two island groups autonomous status in 1976, with their own legislatures and governments.

Bibliography

ALEXANDER, LEWIS M., "Recent Changes in the Benelux-German Boundary," *The Geographical Review*, Vol. 53, (1950), pp. 29–36.

ANDERSON, JAMES, "Separatism and Devolution: the Basques in Spain," in *Shared Space: Divided Space: Essays on Conflict and Territorial Organization*, eds. Michael Chisholm and David M. Smith. London: Unwin Hyman, 1990, pp. 135–156.

BARROS, JAMES, *The Aland Islands Question: Its Settlement by the League of Nations*. New Haven: Yale University Press, 1968.

BOAL, F.W., and J.N.H. DOUGLAS, eds., *Integration and Division: Geographical Perspectives on the Northern Ireland Problem*. London: Academic Press, 1982.

BRADFORD, SAX, *Spain in the World*, Princeton, NJ: Van Nostrand, 1962.

DARBY, J. ed., *Northern Ireland: The Background to the Conflict*. Belfast: Appletree Press, 1983.

FOSTER, CHARLES R., *Nations Without a State: Ethnic Minorities in Western Europe*. New York: Praeger, 1980.

HARTSHORNE, RICHARD, "The Franco-German Boundary of 1871," *World Politics*, Vol. 2 (1950), pp. 2029–2051.

KINGSBURY, ROBERT C., and NORMAN J.G. POUNDS, *An Atlas of European Affairs*. New York: Praeger, 1964.

MALMSTRÖM, VINCENT H., *Norden: Crossroads of Destiny and Progress*. Princeton, NJ: Van Nostrand, 1965.

MEAD, W.R., *The Scandinavian Northlands*, in the series Problem Regions of Europe. London: Oxford University Press, 1974.

MEDHURST, J., "Basques and Basque Nationalism," in

National Separatism, ed. C.H. Williams, Cardiff: University of Wales Press, 1982.

MOHAN, J. ed., *The Political Geography of Contemporary Britain*. London: Macmillan, 1989.

MURPHY, ALEXANDER B., "Evolving Regionalism in Linguistically Divided Belgium," in *Nationalism, Self-Determination and Political Geography*, eds. R.J. Johnston, David B. Knight, and Eleonore Kofman. London: Croom Helm, 1988.

PRINGLE, DENNIS, "Separation and Integration: The Case of Ireland," in *Shared Space: Divided Space: Essays on Conflict and Territorial Organization*, eds. Michael Chisholm and David M. Smith. London: Unwin Hyman, 1990, pp. 157–177.

PRINGLE, D.G. *One Island, Two Nations? A Political Geographical Analysis of the National Conflict in Ireland*. Letchworth: Research Studies Press, 1985.

STEPHENS, MEIC, *Linguistic Minorities in Western Europe*. Llandysul, Wales: Gomer Press, 1976.

4

The Middle Belt of Europe

I N OCTOBER 1990, the German Democratic Republic entered into the German Federal Republic, creating a unified state for the German nation for the first time in forty-five years. Although it would seem "normal" for Germans to enjoy a nation-state comparable to France or the United Kingdom, such a situation is in fact unusual when viewed from an historical perspective. For most of their existence the Germans have found themselves fragmented among several or many political units. A unified German *Reich* appeared only in 1871, and even then, the substantial numbers of Germans living in the Austro-Hungarian Empire were left out, and larger units within Germany, such as Württemberg and Bavaria, retained separate identities until 1920. These entities successfully insisted that the new *Kaiser* ("Caesar") was an emperor *in* Germany, not *of* it.

Italy experienced a similar history, first appearing as a sovereign entity only in 1861. Until that time, the Italian Peninsula, like the German area, was fragmented into a number of small, self-governing units. Gathering all Italian-speakers into a single state likewise was incomplete at the new political unit's inception and remained so for another half century.

The middle belt of Europe from the North Sea to the southern Mediterranean thus constitutes a distinctive region of two states scarcely a century old. It lies between Western Europe, whose political patterns had largely taken shape by 1500, and the "shatterzone" of East Central and Southeastern Europe, where most states appeared only at the end of the second decade of the twentieth century.

In both Germany and Italy national identities emerged before establishment of unitary states. Napoleonic forces occupying each territory spread notions of inherent rights of peoples to form governments of their own choosing. Iconographies grew during the nineteenth century, focused upon exaggerated glorification of a romantic past when groups were united. For Germans it was the medieval Kingdom of Germany within the Holy Roman Empire; to Italians it was triumphs of the classical Empire of Rome. Both saw their contemporary problems to be primarily a result of political fragmentation. Both resented the success of western neighbors and saw nation-states of their own as essential to compete with them effectively (Table 4-1).

Although Germany and Italy became nation states in the second half of the nineteenth century, they retained strong regional differences in culture, political identity, and economic development. Catholics of Bavaria considered the Protestants of northern Germany as arrogant and domineering. Sicilians shared similar views of inhabitants of Italy's industrialized Po Valley. Small farmers in the Rhineland contrasted themselves with the near-serfs on the large *Junker* estates of Prussia, while north Italians considered the *Mezzogiorno* of the south as an economic disaster region.

Although many reformers were initially imbued with sentiments favoring democracy as successfully practiced in Western Europe and Anglo-America, internal and external frustrations led to increasing popular acceptance in both countries of more authoritarian regimes. The parliamentary model of government proved inadequate among peoples who had little or no experience in democratic traditions. The unity so eagerly sought had proven illusory, as particularist regional interests continued to contend in the new forums. Eventually, as internal rivalries persisted and international weaknesses manifested themselves during World War I and its aftermath, both countries adopted totalitarianism as a solution to problems, with disastrous results to themselves and to all of Europe.

Initial policies of the young states were focused upon incorporating unredeemed fellow nationals and collecting colonial territories. Germans immediately gained the Alsatians from France, while Italians pressed for incorporation of Italian-speakers inhabiting parts of France and Austria. Although the informed consensus in established European states in the mid-nineteenth century was that the costs of maintaining and developing colonies exceeded any likely economic benefits, both Germany and Italy set about attaining title to their own overseas territories. They acquired extensive lands, particularly in Africa, but virtually all were marginal in economic promise and had been by-passed by other imperial states. Their efforts did set off a scramble by major European powers to claim interior African territories, however, lest these be acquired by a rival.

Both states were major participants in World War I and World War II. As a consequence of defeat, they were shorn of borderland territories and colonial empires. Since 1945, they have achieved equality and acceptance by their neighbors. Both played prominent roles in European defense against threats from the former Soviet Union and in the steadily growing economic unity of the Continent. Past expansionist aims seem to have been quelled, although Germans have not completely forgotten the loss of historic lands to Poland, and Italians still harbor some lingering sentiments about the northern and eastern shores of the Adriatic.

TABLE 4.1 MIDDLE EUROPE

Italy and Germany were established as states late in the nineteenth century, several decades after distinctive Italian and German nations had emerged among populations divided among numerous small political units. In both cases peripheral states served as organizing forces to consolidate entities that dated from the feudal period. A significant component of these units had been part of the medieval Holy Roman Empire. Both states suffer from major regional dissatisfactions, but the aggrieved groups cannot be said to constitute separate nations. Each state has potential irredentist claims to eastern territories.

State	Total Population	Area (sq. miles)	Distinctive Features of Group
Italy	58,000,000	116,000	
Dominant Nation and % Total			
Italians, 95% (including Northern Italians)			Romance (Italian) language, Roman Catholic
Significant Regional Groups and % Total			
Northern Italians, 45%			Advanced economic development, Romance (Italian) language, Roman Catholic
Sardinians, 3%			Island homeland, Romance (Sardinian) language, Roman Catholic
South Tyroleans, <1%			Germanic (German) language, Roman Catholic
San Marino	23,000	24	
Dominant Nation and % Total			
Sammarinese, 80%			Romance (Italian) language, Roman Catholic
Germany	81,000,000	138,000	
Dominant Nation and % Total			
Germans, 94% (including Bavarians)			Germanic (German) language, Mixed Protestant/Roman Catholic
Significant Regional Groups and % Total			
Bavarians, 15%			Germanic (German) language, Roman Catholic
Wends, <1%			Slavic (Sorbian) language (most bilingual in German), Lutheran

Both states face daunting challenges to raise living standards in lagging regions: Germany in its formerly socialist east and Italy in its semifeudal south. They also must continue to contend with entrenched regional outlooks and aspirations.

Italy

The political borders of Italy conform more closely to linguistic boundaries than is the case for most other states of Europe. Certainly, virtually all people who identify themselves as Italians live within Italy, and only a small fraction of the population, chiefly in the South Tyrol, consider themselves unwillingly incorporated within the Italian state. This is particularly surprising for a territory that originated the term *irredenta*.

For most persons, Italy would seem to be as "natural" a political entity as exists in the world. Set off by the sea on three sides and by high mountains on the fourth, its territory appears clearly defined by physical geography. However, its modern unity dates only from 1860, and it suffers significant regional discord today.

The entire Italian Peninsula was part of the Roman Empire for five centuries, but even then it did not function as an integrated area. The Roman Empire must be seen as an expansion of Rome as a city-state, not of Italy as a peninsular entity. The broad Po Valley of the north was continuously treated as part of Gaul. The southern "heel" and "toe" of the Italian "boot" were considered part of Greater Greece, as was the island of Sicily. Roman control did result in a Latin-based linguistic homogenization of the peninsula's polyglot inhabitants and in the implantation of uniform laws and institutions. This was true, however, for most of the rest of Western Europe. Over its subsequent history the Italian Peninsula experienced fragmentation into numerous political entities. Even today it harbors the microstates of San Marino and Vatican City.

Explanation for the lack of organizational unity of the peninsula is traceable to geographic, historic, and political factors. A significant element is the physical fragmentation of its ecumene. Aside from the broad basin of the Po River in the north, agricultural lands of Italy are confined to limited basins within its Apennine Mountain backbone and along coastlines where streams form river plains and deltas where they enter into the sea. Many of these coastal areas, such as the Pontine Marshes near Rome, have remained marshy and unsuitable for settlement to the present. Developed plains regions on the large offshore islands of Sicily and Sardinia similarly lie fragmented and limited in scope.

The early Romans established themselves in a very small place. The dimensions of the Tiber Valley are only 85 by 25 miles. The Latin-speaking tribal group that ensconced itself there had to contend for territory with Sabines to the east and Etruscans to the north. It is a tribute to their organizational and military skills that the Romans vanquished rivals near at hand and afar and maintained their empire for such a long period.

When Roman authority eventually crumbled, the Italian Peninsula suffered the same barbarian invasions that beset the rest of the empire. German tribes established themselves mainly in the north, but groups wandered through the entire peninsula, sacking Rome itself. Greeks of the surviving eastern Byzantine Empire exerted control for a time over the southern tip of the Italian "boot." Later, Moors from Africa moved into the large offshore islands. Wandering Normans from the north replaced Moorish rule and also took over nearby peninsular coastlands. In so doing, they laid a political basis for a rather long-lasting unity of the south that eventually emerged as the Kingdom of the Two Sicilies.

Charlemagne invaded northern and central Italy in the ninth century, actually making Rome the formal capital of his personal empire. Following his death, this region became the southern bastion of the short-lived Kingdom of Lotharingia and then of the Holy Roman Empire. Charlemagne's successors sought also to maintain control of Rome itself, but it came under the personal authority of its bishop, the Pope, who by tradition and organization was leader of western Christianity. From their base in the city, the popes continuously expanded temporal lands up the Tiber Valley and across the Apennines into the southeastern part of the Po River Plain.

Between the Papal territories and the region controlled by the Holy Roman Empire were a number of small political units. For the most part they functioned as pawns of outside powers, feuding with each other and being wooed by popes and emperors. From the former they gained trade brought by pilgrims, as well as direct papal financial undertakings. They also faced seriously taken threats of religious sanctions for actions considered inimical to the Catholic church. From the emperors, fighting their way to Rome to force papal coronation, the small states received charters of self-government and title to expanded territories.

Gradually the cities of Turin, Milan, Venice, Genoa, and Florence extended their lands to control the north. Although all initially had been within the Holy Roman Empire, they gained virtual independence as the Holy Roman Empire failed. The first three benefitted by trade through passes across the Alps to central Europe. Farther to the south, Florence welded the many small states fronting the southern edge of the Po Valley into a Duchy of Tuscany that became a Habsburg appendage. All grew wealthy and played important roles in Europe's cultural renaissance. Genoa and Venice developed a lucrative trade with eastern Mediterranean lands and became the principal linkages of Western Europe with the Orient. Both acquired remote territories: Genoa over the island of Chios in the Aegean and the coastal ports of Corsica; Venice over the islands and coastal plains of the eastern Adriatic. Both suffered economically when the advance of the Ottoman Turks disrupted their traditional trade ties and the Portuguese discovered a water route around Africa to the Far East.

In the south lay the Kingdom of Naples and to the southwest were the island kingdoms of Sicily and Sardinia. All three had languished since the fourteenth century under remote authority exerted by the Iberian Kingdom of Aragon, which eventually became part of Spain. The region suffered the same problems of economic lag that beset Spain itself. In 1720 the northern Duchy of Savoy acquired Sardinia, principally, it appears, to gain for Savoy the title "kingdom." After a brief period of Austrian control in the early eighteenth century, the kingdoms of Sicily and Naples united to form the Kingdom of the Two Sicilies under personal rule of the Bourbon kings of Spain.

The *Risorgimento*. The inhabitants of Italy were caught up in the nationalist and democratic enthusiasms that had been engendered by the French Revolution and felt throughout the Continent. Napoleon occupied the peninsula, eventually annexing Savoy and Genoa to France and constituting the states north of the Papal territories into a new Kingdom of Italy. After Napoleon's downfall, the 1815 Treaty of Vienna reestablished the previous political fragmentation, even though all segments of the peninsula had come to deplore the consequences of local particularism. A process of political consolidation then began that is generally known by its Italian name, the *Risorgimento*.

The unification of Italian lands into a single state was organized by the Kingdom of Sardinia, which, to

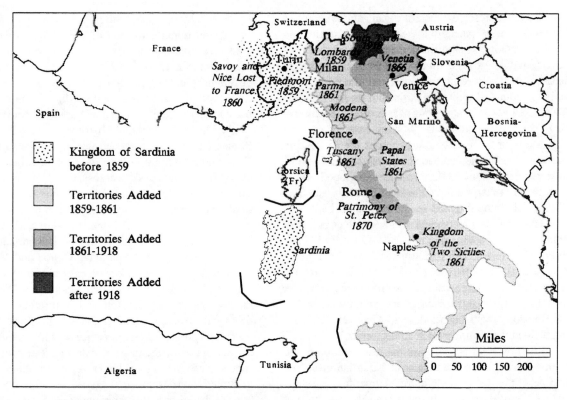

FIGURE 4-1   STAGES IN THE UNIFICATION OF ITALY

avoid confusion with its island possession, usually is identified as "Piedmont," the designation for its core region in the upper Po Valley (Figure 4-1). Piedmont began by encouraging uprisings of Italian inhabitants of the Austrian provinces of Lombardy and Venetia during the revolutionary year of 1848. These were contained by the Habsburgs, but, aided by Napoleon III of France, the Piedmontese attacked Austria directly in 1859. They had great success, gaining Lombardy and unleashing a groundswell of Italian national feeling.

As a price for France's assistance, the Piedmontese had to cede to France substantial parts of Piedmont's home territory. These were the regions of Savoy and Nice, which lay to the west of the Maritime Alps. The loss of these lands had the positive effect for Piedmont of removing suspicions in other Italian areas that it was operating as a pawn of France. Piedmont soon was joined in the *Risorgimento* by the adjacent duchies of Parma, Modena, and Tuscany. The eastern two-thirds of the Papal territories also became part of the expanded political unit. With encouragement and assistance from Piedmont, Giuseppe Garibaldi led revolts in the Kingdom of the Two Sicilies that resulted in its joining the other territories in 1861 to form the Kingdom of Italy, with the Piedmontese King of Sardinia as its monarch.

Although many who had worked for Italian unity sought a federal state that would recognize regional particularism, the political architects of Piedmont adopted a highly centralized form of government modelled after that of France. They extended Piedmont's constitution to the entire state, as well as its system of external tariffs. In addition to instituting political geographic coherence through a unitarian government, the young regime also pressed for a greater Italian homogeneity by a "declaration of war against dialects." The local language of Piedmont itself was among the first to suffer. As might be expected from its region's location, Piedmontese is a bridge between other forms of Italian and the Occitanian language of southern France. The use of Piedmontese in schools was banned in 1864, and teachers and administrators from other regions were hired in great numbers to educate students in the Tuscan dialect of Florence, which had been adopted as the standard form of Italian because of its association with the poet Dante. Other regional dialects and languages that were denied official standing and any further development of literary forms included adjacent Romagnole, the Ladin and Friulian speech of the Alpine slopes, Occitanian spoken in northern Piedmont, and Sardinian. All managed to survive as popular spoken tongues, however.

Italian national areas left outside the boundaries of Italy were principally the Austrian province of Venetia and the Patrimony of St. Peter, as the rump of the Papal territories was known. Italy acquired Venetia in 1867 as part of its ally Prussia's terms of peace imposed upon Austria. In 1870 Italy took over the Patrimony of St. Peter when French troops protecting it were called home to fight the Prussians.

The capital of the Italian Kingdom remained in Turin for the first five years of its existence. It then moved to Florence, which had the advantages of a more central location. Following acquisition of Rome, however, the young regime transferred capital functions to that city, despite inadequacies born of centuries of neglect. Like the twentieth-century capital movements from St. Petersburg to Moscow and from Nanking to Beijing, the transfer reflected a desire for legitimacy based upon a glorious past. Similar so-called historic imitation capital cities can be cited for other areas. The young Italian regime considered the selection of Rome important as a means of binding the diverse Italian regions together. This was because Italy lacked any other territorial precedent for unity that would be comparable, say, to the national allegiance given by Poles to a revived Poland after World War I.

Despite the bringing of most Italian-speaking *irredenta* into the new Italian state, popular feelings sought to incorporate those continuing to live outside the new state. Austria still had many Italian-speakers in its eastern Adriatic regions, although the majority of inhabitants spoke either Slovenian or Croatian. Ticino remained in Switzerland, and Savoy, Nice, and Corsica were parts of France. For the next fifty years a goal of Italian foreign policy was acquisition of these territories.

From its inception, the young Italian state had difficulties functioning. Regional particularism did not end with unification. Notable economic and political problems developed between its rural, semifeudal central and southern regions and its more urbanized and progressive north. Italy could not support a very rapidly growing population. Large numbers of Italians emigrated to North Africa, Latin America, and, especially, to the United States. Before World War I, the annual flow to America exceeded 400,000.

One of the rationales given for the *Risorgimento* was that a unified Italian state would have the opportunity to benefit from acquisition of colonies as France and Britain had done. By the time Italy was ready to expand overseas, however, there were few areas available for imperial endeavor. In 1880 Italy elected to lay claim to footholds on the "horn" of Africa, including the desert regions of Eritrea along the Red Sea and Somalia on the Indian Ocean. It had aims of pushing inland to acquire Ethiopia, but local forces successfully stopped the Italian advance into the interior in 1896. Later, in 1912, Italy took advantage of a weakened Ottoman Empire to seize the desert wastes of Libya and the Greek-inhabited Dodecanese Islands off the south coast of Turkey. Its ventures into colonialism proved a costly extravagance, however. It is estimated that Italy spent four times as much in administering and developing its colonial empire as it received in commercial benefits. Only a very small number of Italians ever settled in Italy's African possessions.

World War I. Italy's colonial expansion was part of a seemingly insatiable hunger for territorial acquisition that began with the *Risorgimento*. The quest for redeeming *irredenta* went beyond simple acquisition of Italian-speakers. Thus, Italians increasingly had come to view the Adriatic Sea as a personal lake. They recalled Venice's long control of Istria and Dalmatia along the eastern shore of the Adriatic, but ignored the fact that the population of these regions was overwhelmingly Slavic. They also viewed the crest of the Alps as a "natural" boundary of Italy, even though Tyrolean Germans had long inhabited the south-facing mountain slopes. Italy's desire for adding these territories was enhanced by the fact that the territories belonged to an Austria still incorporating many Italians in Trieste and elsewhere.

Opportunity came during World War I. Italy first announced a neutral position in the conflict. Then, England, France, and Russia offered a secret treaty in 1915 that would grant Italy extensive Habsburg lands if it would enter the war on the Allied side. Italy did so, but it paid a heavy price in manpower and treasure in fighting the Austrians. At war's end, Italians felt frustrated by the limited gains they made in the treaty of peace. Italy did receive the section of Austria's Tyrol province south of the Alps, the Istrian Peninsula, and some of the Adriatic islands. The Dalmatian coast originally promised by their Allies, however, went instead to the new Kingdom of Serbs, Croats, and Slovenes, as Yugoslavia was first named. Italy gained only a tiny toehold around the port of Zara (Zadar) in the mainland's central region.

Fiume. The secret treaty of 1915 had exempted the Hungarian port city of Fiume (Rijeka) at the head of the Kvarner Gulf from promised postwar rewards to Italy. Instead, it was assigned to a future Croatia, with which it had long been linked historically and economically. Following declaration of its independence from Austria-Hungary in October 1918, Croatia sent armed forces and administrators into Fiume. In the following month, however, after the Armistice was signed, Italy led an Allied force to occupy the city. Only its eastern suburban port of Susak was left directly under the control of Croatia, which itself soon became a component of the Kingdom of Serbs, Croats, and Slovenes.

The majority of Fiume's population was Italian, and, despite the continuing Italian-controlled occupation, their "redemption" became a major nationalist cause in a postwar Italy that viewed itself as suffering defeat by its own allies. In September 1919, an Italian poet and adventurer, Gabriele d'Annunzio, with a small force of supporters, seized the city and proclaimed a "free state," forcing Allied occupation forces to retire to Italian-annexed Istria. The action was enthusiastically welcomed by the local citizenry, even though it meant severing their port facilities from Fiume's economic hinterland in Croatia. The Italian government compelled d'Annunzio to leave Fiume in December 1920, and then required the "free state" government to sign a formal treaty of association with Italy. Italy annexed Fiume in 1924, after reaching reluctant agreement from the Yugoslavs.

As part of its paternalistic view of the Adriatic Sea, Italy also harbored pretensions to Albania, actually signing an agreement with Greece to partition that fractious region. Although treaty makers in Versailles recognized Albanian rights to sovereignty, they did concede Italian control of the offshore island of Saseno, which Italy had occupied militarily since 1914. Italy soon penetrated the small state's economy and politics and, in effect, made it a protectorate by 1926.

The Fascist period. The postwar territorial disappointments added to Italy's internal woes, including continuous regional bickering, strikes by a strong Communist labor movement, and a poorly functioning economy. In 1922 Benito Mussolini and his Fascist Party seized power with an announced aim of instilling order. Party stalwarts took charge of every community. Italy experienced its first true organizational unity since Roman times. Among Mussolini's acts was resolution of Italy's long-standing dispute with the Papacy. After years of papal sulking over Italian seizure of its 17,000 square miles of temporal holdings, relations were normalized in 1929 by a treaty that established Vatican City as a 110-acre sovereign enclave within Italy.

Mussolini's programs were intensely nationalist, both at home and abroad. Internally, the Fascists set about Italianizing Germans and Slavs acquired from Austria after World War I. They replaced local officials by Italians and permitted only the Italian language to be used in public, including newspapers and speeches. Local inhabitants were required to adopt Italianized personal names, and only Italian versions of place names could be utilized.

In the South Tyrol the Fascists even forbade use of the German name *Süd Tyrol*, replacing it by *Alto Adige*. They encouraged German-speakers to emigrate to Austria at the same time that they induced Italians from other regions to come to the area as part of a program for diluting numerical strength of the Germans. Beginning in 1935, the Fascists created a special industrial complex around the local center of Bozen (Bolzano) that hired only Italians. By 1943, the numbers of Italians in the region had increased from 7,000 before World War I to more than 105,000, out of a total population of 350,000. Italians dominated the cities, while Germans remained an overwhelming majority in the countryside.

Fascist linguistic acculturation policies were not confined to Germans and Slavs. They notably also affected French speakers in the northwestern Val d'Aosta and Ladin people of the Dolomite Mountains, whose language was related to the Romansch of Switzerland. The Piedmontese also resented the intensified assaults upon their own regional language. Fascism made few inroads among the Piedmontese, and they created a deeply rooted resistance movement during World War II. The Piedmont capital of Turin saw two massive labor strikes against Mussolini's intransigence in 1943, and a strong partisan force committed to a liberated Italy harassed Fascist authorities from bases in the Alps.

Italy's foreign policy continued its expansionist thrust. In 1936 it successfully defeated Ethiopia, substantially expanding its colonial holdings in East Africa. Three years later Italy occupied its *de facto* economic colony of Albania, and from this base it invaded Greece in 1940. It also attacked southeastern France while that country was being overwhelmed by Nazi Germany. Italy's Greek and French campaigns turned out to be military disasters, but conquests by its ally Germany saved it from absolute defeat. Italy took part with Germany in the 1941 invasion of Yugoslavia and was rewarded by control over much of Slovenia, Dalmatia, Montenegro, and Albanian lands in Serbia. Later that summer it joined in the invasion of the Soviet Union. In 1942 the German army again came to Italy's rescue, this time in its colony of Libya. However, the British army ultimately seized control of that territory as it earlier had claimed Italian East Africa. When Germany decided to move into the unoccupied zone of southeastern France in late 1942, Italy took over the French island of Corsica.

Italian Fascism ended in 1943, when Mussolini was deposed and Italy announced that it was leaving the war. The country continued to suffer destruction, however, as Allied forces advanced slowly up the peninsula from the south, while defending Germans transformed the north into a puppet state called the "Italian Social Republic."

Postwar Italy. In the postwar period Italy found itself shorn of all colonial territories. In addition to loss of wartime gains in the eastern Adriatic, a treaty of peace signed in Paris in 1947 gave most of the former Austrian province of Venetia-Giulia to Yugoslavia, including the Istrian Peninsula, the Isonzo (Soca) Valley, islands in the Kvarner Gulf, and Fiume. It also lost Zara and the island of Pelagosa. The region around the port city of Trieste remained under occupation of Allied and Yugoslav forces for nearly a decade more, until a 1954 agreement conceded the hinterland to Yugoslavia, while retaining for Italy the city of Trieste itself. Italian inhabitants of these territories virtually all emigrated to Italy. It also lost Saseno to Albania and the Dodecanese Islands to Greece. In the west it was required to yield four small frontier districts to France.

A referendum in 1946 ended the Italian monarchy and established a republic. However, voting was close and reflected the state's continuing regional division between north and south. With nearly 90 percent of registered voters casting ballots, the 54 percent in favor of a republic were concentrated mostly in the industrial north. A large majority in the traditionalist south voted to retain the kingdom.

The Mezzogiorno. The continuing economic contrast between the two parts of the peninsula resemble the differences between northeastern Spain and the rest of that state. Like southern Spain, the South long retained a *latifundia* system of land ownership. Rural families possessed little or no land themselves and were dependent upon sharecropping or employment by absentee landowners. Their traditionally large numbers of children competed for a fixed supply of land. Many saw survival only by out-migration, either to the industrial north or overseas. The region also lagged in developing an adequate infrastructure to facilitate enterprise functioning. Long overland distances, rough intervening terrain, and, in the case of Sicily and Sardinia, separation by water added high transportation costs and bottlenecks that handicapped industrial competitiveness.

The central government also has had continuing difficulties in projecting effective control. Southern Italy is notorious for the persistence of organized criminal activity. The Sicilian *Mafia* and the Neapolitan *Camorra* have functioned as regimes of their own, discouraging entrepreneurial initiative by their extortion and other crimes. One of the major accomplishments of the Fascist regime of Mussolini was its suppression of criminal gangs. The republican regime proved unable to maintain control, however.

The postwar Italian government sought to reduce economic inequalities in the southern Mezzogiorno region by a major program of agricultural redevelopment, including land reclamation, erosion control, and crop diversification. Subsequent regimes have encouraged northern companies to invest funds to establish manufacturing facilities in the south. Leverage has come from the significant share of governmental ownership of Italy's two principal financial holding companies.

Unlike Spain, economic contrasts do not reinforce national antagonisms. This is not to say that separate group identities are absent. Northerners consider the Sicilians of the south to be lazy and virtually of another race. They resent government transfer of funds generated by northern industry for futile economic and social programs in the south. Southerners look upon northerners as avaricious "Germans." Both groups see themselves as Italians, however. Neither group harbors secessionist outlooks.

The South Tyrol. Italy does have one major trouble spot. The German-speaking population of the South Tyrol has never accepted its transfer to Italy at the conclusion of World War I. The continuing difficulties caused by this region of 2,800 square miles and 500,000 inhabitants highlight the futility of Italy's insistence upon incorporating it.

Its original motivation appears to have been based upon abstract and erroneous perceptions. Adding more territory to the Italian map was seen in itself a means of relief of a chronic condition of overpopulation. However, the area's mountainous character offered virtually no opportunities for expanded settlement, particularly since suitable valley lands were already occupied. A similar illusion was the notion that a "natural boundary" would be inherently better than a historically established or ethnographically based one. This assumed that a mountain-crest border would provide greater defensive capabilities, but it defied logic. A ridgetop in the technology of early twentieth-century warfare would be inherently more difficult to defend from an aggressor than a position down the far slope of a mountain that would force an enemy to attack uphill. From Italy's point of view, in either case military defensive benefits required weighing the consequences of incorporation of a hostile population that preferred to remain with Austria. Italians would have been better served by continuing to use a border short of the Alpine crest that separated Italians from German-speakers.

Also to be considered is the fact that severing national territory would provide a motivation for taking it back. The South Tyrol had belonged to the Habsburgs since 1353 and had been attached to an Italian state only during the brief Napoleonic period of 1810–1815. Its population was almost entirely an Austro-German peasantry who could be expected to resist any attempt at assimilation into the Italian nation. Although Austria was prostrate at the end of World War I, it had been a major power of prewar central Europe and could be expected to be again, particularly if it became part of an expanded German nation-state.

This, of course, happened in the 1938 *Anschluss* (annexation) of Austria by Germany. The South Tyrol had the potential for serious frictions between the two members of the so-called Rome–Berlin Axis, but Hitler and Mussolini reached agreement in 1939 to allow the German population to emigrate to the Third Reich. It is rumored that one proposal advanced during the war was to transfer South Tyroleans en masse down the Danube and across the Black Sea to become the new hoteliers of a German Crimea. In a referendum some 83 percent of the German population of the region opted to leave. However, by 1943, when the program was suspended, only 30 percent of the South Tyroleans actually had departed for Germany. Most of those who left were workers in towns. Villagers were reluctant to leave ancestral lands, but it meant that their group stayed outside the economic modernization taking place in the region.

Under the peace treaty following World War II, Italy was obliged to give the region a special statute of autonomy, which it did. However, it attached the South Tyrol to the largely Italian-inhabited adjacent Trentino territory, making the Germans a minority in the province. Under terms of the treaty, Italy allowed elementary and secondary education in the German language. It permitted parity of German with Italian and restored the traditional German form of family names. However, the government did not immediately implement key provisions of the statute, particularly the right of return for South Tyroleans who had emigrated to Germany in the Fascist era. Germans were also angered by renewed inducement of Italians to come to the area for employment.

In 1955 Austria ceased to be a divided, occupied territory once a peace treaty with the Allies was signed. Among its early acts was to champion the cause of South Tyrolean leaders who pressed for greater autonomy within Italy. Italy resented what it saw as outside interference in an internal problem. However, the action gave encouragement to local nationalists, who adopted the slogan *Los von Trient* ("Get out of Trentino"), pressing for the South Tyrol German community to have autonomy for itself. In 1957 a massive demonstration of 35,000 South Tyroleans agitated for greater self-rule. The increasingly popular national movement spawned terrorist groups that took on an increasingly neo-Nazi tone. During one June night in 1961 there were no less than forty-seven bombings.

It should be stressed that South Tyroleans shared little sense of common identity with the majority of Austrians. Like the Bavarians of Germany, national feelings tended to be regional in scope. Their ties abroad were to the Tyrolean people of the western Austrian province of Vorarlberg. Both groups tended to be conservative, rural Catholics who took pride in preserving a distinctive German dialect. The Viennese to them were as foreign as the Swiss. Vienna also had

doubts about the consequences of any incorporation of South Tyroleans into Austria. It saw, probably rightly, that what had been an Italian problem of coexistence and assimilation would become an Austrian one.

The increase in demonstrations and terrorism led the Italian government in 1972 to come to terms with South Tyrolean aspirations. It gave the local province of Bolzano the status of "Autonomous Region with Special Statute" that provided for major devolution of governmental powers. The statute released the school system from the need to adhere to national norms and created job quotas for ethnic groups. Programs were established to further bilingualism. The changes had a positive effect upon German-speakers, although it generated deep resentment among the local Italian community. Terrorism decreased in the region and separatist politics waned. The growing economic unity of the European Community may provide a rationale for renewed efforts at independence, however, which could be successful if Italians have lost their illusions about the need for defensive "natural" boundaries.

The Friulans and Slovenes. Italy has four other autonomous regions with special statutes. To the east of the South Tyrol is the autonomous region of Friuli-Venezia-Giulia. Its area of slightly more than 3,000 square miles contains a population of 1,200,000. About 700,000 of these are Friulans, whose language is more closely related to the Romansch of Switzerland than to Italian. They can point to a significant political and literary tradition going back to the early Middle Ages. The Friuli region voluntarily adhered to the new Italian state in 1866, and has not exhibited the separatist tendencies of the South Tyroleans.

Living among them and often speaking the Friulian language are perhaps 40,000 Slovenes. They are a remnant of far larger numbers before the Isonzo Valley to the east was transferred from Italy to Yugoslavia after World War II. Most are concentrated around the town of Gorizia (Gorica). They enjoy a number of cultural rights and evince little of the irredentism prevalent among Slovenes in Austrian Carinthia.

Both Friulans and Slovenes resent the continuing influx of Italians into their regions. Up to 25,000 of those leaving Yugoslav Istria settled in Friuli. There is also some unhappiness that the regional center is in the rather remote and predominantly Italian city of Trieste instead of the more central market town of Udine.

The Valle d'Aosta. Tucked away in Italy's northwestern corner is the 1,200-square-mile autonomous province of the Valle d'Aosta. It lies across the watershed from the rest of Savoy, which went to France in 1860. Among its 110,000 inhabitants, about 70 percent still speak Occitanian French. They have preserved their language in the face of Italian homogenization pressures for more than a century. In 1919 they unsuccessfully petitioned to join Switzerland. Subsequent Fascist linguistic policy was as vicious as elsewhere in Italy.

Charles DeGaulle had sought incorporation of the region into France after World War II, but received only small additions of territory around passes in the Maritime Alps. Although Italy was required to give the region a statute of autonomy in the postwar period, it did not immediately implement all the provisions promised. French is now a required subject in school. Like other minority areas on the fringe of the Alps, the local inhabitants resent the influx of Italians from the south into their area.

Sardinia and Sicily. In contrast to Sicily, which was long linked to Italy's southern peninsula, the island of Sardinia had a quite separate history up to the eighteenth century. The Sardinian language belongs to the Romance family and perhaps is closest to the original Latin. It is spoken by 85 percent of the 1,600,000 residents of the 8,000-square-mile island.

Sardinia's cultural distinctiveness was recognized by postwar Italy's 1948 grant of a statute of autonomy. It has had far less practical significance than those granted to the Alpine minorities, however, since the island has lacked any strong separatist movement.

Sicily also received a special statute of autonomy. This was granted in 1948 to head off an existing strong separatist movement. Subsequently, the population of the island has shown little inclination to change the political status quo, perhaps because the government has faced insurmountable difficulties in attempting to assert central authority. The inhabitants maintain close affinity to those on the adjacent mainland, reflecting long associations under past Catalan rulers.

Southeastern Italy also has several communities that have maintained their Albanian, Croatian, and Greek languages and cultural identities. They have no political significance and remain as ethnic curiosities, although Albanians number a quarter-million.

Germany

Since it was founded as a nation-state in 1871 (Figure 4-2), Germany has seen a reduction in size from its initial 210,000 square miles to 180,000 in 1918 following the Treaty of Versailles, to 138,000 square miles today. It had expanded formally during World War II to

FIGURE 4-2   GERMANY IN 1871

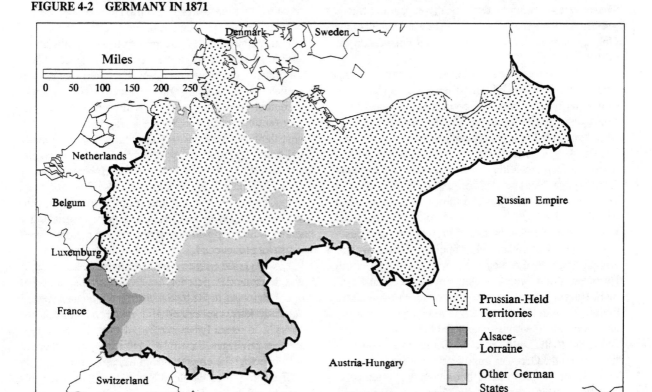

280,000 square miles. Another 2,000,000 square miles were occupied or dominated by Germany during World War II, but in the postwar period up to 1990 Germany lay divided between a German Federal Republic of 96,000 square miles and a German Democratic Republic of 42,000 square miles. These fluctuations in size reflect the complex political-geographic character of the German land space and the changing power relationships of Germans with their neighbors.

Germans had their cultural hearth in southern Scandinavia and the Baltic region. Tribal groups moved southward in the pre-Christian era, conquering and acculturating Celtic tribes whose core area had been the lower Rhineland. Celts farther west escaped being Germanized by Rome's conquest of Gaul, but increasing numbers of Germans moved across the Roman Empire's proclaimed Rhine River border, particularly during the empire's declining years in the fifth century. Although Frankish tribes eventually captured all of Gaul, most who went west were soon themselves absorbed by local Latinized cultures.

The Rhineland and adjacent areas to the east had not experienced Roman governmental organization; the people there retained their customary language, social order, and system of common law. As tribal groups, their political structures tended to be tied to kinship rather than to territory. Many tribes wandered to distant areas, particularly abandoning lands in regions of poor soils and indifferent climates east of the Elbe River. These were taken up by dynamically expanding Slavic groups, whose center of development was located in the Galician region of what is now eastern Poland and the USSR.

In the ninth century Charlemagne created an extensive personal empire, bringing Roman concepts of governmental organization to Germans east of the Rhine. Following Charlemagne's death, the eastern Germans were constituted into the separate Kingdom of the East Franks. A rather constant theme for the ensuing millennium was German cultural and political expansion eastward against the Slavs. This process is often termed the *Drang nach Osten* ("push to the east"). It was not a coordinated effort, but the sum total of piecemeal movements of individuals and groups into territories that generally were sparsely populated. The eastward advance was fostered by the continuity of the North European Plain, which widened out to become European Russia. There were no empty seas or mountain regions to set a logical eastern terminus for expansion, although movement was channeled latitudinally by the Baltic Sea to the north and the high Alps to the south. In the process the Germans imposed their religion and law upon Slavic peoples whom they enveloped, often completely absorbing them into the German-speaking cul-

ture. The Sorbs of the Spree Valley south of Berlin were unusual in being able to withstand Germanization pressures. Governmentally sponsored acculturation began only in the eighteenth century, when the Prussian king Frederick the Great ordered resettlement of German farm families among his Slavic subjects to the east.

The Kingdom of the East Franks, which came to be known as the Holy Roman Empire, expanded westward to incorporate much of short-lived Lotharingia. Within the empire was the Kingdom of Germany, which had rather indeterminate boundaries. Unlike the adjacent Kingdom of the West Franks, which evolved into an increasingly centralized France, the German realm to the east grew ever more fragmented. The kingdom had been subdivided into eight rather arbitrarily defined duchies. These became increasingly independent, particularly after the Carolingian dynasty died out in the tenth century and dukes made their own offices hereditary. Much of medieval German history revolved around ill-fated efforts of Germany's kings from the subsequent Saxon dynasty to dominate the nominally subordinate dukes. In the process, each duchy tended to evolve its own personality. Even today German village patterns, house types, and dialects reflect distinctive cultural strands that had emerged in the old duchies.

Further complicating relationships were quests by Holy Roman emperors to legitimize their positions by being crowned by the popes in Rome. These almost always required military campaigns across the Alps to force recognition. Already having frittered away much of their resources in bribing electors to gain the post of emperor, they found it necessary to raise substantial additional sums to wage their campaigns to reach central Italy. A continuous manner of garnering funds and armies was to bargain rights of local self-government with nobles and city burghers. While French provincial ruling families and towns were losing hereditary privileges, their counterparts in Germany steadily gained local powers. Moreover, the Holy Roman emperors, almost all of whom came from the Habsburg family after 1273, paid little attention to needs of their German realm. Unlike France and Poland, they created no central bureaucracy. By the fifteenth century imperial unity had ended and regional rivalries among the dukedoms had grown pronounced.

Although the empire lacked internal coherence, it was a substantial defensive force against external threat. Beginning in the tenth century, it created special borderland territories termed *Marken* ("marchlands" or "marks"). In return for exemptions from imperial dues and other privileges, their ruling families were charged with protecting the empire from eastern intruders, who over the centuries included Slavs, Magyars, Mongol-Tatars, and Turks. The marchlands formed a belt from the Baltic Sea to Slovenia. The principal ones were Brandenburg, Upper Saxony, Bohemia, and Austria (the "Ostmark"). At a time when traditional duchies suffered declines as local nobility and towns within them gained imperial privileges of self-government, the *Marken* grew more and more powerful by garnering increasing territories eastward inhabited by non-Germans. Brandenburg came to dominate in the north and Austria in the south.

The Reformation of the sixteenth century added further to the disunity of the Germans. The Diet of Augsburg in 1555 allowed princes to select the religion of their subjects. While southerners generally remained Roman Catholic, rulers in the north and east tended to become Protestant. The latter notably gained wealth by being able to sequester church lands. The Thirty Years War from 1618 to 1648 proved disastrous to all. In its wake, each tiny principality took on pretensions of sovereignty. By this time there were more than 300 such units, often fragmented into several bits of territory.

Through the end of the eighteenth century the numerous tiny principalities, bishoprics, and city states of the German realm formed a sharp contrast with the consolidated states in neighboring areas of Europe. However, Brandenburg was pursuing a successful policy of continual territorial aggrandizement. In the seventeenth century it had acquired the territory of Prussia, which at the time was a fief of the Polish kingdom. Originally the home of Baltic tribes speaking a language related to Lithuanian and Latvian, Prussia had been conquered in the thirteenth and fourteenth centuries by German knights of the Teutonic Order. The Poles then had acquired it by defeating the Teutonic knights in 1410 at the Battle of Grunwald. Brandenburg abruptly renounced Prussia's feudal obligations to Poland in 1656 and declared the region a separate kingdom in 1701. A century later it seized other Polish territory in the partitionings of that state in 1772, 1793, and 1795.

All the German lands came under the control of Napoleonic forces at the beginning of the nineteenth century. Napoleon declared an end to the Holy Roman Empire and simplified the political map. A majority of the petty states were brought together into a short-lived Confederation of the Rhine. The lands of Brandenburg remained separate as an enlarged Kingdom of Prussia, but much of its recently acquired Polish territories was lost to Napoleon's new Grand Duchy of Warsaw.

Following defeat of the French forces, the Treaty of Vienna in 1815 preserved Germany's fragmentation, although it did simplify the crazy-quilt pattern of tiny units, consolidating them into about fifty states. The new entities were quite arbitrary, however, and offered little historical or regional basis for the development of

loyalties of their inhabitants in any way comparable to the nationalisms then raging in other parts of Europe. Indeed, a principal concern of treaty makers was to assure that the individual states were viable enough to resist internal revolution. They were linked together in a German Confederation (*Bund*), but it was an association of princes, not of peoples. Brandenburg-Prussia and Austria were the largest units, and each held extensive territories outside Confederation boundaries. Prussia regained western Poland and received a substantial territorial augmentation in the lower Rhineland area.

Continued fragmentation did not stifle the formation of German national awareness, however. The new climate of ideas disseminated by the French legions had taken firm root. In 1807 the influential scholar J.G. Fichte had declared the necessity for all the German-speaking lands to unite. Others expanded the concept to include all areas where Germans had set their mark. Leading elements of society everywhere railed at the consequences of parceling out the German lands and called for a more unified state. In 1848, the year of revolution in Europe, an all-German council met in Frankfurt with high hopes of creating a united national state based upon liberal parliamentary institutions. However, it proved incapable of mobilizing support to overturn the entrenched princely families.

Prussia then assumed the task of welding the separate German units into a modern nation-state. It had managed to avoid the turmoil besetting other German units and set about its own internal revolution whose consequences were as great as those that occurred earlier in France. Prussia emancipated its serfs, reformed its taxes, and streamlined its bureaucracy. It promoted the growth of industry and commercialized agriculture. It took the lead in forging a *Zollverein* (customs union) in 1833 linking most of the German states. The *Zollverein's* high external tariffs coupled with an open internal market for indigenous entrepreneurs yielded many of the benefits enjoyed by the large unitary states of Europe. In addition to expanded economic activity, the regional interdependence that resulted reinforced the growing sense of pan-German identity.

Under the leadership of Otto von Bismarck in the second half of the nineteenth century, Prussia contrived three wars with neighbors that had the effect of promoting an image of it as guardian of German national interests while negating the influence of Austria and France, Prussia's rivals for power in the German lands. A war with Denmark in 1864 "rescued" the Germans of Schleswig-Holstein and legitimized Prussia as defender of the German nation. Two years later Prussia enticed Austria into a fight, ostensibly over the outcome of the earlier war with Denmark, and defeated it. The peace treaty required termination of the inactive 1815 Austrian-led Confederation of Germany and its replacement by an organization excluding Austria and its Kingdom of Bohemia, which had been part of Germany since the early Middle Ages. Prussia then proceeded to annex the states of Hannover, Hesse-Kassel, and Nassau, giving it 90 percent of the territory and population of the new North German Confederation. Finally, in 1870, it drew France into a war that brought Prussia national support from the inhabitants of the Catholic German states to the south. The war's successful conclusion led those states into the Confederation, together with German-speaking Alsace and Lorraine acquired from France. Still, the Germans in the Austrian and Bohemian lands remained outside the association. The Prussian territory also contained substantial non-German minorities, chiefly Poles acquired in the eighteenth century partitionings of that state.

The establishment of a unified German state was formalized by the 1871 inauguration of the second German Reich under a *Kaiser* who was the king of Prussia. Although nominally a federal unit, the new Germany was in fact a highly centralized super-Prussia. It soon challenged the British in the oceans and embarked upon an active policy of colonial expansion. It developed an integrated economy that became the best in Europe in food production, mining, industrial development, and internal transportation.

Disaster then struck when Germany was drawn into World War I by its old rival and new ally, Austria-Hungary, against the forces of Russia, France, England, and, ultimately, the United States of America. The war was lost and the victors sought to punish the vanquished. They took away substantial German-speaking territories in Alsace-Lorraine, the Saarland, Luxemburg, Schleswig, Posen, Upper Silesia, Danzig, Memel, and a corridor across Pomerania created for access to the sea by a reestablished Poland. Despite the common German national identity long felt by Austrian and Bohemian Germans in the collapsed Habsburg Empire, the victorious Allies forbade these groups to become part of the postwar German state. They also required that the Rhineland region be demilitarized and that Germany pay heavy reparations. Subsequently, a disastrous inflation wiped out the accumulated wealth of the German middle class.

The German Reich was replaced by the Weimar Republic. It was shorn of any nationally unifying trappings of monarchy, although it did retain much of the Prussian centralization of its predecessor government. Democratic institutions borrowed from the French, British, and Americans soon proved inadequate. Germany's internal economic and political problems led to active Communist and Fascist movements in the 1920s.

The National Socialist Workers Party of Adolf Hitler grew dominant in Prussian politics and from this base, in 1933, over all of Germany.

Germany again became a super-Prussia as the so-called Third Reich, although its leader, Hitler, was from a Catholic background in Austria. Part of the success of the Nazis in gaining broad popular support was identification made with deeply felt sentiments of the German nation. The Nazis announced a program to reverse the punishing aspects of the Treaty of Versailles by bringing the forcibly separated Germans back together into a single state. The Nazis also fanned the flames of anti-Semitism, portraying Germany's Jews as a parasitic caste and calling for a Jewish-free society. In addition to continuing a traditional European utilization of Jews as scapegoats for internal economic and political problems, the hatred of the Nazis appears also to have been motivated by the significant role played by German Jews in the rival Communist movement.

The Nazis sought to regain and maximize the status of Germany as a world power. Their propagandists rationalized aggression toward neighbors by promoting a pseudo-science of *Geopolitik*, which asserted that territorial expansion was essential for a state to thrive. Governments had to provide increasing *Lebensraum* ("living space") for their inhabitants if they were to be successful. In this regard it is interesting to note that the postwar German Federal Republic provided ever higher living standards for a population that grew to exceed that of prewar Germany, yet it had an area barely half that of its predecessor. Its agricultural land declined substantially in amount as marginal farms were abandoned to meadows and forests.

German national feelings received gratification in 1935 when a plebiscite in the Saarland resulted in an overwhelming majority of the people voting to join the German state. A year later the Nazis brought German military forces back to the Rhineland. In 1938 they peacefully incorporated the Austrians and Sudetenland Germans into the Third Reich, and later in the year made remaining Bohemia and Moravia a German "protectorate." Germany then launched World War II in 1939 by attacking Poland on flimsy grounds of "persecution" of its German minority.

Germany's military operations were successful at the beginning of the war. The armed forces quickly defeated Poland by a "lightning war" (*Blitzkrieg*) in which they were joined by the Soviet Union. The Third Reich annexed directly the German-inhabited regions of the Polish Corridor, Posen, Danzig, and Upper Silesia, all of which had substantial Polish minorities. The Soviet Union incorporated extensive Polish eastern territories that had Ukrainian, Byelorussian, and Lithuanian majorities. What remained of Poland was occupied by German forces and designated simply as the "Government General of Poland."

The invasion of Poland brought France and the United Kingdom into the war. Germany quickly overran Denmark, Norway, and the Low Countries in 1940. It then defeated France, dividing it between a German-occupied north and west and an unoccupied, but submissive, southeast. The British managed to withstand German air and sea attack, however, and were able successfully to engage forces of Germans and their Italian allies in the eastern Mediterranean and North Africa. Apart from the announced neutral states of Switzerland, Sweden, Spain, and Portugal, Germany established dominance over the rest of Europe by forging military and political alliances or, in the case of Yugoslavia and Greece, conquest. In 1941 it went to war with the USSR, its armed forces reaching the Volga River and coming within twenty miles of both Leningrad and Moscow by the following year. It subsequently suffered a series of reverses, particularly after entrance of the United States into the war at the end of 1941. Germany was forced to surrender unconditionally in 1945.

As a result of agreements between the United States, the United Kingdom, and the USSR, the political map of Germany changed substantially after World War II. It lost all of its wartime territorial gains. Austria was severed once again and treated as a separate entity under occupation by the victorious Allies. Poland and the USSR annexed the ancient German regions of East Prussia, Pomerania, and Silesia. Remaining German territory was divided into four occupation zones administered by the Soviet Union, the United Kingdom, France, and the United States. The German capital of Berlin, lying inside the Russian zone, was also divided into four separate occupation districts.

These temporary occupation arrangements hardened into long-run partitionings, as frictions developed between the Soviet Union and the Western Allies. By 1947 the Americans and British had decided to merge their two occupation zones, and the French zone joined in the following year. The Allies called for the drafting of a constitution for their territories, and the German Federal Republic began functioning in 1949, becoming fully sovereign in 1955. The Soviet Union reacted by creating a German Democratic Republic in its occupation zone. Each republic claimed to be the legitimate state of the entire German nation. Austria remained under four-power occupation until 1956, when an agreement between the Western Allies and the Soviet Union permitted reestablishment of sovereignty but prohibited any future union with a German state.

The status of Berlin created special problems under the increasingly hostile relations between the Western Allies and the USSR. The occupation arrangements, initially assumed to be temporary, vaguely provided for access to their sectors of that city by American and British forces from their western zones. However, in 1948 the Soviet Union cut surface connections from the west to Berlin. The Allies then undertook to supply their forces and the 2,000,000 inhabitants of West Berlin by air transport. It was a costly operation, but the Berlin Airlift resulted in a 1949 agreement with Soviet occupation authorities that reopened surface access by a limited number of roads, rail lines, and canals.

West Berlin became a primary route by which East Germans fled to an increasingly more attractive West Germany. Communist authorities felt the necessity to end this flight in 1961 by erecting a fortified wall completely around the western-occupied zones of the city. To maintain legitimacy of their control of West Berlin, the Allies did not allow Berlin to become a formal part of the German Federal Republic. Berlin functioned as an outpost of that state, however, and was the recipient of substantial subsidies to alleviate its precarious financial situation.

The Germans thus remained fragmented among four governmental units for more than four decades following World War II. Although separation led to establishment of a distinctive Austrian sense of nationhood, a unified German national identity remained strong in the other three units. Just as during the first two-thirds of the nineteenth century, ties of language, culture, and perceived joint historical experiences bound politically fragmented Germans together. A decision by the USSR to withdraw from military domination of Eastern Europe led to reestablishment of a unified German nation state in 1990, symbolized by dismantling of the heavily fortified border between the Federal and Democratic republics and the tearing down of the wall around West Berlin (Figure 4-3).

Forty-five years of enforced separation had left substantial political and economic problems facing the new state, however. Although the Communist government in the east had built up an impressive industrial machine with higher living standards than elsewhere in the Soviet bloc, its competitiveness was no match for the dynamic economy of the West. Its factories were overmanned and technologically inferior. The infrastructure of transportation and communication had been allowed to deteriorate substantially. Workers lacked incentive to produce efficiently and were not accustomed to taking responsibility for making decisions. Although politicians in western Germany had initially seen economic problems as easily surmountable, the reality of integration demonstrated that the costs of bringing the east up to western economic levels annu-

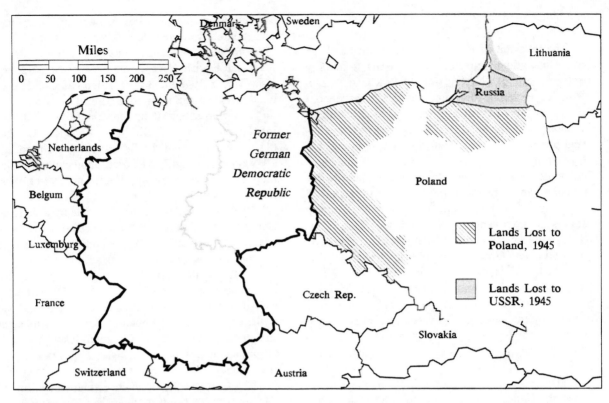

FIGURE 4-3   GERMANY IN 1994

Map labels: Miles, 0 50 100 150 200 250, Denmark, Sweden, Lithuania, Netherlands, Former German Democratic Republic, Russia, Belgium, Poland, Luxemburg, France, Czech Rep., Lands Lost to Poland, 1945, Lands Lost to USSR, 1945, Slovakia, Switzerland, Austria

ally would require more than a hundred billion dollars of investment and subsidy for at least a decade.

Redressing the economic lag of its old Prussian and Saxon territories is now the major regional problem facing the German state. Its political leaders also still have to contend with localisms that impinge upon national unity, particularly in the Catholic south. Although religious issues no longer directly affect internal relations, they provide a basis for group identity comparable to the contending forces in Northern Ireland. A Catholic heritage played no little part in the separate nationalism adopted by Austrians after the war. Their relationship to the German nation has become somewhat analogous to that of Canadians with Americans. Bavarians particularly feel a strong regional particularism, reinforced by their awareness of ten centuries of more or less continuous existences of a political unit called "Bavaria."

Regional minority problems are minor in comparison with almost every other European state. There are small groups of Frisians along the North Sea coast and the remnant Sorbs retain their Slavic traditions south of Berlin. The German Democratic Republic supported

the latter's resistance to acculturation. Neither group currently appears unhappy at being included within a German nation-state.

A potential problem externally is the future of German lands lost in the east to Poland and the Soviet Union, as well as the formerly German-settled Sudetenland of the Czech Lands and Slovakia. Virtually all German inhabitants of these territories, more than 10,000,000, fled or were expelled westward at war's end. They constituted a quarter or more of the population of the two German republics in the immediate postwar decades. Although they once represented a vociferous force in West Germany calling for return of their home regions, pressures have abated with economic integration into their new homes, intermarriage, and the passing of generations. Lingering sentiments remain, however, and have been stirred by a belated finding of voices by the small numbers of Germans remaining in the east, particularly in Polish Silesia. Poland, the Czech Lands, and Slovakia are mindful of a potential threat to their territories from a united future Germany beset by internal economic and political problems comparable to those it experienced after World War I.

Bibliography

BECKINSALE, MONICA, and ROBERT BECKINSALE, *Southern Europe: A Systematic Geographical Study*, New York: Holmes & Meier, 1975.

DICKINSON, ROBERT, *Germany*. New York: Dutton, 1953.

EAST, W. GORDON, *An Historical Geography of Europe*. London: Methuen, 1962.

POUNDS, NORMAN J. G., *Divided Germany and Berlin*. Princeton, NJ: Searchlight Books, 1962.

POUNDS, NORMAN J. G., *An Historical Geography of Europe: 1800–1914*. New York: Cambridge University Press, 1985.

PRISTINGER, FLAVIA, "Ethnic Conflict and Modernization in the South Tyrol," in Charles R. Foster, ed., *Nations Without a State: Ethnic Minorities in Western Europe*. New York: Praeger, 1980, pp. 153–188.

5

The States of East-Central Europe

The Demise of Eastern Europe

Among the many consequences of the collapse of Communist regimes in Eastern Europe during the winter of 1989/90 was the restoration of traditional regional cultural/political associations within the area. Central Europe and the Balkans reappeared once more, after forty-five years of suppressed identity within a bloc of states whose functioning had served to sever them from much of their European heritage and to orient their societies and economies to the interests of Russia.

"Eastern Europe" had become a customary and seemingly permanent regional designation for those eight states in which Marxist-Leninist regimes were established under Soviet occupation or influence in the wake of defeat of the Axis powers in World War II: Poland, the German Democratic Republic, Czechoslovakia, Hungary, Romania, Bulgaria, Yugoslavia, and Albania. Although Yugoslavia had separated itself from the others in 1948, and Albania had pursued an independent course since the 1960s, both had retained, like the other states, sets of political, social, and economic institutions modeled after counterparts in the USSR. (See Table 5-1.)

In addition to the homogeneity of political cultures and organizational forms, Eastern Europe also had a high degree of political-geographic coherence. Under Russian direction, the states had oriented their trade linkages and other patterns of circulation to the USSR and to each other, with a degree of coordination by the Council for Mutual Economic Assistance (CMEA or COMECON). Militarily, their armed forces were organized through the Warsaw Pact.

Eastern Europe foundered as a socialist territorial commonwealth, however. With the possible exception of Yugoslavia, its regimes were never able to elicit the positive allegiances of their peoples. To a degree this was because they were never able to come to terms with the phenomenon of national identities. To the extent that they had any freedom of action, the loyal Communists initially installed under Red Army supervision were antithetical to the sentiments of nationalism. Often drawn from minority groups that had felt oppression within the states before World War II, the new rulers had few sympathies for the customs and aspirations of the past. Their vision of the future was one of the establishment of an international socialism that transcended the inherited social and political cultures.

In succeeding decades, as Soviet control relaxed, the newer leaderships sought closer identity with their nations, particularly as economic and social policies foundered. National figures who had once been castigated were again honored. Even the equestrian statue of Frederick the Great reappeared in downtown East Berlin after forty years of storage. On a darker side, traditional enmities toward minorities and neighboring nations were allowed to reestablish themselves. Zhivkov, the Communist leader of Bulgaria, gained some popular support for efforts to Bulgarianize the state's rapidly multiplying Turkish population. Ceausescu similarly won plaudits from Romanians for measures to denationalize the Magyar minority.

Despite such attempts to appeal to national sentiments, the dependence of the East European regimes upon the support of the Soviet Union was painfully evident. When the USSR decided to pull back from its long-standing involvement in Europe, the Communist leaderships fell. Only the independent regimes in Yugoslavia and Albania held on, and their futures are problematical. The successor governments from the start strove to reestablish regional positions that had been lost in World War II and its aftermath. The northern states began the process of reconstituting themselves into Central Europe, and those in the south displayed increasingly "Balkan" traits.

The Region of East-Central Europe

Before World War II, "Central Europe" conventionally was seen as Germany, Switzerland, and Austria plus the adjacent states that shared commonalities as a result of centuries of cultural and penetration from the Germanic lands: Poland, Czechoslovakia, Hungary, Lithuania, Latvia, Estonia, Romanian Transylvania, and Yugoslav Slovenia and Croatia. The "Balkans" embraced the remaining territories of southeastern Europe that had been heavily influenced politically, economically, and culturally by long association with the Ottoman Empire.

The area of Central Europe expanded in size during 1991 with the breakup of the USSR and Yugoslavia. Estonia, Latvia, and Lithuania in effect rejoined the region when they regained their independence. Similarly, the emergence of independent Slovenia and Croatia again moved the borders of Central Europe to the Sava River. The cultural contrasts between the Central European Slovenia and Croatia and the Balkan Serbia played a major part in the fragmentation of Yugoslavia.

TABLE 5.1 EAST CENTRAL EUROPE

Five medium-sized, predominantly Roman Catholic states make up the region of East-Central Europe. They were created in the twentieth century out of the ashes of the Austro-Hungarian, German, and Russian empires (Lithuania also is a part of this group, but is considered with other former parts of the USSR). Each state formerly dominated substantial regional minority groups, but now all are much more homogeneous. They face pressures internationally from both Germany and Russia.

State	Total Population	Area (sq. miles)	Distinctive Features of Group
Austria	7,800,000	32,400	
Dominant Nation and % Total			
Austrians, 96%			Germanic (German) language, Roman Catholic
Significant Regional Groups and % Total			
Slovenes, 2%			South Slavic (Slovenian) language, Roman Catholic
Poland	39,000,000	120,700	
Dominant Nation and % Total			
Poles, 99%			Western Slavic (Polish) language, Roman Catholic
Potential Trouble Areas and Possible Adversaries			
Silesia, Pomerania (Germany) and Southern East Prussia (Russia, Lithuania, Germany)			
	12,000,000	44,000	
The Czech Lands	10,500,000	30,450	
Dominant Nation and % Total			
Czechs, 90%			Western Slavic (Czech) language, Anticlerical Roman Catholic
Significant Regional Groups and % Total			
Moravians, 9%			Western Slavic (Czech) language, Anticlerical Roman Catholic
Slovakia	5,300,000	18,500	
Dominant Nation and % Total			
Slovaks, 85%			Western Slavic (Slovak) language, Devout Roman Catholic
Significant Regional Groups and % Total			
Magyars (Hungarians), 10%			Finno-Ugrian (Hungarian) language, Roman Catholic
Ruthenians, 7%			Eastern Slavic (Ukrainian) language, Uniate Catholic
Potential Trouble Areas and Possible Adversaries			
Southern Slovakia (Hungary)	500,000	2,000	
Hungary	10,300,000	36,000	
Dominant Nation and % Total			
Magyars (Hungarians), 97%			Finno-Ugrian (Hungarian) language, Roman Catholic and Calvinist

Germany (including East Germany) and Switzerland have been examined previously. In this chapter Hungary, the Czech Lands, Slovakia, Poland, and the Baltic States are examined as parts of "East-Central Europe." Because of Austria's common history and close economic and cultural ties with the East-Central European states, it also is included in this section. Slovenia and Croatia are considered in the following chapter on the Balkans because of the effects of seventy

years within Yugoslavia. For similar reasons, Transylvania also is included in the next chapter owing to its seven decades of inclusion within Romania.

The population of East-Central Europe, including Austria, numbers some 72,000,000 people and occupies an area of approximately 240,000 square miles. The northern part of the region is dominated by Poland's section of the East European Plain, which has provided few impediments to movement of invaders from either east or west. The southern portion consists of low mountains and hills surrounding the productive interior basins of Bohemia and Pannonia.

The territory is rather continuously settled, without the extensive non-ecumene to be found in the Norden states or the USSR. Low population densities are found scattered in areas marginal for farming, including the glacially created wetlands of northeastern Poland and the thin soils of the Carpathian Mountains and the uplands of Bohemia.

Polish, Czech, and Slovak form a Western Slavic branch of the Slavic languages. Magyar is a Central Asian Finno-Ugrian language, quite different from most languages of Europe, which are derived from an Anatolian Indo-European parent.

National consciousness developed among the bulk of the inhabitants of East-Central Europe only during the nineteenth century. Before this period, as in the rest of Europe, identities were vaguely based upon religion, which was principally Roman Catholic. The Protestant Reformation had permanent effects mainly among the scattered colonies of Germans and in certain eastern areas of Hungary. In this regard, however, it should be noted that while the so-called Hussite Protestant rebellion in Bohemia and Moravia was eventually suppressed brutally by the Roman Catholic Habsburgs, the Roman Catholic church never was able to regain the allegiance of the Czechs.

In the sixteenth century substantial numbers of Ashkenazi Jews were welcomed into Poland following persecutions in the German Rhineland. The invading French armies of Napoleon are generally seen as the catalyst for the development of national consciousness in nineteenth-century East-Central Europe. Imbued with a Jacobin ideology, they presented a challenging alternative political philosophy to the prevailing view of a divine right of kings.

In the interwar period it was fashionable to see this area as part of an eastern "shatterbelt" of Europe. This was because nationally based states appeared in the region only at the end of World War I. Before that time, virtually all of the territory was attached to four externally based empires: German, Russian, Habsburg, and Ottoman (although Serbia, Romania, and Bulgaria had been able to break away from Ottoman control by the middle or end of the nineteenth century). All four empires managed to lose the war.

The young states exhibited a number of common problems associated with their newness. A principal difficulty was the presence of significant national minorities in each. This was a legacy of the long intermingling of peoples within the old empires that made it impossible to draw new boundary lines that did not incorporate substantial numbers of individuals outside of the state that was designated for their nation. They also had to develop self-contained modern economies after being parts of broader imperial common markets or languishing for centuries as subsistence agricultural areas.

During succeeding decades a remarkable change has occurred in the region. Currently the states of East Central Europe are among the most homogeneous in the world. In Poland, the percentage of inhabitants identifying themselves as Poles has risen from 60 percent in 1918 to 95 percent today. This is explained by its loss of Byelorussian- and Ukrainian-inhabited territories to the USSR, the horrendous extermination of three million of its Jewish citizens during World War II, and the expulsion of most Germans at the end of the war, including millions from newly gained lands of East Prussia, Pomerania, and Silesia. Similar eviction of Germans from the Sudetenland eliminated a major minority problem in Czechoslavia. Its amicable division in 1993 into separate Czech and Slovak states continued the trend toward increasingly homogeneous nation states in East-Central Europe, although Slovakia contains a 10 percent Hungarian minority and 7 percent Ruthenian.

The Habsburg Lands

A dominant force in the region, with a legacy that remains substantial at the end of the twentieth century, is the Habsburg lands, which in East-Central Europe stretched from Krakow in Poland to the borders of Montenegro, and from Upper Austria to Eastern Transylvania (Figure 5-1). The Habsburg family first rose to prominence in 1273, when a member was elected emperor of the Holy Roman Empire. Habsburgs remained in control of the title for most of the ensuing five centuries, gathering extensive personal territories by carefully arranged marriages, effective diplomacy, and a strong military force. They also found a strong ally in the Roman Catholic church.

The Habsburg territories grew from a nucleus on the upper Danube in the vicinity of Vienna known as the *Ostmark*, or "Eastern Marchland." German families ruling the Ostmark had been given special privileges by the Holy Roman Empire in return for serving as a bulwark against military threats from the east. The Habsburgs came to rule the Ostmark and gathered in their hands substantial non-German territories eastward and southward, including the Slavic Kingdom of Bohemia and the Magyar Kingdom of Hungary. The latter was gained in the sixteenth century after it had lost much of its area and population to the advancing Turks. Twice the Turks besieged Vienna, but with the aid of the Poles and other allies, the Austrians repulsed the threat.

The Habsburg family held extensive territories elsewhere in Europe for long periods, including the Low Countries and Spain. Although popularly termed

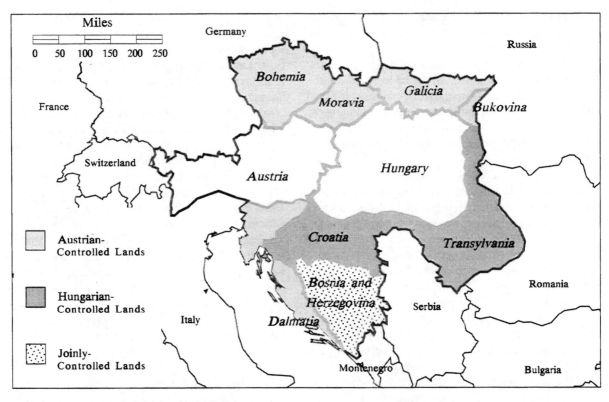

FIGURE 5-1 THE HABSBURG EMPIRE

an "empire," the Habsburg-controlled lands did not actually receive that designation until threatened by the forces of Napoleon in the first decade of the nineteenth century. Even then, the ruler's new title of "Emperor of Austria" clearly meant "of the Ruling House of Austria" rather than "of the Austrians."

The Habsburg lands constituted one of the largest and most formidable states of Europe. However, the state fell victim to increasing centrifugal pressures for sovereignty by the multitude of nations that emerged within it during the nineteenth century. After participating in the unsuccessful series of revolts that shook the state in 1848, the Hungarians eventually forced the dominating Austrian Germans in 1867 to concede them an equal partnership role in managing the empire, which was essentially divided into two parts. The Austrians retained control over the German, Czech, Polish, Italian, Slovene, and Dalmatian segments of the empire; the Hungarians gained domination over the Slovaks, Ruthenians, Romanians, Serbs, and Croatians. However, the Hungarians proved to be less tolerant of the development of local nationalisms within their allotted territory than the Austrians had been.

The southern limits of the empire facing the Turks were stabilized in the eighteenth century along the Kupa-Sava-Danube rivers. In 1878 this boundary was shifted southward when the empire seized the Turkish provinces of Bosnia and Herzegovina, containing a mixed population of Serbs, Croats, and South Slavic Muslims. Ultimately this proved the undoing of the state, since it led to the assassination of the heir to the throne in 1914 by Serbian nationalists, and thence to World War I, which proved to be a military and, ultimately, a political disaster to Austria-Hungary.

As Habsburg power collapsed in 1918, national leaders in the borderlands succeeded in securing separation from the empire (Figure 5-2). They were aided by the policy of "self-determination of nations" enunciated by President Wilson of the United States of America. The Czechs, Slovaks, and Ruthenians gained a new state of their own that was named Czechoslovakia. The Croats and Slovenes, after proclaiming their independence, joined with the Serbs and other South Slavic peoples in the Kingdom of Serbs, Croats, and Slovenes, that was officially renamed Yugoslavia in 1930. The empire's Poles joined with their fellow nationals situated in Germany and Russia to establish a revived Poland, and the Transylvanian Romanians united with countrymen in Bessarabia and the Kingdom of Romania to form an expanded Romanian nation-state. The Austrian Germans and Hungarians also found themselves with states of their own.

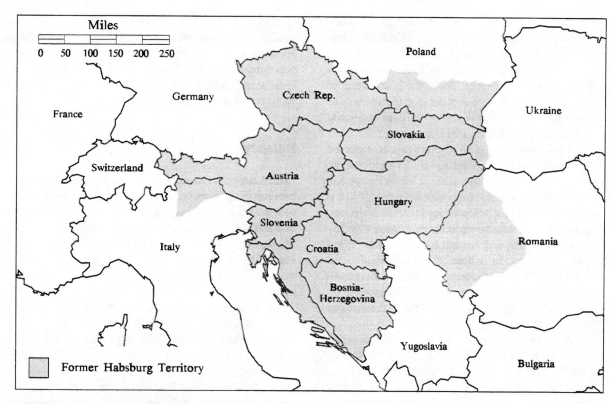

FIGURE 5-2 SUCCESSOR STATES TO THE HABSBURG EMPIRE

For all of its problems of national antagonisms, the Habsburg Empire had functioned quite well as a state for its citizens. Economically, its far-flung, contrasting parts had developed regional productive specializations that were complementary and mutually beneficial. A system of institutions had emerged that guaranteed fair procedures and personal rights and freedoms. Unfortunately, the economic and political situations within the postwar successor states (aside from pre-World War II Czechoslovakia) tended to be far less positive. Their individual policies of economic self-sufficiency (autarky) disrupted the evolved productive system of specialization and exchange based upon regional comparative advantage, leading to declines in productivity and living standards. Most adopted Fascist forms of government, in part to counter fractious national minorities and class conflicts.

Austria

The successor state most disrupted by the breakup of the Habsburg Empire was Austria itself. It is considered in this section because of its intimate linkage to the East-Central European states. Moreover, until a peace treaty was signed in 1956, much of its productive

eastern fringe after World War II was occupied and administered by the Soviet Union.

Post-World War I Austria was confined to a territory of scarcely 32,000 square miles, only a quarter of which was cultivated. Forty percent of the young Austrian state consisted of forested mountains. Nearly a third of its population of 6,500,000 was concentrated in Vienna, which had grown large as the primate city of an empire containing more than 50,000,000 inhabitants. Vienna became a "head-without-a-body" in 1918, cut off from its former markets, its sources of raw materials, and its constituencies for an administrative machine that employed a substantial segment of its working force.

Austria suffered a profound economic depression. Its two western provinces of Vorarlberg and Tirol even unsuccessfully attempted to seek relief by joining Switzerland. To redress the impossible economic situation, the Austrian National Assembly on three occasions between 1919 and 1921 sought to join the new German Republic. This solution reflected the fact that Austrians still saw themselves as members of a German nation, despite being excluded by Bismarck in the 1871 formation of a German national state. Their national feelings toward other Germans, including Prussians and Saxons, were little different from those of the Bavarians who had become incorporated in Germany. However, pressure from the Allied powers, particularly France, prohibited political union (*Anschluss*). Austrians were even forbidden to continue to use the designation *Deutschösterreich* ("German Austria") as the name of their new state. Austria's economic difficulties continued through the decade of the 1930s, until *Anschluss* was achieved in 1938 with Nazi Germany.

The German defeat in 1945 saw again an enforced separation of Austria from the rest of the Germans. Its territory was divided among the four victorious Allied powers and occupied for more than a decade. When it was allowed to sign a peace treaty in 1956, the provisions appeared to forbid even economic union with any other German state, and Austria did not join the European Community in which the German Federal Republic was a major partner. Austria did become a member of the European Free Trade Association, however, together with the United Kingdom, the Norden countries, Switzerland, and Portugal.

A distinctive Austrian national identity has established itself since World War II. Its iconography includes its Roman Catholic heritage and its lingering associations with the former subject peoples of the old empire. With the 1989 fall of Communist regimes in Eastern Europe, Vienna has again assumed a role as a focal point for spatial interaction in the Danube Basin.

Austria has few problems with national minorities. Groups of Hungarians and Croats live in its small eastern province of Burgenland. This territory was awarded to Austria after World War I from lands of the Kingdom of Hungary that traditionally had commenced at the Leitha River. The bulk of the population of Burgenland consists of Germans whose forebears migrated to the area after the Turks were repulsed from Vienna. The Croats are descendants of refugees who fled to Burgenland during the Turkish invasions of the Balkans. They retain an archaic Croatian language, although substantial numbers have been assimilated into the Austrian nation.

In the southeast a significant minority is the Slovenian-speaking population of the Klagenfurt Basin of the province of Carinthia. They can be seen as a last remnant of a formerly continuous Slovenian population of eastern Austria that over the centuries was assimilated into German culture. As in several other areas of mixed populations, a post-World War I plebiscite was held to determine the state preference of the local residents. The 1920 results favored the area being part of Austria.

Despite a continuing assimilation, a group of Austrian Slovenes has retained its identity and increased its linkages across the border with the Slovenes of Yugoslavia. Resentment by German-speaking Carinthians against Slovene demands for recognition of their cultural distinctiveness has led to some local conflict. Thus, in desperation at the vandalism of the Slovenian portions of dual-language traffic signs required by peace treaty in areas inhabited by Slovenian speakers, local authorities finally decided simply to remove all such road signs completely.

Hungary

Like Austria, the modern state of Hungary dates to the breakup of the Habsburg Empire in 1918. However, the new entity was a successor to a Kingdom of Hungary that had been founded in the ninth century by nomadic Magyar (Hungarian) invaders of the Middle Danubian Plain. The Magyars subdued and assimilated the primarily Slavic peoples inhabiting the plain and developed a strong political entity. Under pressures from Turks moving up the Balkan peninsula, the Magyars lost much of their territory. The nobles of the remaining rump state named the Habsburg emperor of Austria as their king in 1526, beginning a linkage of nearly four centuries.

The Magyars gained equal status with the Austrian Germans within the empire in 1867. They had their own parliament with substantial control of internal affairs of their portion of the empire. However, within this area they numbered only half of the some 20,000,000 inhabitants. By restrictive policies on suffrage, on the use of non-Magyar languages, and on control of schools, they sought to promote a predominance of Magyar culture.

Such measures engendered a reaction from the subject peoples, who were caught up in their own flowerings of national identity. National manifestations were violently suppressed, paralleling what the Austrians had done to Magyars in an earlier era. During the stress of World War I, the Magyars attempted to appease national sentiments. They belatedly allowed non-Hungarians to wear their own national colors and emblems, extended the right to vote, reformed the school laws, and allowed use of local languages in official business. Such concessions did not curb national feelings, however. Although most of the non-Magyar military units fought valiantly for the Habsburg Empire, at war's end the subject peoples were near-unanimous in wanting to separate from Hungary. Only the Slovaks showed some ambivalence about leaving the Hungarians.

In the drawing of postwar boundaries, the successor states—expanded Romania, Czechoslovakia, and Yugoslavia—received territories that included more than 3,000,000 Magyars. Within Hungary itself the non-Magyar population constituted barely 800,000 of a total population of 8,000,000. Hungarians considered this situation intolerable, and adopted a policy toward the lost territories expressed in the slogan "No,

No, Never!" ("*Nem nem soha!*"). Magyar pressures to revise the boundaries were met by the formation of the contra-Hungarian "Little Entente" military alliance of Czechoslovakia, Romania, and Yugoslavia.

Hungarian irredentist aspirations were eventually successful, however, as that country was rewarded for joining with Germany and Italy in World War II. It gained substantial Magyar-inhabited territories in northern Transylvania, southeastern Czechoslovakia, and northern Yugoslavia. The defeat of the Axis powers, including Hungary, in 1945 saw a return to the pre-World War II status quo.

Although the population of Hungary now appears reconciled to the permanent alienation of these territories, sensitivities to the situation of their Magyar inhabitants remains. In the final months of the Romanian Ceauşescu regime in 1989, Hungary made known its grave concerns about the de-Magyarization campaign of that regime in Transylvania.

The Czech Lands and Slovakia

The economically and politically most successful of the Habsburg successor states in the interwar period was the Republic of Czechoslovakia (Figure 5-3). Its 55,000-square-mile area was composed of the former Bohemian and Moravian provinces of Austria and the Slovakian- and Ruthenian-inhabited areas of Hungary. More than a third of the 14,000,000 inhabitants of the young state were neither Czechs nor Slovaks, however. Among them were 3,100,000 Germans, 750,000 Magyars, 460,000 Ruthenians, and 75,000 Poles.

The Czechs are a Slavic people, who number some 9,000,000. They occupy the Bohemian Basin of the Elbe River and its tributaries and the lowland Moravian Corridor in western Czechoslovakia. They had prospered under Austrian control, becoming the workshop of the Habsburg Empire. The Slovaks total somewhat less than half the Czech population. Their language is similar to Czech, and both groups can readily understand each other. They principally inhabit valleys in the northern wing of the Carpathian Mountains. The Slovak historical experience was with the Hungarians, however, and at independence they enjoyed much less economic and cultural development than did the Czechs. The same can be said for the Ukrainian-speaking Ruthenians.

The Czechs made a valiant effort to accommodate the young state's minorities. They sent large numbers of teachers and economic experts to Slovakia to raise cultural and productive levels of that region. Special rights were extended to all minority groups. In one of its last acts before the onset of World War II, the gov-

FIGURE 5-3 CZECHOSLOVAK MINORITIES AFTER WORLD WAR I

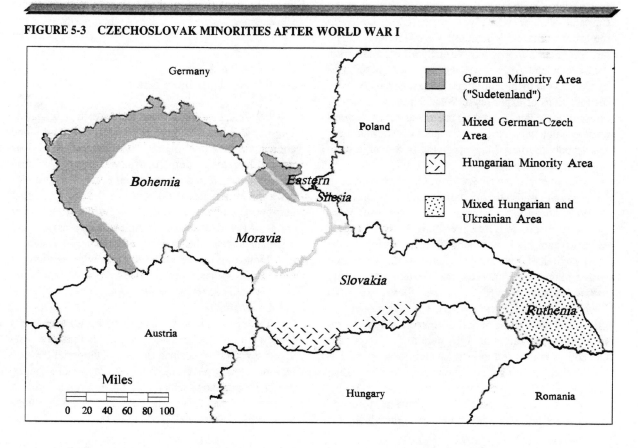

ernment even sought to appease the Slovaks by changing the official name of the country to a hyphenated Czecho-Slovakia.

However, in attempting to find ethnic accommodation the Czechs faced severe odds. Most troublesome were the Germans, who outnumbered the Slovaks. The Germans lived primarily in the Sudetenland—a ring of hills and low mountains surrounding the Bohemian Basin. The dramatic rise of the Nazi Party in Germany in the 1930s was accompanied by agitation among the Czechoslovak Germans for *Anschluss* with the Third Reich, even though throughout history their ancestors had never found themselves living inside a German nation-state. Similar irredentist agitation occurred among the Magyars of southern Slovakia.

In the famous Munich Agreement of September 1938, Czechoslovakia was forced to give up the Sudetenland to Germany and the Magyar areas to Hungary. It was also forced by Poland to cede to it the south Teschen area. Six months later, in March 1939, Germany occupied the remaining Czech territories, declaring them to be a German "Protectorate of Bohemia and Moravia." Slovakia at the same time declared its independence and signed a treaty with Germany recognizing that country's "protection" for twenty-five years. The Carpatho-Ukraine also declared independence, but immediately was occupied and annexed by Hungary.

At the conclusion of the war Czechoslovakia was reestablished with its prewar borders, aside from the Carpatho-Ukraine, which was annexed by the USSR on the grounds that its inhabitants were Ukrainians. The large German minority was virtually all expelled from the Sudetenland. Its factories and farms were taken over by Czechs and by in-migrating Slovaks. For many years organizations of expellees in West Germany called for return of these lands, but their cause was never championed as a policy by the government of the German Federal Republic. Many Magyars living in Slovakia were also expelled to Hungary.

Communists seized power in Czechoslovakia in 1948, creating a Soviet-modelled state that continued to 1989. During that period national tensions were generally suppressed. However, Slovaks never ceased to view themselves as a subjugated minority. In the brief period of a relaxed Czechoslovak "socialism with a human face" in 1968, the Slovaks successfully demanded and received a separate "Slovak Socialist Republic" within Czechoslovakia. The Magyars in Slovakia used the fleeting period of freedom to assert their own calls for greater cultural autonomy. Among their demands was the right to identify their local communities by their traditional Hungarian place names, rather than by the long-imposed Slovak ones.

The Soviet invasion of Czechoslovakia, followed by implementation of a policy termed "normalization,"

did not put an end to Slovak and Magyar nationalist sentiments. Slovakia received disproportionate industrial investment funds from the Soviet-imposed Czechoslovak regime that finally redressed the inherited disparities in development. It continued its separate regional government.

Further national unrest emerged with the overthrow of the Communist regime. Slovaks resented what they believed to be a second-class status within the state; Czechs came to view Slovaks as parasites who could never be satisfied, no matter how many funds were transferred to them from the west. In one of the new government's first contentious debates, Slovaks again forced the renaming of the state as "Czecho-Slovakia" and, a month later, "The Czech and Slovak Federal Republic." Finally, the two groups decided to go their separate ways. On January 1, 1993, the western territories became the Czech Republic and the east again became an independent Slovakia. In contrast to the fighting that erupted in the former Yugoslavia, the separation occurred in an orderly manner.

Both new states have internal regional problems. The Czech Republic must contend with the emergence of a long-simmering regionalism of the Moravians, who seek separate local control over their area. Such regional sentiments have particularly been strong in the Moravian city of Brno and may lead to the creation of a new European nation. Slovaks face possible irredentism from Hungarians living in their southern margins and Ukrainian-speaking Ruthenians in their northeast.

Cooperation Among the Former Habsburg Lands

In 1989, Zita, the last Empress of the Austro-Hungarian Empire, died in her 97th year. Her husband, Karl I, had abdicated the throne in 1918. State memorial services were celebrated in both Austria and Hungary. These ceremonies reflected a substantial change of attitudes toward the monarchy, not only in the two principal components of the empire, but also in the successor states. After decades of Communist oppression and mismanagement, the once-detested imperial system is now looked upon with nostalgia by new generations of Central Europeans. Portraits of the imperial family are frequently to be seen on public display in many cities of the former empire.

Throughout the former Habsburg lands the empire's legacy is in institutions and procedures that have survived seven decades since the end of imperial control. Organization of government ministries, postal services, and law courts shows remarkable uniformity across much of Central Europe. Even the color of official buildings more often than not still tends to be the "Maria Theresa yellow" favored by the old regime. Despite substantial inroads by the English language, German remains the *lingua franca* for communication by the empire's former Slavic, Magyar, and Romanian subjects.

It is not surprising, then, that in the wake of the 1989 toppling of the Communist regimes, proposals were advanced for an economic confederation of the former Habsburg lands, particularly if their socialist patterns of ownership and management would exclude them from the European Community. An Alps-Adria consultative body has functioned for several years to address mutual problems of southeastern Austria, northeastern Italy, southwestern Hungary, and Slovenia.

Poland

The Habsburg Empire had extended northward to include the Galician region of Poland. However, the greater part of Poland had been within the German and Russian empires. Poland, in union with Lithuania after 1386, had been one of the largest of the European states in the Middle Ages. Its territory stretched from the Oder to the Dnieper rivers, and from the Baltic Sea to the Carpathian Mountains. Unfortunately, it was continuously beset by external and internal problems. Avaricious neighbors and a quarreling nobility increasingly weakened its capacity to maintain itself. Finally, at the end of the eighteenth century, Poland disappeared completely from the map of Europe. The Prussians, Austrians, and Russians apportioned it among themselves in three partitions in 1772, 1793, and 1795. As part of the Treaty of Vienna of 1815, a so-called Congress Poland with its capital in Warsaw was established as an autonomous subdivision of the Russian Empire. Its autonomy was terminated after the crushing of an 1863 uprising against Russian domination, however. Despite the lack of a sovereign state of its own, a Polish nation thrived during the nineteenth century. It again achieved statehood in 1918.

Reconstituted Poland again became one of the larger states of Europe in 1918, with an area of 149,000 square miles and a population of 27,000,000. It contained most of Europe's Polish-speakers, but a third of the population was not Polish. These minorities consisted of 14 percent Ukrainians, 10 percent Jews, 3.5 percent Germans, 3.5 percent Byelorussians, and 1 percent Lithuanians.

The large number of minorities can be traced to three principal causes: the mixing of populations in border zones, the achievement of a corridor to the sea across areas with large German populations, and military conquest at the expense of the young Soviet state.

As elsewhere in Eastern Europe, boundary-makers for the new Poland faced the general impossibility of drawing lines that would neatly divide contrasting national groups across a long-settled area. In the west and north, Polish and German populations were greatly interspersed. Moreover, many Polish-speakers in border areas were not anxious to leave a German state. These included a number of Polish Protestants in East Prussia and Polish industrial workers in the coal-rich Silesian region. Plebiscites were held in both areas that resulted in more than a half-million Poles remaining on the German side of the border. Poland, though, received three-quarters of the coal-mining capacity of Silesia, which substantially bolstered its economy.

The Poles also pressed for incorporation in Poland of Teschen, Orava, and Spis, three small territories that were also claimed by Czechoslovakia. An inter-Allied Commission called for a plebiscite for the region, which collectively was known as "Eastern Silesia." In 1920, however, the commission decided to award 611 of the 1,553 square miles of the disputed territory to Poland without a plebiscite. The Czechs received the principal areas of Czech and Slovak population and the main coal mines of the region. The Poles gained the headwaters of the Vistula River and the main areas of Polish population, but never completely accepted the commission's decision.

No plebiscites likewise were held as a basis for the decision to give Poland an access to the Baltic Sea. Despite the fact that Germans were the principal population in the regions along the Baltic Coast, a "Polish Corridor" was established along the Vistula River to the seaport of Danzig (Gdansk in Polish). The territory chosen for the Corridor was twenty to fifty miles wide and had roughly equal proportions of Poles and Germans, although most of the arable land was owned by German landowners.

Opposition by the 400,000 predominantly German citizens of Danzig led the League of Nations to decide not to incorporate that city into Poland, but to create a "free city" independent of both Poland and Germany. However, the continuing Danzig demands to be joined to Germany led Poland to create an entirely new port city of Gdynia within its allotted corridor territory to the north of Danzig.

The effect of the corridor was to interpose Polish territory between the main part of Germany and the province of East Prussia, with its capital in Konigsberg. The separation was more apparent than real, with parallels to the separation of Alaska from the main body of the United States. In addition to ready access between the two parts by ships and planes, sealed German trains were allowed to cross the Polish salient easily. However, the separation of the state territory with its border-crossing inconveniences was never accepted by the Germans, and this was a continuing source of friction between the two governments.

A third element accounting for the large non-Polish minority population was the postwar acquisition of substantial territory in the east. This was beyond what Lord Curzon, a British expert at the Paris Peace Conference, had proposed for the new Poland. His "Curzon Line" was based upon analysis of the ethnic patterns of the Polish-Russian borderland. In a struggle with the Soviet Red Army, which at one point had reached the gates of Warsaw, the Poles seized substantial lands that had been part of historic Poland up to 1772, but which were inhabited primarily by Ukrainians and Byelorussians, although the cities were predominantly Polish and Jewish.

In the turmoil besetting the former Russian Empire after the Bolshevik Revolution, short-lived governments had been established in this border zone by the Ukrainians in Kiev and the Byelorussians in Minsk. In the former Galician region of the Habsburg Empire an independent Western Ukrainian state with capital in Lwow also had been proclaimed, which later joined itself to the former Russian Ukraine. Despite their strivings, however, these national groups lost their quest for sovereignty, and they were ultimately partitioned when Poland and Russia agreed to a peace treaty that was signed in Riga in 1921. Under the treaty Poland gained 4,750,000 Ukrainians and Byelorussians.

Poland also gained a territory of some 11,000 square miles around the city of Vilnius (Vilna). It had been a part of the area of Lithuania that became independent of Russia in 1918. It was claimed by the Lithuanians as their historic capital and largest city, although the Lithuanian population of the area was exceeded substantially in numbers by Poles, Byelorussians, and Jews. The Poles sought it because of its large Polish population and its historic significance to the Kingdom of Poland. The two sides were involved in several armed clashes over the region. Attempts by the Western Allies to settle the dispute peacefully were to no avail. At length the Poles successfully incorporated Vilnius in Poland in 1922. This was later recognized by the League of Nations, but never accepted by the Lithuanian government, which found itself powerless to change the status quo.

The unity of interwar Poland was tested by the large numbers of non-Polish minorities, by pressures from its neighbors, and by some basic differences among the Poles themselves. The latter included the separate paths of Polish economic development within the antecedent empires. The Poles in the former German lands were much more advanced in education and productive resources than those who had been within the Russian Empire. Moreover, the young state had problems of coherence because its railroads were the products of three distinct networks that focused, respectively, on Berlin, Moscow, and Vienna, and

which had limited interconnections. The situation of the Poles was made worse by the ravages of the global economic depression.

World War II saw the partitioning of Poland between its western and eastern neighbors. In a secret agreement signed in 1939 between Ribbentrop and Molotov, who were the foreign ministers of Germany and the USSR, respectively, Poland was divided into areas of interest roughly along the Curzon Line. The two states then invaded and subdued Poland. The Germans incorporated Danzig, the Polish Corridor, and other Polish borderlands into the Third Reich and declared remaining territory as a "Government General of Poland" under military occupation. A large number of the Poles in the annexed territories were expelled from their homes to the General Government. Substantial numbers perished from privations and organized genocide, including most of the Jewish and Gypsy minorities.

The defeat of the Germans led to Soviet domination of all of Poland. At a summit conference in Yalta in February 1945, the Western Allies recognized the Curzon Line as the basis for Poland's postwar border with the Soviet Union. Nearly 70,000 square miles of prewar Polish territory, with 11,000,000 inhabitants, were lost to the USSR. These included Ukrainian-speaking Galicia, western Byelorussia, and the Vilnius region. Some 4,000,000 of the inhabitants of these areas were Poles, and most of these were resettled westward in former German lands east of the Oder and Neisse rivers that had been awarded to Poland, including Lower Silesia, Eastern Pomerania, Danzig, and the southern half of East Prussia. The new lands totaled some 44,000 square miles (Figure 5-4). Indigenous Germans were largely expelled and their homes taken over by the incoming Poles. Thus, an emptied city of Breslau was renamed Wroctaw and became populated primarily by former Polish inhabitants of the Galician capital of Lwow.

Postwar Poland in this way had lost most of its prewar minorities. However, a small concentration of Ukrainians was left in the mountainous territory of its southeastern corner. Many of these were encouraged in the immediate postwar period to move to the Soviet Union. The continuing antiregime guerrilla activities of Ukranians who remained in Poland led the Soviet-installed Polish government forcibly to resettle them in the newly gained northern and western lands.

After the toppling of the old regime, the new government of Poland appeared to face the restructuring of its economic and social system without the regional minority difficulties that beset other East European countries. However, it was not completely free of such problems. In the Opole (Oppeln) region of Lower Silesia a significant group demanded recognition of

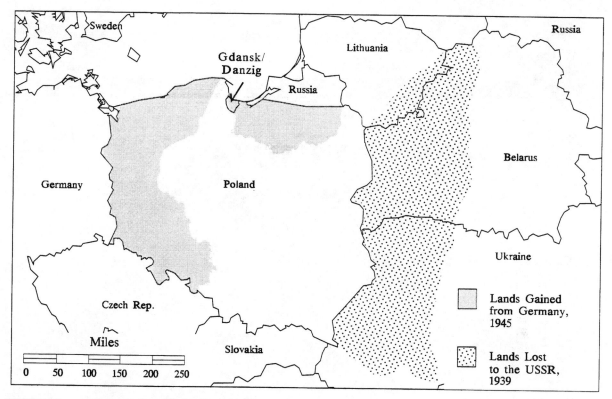

FIGURE 5-4 CHANGING TERRITORIES OF POLAND

their German heritage. This contributed to the fueling of long-dormant irredentist fires in the German Federal Republic, where the bulk of the expellees from Poland had settled after the war. The Poles are mindful of the ever-present potential of demands for return of the former German territories. At the same time, they have expressed their own interest in events in the small Polish-inhabited lands to the east, including the Polish minority areas around Vilnius in Lithuania.

Bibliography

JELAVICH, B., *Modern Austria: Empire and Republic, 1815–1986.* New York: Columbia University Press, 1987.

KOVAKS, Z., "Border Changes and Their Effect on the Structure of Hungarian Society," *Political Geography Quarterly*, Vol. 8 (1989), pp. 79–86.

LEFF, C.S., *National Conflict in Czechoslovakis: The Making and Remaking of State.* Princeton, NJ: Princeton University Press, 1988.

MELLOR, ROY E.H., *Eastern Europe: A Geography of the Comecon Countries.* New York: Columbia University Press, 1975.

MOODIE, ARTHUR, "The Eastern Marchlands of Europe," in *The Changing World: Studies in Political Geography*, W. East and A. Moodie, eds., Yonkers, NY: World Book Co., 1956, pp. 111-137.

POUNDS, NORMAN J. G., *Eastern Europe.* Chicago: Aldine, 1969.

RAMET, P., *Religion and Nationalism and Soviet and East European Politics.* Durham, NC: Duke University Press, 1988.

RUGG, D. S., *Eastern Europe.* The World's Landscapes Series. London and New York: Longman, 1985.

SIMMONDS, G., ed., *Nationalism in the USSR and Eastern Europe in the Era of Brezhnev and Kosygin.* Detroit: University of Detroit Press, 1977.

SUGAR, P., ed., *Ethnic Diversity and Conflict in Eastern Europe.* Santa Barbara, CA: ABC-Clio, 1980.

SUGAR, P. and I. LEDERER, eds., *Nationalism in Eastern Europe.* Seattle: University of Washington Press, 1969.

THADWICK, H.M., *The Nationalities of Europe and the Growth of National Ideologies.* London: Cambridge University Press, 1945.

WANKLYN, HARRIET, *The Eastern Marchlands of Europe.* London: George Philip, 1941.

6

Southeastern Europe

SOUTHEASTERN EUROPE has an area of just under 300,000 square miles, which makes it 50 percent larger than France. Its population of some 60,000,000 is nearly half that of Japan. The region lacks the cultural and political homogeneity of those two countries, however. For most of the twentieth century, Southeastern Europe has been divided into five sovereign states—Yugoslavia, Romania, Bulgaria, Albania, and Greece. Moreover, the territory of those states has harbored the homelands of at least fourteen different nations, each of which has developed profound grievances against some or all the national groups that neighbor it. Tensions over territory are numerous. This was the area that nurtured the spark that led to World War I and manifested some of the most vicious fighting between ethnic groups during World War II.

During 1991 the internal Yugoslav republics of Slovenia, Croatia, Macedonia, and Bosnia-Herzegovina each declared independence (Table 6-1). Their actions were contested by the Yugoslav People's Army. Although the Slovenes and Macedonians achieved their sovereignty with a minimum of fighting, Croatians and Bosnian Muslims found themselves subject to prolonged hostilities that destroyed a significant part of their cultural heritage.

The Yugoslav army's attempt to suppress secession reflected two deep motivations. The army had become a major self-perpetuating institution, dependent to a high degree upon financial support from the profitable industries of Croatia and Slovenia. Moreover, its commissioned and noncommissioned officers were overwhelmingly Serbs and Montenegrins, most of whom had developed antipathies toward Croatians and Muslims for reasons grounded in history.

The origins and the character of this strife are a microcosm of the political tensions that long have beset Southeastern Europe. Throughout its history the Balkan peninsula has been the scene of warfare. The forty-five years of peace following the conclusion of World War II, in fact, were a major anomaly in the region's evolution. Authoritarian Communist governments within each state and an external domination by the Soviet Union put a damper upon group tensions persisting since Roman times and even earlier. Weakening of these controlling forces released pent-up emotions that climaxed in Yugoslavia's vicious struggles.

The diversity of the region has contributed a major term to the English language—"Balkanization"—which is now employed to describe similar areas of geopolitical fragmentation in West Africa, Central America, and Southeast Asia. Paradoxically, contemporary historians and social scientists have dropped the term "Balkans" as a designation of the region in favor of the more value-free "Southeastern Europe." Most now use "Balkans" only in a physical geographic sense to designate the rather broad peninsula that the five states occupy, or, in usage even more limited, the mountain range forming the backbone of Bulgaria (which the Bulgarians themselves term the *Stara Planina* ["Old Mountains"]). This does not mean that the region is any less Balkanized now, however, than in the nineteenth century, when it gave rise to that term.

Southeastern Europe is mountainous territory. Unlike the extensive plains and broad basins of East-Central Europe, this is an area intensively compartmentalized by rough terrain. As in other European lands fronting the Mediterranean, pressures of continental plate movement from land masses to the south have heaved up the terrain in relatively recent geologic time, creating highlands sculptured by running water and gravity into intricate masses of mountains and valleys.

The complexity of the uplands has lent particular historical significance to the few low-level routes that traverse them. Most notable are the Vardar-Morava corridor and the Iron Gates of the Danube. The former is a passageway that follows the Vardar River from the Aegean Sea to its headwaters and then passes down the abutting Morava River headwaters to that river's junction with the Danube. This route has been a line of constant linkage between Mediterranean and Central European civilizations since ancient times. The Iron Gates is a narrow gorge carved by the Danube through the Carpathian Mountains, connecting Central Europe with the Black Sea. The Roman emperor Hadrian caused an ancient road to be built along its south side. Its swift-flowing waters discouraged extensive navigation until a giant hydroelectric project built by Yugoslavia and Romania tamed the Danube in the 1960s.

A distinctive terrain has developed in a hundred-mile wide belt of Southeastern Europe paralleling the length of the Adriatic Sea. Lateral forces wrinkled ancient horizontal seabeds as if they were rugs on a floor. Weathering and erosion gradually abraded uplifted surfaces of sandstone and shale. Limestone layers tended to resist degradation, however. Instead of forming streams on the surface, precipitation found ways to penetrate cracks in the easily dissolved limestone and to form

TABLE 6.1   SOUTHEAST EUROPE

Southeastern Europe consists of nine relatively small states, divided among Eastern Orthodox, Roman Catholic, and Muslim traditions. Created in the twentieth century from the Austro-Hungarian and Ottoman empires (Moldavia also is properly a part of this group but is considered with other former parts of the USSR), nearly all of the countries had developed strong national identities during the nineteenth century before achieving statehood. National iconographies are closely tied to traditional religions; most states have significant regional minority groups and long-standing animosities toward neighbors.

State	Total Population	Area (sq. miles)	Distinctive Features of Group
Yugoslavia (Serbia and Montenegro)	10,350,000	40,000	
Dominant Nation and % Total			
Serbians, 63%			South Slavic (Serbocroatian) language, Eastern Orthodox
Significant Regional Groups and % Total			
Albanians, 14%			Illyrian (Albanian) language, Muslim
Montenegrins, 5%			Tradition of independence, South Slavic (Serbocroatian) language, Eastern Orthodox
Magyars (Hungarians), 4%			Finno-Ugrian language, Roman Catholic
Potential Trouble Area and Possible Adversary			
Kosovo (Albania)	2,000,000	4,200	
Slovenia	2,000,000	7,800	
Dominant Nation and % Total			
Slovenes, 90%			South Slavic (Slovenian) language, Roman Catholic
Croatia	4,800,000	21,800	
Dominant Nation and % Total			
Croats, 75%			South Slavic (Serbocroatian) language, Roman Catholic
Significant Regional Group and % Total			
Serbians, 11%			South Slavic (Serbocroatian) language, Eastern Orthodox
Potential Trouble Areas and Possible Adversaries			
Krajina (Serbia)	250,000	7,000	
Eastern Slavonia (Serbia)	150,000	2,000	
Bosnia and Herzegovina	4,300,000	19,800	
Dominant Nation and % Total			
Bosnian Muslims, 40%			South Slavic (Serbocroatian) language, Muslim
Significant Regional Groups and % Total			
Serbians, 32%			South Slavic (Serbocroatian) language, Eastern Orthodox
Croats, 18%			South Slavic (Serbocroatian) language, Roman Catholic
Active Trouble Areas and Adversary States			
Western Herzegovina (Croatia)	600,000	4,000	
Eastern Bosnia (Bosnia and Serbia)	800,000	8,000	

State	Total Population	Area (sq. miles)	Distinctive Features of Group
Macedonia	2,000,000	10,000	
Dominant Nation and % Total			
Macedonians, 67%			South Slavic (Macedonian) language, Eastern Orthodox
Significant Regional Group and % Total			
Albanians, 20%			Illyrian language, Muslim
Potential Trouble Area and Possible Adversary			
Western Macedonia (Albania)	200,000	2,000	
Romania	23,000,000	92,000	
Dominant Nation and % Total			
Romanians, 78%			Romance (Romanian) language, Eastern Orthodox
Significant Regional Group and % Total			
Hungarians (Magyars), 11%			Finno-Ugrian language, Roman Catholic and Calvinist
Potential Trouble Area and Possible Adversary			
Northern Transylvania (Hungary)	2,000,000	25,000	
Bulgaria	9,000,000	42,855	
Dominant Nation and % Total			
Bulgars, 85%			South Slavic (Bulgarian) language, Eastern Orthodox
Significant Regional Groups and % Total			
Turks, 9%			Altaic language, Muslim
Macedonians, 3%			South Slavic (Macedonian) language, Eastern Orthodox
Albania	3,300,000	11,000	
Dominant Nation and % Total			
Albanians, 98%			Illyrian language, Muslim and Roman Catholic
Greece	10,500,000	51,000	
Dominant Nation and % Total			
Greeks, 95%			Hellenic language, Eastern Orthodox

NOTE: Up to 20% of the total population, living mainly in the north, may consider themselves to be Slavic Macedonians, but the Greek government suppresses any expression of distinctiveness.

channels underground. The result is an area where sandstones and shales have eroded away to form closed basins ("polyes") encircled by rugged limestone hills that are honeycombed by caves and underground rivers. This so-called karst topography in Yugoslavia contributes to an extreme parcelization of land suitable for growing crops and supporting high densities of population.

Historical Evolution

The bulk of the inhabitants of Southeastern Europe traditionally have lived apart from each other in concentrations nestled in favored agricultural sites in basins and plains. Their relative isolation has permitted resistance to pressures for ethnic homogenization that forged the broadly based Germanic peoples and Western Slavs in the plains regions of the north. Inhabitants of the highlands traditionally have been seminomadic, moving domestic flocks across sparse grazing lands. Often these herders differed markedly in culture from adjacent dirt farmers. Today one still finds settlements of Romance-language Vlachs in hills and mountains above lowland agricultural villages of Slavs, Greeks, and Albanians.

Relative isolation resulted in the perpetuation of distinctive cultural and even physical traits in the region's dispersed patches of settlement. Albanians preserved their version of the early Thraco-Illyrian language family that died out in the east under pressures from seventh-century Slavic migrations. Albanians and the Montenegrin Slavs still owe allegiances to terrain-based tribal identities. Montenegrins are also noted for their unusually high incidence of individuals who are more than six feet tall.

Like East-Central Europe, this is a region whose history has been determined as much by external forces as by indigenous ones. It is part of the frontier between Western and Eastern European civilizations and also the zone where Christianity and Islam come together. The many societies in its core have lacked a regional unity to withstand a stream of external assaults coming from Romans, Central Asians, Byzantines, Turks, Venetians, Habsburgs, and Russians.

These aggressive neighbors have left a legacy of geographic discontinuities that continue to sunder the region. They include sharp lines between Roman Catholic and Eastern Orthodox Christians; between both Christian groups and Muslims; between Central European and Mediterranean ways of living; and between landsmen and coastal peoples.

The ancient Greeks established colonies along both the Adriatic and Black seas as part of a sea-girt trading empire that extended the length of the Mediterranean. The Greek impact was ephemeral, expressed today mainly in the excavated ruins of their settlements. The Greeks coined the term "barbarian" from the unintelligible "bar-bar" sounds they perceived in the indigenous Thraco-Illyrian languages. In the fourth century B.C. a Balkan leader, King Philip II of Macedonia, subjugated the principal Greek city-states. His successor, Alexander the Great, advanced an empire to Egypt and India.

The Romans

The Romans began their conquest of the Balkan Peninsula in 146 B.C. Their impress was more lasting. They planted colonies throughout the region. Along the Adriatic coast one can still see the stone-marked margins of carefully surveyed Roman fields. Their Latin language is preserved in the speech of the Romanians and also of the Vlachs, whose ancestors fled into the mountains when Huns and Avars from Central Asia swept through Dalmatia. As elsewhere in Europe, the Romans also built excellent roads that continue to serve as routes through the region. In some cases, especially in Albania, ancient pavements are still in use. Numerous Roman-founded cities have flourished to the present, albeit under different names: Singidunum (Belgrade), Napoca (Cluj), Emona (Ljubljana).

The Roman emperor Diocletian, pressured by German tribes, found it necessary to split the Roman Empire into western and eastern parts in A.D. 293. The north-south dividing line passed through the heart of Southeastern Europe. The Christian religion, like other imperial affairs, came to be organized from competing centers in Rome and Constantinople, although formal schism between Roman Catholicism and Eastern Orthodoxy waited until the late eleventh century. Diocletian's line still marks the divide between Catholic Croatians and Hungarians to the west and Orthodox Montenegrins, Serbs, and Romanians to the east.

Although the eastern (Byzantine) wing of the Roman Empire continued a formal existence for more than a millennium, until final conquest by the Turks in 1453, in its later stages it consisted of only limited territory around Constantinople itself. Beginning in the fifth century A.D., waves of migrant tribes moved into the Balkan Peninsula from the north and east. They included Visigoths, Huns, Ostrogoths, and Avars. Their influence was transitory, as they passed through and pillaged. However, large areas were depopulated in their wake, particularly in Romanized Dalmatia.

In the sixth and seventh centuries Slavic tribes moved into the region from East-Central Europe, subjugating and acculturating a large proportion of the indigenous Thracian- and Illyrian-speaking inhabitants. The Slavs in turn were subjected to new cultural influences emanating from the old imperial capitals, most notably in religion. Peoples from homelands in Central Asia also came into the Balkan Peninsula. The nomadic Bulgars settled in the Maritsa Valley in the seventh century. Hungarians entered the Pannonian Basin in about the year A.D. 900.

At times, usually when powerful neighbors were engaged elsewhere, the Slavic peoples established their own broad-based states. Most notable were medieval Bulgaria, Croatia, Raska, and Bosnia. The Central Asian rulers of Bulgaria, who had adopted the Slavic speech of their subject peoples, were dominant in their segment of the Balkan Peninsula for four centuries until a decisive defeat by Byzantium in 1018. The Croats had less than 200 years of self-rule in their kingdom founded by King Tomislav in A.D. 924 before coming under Hungarian control. The Serbian Kingdom of Raska at its height in 1335 commanded territory from the Vardar-Morava passage to the Adriatic Sea and the Aegean coasts of Greece, but then succumbed to the Turks. A Bosnian state developed as early as the eleventh century. Its population lived on the frontier between Roman Catholicism and Eastern Orthodoxy. It adopted the heretical Bogomil Christianity, which rejected teachings and symbols of the established churches to east and west. Bosnia expanded as a state to incorporate much of what is modern Bosnia, Herzegovina, Dalmatia, and Montenegro, before disintegrating about the year 1400.

The Turks

The Ottoman Turks swept out of Central Asia into the Anatolian Peninsula of Turkey in the thirteenth century. A century later they pushed into Europe, shattering the Serbs at the battle of Kosovo in 1389. The Turks continued to move northward, reaching beyond the Danube into Hungary and Romania. They defeated the Hungarians at the Battle of Mohács in 1526 and twice laid siege to Vienna, in 1529 and 1683. The Ottoman advance caused entire Christian settlements to flee northward. Many villages in Bosnia and Croatia can trace the origins of their inhabitants by oral tradition to original sites in medieval Serbia and Macedonia. Some ethnic Turks moved into abandoned Slavic villages in northeastern Bulgaria, Thrace, and Macedonia, establishing communities that have endured to the present. However, the presence of Turks in most of the Balkan Peninsula was confined mainly to scattered military garrisons.

Administration in the Ottoman Empire was weak. The Turks relied upon Greeks and Islamicized Slavs to handle most administrative affairs. Many of the latter were from the ranks of teen-aged boys collected as a tax from Christian village households and forcibly converted to the Muslim religion. They were organized militarily into the dreaded Janissary legions that often involved themselves in imperial politics.

Ottoman sultans used the organization of the Eastern Orthodox church to control their Christian subjects. Other than the Janissary recruitments, few instances of forced conversion to Islam occurred. There were voluntary conversions, however. A major one with lasting significance was the acceptance of the Muslim faith by the Bosnian Bogomils. They had longstanding grievances against the Catholic and Orthodox religions that had persecuted them as heretics, and their nobles saw the personal benefits of retention of land holdings by becoming Muslims. A similar situation occurred in southern Bulgaria, where substantial numbers of Slavic-speaking "Pomaks" ("Helpers") retain an Islamic faith to this day.

Christian Greeks played a major role in running the Ottoman Empire. The Phanariot Greeks, named for their native Phanaros district in Constantinople, were particularly noted for rapaciousness in administering Romania after being placed in power by the Ottoman sultan in 1711. Greek merchants dominated commerce. Efforts by Greek Orthodox clergy to make Romanians, Macedonians, and Bulgarians a part of the Greek culture world led to strong reactions by those groups.

Sephardic Jews were another people who played a significant role in managing the empire. They had developed prominent positions in trade and the arts in the Muslim Moorish Kingdom of Spain ("Sepharad" was the Hebrew name for Spain). The triumph of Christians over the Moors in 1492 led to expulsion of the Jews from Spain. Most found haven in the Ottoman Empire. Particularly noteworthy concentrations of Sephardic Jews developed in the commercial port towns of Salonika on the Aegean and Ragusa (Dubrovnik) on the Adriatic.

Some historians have suggested that the role played by Ottoman Turks in the empire can be traced to their pastoral origins. They lacked interest in commerce and had few ties to the land. They were content to allow their Christian "flocks" in the Balkans to pursue their own endeavors, as long as tax collectors could shear off whatever wealth was generated. They did little to build roads or otherwise foster modernization by creating an infrastructure. They also made little effort to control extensive areas where local economies showed few prospects for producing riches, including major parts of Albania, Montenegro, and Romania. The economic backwardness of the Balkan Peninsula was due more to sins of omission than of commission. The role of the Turks in Southeastern Europe is perhaps best seen as a preservation of an unsatisfactory system originating in the Byzantine Empire than as interruption of an otherwise progressive development.

Turkish influence waned in the eighteenth century. The Habsburgs, after successfully defending Vienna, began to drive the Ottoman forces southward. By 1800 they had reclaimed Pannonia as far south as the Sava and Danube rivers. The Austrians instituted a program of planned colonization in the virtually depopulated lands of the Hungarian Basin, bringing peoples from all parts of their empire. Even today one finds a polyglot of villages in southeastern Hungary and adjacent areas of the Romanian Banat of Timişoara and Yugoslav Vojvodina. As to demands that their subjects be Roman Catholic, however, the Habsburgs proved to be significantly less tolerant than were the Turks.

Emergence of the Modern Balkan States

As in the rest of Europe, fires of nationalism began burning in Southeastern Europe early in the nineteenth century. Napoleon's forces garrisoned in his "Illyrian provinces" along the eastern Adriatic coast were a catalyst to the development of Slovenian and Croatian national identities.

Further east, national consciousness also grew in Ottoman-held lands. The Serbs revolted in 1804, and, after a period of uprisings and suppressions, by mid-century they had gained recognition of the right to rule themselves within the empire. Their success came in large part from support by the Russians, who also subsidized the continuing independence of the Montenegrins, who were never conquered by the Turks.

Russian influence was felt elsewhere in the Ottoman Empire. In addition to acquisitions of the Crimea and Caucasus regions at the turn of the nineteenth century, Russia acquired Romanian-speaking Bessarabia in 1812. At this time Romanians still remaining within the Ottoman Empire in Moldavia and Wallachia succeeded in forcing out the hated Phanariots, replacing them by native princes. In 1878 the Russians again went to war with Turkey, and the end result was complete independence for Serbia, Bulgaria, and Romania. The Habsburg Empire expanded southeastward against the Turks also in 1878, occupying and later annexing Bosnia and Herzegovina.

Problems of Irredentism

The new states in Southeastern Europe at the end of the nineteenth century fell far short of national aspirations of their peoples, however. Large numbers of Serbs remained outside Serbia in Hungary, Bosnia, and the Ottoman Sanjak of Novi Pazar. Romanians were local majorities in Russian Bessarabia, Austrian Bukovina, and parts of Hungarian Transylvania and eastern Pannonia. A substantial fraction of the Bulgarians remained in Turkish hands in a territorial unit designated as "Eastern Rumelia." The Bulgarians also saw the inhabitants of Greek- and Turkish-controlled Macedonia as *irredenta*, although this view was not necessarily shared by the Macedonians themselves. Western Europeans were responsible for limiting the territorial expansion of the new states because of fears of Russia's growing influence among Southeastern Europe's Eastern Orthodox Christians.

As a consequence of the unfulfilled expectations of their national groups, the states of the Balkan Peninsula fought with each other in two bloody Balkan wars before the outbreak of World War I. In 1912 the Bulgarians gained southern Dobrogea, Eastern Macedonia, and a foothold on the Aegean Sea. However, they were repulsed in attempts to expand their state's boundaries westward to Albania and the Adriatic. Serbia captured the Vardar Valley of western Macedonia and advanced into the legendary Serbian homeland of Albanian-inhabited Kosovo. Greece gained the island of Crete and pushed northward into southern Macedonia and Albanian Epirus. The tribal Albanians, frightened by Serbian and Greek aspirations for their traditional lands, developed a belated national unity and successfully gained independence from the Ottoman Empire in 1913. The troubled Turks eventually were left with only the 9,000-square-mile area of Turkey-in-Europe.

The disintegration of the Habsburg and Ottoman empires as an aftermath of World War I resulted in substantial further revisions of the political map. Romania acquired Bessarabia, the Bukovina, and Transylvania, together with a substantial part of Hungary's Banat. Greece captured Bulgaria's foothold on the Aegean, but lost other temporary territorial gains in European Turkey and Anatolia. Italy became a new player in Southeastern Europe, acquiring Turkey's Dodecanese Islands and substantial Austrian territories on the eastern shore of the Adriatic, including the Istrian Peninsula, western Slovenia, and the Dalmatian port of Zara (Zadar). A group of Italian adventurers additionally seized the port of Fiume (Rijeka) at the head of the Kvarner Gulf, and it eventually also became part of Italy. The most profound change in the region, however, was the creation of a new multinational South Slavic state. The Kingdom of Serbs, Croatians, and Slovenes linked together the earlier independent Balkan states of Serbia and Montenegro and former Habsburg lands inhabited by Slovenes, Croats, Serbs, and Slavic Muslims. The young country was to be renamed "Yugoslavia" within a decade.

Yugoslavia

Travelers to Yugoslavia after World War II frequently heard a capsule recitation of its political geography: "One state, two alphabets, three religions, four official languages, five nations, six republics, seven hostile neighbors, and eight separate countries." This litany had more than a little truth. Yugoslavia did employ Latin and Cyrillic alphabets; it was home to Roman Catholics, Eastern Orthodox, and Muslims; its Slavic groups did speak Serbian, Croatian, Slovenian and Macedonian; they identified themselves as Serbs, Montenegrins, Croats, Slovenes, and Macedonians; each had its own republic, with an additional Republic of Bosnia and Herzegovina for a mixed population of Serbs, Croats, and Serbo-Croatian-speaking Muslims; Yugoslavia was bordered by Italy, Austria, Hungary, Romania, Bulgaria, Greece, and Albania, all of whom harbored some grievances against it; and the "autonomous regions" of Hungarian Vojvodina and Albanian Kosovo within Serbia functioned until 1990 in an independent manner comparable to that of the six formal republics. This was indeed a diverse state. One might note the additional observation that Yugoslavia had been "a geographic impossibility, tied together by railroads, highways, and a Serbian-dominated army."

Yugoslavia was, in fact, a microcosm of all Southeastern Europe. Across its borders passed European frontiers between Eastern and Western cultures, between Christian and Muslim faiths, between development and underdevelopment. Its diverse peoples never were able to find a truly common identity. No other country on the Continent was host to so many internal quarrels and, with the exception of Germany, to so many external disputes. Yugoslavia came crashing down in 1991 as centrifugal forces gained the upper hand over centripetal ones. Slovenia and Croatia declared independence. The Serbs, who played a pre-eminent role in the state by virtue of their numbers, reacted by challenging the breakaway republics with the armed might of the Yugoslav army, whose officer corps they dominated. The army quickly was defeated in Slovenia, but engaged in a punishing struggle with the hastily organized Croatian militia. Ancient group antagonisms became manifest in the attack, as Serbian-led forces destroyed churches and other historical monuments dear to the Croatians. Despite its lack of any modern military significance, even the Croatian medieval walled tourist center of Dubrovnik, which had been spared attack during both World War I and World War II, suffered severe artillery bombardment from land and sea.

Yugoslavia had emerged in 1918 as a consequence of opportunity, idealism, and pragmatism. The wartime collapse of the Habsburg and Ottoman empires had made self-determination possible. Despite the many contrasts and enmities among its principal groups, their cultural and intellectual leaders saw a common Pan-Slavic bond holding promise for mutual progress through a merger. Their political leaders saw strength in union against continuing postwar threats from Italy, Hungary, and Bulgaria. Their economic leaders saw benefits to all by combining the industrial development of the Habsburg regions with the resources and markets of the former Ottoman lands. All ultimately found themselves disappointed. Cultures did not harmonize, greedy neighbors were not held at bay, and economies did not prosper. Yet Yugoslavia continued to function for more than seven decades, despite a period of dismemberment during World War II and continuing threats to unity and territorial integrity.

Internal conflicts. Fundamental differences in outlooks troubled the young state from the very beginning. Croats, long submerged in an unequal partnership with the Hungarians within the Habsburg Empire, sought desperately to run their own cultural and economic affairs. Slovenes, whose Slavic culture had been suppressed by the Austrians, harbored similar feelings. Serbs, with a 40 percent plurality in Yugoslavia, were conscious of a millennium of humiliations at the hands of enemies. They viewed the new state as their rightful reward for triumphing in the Great War (which World War I was then called). Thus, it was only proper that Yugoslavia should have their king as its king, their capital as its capital. Hungarians and Albanians felt outrage at being cut off from their nation-states, the Albanians particularly aggrieved at not-too-subtle Serbian encouragement to emigrate to Albania or Turkey from their home territory in Kosovo, which Serbs regarded as their own cultural hearthland.

In 1918 the Slavic-speaking Bosnian Muslims, Montenegrins, and Macedonians better were identified as peoples than as modern nations, but they too soon developed resentment at what were perceived as Serbian hegemonistic proclivities. The Bosnians, like the Albanians, reacted to Serbian pressures for them to leave the young state for Turkey. Montenegrin tribesmen reacted negatively to the loss of centuries of sovereignty to a distant bureaucracy in Belgrade, as well as to a Serbian tendency to dismiss them as "Mountain Serbs." The Macedonians, whose linguistic and cultural linkages had been closest to the Bulgars, were similarly distressed to find themselves designated as "South Serbs."

Unifying elements. Some countervailing unity came from continuing external threats, however. Bulgaria never gave up its claim to Macedonia, and in 1934 it was involved in assassination of the Yugoslav king. The citizens of Yugoslavia feared continuing Italian designs upon Montenegro and Dalmatia and never accepted Italian annexations of Istria, Fiume, and Zara, where large numbers of Croatians and Slovenians lived. They also reacted to Germanization pressures upon Slovenes living across the border in Austrian Carinthia and Hellenization pressures upon Slavic-speakers in Greek Macedonia. Resistance to Hungarian irredentism for its separated brethren in Yugoslav Vojvodina similarly served to bind the southern Slavs.

Centrifugal forces ultimately overcame centripetal ones, however, particularly under stress of the worldwide economic depression of the 1930s. Croatian antagonism against Serbs earlier reached a high in 1928 when two of the foremost Croatian political leaders were gunned down by a Serbian deputy in the Belgrade parliament building. Ensuing unrest led Yugoslavia's Serbian king to declare a royal dictatorship. In an attempt to minimize national antagonisms, he changed the state's name from "Kingdom of Serbs, Croatians, and Slovenes" to the less specific "Yugoslavia." (*Yug* is the word for "south" in most Slavic languages.) He also recast the territorial components of the state into new provincial *banovinas* that were neutrally named for principal river valleys or coastal position, rather than by traditional ethno-political designations. These acts did little to weaken national identities, however. In 1939, attempting to pacify increasing political agitation by the Croats, the regime established a specifically Croatian *banovina* by combining the short-lived Maritime and Sava River provinces.

Wartime fragmentation. In March 1941, Yugoslavia was caught up in World War II. German, Italian, Hungarian, and Bulgarian troops moved against it from all sides. Under attack, the state quickly succumbed both to its external adversaries and its internal antagonisms. The Croats immediately took the opportunity to declare independence and form an "Independent State of Croatia" under a Fascist leadership. The occupying Axis forces permitted them to annex all of Bosnia and Herzegovina, although Croatia had to concede to Italians and Hungarians substantial traditional territories in Dalmatia and Pannonia (Figure 6-1).

Each of the victorious invaders seized parts of defeated Yugoslavia. Germans appropriated northern Slovenia into Austria and imprisoned or expelled to occupied Serbia large numbers of Slovene cultural and political leaders. They also established direct German rule in the Banat region of the Pannonian plain, where many Germans had settled and become prosperous following the eighteenth-century expulsion of the Turks. Hungary acquired the Bavka region of the Vojvodina and a sliver of Slovenian territory. Italy took the rest of Slovenia, the Adriatic islands, and the Croatian coast as far south as Split. Montenegro became an Italian puppet state. The Italians also added Albanian-inhabited territories of Kosovo and western Macedonia to the Albanian state that they had occupied in 1939. Bulgarians claimed the remainder of Macedonia and several Serbian border regions. The Germans also directly occupied the remainder of Serbia, managing civil affairs through a collaborationist puppet government.

Unlike occupied Poland or France, dissection by external forces did not lead the peoples of Yugoslavia immediately to a greater sense of common unity. National antagonisms were too deeply rooted. Serbs had enmity toward Muslims and Croats as much as toward invading Germans. Serbian "Chetnik" resistance forces attacked Croatian settlements as often as they harassed German troops. Croats, spearheaded by their Fascist-modelled "Ustša" party organization, committed atrocities against long-established Serbian settlements in Croatia's southern military borderland and in Bosnia. Albanians, Montenegrins, and Bosnian Muslims similarly fought with neighbors while under the foreign occupation. The horrendous massacres ultimately claimed a significant proportion of the prewar Yugoslav population.

The Yugoslav partisans. The one unified Yugoslav resistance force was the Partisan army organized by the Communist leader Josip Broz, who used the pseudonym "Tito." Although leadership came from a small urbanized and educated clique nourished in the prewar years by the Soviet Union, the Partisans gained adherents from all segments of Yugoslav society by their relentless attacks upon the occupying powers. Partisan action contrasted with the reluctance of Chetniks and other ethnically based resistance forces to attack Germans and thereby invite huge retaliatory shootings of civilian populations. In their relentless determination to be on the offensive against occupation forces, the Partisans were motivated not only to liberate Yugoslavia but also to tie down Axis troops who otherwise would be engaged in the Axis invasion of their political motherland in the Soviet Union.

Utilizing the rough terrain of the central part of the state for shelter and base camps, the Partisans succeeded in creating a substantial "liberated zone." When Soviet forces swept in from Romania and Bulgaria, the Soviets found that the occupiers had already been expelled from most Yugoslav territory.

The defeat of the Axis powers saw the reestablishment of Yugoslavia's prewar borders. In addition, the state gained nearly all the Italian-held Slavic territories on the Adriatic coast, including Zara, Fiume, and Istria. Yugoslavia pressed also to annex the port city of Trieste, but was rebuffed by the Americans and western Europeans. A "free territory" was created for Trieste, divided between an "Allied Military Government" in the city itself ("Trieste Zone A") and an area of Yugoslav occupation in the villages of the surrounding heights ("Trieste Zone B"). Eventually, in 1954, Yugoslavia and Italy reached an agreement that resulted in the incorporation of the respective military zones into each state.

The immediate postwar months remained chaotic. Although numerous Croats and Slovenes had rallied to

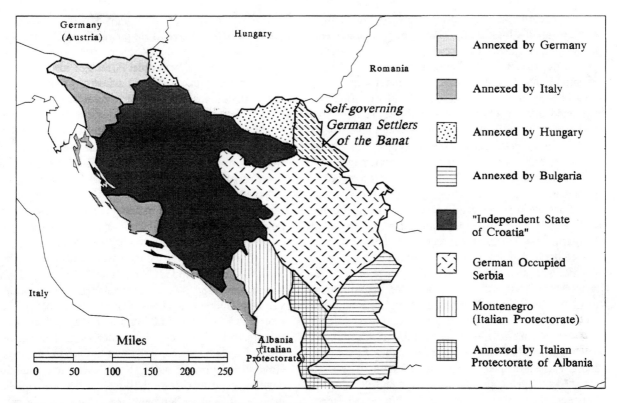

FIGURE 6-1 PARTITIONING OF THE FIRST YUGOSLAVIA, 1941

Map legend:
- Annexed by Germany
- Annexed by Italy
- Annexed by Hungary
- Annexed by Bulgaria
- "Independent State of Croatia"
- German Occupied Serbia
- Montenegro (Italian Protectorate)
- Annexed by Italian Protectorate of Albania

Map labels: Germany (Austria), Hungary, Romania, Self-governing German Settlers of the Banat, Italy, Albania (Italian Protectorate), Miles, 0 50 100 150 200 250

the Partisan cause, the guerrilla army was principally a Serbian and Montenegrin force. The victorious Partisans wreaked revenge upon those they believed had actively collaborated with the enemy. Croatians particularly were singled out. A large contingent of the Croatian national guard had retreated with the Germans and surrendered at war's end to British forces in Austria. The British proceeded to repatriate them to Partisan military commanders, who marched the Croats overland to Belgrade, causing many to perish in the process. A Partisan reign of terror prevailed throughout Yugoslavia for months. Only recently has the magnitude of indiscriminate killings become generally known.

The Postwar federation. Reconstituted Yugoslavia's new leaders, drawn from the prewar Communist party, elected to use the USSR model in dealing with the state's complex national situation. They organized Yugoslavia formally as a "federation," with Soviet-style "republics" for the principal nations. For the first time Macedonians gained recognition as a national group by other Yugoslavs. The Communist regime also established two "autonomous regions" within Serbia for Hungarian and Albanian national minorities.

Despite such concessions to national identity, the government was intolerant of open popular manifesta-

tions of nationalist feeling. Like their fellow Communists in the Soviet Union, they believed that nationalist sentiments were part of an obsolete social superstructure doomed to disappear. However, Serbs had dominated the Partisan movement, and a number of postwar government actions occurred that paralleled Serbian nationalist policies of the prewar regime. These particularly affected the Croatians, Bosnian Muslims, and Albanians. Serbs received disproportionate roles in administering non-Serbian republics. A Soviet-styled secret police organization headquartered in Belgrade tightly controlled civil affairs. It proved particularly oppressive in the newly established Albanian Autonomous Region of Kosovo-Metohija in southwest Serbia, prompting many Albanians to emigrate to Turkey.

As in the Soviet Union, the creating of ethnic-based republics had long-term centrifugal effects upon Yugoslav unity, however much they met any short-run aims of defusing national tensions. Each nation was legitimized with a clearly defined territorial homeland. Mixed frontier zones between major groups were reduced to boundary lines, creating potentially irredentist minorities outside their designated republics. Fully 10 percent of the population of the Croatian Republic was Serbian, and more than 20 percent of the Macedonian Republic was Albanian (see Figure 6-2).

As occurred at its inception following World War I, Yugoslavia's long-standing internal problems were somewhat mitigated in the postwar period by external pressures. In 1948 the Communist camp in effect excommunicated the Yugoslav regime following a quarrel between Tito and Stalin. The latter confidently expected that cut-off of Soviet political support together with its markets, raw materials, and investment funds would quickly cause a termination of Tito's rule. However, Yugoslavia's Communist government received substantial aid from the United States and managed to persevere.

Yugoslavia subsequently faced continuous threats of Soviet-initiated invasion from Hungary, Romania, Bulgaria, and Albania for many years. This situation helped draw its diverse nations together and lasted into the 1960s. It also allowed the state to develop a more successful economy that was based upon opportunities to trade with Western Europe and America. Retaining its Communist form of government, Yugoslavia gained international recognition for leadership of a group of self-proclaimed nonaligned states, including Egypt and India. These attempted to stand apart from both "West" and "East" during the cold war that had developed between the Soviet Union and its former Western Allies.

Another major force for unity was the charismatic presence of Tito himself. He proved himself a pragmatist, forsaking past ideological positions for concrete solutions to looming problems. Although his regime had relentlessly pursued collectivization of farming and nationalization of businesses for several months after the break with the USSR, Tito had the foresight and courage to reverse these policies as their inherent inefficiency became apparent. In 1966 he sacked the head of the secret police, a close wartime colleague who had been responsible after the war for supression of the Albanians of Kosovo-Metohija. Tito continued to remain intolerant of overt nationalist manifestations, however, and ruthlessly suppressed massive demonstrations by Croatian students in Zagreb in 1971.

Those events reflected increasing dissatisfaction by industrially developed Croatia and Slovenia with transfer payments they were forced to make to underdeveloped southern republics. Communist ideology and intergroup politics had led the postwar Yugoslav regime to seek to remove territorial inequalities in income by industrializing the former Ottoman regions. However, ingrained cultural attitudes and a weakly developed infrastructure inhibited productivity of the new factories in the southern areas. They required substantial continuing subsidies from the federal govern-

FIGURE 6-2   THE SECOND YUGOSLAVIA, 1945–1990

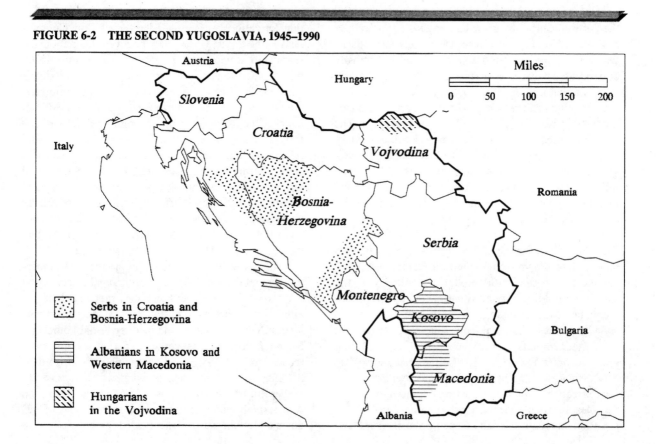

ment in order to operate. Their establishment also did not end regional economic differentials. Per capita incomes in Slovenia remained twice those of Yugoslavia as a whole, whereas earnings in Kosovo barely reached 20 percent of the statewide average.

The death of Tito in 1980 marked a turning point in Yugoslav unity. No strong individual had been groomed to succeed him. Instead, a collective presidency with a rotating leadership from each of the republics administered the state. The League of Yugoslav Communists, as the ruling party styled itself, saw continuing erosion of its own cohesiveness. Each party organization sought control over its own territorial unit. The weakness in central authority fostered development of political and economic exclusiveness of governmental organizations within each republic and autonomous region. A reflection of this situation was the complete change of railroad crews that occurred when trains crossed each republic's borders.

Accompanying the increase of local authority in republics was an upsurge of nationalist sentiments. Although transfer payments to the southern republics had become substantially reduced, Croats and Slovenes demanded yet higher retention of the profits of their industry and agriculture. Calls for greater autonomy and even independence became manifest at the highest levels of the regimes of the two republics.

In poverty-stricken Kosovo, Albanians pressed demands for upgrading their autonomous region to full republic status. Actually, they already enjoyed such a status *de facto*, since the Yugoslav federal government allowed the Serbian Republic regime to exercise virtually no authority within the province. Kosovo's officials reported directly to the federal government. Albanians also put various kinds of pressures upon Serbian families settled in Kosovo to sell off their lands and emigrate to Serbia. Because of awareness of the frightful economic and political situation in Albania, however, few Albanians expressed irredentist sentiments for incorporation within that state.

The Serbian population reacted with vehemence to the political activities of the other groups. Huge mass demonstrations decrying events took place in Serbian cities in 1989 and 1990. Serbian newspapers and television exaggerated reports of anti-Serbian incidents, particularly in Kosovo. An increasingly nationalist Serbian political leadership succeeded in gaining direct administrative control over its two autonomous regions after their decades of *de facto* self-rule. The Serbian-dominated Yugoslav national army subjected Kosovo to martial law.

The 1991 eruption of hostilities. The Slovenes and Croats had prospered most in Communist Yugoslavia, yet they saw that economically they lagged behind their Austrian, Italian, and even Hungarian neighbors. They attributed this to relentless transfers of Slovenian and Croatian enterprise profits to southern republics. During the decade of the 1980s they began manifesting strong anti-Serbian sentiments, with many calling for separation from Yugoslavia. Nationalist feelings were intensified in 1990 in Slovenia by a Serbian economic boycott of Slovenian products, retaliating for Slovene expressions of separatism and their championship of the Kosovo Albanian cause.

In reaction, Slovenians declared independence in the summer of 1991. The Yugoslav federal army attempted to suppress the Slovene declaration of sovereignty. The overwhelmingly Serbian officer corps was mindful that financial support for army salaries, equipment, and pensions disproportionately came from the advanced economies of Slovenia and Croatia. However, Slovenian militia forces defending their homeland quickly humiliated the federal army, suffering losses of only fifty dead.

To arguments that their territory of 12,000 square miles was too small for state functioning, Slovenians cited the economic success of similarly sized Belgium within the unified European Common Market. Some called for political union with prosperous Austria, to which Slovenia has strong historic ties. Slovenia's prospective border disputes are minor, although a potential still exists for irredentist claims against Italy for so-called Venetian Slovenia, and also against Austria concerning Slovenian-speaking areas of Carinthia. Reportedly, Yugoslavia's federal government sought to play on Italian pretensions to Slovene coastal areas by suggesting a return of the Istrian Peninsula to Italy in return for allowing Yugoslav army troops and equipment to evacuate Slovenia through the Italian port city of Trieste, since overland withdrawal by road or rail through Croatia to Serbia faced ambush and destruction.

Anti-Serbian sentiments had long been part of the Croatian national iconography. They had come to the fore in the 1970s over Croatian financial support of the former Ottoman lands in Yugoslavia and were aggravated in the 1980s by widespread publicity concerning Serbian-led Communist atrocities in Croatia following the end of World War II. There was strong resentment at the disproportionate role played by Serbs in Croatian governmental and economic affairs. All these factors contributed to separatist outlooks similar to those of the Slovenians. By the summer of 1991 the Croatians also felt impelled to declare independence.

A sovereign Croatia faced a number of internal and external political geographic problems, however. It had a Serbian minority of more than one-half million, constituting 11 percent of Croatia's total population. Serbs dominated the Kordun and Lika regions of the former

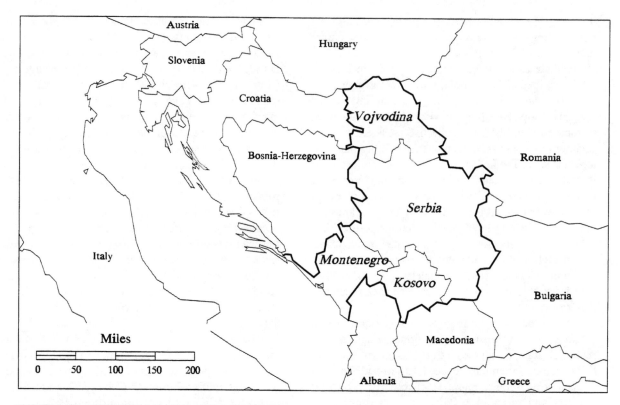

FIGURE 6-3 THE YUGOSLAV LAND AFTER 1990

Austrian military border area, and many lived in parts of Dalmatia, particularly around the town of Knin. Most Serbs of Croatia were concentrated in Zagreb and other large cities, however.

As Croats increasingly called for separation, Serbian groups in the southwestern border area held an unofficial referendum in 1990 for national autonomy. The Croatian leadership rejected their demands, however, and differences escalated into a rebellion by Serbian irregulars that quickly was joined by the Yugoslav army. The army also reacted to Croatian sieges that cut off food, water, and other supplies to military installations within Croatia. Repeated attempts at a cease-fire failed over Serbian insistence on attachment to Serbia of Serb-inhabited regions in Croatia. The Yugoslav army and Serbian irregulars managed to hold peripheral parts of Croatia inhabited by Serbs. Croatians succeeded in capturing areas of Serbian rebels in the interior, however. Most Serbs in urban areas fled eastward to Serbia.

The Serb-Croatian conflict expanded to Bosnia-Herzegovina in 1992. Its mixed population of Serbs, Croats, and Muslims became polarized by fighting in adjacent Croatia. The Bosnian government sought to preserve the republic's territorial integrity from Serbian and Croatian irredentist pressures by declaring its independence. Many of its Serbs, particularly those in rural areas, reacted vehemently, pressing for annexation to Serbia. With the aid of Yugoslav army detachments, they set about driving Muslims and Croats from areas that they could dominate. From high ground around the historic city of Sarajevo they blockaded and reigned terror upon the inhabitants. Military units from Croatia joined in the fray to help protect the republic's nearly 800,000 Croats. The western (Herzegovina) section is heavily settled by Croatians, whose speech is generally recognized by other Croats as setting the Croatian national standard for pronunciation and usage.

Other potential problems. By the 1980s, Yugoslavia's 1,800,000 Albanians had exceeded the numbers of its Slovenes, Montenegrins, Bosnian Muslims, or Macedonians. Although Albanians were scattered throughout the state, more than two-thirds were concentrated in the 4,200 square miles of Kosovo, lying adjacent to the Albanian People's Republic. Serbs had strong concerns about Kosovo because it was seen as the core area where their culture had developed. It was also the site of their tragic medieval defeat by the Muslim Turks. They felt particularly outraged at reports of Albanian harassment of the region's small Serbian minority, who totaled less than one-sixth of the population of the autonomous province. Albanians, in turn, were infuriated at their treatment as second-class citizens within their own homeland. They grew bitter at the central government's refusal to grant Kosovo the status of a full republic, and, later, by the loss of the autonomy in local affairs that they had enjoyed in previous years. Although Kosovo Albanians initially were not irredentist, the emergence of a less oppressive Albania in 1991 changed attitudes of many.

The Vojvodina Autonomous Region of Serbia north of the Danube has a mixed population, among whom Serbs make up barely half the total. Nearly 20 percent are Hungarians. Croats, Slovaks, and Romanians constitute the rest. Although Hungary appeared more reconciled to the alienation of this Magyar-inhabited territory than it was for Romanian Transylvania, concern developed in 1991 after the Serbian government abolished Magyar minority rights in the Vojvodina. An interesting division exists between the bulk of the Vojvodina's Serbian population and those living in Serbia proper. The Vojvodina Serbs, like the Slovenes and Croats, had developed their culture and economy within the Habsburg Empire. Their university in Novi Sad was far advanced over its counterpart in Belgrade in the former Ottoman realm. They did not join in the 1980s Serbian popular demonstrations over Kosovo and Slovenia. On the contrary, they expressed deep resentment at their own loss of local governmental control over their home region. Their sentiments are perhaps best compared to those of the Moravians in Czechoslovakia.

Macedonia. Macedonians, mindful of continuing pretensions to their territory by Bulgarians and Serbs, also declared their independence in 1992 from what remained of Yugoslavia. They did not suffer immediate attack by the Yugoslav army because of the latter's preoccupation with struggles in Croatia and Bosnia. Their sovereignty came into question immediately from an unanticipated quarter, however. The Greek government was able to delay formal recognition of Macedonia by member states of the European Community on the grounds that the name Macedonia could only be used to designate a section of Greece. It insisted that the regional term had been unilaterally appropriated by Tito as a means to further eventual expansion of the Yugoslav state southward.

Independent Macedonia faces a major internal problem from a rapidly growing Albanian minority, which constitutes more than 20 percent of its population. Albanians are the dominant group in western Macedonia and, like Kosovo, this region would likely be a focus of future irredentist claims by an aggressive Albania. Macedonians generally believe that the inhabitants of the Greek seaport of Salonika are predominantly of Slavic Macedonian origin and, in a situation of future sovereignty, Macedonia might well attempt to claim the area as an historic outlet to the Aegean Sea.

Montenegro. Montenegro remained joined to Serbia in the rump Yugoslavian state after the other republics broke away. Montenegrins have generally found common cause with Serbs, with whom they share a common Eastern Orthodox faith. They have actively supported the Yugoslav army's attempt to suppress secession by the other republics. Montenegrin guerrillas are blamed for the bombardment of Dubrovnik.

Montenegrins are concerned about Croatian historic claims to their seacoast, including spectacular Kotor Bay. They also fear irredentist pressures from Bosnian Muslims, who constitute 20 percent of the republic's population and are concentrated on Montenegro's northern fringe. The Montenegrins have also taken pains to insulate their 10 percent Albanian minority from nationalist agitation in Kosovo. Montenegrins have some pretensions to the bordering Albanian port city of Scutari (Skadar), but development of their own port city of Bar as terminus of a railroad to Belgrade probably has precluded future agitation for the "return" of Scutari.

Romania

Although Romania had little military success during the Balkan Wars and World War I, it emerged in 1918 as one of the most successful states of Southeastern Europe in achieving national territorial aims. It expanded its boundaries at the expense of Austria, Hungary, Bulgaria, and Russia, virtually doubling in size from its prewar situation.

The emergence of Romania is usually dated to the establishment of typical medieval principalities in Romanian-speaking Wallachia and Moldavia at the end of the thirteenth and beginning of the fourteenth centuries, respectively. The leaders of these feudal units had far less authority than rulers in Slavic states of the time, however. In the fifteenth century both principalities were forced to accept Ottoman suzerainty. Local authority was exerted by *boyars* (local nobility), led by a prince who usually was weak politically. From 1711 to 1821, Greek Phanariots dominated the principalities.

The subsequent emergence of the Romanian state owed much to Russian support for change. Catherine the Great in the eighteenth century had enunciated a doctrine that Russia was the protector of all Orthodox Christians in the Ottoman Empire, with particular interest in "protection of the Romanian Principalities." Russians were directly involved in the anti-Phanariot revolution that restored native Romanian princes to the throne in 1821. Its leader, Tudor Vladimirescu, was a Romanian officer in the Russian army. The Russians established a protectorate over the principalities in 1828 as a result of a war with Turkey.

Russians occupied the Romanian principalities from 1828 to 1834. Their administration was enlightened and led to the development of a rational government organization and a progressive educational system. It also fostered the development of a Romanian national identity, much as Napoleon's occupation had led to the flowering of nationalism among Germans, Poles, Croats, and Slovenes. The fires of nationalism glowed throughout the principalities and also in Hungarian-controlled Transylvania. Romanians took part in the nationalist revolts that shook Europe in 1848. However, Hungarians suppressed Romanian disturbances in Transylvania, and Russian troops intervened to quell revolutionary manifestations in Moldavia and Wallachia.

The modern state. Following Russia's defeat in the Crimean War in 1855, France took up the Romanian cause. The French facilitated union of the two principalities under a single ruler in 1859. Romania became completely independent of the Ottoman Empire in 1878, its prince receiving the title of king. Romania played a minor role in the ensuing Balkan Wars. It gained the Bulgarian-held territory of Dobrogea, but it was only after World War I that the state gathered together virtually all of Southeastern Europe's Romanian speakers into one nation-state. It gained territory from all its neighbors. Bessarabia was taken from the Russians, who had seized it from the Ottoman Empire in 1812. The Bukovina, lost by the Moldavian principality to Austria in 1775, was taken back. Transylvania, which had been part of the Hungarian Kingdom since the ninth century, became part of Romania, as did the eastern section of the Hungarian-held Banat of Timisoara (Timesvar) in the Pannonian Plain. Dobrogea, which had been reattached by Bulgaria during the war, also was confirmed by the peace treaties as Romanian territory.

Romania had overextended itself, however. In addition to "redeeming" Romanian kinsmen, it had acquired substantial numbers of Hungarians, Germans, Ukrainians, Jews, and Bulgarians. This led to increasing irredentist pressure from its neighbors. The regime also had difficulty in integrating the Transylvanian Romanians, whose educational levels and economic development were notably higher than those of the population in the principalities, which had come to be known as the *Regat,* or "Old Kingdom." Romanian exasperation at contentious minorities led to emergence of a strong Fascist movement that briefly came to power.

In June 1940, at the beginning of World War II, the Soviet regime forced cession of Bessarabia and the northern part of the Bukovina to the USSR. At the end of August, Adolf Hitler, in what is known as the "Vienna Diktat," similarly pressured Romania to yield northern Transylvania to Hungary. He is reported to have told Romanian representatives that refusal "would mean Romania's annihilation sooner or later, probably sooner." The lost area totaled 16,000 square miles. The Hungarian government immediately began implementation of a provision of the Vienna Diktat for exchange of populations. More than 200,000 Romanians were sent to the south. A comparable number of Hungarians moved northward from southern Transylvania. On September 5, 1940, Hitler additionally forced Romania to cede southern Dobrogea to Bulgaria (Figure 6-4).

As an ally of Germany, Romania was allowed during the war to reincorporate both Bessarabia and the Bukovina from the USSR and to control additional Soviet territory east of the Dniester River, including the port city of Odessa. Under the territorial settlement at the end of the war, Romania again lost Bessarabia and northern Bukovina to the Soviet Union, but gained back northern Transylvania from Hungary. From a prewar area of 114,000 square miles, Romania shrank to just under 92,000 square miles. The Soviet Union also imposed one-party Communist rule upon the Romanians.

The minorities problem. Romania's population of 23,000,000 continues to incorporate a large number of minorities. These include 2,300,000 Hungarians (10%), 1,000,000 Gypsies (4%), and 280,000 Germans (1%). The Hungarians have a major concentration in eastern Transylvania, but are found scattered throughout Transylvania and the Banat. Romania's Germans are divided into two groups: Saxons, living primarily in southern Transylvania, and Swabians in the Banat.

The Communist regime initially sought to denationalize Romanian national identity. The occupying Red Army put into power Romanian Communists primarily of Hungarian and Jewish background who had little love for the prewar nationalist regime that had forced them to spend years of exile in the Soviet Union. Scholars were given tasks of de-mythologizing Romanian history, particularly its asserted ties to Western Europe. They stressed the commonalities of all peoples of the Balkans. The regime established a Soviet-type "autonomous Hungarian region" in 1952 for the area of principal Hungarian concentration in eastern Transylvania.

A palace revolt within the Communist party leadership reversed this policy in the 1960s. Romania became one of the first of the Communist governments to seek popular support by appealing to traditional nationalist values and goals. Internal propaganda began to stress a Romanian heritage from the west, again emphasizing

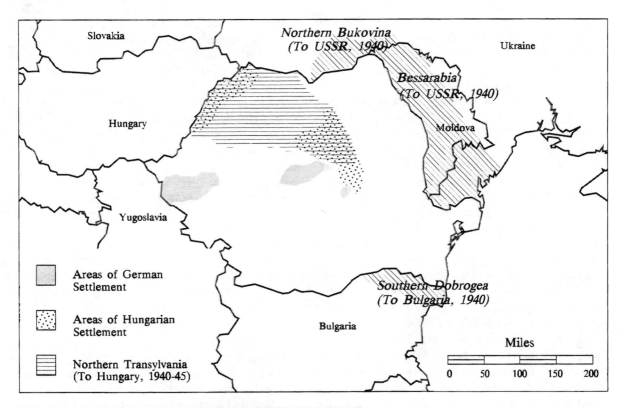

FIGURE 6-4   ROMANIA: MINORITIES AND LOST TERRITORIES

ancient ties to Rome. It openly criticized Soviet policies and courted support from Western Europe and the United States.

Transylvania and the Banat. The resurgence of Romanian national identity had an impact upon the large minority groups within the state. This was particularly felt by the Hungarians. The new regime abolished their autonomous region in Transylvania and the Hungarian-language university in the city of Cluj. Hungarians came under increasing pressures to sever any cultural and family linkages with Hungary itself. The importation of newspapers and magazines from Hungary was forbidden, and impediments were placed upon visits from relatives living in that state. In attempts to break up the large Hungarian concentration in eastern Transylvania, young workers from that region were often given posts in distant parts of the state. By 1989 the attempts at denationalization of the Hungarian minority had led to substantial illegal emigration to Hungary and exceptionally strained relations between the two regimes. Events leading to the downfall of the Romanian Communist leader Nicolae Ceauşescu began with a massacre of Hungarians in the Banat city of Timişoara demonstrating against the announced deportation of a local religious leader.

Although the post-Communist regime reduced pressures upon Romania's Hungarians, group enmities persist. The Hungarian minority took particular exception to a 1990 visit by the Romanian prime minister to northern Transylvania to commemorate the fiftieth anniversary of the Vienna Diktat and the 900 Romanians who lost their lives in the initial stage of the Hungarian occupation.

A German minority also persists in Transylvania and the Banat, although its numbers are now less than 40 percent of the total before World War II. It is estimated that more than 200,000 Germans left Romania for Germany by the end of World War II, and another 70,000 were deported to the Soviet Union. Many who had remained in Romania later emigrated to West Germany. The Ceauşescu regime claimed a head tax of several thousand marks from the German Federal Republic for each German allowed to leave. Germans are particularly concentrated in southern Transylvania. Their principal cities of Kronstadt and Herrmanstadt now go by their Romanian names of Brasov and Sibiu.

Bessarabia. In addition to internal concerns with Hungarian and German minorities, the Romanian regime also has an external interest in the future of Bessarabia, much of which was made a part of the Moldavian

Soviet Socialist Republic following its forced transfer from Romania to the USSR in 1940. The Moldavian SSR was declared the independent state of Moldova in 1991. Two-thirds of its 4,200,000 inhabitants speak Romanian, although a distinctive regional dialect was employed in radio and television transmissions during the Soviet period, and the Cyrillic alphabet was required in writing the language. Among remaining inhabitants of the 13,000-square-mile territory, 14 percent are Ukrainians, 13 percent are Russians, 3.5 percent are Gagauz, and 2 percent are Jews.

The Romanian majority regime of Moldova provoked bitter resistance from the other groups in 1991 by declaring Romanian the official language of the territory. It also adopted the traditional blue, yellow, and red Romanian flag and other elements of Romanian iconography. In strong reaction, the Gagauz group, who are Turkic-speaking Christians, called for a separate self-governing territory for themselves. Romanians also raised claims to southern parts of Bessarabia that had been settled by Slavs and annexed to the Ukrainian SSR and to lands east of the traditional Bessarabian boundary of the Dniester River that had been part of the short-lived Moldavian Autonomous Soviet Socialist Republic set up within the Soviet Ukraine in the interwar period. This area reverted to the Ukrainian Republic after the Soviet Union gained Bessarabia and created the Moldavian SSR. The regime of Moldova has not openly called for union with Romania, perhaps being mindful of that country's severe economic and political problems. For Romania, a union with Moldova would add to its substantial existing minority problems.

Bulgaria

Bulgarians have played a disproportionate role in generating difficulties on the Balkan Peninsula ever since they gained independence from the Turks in 1878. At the same time, their national aspirations have been the least satisfied in struggles over territory. They have managed ultimately to lose all of the wars in which they were engaged, and in the process they alienated all their neighbors. Their closest ally has been the Soviet Union, and that strong tie has been weakened, if not broken. In the liberation year of 1990 they created opprobrium from the rest of the world for vicious treatment of the Muslim minority.

Bulgaria was among the last of the European holdings of the Ottoman Empire to become independent. Its proximity to the Ottoman capital at Istanbul led to greater Ottoman concern about its status than was the case for other Slavic Christian territories in the empire. Independence came as a result of Russian military vic-tory when that power intervened in the seething cauldron of Balkan politics in 1878.

Bulgarian national identity had been kindled during the nineteenth century. It developed as much from reaction against Greek domination of religious and cultural affairs as from obvious Ottoman misrule. It was encouraged by the example set by the Serbs. Bulgarian clergy and laity began pressures to establish a separate Bulgarian Orthodox church in 1860. They were supported by the Turks, who had increasing concerns about their Greek minority ever since the independence of Greece in 1829. The Russians also backed the Bulgarian quest, which was successful in 1870. Emancipation of their church encouraged the Bulgarians to press for freedom in the political sphere. Insurgency against Ottoman rule began in 1875, but it was ruthlessly repressed. Russian military intervention led to independence in 1878, as it did for neighboring Romania and Serbia.

Under terms of a peace treaty signed at San Stefano, Bulgaria emerged as a state stretching from the Danube to the Aegean, and from the Black Sea to Lake Ohrid and the mountains of Albania. It had an area of 63,000 square miles and a population of 4,500,000. Its nationalist leadership was overjoyed at attaining boundaries that embraced most of the lands that had been part of tenth-century Bulgaria. In their hubris they rejected the traditional eastern mountain capital of Tirnovo in favor of Sofia, on grounds of the latter's more central position for administering the expansive young state.

The Western European powers, alarmed by Russia's growing penetration of the Balkans, abruptly dashed their enthusiasm. France and the United Kingdom insisted upon preserving a far greater Ottoman presence in Southeastern Europe. A new treaty, signed in Berlin four months later, reduced Bulgaria to an autonomous Christian principality of 25,000 square miles and a population of 1,850,000. It was required to remain within the Ottoman Empire. Macedonia stayed under direct Ottoman control, together with Bulgarian-inhabited areas south of the Stara Planina that were constituted as the new East Rumelian province of the empire, with local self-rule. (The toponym Rumelia is derived from the Turkish term for Rome.) In addition, Bulgaria lost part of Dobrogea in the northeast as a European compensation to Romania for Russia's continuing control of Bessarabia.

Bulgarians never accepted the loss of the lands granted by the treaty of San Stefano. Despite several wars, however, they were able to gain on a permanent basis only Eastern Rumelia, which they seized in 1885 after a dispute with Serbia. Later, in 1908, they successfully proclaimed their complete independence from the Ottoman Empire, and their prince assumed the title of tsar. An alliance with Serbia in 1912 forced the Turks to relinquish control of all European holdings aside from a wedge of territory north of Istanbul. However, during a second war in 1913, Bulgaria found itself on the defensive against combined forces of Serbia, Montenegro, Romania, Greece, and Turkey. Its neighbors obliged it to give up much of the spoils it had gained the previous year. Montenegro and Serbia divided the Sanjak of Novi Pazar. Northern Macedonia also went to Serbia, southern Macedonia to Greece, and most of the Aegean coast to Turkey. In addition, Romania seized the southern section of Dobrogea (Figure 6-5).

Bulgaria's frustrated territorial ambitions led it to ally itself with Turkey and the Central Powers in World War I. Their defeat resulted in Bulgaria's complete loss of the Aegean coast and southern Dobrogea. It also had to cede to the Kingdom of Serbs, Croatians, and Slovenes several small Bulgarian-inhabited areas along the railway between Belgrade and Salonika, leaving its once centrally located capital of Sofia only thirty-five miles from an international border. For Bulgarians, however, the most bitter loss was the division of the greater part of Macedonia between the Greeks and Yugoslavs.

Macedonia. The territory of Macedonia has been one of the most contentious areas in all of Europe. It occupies about 25,000 square miles and has a population approaching 2,000,000. It is a frontier where Greek, Albanian, Serbian, Turkish, Bulgarian, and even Romanian interests overlap. All groups have historic claims to the region dating from before the fourteenth century. It remained Ottoman territory until 1913. Currently it is divided among Bulgaria, Yugoslavia, Albania, and Greece (Figure 6-6).

The largest population group consists of Orthodox Christians who speak a South Slavic language containing both Serbian and Bulgarian elements. It also is home to significant numbers of Greeks, Albanians, Gypsies, and Vlachs. Greek influence has been strong in religion and education throughout the region. Each of the occupying powers has sought to assimilate the local population into its dominant national identity. Greece has forbidden public use of the Macedonian language, and Bulgaria has refused to give recognition to any separate Macedonian identity of the inhabitants of its southwestern Pirin Mountain region. Before World War II, Yugoslavia, dominated by Serbia, classed Macedonians simply as "South Serbs."

After Bulgaria's frustratingly repeated losses of Macedonia following the San Stefano treaty, the Balkan Wars, and World War I, it occupied the Yugoslav portion of the region during World War II. Once more it was on the losing side, however, and found itself forced to relinquish the territory back to Yugoslavia after the war. Bulgaria's heavy-handedness during the occupa-

FIGURE 6-5 BULGARIAN TERRITORIAL CLAIMS

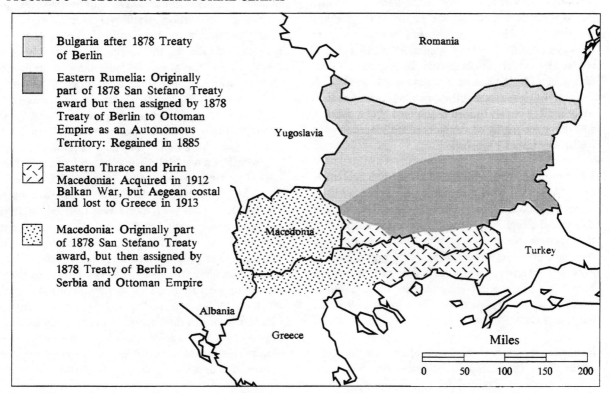

Bulgaria after 1878 Treaty of Berlin

Eastern Rumelia: Originally part of 1878 San Stefano Treaty award but then assigned by 1878 Treaty of Berlin to Ottoman Empire as an Autonomous Territory: Regained in 1885

Eastern Thrace and Pirin Macedonia: Acquired in 1912 Balkan War, but Aegean costal land lost to Greece in 1913

Macedonia: Originally part of 1878 San Stefano Treaty award, but then assigned by 1878 Treaty of Berlin to Serbia and Ottoman Empire

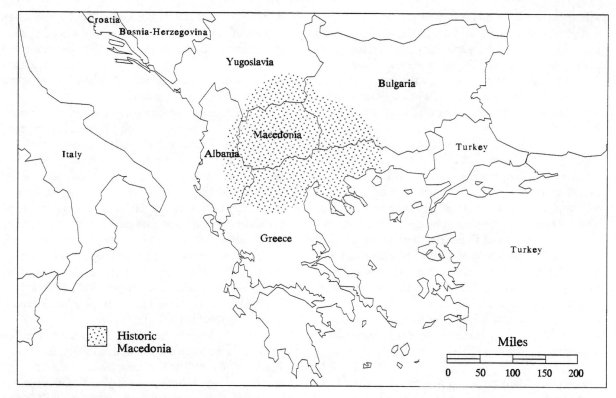

FIGURE 6-6   THE MACEDONIAN REGION

tion had led to strong resistance by the local population, who, by war's end, had crystallized into a separate national identity. The postwar Yugoslav Communist decision to establish a Macedonian republic facilitated this development, as did the creation for the first time of a Macedonian literary language, largely through the efforts of a Slavic linguistics professor at Harvard University. Bulgarians retain their national pretensions to Macedonia, but anti-Bulgarian sentiments play a major role in the iconography of members of the Macedonian nation living within Yugoslavia.

Eastern Thrace. Bulgarian ambitions for direct outlets to the Aegean Sea were thwarted by the peace settlements after both world wars. In both cases the victors awarded the region of eastern Thrace to Greece after Bulgarian wartime occupations. Distressed Bulgaria rejected a post–World War I offer of the port of Dedeagach as a free port. Bulgarian claims to both eastern Thrace and Macedonia were weakened by post–World War I mass emigration to Bulgaria of its supporters living in the areas.

Bulgarian Muslim areas. In addition to the Macedonians of its Pirin region, Bulgaria has substantial

minorities of Muslims in both its northeastern hills and its Rhodope Mountain area. Those in the northeast are descendants of Turkish agricultural colonists who came during the period of Ottoman rule. Their native language is Turkish and they consider themselves to be ethnic Turks. The groups in the southwestern mountains are generally identified as "Pomaks" ("Helpers") and speak only Bulgarian. They are descendants of Slavs who accepted Islam in the seventeenth century. In this regard they should be seen as similar to the Muslims of Yugoslav Bosnia. They number about 200,000.

Muslims have felt pressures to emigrate to Turkey ever since Bulgaria gained its independence. An estimated 50,000 fled during the Balkan Wars, and another 100,000 left in the post–World War I period. In 1950 Bulgaria announced that 250,000 of its remaining 800,000 Turks would be expelled over a three-month period. It then proceeded to carry out the order. The Bulgarian regime appears to have been motivated to put economic pressure upon Turkey by having it absorb refugees. At that time Turkey and Greece, with American support under the Truman Doctrine, were successfully resisting Communist world threats in eastern Anatolia and Greek Macedonia. This may also be the reason for similar Yugoslav coercion of its Muslim Turks and

Albanians to emigrate to Turkey. The Bulgarians may also have sought productive Turkish lands for establishing collective farms.

The Bulgarian regime renewed pressures upon its Muslims in the 1980s. It closed many mosques, outlawed circumcision and Islamic burial customs, and forbade the speaking of Turkish in public. It also set about a policy of requiring the adoption of Bulgarian (Christian) names. Bulgaria's tight restrictions on travel abroad were simultaneously eased for Turks, resulting in a new exodus to Turkey.

The actions proved popular with the majority of Bulgarians, who had long fretted about the exceptionally high birthrates of the Muslim minority. After the ouster of the Communist regime in 1990, the new government declared an end to discrimination against Muslims. It was rewarded by mass demonstrations in Sofia and elsewhere protesting the easing of pressures upon the Turks and Pomaks.

Albania

One of the smallest of the European states is Albania, with barely 11,000 square miles. It is also the most isolated and economically undeveloped. It is beset by internal tensions derived from tribe, language, and religious heritage, and it has major quarrels over territory with its two neighbors, Yugoslavia and Greece.

Although wracked by most of the major historical events that have given character to the Balkans, Albanians have managed to preserve both their ancient Illyrian language and their tribal social order to the present. Tucked away in deep mountain valleys, the Albanians resisted acculturation processes that Slavicized and otherwise homogenized inhabitants of other areas.

The Albanian language is divided into two distinct but mutually intelligible parts: Gheg in the north and Tosk in the south. Differences in vocabulary and pronunciation are significant. They are reflected in toponyms. Thus the city generally known in Europe by its Italian name Valona is Vlona in Gheg and Vlorë in Tosk. The linguistic division was likely perpetuated by the late development of an Albanian literary language. Although some Albanian appeared in written form as early as the sixteenth century, Albanians were illiterate in their native tongue until quite recent times. The few who were educated wrote in Greek. A major problem existed in trying to adapt the Greek, Latin, or Arabic alphabets to Albanian sounds. A literary language using the Latin alphabet became standard only in the early twentieth century.

The Albanians have also preserved their traditional tribalism. Each valley has its own tribe operating under an ancient code relating to marriage and customary relations with others. Even the Communist bureaucracy of the postwar era has been beset by tribally based nepotism.

Religion never achieved the profound cultural role among Albanians that it played elsewhere in Southeastern Europe. The dividing line between Roman Catholicism and Eastern Orthodoxy passed through Albania. Northern and mountainous areas were linked to Rome, whereas the south was dominated by Greek missionaries. However, Albanians saw both religions as foreign, and thus they had few problems in accepting Islam following Ottoman conquest of 1385. It promised local landowners a continuation of their control. There was similar general acceptance of the secular religion of Marxism following World War II, with only minor resistance to the closing of all mosques and churches during a mini-cultural revolution in the 1970s while Albania was allied with China. About 70 percent of contemporary Albanians come from Islamic families, 20 percent from Greek Orthodox ones, and 10 percent from Roman Catholic homes.

Albania was part of the Ottoman Empire for more than six centuries. However, the Turks seldom were able to control its tribal groups. The Albanian tribes did unite for twenty-five years, following successful rebellion against the Ottoman Turks in 1443. The revolt was led by George Kastriotis, who adopted the name Skënderbeg. He remains a national hero. Although the Ottoman Empire eventually reestablished its nominal authority, it seldom attempted to control interior tribes. In contrast to the flowering of national identities elsewhere in the empire during the nineteenth century, Albania remained quiescent, the population seemingly content with the status quo. Manifestations of nationalism began only in the 1870s, as Albanians grew aware of designs on their homeland by Bulgarians, Serbs, Greeks, and Montenegrins.

The Albanian state. The first shock was a provision of the 1878 Treaty of San Stefano that allotted to Bulgaria Albanian-inhabited territory as far west as Lake Ohrid. Although that document was countermanded a short time later by the Treaty of Berlin, the Albanians were then confronted by the subsequent treaty's award of substantial Albanian traditional territories to Montenegro. The weak Ottoman Empire found itself forced to accept the Berlin demands. Albanian leaders realized that separate statehood was necessary if they were to resist pressures by the Slavic states and Greece for their ancestral lands. The Turks grew alarmed at resulting Albanian nationalist activities, and their ensuing repressions served to intensify Albanian feelings into full nationhood.

In 1912 the Albanians staged a successful revolt against Ottoman rule and proclaimed a republic. For a variety of external reasons, their independence was recognized by a Council of Ambassadors, who met to draft a treaty following the first Balkan War. They gave the new country a German king, although he had to leave after only six months of rule. They also gave the state "natural boundaries" that generally followed mountain ridge crests. Their delimitation involved little consideration of patterns of ethnicity. Large numbers of Albanians were left in Serbia, Montenegro, Turkey, and Greece, and substantial enclaves of other groups were incorporated within Albania.

During the subsequent World War I, Albania witnessed Serbs, Austrians, Italians, Greeks, and even Frenchmen fighting through its territory. It also faced internal struggles by contending tribal groups. After witnessing such civil quarrels, its neighbors after the war saw little hope in Albanian ability for self-government, and they sought to rule its territory. Italy and Greece actually signed an agreement to divide the country between themselves. The Albanians managed to form a postwar government of their own, however, and to prevail upon treaty makers in Paris to recognize Albania's continuing independence. They were successful. Albania was reaffirmed in its 1913 boundaries.

The folly of utilizing avowed "natural boundaries" has never been more evident than in independent Albania's resultant problems of disaffected minorities and irredentism. Some 200,000 Greeks were incorporated in the Albanian areas of Koritsa and Girokaster, termed "northern Epirus" by Greeks. Numerous Albanians, in turn, were included in Greece as far south as the western city of Ioannina. Hundreds of thousands of Albanians also became unwilling subjects of the Kingdom of Serbs, Croatians, and Slovenes in the Serbian traditionalist homeland of Kosovo.

Albania continued to be beset by internal political and economic difficulties after the war, and it turned to Italy for assistance. By 1928 it had become a virtual Italian protectorate. A decade later, in 1939, Italy took full control, ousting despotic King Zog. Italians supported Albanian territorial claims, however, and were in turn supported by most Albanians when Italy went to war with Greece in 1940.

Italy's Albanian campaign went badly, and Greek forces captured substantial areas of southern Albania. Fortunes of the Albanians changed, however, when Italy's ally Germany invaded and overpowered Yugoslavia and Greece. It severed Serbian Kosovo and a strip of southern Montenegro from Yugoslavia and added them to the Italian puppet Albanian state. Greeks were ousted from northern Epirus. Albanian allegiances nevertheless were divided during World War II, particularly after Italian withdrawal from the war in 1943. A German takeover of Italian-occupied areas in Southeastern Europe prompted development of Albanian resistance movements. The strongest proved to be that of the Communist partisans, working closely with their Yugoslav counterparts. By the end of 1944 they established control over the entire country.

The Yugoslav Partisans dominated Albanian affairs for nearly four years into the postwar period. Despite Albanian unhappiness, the Yugoslavs forced a return to prewar boundaries, including Serbian retention of Kosovo. The break between Yugoslavia and the Soviet Union provided an opportunity for Albania to renounce its treaties and agreements with the Yugoslavs. The USSR became its protector. Albania gained little from the relationship, however, and in 1961 broke with the Soviet Union in favor of close alliance with Communist China. In 1977 the Albanians decided also to break with the Chinese.

Continuing internal problems. Albania distinguished itself during the Communist era by establishing the most repressive regime in Europe. In addition to minimizing influences from Western societies, the tight system also suppressed the divisiveness that had been so endemic in prewar Albania. It stifled rivalry between Ghegs and Tosks, even though the leadership appeared to favor Tosks in such matters as official language style. Disputes between tribes were not permitted to escalate into open clashes. Religious rivalries were silenced by pressures on all three major faiths. In 1967 all houses of worship were closed and put to other uses. Minorities lost all interactions with their homelands across the borders, as well as all rights to agitate for their own interests.

Antagonisms and allegiances that for long had been imbedded in the landscape did not disappear, however. As Albania at the end of the 1980s sought a more workable system along with expanded ties to other countries, it felt the rebirth of popular feelings so long held down. Tribal antagonisms surfaced, and Ghegs blamed Tosks for negative aspects of the old regime. The Greek minority of some 200,000 found its self-identity again, despite having been required to master Tosk Albanian speech. The decision of the socialist government of Greece in 1987 to renounce all territorial claims to northern Epirus reduced the threat of irredentism. Albania also benefitted by Serbian repressions of the Albanians in Kosovo that began in 1990, since news of outrages strengthened bonds of national feeling within the country.

Greece

Greece occupies the southern tip of the Balkan Peninsula. Twenty percent of its 51,000 square miles lies on rocky islands. Barely 30 percent consists of plains, and much of that area is in swampland unsuitable for agricultural development. Population clusters are widely separated along the mainland seacoast, in interior basins, and on the islands. Although a common modern Greek national identity has flourished since the early nineteenth century, the Greeks are fragmented by regional allegiances that reflect their physical and psychological separation from each other. Even in emigration to America or Australia, Greek communities tend to divide themselves according to ancestral home territories. Regional divisiveness within Greek society has been tempered, however, by common reaction to historic claims to parts of its territory by each of its neighbors.

The iconography of the modern Greek nation celebrates a descent from the classical Greeks. As often is the case, image departs somewhat from historic reality. Ancient Greek civilization was a glorious achievement. Its language and culture dominated the eastern Mediterranean and resisted Latin acculturation that occurred in other Roman conquests. The Greek-based Byzantine Empire did persist to the mid-fifteenth century, when its last sliver of territory was conquered by the Ottoman Turks. The Greek Orthodox church maintained a continuity to the present. However, over the course of centuries the inhabitants of Greece substantially changed. Slavs and other barbarian groups settled in the area. Although most immigrants were Hellenized, they contributed significantly to changes in Greek culture. Language increasingly departed from its classical form as much as Italian did from Latin. Four centuries of Turkish domination had even more profound impact.

National passions developed among Greeks early in the nineteenth century. A weakened Ottoman Empire could not contain a rebellion that lasted from 1821 until Greek self-rule was recognized in 1829. However, the young Greek state fell far short of Greek-inhabited territory within the empire. It included only the Peloponnesus Peninsula with a narrow strip of land to the north of the Bay of Corinth and a handful of islands in the Aegean Sea. Its total population was 700,000, with only 5,000 residents in its new capital of Athens. Substantial concentrations of Greeks remained under Ottoman control in adjacent areas of the Balkan Peninsula, the islands of the eastern Mediterranean, the Anatolian coast, and, of course, the Ottoman capital of Constantinople itself. Greek clergy, merchants, and bureaucrats were to be found throughout the rest of the empire, and also in southern Russia.

Greece expanded gradually during the ensuing century. In 1864 the United Kingdom ceded the Ionian Islands to Greece. Much of Thessaly was gained in 1881. Greeks in Crete staged several rebellions against Ottoman domination during the nineteenth century. In 1898 they attained an autonomous state under Turkish sovereignty. A decade later they proclaimed union with Greece, but the Ottoman Empire formally accepted this status only in 1913. At this time it also confirmed Greek gains during the Balkan Wars, including Epirus, southern Macedonia, and Thrace (Figure 6-7).

After World War I, Greece sought additional territory from the young Turkish nation-state that had emerged from the ruins of the Ottoman Empire. Greek demands included eastern Thrace, the Straits between the Black and Aegean seas with Constantinople itself, and much of western Anatolia and adjacent islands. In 1922 the Greek army invaded the latter, claiming Turkish threats to the local Greek population. They particularly sought the largely Greek-inhabited city of Smyrna, which at that time had twice as many citizens as Athens. The move was disastrous. In the subsequent peace treaty Greece not only had to renounce claims to the mainland and the islands within three miles of the coast, but also had to agree to an exchange of populations. More than 1,750,000 Greeks left Turkey and 350,000 Turks emigrated from Greece. The problem of Greek *irredenta* in Turkey thus became minor, but there still remained 100,000 Greeks in the Dodecanese Islands gained by Italy from Turkey after the war, and another 250,000 in Cyprus, which the United Kingdom had held since 1878.

The Greek acquisition of Macedonia led many Macedonian- and Bulgarian-speaking inhabitants to move northward. In turn, more than a half million of the Greek refugees from Turkey settled in their abandoned villages, fundamentally changing the character of the regional population. Slavic-speakers remaining in Greek Macedonia were forbidden to use their native language in public, a situation remaining to this day. In eastern Thrace a number of non-Greeks also emigrated to Bulgaria and Turkey, but many remained in their rural villages. They included Bulgars, Pomaks, Turks, and Gypsies. Their numbers are uncertain because census returns in Greece have omitted references to language and religion. The largest group appears to be ethnic Turks, whose total is estimated at more than 100,000. Muslim Bulgarian-speaking Pomaks and Gypsies number about 40,000. Their numbers were sufficient to elect two Muslim deputies to the Greek parliament in the 1980s, until election laws were changed to eliminate minor political parties. Eastern Thrace has remained one of the most poverty-stricken regions of Europe. In 1991 the Greek government announced

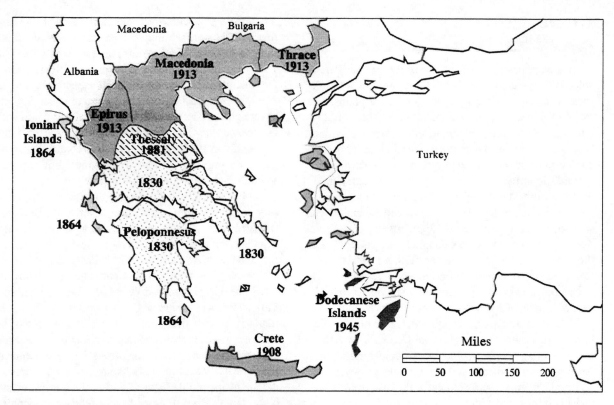

FIGURE 6-7 THE TERRITORIAL GROWTH OF GREECE

plans to resettle in eastern Thrace several thousand so-called Pontic Greek immigrants from the Black Sea shores of the former Soviet Union.

In the interwar period the Greeks manifested concerns for members of their nation in other states. When Italy invaded Greece from Albania in 1940, the Greek army was successful in repelling the enemy and occupied virtually all of the Greek-inhabited northern Epirus region of southern Albania. German forces then completely subdued Greece. In the postwar period northern Epirus reverted to Albania. Greece also endured a civil war in Macedonia supported by the newly installed Communist regimes of its three northern neighbors. That movement ended when Yugoslavia ceased to support and give haven to the rebellious guerrillas following Yugoslavia's 1948 ouster from the Soviet bloc. Greek sensitivities to potential problems in Macedonia manifested themselves in 1992, when the government waged a concerted effort to induce other European states not to recognize the declared independence of the Yugoslav Macedonian Republic until it renamed itself the "Republic of Skopje" or a similar name that had no allusions to the Greek patrimony.

Tensions with other neighbors have remained high, however, particularly along the Albanian border. This area has a mixed population whose allegiances are diffi-cult to discern. Greeks claim that 40 percent of the 320,000 inhabitants of northern Epirus were Greek. Albanians put the figure at less than 10 percent, and claimed 100,000 Albanians lived in adjacent parts of Greece. Both sides suppressed the national identities of their minorities. In 1987 Greece led the way in relaxing tensions by formally renouncing its claims to northern Epirus and by permitting Albanian Greeks to enter its territory to meet with long-separated family members.

Two other territorial problems have inflamed Greek national passions in recent times: Cyprus and the Aegean seabed. Both have strained relations of Greece with Turkey.

Cyprus. The island of Cyprus lies in the eastern Mediterranean Sea some fifty miles off the coast of Turkish Anatolia and sixty-five miles from Syria. It has an area of 3,500 square miles and a population of 700,000, some 80 percent of whom are Greeks and about 18 percent Turkish.

The island's pivotal location in the eastern Mediterranean has attracted imperial interests for millennia. It has been part of the Persian, Roman, Byzantine, Ottoman, and British empires. The British gained control in 1878, when the Sultan in Constantinople ceded to them the right to administer the territory. The outbreak of World War I led the United Kingdom to annex Cyprus in 1914. It was a Crown colony until 1959, when a guerrilla war initiated by Greek Cypriots in 1955 culminated in a British decision to allow the establishment of an independent republic. The leaders of the rebellion had sought *enosis* (union) of Cyprus with Greece. However, a treaty signed by the prime ministers of the United Kingdom, Greece, and Turkey forbade such *enosis* and also any partition of the island between its Greek and Turkish communities. The British received the right to continue to operate their military bases on the island without interference.

Cypriot Turks reacted violently in 1963 to Greek Cypriot attempts to modify some provisions of the agreements that established the republic. Fighting led to a joint force of British, Greek, and Turkish troops being dispatched to the island to keep the peace. Their role subsequently was assumed by the United Nations.

In 1974 the military regime that ruled Greece encouraged a coup d'etat in Cyprus by a Greek Cypriot faction that had continued to press for *enosis*. The coup was short-lived, but it provoked an invasion of the island by the Turkish army. Its 40,000 troops occupied nearly 40 percent of the territory. More than 200,000 Greek Cypriots fled the occupied area to refugee camps in the area held by republican forces. This represented two-fifths of the Greek community. Some 50,000 Cypriot Turks moved to the Turkish-held territory. The United Nations established a buffer zone between the two areas.

An autonomous Turkish Cypriot Administration established itself in the Turkish-controlled area. In 1975 it proclaimed itself a "Turkish Cypriot Federated State" and in 1983 "The Turkish Republic of Northern Cyprus." It has not sought international recognition outside of Turkey. Its population of 175,000 includes more than 27,000 Turkish troops and at least 40,000 mainland Turks who moved to Cyprus after the invasion.

The Greek Cypriots have never accepted the *de facto* partition of the island. Most remain bitter over homes and lands seized by the Turks. Various efforts have been advanced to unite the two parts into a federal state, but this has not occurred. The potential remains for renewed fighting between the two communities. The dispute has also soured relations between Greece and Turkey.

The Aegean seabed dispute. Turko-Greek relations have also suffered from conflicting claims to the bed of the Aegean Sea off Anatolia. The Turks claim the entire continental shelf, acknowledging Greek control only of submerged lands extending six miles from the Greek-held islands. Greece maintains that the entire seabed between islands is Greek territory. The significance of the dispute has grown in recent decades with improvements in the technology of undersea mining. Periodic crises have occurred as one side has disputed the other's right to drill through the seabed floor to explore the presence of oil and other minerals.

Bibliography

BOWMAN, ISAIAH, *The New World—Problems in Political Geography*. London: Harrap, 1928.

FISCHER-GALATI, STEPHEN. *Romania: East-Central Europe Under the Communists*. New York: Praeger, 1957.

FISHER, J., *Yugoslavia: A Multinantional State: Regional Differences and Administrative Response*. San Francisco: Chandler Publ. Co., 1966.

HOFFMAN, GEORGE, and F. NEAL, *Yugoslavia and the New Communism*. New York: Twentieth Century Fund, 1962.

HOFFMAN, GEORGE, *The Balkans in Transition*. Princeton, NJ: Van Nostrand, 1963.

KOSTANICK, H.L., "Turkish Resettlement of Bulgarian Turks 1950-1953," *University of California Publications in Geography*, Vol. 8, No. 2 (1957).

MOODIE, ARTHUR, *The Italo-Yugoslav Boundary*. London: Philip, 1945.

MOODIE, ARTHUR, "States and Boundaries in the Danubian Lands," *Slavonic and East European Review*. Vol. 26 (1948), pp. 422–437.

MOODIE, ARTHUR, "The Eastern Marchlands of Europe," in *The Changing World: Studies in Political Geography*, W. East and A. Moodie, eds. Yonkers, NY: World Book Co., 1956, pp. 111–137.

7

Russia and
the Commonwealth
of Independent States

AFTER seven decades of functioning as the largest and most highly centralized state in the world, the Union of Soviet Socialist Republics formally ceased to exist in December 1991. Over the preceding several months, local authorities in each of the USSR's fifteen "constituent republics" had declared some form of self-rule. Seeking to arrest further weakening of the Soviet Union, a group of Communist party, military, and secret police officials attempted a coup d'etat in August 1991. Their aim was to reestablish the USSR's highly centralized political and economic command systems. Following failure of that coup, the principal institutions binding the diverse peoples of the Soviet Union together collapsed. The republics quickly became sovereign units. Subsequently, eleven republics agreed to form a "Commonwealth of Independent States" that would maintain a common currency and share other joint functions. Only Georgia and the Baltic republics of Estonia, Latvia, and Lithuania did not immediately join (see Table 7-1).

The demise of the USSR and its replacement by fifteen separate nation-states has had a profound impact upon the political and economic geography of the continental-sized region lying between Europe and China. Instability suddenly appeared in what had been one of the most stable of the world's realms. Long-suppressed group antagonisms again flourished. No central forces remained to protect the fates of minorities. Customary linkages among enterprises, resources, and markets were sundered. An uncertain free-enterprise system replaced a predictable, albeit inefficient, managed economy.

A particular political-geographic consequence of the changes was the reemergence on the world scene of Russia. Moscow again was a Russian capital city. The world community acknowledged the new democratically elected Russian government as successor to the Soviet Union. Russia's leadership appropriated the role and facilities of the Soviet Union in the Security Council of the United Nations and in diplomacy with other states. Although the USSR had functioned in many ways as a continuation of the Russian Empire that it replaced in 1917, its Communist regimes had generally suppressed Russian national feelings in keeping with their internationalist ethic. In contrast to the toleration, if not encouragement, of separate national identities in non-Russian areas, the Communist-controlled media gave little support to open pride in being Russian. However, the Russian nation survived more

than three generations of internationalist indoctrination, and, despite concerted efforts, the vaunted new "Soviet man," *Homo sovieticus*, did not emerge.

Aside from the period of World War II, when the hard-pressed regime found it necessary to make patriotic appeals to defend "Mother Russia" and to permit the Russian Orthodox church to function comparatively freely, strictly Russian sentiments were not allowed to flourish in the Soviet Union. The governmental structure and other institutions of the Russian Soviet Federated Socialist Republic were notably less separated from the "all-Union" organizations of the USSR than were counterparts in other republics. All this changed in 1991. The political severing from Russia of the majority of non-Russian areas, the elimination and discrediting of the Communist party, and the adoption of a democratic system opened the way for a return to traditional Russian values and goals.

The Russian republic itself embraces 6,500,000 square miles, twice the area of the United States or of Europe west of the Commonwealth of Independent States frontier. It spreads over eleven time zones. The distance from St. Petersburg (Leningrad) to Vladivostok is more than twice that from San Francisco to Boston. Trans-Siberian express trains require seven days to travel from Moscow to the Pacific coast.

The huge size of Russia can be misleading. Virtually three-quarters is unpopulated. The Arctic tundra and the great northern forest zone stretching across the country from the border with Finland to the Pacific shores of Siberia have only minor roles to play. Developed land occupies a bit more than 1,000,000 square miles, or roughly one-sixth of the state. This is equivalent to half the developed area of Europe or the United States. The ecumene consists mainly of a wedge running from St. Petersburg in the northwest, to Novosibirsk in central Siberia, to the Black Sea and Ukrainian border. Even this settled region is marginal for agricultural production. Its southern fringes suffer from inadequate and undependable rainfall, while the rest is characterized by poor soils and limited summer warmth. Siberia east of Novosibirsk is a harsh land. Its isolated concentrations of population are to be found almost entirely within a few miles either side of the Trans-Siberian railroad line.

The other states of the Commonwealth have a combined area of 2,000,000 square miles and a population of 120,000,000. Only Ukraine, Moldova, and Belarus can be said to be completely settled. Mountains and deserts occupy more than three-quarters of the territory of the republics of Central Asia and the Caucasus.

TABLE 7.1   THE FORMER SOVIET UNION

The internal collapse of the Union of Soviet Socialist Republics in 1991 led to the political independence of all fifteen of the USSR's former constituent republics. The Russian Empire had conquered the non-Russian areas during the eighteenth and nineteenth centuries. Although Ukrainians (under Austrian manipulation) had developed a national identity by the mid-nineteenth century, most other ethnic groups attained strong national awareness only after the Communist Revolution of 1917. Since their recent independence, most states have begun to gravitate to neighboring states with which they share common cultural features. Their long association with each other within the USSR and their common economic and political problems continue to bind them together as a bloc, however.

State	Total Population	Area (sq. miles)	Distinctive Features of Group
Russia	149,000,000	6,600,000	
Dominant Nation and % Total			
Russians, 81%			Eastern Slavic (Russian) language, Eastern Orthodox
Significant Regional Groups and % Total			
Tatars, 4%			Turkic (Tatar) language, Sunni Muslim
Chuvashes, 1%			Turkic (Chuvash) language, Eastern Orthodox
Bashkirs, 1%			Turkic (Bashkir) language, Sunni Muslim
Buryats, <1%			Mongol language, Buddhist
Tuvinians, <1%			Turkic (Tuvinian) language, Buddhist
Chechens, <1%			Nakh (Chechen) language, Sunni Muslim
Yakuts, <1%			Turkic (Yakut) language, Animist/Eastern Orthodox
Ukraine			
Dominant Nation and % Total			
Ukrainians, 72%			Eastern Slavic (Ukrainian and Russian) languages, Eastern Orthodox and Uniate Roman Catholic
Significant Regional Groups and % Total			
Russians, 22%			Eastern Slavic (Russian) language, Eastern Orthodox
Potential Trouble Areas and Possible Adversaries			
Crimean Peninsula (Russia)			
Belarus	10,500,000	80,000	
Dominant Nation and % Total			
Belorussians, 78%			Eastern Slavic (Belarus) language (although most are bilingual in Russian), Eastern Orthodox and Uniate Roman Catholic
Significant Regional Groups and % Total			
Poles, 4%			Western Slavic (Polish) language, Roman Catholic
Estonia	1,600,000	17,500	
Dominant Nation and % Total			
Estonians (62%)			Finnic (Estonian) language, Lutheran
Significant Regional Groups and % Total			
Russians (32%)			Eastern Slavic (Russian) language, Eastern Orthodox
Potential Trouble Areas and Possible Adversaries			
Narva Region (Russia)			
Latvia	2,700,000	25,000	
Dominant Nation and % Total			
Latvians, 52%			Baltic (Latvian) language, Lutheran
Lithuania			
Dominant Nation and % Total			
Lithuanians, 80%			Baltic (Lithuanian) language, Roman Catholic

State	Total Population	Area (sq. miles)	Distinctive Features of Group
Moldova	4,400,000	13,000	
Dominant Nation and % Total			
Moldovans, 65%			Romance (Romanian) language, Eastern Orthodox
Significant Regional Groups and % Total			
Russians/Ukrainians, 26%			Eastern Slavic (Russian/Ukrainian) languages, Eastern Orthodox
Gagauz, 4%			Turkic (Gagauz) language, Eastern Orthodox
Potential Trouble Areas and Possible Adversaries			
Transdnistria			
(Ukraine, Russia)			
Georgia	5,500,000	27,000	
Dominant Nation and % Total			
Georgians, 70%			Kartvelian (Georgian) language, Eastern Orthodox
Significant Regional Groups and % Total			
Ossetes, 3%			Iranian (Ossetian) language, Sunni Muslim
Abkhazians, 2%			Adygo-Abkhaz language, Mixed Muslim/Eastern Orthodox
Adzhars, <1%			Kartvelian (Georgian) language, Muslim
Armenia	3,500,000	11,500	
Dominant Nation and % Total			
Armenians, 94%			Unique Armenian language, Eastern Orthodox
Significant Regional Groups and % Total			
Azeri Turks, 3%			Turkic (Azerbaijani) language, Shiite Muslim
Potential Trouble Areas and Possible Adversaries			
Nakhichevan (Azerbaijan)			
Azerbaijan	7,200,000	34,000	
Dominant Nation and % Total			
Azeri Turks, 83%			Turkic (Azerbaijani) language, Shiite Muslim
Significant Regional Groups and % Total			
Armenians, 6%			Unique Armenian language, Eastern Orthodox
Turkmenistan	3,750,000	190,000	
Dominant Nation and % Total			
Turkmen, 72%			Turkic (Turkmen) language, Sunni Muslim
Uzbekistan	21,000,000	175,000	
Dominant Nation and % Total			
Uzbeks, 72%			Turkic (Uzbek) language, Sunni Muslim
Significant Regional Groups and % Total			
Tajiks, 5%			Iranian (Tajik) language, Sunni, Shiite and Izmaili Muslim
Kazakhs, 4%			Turkic (Kazakh) language, Sunni Muslim
Karakalpaks, 2%			Turkic (Kazakh) language, Sunni Muslim
Potential Trouble Areas and Possible Adversaries			
Karakalpakia (Kazakhstan)			
Tajikistan	5,500,000	55,000	
Dominant Nation and % Total			
Tajiks, 62%			Iranian (Tajik) language, Sunni and Izmaili Muslim
Significant Regional Groups and % Total			
Uzbeks, 24%			Turkic (Uzbek) language, Sunni Muslim
Potential Trouble Areas and Possible Adversaries			
Fergana Valley	1,000,000	1,000	
(Uzbekistan)			

Continued

State	Total Population	Area (sq. miles)	Distinctive Features of Group
Kirgizstan	4,500,000	77,000	
Dominant Nation and % Total			
Kirgiz, 52%			Turkic (Kirgiz) language, Sunni Muslim
Kazakhstan	17,000,000	1,000,000	
Dominant Nation and % Total			
Kazakhs, 40%			Turkic (Kazakh) language, Sunni Muslim
Significant Regional Groups and % Total			
Russians and Ukrainians, 42%			Eastern Slavic (Russian and Ukrainian) languages, Eastern Orthodox
Uighurs, <1%			Turkic (Uighur) language, Sunni Muslim
Potential Trouble Area and Possible Adversary			
North Kazakhstan "Virgin Lands" region (Russia)			
	4,500,000	170,000	

These empty stretches long served to separate and insulate Russia from its former overland colonies, much as the Mediterranean Sea divided France from Algeria (see Figure 7-1).

The Russian Empire

Over a period of four centuries, beginning in the 1500s, Russia's rulers from a core in Moscow built one of the world's greatest empires (Figure 7-2). Before that time, most Russian territory had been part of an empire of Mongols and Tatars (Turks) forged by Genghis Khan. The Mongol-Tatars had conquered an earlier state of Russian-speaking people, the Kievan Rus, that had existed on the East European Plain from the ninth to the twelfth centuries A.D. Scandinavian Varangians had organized that unit along the nearly continuous waterways linking the Baltic Sea with the Black Sea. Its capital was the Dnieper River town of Kiev, located on the margin between woodlands and the dangerous open grasslands of the nomadic-inhabited steppes. The Kievan Rus was a successful state, comparable in size and functioning to the Kingdom of France of the time. The origin of the name "Rus" is controversial. Many believe it is a corruption of "Rurik," the name of the legendary Varangian founder of the Kievan state.

The people of Russia acquired distinctive perspectives and institutions during four centuries of subordination to the Tatars. They did not participate in many of the developments of European civilization, although they did retain their Eastern Orthodox Christian traditions during their long period under the "Tatar Yoke." After Byzantium fell to the Ottoman Turks, Russian clergy saw themselves as the leaders of the Christian religion. A recurring theme in Russian self-perceptions and iconography is that Moscow, following barbarian captures of Rome itself and the "second Rome" of Constantinople, became the world's "Third Rome," with a destiny to become savior of all of Christendom.

Some interpret this sense of destiny as a primary motivation for Russia's outward political expansion. Others cite far more mundane rationales. They ascribe Moscow's twelfth-century drive to acquire dominion over neighboring Russian-speaking principalities to simple ambition and greed. This upstart community had not been mentioned in Russian chronicles before the year 1147, in contrast to Novgorod, Smolensk, and other older centers that had arisen as early as the eighth century. However, when Muscovite princes acquired the role of tax collectors for the Tatars, Moscow supplanted the sacked and ruined Kiev as the leading city of the Eastern Slavs. In the process of gathering tribute for the Tatars from its neighbors, Moscow gained wealth and power sufficient to enable it to absorb and dominate them. Eventually, by the fifteenth century, the Muscovites had defied the Tatars themselves, refusing to pay them the monies that they continued to collect from former Rus principalities. In 1552 Moscow symbolically ended its formal subjugation to the Tatars when it conquered the city of Kazan, a capital of one of three major principalities into which the empire of Genghis Khan had fragmented.

There ensued a period of rapid expansion eastward across Siberia that saw the Russians reach the Pacific Ocean in less than a century. (During a comparable period in North America, the Pilgrims and Puritans managed to press inland hardly further than the Connecticut River.) The movement into Siberia was motivated by promises of riches in gold, salt, and other minerals, and by a quest for furs. Siberian conquest was relatively easy, for few organized groups were strong enough to contest the Russians in this sparsely populated forested region. Only when they reached Manchuria did they find

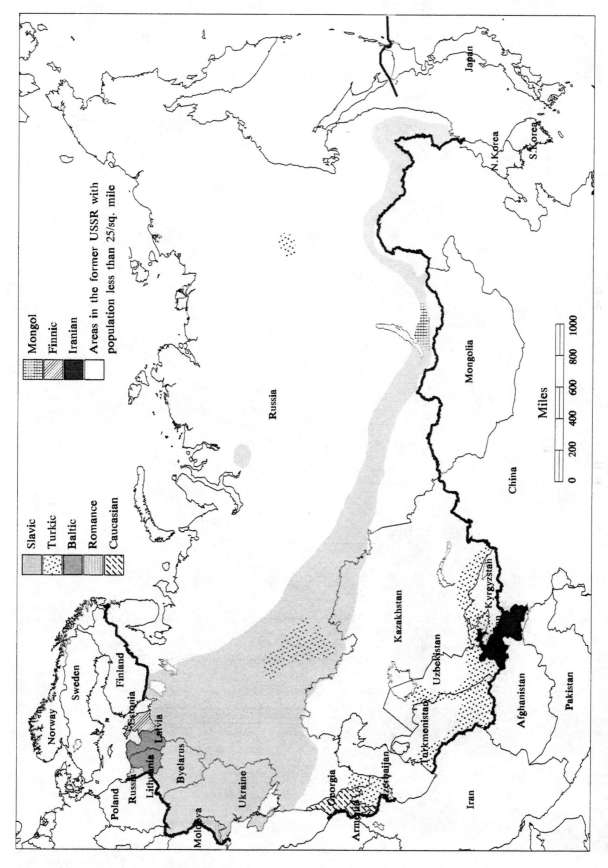

FIGURE 7-1 LANGUAGES AND ECUMENES OF THE FORMER SOVIET LANDS

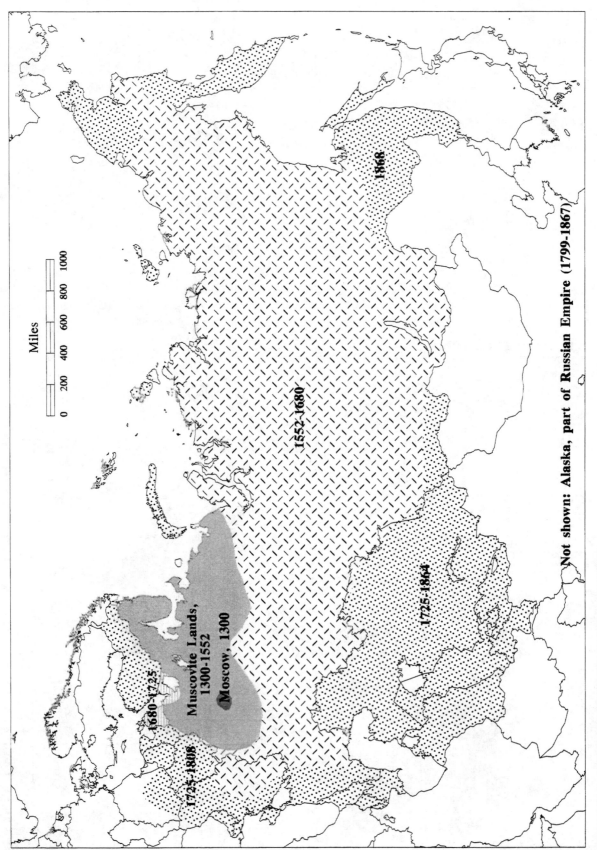

Miles

0   200   400   600   800   1000

Moscow, 1300

Muscovite Lands,
1300-1552

1552-1680

1680-1725

1725-1808

1725-1864

1868

Not shown: Alaska, part of Russian Empire (1799-1867)

FIGURE 7-2 EXPANSION OF THE RUSSIAN EMPIRE

themselves confronting a superior force, the Chinese. The latter forced the Russians to sign a treaty at Nerchinsk in 1687 that specified their mutual border to be the Stanovoy Mountains on the northern margins of the Amur valley watershed. The Russians did assert their presence over the remainder of Siberia, however, and in the eighteenth century claimed all of Alaska as a consequence of explorations by Vitus Bering.

By this time the princes in Moscow had proclaimed themselves "Tsars [Caesars] of All the Russias." However, stronger neighbors blocked them from recovering former Kievan lands lying to the south and west of their domain. Poland controlled the Ukraine and Byelorussia, the Ottoman Empire ruled the Black Sea littoral, and Sweden dominated the eastern Baltic coast. Between the fifteenth and seventeenth centuries, Russia and Poland were continuously at war, the Poles at one period even capturing Moscow.

During the second half of the seventeenth century Russia began to expand westward. The Tsar Alexis captured from Poland a swath of territory that included the towns of Smolensk and Kiev and extensive Ukrainian lands east of the Dnieper River. Alexis's son, Peter, later known as Peter the Great, moved southward against the Turks in the Caucasus and also pushed the Swedes out of Estonia, northern Latvia, and the Karelian region adjacent to Finland. In 1702 Peter ordered the creation of a new capital city, St. Petersburg, in the swampy delta of the Neva River at the east end of the Gulf of Finland.

Peter's successors continued to expand the Russian Empire. They joined with Austria and Prussia in the famous three partitionings of Poland in 1772, 1793, and 1795. They forced the Swedes to cede all of Finland to Russia in 1809. During the early nineteenth century they pushed Turkey out of the Black Sea region as far west as the Danube Delta and as far east as the Transcaucasus. In the first half of the nineteenth century Russia absorbed several non-Slavic Christian groups, including Romanian-speaking Moldavians of Bessarabia and the Georgians and Armenians of the Transcaucasus. It also incorporated substantial Muslim-inhabited territory in the northern Caucasus region and Azerbaijan. In the 1860s Russians conquered the Muslim native states of Bukhara, Kokand, and Khiva in Central Asia at a time when the British were moving into northwest India. The Russians also pushed into the northeastern Chinese realm, after China's 1840 Opium War with Britain had demonstrated its fundamental weaknesses. Despite the earlier Treaty of Nerchinsk, Russia in the 1860s proceeded to annex all territories lying north of the Amur River and east of the Ussuri River to the shores of the Pacific. It also built a railroad across Manchuria, although it recognized that region nominally to be Chinese. At the same time Russia decided to relinquish its remote North American holdings, selling Alaska to the United States in 1867.

In attempting to account for Russia's persistent outward territorial expansion, some scholars have identified a constant urge for the state to acquire effective access to the world's oceans. It should be noted, however, that during four centuries of empire-building, records of deliberations by Russia's leadership never mention as a motivating force the acquisition of ports, and particularly ones that would be free of ice throughout the year. Peter the Great's desire to found St. Petersburg as a "window on the west" may constitute an exception, but even there a rational goal existed of neutralizing the threatening force of Sweden. Most expansion can be understood by reference to such conventional considerations as the opening up of new sources of wealth, the neutralizing or elimination of traditional enemies, and the rescue of Christian peoples from the Muslim Turks.

In the early part of the twentieth century Russia suffered a notable reduction in territory. Defeat by Japanese forces in 1904–1905 forced it to abandon its developing economic interests in Korea, its domination of Manchuria, and its sovereignty over the southern half of Sakhalin Island. The catastrophe of World War I saw the revolutionary government of newly styled Soviet Russia also forced to recognize the separate independence of Finland, Estonia, Latvia, Lithuania, and Poland, and to concede Bessarabia (Moldavia) to Romania and other minor borderlands to Turkey. By 1945, however, the USSR had regained all but Poland, Finland, and the Turkish territories, and among these it had annexed to itself a substantial strip of eastern Poland plus Finland's former northern corridor to the Arctic Ocean. Following the end of World War II it also seized Czechoslovakia's eastern Carpatho-Ukraine region, the remote East Asian territory of Tannu Tuva, and the Kurile Islands lying north of Japan.

Four centuries of Russian expansion resulted in the building of an empire in which the population had a multiplicity of languages, religions, and cultural traditions. Russian-speakers were dominant, numbering about half of the population. Another 20 percent, the Ukrainians and Byelorussians, spoke similar Eastern Slavic languages. The Poles also had a Slavic language, but from the notably different Western branch of that group. Remaining minorities in the empire conversed in at least 90 other non-Slavic languages.

The main body of Eastern Slavs were Orthodox in religion. However, virtually all Poles and significant numbers of Ukrainians and Byelorussians were Roman Catholic. Scattered throughout eastern Poland and the cities of Russia were large numbers of Jews. There were also many Catholic and Protestant Germans concentrated in the lower Volga region and the Ukraine. In the middle Volga heart of Russia and in the borderlands of Central Asia and the Caucasus were substantial numbers of Muslims.

The Finns and Estonians were Lutheran peoples whose languages derived from the non-Indo-European Finno-Ugrian family. Similar tongues were used by the Eastern Orthodox Karelians and a host of small groups scattered across northern European Russia and Siberia. Latvians, too, were Lutheran in religion. They and the Roman Catholic Lithuanians spoke similar Baltic languages, which many scholars argue have changed least among languages of Europe from the parent Indo-European. Moldavians spoke Romanian, a Romance language strikingly similar to Italian, and, like the Romanians, the Moldavians were Eastern Orthodox in religion.

In the Caucasus region a bewildering array of linguistic groups had preserved their identities in the fastness of the mountains. The principal ones were the Orthodox Christian Georgians and Armenians, and the Shiite Muslim Azeri Turks. The Central Asians east of the Caspian Sea were Sunni Muslims and spoke mainly a Turkish dialect, although the Tajiks of the south had an Iranian-based language. The Sunni Muslim Tatars and Bashkirs, living between the middle bend of the Volga and the southern Ural Mountains, were also Turkic speakers, as were the animist Yakuts of northeastern Siberia. The Kalmyks of the lower Volga region and the Buriat Mongols around Siberian Lake Baikal were Buddhists and spoke East Asian languages.

The Nations of the Commonwealth

Virtually all the major ethnic groups of the Russian Empire and many of the minor ones became true nations during the nineteenth and twentieth centuries. National identities, as in the rest of Europe, emerged following contact with the legions of Napoleon I. Fighting a "patriotic war" against the French invaders, the Russians may be said to have become a unified nation early in the 1800s. Association with the radical ideas of the French troops also began incubation of national identities among other peoples within the Russian state, most notably the Poles, who revolted against Russian imperial domination in 1830 and again in 1867. The Finns likewise became a nation in the nineteenth century, in part because the Russians, after acquiring Finland from the Swedes, had initially preserved it as a local self-governing unit. Its citizens enjoyed more freedoms in the empire than even the Russians. Attempts to repress Finnish national identity at the end of the century only solidified the group's sense of nationhood. However, by the beginning of World War I national movements among peoples in the empire were notably less developed than the ethnic unrest endemic in the Habsburg

lands. The Russian Empire's slowness in economic and cultural modernization probably accounts for the lag in national awareness.

During the hardships and defeats of World War I and the subsequent civil war in Russia, strong national identities emerged rapidly among the empire's peoples. The necessity for local groups to supply basic needs in conditions of breakdown of transportation and production was accompanied by the growth of national passions. Communist forces galvanized such sentiments by proclaiming a policy of national self-determination. Their program was part of a series of desperate attempts to hold onto power in the early months following their coup d'etat of November 1917. (This seizure of control was romantically called "The October Revolution," reflecting the fact that the Russian Empire still used the Julian calendar, which had grown to lag two weeks behind the Gregorian calendar used in Europe and much of the rest of the world.) At one point Communist forces controlled little more than the territory between St. Petersburg and Moscow. Seeking at least the neutrality of the non-Russian minorities during the struggle with supporters of the tsarist regime, the Bolsheviks promised each national group that it would have the right to form a government of its own. These entities could either join with Soviet Russia in building a new socialist realm or go their independent ways. Bolshevik-sponsored nationality units soon appeared, beginning with a Bashkir territory designated as a "republic" in 1919.

Many national groups did not need Bolshevik inducement to consider separating from Russia, however. Prewar Austrian encouragement of Ukrainian nationalism in its Polish province of Galicia had well served its purpose of developing nationalist sentiments in adjacent Ukrainian-speaking territories of Russia. Ukrainians declared their independence from the Russian Empire in January 1918, signing a peace treaty with Austria and Germany a month later. Following collapse of those powers in November, Red Army forces seized Kiev in January 1919, compelling the young Ukrainian government to flee to Polish-controlled territory. The Bolsheviks then declared establishment of a Ukrainian Soviet Republic in March of that year. In December 1920, the government of the Ukraine signed a formal alliance with Soviet Russia.

National republics appeared in the Transcaucasus region. Armenians, Azerbaijanis, and Georgians each declared independent states of their own in May 1918. Sovereignty was short-lived, however. The Red Army conquered them during the winter of 1920/21. In March 1922, the three states were merged into a "Transcaucasian Federation," which subsequently became part of the USSR in July 1923.

More durable independence was achieved by national groups in the northwest. Finland became a separate state in December 1917. Despite local attempts to establish Bolshevik authority, the three Baltic lands of Estonia, Latvia, and Lithuania achieved sovereignty at the end of the war. They were supported by foreign forces, including the British and the French. After more than a century of being partitioned among Russia, Austria, and Prussia, the Poles also were able to reestablish their own sovereignty in 1918.

Within what remained of the former Russian Empire the Bolsheviks implemented their pledge to allow groups to form their own self-governing units, although the autonomy of these bodies remained largely illusory. On December 30, 1922, the Union of Soviet Socialist Republics was proclaimed. Its administrative map was complex. The largest borderland groups received the status of "Soviet Socialist Republics" (usually abbreviated as "SSRs"). Through processes of division, together with new conquests in the west, sixteen such "republics" had emerged by 1940. This number was reduced to fifteen in 1956 when the Karelo-Finnish SSR was assigned a lesser status as part of an accommodation with Finland. Russia was the largest of the constituent republics, embracing much of the European territory west of the Urals and all of Siberia. Its official title was the Russian Soviet Federated Socialist Republic (RSFSR).

Each SSR had the constitutional right to secede from the USSR. Smaller groups located away from state boundaries were organized into "Autonomous Soviet Socialist Republics" ("ASSRs") within the constituent republics. These also had the right of formal self-government, but separation from the USSR was deemed impossible because of their internal locations and small sizes. Minor groups received a status of "autonomous oblasts [regions]" ("AOs"), or units of lower rank.

Image and Reality
in Soviet Nationality Policy

The Soviet Union had managed to hold its diverse peoples together for more than seven decades after the Revolution of 1917. It was, in effect, the last of the world's great empires. During this period the British, French, Dutch, Belgians, and Portuguese saw their formerly huge imperial realms break up under pressures from subject peoples. The continued integrity of the Communist empire rested on several factors, including cosmetic concessions to national sentiments, centralized political control, economic interdependence, and coercion. All these centripetal forces weakened during the 1980s, leading eventually to disintegration of the USSR as a unified, coherent state.

Early Bolshevik nationality policy permitting establishment of the republics and other autonomous units initially dampened national passions for sovereignty. The nations of the former Russian Empire received a recognition and legitimacy that they had not enjoyed under the tsarist regime. They had their own formal governmental institutions embodying many traditional elements, including historic emblems of group identity and customary names for legislative bodies. More significantly, they had the right to utilize native languages in education and public affairs. They also had clearly marked territories designated as their own homelands.

Such concessions to national sensitivities were limited, however. The Soviet regime established a number of instrumentalities to assure that national feelings would not lead to separation from the state. A widely propagated slogan declared that the republics were "national in form, socialist in content." Chief among forces holding the country together was the Communist Party of the Soviet Union (CPSU).

The CPSU enjoyed a monopoly status in political activities. Opposition parties were forbidden. The alternative to CPSU membership was simply to be a "nonparty" person. Moreover, the CPSU maintained itself as a highly centralized body. Although up to 10 percent of the population belonged to the Communist party, an elite group of a half million worked full time on party affairs in the organization's Secretariat. It was this body that actually made decisions and ran the country. The General Secretary of the CPSU commanded the Secretariat and was, in effect, leader of the country, despite the existence of a formal governmental head of state. Joseph Stalin, Nikita Khrushchev, Leonid Brezhnev, Mikhail Gorbachev, and other Soviet leaders all achieved their dominant roles in the state by becoming party First Secretaries, although most subsequently assumed the formal governmental titles of Chairman of the Council of Ministers or President. The CPSU Secretariat maintained branches in all the nationality designated administrative divisions, but these were subject to exactly the same centralized controls and regulations of the CPSU's Politburo in Moscow as party units in provinces and districts of the sprawling RSFSR.

The CPSU organization dominated the rest of Soviet society. It reserved to itself the right to make all policy decisions, which then were ratified by corresponding formal governmental institutions. It also controlled the naming of key personnel in the government and economy. This *nomenklatura* of managers and officials was dependent upon continuing approval by local and central organs of the Secretariat. Such control served to minimize unwanted manifestations of national feelings in republics and autonomous areas. The Russian-dominated CPSU selected trusted natives to run regional and local organizations and to otherwise administer the non-Russian borderlands. As a precaution, it usually named a Russian to be second in command.

Another factor binding the national areas to each other was the development of interdependent regional economies. Areas that had traditionally raised their own food supply became highly specialized in a restricted number of crops that were traded with other regions. Formerly self-sufficient in food, Central Asia, for instance, came to devote most of its farmland to the raising of cotton. Its farmers were dependent upon the textile-producing region around Moscow as a market for their goods and upon Russian grain farms in the Volga region and western Siberia as the source of food supply. Major manufacturing industries in the national borderlands received economic commands, allocations of materials, and capital for equipment from ministries in Moscow. Most goods available to local populations were produced elsewhere and distributed through a cumbersome system of centralized planning and management. All regions of the Soviet state became dependent upon all others.

Fear was a significant element keeping national areas in line. During the 1930s Joseph Stalin destroyed virtually all his opponents. This period of purges witnessed execution of most national leaders. Subsequently, the Committee of State Security (KGB) maintained a substantial apparatus to detect and quell manifestations of nationalism. This body showed no hesitation to neutralize "harmful tendencies." The famed novelist Alexander Solzhenitsyn coined the term "Gulag Archipelago" to describe the extensive network across the USSR of forced-labor camps to which KGB victims were committed. People were fearful of any political expression. They could remember relatives and neighbors who disappeared after being denounced for uttering allegedly seditious statements.

Non-Russian nationality groups were also mindful of the forced removal from homelands of entire nations. In 1937 Stalin ordered that all 200,000 Koreans in the Soviet Far East be transported to the deserts of Soviet Central Asia on grounds that they were spies for Japan. At the end of World War II, he accused Crimean Tatars, Volga Germans, Kalmyks, Chechens, Meshketians, Ingush, Balkars, and others of group disloyalties. Special forces shipped them literally in boxcars from their traditional homelands to desolate areas in Central Asia. Victims included everyone—infants, the elderly, Communist party members, war heroes. All references to the existence of such groups were expunged from history books and encyclopedias. Party General Secretary Nikita Khrushchev, in a famed 1956 secret speech denouncing Joseph Stalin, reported that his predecessor had even considered expelling the 40,000,000 Ukrainians, but at length decided that they were simply too numerous.

A high proportion of these peoples perished during the forced migration and the privations found in their places of relocation. For many years they were not allowed to travel outside their places of resettlement. After more than a decade of exile, survivors were finally "rehabilitated" following Khrushchev's speech. Most were allowed to return to their traditional territories, but they then had to contend with Russians and others who had settled in their homes. The Crimean Tatars, Koreans, Turkic Meshketians of Georgia, and Volga Germans were not extended the privilege of return, however, and those who attempted to reenter their former areas were unceremoniously expelled. The fate of the deported nations had an effect upon other ethnic groups. Until the mid-1980s there were virtually no outward manifestations of national unhappiness.

The success of the Soviet Union in maintaining itself for so long in a world era of minority nationalism can also be attributed to inertia. For all its economic inefficiency and shortcomings, the USSR was an entity that managed to provide a relatively satisfactory life for its inhabitants. Its image of success was constantly reinforced by the regime's monopoly control of media that continually stressed attainments and ignored or minimized failings.

The Impact of Perestroika and Glasnost

Economic problems began to grow during the decade of the 1980s. The costs of a disastrous war in Afghanistan, the long neglect of an antiquated transportation and communications infrastructure, the decline in the profitability of export commodities, and the inefficiencies of a command economy combined to create serious shortages of food and other goods within the Soviet state. A change in direction was clearly needed. A reform-minded leader, Mikhail Gorbachev, at length achieved the post of Party First Secretary. His prescription for improving the situation was a fundamental restructuring (*perestroika*) of the system. He concluded that to accomplish such reorganization required a general candor (*glasnost*) in facing up to specific problems. Unlike his predecessors, he showed an unwillingness to use coercion to achieve goals.

The result was a revolution from above. Although the initial years of the Gorbachev regime saw few actual changes in the system's structure, openness became a watchword everywhere—there was little *perestroika* but an abundance of *glasnost*. No longer were harsh facts ignored or papered over. Everything could be examined and discussed. Such openness could not be confined to economic problems. For the national minorities it meant the ability for the first time to talk openly of what had happened in the past and to debate alternatives for the future. As seems to occur with the quickening of national awareness everywhere, a consensus quest for sovereignty emerged among all groups.

The groundwork for national separatism paradoxically had been created during the restrictive Brezhnev years (1964–1982). When Leonid Brezhnev came to power the Soviet regime had few concerns about national unrest. The principal manifestations were in the western Ukraine and Baltic states, and dissidents could rather easily be controlled. The Brezhnev regime placed an emphasis upon stability of institutions and personnel as a reaction to the "hare-brained" innovations of the preceding Khrushchev era, when a goal to make the economic system more efficient had led to an attempt to diminish the influence of central ministries and a proposal regularly to change top CPSU officials.

Under Brezhnev, a "corporatist state" emerged in which major governmental units were allowed to function as monopolies within their own spheres of activity. Leaders of each bureaucratic unit received greater authority over internal organization, and they found themselves contending with each other for investment funds as more-or-less equals. Although there were strong pressures to create greater economic and political centralization in Moscow, the regime also decided to support regional CPSU and governmental establishments in the quest for institutional stability. Among these were the cadres who ran the national republics.

Local Communist party organizations gained substantial new powers of patronage to fill key positions. They generally tended to adopt affirmative-action programs favoring their own titular nationalities. They championed local interests, including more industrial investment and restrictions on in-migration of Russians. They retained higher proportions of the so-called turnover tax, which gave them greater abilities to finance local projects and welfare programs. They gained wider latitude in running local affairs, which often meant a greater toleration of the "second economy" (black market). For some local elites these broader prerogatives constituted a license to steal. Top officials of the Uzbek SSR are estimated to have pocketed more than four billion rubles during the Brezhnev era, using such techniques as overreporting the amount of raw cotton delivered to state procurement agencies.

Within this greater toleration for local initiative, new native elites emerged, particularly in education and cultural affairs. They replaced past ill-prepared token native time-servers who had achieved their positions primarily by acts of loyalty to the Russian-dominated CPSU. Particularly concerned with the preservation of their languages and cultures, the new local leaderships reversed earlier pressures to assimilate their national groups. They provided organizational leadership for national movements as central coercive power declined.

By encouraging popular pressures from below, Gorbachev had sought to destabilize the fossilized bureaucratic system that he inherited. This was certainly accomplished. A key casualty, however, was the prestige of the Communist party itself. Everywhere there was a decline in respect for the party and its national and local leadership. The government's image also suffered. The unwillingness of the regime to use force was taken, perhaps justifiably, as evidence of a weakness under stress. Within this changed situation nationalism flourished. By mid-1990, thirteen of the fifteen SSRs had declared that their local laws superseded those of the USSR.

Gorbachev instituted *glasnost* particularly as a means to expose irrationality and fraud. In doing this he also opened up a past that had long been swept under the rug. Hitherto taboo topics became energizing pursuits in non-Russian areas. In the Baltic republics public attitudes focused on the Molotov–Ribbentrop pact between Germany and the USSR of August 23, 1939, which resulted in the incorporation of Latvia, Lithuania, and Estonia within the Soviet Union the following year. Popular discontent also was voiced over the constant immigration of Russians into the Baltic region in search of better jobs and living conditions.

Calls for separation occurred among all groups. They were fueled not only by national sentiments but also by a general reaction to the discredited Communist party and system of central planning. A concern to preserve local resources and to utilize domestic production for the benefit of home populations was widespread. There were even strong sentiments among Russians living on the Pacific seaboard to terminate Moscow's bureaucratic authority, perhaps in a Far Eastern Republic that had its precedent in a short-lived entity during the civil war.

The weakening and discrediting of central authorities, coupled with increasingly difficult economic times, led to *de facto* self-government in each of the republics. After a period of uncertain relationships between central and local bureaucratic organizations and the attempted coup led by the KGB to reassert Moscow's authority, the elected President of the Russian Republic, Boris Yeltsin, took the lead in forging an agreement with Ukraine and Belarus in December 1991, to create a Commonwealth [*Sodruzhestvo*] of Independent States. Although the Baltic states insisted upon complete independence, the leadership of eight of the remaining nine former Soviet republics agreed to join the founding trio. Only Georgia, beset by acute internal struggles for power, stayed out. The end of the Union of Soviet Republics was formalized on Christmas Day, 1991, by the resignation of its last president, Mikhail Gorbachev.

Problem Areas within the Russian Republic

Russia became an independent state with more than half the population and three-fourths of the territory of the former USSR. Although it no longer incorporated the majority of non-Russian territories acquired during the tsarist period, Russia continued to appear as an imperial entity to the 20 percent of its population who were not of Russian origin. The political forces that led to the independence of the fourteen SSRs continued to weigh upon virtually all the peoples of the sixteen so-called Autonomous Republics (ASSRs) and thirty lesser-ranking Autonomous Regions (*oblasti*) within the Russian Republic. Among the most vociferous demands for separation were those of the Chechens and Ingushes, the Tuvinians, and the Kazan Tatars.

Chechens and Ingushes. As the USSR disintegrated, leaders of the Chechens and Ingushes called for complete independence of their national groups. The two Muslim peoples live on the north slope of the Caucasus Mountains and adjacent plains region, and they speak variants of the distinctive Nakh Caucasian language family. Chechen and Ingush tribal groups grew apart during the nineteenth century when the more militant Chechens to the east resisted for several decades imperial incursions into their homeland, while Ingushes to the west tended to be more abiding of the Russians. The Chechens, commanded by their extraordinary leader Shamil, were finally subdued by Russian forces only in the 1850s. In 1918 each group formed its own National Soviet within a short-lived Terek Republic. Following territorial reorganizations, the Soviet regime eventually united the two into a Chechen–Ingush Autonomous Soviet Socialist Republic in 1936. Their ASSR prospered in the interwar years from development of a major oil field.

In 1944 the Soviet regime expelled all Chechens and Ingushes from their Caucasian homelands to the barren lands of northern Kazakhstan, charging group disloyalty during the German invasion. Of some 500,000 who had lived in the 7,000-square-mile Chechen–Ingush Republic on the eve of World War II, only 232,000 returned after its restoration in 1957. Those who came back had to accommodate to thousands of foreigners who had moved into their emptied towns and villages. In the 1989 census more than a quarter of the inhabitants of the restored republic were Russians.

In the uncertainties of the USSR following the August 1991 coup attempt, Chechens held massive demonstrations in their capital city of Grozny, calling for complete independence. Resistance to continued Russian domination did not heal long-standing differences between Chechens and Ingushes, however. Leaders indicated that each group wanted its own separate sovereignty. In 1992 Ingushes became involved in a bitter contest over territory with the North Ossetians, another North Caucasus Muslim group. Hundreds died

in the fighting. The Russian government sent 5,000 troops to patrol the region and maintain the peace.

The Tuvinians. The Tuvinian ASSR has an area of 66,000 square miles and a population of 300,000, one-third of whom are Russians. Tuvinians traditionally have engaged in nomadic cattle herding. They speak a Turkic language and have a Lamaistic Buddhist heritage. Tuva was treated by the Chinese and others as a part of Outer Mongolia. However, the Russian Empire made it a protectorate in 1914, following settlement there by a number of Russian traders. Tuvinians declared their independence during the turmoil of 1918, but found themselves caught between contending Bolsheviks, White Russians, Mongols, and Chinese. In 1921 the Red Army prevailed. The victors proclaimed establishment of the Tuvinian People's Republic (Tannu Tuva) as an independent state under Russian protection. An international commission recognized this status in 1926.

The USSR decided to annex Tannu Tuva in 1944. This was likely done to forestall possible future Chinese pretensions to the area. Initially the territory received a lower-order nationality status as the Tuvinian Autonomous Oblast. In 1961 it was raised to ASSR level. As part of the USSR, Tuvinians found themselves subject to abrupt transformations of their way of life. Traditional nomads were forcibly settled on the land. Buddhism was suppressed. By 1991, the republic had only one lama, and he was 94 years old. The number of Russians grew rapidly, reaching 40 percent of the population by 1959. They came to develop pioneer collective farmlands and to work in new mines and factories established by Soviet authorities. Thirty years later, despite a rather steady increase in numbers, their proportion had dropped to 32 percent. This reflected both a high Tuvinian rate of natural increase and mounting pressures by natives for Russians to leave the republic.

The nationalist winds of change of the 1980s in the USSR and adjacent Mongolia affected the Tuvinian ASSR. Tuvinians manifested deep resentment at injustices occurring under Soviet control and the large-scale in-migration of Russians. They became increasingly militant. By mid-1990, the Soviet government determined that it needed to counter increasing inter-ethnic clashes by deploying special Soviet "Black Beret" militia units to maintain order within the republic. Prominent Tuvinian political leaders demanded that the republic be raised from ASSR to SSR status. More radical elements questioned the validity of the original incorporation of Tuva within the Soviet Union and called for a return to independence. They also demanded the addition of territories of traditional grazing lands in adjacent Krasnoyarsk Krai and the Gorno–Altai region.

The Kazan Tatars. Despite being completely surrounded by Russian territory and having nearly as many Russians as Tatars among its inhabitants, the Tatar ASSR witnessed demands of its titular group for complete independence in 1991. The republic has a territory of 26,000 square miles and a population of 3,500,000. It lies at the great eastern bend of the Volga River, about 800 miles east of Moscow. Tatars dominate the countryside while Russians are a majority in the towns.

The Tatars speak a Turkic language. Their ancestors appeared in the Volga region in the seventh century, forming the successful state of Bolgar that included a substantial part of the Ural Mountains. In A.D. 922 they accepted Islam. Troops of Genghis Khan incorporated the Tatars into the famed Golden Horde in the early 1200s. Three centuries later they became the first major foreign group to be absorbed by the Russian state when Ivan the Terrible conquered them in 1552. After an initial period of persecution for their religion, they gained a degree of official toleration by the end of the eighteenth century and received special rights to trade with the Chinese, Central Asians, and Iranians. Their economy and culture prospered, and they developed a national consciousness during the second half of the nineteenth century. In the 1860s they were able to resist renewed Russian efforts toward Christianization and Russification.

In 1917, during the turmoil of the Russian Revolution, Tatar leaders proclaimed creation of an Idel–Ural state incorporating the similar Turkic-speaking Muslim Bashkirs of the southwestern Urals. However, the Bolsheviks divided the Tatars and Bashkirs into separate ASSRs in 1919/20. Three-quarters of the Tatars were left outside their nominal republic, mainly in Bashkiria. Most Tatar leaders viewed this as an attempt to weaken Muslim unity in the Volga–Ural region, although a wide gulf already existed between the seminomadic Bashkirs and the more settled Tatar farmers.

The present demands for complete independence in an enclave surrounded by Russian territory reflect long-suppressed Kazan Tatar unhappiness with a low-ranking ASSR status within the USSR, despite the fact that their numbers were greater than those of the Estonians, Latvians, Tajiks, Turkmens, or Kirgiz, all of whom enjoyed constituent republic rank. The weakening of Soviet controls over nationalist expression also permitted Tatars open expression of long-standing covetousness for neighboring Bashkiria. As part of their demands for Tatar sovereignty, the Tatars insisted upon annexation of the territory of the Bashkir ASSR. Not to be outdone, Bashkir leaders demanded incorporation of the Tatar ASSR within their own republic. Potentials for conflict resemble such traditional Balkan problems as antagonisms between Macedonians and Bulgars or Serbs and Croats.

The Russian regime has responded to declarations of independence by its ethnic enclaves by proposing a new system that would eliminate the complex internal pattern of autonomies inherited from the Soviet Union. A draft plan for a federal constitution plan was offered in November 1993 that would make the twenty-one ethnic units equal in status to the sixty-seven predominantly Russian provinces (*oblasti*) in the state. It replaced an earlier draft that would have declared each ethnic territory a "sovereign state." In part the proposal addressed concerns for regional autonomy surfacing in the Russian provinces. Some units, such as Sverdlovsk (Yekaterinburg) Oblast, had declared themselves "republics." Particularly strong feelings emerged in the remote provinces on the Pacific slope.

Pressures for border revision. During the disintegration of the Soviet Union in 1990/91, a number of ethnic groups within the Russian Republic called for revision of homeland boundaries. Karelians sought the southern part of Murmansk Oblast, and Kalmyks demanded parts of Rostov Oblast and Stavropol Krai. In Siberia, Buriats demanded control of a Buriat enclave within Chita Oblast. Yakuts sought rectifications of their ASSR border with Magadan Oblast. Even the 150,000 so-called Northern Peoples, consisting of at least twenty-six separate groups, demanded greater control of their environment and natural resources, which included much of Russia's diamonds, gold, petroleum, and coal.

Ukraine

Second largest of the successor states to the USSR is Ukraine. Its 230,000 square miles and 52,000,000 inhabitants make it comparable in size and population to France. Unlike that state, however, Ukraine has not enjoyed the prerogatives of being a sovereign entity. Its name literally means "borderland," and its fate has been to serve as a frontier zone contested among Russians, Poles, Habsburgs, and Turks. Its inhabitants have found themselves the recipients of contending pressures for assimilation by their neighbors, which have resulted in significant regional differences in Ukrainian culture. Although a sense of national identity developed among Ukrainians during the nineteenth century, it took quite different directions in the Habsburg and Russian empires.

Ukrainians east of the Dnieper River generally acknowledge a Russian heritage. Individuals running away from serfdom in the sixteenth and seventeenth centuries formed communities beyond tsarist control in the rich grasslands of central and eastern Ukraine. They adopted the name Cossacks, a term derived from a Turkic term meaning "free man" and related to the Central Asian designation "Kazakh." The Cossacks borrowed techniques and life styles from Tatars and other groups with whom they contended for territory. Following establishment of an effective presence by Russia in the early nineteenth century, the region saw settlement by new Russian immigrants and also by Serbs, Bulgars, and other Balkan peoples. In the 1850s the southern margins of the Ukraine were actually identified as "New Serbia." Development of the mineral-rich Donets Basin brought further waves of Russians. From Kiev eastward, Ukrainians largely came to use the Russian language and cherish their Russian Orthodox religious heritage.

Western Ukrainians developed their distinctive culture during centuries of subordination to Roman Catholic Lithuanians, Poles, and Austrians. Although part of the Eastern Orthodox religious world, their clergy found it desirable to acknowledge the spiritual supremacy of Rome. The resulting "Uniate" religion retained Eastern Orthodox Christian rituals while accepting papal authority. Western Ukrainians developed a strong sense of national identity after becoming part of the Habsburg Empire at the end of the eighteenth century. The Austrians encouraged this as a means of weakening Russian authority in the eastern Ukraine.

The two Ukrainian groups were united in 1940 when the Soviet Union annexed 171,000 square miles of territory from Poland and Romania. Ukrainians in the west lived mainly in rural villages, the towns being inhabited primarily by Poles and Jews. The majority of the latter did not survive the war, and the Soviet regime pressed Poles to emigrate westward. Most needed little encouragement, moving to towns and villages in western lands newly annexed to Poland from which the former German inhabitants had been expelled. Thus, a high proportion of the Polish population of the city of Lviv resettled in the Silesian city of Wroclaw (Breslau), whereas Russian immigrants moved into their former homes and enterprises in Lviv.

Western Ukrainians actively resisted their incorporation in the Soviet Union. In 1941 crowds actually welcomed invading Nazi troops as liberators from Communist tyranny. However, their enthusiasm was short-lived, for the Germans preserved the hated communist collective farms and otherwise ruled Ukrainians with an iron fist. Many were drafted for factory work in the Third Reich. Following conclusion of the war, western Ukrainian guerrillas fought reestablishment of Soviet authority for many months. As a consequence, the regime discriminated against the entire population of the region for many years after the war.

The Ukrainian SSR conspicuously remained on the sidelines during the ferment at the end of the 1980s leading to the breakup of the Soviet Union. Its Communist leadership suppressed the types of nationalist manifestations that came to dominate the Baltic republics, the Transcaucasus, and even Russia itself. The republic had an ethnically diverse population, and few responsible individuals could visualize a future separate from the markets and raw materials of Russia. Following the August 1991 attempted coup in the USSR, however, Ukrainian leaders reversed their course and opted for complete independence. Sweeping manifestations of nationalism followed, including official adoption of the Ukrainian language, despite its unfamiliarity to some 30 percent of the republic's inhabitants who considered themselves Ukrainians. Sovereignty also brought an intensification of problems with the additional quarter of the population that did not see themselves as Ukrainian.

Russian-inhabited areas of Ukraine. The declaration of Ukrainian independence made inhabitants of eastern and southern parts of Ukraine uneasy. Most saw themselves as Russians. Few had sympathy with the militant Ukrainian nationalism of the west. Many Russians feared their own change in status from being members of the USSR's dominant nation to becoming minorities in a Ukrainian nation state.

Particularly aggrieved were residents of the Crimean Peninsula, whose oblast the Soviet regime transferred from the RSFSR to the Ukrainian SSR only in 1954 in commemoration of the three hundredth anniversary of the declaration of affiliation with Russia by Bohdan Khmelnitsky, an early Cossack leader. Soviet authorities had designated the peninsula a Crimean Tatar ASSR in 1920, but the unit was abolished in 1944 on grounds of group collaboration with the Germans. The regime deported a quarter million Crimean Tatars, Bulgarians, Greeks, and others to Uzbekistan and other parts of Central Asia. Nearly 8,000 died in transit and another 44,000 perished during the first five years of exile.

The Tatars remained in limbo long after similarly exiled groups officially had been "rehabilitated." By 1990 their numbers had grown to 300,000. They were noted for public demonstrations in Tashkent, Moscow, and elsewhere, calling for the right to resettle in their homeland. This right was denied them until nearly the end of the Soviet era. After Ukraine declared its independence, however, it was the peninsula's preponderantly Russian inhabitants who were in the forefront in demands for a return to autonomous status or even Crimean sovereignty. Their cultural and economic ties had always been to Moscow rather than Kiev, Ukraine's capital. Even inhabitants who were of Ukrainian origin had become Russianized. Ukraine did grant autonomous status to the Crimea, recognizing its overwhelmingly Russian character. In early 1994 the region elected as president an advocate of union with Russia.

Russians also predominated in the southern part of the former Bessarabian region of Romania between the port city of Odessa and the Danube. They too grew uneasy about living in an independent Ukraine, although they also worried about pretensions to their territory by both Romania and the ex-Soviet state of Moldova. Romania also has raised claims to the Ukrainian territory of northern Bukovina, which was, like Bessarabia, annexed by the Soviet regime in 1940. Ukraine also has inherited a potential dispute with Poland over the western Ukraine and contending Hungarian and Slovak claims to the Ruthenian lands of the Carpathian Mountains. On the other hand, it is mindful of Ukrainian historic interests in northern Moldova and eastern Slovakia.

Moldova. The Russian Empire acquired large numbers of Romanians in 1830 when it pushed its borders against the Ottoman Empire southwestward to the Prut River, incorporating the province of Bessarabia. Romania seized the region in 1918. Subsequently, the Soviet regime exerted continuous political pressure for its return. This included establishment of a Moldavian ASSR within the Ukrainian SSR in 1924 to serve as a socialist alternative to the Romanian state, even though Romanians constituted only a small part of the new ASSR's population. After finally gaining Romania's return of Bessarabia in 1940, the USSR constituted its northern part as a Moldavian SSR, to which were added several parts of the former ASSR where Romanian was spoken. The rest of the ASSR reverted to the Ukraine.

During the decade of the 1980s Moldavian nationalism began to flourish. Symbolically, the local regime replaced the Cyrillic alphabet by the Latin orthography used by the Romanians. However, given the distressing economic and political regime in Romania, Moldavian nationalists did not exhibit an irredentist stance. The Moldavian SSR finally declared independence in 1991, insisting that its territory be identified internationally by its Romanian-language form, "Moldova." (Northeastern Romania is also known as Moldova.)

While Moldovans happily saw an end to their domination by Moscow, they showed little tolerance for non-Moldovan national sentiments within their young state. Particularly resistant to being part of an independent Moldova were the Gagauz, a Turkish-speaking Christian group in the southern part of the SSR. Their origins appear to have been in Bulgaria. Although they numbered only 175,000, the Gagauz agitated for their own separate republic in 1990. The Moldova government used force to suppress the protests, and it subsequently had to contend with efforts of Russians and Ukrainians in its northern section to declare their area of settlement a separate republic. Russians in units of the army of the former Soviet Union gave support to the separatists, who were resisting incorporation into both Moldova and Ukraine.

The Baltic States

As the Soviet empire weakened during the 1980s, the three Baltic republics were among the most adamant in pressing for local control of their own affairs. Even leaders of the Communist parties of Estonia, Latvia, and Lithuania sought increasingly to separate themselves from interests perceived as Russian and to call for true autonomy if not actual political separation. Popular opposition to external domination provoked a number of conflict situations during the period immediately preceding the USSR's collapse. Attempts by authorities in Moscow to intimidate the Baltic peoples resulted instead in strengthening local resolve. In the immediate aftermath of the failed Soviet coup of August 1991, which had sought to reimpose strong central authority throughout the state, the three constituent Baltic republics were among the first to declare complete independence from the USSR. Their leaderships adamantly refused to join their countries with Russia in the proposed post-Soviet "Commonwealth of Independent States."

Estonia, Latvia, and Lithuania, together with Finland and Byelorussia, form the northern wing of what frequently has been termed the "shatterbelt" of Eastern Europe. Like Poland and the former Czechoslovakia and Yugoslavia, they occupy areas intermediate between powerful and covetous societies that long have sought to dominate them. They likely will retain such an unenviable situation well into the future. Over the past thousand years the Baltic territories have been fought over by Danes, Swedes, Germans, Poles, and Russians. The Baltic peoples constituted the last bastion of European paganism before their conversion to Christianity in the thirteenth century, and they then became a zone of contention among Eastern Orthodox, Roman Catholic, and Protestant religions. Despite centuries of impress by foreign conquerors, the Baltic peoples managed to maintain their distinctive cultures and, during the nineteenth century, to develop strong senses of national identity.

Their languages are some of the oldest and least modified tongues to be found in Europe. Estonian is part of the Finno-Ugrian linguistic family that extends across Eurasia from northern Scandinavia to the Taimyr Peninsula and includes Finns, Lapps, Karelians, Magyars, Udmurts, and Mordvinians. The Latvian and Lithuanian languages are surviving members of the quite different Indo-European Baltic family that once included the now extinct Prussian language. Many linguists believe that the Baltic languages are closest to the speech of the original proto-Indo-European culture hearth. They represent the nearest European languages to the ancient Sanskrit employed in holy writings of the Hindus. Over the centuries Latvian has grown apart from Lithuanian, reflecting a split in allegiances between the Scandinavia/Lutheran realm and the Polish/Roman Catholic world.

All three peoples had national awakenings during the nineteenth century. Their differing languages and cultural traditions precluded emergence of a joint Baltic national entity, but they have cooperated with each other economically and politically much as the Dutch, Flemings, and Walloons in the similar Lotharingian shatterzone. Their populations reflect a history of outside domination. Many Baltic individuals proudly trace their ancestry to past Swedish or German implanted families. The large Russian minority is a legacy of the most recent overlordship of the region.

The combined area of the three states is under 70,000 square miles, and their populations total approximately 7,000,000. The Baltic states occupy a stony glaciated section of the north European plain in a high-latitude climate rather marginal for commercial farming. Aside from oil shales in northeastern Estonia, they notably lack mineral resources and fuels. Their position well north of Europe's belt of high population density has precluded land improvement comparable to the poldering (land reclaimed from the sea) of the more favorably situated Netherlands and Flanders. The position of the Baltic states was more favorable in an earlier era when their port cities of Riga and Tallinn participated in the medieval Hanseatic League of communities that traded around the Baltic Sea.

In contrast to the intermingling of peoples characteristic of the Balkan lands, the three Baltic groups occupy rather discrete territories. There are few situations of minorities living on the "wrong" side of a political border. This is rather remarkable, for traditional territorial units generally did not correspond to ethnolinguistic patterns as they did in historic Croatia or Bohemia. Although a strip of territory along the Gulf of Finland historically was known as Estonia, Estonians also lived with Letts (Latvians) in the adjacent territory of Livonia to the south. Lithuanians lived mainly in what became the great medieval state of Lithuania, but many lived among Letts in the historic Courland territory lying south of the Dvina River between Livonia and Lithuania.

The Baltic peoples were organized into pagan tribal entities well into European history. The Roman writer Tacitus notes the existence of their thriving trade in amber with the Mediterranean region. They often were subject to struggles with adventurers from Scandinavia and Finland. In the thirteenth century Estonians and Letts came under control of the Brothers of the Sword, a group of German crusaders who eventually merged into the medieval Teutonic Order that came to control the eastern Baltic coast. Lithuania grew into a large and powerful state following unification of its tribes in the thirteenth century and acceptance of Western Christianity. It acquired vast lands to the south and east in the wake of destruction of the Kievan Rus state by forces of Genghis Khan.

The Estonians and Letts eventually became part of Sweden and then, during the eighteenth century, they were acquired by Peter the Great of Russia. The Russians decided to allow members of the existing German ruling class to retain privileges and positions. Lithuania remained part of the Kingdom of Poland until Poland's dismemberment in the 1790s, when it too became part of Russia. For much of their existence within the tsarist empire the Baltic peoples enjoyed greater privileges and liberties than did Russians themselves. Their favored position ended in the 1890s as the beleaguered empire increasingly attempted to Russify its diverse peoples.

Baltic independence came with the Russian Empire's collapse in 1917. It was backed by German and, later, British and French military support. There followed two decades of self-rule during the perilous economic and political times of the 1920s and 1930s. Germany conceded the Baltic lands to the USSR in a secret protocol of the 1939 Molotov–Ribbentrop nonaggression pact that apportionioned Eastern Europe between Germany and the USSR. The Soviet Union then invaded the Baltic states in the summer of 1940 and declared them internal republics of the USSR. Collectivized agriculture and other Soviet institutions were imposed, and large numbers of educated citizens were deported to remote parts of the Soviet Union. In the following year Germans occupied the territories during their invasion of the USSR, only to be ousted in 1944. The Baltic populations suffered great losses of life at this time, including extermination of virtually all the region's Jewish inhabitants.

As Soviet troops approached from the east, large numbers of Baltic peoples retreated with German forces or sought refuge across the Baltic Sea in Sweden. The Soviet reoccupation saw significant resistance by Baltic guerrilla fighters until the 1950s. Additional massive deportations of intellectuals occurred after the war. For many years fear of the region's vulnerability to Western invasion led the Soviet regime to invest few funds for economic development. At length, investments were poured into the region to build factories and other facilities to take advantage of the skills and work ethic of the populations. The Baltic region then became the most thriving part of the Soviet Union, principally because of its high labor productivity and its access to undervalued raw materials from other parts of the USSR.

In the 1960s the noticeably higher living standards of the Baltic republics began to draw many Russians and Ukrainians to the region, where they found ready employment in lower status activities. As a result of the early deportations and this large influx of Slavs, the proportion of ethnic Latvians in Latvia dropped from 75 percent before World War II to barely half the population by the early 1990s. Estonians similarly were diluted from 90 percent to barely 60 percent of their territory's inhabitants. Lithuania suffered the least from an influx of foreigners, and Lithuanians now make up 80 percent of its population.

Since the fall of the USSR the future of Slavs living in the Baltic states has become a source of friction with Russia. The new governments have sought to restrict citizenship to those who inhabited the states before World War II or to their direct descendants. Opportunities to acquire citizenship remain open to all who reside in the new countries, but only after passing examinations demonstrating knowledge of the local language. This provision reflects anger by the Baltic peoples that Russians and Ukrainians generally did not attempt to learn local vernaculars.

Although the new Baltic regimes made clear their opposition to continued association with the Russians in the post-Soviet Commonwealth of Independent States, they became painfully aware of how dependent they were upon markets and low-cost raw materials of other parts of the former USSR. In particular, they came to understand that they were in no position to pay world market prices for oil and natural gas. Like other former Soviet republics, they found it necessary to expand economic ties with the Russians. In Lithuania the strong national political movement that assumed power with the breakup of the USSR lost out in a subsequent election to a party principally composed of former Communist officials.

Estonia

Estonians witnessed Varangian adventurers from Sweden as early as the ninth century, and Swedes and Danes unsuccessfully sought to Christianize them in both the eleventh and twelfth centuries. Knights of the Sword pushed northward into Livonia in the thirteenth century at a time that Danes were establishing their own authority along the north coast and offshore islands. (The name of the Estonian capital, Tallinn, means "Dane town.") The Danes sold their interests to the Teutonic Knights in 1346, and Germans ran the country thereafter.

Ivan the Terrible of Russia seized northeastern Estonia in the sixteenth century, but he was forced to yield it to Sweden several years later. Swedes later encroached upon Estonia from the west and Lithuania pushed from the south, following the dissolving of the Order of Teutonic Knights. By 1629 all Estonian lands had come under Swedish control. Estonians accepted Sweden's reformed Evangelical Lutheran faith and adopted many Scandinavian attributes. (From the point of view of national iconography it is interesting to note that some of independent Estonia's first postage stamps after World War I featured a Viking sailing ship.) In 1709, the Russians under Peter the Great acquired Estonia and held it until 1917.

Estonia, with backing by occupying Germans, proclaimed its independence following the Bolshevik coup in Russia and sustained it with the support of Finns and a British naval squadron after Germany's capitulation in the ensuing year. After two decades of independence Estonia became part of the USSR in the summer of 1940. More than 60,000 of its citizens were immediately deported or killed, 10,000 in one night. It sustained substantial additional losses in the ensuing German invasion and reoccupation by the Red Army.

Since becoming independent, Estonia has received economic assistance from Sweden and Finland, and in many ways the country is reclaiming its Norden heritage. It has also found it necessary to achieve some kind of accommodation with Russia. However, some political-geographic problems remain with its large neighbor to the east. These include territories transferred to adjacent Pskov Oblast after Estonia's incorporation into the USSR and the future of the large Russian minority, which actually forms a majority in the northeastern regions of Estonia.

Latvia

The Latvian lands endured much the same history of foreign occupation as their Estonian neighbors. The historic territories of Livonia and Courland were controlled for centuries by the German Brothers of the Sword and their successors, the Teutonic Knights. Latvians also endured periods of domination by Lithuanians and Swedes. From the latter, like the Estonians, they acquired their Evangelical Lutheran faith and many other Scandinavian traditions. Russians acquired much of Livonia including the Latvian capital of Riga from Sweden in 1711 and annexed the rest of the territory in the three partitions of Poland at the end of the eighteenth century. As in Estonia, landlords and the ruling class remained mainly German.

Latvians proclaimed their independence after the 1917 Bolshevik coup in Russia, but immediately faced a rival Communist government advanced by the Soviet regime. German occupation armies remained to defend the region and German East Prussia against the Red Army with Allied approval after the armistice that ended World War I. Following German withdrawal, Latvia's independence was supported by troops from Estonia and a British naval squadron. The Soviet government renounced all claims to Latvia in 1920.

Like Estonia, Latvia suffer massive deportations of its citizens following invasions by the Soviet Union in 1940 and again in 1944, after a period of German occupation. It is estimated that more than 100,000 Latvians fled to Germany and Sweden with the Soviet advance, after which 100,000 more were deported to northern Russia and Siberia. Since reestablishment of independence in 1991, Latvia faces pressures from Russia about the status of its large Slavic minority, but it appears to have no outstanding territorial questions with its neighbors. It too has received economic assistance from the Norden countries and is gradually again becoming a part of that European region.

Lithuania

Unlike the two neighboring Baltic peoples who accepted Evangelical Lutheran Protestantism during a period of Swedish control, Lithuanians through their long association with Poland remained loyal to Roman Catholicism. Their ancestors were the last pagans in Europe, converting to Christianity only in the year 1387. This act removed the principal reason for existence of the Teutonic Knights, who disbanded not long afterward. Some obviously pagan traditions still persist in the countryside. Lithuanians notably lack the Scandinavian traditions found in Latvia and Estonia, but since independence in 1991 they are reclaiming their Central European heritage.

After establishing a formal kingdom from a union of several tribes in 1253, Lithuanians built a huge empire in the fourteenth and early fifteenth centuries, principally from Kievan Rus lands that had been ravaged by the forces of Genghis Khan. During the sixteenth century they struggled with Muscovites, who claimed rights to all former Kievan territory. This prompted a strong Lithuanian union with Poland and saw Lithuanian nobles increasingly Polonized. At the end of the eighteenth century Russia acquired Lithuania's Slavic-speaking lands in the first two partitions of Poland. In the third partition, in 1795, all of Lithuania became part of the Russian Empire, aside from a small region in the southwest that went to Prussia. Russianization became particularly harsh for the Lithuanians after Polish rebellions against Russian rule in the 1830s. They could not use their language in public and any printed publications in Lithuanian had

to be in the Cyrillic alphabet. This regulation lasted until 1905.

Like the other Baltic states, Lithuania proclaimed its independence at the end of World War I while under German occupation. In 1919 the Soviet army invaded the country, but Polish forces expelled it by midyear. Although Soviet Russia soon conceded Lithuanian independence, the young state early faced problems with its southern and western neighbors. Many Poles considered Lithuania to be a rightful part of Poland. In 1919 a Polish army seized the traditional capital of Vilnius with its environs, and in the following year established a separate government of Central Lithuania with jurisdiction over a 5,000-square-mile territory. Poland annexed the region in 1922, but Lithuania never recognized Polish control. Lithuania also antagonized the Germans in 1923 by seizing the East Prussian port town of Memel (Klaipeda) to provide an outlet to the sea, although Memel had never been part of a Lithuanian state. One of the first acts of World War II was German reacquisition of Memel.

The Soviet Union imposed itself upon Lithuania in 1939 at the time of its joint invasion of Poland with Germany. In partitioning the Soviet share of the conquered Polish territory among its Ukrainian and Byelorussian republics it granted the Vilnius area to Lithuania. This seemingly magnanimous gesture was followed a year later by Soviet annexation of all of Lithuania, deporting 35,000 intellectuals and others to the USSR's northern and eastern territories. Germans entered Lithuania in 1941.and held it until 1944. A quarter-million Lithuanians perished during this period, mainly Jews sent to German death camps. The Soviet Union's return was followed by deportations eastward of at least 200,000 additional Lithuanians.

Since attainment of independence in 1991 Lithuania has faced problems similar to those of its Baltic neighbors. Its relations with Russia have not faced as great strains over the future of Slavic minorities, since far fewer Russians and Ukrainians had moved into the country. A potential problem existed over future Russian linkages with Kaliningrad Oblast, the former USSR's share of East Prussia annexed from Germany after World War II. That 6,000-square-mile entity was separated from overland connection with the main body of Russia by Lithuanian territory, a circumstance not unlike the position of Alaska with the rest of the United States. Agreement was reached in 1992 that allowed easy movement of Russian rail and truck transport across Lithuanian territory.

More acrimonious were frictions with Poland over the rights of settlements of Polish farmers living within its southern border region. Although the Poles did not raise claims to the city of Vilnius, the newly independent Belarus state did. It is ironic that throughout much of its history Vilnius did not witness majorities of Lithuanians, Poles, or Byelorussians, but rather principally was home to a large Jewish population.

Belarus

The government of the newly independent state of Belarus has successfully pressed for adoption of a transliteration of its name from the local language. Before 1991, Belarus was known as Byelorussia, a designation based on transliteration from the Russian language. Like Lithuania, the territory of Belarus has long been a zone of contention between Poland and Russia. This 80,000-square-mile republic derives its name from the breakup of the Kievan Rus into four parts after the Mongol conquest in the thirteenth century. The term means "White Russia," and the area was distinguished from Lithuanian-held "Black Russia" to the north. To the east lay "Great Russia" and to the south "Little Russia," or the Ukraine. The Belarus population speaks a Slavic language that is transitional between Polish and Russian. It had no written form until the Soviets created one in the 1920s. Before that time its educated populace wrote in either Russian or Polish, and many continued to do so after the October Revolution. Even today, the standard language in towns is Russian, although nationalists now are pressing for more general use of the Belarus language.

Long control of parts of Belarus by the Roman Catholic Lithuanians and Poles is evident in the continuing presence of the Uniate religion, which retains Russian Orthodox forms of worship but acknowledges the primacy of the Roman Catholic pope. The majority of Belarus citizens, however, retain allegiance to traditional Russian Orthodoxy.

The Belarus population long was outside the mainstream of Russian nationalist development. Its populace began thinking of itself as a distinctive group mainly in the aftermath of the Bolshevik assumption of power and creation of the Belarus Soviet Socialist Republic in 1919. Although occupying Germans had fostered a Belarus declaration of independence the previous year, the Soviet action appears to have been done particularly to weaken Poland's grip on its Belarus minority, much as the Moldavian and Karelo-Finnish SSRs were founded to create problems for Romania and Finland, respectively. Poland annexed the western part of the Belarus Republic in 1921, reinstating a boundary established in the first eighteenth century partition of Poland. Poland's claim was based on the predominantly Polish population of towns, which also had large numbers of Jewish inhabitants. Rural areas were almost entirely inhabited by the Belarus population, however. The rump Belarus territory left to the USSR subsequently was augmented by additions of substantial Belarus-inhabited regions that in the past had been considered parts of Russia proper.

In 1939 the Soviet Union reannexed the Belarus lands that earlier had been lost to Poland. The German invasion of the USSR followed in 1941, and all Belarus lands were occupied. Significant partisan guerrilla activity based in the country's dense forests hampered German supply of front lines to the east.

Three quarters of the population identifies itself as members of the Belarus nation. Small numbers of Poles and Russians live in Belarus. Most Poles were expelled westward to Poland at the end of World War II. The Russian minority increased significantly by migration that began in the 1960s. Large numbers of Jews had emigrated to America and other countries at the turn of the twentieth century, and those who remained largely were lost in the holocaust of World War II.

Post-Soviet Belarus has few frictions with its neighbors. It signed an accord with Poland that recognized their present boundary as permanent and it has sought greater alliance with the Poles. Frictions exist with Ukraine over the aftereffects of the Chernobyl nuclear incident in northern Ukraine that rendered uninhabitable large tracts of southeastern Belarus.

Central Asia

The vast Central Asian realm of the former USSR contains primarily Muslim peoples speaking a Turkic language (Figure 7-3). Before the Russian conquest of the 1860s, political allegiances were to clan or tribe. Nominal control of the area was exerted by three feudal emirates. The Russians preserved two of these, Bukhara and Khiva, as "protectorates" and organized the remainder of the region, including the Kokand emirate, into a Governor-Generalship of "Turkestan." Identity of the local inhabitants beyond clan or tribe was essentially religious, although there was general recognition of Central Asian lands being part of a broad realm known as Turan with a spiritual center in the ancient silk-route town of Samarkand. The educated found common cause with fellow Muslims in Russia, Iran, the Ottoman Empire, and Arabia. Like other peoples of the Russian Empire, Central Asians rapidly developed political consciousness during the turmoil of Russia's Revolution and civil war. A significant part of the emergent militant national feelings reflected resentment at the acquisition of lands and authority by Russians who came into the area in the wake of conquest. A variety of local self-governing units emerged.

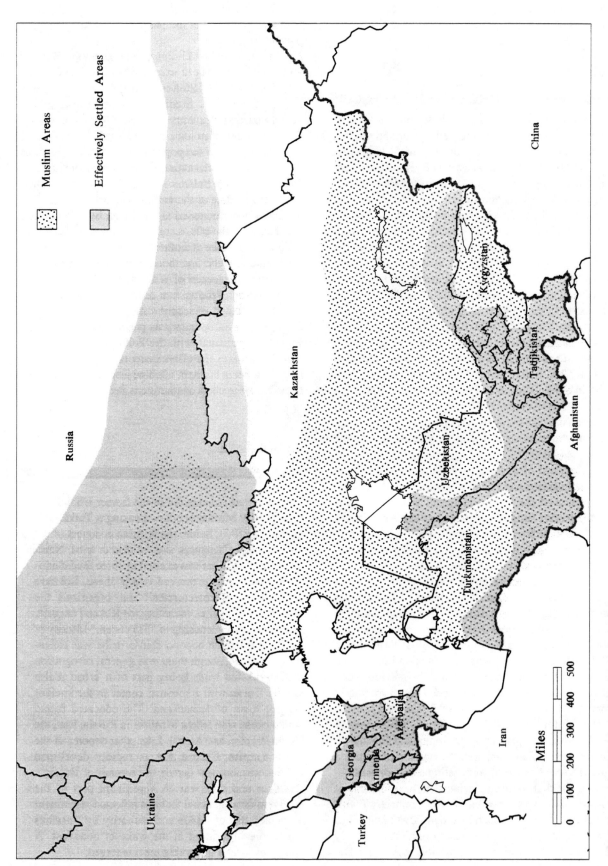

FIGURE 7-3 MUSLIMS IN THE FORMER SOVIET LANDS

In 1924 the Soviet regime redrew the map of Central Asia, giving separate territorial recognition to a number of groups. Settled peoples along the Syr Darya and Amu Darya rivers of the former Bukhara and Khiva emirates were organized into an Uzbek SSR. Nomadic tribes to the west were organized into a Turkmen SSR and Iranian-speaking Tajik tribes of the southern mountains and valleys into a Tajik SSR. The northern deserts and steppelands with their nomadic herdsmen were incorporated into the Russian republic as the Kazakh ASSR, within which was an autonomous region (oblast) for the Karakalpaks, who lived near the Aral Sea. Nomadic tribal groups of the eastern mountains also were made a part of the RSFSR, first as a Kirgiz Autonomous Region and then, in 1926, as a Kirgiz ASSR. A second territorial reorganization in 1936 saw Kazakh and Kirgiz republics raised to SSR status, while the Karakalpaks were transferred to the Uzbek SSR as an ASSR. As in the states of Eastern Europe, the drawing of new boundaries to separate ethnic groups was exceedingly difficult. Problems were particularly complex in the enclosed Fergana Valley region of the south, where the borders of Uzbekistan, Tajikistan, and Kyrgyzstan were quite irregular, including several detached enclaves in mountainous regions. The superimposed lines disrupted established economic interdependence within a number of local regions, since, under the Communist system, decision making was transferred from localities to bureaucracies in widely separated republic capitals.

Secular national identities developed within the new republics, as traditional forces binding peoples of Turan to each other and to other Middle Eastern peoples were severed. The common territory in which groups had interacted with each other for centuries became fragmented into separate administrative areas. Individuals found themselves natives in only one of these parts and foreigners in all the others. In 1928 the Soviet government replaced by Latin script the Arabic alphabet used in writing indigenous literary languages and also the Persian and Turkish languages. The Latin alphabet also had been adopted in post-Ottoman Turkey. Perhaps to distance Central Asia from Turkic cultures abroad, the regime subsequently replaced the Latin alphabet by Cyrillic in 1940. Islam suffered severe repression similar to that which befell other religions in the Soviet Empire. Mosques were closed and turned into warehouses or cinemas. Pilgrimages to Mecca became impossible for all but token groups drawn from loyal supporters of the Communist regime.

Despite the repressions, Central Asia prospered economically as much as any part of the USSR during the Communist era. Farmers received high prices for the cotton they raised. Factories appeared throughout the region. Cities and towns expanded, Tashkent overtaking Gorky (Nizhnii Novgorod) as the fourth largest city in the Soviet Union. Public health measures ended endemic scourges and prolonged longevity.

As in other colonial areas, modernization did not bring local gratitude, although it did encourage national identity. Native intellectuals, all of whom owed educations and opportunities to the Russian-led Communist system, began dwelling on past glories under leaders such as Tamerlane, who conquered much of India (although, in fact, he was regarded as an enemy by Central Asian inhabitants of the time). They reminded their peoples of illustrious histories. They restored architectural monuments and called attention to medieval Turanian attainments in culture, science, and engineering. They pressed for increasing ties with Muslims outside the Soviet Union. Some demanded a return to the Arabic alphabet. Intellectuals also were in the forefront of agitation directed against Russians living in the area who were perceived as having privileged positions. Many Russians responded to such pressures by leaving the region.

The deterioration of central controls further encouraged the Central Asian nationalists. However, they showed less inclination toward separation from Russia than occurred in the Baltic or Caucasus republics. Most were mindful of their economic dependence upon the rest of the Soviet state. It was really Russia that separated itself from Central Asia. Russian president Boris Yeltsin effectively terminated bonds by engineering an agreement with the two other Slavic republics to end the USSR and to make the Soviet republics independent states with options of joining a loose commonwealth.

As in the new states of Eastern Europe between the world wars, achievement of sovereignty brought its own problems. The peoples of Central Asia had become true nations. Their homelands had unquestioned cores, but mixed-population borderlands were subject to conflicting claims. Proof for one nation based upon an area's preponderance in numbers of its group was contested by a neighboring group on the basis of historic associations with ancestral states. For such reasons, Tajiks sought annexation of the adjacent southern tip of Uzbekistan, and Kazakhs pressed claims to a substantial part of northern Kyrgyzia and to the Karakalpak ASSR.

Divisions exist also within the new states. Tajikistan experienced internecine struggles almost immediately after achieving independence. Differences appear based upon clan and religious affiliations. The new regime in the capital Dushanbe represented the republic's population that became urbanized and secularized during the Soviet era. It was challenged by outlying clans avowedly seeking a more fundamentalist Islamic state. Tens of thousands died in a bloody civil war. Particularly strong opposition came from Ismaili Muslims on the border with Afghanistan. They were aided by Afghan Tajiks who had been guerrilla fighters against Soviet forces in the Afghanistan war and who see the present Tajik regime as Russian-inspired. Russia sent a rifle division and a division of border guards armed with helicopters, tanks, and heavy artillery to aid the Tajik government. It clearly worried about the prospect of Muslim fundamentalism spreading to its other former colonial areas of Kyrgyzstan and Uzbekistan, threatening future economic ties to the Russian Republic.

At least one prominent leader from Uzbekistan sought in 1990 to unite Central Asians by reorganizing the region into a single state of Turan. He cited their common history, Muslim heritage, and similar languages. His proposal called for a capital city to be located not in the dominant metropolis of Tashkent, but in the traditional regional center of Samarkand. It is doubtful that general acceptance of a common state could be attained, however. More than six decades of territorial segregation have reinforced or created separate national identities that would resist merger more strongly in the decade of the 1990s than at the time of the Russian Revolution. The negative experience of efforts to establish a somewhat similar Mali Federation among mainly Muslim former French West African colonies does not lend optimism for such a project. Ultimately, local leaders led each French colony to separate independence.

The Transcaucasus

The area of greatest political geographic complexity in the post-Soviet era is the Transcaucasus region. It was this part of the Soviet Union where traditional enmities first erupted into bitter strife. In 1989 Armenians confronted Azeri Turks over the future of the 1,700-square-mile enclave of Nagorno–Karabakh in Azerbaijan. Armenians claimed the territory on the basis of the majority Armenian population there. Azeris resisted any change in control, citing traditional association of the region with the other Azeri lands and stressing that Armenians are relative newcomers to the area. Many Azeri political and cultural leaders trace their families to Nagorno–Karabakh. There are many parallels with the dispute between Albanians and Serbs over the territory of Kosovo.

The fierceness of hostilities reflected deeper elements of national iconographies of the contending groups. The Shiite Muslim Azeri Turks traditionally have expressed contempt for Armenians, who, in the third century A.D. were among the first groups to adopt Christianity. Armenians see Azeris as part of the Turks who perpetrated mass genocide against their forebears in the early part of the twentieth century.

Similar long-standing animosities poison relationships between both national groups and the Georgians. Each has claims to territory awarded to the others when

SSR boundaries were established in the 1920s. Azeris accuse the Christian Georgians of persecuting Muslim minorities inhabiting their eastern border region. Georgians cannot forget Armenian domination of their cities and society during the tsarist era.

Severe internal ethnic problems face independent Georgia. The republic during the last years of the Soviet Union found itself suppressing separatist drives by three ethnic groups within its borders. The Abkhaz live in northwestern Georgia. They speak a Circassian language similar to the Kabardinians and other peoples living on the north slopes of the Caucasus Mountains. Religiously, they are divided between Sunni Muslims and Orthodox Christians. They became a protectorate of Russia in 1810. During the early 1920s they briefly had their own SSR at the time the Soviet Union annexed Georgia. It 1930 their 3,000-square-mile area was confirmed as an ASSR within Georgia. Beginning in the late 1980s, leaders agitated for a return to SSR status, even though half the population of the ASSR identified itself as Georgian, 16 percent as Russian, and only 17 percent as Abkhazian.

Agitation continued after the breakup of the USSR. During 1993 Abkhaz militants, joined by volunteers from minority groups from the north slopes of the Caucasus Mountains, engaged in rebellion against Georgian authority that resulted in a complete victory and flight southward of the region's resident Georgians.

In northeastern Georgia the Soviet regime created a South Ossetian Autonomous Region. The titular group was descended from Iranian-speaking Alans driven across the Caucasus Mountains in the thirteenth century by the Mongols. The Soviet government also created an ASSR in the Russian Republic for Ossetians living north of the mountains. The autonomous oblast in Georgia has an area of 1,500 square miles and a population of 100,000, two-thirds of whom are Ossetian. As Georgia became more nationalist in the 1980, the South Ossetians pressed for attachment of their area to the North Ossetian ASSR. The Georgian regime resisted their efforts and attempted to suppress them, leading to major strife.

A third unhappy group in Georgia is the Adzhar community. They speak Georgian, but their ancestors were converted to Islam following Ottoman annexation in the mid-sixteenth century. They became part of the Russian Empire in 1878, long after the acquisition of Georgia at the beginning of the nineteenth century. Although an independent Georgian state emerged in 1918 that considered Adzharia part of its territory, the Soviet government conceded the region to Turkey in the Treaty of Brest Litovsk. Following Soviet conquest of Georgia in 1921, agreement was reached with Turkey that the area should again become part of Georgia. Because of the distinctiveness of its people, it was given separate status as an ASSR.

Clashes of Adzhar militants with Georgian troops began in late 1988 and have continued. Following independence in 1991, Georgian leaders called for abolition of the ASSR on the grounds that the separate government bureaucracy was costly and that Adzhars were not different from other Georgians—few actually practiced Islam, which was the basis of the original distinction. Nationalists reacted strongly, stressing that all Adzhars have a Muslim heritage, whether or not they practice their religion. Strong sentiments exist for attachment to Turkey.

Among ethnic Georgians themselves regional sentiments run high. The first elected president of Georgia was from the western region of Mingrelia. He was deposed by a violent military coup that resulted in substantial damage to the central part of Tbilisi, the Georgian capital. The successor Georgian government soon was confronted by rebellion in Mingrelia led by the deposed president. The uprising was suppressed in late 1993 with the assistance of troops from Russia. Local sentiments remain volatile, however.

The Legacy of Soviet Centralization

Although virtually all non-Russian national groups expressed objections to domination by the Russians, they also opened old wounds involving each other. The situation is somewhat less ambiguous than in the Habsburg and Ottoman empires because in the early years of the Soviet regime each major national group received a specific territory of its own. Each had borders that became discontinuities in cultural, economic, and political affairs. Administrative regions in the USSR were far more important than their counterparts in other states because the role of government was so pervasive. All government ministries devolved authority downward on the basis of the network of administrative regions, including the republics and their subdivisions. Unlike the borders of counties in the United States or the boundaries of departments in France, patterns of everyday life changed abruptly when crossing administrative lines, even if populations were ethnically mixed on both sides. Local newspapers, for instance, were easily obtained only in the province or district where they were published, and were either in the language of its dominant national group or in Russian. Adjacent farms on opposite sides of an arbitrary administrative line sent crops to different procurement centers located in their respective administrative centers.

Boundaries between Soviet republics thus became meaningful for future nation-states not present in the historic provincial borders of East-Central and Southeastern Europe. Nevertheless, as detailed above, many boundaries remain contested. It would seem wise for the successor states to the Soviet Union to adopt the policy of *uti possedetis* utilized by the new states that replaced former colonies in South America and tropical Africa (see page 330). That is, they should jointly recognize that all groups have potential claims against their neighbors, but that no group would ultimately benefit from any such conflict. They should treat present boundaries as not subject to modification. This policy has worked well elsewhere. The Somalis, for instance, received no support from others for irredentist claims against Kenya and Ethiopia, even though substantial numbers of Somali tribesmen live in those states.

Active and potential troubles between the component national groups within the Commonwealth of Independent States are matched by foreign claims to borderland territories. The land boundary of the Soviet Union was not only the longest one in the world but it also was the most contested. Every one of its neighbors has harbored territorial grievances.

Bibliography

BATER, JAMES H. and R.A. FRENCH, eds., *Studies in Russian Historical Geography*, (2 vols.). London: Academic Press, 1983.

BATER, JAMES H., *The Soviet Scene: A Geographical Perspective*. London: Edward Arnold, 1989.

BEISSENGER, M. and L. HAJDA, eds., *The Nationalities Factor in Soviet Society and Politics: Current Trends and Future Prospects*. Boulder, CO: Westview Press, 1987.

BROWN, A., *The Cambridge Encyclopedia of Russia and the Soviet Union*. Cambridge: Cambridge University Press, 1982.

COLE, J. P., *Geography of the Soviet Union*. London: Butterworths, 1983.

CONQUEST, R. *The Harvest of Sorrow: Soviet Collectivization and the Terror-Famine*. New York: Oxford University Press, 1986.

LYDOLPH, P.E., *Geography of the USSR*, 5th ed. Elkhart Lake, WI: Misty Valley Publishing, 1990.

PALLOT, J. and D.J.B. SHAW, *Planning in the Soviet Union*, 3rd ed. London: Croom Helm, 1981.

SMITH, GRAHAM, "The Soviet Federation: From Corporatist to Crisis Politics," in *Shared Space, Divided Space: Essays on Conflict and Territorial Organization*, Michael Chisholm and David M. Smith, eds. London: Unwin Hyman, 1990, pp. 84–105.

SYMONS, L. et al., *The Soviet Union: A Systematic Geography*. Totowa, NJ: Barnes & Noble, 1983.

WIXMAN, R., *The Peoples of the USSR: An Ethnographic Handbook*. New York: M.E. Sharpe, 1984.

8

The Middle East and North Africa

WHEN the United States led a coalition of United Nations forces to attack and decisively defeat the troops of Iraqi dictator Saddam Hussein in early 1991, many Westerners were fearful that the event would set astir the Arab-Muslim world and result in untold consequences for world peace and economic development. Substantial numbers of individuals curtailed customary activities, including overseas flights for business or vacation, apprehensive of the likelihood of a global expansion of the war and a resurgence in international terrorist activities.

With minor exceptions, projected fears did not materialize. Arabs did not rise en masse against Americans and Europeans. Only Palestinians and Yemenis joined the Iraqis in exhibiting genuine regret for Saddam's catastrophic defeat. Virtually none rallied to his call for an Arab *jihad* ("holy war") against the foreign infidels, despite exhortations of his propaganda media throughout the region. Terrorist activities were few and in keeping with what had become long-standing patterns.

A principal explanation for such low-keyed response is that the notion of a common Arab-Muslim nation is greatly exaggerated. Despite more than a century of proclamation of a regionwide pan-Arab unity, inhabitants of the Middle East and North Africa for the most part have evolved parochial national identities within the specific states in which they live. Individuals are "Syrians" or "Algerians" much more than they are "Arabs." Such national commitments often are further tempered by loyalties to such substate minority groups as Berber tribes and Druze religious communities. Increasingly, the concept of being "Arab" has become something as abstract and remote from daily thought as being "European." The situation is illustrated by the fact that the Arab states of Saudi Arabia, Egypt, and Syria were major partners in the American coalition, which ostensibly was forged to wrest the Arabic state and people of Kuwait from forced incorporation into Iraq.

This is not to say that the territory which extends across the Sahara, through the Arabian Peninsula, and to the interior of Asia does not enjoy a degree of cultural homogeneity sufficient to set it apart from neighboring areas as a distinctive political-geographic territory. From the Atlantic shores of Morocco and Mauritania to the outliers of the Himalaya Mountains stretches a continental-sized area that rivals Latin America in its commonality of language, religion, and mutual historical experience. At the same time, it also resembles Latin America in its seemingly permanent fragmentation into more than twenty different states, none of which rests completely easy with its neighbors (Figure 8-1).

The area discussed in this section cannot be termed "The Arab World" because less than 60 percent of its inhabitants actually speak the Arabic language and identify themselves as Arabs. Large numbers are Turks, Iranians, Kurds, Berbers, and Jews. It cannot be called "The Muslim World," if only because no more than 25 percent of the world's Muslims live in the North African and Middle Eastern states. Three of the largest Muslim states—Indonesia, Bangladesh, and Pakistan—lie clearly in other world regions. Moreover, it should be noted that the cleavage between Sunni and Shia branches of Islam rivals divisions among Roman Catholic, Protestant, and Eastern Orthodox branches of Christianity. Furthermore, the area is the cultural hearth not only of Islam but also of Judaism and Christianity, both of which retain significant representation within it.

The region is sometimes identified as "The Dry World," a concept descriptive of much of its physical geography, but even then the term falls short. Most of the inhabited part is climatically comparable to regions of Southern Europe across the Mediterranean Sea, whereas the area's belt of dryness extends southward into the Sub-Saharan African realm and eastward well into China.

Despite individual inadequacies of each of these designations, they collectively serve to set apart a broad territory that is not "European," "Sub-Saharan African," "Russian," nor "South Asian." It is a crossroads among those four civilizations, and has affected—and been affected by—each of them. It adjoins its neighbors in frontier zones that share characteristics of both realms.

This chapter considers the core of the area, conventionally termed "The Middle East and North Africa." Despite the inadequacies cited above, the designation "Arab-Muslim World" also is sufficiently descriptive to be useful. Many of the region's characteristics are to be found in the adjacent Baluchi and Sindhi regions of Pakistan, in the Sahel frontier of Sub-Saharan Africa, and in the Central Asian deserts. With the collapse of the USSR, its former Muslim areas once again are becoming unambiguous parts of the Middle East, resembling the shifted status of Estonia, Latvia, and Lithuania, which, since leaving the former Soviet Union, have become once again components of "East-Central Europe."

The Middle East and North Africa constitute an area of more than 5,000,000 square miles. This is more

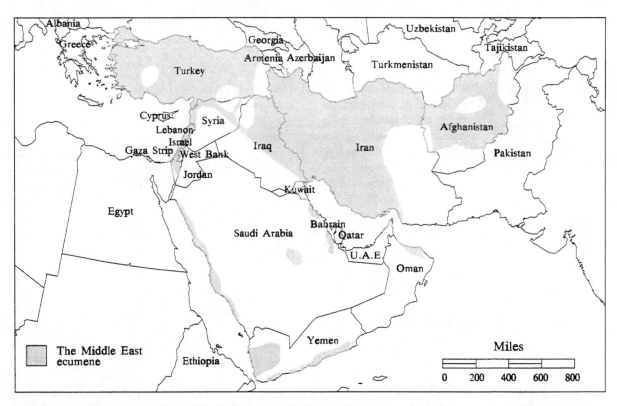

FIGURE 8-1   STATES AND SETTLED AREAS OF THE MIDDLE EAST

than twice the territory of Europe west of the Russian and Ukrainian borders. The total population of 350,000,000 is equal to that of the former USSR and is three-fifths that of Europe. However, the region's ecumene constitutes but a fraction of its total area. For example, virtually all of Egypt's 50,000,000 inhabitants are concentrated in the 5 percent of its territory that lies in the valley and delta of the Nile River.

The pattern of population is closely tied to the area's physical geography. The dry deserts of Arabia and the Sahara, which occupy the southern two-thirds of the region, receive less than four inches of precipitation annually. In this region people cluster where irrigation is feasible—principally along rivers whose headwaters originate in zones of greater precipitation. An exception is to be found in the Persian Gulf region, where affluence from developed petroleum resources has made feasible the desalinization of seawater for household use and consequent support of large populations.

The majority of inhabitants of the Middle East and North Africa is to be found along the region's northern fringes, adjacent to the Mediterranean, Black, and Caspian seas. The desert climate characterizing the south extends across these territories during the summer, but the winter period brings a modest rainfall suf-

ficient for raising grain. The seas tend to moderate temperature extremes, cooling by absorption of solar energy in the summer and warming by release of stored heat in the winter. The result is a so-called dry-summer subtropical or Mediterranean climate similar to that found in southern Italy or California. Northern Iraq marks the furthest extent inland of this moderate climate. In the eastern margins of the region, the higher mountains wring moisture from the air, permitting local spots of high agricultural density. However, remoteness from the seas leads to a more continental climate, with greater extremes of summer heat and winter cold.

The terrain of the region is varied. More than 100 peaks in the eastern mountains reach elevations in excess of 10,000 feet. Mt. Ararat on the Turkish border with Armenia rises 17,000 feet, and Mt. Demavand is 19,000 feet high. Between the mountain ranges stand high plateaus. Plateaus also dominate the landscapes of the Arabian Peninsula and North Africa, although the Atlas Mountains of Morocco and the ranges of Yemen rise up to 10,000 feet above the land.

The population living within this expanse of generally subhumid territory is by no means uniform. Like Europeans, Arabs are not descended from a common racial strain. Rather, present inhabitants reflect a variety of origins and contacts throughout time. Southern

Arabia, for instance, has a significant proportion of individuals with African features, a legacy of the area's long role in the slave trade. Blond and blue-eyed attributes found in many Turkic areas suggest slave-raiding and other interactions with European stock.

Coexisting in the region are three characteristic societies—nomads, peasant farmers, and urban dwellers. Nomads, although steadily decreasing in numbers, continue to roam vast empty spaces with their bands of sheep and goats. Peasant farmers use irrigation to wrest crops from river-bottom soils in areas where water is adequate. In regions of better rainfall the farmers raise grains by dry-farming techniques. The inhabitants of the cities have long served as markets for food producers. All three groups are interdependent, yet they also find themselves competing rivals. In the twentieth century two additional significant occupations have become manifest: petroleum workers and military personnel.

The population of the Middle East and North Africa is one of the most rapidly growing in the world, doubling every twenty-five years. The harshness of the region's predominantly desert environments meant, in the past, a relatively short lifespan for most inhabitants. Families had large numbers of children to assure survival. The spread of public-health measures and assured food supplies in the twentieth century increased the lifespan and thereby reduced annual death rates. However, birthrates continued to remain high. The result has been increasing population pressure upon a limited environmental base.

Regional Unity

The remarkable cultural similarities of the region cannot be ascribed solely or even principally to the homogeneity of its physical geography. Its inhabitants have always had contrasting ways of life, and significant groups have been able to resist assimilation for millennia. The area's commonality must be seen in the context of political organizations and integrations, much as similarities throughout Western Europe are traceable to the impact of the Roman Empire and the long-standing dynastic states. Over the centuries, the region has seen a succession of groups organizing sizable agglomerations of territory, although none ever was able to bring the entire Middle East and North Africa together at any one time. Dominating significant parts of the region over various periods have been Assyrians, Egyptians, Phoenicians, Persians, Greeks, Romans, Arabs, Mongols, Turks, and the modern-day French and British. Each contributed to the unity of those areas that it controlled, but the outer limits of its area of authority also tended to become lasting spatial discontinuities within the region.

The Arab Empire's Legacies.

The empire most widely celebrated in the Middle East and North Africa was that of the Arabs, which reached its zenith about A.D. 750. From a core in the Arabian Peninsula, the Arab Empire quickly spread during the seventh century to the Atlantic and then across the Strait of Gibraltar as far as southwestern France. To the east it extended well into east Turkestan on the frontiers of China, a few relic Arabic-speaking villages testifying to the greatness of its former extent. In this respect it exceeded the Roman Empire, which earlier covered substantial territory in the region, although it did not extend beyond Mesopotamia (modern Iraq). Lasting legacies of the Arab ascendency are the Arabic language and Islam.

Language. Arabic belongs to the Semitic family of languages, of which Hebrew is also a member. Conquerors based in its hearth region in central Arabia imposed its use northward and westward along the entire southern fringe of the Mediterranean Sea, replacing a complex web of indigenous Semitic, Hamitic, and Berber tongues. Its adoption derived both from the supremacy of the Arab forces and from the legitimacy Arabic gained as the language of the sacred Koran. Also, like the Latin of the Romans, it was the vehicle for learning. Although Europe had plunged into the Dark Ages, the accumulated wisdom of classical scholars was kept alive in the Arab Empire through dissemination of Arabic translations from the Greeks and Romans.

However, just as Rome conquered Greece but not Greek culture, Arabs were able to impose authority upon Persians and Turks to the east, but had less success in impressing cultural attributes upon those subject peoples. Actually, the Arabs were not able to conquer all of Asia Minor, and their impact farther east was transitory. The Turks retained much of their traditional language and culture, although it should be noted that perhaps 75 percent of the Turkic population was descended from Middle Eastern peoples who had lost indigenous languages and traditions through acculturation by conquerors from east Turkestan.

Arabs did leave linguistic legacies throughout the Turkic realm, however. Many Turkic words are of Arabic origin. A number of Turks adopted classical Arabic as a medium for writing. Those who transformed their vernacular into a literary language generally employed the Arabic alphabet to write it. During the World War I era and its aftermath, Turks in Turkey and east

Turkestan switched to the Latin alphabet. This action was part of ambitious programs for modernization following revolutionary upheavals, although Turks living in the Soviet Union were required to shift alphabets once again in the 1930s and accept modified versions of the Cyrillic alphabet used by the Russians. Persians and Kurds also early adopted the Arabic alphabet for writing their languages.

Although a standard literary Arabic language dominates the Arabian Peninsula and North Africa, Arabic speech patterns differ markedly from locality to locality, reflecting the relative isolation of nodes of settlement. It is interesting to note that discussions at the founding conference of the Arab League in 1945 were conducted in French.

Islam. In addition to their language, the conquering Arabs brought with them a dynamic new religion—Islam. It has remained as a unifying force throughout the region, distinguishing an overwhelming majority of its inhabitants from peoples of neighboring realms. Like other great world religions, Islam has stamped the peoples of the Middle East and North Africa with common perceptions, beliefs, and rituals that bind them together and distinguish them from non-Muslims. A particularly significant unifying element is the Islamic notion that all Muslims are brothers. The Muslim obligation to visit Mecca has also produced one of the few elements of coherence in the territory.

In Arabic Islam means literally "submission" (to the will of God). It is a belief system proclaimed by the prophet Mohammed, who was born about A.D. 571 in Mecca. He grew up in a polytheistic pagan community and was familiar with both Judaism and Christianity. At about the age of forty Mohammed began periods of religious meditation during which, he avowed, he received revelations of religion—void of error—from God, who commanded him to recite these pronouncements to the community. He preached the oneness of God and the certainty of the Last Judgment of heaven or hell. Arab tribal groups rallied to his teaching, and by the time of his death in 632, he had become caliph—spiritual and temporal ruler—of most of Arabia. Mohammed may not have been able to read or write, at least not skillfully, and the divine oral communications that he recited in rhymed prose were written down by literate converts and subsequently assembled into the Koran ("recitation"), a book of 114 chapters, which Muslims accept as the precise Word of God. A key element of the Koran is a list of five obligations for all Muslims, sometimes called the "pillars" of Islam. These include (1) a profession of faith, (2) prescribed prayers, (3) giving of alms, (4) fasting during the month of Ramadan, and (5) a pilgrimage to Mecca. Although he called upon his followers to convert the unbelievers,

Mohammed recognized a special status for Jews and Christians. He saw their revealed Scriptures as predecessors to the Koran, and he called for them to live according to their own religious laws as "people of the book."

Mohammed left no provision for a successor after his death. Three rival groups sought control of the caliphate. His companians wanted an election, and they prevailed. Another group wanted his son-in-law, Ali, to be caliph through the right of inheritance. Ali became the fourth of the caliphs in 656. The third group was the Umayyed family, which had long dominated Mecca. They assumed control of the caliphate after Ali's assassination. Their tradition of Islam is known as the Sunni branch, and counts a majority of Muslim adherents. The supporters of Ali did not accept Umayyed control and formed a separate religious and political body called the *Shiat Ali*, or "Followers of Ali." The Shia tradition of Islam derives from this group. It is fragmented into several sects.

Islam has tended to be much more involved in the political realm than has Christianity. It embodies a customary law, *shariah*, that serves as a legal base in most Islamic states. It lacks a tradition of separation of church and state comparable to the Christian admonition to "render unto Caesar that which is Caesar's." Both the legitimacy and the power of many rulers in the region stem from religious roles. The king of Saudi Arabia gains prestige and legitimacy as protector of Mecca. Popular demand supplanted the secular Shah of Iran by the religious Ayatollah Khomeini. The Imam of Oman controls a broad territory by virtue of his leadership of the Ibadi sect of Islam. The ruling family of Morocco derives its authority by its claimed direct descent from the prophet Mohammed.

The role of Islam as a unifying force is limited by the continuing presence in the region of Christians, Jews, and other "people of the book" and by division of the Muslim faith among two major and several minor branches. The principal schism is between Sunni and Shia segments. Sunni Muslims predominate in most areas, but Shias constitute a major force in Iran and Iraq, and are to be found in eastern Saudi Arabia and elswhere in Sunni-dominated territory. Among minor Islamic sects are the Druze and Alawites of Lebanon and Syria, and the Izmaili and Zayadi groups of southern Arabia.

The Ottoman Empire. The Arabian Empire gave way to the Empire of the Ottoman Turks. Their domain reached its zenith in the sixteenth century and then fell into steady decline. At its peak it embraced most of North Africa and much of Arabia, as well as Turkey and a substantial part of the Balkans. It operated in a decentralized fashion, with many of its nominal parts, including Egypt and Algeria, for all practical purposes being independent. Islam was the Ottoman state religion, but non-Muslims received official status by being organized into recognized communal bodies under the so-called millet system.

The Ottoman Empire never embraced Persia or the interior and southern reaches of the Arabian Peninsula. Its territorial contact with Persia was through a fifty-mile-wide frontier zone where associations were determined by shifting allegiances of tribal groups. The Ottoman Turks were able to impose their language and other aspects of culture only upon a limited number of groups in Asia Minor and the southern Balkan Peninsula. Arabs, Armenians, and Kurds retained their linguistic and cultural identities. One lasting legacy of Ottoman rule was the perpetuation of many of the empire's administrative regions as independent states after World War I.

European colonialism. A principal basis for the degree of unity that exists in the Arab-Muslim world is the common reaction of its peoples to the experience of colonial rule by Europeans. The populace is resolved not to permit reimposition of such domination. Part of the common antipathy toward Israel, which itself serves also as a major binding force, is a general perception that the Jewish state is an imperial enclave imposed upon the region by Western powers.

Virtually all of the Middle East and North Africa, aside from Turkey and central and southern Arabia, came to be controlled by European powers by 1920. European colonialism actually begin in the region in 1450, when the Portuguese established footholds in northwest Africa. However, imperialism in the region was principally a nineteenth-century phenomenon, motivated particularly by rivalry between France and the United Kingdom. In 1798 Napoleon invaded Egypt to challenge the British position in India, although he found it necessary to withdraw after thirteen months. A more lasting French thrust into the region was the conquest of Algeria, begun in 1830 and completed by 1847. In the 1860s France established a position in Lebanon, where it intervened to protect the Maronite Christian community from massacre by the Druze. It also cultivated relations with Egypt, building the Suez Canal in 1869. In 1882 France made Tunisia a protectorate, and in 1912 it established a presence in Morocco.

British involvement in the Middle East and North Africa began in 1820 when the United Kingdom signed treaties with the so-called Trucial States along the eastern shore of Arabia. British motivation was to shore up the flanks of its empire in India. In 1839 the United Kingdom established control over Aden on the southwestern tip of Arabia. It acquired Egypt's shares of the Suez Canal in 1875, and control over Egypt itself in

1882, although Egypt continued to remain a nominal part of the Ottoman Empire. In 1899 the British established a protectorate over Kuwait.

Both France and the United Kingdom expanded involvements in the Middle East during and after World War I. The French received "mandates" from the League of Nations over Syria and Lebanon, and the British gained similar authority over Palestine and Mesopotamia. Two other European states played minor colonial roles in the region before World War I. Spain established bases in the Moroccan port cities of Ceuta and Melilla in the sixteenth century and continues to hold them. In 1912 it joined with France in dividing Morocco into protectorates. Italy moved into Eritrea in 1882 and seized Libya in 1912.

European imperialism had revolutionary effects on the Middle East and North Africa. New technologies and intellectual concepts diffused throughout society. Western ideas provided alternatives to traditional forms and processes of political organization, particularly in the separation of religion from government. Through expansion of educational opportunities colonialism created a means for diffusion of the notion of group national identity beyond that of a common religious heritage. These new perspectives led a significant number of people throughout the region to begin to see themselves as "Arabs" beyond being "Muslims."

Ottoman leaders grew alarmed at the emergence of such Arab nationalism because it threatened the empire's principal unifying force of Islam. As happened also in the Habsburg and Russian empires, attempts to suppress national feeling only reinforced it. Arabs became anti-Turkish as well as anti-European. World War I served as a catalyst for Arabs to sunder ties with the Ottoman Empire, although, to their dismay, a majority found Turkish domination immediately replaced by British or French authority.

Disunity among the Arabs. Arab intellectuals generally blame the European colonial powers for frustrating the development of a single Arabic nation-state following disintegration of the Ottoman Empire. They are certainly correct that the victorious British and French partitioned most of Ottoman Arabia for their own purposes. During the course of World War I the two imperial states had entered into a secret treaty for division of Arabs of the Middle East between them. Britain and France implemented this secret agreement by leading the newly formed League of Nations to grant them mandates over former Ottoman territories with the stated purpose of preparing local inhabitants for eventual self-government.

The mandated Arab territories quickly grew apart from each other. France and England established new sets of institutions modelled after their respective systems of government and standard operating procedures. Arab inhabitants had to adopt differing European languages to conduct public affairs and commercial activities. Both France and Britain found it expedient to introduce further fragmentation of Arab territory to meet local problems or challenges to authority. Thus, the French separated predominantly Christian Lebanon from the rest of their Syrian mandate. Later, they created self-governing regions for areas of the Alawite and Druze minorities. The British separated Bedouin Arabs from settled Arabs (and Zionist Jewish colonists) by creating the Kingdom of Transjordan east of the Jordan River.

The British also chose not to link their established protectorate of Kuwait near the mouth of the Tigris–Euphrates River system to their mandate of Iraq. The British also prevented the recently established Saudi Arabian state from annexing the numerous sheikdoms situated along the shore of the western Persian Gulf. Likewise, the British maintained the separation of the independent kingdom of Yemen from their naval base at Aden and tribal areas adjacent to it along the Indian Ocean.

However, even if European colonialism had not occurred, it is doubtful that a single Arab nation-state would have emerged during the twentieth century. Despite all the political-geographic elements of homogeneity cited above, the peoples of the Middle East and North Africa have not been able to forge an areawide sense of national identity. In particular, profound religious differences have kept apart major territorial groups in the Fertile Crescent stretching from the Levant coast of the Mediterrean to the Persian Gulf.

The area has also consistently lacked the degree of economic and political coherence necessary for effective state functioning in the modern world. Even though its nominal authority extended as far west as Algeria, the Ottoman Empire had witnessed the fragmentation of its North African holdings into several completely self-governing units long before the advent of European colonialism. The Middle East displayed similar parcelization, both within and without the Ottoman realm. Arabs living in Nejd and the Hejaz, which lay in the interior of the Arabian Peninsula outside the Ottoman Empire, were never able to establish political unity with the adjacent mountain kingdom of Yemen in the southwest corner.

The fragmented ecumene. A principal reason for such lack of coherence was the wide longitudinal extent of the ecumene, coupled with its fragmentation into separated parts. The Roman geographer Pliny described the peoples of the Mediterranean Basin as "sitting like frogs around a pond," and this description remains apt today. The Arabs and associated groups live principally in clusters in favored regions along the northern fringes of North Africa and Arabia, and in the well-watered valleys of the Nile River and Tigris–Euphrates system of Iraq. Empty desert lands separate areas of settlement. Like the isolated population clusters of Latin America, each region has evolved its own identity and personality.

Although sea communications in the past continuously linked these far-flung areas, such ties were episodic. The Arabs were not able to maintain a common culture over their isolated ecumenes comparable to the homogenization occurring where peoples were in constant daily contact with each other across contiguous broad land areas. Regional differences in vocabulary and pronunciation gradually developed like those that emerged from the once-uniform Germanic language of the Norden peoples. Furthermore, contact by sea with neighbors too often was in the form of piracy and pillage, doing little to bring groups together. Landward, nomadic bandit tribes tended to discourage communication overland.

This lack of political coherence of the Middle East and North Africa is also traceable to the fact that no region emerged as a "core" welding disparate parts together as did the Paris Basin in France or the Vienna Basin in the Habsburg Empire. The original Arab expansion in the seventh century A.D. had its base in Damascus. A century later, Baghdad assumed this role. Neither city established clear-cut dominance over other regions, however, and eventually both found themselves eclipsed by the ascendency of Constantinople under the Ottoman Turks.

The absence of economic coherence reflects the fact that commerce has largely been an endeavor with outside regions. Both Arab and Ottoman empires witnessed some trade among their constituent parts, but populations overwhelmingly were self-subsistent, and largely remain so today. Commercial linkages traditionally were stronger with states lying outside the region. The Middle East particularly prospered from a position intermediate between Europe and eastern and southern Asia. North Africa and southern Arabia also benefitted from their roles as intermediaries for Europeans in the African slave trade.

The similarity of environments resulted in little regional specialization and exchange within the area itself. Agricultural economies were competitive rather than complementary. Virtually all territories produced grain and dates. Most areas competed with each other for the same customers in world markets. In the modern era, similarly, markets for petroleum production all lie outside the region.

European colonialism further discouraged areawide coherence. Economic development of colonies and mandates usually began with building railroads from interior areas to coastal ports. Mother countries encouraged trade principally with themselves and with other parts of their empires. Commercial firms established working relationships with mother-country partners that generally continued after the achievement of independence.

The British and French did not intend to foster group antagonisms within their Middle Eastern territories. Their mandates were not arbitrary partitionings of space but traditional Ottoman provinces in which diverse peoples had coexisted for centuries. The effect of twentieth-century European control reinforced existing parochialisms rather than creating them. Neither Iran nor Turkey suffered European rule, yet both had internal problems as complex as those in the mandated territories. Group awareness and mutual enmities had long existed between the Arabs of Syria and those of Iraq, between Maronite Christians and Muslims in Lebanon, and between Palestinian farmers and Bedouin nomads.

Political processes at the end of the twentieth century may reverse Arab political fragmentation. After decades of subordination to European-style parochial secularism, Islam is regaining prestige in the postcolonial Middle East and North Africa. Fundamentalist religious movements challenge governments in northwest Africa and Egypt. Through Islam's revival it may be possible for Arabs to achieve a unified nation comparable to the emergence of German and Italian identities amid political fragmentation in the nineteenth century.

Modern States and Nations

Like Sub-Saharan Africa, South Asia, and Southeast Asia, the independent states of the Middle East and North Africa are mainly products of the era following World War II. Prior to that war, only seven territories had achieved a semblence of sovereignty: Egypt, Turkey, Iran, Iraq, Saudi Arabia, Oman, and Yemen. Syria and Lebanon declared independence in 1941 following defeat and occupation of France by Germany. Remaining colonial areas achieved statehood over ensuing years.

The contemporary states of the Middle East and North Africa reflect the uniqueness of their historical experiences, their cultures, and their economic development. A majority population within each state shares a sense of common identity and constitutes a nation comparable to those found in Europe. Most national feelings can be traced to secular influences emanating from contact with European societies. As elsewhere in the developing world, students and others who found themselves living in a mother country absorbed there the political ideas of the prevailing nation. They gained European perspectives on the role of government and the rights of the governed. As a result of social discrimination and contact with dissident political groups, many often developed a determination to oppose colonial authority and to achieve sovereignty for their people. Such secular nationalism particularly characterized Algerians in France.

Traditionalism also has played a role in the evolution of modern national identities. Both Morocco and Egypt had long functioned as independent units within the Ottoman Empire. Their peoples saw independence from France and the United Kingdom, respectively, as a resumption of lost sovereignty. In other areas, historic religious traditions formed a basis for modern national identity. Sunni Muslims of the Arabian Peninsula long have been split between the sects of the Wahhabis dominating Saudi Arabia, the Ibadis of Oman, and the Zayadis of Yemen. The contemporary national groups of these states continue to see the others as fundamentally different from themselves. Inertia also has been a factor. Linkages of settlements within each administrative subdivision of the Ottoman Empire to a certain degree developed a sense of community. In the cases of Syria and Iraq, the post-Ottoman mandates reinforced internal unities while increasing separation from each other.

Minorities. At the same time that majorities in each state evolved national identities, minorities also emerged as distinctive nations. In the Arabian Peninsula, communities of Shia Muslims constitute distinctive regional groups in several states. A compact body of Kurds plays a significant role in the region where Turkey, Iran, and the Fertile Crescent states come together. Berber-speaking tribes live scattered throughout the Maghreb of northwest Africa. In some states, such minorities have gained dominance over majority groups. Thus the Alawite Islamic religious minority has controlled the far more numerous Sunni Muslims in Syria for many years, and Sunnis dominate Iraq although they constitute barely a quarter of that country's population.

Boundary problems. Establishment of mandated territories in the Arabic regions of the Ottoman Empire resulted in surprisingly few economic dislocations and border disputes. Several cities in Syria and Palestine found customary outlets to the sea in foreign territories, and railroad lines now crossed boundaries that had become international.

For the most part, present boundary problems in the Middle East and North Africa reflect disputes that did not develop in the colonial era, but either had their origins in Ottoman times or developed after independence.

TABLE 8.1   THE MIDDLE EAST AND NORTH AFRICA

A vast area with limited islands of ecumene, the region encompassing the Middle East and North Africa is characterized by a predominantly Muslim population living in a harsh, arid environment. An Arab heritage dominates the Arabian Peninsula and North Africa, while Turkish and Iranian influences govern the northeastern regions. Three modes of life have long coexisted throughout the region: nomadic herders, peasant dirt farmers, and inhabitants of cities. More recent additions in many parts of the region are petroleum workers and major military establishments. Several ancient and medieval empires united large parts of the territory. During the nineteenth and twentieth centuries virtually all areas were subject to the humiliations of European colonialism. Despite the high degree of homogeneity of the region's inhabitants, no common national identity has emerged. The numerous nations are in part a product of widely spaced ecumenes, isolated from each other by empty insulating barriers of deserts and seas. Although all parts of the area have gained sovereignty, the new states suffer minority problems and disputes with neighbors comparable to their older counterparts in Europe. Despite the cultural homogeneity and common history of the Middle East and North Africa, it is useful to view the region in terms of five distinctive areas: The Fertile Crescent, the Arabian Peninsula, the Northeastern Periphery, the Nile River States, and the Maghreb.

Subregion	Total Population	Area (sq. miles)
Fertile Crescent	43,000,000	295,000
Component States		
Iraq, Kuwait, Syria, Lebanon, Jordan, Israel		
Arabian Peninsula	34,000,000	1,200,000
Component States		
Saudi Arabia, Bahrain, Qatar, United Arab Emirates,		
Oman, Yemen		
Northeastern Periphery	120,000,000	930,000
Component States		
Iran, Turkey		
Nile River States	90,000,000	1,355,000
Component States		
Egypt, Sudan		
The Maghreb	67,000,000	1,850,000
Component States		
Morocco, Algeria, Tunisia, Libya		
Total	354,000,000	5,630,000

Long-standing arguments include rival claims between Arabs and Persians over the Shatt-al-Arab waterway, Bahrain, and some islands in the Strait of Hormuz. Among postcolonial controversies are Iraq's claim to Kuwait, Algeria's dispute with Morocco, and Saudi Arabia's aspirations for the emirates along the Persian Gulf. The most serious postcolonial disputes have revolved around the formation and expansion of the new state of Israel at the expense of its Arab neighbors. Many old quarrels gained new currency with discovery of oil.

The impact of petroleum. The generally inhospitable qualities of the environment of the Middle East and North Africa have been mollified by the region's rich endowment of petroleum beds. No other region of the world can claim such resource wealth beneath its surface. The development of petroleum production has had profound effects upon all aspects of the region's economic, cultural, and political geography. Wealth has poured into the region from the rest of world, creating employment and leading to exceptionally high living standards in a few favored territories, particularly those around the Persian Gulf. Formerly isolated societies have become integrated into the international network of trade and communication. Because of world dependence upon its petroleum production, the government of such an otherwise tiny and weak political entity as Kuwait could enlist aid from the United States and major European powers in 1991 to restore its sovereignty after conquest by neighboring Iraq.

Control of the world's oil supply has served to bind the region's states together. Membership in the Organization of Petroleum Exporting Countries (OPEC) is overwhelmingly from the area. Even during the long war between Iran and Iraq in the 1980s, representatives from both warring states managed to sit together in OPEC meetings to allocate production shares and otherwise bolster the world price of crude oil.

Petroleum also has had centrifugal effects upon the region. Great economic and political contrasts exist between those states blessed with oil and those that lack it. Wealthy entities such as Saudi Arabia and Abu Dhabi have mitigated some regional economic disparities by generous transfer payments to states bereft of petroleum. Resource-poor Jordan has particularly benefitted from such subsidies. The chronic need for foreign workers in the petroleum industry has also benefitted have-nots in the Muslim world, including Pakistanis, Yemenis, and stateless Palestinians.

Major Regional Groupings

In examining characteristics of states of the Middle East and North Africa it is useful to consider them in terms of five distinctive regions: the Fertile Crescent, the Arabian Peninsula, the Eastern Periphery, Northeastern Africa, and the Maghreb (northwestern Africa).

The traditional core of the region is the so-called Fertile Crescent area of rain-fed and irrigated farming stretching from the eastern Mediterranean coast around the Syrian Desert to the head of the Persian Gulf. It includes the states of Iraq, Kuwait, Syria, Lebanon, Jordan, and Israel. Adjoining it on the south, the Arabian Peninsula embraces Saudi Arabia, the oil-rich tiny sheikdoms and emirates facing the Persian Gulf, Oman, and Yemen. The Northeastern Periphery includes Iran and Turkey. The Nile River states incorporate Egypt and Sudan, and the Maghreb includes Morocco, Algeria, Libya, and Tunisia (see Table 8-1).

The Fertile Crescent States

The territory of the Fertile Crescent has played a major role in the evolution of civilization (Table 8-2). Stable, large-scale territorial entities have existed in the region ever since the establishment of ancient Babylon. Despite cultural commonalities, however, the area has seldom seen internal political coherence. As in the history of the Indian subcontinent, political unity generally has come from the outside, most notably during nearly five centuries of Ottoman Empire authority. Rivalries between the region's western and eastern wings particularly have rent it. The classical city states of Ninevah and Tyre were at odds with each other. Damascus and Baghdad competed for Arab leadership. The twentieth-century states of Syria and Iraq perpetu-

ate age-old antagonisms in the Fertile Crescent.

The present political map of the region is a consequence primarily of decisions taken in Europe during and after World War I. The British promised sovereignty to the Arabs in 1915 in return for action against Ottoman forces. A year later, however, in the secret Sykes–Picot agreement with the French they forecast partition of the Middle East into respective spheres of influence. In 1917 the British also promised a homeland for Europe's Jews in Palestine as a reward for Jewish support of the Western Allies, although the so-called Balfour declaration specifically stated that "it being clearly understood that nothing shall be done which may prejudice the civil and religious rights to existing non-Jewish communities in Palestine."

The postwar division of the Ottoman Empire reflected the 1916 agreement between the United Kingdom and France. The newly founded League of Nations was led to create "mandated territories" from historic Ottoman administrative divisions of the region. The British received the right to control mandates in Palestine and Mesopotamia, and the French were given authority over Syria. Both European powers then proceeded further to fracture the region's political unity. The British separated the territory of Palestine east of the Jordan River into a new unit to be named Transjordan. The French recognized the separateness of Christian Lebanon. The British proclaimed Iraq to be an independent state in 1932 and Transjordan to be independent in 1946. Syria and Lebanon declared their independence in 1941 following German defeat of France, and the French formally recognized this status in 1946. Jewish immigrants to Palestine declared formation of the state of Israel in 1948 and successfully defended its independence against Arab armies from adjacent territories.

The modern political geography of the Fertile Crescent has revolved around its ethnic and cultural diversities. Two non-Arabic-speaking groups have played particular roles: the Jews and the Kurds.

The Jews

Although never in control of an empire comparable to those of the Egyptians, Arabs, Turks, or Iranians, the Jewish people have been a fixture in the Middle East for millennia. They are recorded as having moved into Palestine from Mesopotamia about 1200 B.C. They remained a collection of warring tribes until King Saul established a unified state in the tenth-century B.C. It lasted for barely two centuries before breaking apart into separate kingdoms of Israel and Judah. Assyrians captured Israel in 721 B.C., and Babylon acquired Judah in 586 B.C. In the mid-first-century B.C., these territo-

TABLE 8.2 THE FERTILE CRESCENT

The Fertile Crescent extends from the Mediterranean shores of the Levant to the Persian Gulf. It was the cradle of ancient civilizations. Although predominantly Arab in language and culture and Muslim in religion, the region seldom has seen political unity. Rivalries between its eastern and western settled areas have characterized it for most of its history. Its political units continually have had to contend with a large minority of Kurds, who speak an Indo-European language. The region has also been subject to conflicting influences from its neighbors: Egypt to the west, Iran to the east, and Turkey to the north. For several centuries its restless areas were parts of the Ottoman Empire. In 1918 British and French colonialism replaced Ottoman authority. Their mandates reinforced regional rivalries. Jewish immigration to Palestine created a new force in the region during the twentieth century, culminating in the establishment of the state of Israel.

State	Total Population	Area (sq. miles)	Distinctive Features of Group
Iraq	18,000,000	168,000	
Dominant Nation and % Total			
Iraqi Sunnis, 34%			Semitic (Arabic) language, Sunni Muslim
Significant Regional Groups and % Total			
Iraqi Shiites, 62%			Semitic (Arabic) language, Shiite Muslim
Kurds, 19%			Iranian (Kurd) language, Sunni Muslim
Potential Trouble Areas and Possible Adversaries			
Shatt-al-Arab Waterway (Iran)			
Kuwait	1,700,000	7,000	
Dominant Nation and % Total			
Kuwaiti Arabs, 52%			Semitic (Arabic) language, Sunni Muslim
(Although not regionally segregated, 43% of the population consists of non-Kuwaiti Arabs.)			
Syria	13,000,000	72,000	
Dominant Nation and % Total			
Syrian Arabs, 89%			Semitic (Arabic) language, Sunni Muslim
Significant Regional Groups and % Total			
Kurds, 6%			Iranian (Kurd) language, Sunni Muslim
Alawites, 3%			Semitic (Arabic) language, Alawite Muslim Sect
Druze, 3%			Semitic (Arabic) language, Druze eclectic religion
Lebanon	2,200,000	4,000	
Dominant Nation and % Total			
Lebanese Maronite Christians, 15%			Semitic (Arabic) language, Uniate Christian
Significant Regional Groups and % Total			
Lebanese Shiite Arabs, 40%			Semitic (Arabic) language, Shiite Muslim
Lebanese Sunni Arabs, 25%			Semitic (Arabic) language, Sunni Muslim
Palestinian Arabs, 10%			Semitic (Arabic) language, Mixed Sunni Muslim and Christian
Druze, 6%			Semitic (Arabic) language, Druze eclectic religion
Armenians, 4%			Indoeuropean (Armenian) language, Armenian Orthodox Christian
Palestinian Arabs, 10%			Semitic (Arabic) language, Sunni Muslim and Christian
Jordan	3,500,000	35,000	
Dominant Nation and % Total			
Jordanian Arabs, 50%			Semitic (Arabic) language, Sunni Muslim
Israel	4,500,000	8,000	
Dominant Nation and % Total			
Israelis, 82%			Semitic (Hebrew) language, Jewish
Significant Regional Groups and % Total			
Palestinian Arabs, 18%			Semitic (Arabic) language, Sunni Muslim and Christian
Potential Trouble Areas and Possible Adversaries			
West Bank (Jordan)	850,000	2,270	
Gaza Strip (Egypt)	550,000	360	
Golan Heights (Syria)	20,000	440	

ries became part of the Roman Empire. Jews migrated throughout the Mediterranean region, forming a trading diaspora. Three uprisings against Roman authority in their homeland province of Judea led Romans to enslave or resettle the Jews elsewhere in the empire. For the next 1,800 years very few Jews lived in Palestine.

Despite oppression and pressures to assimilate, Jews managed to maintain their distinctive religious traditions within the alien societies in which they found themselves. Islam accepted them as "people of the book," and they played significant economic roles throughout the Arab Empire and the subsequent Ottoman Empire. When Christian forces conquered Granada, the last Islamic state on the Iberian Peninsula, the victors forced Muslims and Jews to renounce their religions or be expelled. Most left, finding haven elsewhere in the Middle East and North Africa. Descendents of expelled Iberian Jews form a distinctive branch of world Jewry known as the Sephardim. They maintain a distinctive Spanish-derived language, Ladino, and otherwise distinguish themselves from the other main European branch of Judaism, the Ashkenazim. The latter are characterized by their use of Yiddish, a Germanic language. Both groups employ Hebrew as a literary and religious language.

The Ashkenazim suffered persecution during the Middle Ages, particularly in the Rhineland region where most were concentrated. Large numbers fled eastward to Poland, whose kings welcomed them for their technical and commercial skills. However, they endured a number of disabilities. They could not own land and often had to live in segregated areas of cities that were termed "ghettoes."

Following the partitions of Poland at the end of the eighteenth century, its Jews found themselves within the Russian, Prussian, and Austrian empires and facing increasing degrees of prejudice and discrimination. The Russian government ordered its newly acquired Jewish inhabitants to be confined to a designated "pale" of settlement within former Polish territory. The regime also appeared to tolerate pogroms against Jews in Bessarabia and Poland.

The nineteenth-century emergence of national identities among peoples of the three empires tended to reinforce their long-prevailing religious intolerance of Jews, who increasingly became unwanted foreigners in territories where their families had coexisted with Christian groups for centuries. Like their neighbors, the Jews themselves began to develop a secular national identity based upon their religious and cultural heritage. However, unlike the citizens of Central Europe's other nations, they could not press for sovereignty because they were dispersed in small communities with no contiguously inhabited territory to serve as a possible homeland. To escape increasing problems, an estimated 2,500,000 Jews fled East-Central Europe in the period between 1880 and the beginning of World War I, mostly to the United States of America.

It was in this context that Zionism appeared at the end of the nineteenth century as a national political movement among European Jews. Zionism called for reestablishment of a Jewish homeland in the Middle East. Jewish religious practice traditionally celebrated the glories of the kingdom of Solomon. Passover prayers included the phrase "Next year in Jerusalem!"

Zionists began their program by establishing collectivist agricultural colonies in Palestine. With financial aid from supporters throughout Europe, groups purchased tracts of land, mostly from absentee Turkish owners. By the outbreak of World War I, they had created forty-six Ashkenazi Jewish colonies (*kibbutzim*) inhabited by some 12,000 immigrants, which amounted to about 10 percent of the Palestinian population. This number was quite small in comparison with Sephardic Jews in Iraq (120,000), Iran (100,000), Turkey (90,000), and Yemen (70,000).

More European Jews migrated to Palestine following World War I. They came mainly from Poland, Russia, and Romania. By 1922 they numbered 84,000. At that time Arabs in Palestine totaled 700,000, and more than 3,000,000 Jews lived in the United States. The advent of the Nazi regime in Germany prompted an increased exodus to Palestine. Some 174,000 Jews arrived between 1932 and 1936. The proportion of Jews in Palestine reached 28 percent by the end of the 1930s. Serious frictions developed with indigenous Arab sharecroppers, who lost traditional lands after absentee landlords in Beirut and Damascus sold holdings for exhorbitant prices to the Jewish National Fund. The fund's leases of land to agricultural colonies specified that only Jewish labor could be employed. In 1939 Arab leaders successfully persuaded the British government to limit future Jewish immigration to 15,000 annually.

The start of World War II temporarily curtailed the flow of refugees. However, following war's end, the British found they could not stanch the movement into Palestine of Jews seeking refuge after the trauma of the Holocaust. By 1946, Jews numbered 583,000 and accounted for a quarter of the mandate's inhabitants. Despite the original rural agricultural thrust of Zionism, most Jews settled in cities.

The British sought to disentangle themselves from increasing frictions between Jews and Arabs. Following British announcement of their intention to surrender the Palestinian mandate, the newly formed United Nations created a Palestinian Commission to develop an equitable program for future independence. At length it proposed a partition of Palestine into three Jewish and three Palestinian Arab regions. The proposal received approval by the United Nations General

Assembly and by Jewish leadership. However, Arab leaders vehemently rejected it.

In May 1948, the United Kingdom began its withdrawal from Palestine. The territory's Jews immediately proclaimed establishment of the independent state of Israel. Arab states reacted by sending their armies into the region. Their forces included many Palestinian Arabs who were motivated to defend their homeland. The Israelis prevailed, and eventually truce lines were arranged with Israel's Arab neighbors. The resulting Jewish state incorporated slightly more than 8,000 square miles. This constituted 77 percent of the original Palestinian mandate and an area substantially larger than that proposed in the original UN partition plan. (See Figure 8.6.)

When fighting began, more than 700,000 Palestinian Arabs fled their homes, fearful of atrocities and buoyed by belief that Arab forces would soon prevail. Some 350,000 Palestinians went to Jordan, 200,000 to the Gaza Strip held by Egypt, 100,000 to Lebanon, and 75,000 to Syria. The Israeli government barred their return after hostilities ended. Most Palestinian families then spent decades in refugee camps, their numbers ballooning to 3,000,000.

Up to a quarter million exiled Palestinians subsequently found themselves under Israeli control following the latter's victory in the so-called Six-Day War of 1967. Another 350,000 fled to what remained of Jordan. The Israeli government did not allow newly acquired Palestinians to reclaim family homes and land, however, but required them to continue living in the occupied territories. These included the West Bank occupation zone between Jerusalem and the Jordan River, with an area of 2,300 square miles and 900,000 inhabitants, and the Gaza Strip on the south Mediterranean coast adjacent to Egypt, covering 140 square miles and a population of 600,000.

The number of Jews in Israel grew rapidly after statehood when a "right of return" was proclaimed for all Jews in 1948. Within three years nearly as many Jews immigrated into Israel as the number of Palestinian Arabs who had fled. Most immigrants initially were from Europe and the United States. They were soon joined by Sephardic Jews from Arab lands fleeing persecution that followed Israel's establishment. Over succeeding decades nearly 2,000,000 additional Jews entered Israel, two-thirds from Africa and Asia. Additional immigrants are anticipated from Russia and Ukraine following the greater opportunities to leave those areas after dissolution of the USSR in 1991. The present population of Israel within its boundaries of 1948 is 4,500,000.

The inflow of Jews into the Middle East has tended to submerge many antagonisms that long divided the region's Arabic-speaking populations. Fundamental schisms between Sunnis and Shias remain, however, together with animosities between Bedouins and farmers and age-old regional rivalries between the Levant and Mesopotamia.

The Kurds

In contrast to the relatively recent inflow of Jews to Palestine, Kurds for millennia have formed a compact territorial group of non-Arabic speakers in the Fertile Crescent (Figure 8-2). The colonial partitioning of the Ottoman Empire after World War I divided Kurdish tribesmen among Turkey, Iran, Iraq, and Syria. Their distinctive Indo-European language set them apart from dominant national groups in the four states they inhabited, and their Sunni branch of Islam further marked them as different from the majority Shia groups in Iran and Iraq.

Many scholars consider Kurds to be descendants of the ancient Medes, who were allies of the Persians. They now number about 8,000,000 and have rather continuously inhabited a 75,000-square-mile section of the western Zagros Mountains. The term "Kurdistan" was in use as early as the seventh century A.D. Most Kurds identify themselves by tribal affiliations that preserve animosities that serve to divide them. They also are divided by language. Three main dialects exist, which are not mutually completely understood. However, an increasing sense of a common nationhood has emerged over the past century. Although a number of Kurds have become urbanized, the majority maintain a seminomadic existence that involves patterns of seasonal migration.

Kurds early developed reputations as fierce warriors. Saladin, the conqueror of the Crusader kingdoms, was a Kurd. Different Kurdish tribes often hired themselves to opposing sides in major struggles, depending upon the best arrangement each could strike with the contenders. They lived in a virtual state of anarchy among themselves within the Ottoman Empire, a situation not unwelcome in Constantinople because it kept any one tribe from gaining dominance. Patterns of tribal groups changed over time, with new ones often emerging among disparate followers of dynamic religious leaders.

Nineteenth-century nationalist ideas began to supplant traditional Islamic and tribal identities among Kurds during the 1880s. Several Kurdish political movements emerged in reaction to growing national awareness among Turks, Armenians, and Iranians. All Kurdish movements sought autonomy in local affairs and the right to use their own language in schools. The Ottomans used nascent Kurdish national feelings to their own ends. They encouraged their Kurds to travel to Persia to foment minority problems for that rival

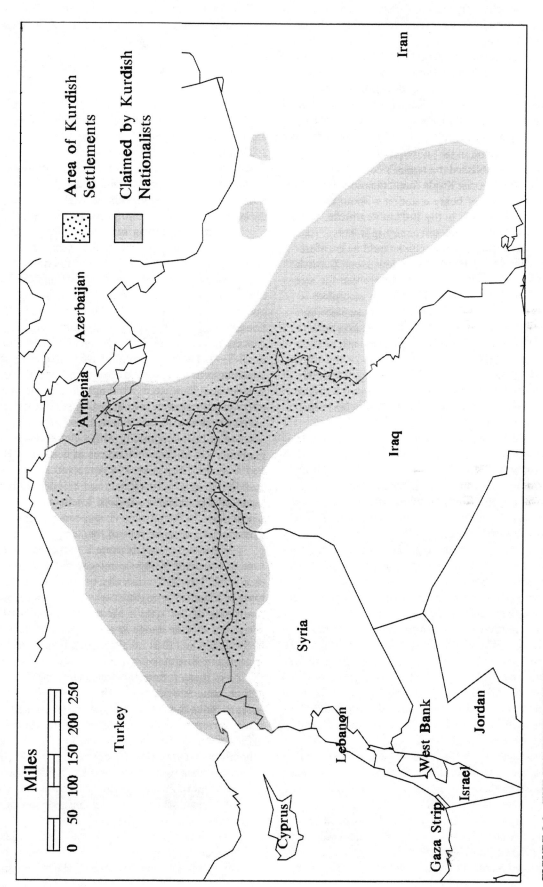

FIGURE 8-2 THE KURDISH REGION

state. Kurdish cavalry units in the Ottoman army played principal roles in massacres of Armenians in the early twentieth century.

The victorious Western Allies initially recognized Kurdish national aspirations in the 1920 Treaty of Sèvres, which made provision for Kurdish autonomy in the former Ottoman lands. Kemal Atatürk's successful efforts to resist any further erosion of Turkish territory, however, led the European powers to ignore completely the Kurdish question in the subsequent 1923 Treaty of Lausanne that established the region's boundaries.

The result was that Kurds found themselves in the unhappy situation of being a nation without a state. Like the Macedonians in the Balkan Peninsula, they had emerged in the twentieth-century split among four different countries, none of which could be comfortable with the existence of any independent Kurdish national entity because of irredentist problems it was likely to engender. Each state sought to assimilate its Kurds into broader Arab, Turkish, or Persian identities. Turkey, especially, refused to make any concessions to Kurdish distinctiveness, and banned any use of their language. The Turks even forbade use of the term "Kurd," insisting upon calling the group "Mountain Turks." Turkish suppression led to several Kurdish revolts and the emigration of many Kurds to the French mandate of Syria.

Turkish repression of Kurds does not appear to have been the result of an ethnic hatred comparable to Turkish attitudes toward Christian Armenians. Rather, it seems to have stemmed from simple annoyance at the constant troubles Kurds presented as a group. The popular image of Kurds in the Middle East is that of a backward, slow-witted people with a proclivity to petty thievery. They stand out from other groups by their language and the distinctive dress of their women. For their part, the Kurds have remained aloof from their neighbors amid the swirling currents of Pan-Arabianism, Pan-Iranianism, and Pan-Turkism.

In addition to tribal divisions, the Kurds have faced other internal problems. Many have adopted the Arabic, Iranian, or Turkish languages, although they retain personal identities as Kurds. A group of some 60,000 Kurdish-speakers in Iraq, the Yazidis, have adopted a heretical religion rejected by other Kurds as "devil worship." Small numbers are to be found in adjacent states.

The Kurds briefly gained a state of their own in Iran at the end of World War II. The Soviet Union had occupied northern Iran during the war, and it facilitated there the formation of a "Kurdish Autonomous Republic of Mahabad" in January 1946. However, pressure from the United States and Western European powers forced the USSR to withdraw from Iran, and the Soviet-Sponsored Kurdish republic collapsed that December.

The Shah of Iran bought a degree of peace with the Kurds, however, by giving support to continuing Kurdish rebellion in neighboring Iraq.

Iraq

The British captured the Ottoman Mesopotamian provinces of Baghdad, Basra, and Mosul in 1916. In 1921 the League of Nations made the territory a mandate of the United Kingdom. The British organized it into the Kingdom of Iraq and installed a member of the Hashemite family of central Arabia as king. They declared Iraq a self-governing protectorate in 1932.

The young kingdom suffered several immediate problems. Its peoples shared little sense of commonality. Although nearly four-fifths were Arabs, they were regionally divided between the three-quarters living in the southeast who were Shia Muslims and the one-quarter in the northwest who were Sunni. An additional 20 percent were Sunni Muslim Kurds, who were concentrated in the Zagros Mountains in the north (Figure 8-3). The Kurds would have preferred continuing attachment to Turkey if they could not be part of an independent Kurdistan. Although Iraq's main area of effective settlement was in the valleys of the Tigris and Euphrates rivers, its inhabitants lacked the Egyptians' sense of political continuity with a glorious past. They generally did not see themselves as heirs of Babylon and Assyria. They generally perceived their British-installed king as a foreigner, and he could not command loyalty from his subjects. Intellectuals, most of whom shared a Pan-Arabic vision, considered the very existence of a separate state of Iraq to be illegitimate.

Nevertheless, Iraq became a successful modern state. It was aided by increasing wealth from oil discovered in 1923 in the Kurdish area of the north around the town of Mosul. The regime early began inculcating an awareness of the state's Mesopotamian heritage. It adopted a secular stance to override the cleavage between Sunni and Shia inhabitants. It also played upon general anti-British feelings.

As in many former colonial territories, a one-party regime came into power in Iraq. In the years following independence the military had early assumed a major role in government. Army officers were responsible for five coups d'etats in the 1930s. In 1958 the military once again overthrew the government. The king and crown prince were killed, and a republic proclaimed. Several more military coups then occurred, until the Baath ("renaissance") party established monopoly control over the army and the state in 1968.

The Baath party exhibits many similarities to the former Communist party of the Soviet Union. Its leadership sets policy, and a professional party organization

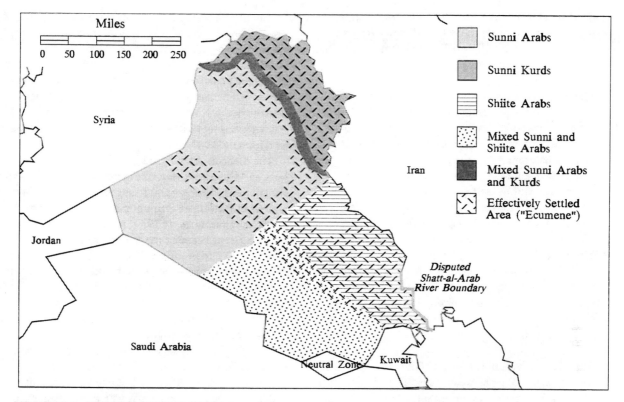

FIGURE 8-3   ETHNIC GROUPS OF IRAQ

plays a major role in resolving problems. The functions of the formal organs of government are largely administrative. Baath ideology is vaguely socialist, with announced goals of leadership of the Arabs against foreign imperialism and of redistribution of wealth among the poor.

The many governments of Iraq have had to contend with four chronic regional problems. These involve (1) constant rebellion by the Kurdish minority in the north, (2) disaffection of Shias in the south at dominance by the Sunni minority, (3) a long-simmering quarrel with Iran over their riverine boundary on the Shatt-al-Arab, and (4) a quest for the oil-rich territory of Kuwait located on Iraq's southern margins.

Iraq's Kurds. Kurds now number about 3,000,000 in Iraq. They have been in more-or-less continuous rebellion since 1919, when they resisted their initial incorporation into the League of Nations mandate. The British sought their territory for Iraq because of oil discovered around Mosul. They also wanted to offset the Shia Muslim majority faced by the Sunni regime that they installed. The Turkish government supported a revolt by Iraqi Kurds in 1922, but the British air force soon quelled the insurrection. The Kurds staged another major revolt in 1931. Much of Kurdish-inhabited terri-

tory remained outside effective Iraqi government control well into the 1970s.

After the repeated failures of his predecessors to come to terms with Kurdish insurgency, a new Iraqi head of state, Saddam Hussein, signed an agreement with Kurdish leaders in 1970 that gave them an autonomous Kurdish region and allowed the Kurdish language to be taught in schools. The agreement soon collapsed, however, and the Kurds again rebelled in 1974, receiving aid from Iran, Israel, and the United States. To cut off Iranian assistance to the Kurds, Iraq made made a boundary concession to Iran in 1975. Without aid from the Iranians, the Kurdish revolt faltered and tens of thousands fled to Iran and elsewhere. The Iraqi regime executed 227 Kurdish leaders and announced plans to move 300,000 Kurds to southern parts of the state. It encouraged thousands of Arabs to resettle in Kurdish areas. The regime completely destroyed more than sixty Kurdish villages situated in the border zone with Iran.

Subsequently, Iraq became involved in a drawn-out war with Iran. Renewed Iranian support for the Kurds led the Iraqi regime to move ruthlessly against the Kurds, employing chemical weapons, burning more of their villages, and forcibly transferring many to areas outside their homeland. Although the regime crushed

Kurdish rebellion once more by using draconian tactics, fighting started anew in 1991 following Iraq's catastrophic defeat by UN coalition forces, which had reversed Iraq's occupation of Kuwait.

The Shia majority. Some 55 percent of Iraq's inhabitants are Arabs professing the Shia branch of Islam. Most are subsistent farmers living in villages and small towns in the south. In religious matters they tend to be more impassioned than the more secular Sunni Arabs of the north. Far fewer Shias than Sunnis have achieved higher educations and professional positions from which the state's elite are drawn. Iraqi Shias long have interacted with co-religionists in neighboring Iran.

That state anticipated their support for its fundamentalist Shia regime when Iran and Iraq went to war in 1980. However, Iraq's Shias remained loyal or inert during the eight years of bitter warfare. Iraq's defeat in the Gulf War of 1991 temporarily led to Shia separatist manifestations, but the Saddam Hussein regime was successful in quelling them.

The Shatt-al-Arab waterway. Rivers tend to be the worst type of border between states. They do not inherently divide territories or establish discontinuities. Rather, their traditional function has been to link together lands through which they pass. The precise location of a boundary line following a river is subject to challenge, particularly if more than one channel is present. Changes in the course of a river often lead to new frictions between states. One of the world's least satisfactory boundaries is the fifty-mile-long Shatt-al-Arab, which has long served to divide Iraqi from Iranian territories. It was the basis for the quarrel that led to the devastating eight years of warfare between Iran and Iraq during the 1980s.

The Shatt-al-Arab is formed by the merger of the Tigris and Euphrates rivers (Figure 8-4). It is several hundred yards wide and has long served as a border between the Ottoman Empire and Iran. A number of treaties, beginning in 1639, confirmed its boundary role. Agreement between the two states in 1847, supervised by the Russians and British, conceded to Iran the major island of Khizr at its mouth but specified that the channel belonged to the Ottoman Empire. This effectively placed the boundary line on the river's eastern shore. This siting of the border was reconfirmed in a 1913 protocol between the two states.

In 1937 Iraq made the concession to Iran of a four-mile midstream border in the vicinity of the growing Iranian oil port of Abadan. The two states remained at odds over the river boundary, which reflected tensions between them over other matters. Iranians often ignored Iraqi sovereignty over the lower course of the river

FIGURE 8-4   THE SHATT-AL-ARAB WATERWAY

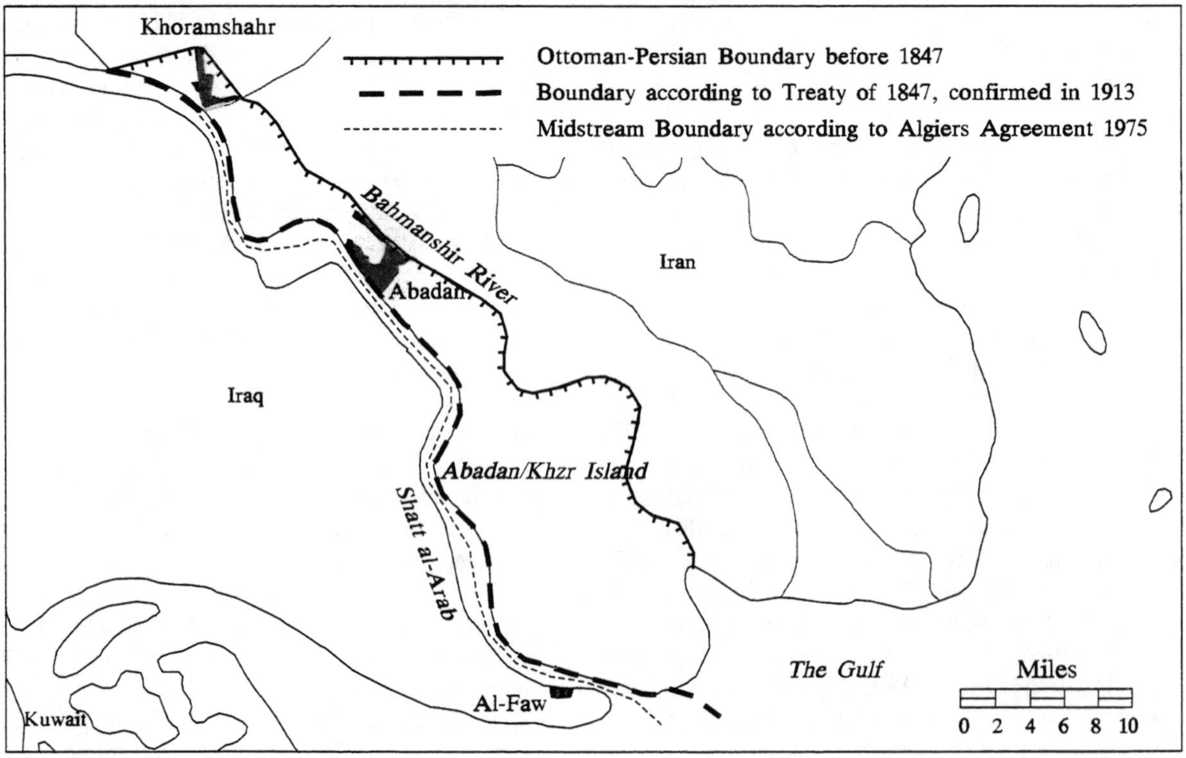

below Abadan. Iraq would retaliate by harassing or even confiscating Iranian ships using the waterway. It became a matter of Iranian foreign policy to achieve a midstream border.

Iran's opportunity to realize this aim occurred in 1975. Weary of the never-ending Kurdish insurgency, Saddam Hussein's regime, prodded by the U.S. Department of State, reluctantly agreed to recognize a midstream boundary in return for Iran's commitment to cease aiding Iraq's Kurdish rebels. In 1979 an intensely fundamentalist Shiite regime drove from office the Shah of Iran and assumed power in Iran. Its leader, Ayatollah Khomeini, harbored deep resentments against Saddam Hussein, who reciprocated the same animosities. Frictions between the two leaders were reflected in increasing incidents along the Shatt-al-Arab. Iraq reported more than 500 such actions in the months immediately following the revolution in Iran.

As the Iranian revolutionary regime began to founder in 1980, the Iraqis went to war against Iran. Although reestablishment of the traditional boundary served as a pretext for the Iraqi attack, acquisition of Iran's Arabic-speaking province of Khuzistan and its rich petroleum beds and facilities was clearly a motivation. Neither state was able to prevail over the other during the many years of warfare, despite frightful costs in human lives and treasure. The United Nations finally arranged a cease-fire in mid-1988. By that time the Iraqis had driven out Iranian forces who temporarily had seized the Faw Peninsula on the west bank of the Shatt-al-Arab. In turn, Iraq had lost most of the territory it had gained east of the waterway. In a futile gesture for Iran's support at the onset of the Gulf War in 1991, Saddam Hussein abruptly relinquished to Iran the few territorial gains it had retained from the war and recognized once again a midstream boundary.

Kuwait

A constant goal of Iraqi governments since establishment of the British mandate has been to incorporate the emirate of Kuwait. The Iraqis have sought this 7,000-square-mile territory for several reasons, including desires to expand a precarious 38-mile coastline on the Persian Gulf, to protect approaches to its inland ports, and to gain the rich oil resources both of Kuwait itself and the seabed territories offshore. Iraq bases its claims on the presumed fact that the territory was part of Basra Province of the Ottoman Empire. Iraqi regimes have also found it useful to manifest interest in the territory to capitalize upon anti-British and anti-traditionalist sentiments among the Iraqi people.

The development of modern Kuwait began in 1716 when famished tribes from central Arabia established

themselves in the area and in the nearby island of Bahrain. They functioned independently like other Arab sheikhdoms along the Persian Gulf until 1899, when they signed a treaty with the United Kingdom. The Kuwaitis were concerned about increasing Ottoman pressures upon them. The British were worried about a German role in the Gulf region following building of a railroad across Ottoman territory to the port of Basra. They also sought to counter Russian interests in building a naval base at the head of the gulf.

Under British protection, the territory claimed by Kuwaiti rulers doubled in size. After World War I, the United Kingdom chose to maintain Kuwait as an entity separate from its mandate over Iraq. The British confirmed Kuwait's separate status in the 1932 agreement that granted self-governing protectorate status to Iraq. Saudi Arabia also protested continuing British protection of a separate Kuwait and closed its land border with the territory from 1919 to 1939. However, an agreement in 1922 established a "neutral zone" between the two entities to provide access to water and pasture for Arab tribal groups.

Kuwait's significance to the United Kingdom grew in the decade preceding World War II, as oil was discovered in 1938 and Iraq's regime developed alarming ties with the Nazi leadership of Germany. The onset of war delayed development of the petroleum industry, but wells began producing in 1946. Subsequently, Kuwait became one of the wealthiest per capita regions in the world.

The United Kingdom conceded full independence to Kuwait in 1961. Iraq immediately attempted to invade the new state. However, the British deterred the threat, and subsequently Arab League forces kept the Iraqis at Bay. Iraq did not end pretensions to Kuwait, however. It was rebuffed in a 1972 attempt to build a road to the Persian Gulf through Kuwaiti territory, and in 1973 it seized a border post and held it for a year. Kuwait meanwhile had normalized its relations with Saudi Arabia. Iraq turned renewed interest to Kuwait in 1990, following the end of its disastrous war with Iran. It claimed that Kuwaitis were removing more than their share of crude oil from the Rumaila field that extended across their mutual border. It also demanded cession to Iraq of Bubiyan Island, which could protect access to Iraq's naval base at Umm Qasr and give it claim to a greater share of undersea oil resources in the Persian Gulf. Kuwait rejected these claims, although it offered to lease Bubiyan Island to Iraq for ninety-nine years.

Despite somewhat ambiguous warnings from Europe and America to refrain from attack, Iraq invaded and occupied Kuwait in August 1990. It had amassed the sixth largest army in the world during its struggle with Iran. Once it subdued Kuwait, it could easily advance down the Persian Gulf coast and seize the weakly defended oil fields of Saudi Arabia and the emirates farther south. This would mean Iraqi control of the world's major source of petroleum. The United States immediately announced support for Kuwait and threatened war with Iraq if it did not withdraw. In the face of Iraqi adamancy, the United States forged a coalition of Arab and European states that soundly defeated Iraqi forces and drove them out of Kuwait in early 1991.

Kuwait suffered profoundly from occupation by the Iraqis, who, in their retreat, set ablaze virtually every oil well in the emirate. Nearly a year was required to extinguish the fires. In addition to the economic and ecologic losses, Kuwait suffered an internal crisis. Before the invasion, fully 60 percent of its inhabitants had been foreigners. Their labor was needed for industry and services.

Nearly half the foreigners were Palestinian Arabs. Kuwait's government always had been uneasy over their loyalty. Although many had been born and had lived their entire lives in Kuwait, all were denied the possibility of Kuwaiti citizenship. Indeed, voting was restricted to a small group of 32,000 men who could trace ancestry in Kuwait before 1920. Many Palestinians willingly collaborated with the 1990 Iraqi invaders. Harsh postwar retributions were met with dismay by the governments that had freed Kuwait.

Syria

The western limb of the Fertile Crescent shares many political-geographic attributes of the eastern limb. Like Iraq, Syria lacks historical legitimacy. When the League of Nations established it as a mandate of France, the territory's only precedent as a political entity was that it had functioned as an administrative subdivision of the Ottoman Empire. Its population saw themselves occupying but a part of a broad Arab national territory. Syria suffers much the same disunity as Iraq, with regionally based religious minorities and a segment of Kurds. It also harbors claims to territory across its international boundaries. Like Iraq's obsession with Kuwait, Syrians have never really accepted France's creation and support of a separate state of Lebanon. Indeed, they have vague pretentions to a Greater Syria embracing the lands of Jordan and Israel and the Hatay (Latakia) region of Turkey.

The eastern shore of the Mediterranean has long been host to political turmoil. This territory, often known as the Levant, was the core of the Phoenician Empire, which for centuries dominated the western Mediterranean region. The area gave birth to the great universalizing religions of Judaism and Christianity, and, in A.D. 636, it saw Islam established as a dominant force when Muslim armies captured Damascus. From their headquarters there, Arabs built an empire stretching to Iberia and to Central Asia. Arabic replaced older Semitic languages of the region. Although Romans had dispersed most Jews from their homeland in Judea long before the Arab conquest, Christian communities survived the Muslim conquest and maintained themselves as distinctive bodies. Islam underwent several heresies, whose adherents formed self-governing strongholds in mountain regions. European crusaders sought vainly to rescue the Holy Land from the infidels, and for a period maintained independent Christian states until driven out by Muslim forces.

Ottoman Turks established ascendency over the Levant in 1516, although they were unable to maintain effective control of the groups living in the mountains. During the 1830s Egyptian forces occupied the region for a decade until Ottoman troops reestablished authority. In 1860 the Turks set Maronite and Druze minorities against each other in a civil war. Western powers under French leadership decided to intervene to protect the Christian Maronites. They forced the Ottoman government to recognize the Lebanon mountain region as a self-governing province under a Christian governor.

France supported Lebanon as a protectorate for the next half century, investing in its infrastructure and subsidizing its educational and cultural development. It also extended its influence northward into the Muslim-inhabited Levant. Other powers came to regard the entire region as a French zone of operations. Newly founded universities and colleges in Lebanon spread European perspectives throughout the Middle East. Although Maronite Christian Arabs tended to adopt an identity focused upon Lebanon, most other inhabitants became imbued with a more general sense of Arab solidarity.

Beginning in 1910, "Young Turks" in Constantinople tried to establish stricter centralized rule over other parts of the multinational Ottoman Empire. Their program fueled Arab nationalist passions. During World War I the British successfully played upon these feelings to promote an Arab revolt against the Turks in 1916. Ottoman forces fiercely retaliated. In Lebanon they terminated autonomy and harshly repressed the population.

British and French troops were stationed in the Levant following Allied victory in the Great War. After the British departed in 1919, Arab leaders in Damascus declared formation of an independent Syrian state. France responded by moving into the interior and ousting the self-proclaimed government. The League of Nations later legitimized the French role by awarding France a mandate over the region in 1923.

Arabs felt betrayed. Politicians and intellectuals in Muslim areas held an image of being part of a "Greater Syria" vaguely embracing the present territories of

Syria, Lebanon, Israel, and Jordan. They did not perceive it as a discrete political entity, but rather as a historic region within a larger Arab homeland. They shared aspirations for creating a broad Arab state for which Syria would be a "beating heart" guarding Islamic ideals.

The Syrian leadership strongly resented the separation of Palestine as a mandate under British authority. To this sense of loss was soon added resentment at French reestablishment of Lebanese autonomy in 1920 followed by creation of a separate Republic of Lebanon in 1926. The Syrians also grew bitter over subsequent establishment of separate autonomous areas for Alawite and Druze religious communities and the transfer to Turkey of the Latakia region around the port city of Alexandretta.

Syrians maintaintained Pan-Arabic outlooks long after achieving independence from France during World War II. Arab activists had founded the Baath party in the 1940s with the announced goal of putting an end to the fragmentation of the Arab people by European-imposed states. The Baathists themselves splintered, however, developing deep animosities between the wings established in Syria and Iraq. In 1958 a group of army officers engineered union of Syria with Egypt into a new entity termed the United Arab Republic (UAR). Tribal Yemen also initially adhered to the combined state. Other Arab states showed little interest in joining, however. Moreover, instead of seeing Syria as the focal point of future Arabic unity as its military leaders envisioned, the far more numerous Egyptians treated Syria as a minor and distant province. Syria seceded from the UAR in 1961 and its leadership gave up illusions of eventual Arab unity.

Syria suffers a number of centrifugal forces. Among these is lack of a clear regional focus. Inhabitants of the cities of Aleppo and Damascus long have been rivals for dominance of the state. Syria also contains a number of distinctive minority groups. These include up to 5 percent of the population who are Kurds, many descendant from refugees fleeing Turkish oppression. It also has small groups of Armenians, Circassians, Druze, and Turkomans.

Religious diversity also besets the Syrian state. Although 85 percent of the population identifies itself as Muslim, the Christian minority does not constitute a significant divisive factor. It is small and divided among numerous sects. Christians have earned acceptance by Muslims because of their constant support of Arabism. They also are dispersed throughout society rather than being regionally concentrated.

Divisions within Islam pose greater threats to Syria's coherence, however. Most Syrian Muslims are Sunni, but other Islamic sects exist. The Alawites and Druze are particularly significant. Alawites tradition-

ally have been Syria's most impoverished and disadvantaged group, eking out a subsistence living in the mountains along the border with Turkey. Many Sunnis do not consider Alawites to be Muslims at all, showing less toleration for them than for Christians and Jews, whom they view forbearingly as "people of the book." The Druze suffer discrimination similar to the Alawites. Numbering only 3 percent of the population, they make up 90 percent of the population of Syria's southwestern highlands.

Currently, Alawites dominate Syria, despite constituting barely 15 percent of the population. After more than four decades of Sunni governments, Alawites came to power in 1963. They accomplished this by gaining influence in the armed forces and the Baath party. They early had benefitted from French recruitment of minorities for the Syrian armed forces as a means of containing subversive activities among Sunnis. Military service brought income to the Alawites and permitted them to achieve upward mobility. The Baath party appealed to them because it promised a secular and egalitarian state.

Despite three decades of rule, the Alawite regime still lacks legimacy in the eyes of many Syrian Muslims. They perceive Alawites as heretics who maintain power by ruthless measures. They remember that Alawites showed no hesitation in quelling an uprising in the city of Hamah that resulted in the deaths of more than 10,000 inhabitants. There is widespread anticipation of a bloodbath of Alawites should members of the Sunni community again regain power.

Baath party domination has had a paradoxical effect upon Syria. Although the party was founded to promote unity among all Arabs, it has been a force chiefly responsible for developing a strong Syrian parochial identity. This perhaps reflects the party's control by a minority less deeply imbued with Pan-Arab sentiments than the Sunni majority and which sees its own greater stake in the separate functioning of a Syrian state. A primary focus upon Syrian interests has also come from quarrels with the other Arab states, including bitter enmity with the Baath regime in neighboring Iraq. The party's development of a strong Syrian military machine has contributed to a Syrian sense of pride. Its building of an infrastructure to foster economic development has reduced regional inequalities. Still, the Baath party has increased sectarian animosities within Syria by its Alawite domination and its resort to force and violence to achieve policies.

Lebanon

The southern mountains of the Levant long have given shelter to groups fleeing foreign capture of their coastal

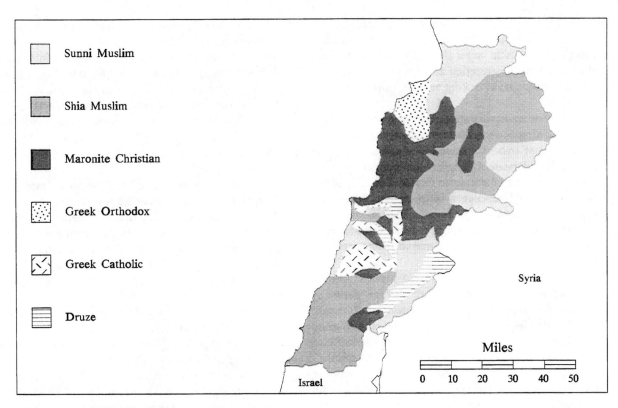

Sunni Muslim

Shia Muslim

Maronite Christian

Greek Orthodox

Greek Catholic

Druze

Syria

Miles

0   10   20   30   40   50

Israel

FIGURE 8-5   ETHNIC GROUPS OF LEBANON

lowland homes (Figure 8-5). Mt. Lebanon and the Shuf Mountains traditionally have played a haven role similar to that afforded by the Caucasus Mountains in the former USSR. The result is an intricate patchwork of peoples preserving distinctive languages, customs, and religious beliefs. Sunni Arabs took control of the Mediterranean shore region in the seventh century A.D. Its former inhabitants were mainly Maronite Christians, who joined earlier refugees in the mountains. More recent settlers in the region include Shia and Druze Muslims, Armenians, and, in the mid-twentieth century, Muslim and Christian Arabs fleeing their Palestinian homeland to the south.

Some 93 percent of the present Lebanese population speaks Arabic, among whom some 15 percent are Palestinian in origin. Arabs are divided by differences in religion. Approximately one-quarter are Maronite Christians, one-third are Shia Muslims, and one-fifth are Sunni Muslims. Others are Orthodox Christians and Druze. The remainder are a number of linguistic and religious groups, including Aramaic-speakers, Samaritans and Armenians. The state officially recognizes seventeen different "confessions" (religions), each of which tends to be dominant in a home area of its own. All have developed greater or lesser grievances against their neighbors. Territorial segregation extends even to

neighborhoods within cities. The capital Beirut is divided by a "green line" between an overwhelmingly Muslim west and a Christian east.

Maronite Christians were a majority in Lebanon when the French established their protectorate in 1864. They viewed themselves as descendants of the ancient Phoenicians and distanced themselves from other inhabitants of the region, even to the extent that many adopted the French language in preference to Arabic. After suffering severe repression by Ottoman forces during World War I, they regained autonomy under the subsequent French mandate. France doubled the size of Lebanon when it made the entity a republic separate from Syria. This act added substantial numbers of Sunni and Shia Muslims to Lebanon's population, thus contributing substantial political problems for Maronites in later decades.

French tutelage ended with France's defeat and occupation by Germany in World War II. The Lebanese, like the Syrians, declared independence in 1943. Ethnic divisions were resolved by allocating governmental positions on a confessional basis. A national pact reserved the presidency of the state for a Maronite Christian, the prime minister's post for a Sunni Muslim, and the speaker of parliament for a Shia Muslim. Under this arrangement Maronites were able to maintain a powerful voice in political and economic affairs. Success of the pact rested upon the roughly equal numbers of Muslims and Christians in Lebanon. Over subsequent years Muslim groups grew disproportionately large. To avoid confronting this reality, the government decided simply not to take a census of population. The last Lebanese census was held in 1932.

A high degree of autonomy in internal affairs was established for each confession. This included the ability of each religious group to raise its own militia to provide group security. Little melding of peoples occurred. Differences in class and economic well-being reinforced differences based upon religious belief. Intermarriage was rare, and for the most part people remained separated geographically. Sunnis dominated the coastal plain, Maronites and Druzes had bastions on Mt. Lebanon or the Shuf Mountains, and Shias formed enclaves along the southern border and in the Beqaa Valley.

It should be stressed that for most groups, religion, as in Ireland, served more as a basis for identification rather than as a motivational force for action. Members of different confessions took different stances on national identity. All resented efforts by Syrians to dominate them. Maronites came to see themselves as a separate nation, with few ties to Arabism. Sunnis in Lebanon shared Pan-Arabic visions, and tended to identify with Iraqis. The Shias, who had become the most numerous group, felt a lack of power. Most identified with co-religionists in Iran.

An influx of Palestinians after World War II upset the precarious balance between confessions. Refugees first streamed into Lebanon in 1948, as they did into other Arab states bordering Israel. In Lebanon they became yet another parochial group in the panoply of peoples there. The Palestinians were housed in temporary camps that became permanent settlements. Their numbers increased in 1970, when Jordan expelled Palestinian fighters who were complicating its coexistence with Israel. Lebanese attempts to control the Palestinians led in 1975 to open fighting that lasted for more than a year until invading Syrian troops again restored order.

Israel invaded southern Lebanon in 1978, allegedly to counter Palestinian incursions into Israeli territory. During the turmoil, Lebanon's religious and ethnic communities assumed differing stances toward the Israelis. Christian groups generally supported them, whereas Sunni Muslims were bitterly opposed. When Israeli forces withdrew, they installed friendly Lebanese militia units in power in the border region. Israel invaded southern Lebanon again in 1982, determined to put an end to the growing economic and political power of the Palestine Liberation Organization (PLO), which supported 15,000 trained guerrilla fighters and managed an industrial complex employing 10,000 workers. Israel at length

forced Palestinian troops to evacuate Lebanon. Another consequence of the invasion was the development of intense fighting between rival Lebanese militia groups.

After Israel's withdrawal, Syrian forces played an increasing role in minimizing strife among the various militias. Although Lebanon's government had lost effective control over much of the state, it was able eventually to consolidate power again. By 1991 it had become sufficiently strong to force abolition of sectarian militias. Lebanon still had to face the fact of Israel's continued control over south Lebanon through its allies.

Lebanese are concerned about the future of their state. Many worry that a possible agreement between Israel and Syria would result in partition of Lebanon between the two. One widely held Lebanese proposal is to adopt a government organization similar to Switzerland's, reserving a limited range of functions for central authorities and granting each group its own self-governing territory similar to a Swiss canton.

Jordan

Among the political entities created after World War I in the Fertile Crescent zone, Transjordan had the least precedent for independent statehood. It occupied less than 35,000 square miles, most of which was empty desert. Not quite 3 percent of the territory was cultivated. Even today 90 percent of the population lives within a fifty-mile radius of the capital city of Amman. During the Ottoman period its northern area was part of Syria and its south belonged to Hejaz. Most Arabs viewed it as a territory of Syria. Zionist colonists and the British government considered it part of Palestine. Its 200,000 seminomadic Bedouin inhabitants saw themselves mainly in tribal terms. Few believed the region to be a distinctive territory deserving of self-government.

Nevertheless, the British government decided in 1923 to form a semiautonomous principality of Transjordan from lands east of the Jordan River detached from the rest of the Palestinian mandate. The British were motivated principally to confine the increasing numbers of Zionist colonies to areas west of the Jordan. As they had done in Iraq, the British chose a member of the Hashemite family of central Arabia to head the new entity. Unlike the Iraqis, the inhabitants of Transjordan almost immediately accepted the legitimacy of their ruler.

Full sovereignty came to Transjordan in 1946 under a treaty signed in London. Its leader renamed the country the Hashemite Kingdom of Jordan and assumed the title of king. Two years later the state of Israel came into being over armed Arab opposition. After several months of fighting, an armistice was arranged in 1949. Except for the small Gaza Strip in the southwest, Palestinian lands held by Arab forces west of the Jordan River were placed under Jordanian administration. This area of 2,300 square miles came to be called the West Bank territory. Jordan annexed it in 1950. An exchange of territory with Saudi Arabia altered Jordan's boundaries in 1965. The swapped areas were empty desert zones, but gave Jordan a frontage of fifteen additional miles on the Red Sea Gulf of Aqaba.

The acquisition of the West Bank population of 400,000 and the influx of an additional 100,000 Palestinian Arab refugees into other areas transformed the demography of Jordan. Palestinians were accorded citizenship and became an overwhelming majority. However, the Jordanian regime continued to operate very much as if it ruled a totally Bedouin state. In 1967, the Six-Day War between Israel and the Arab states resulted in Israeli occupation of the West Bank territory.

An additional 350,000 Palestinians fled the West Bank to Jordan. Disillusioned by the defeat of the Arab forces, the Palestinians of Jordan increasingly saw that the only hope of regaining their lost homeland lay in organizing themselves to do the job. They created armed communities outside the control of the Jordanian government. Their raids into Israel provoked Israeli retaliation against Jordanian targets. This led the Jordanian regime to suppress the Palestinians, driving many guerrilla detachments to Lebanon. For two decades Jordan continued to maintain a claim to the West Bank, but in 1988 it abandoned its pretentions and assigned responsibility for the area to the Palestine Liberation Organization (PLO).

Jordan lacks the regional cleavages that beset other Fertile Crescent states. Contrasts remain between the dwindling numbers of Bedouins and people settled on farms and in cities. Differences in self-identification continue to exist between Jordanian and Palestinian Arabs, but these take place mainly in a social rather than a territorial context.

Without oil and other marketable natural resources, Jordan has managed to support its population of 3,000,000 only with direct aid from other Arab states and the United Kingdom and a continuing inflow of family support funds from a Palestinian diaspora working in Persian Gulf oil fields and elsewhere. Arab financial assistance was interrupted when Jordan's population supported Iraq's occupation and annexation of Kuwait, where Palestinians constituted up to 25 percent of the work force.

Israel

The establishment of the formidable state of Israel within territory of the former British mandate in Palestine has been traced earlier. The immigration of millions of Jews from Europe, Anglo-America, and other parts of the Middle East and North Africa, together with massive inflows of funds from governments and individuals, dramatically transformed a marginal segment of the Fertile Crescent region into a dynamic outpost of the developed world.

As a result of a series of wars that began with its birth in 1948, Israel expanded its territory substantially beyond what its most ardent supporters initially had envisioned for the new state. In doing so it incorporated a substantial Arab population that developed its own strong parochial national identity. It also generated deep enmity on the part of neighboring states (see Figure 8-6).

The result of the initial war for independence was an Israel occupying more than three-fourths of the Palestinian mandate, instead of a roughly equal division between Jewish and Arab territories proposed in the original United Nations partition plan. Subsequent territorial expansion reflected an understandable Israeli preoccupation with security. Terrorist incursions from neighboring lands prompted actions to control those areas. The result was even greater Arab hostility and attacks upon occupation forces and new settlements by groups based beyond the newly established borders, leading to further military expansion and control. Eventually, Israel grew to seven times the size of the Jewish state anticipated at the end of World War II. The process of outward expansion was not unlike actions undertaken to "pacify" Plains Indians in nineteenth-century America, differing principally in scale.

The 8,000 square miles of Israel at the time of the 1949 armistice was vulnerable to guerrilla activities and conventional warfare. Four-fifths of the population was squeezed into a coastal plain barely a dozen miles wide. In the north, Syrians looked down upon Zionist agricultural settlements from the Golan Heights and often exchanged gunfire with them. In the south, the Egyptian-controlled Gaza Strip lay but thirty-five miles from the Israeli capital at Tel Aviv. Israel's precarious foothold in the port of Eilat on the Gulf of Aqaba, giving it access to southern Asia and the Far East, was less than a half dozen miles from Egyptian and Jordanian territory.

The Six-Day War of 1967 resulted in a trebling of Israel's size. It gained the Palestinian West Bank core area, the Gaza Strip, the Golan Heights, and all of the Sinai Peninsula. Israel found itself at war again in 1973. After temporarily gaining even more territory at the expense of Egypt, it gradually withdrew from the Sinai by 1982. This came after Eygpt in a dramatic gesture became the first Arab state to recognize Israel as a legal state.

Although many inside and outside Israel saw retention of Arab territories following the Six-Day War as an Israeli bargaining chip to be traded for peace and recognition from its neighbors, the Israeli regime increasingly viewed the region as a permanent addition to the state. It immediately set about preparing plans to

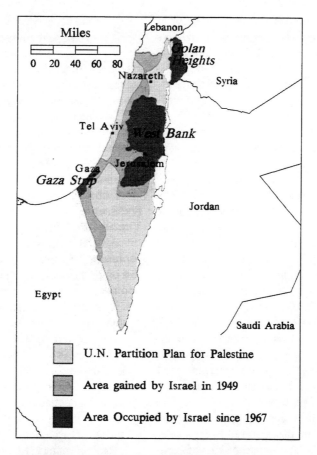

Miles

0 20 40 60 80

Lebanon

Golan Heights

Nazareth

Syria

Tel Aviv

West Bank

Gaza

Jerusalem

Gaza Strip

Jordan

Egypt

Saudi Arabia

☐ U.N. Partition Plan for Palestine

▨ Area gained by Israel in 1949

■ Area Occupied by Israel since 1967

FIGURE 8-6   ISRAEL'S CHANGING BORDERS

establish Jewish settlements throughout the area. Although a third of the West Bank Palestinian Arabs had fled into Jordan, some 700,000 remained under Israeli occupation. Over the next quarter century 150,000 Jews settled among them, two-thirds in the environs of Jerusalem. Officials increasingly referred to the area by its biblical designation "Judea and Samaria" and viewed it as the western limb of legendary "Eretz Israel," seen also as encompassing all of Jordan.

Israeli settlements in the West Bank were achieved through questionable manipulations of owndership laws dating from the periods of the British mandate and Ottoman Empire. By such means the government of Israel acquired title to more than 65 percent of total land in the region. Arab villages saw traditional common grazing lands alienated to become clusters of Jewish-occupied apartments. A north-south string of barren hilltops became a corridor of Israeli settlements, connected by a new highway and effectively splitting the West Bank in half. For the most part the newcomers did not engage in agriculture, but essentially lived as sub-urbanites commuting to jobs in Jerusalem and Tel Aviv. Plans were made for massive further settlement of the West Bank by Jews fleeing discrimination in Russia

and other parts of the former Soviet Union, although the United States and various European states denounced Israeli settlement in the occupied West Bank as violations of international law.

In the Golan Heights, more than 100,000 Syrians fled Israeli occupation in 1967. Following agreement with Syria in 1974, Israel withdrew from a portion of the Golan Heights, as well as from gains of the previous year's war. Israel purposefully destroyed every structure in the repatriated area, however, including the town of Qunaytirah. In 1981 Israel formally annexed its remaining territory in the Golan Heights and accelerated establishment of Israeli settlements there. It anticipated locating up to 20,000 Jewish settlers in the region. The Gaza Strip was too small and densely settled by Arabs to permit a significant Jewish presence. However, the regime encouraged construction of a number of settlements beyond the strip in the adjacent area of the Sinai Peninsula, although these were destroyed and relinquished following the 1977 settlement with Egypt. Subsequently the Israeli regime set a goal of settling 4,500 Israelis among the 750,000 Palestinians crowded in the 124-square-mile territory. The government has acquired title to 34 percent of the land in the Gaza Strip.

A remarkable achievement was the forging of an Israeli nation from the variety of peoples of Jewish religious heritage who streamed into Palestine and Israel. Unlike the nations of Europe that emerged at the beginning of the nineteenth century from peoples sharing common linguistic bonds, the immigrants spoke numerous languages, including Ladino among Sephardic Jews and Yiddish among Ashkenazis. Many knew only the prevailing language of the state from which they emigrated. Public education and the mass media immersed all in a modernized and simplified version of classical Hebrew.

Paralleling linguistic divergences were fundamental differences in attitudes. Immigrants from Europe made up more than 90 percent of pre-independence settlers in Israel. They shared common experiences of anti-Semitism and the Holocaust. Most identified with a secular Zionism that emphasized socialism and a return to the land. They initially sought a mutually beneficial *modus vivendi* with the Arabs. Sephardic Jews had not experienced the historic traumas and ideological development of the Ashkenazis. They had traditional outlooks and were deeply religious. They traditionally had been artisans and merchants, and they shared a disdain for tillage of the land. Although few had suffered overt anti-Semitism in Arab lands before creation of Israel, they harbored strong anger against Arabs for harsh persecution that followed Israel's independence. Most lacked the education and skills of European immigrants and resented having noticeably lower standards of living.

Distinctions and antagonisms continue between Ashkenazi and Sephardic Jews. However, differences have abided with the passing of generations. Up to 20 percent of marriages now are between members of the different groups. The external and internal Arab threats to the preservation of Israel have created among Israelis a common feeling of the need for unity. Conversely, the existence of Israel has for decade been one of the few bonds holding the divergent Arabic-speaking peoples together.

The Arabian Peninsula

The states of the Arabian Peninsula differ from Arab states of the Fertile Crescent in a number of characteristics (Table 8-3). Chief among them is a traditionalism that contrasts with the secularism of Syria and Iraq. Islam plays a fundamental role in the lives of most inhabitants. The peninsula is the birthplace of the Prophet Mohammed and the site of the sacred cities of Mecca and Medina, which are host to more than 2,000,000 Muslim pilgrims annually. A particularly strict and conservative form of Sunni Islam dominates Saudi Arabia, the largest state of the peninsula. Shia Islam is characteristic of the Persian Gulf area, and other Muslim sects are to be found there. However, the regional diversities in language and religion that dominate the Fertile Crescent states are minor in the south.

The region is also much more prosperous. Aside from poverty-stricken Yemen, states of the Arabian Peninsula enjoy some of the highest per capita living standards in the world, derived from discovery and exploitation of petroleum beneath their lands. Although most inhabitants have come a long way from grazing flocks, up to 20 percent still practice pastoral nomadism. Virtually all inhabitants are conscious of tribal origins.

Affluence and strategic position have brought peninsular Arabs into contact and integration with the rest of the world. Such linkage has challenged cultural tradition in such matters as the role of women in society. It also has brought most southern Arabs into daily contact with more secular Palestinians and Pakistanis, whose labor is needed in the oil fields. Before they were repatriated by petroleum states for Yemen's siding with Iraq in the 1991 Gulf War, large numbers of Yemenis working in the Persian Gulf region also came into contact with nontraditional ideas and viewpoints.

Rivalries exist within and among peninsular Arab states that have led to strife in the second half of the twentieth century. Many of these rivalries have at their roots a clash between traditionalists and modernists. For many years Oman was the scene of a left-wing insurrection. Military confrontations frequently characterized relations between the semifeudal Yemen Arab Republic and the Communist-supported People's Democratic Republic of Yemen, which formerly was known as Aden.

Saudi Arabia

More than two-thirds of the Arabian Peninsula is occupied by Saudi Arabia. This arid land of 850,000 square miles has a population of 12,000,000, roughly equal to Syria's and substantially less than the 17,000,000 inhabitants of Iraq. Saudi Arabia is a product of the twentieth century. A remarkable personage, Ibn Saud, welded its tribes together and declared himself king of Nejd and Hejaz in 1927. Five years later he renamed the state Saudi Arabia.

Ibn Saud had been sultan of Nejd, a large political entity in central and eastern Arabia that had never come under Ottoman or European domination. The Saudi family enjoyed great prestige among central Arabian tribes because of its close association with Ibn Abdul Wahhab, a noted eighteenth-century religious reformer

TABLE 8.3   ARABIAN PENINSULA

The Arabian Peninsula consists of one large territorial entity dominating the interior (Saudi Arabia) and a number of smaller states stretching along the eastern and southern periphery. Although nearly all the population is Arabic-speaking and Muslim, it is beset by tribal and state rivalries and deep religious divisions. The states fronting the Persian Gulf have been blessed with rich resources of petroleum.

State	Total Population	Area (sq. miles)	Distinctive Features of Group
Saudi Arabia	15,500,000	865,000	
Dominant Nation and % Total			
Saudi Arabs (Sunni), 82%			Semitic (Arabic) language, Sunni Muslim
Significant Regional Groups and % Total			
Saudi Arabs (Shiite), (5%)			Semitic (Arabic) language, Shiite Muslim
Potential Trouble Areas and Possible Adversaries			
Hasa (Iraq, Iran)	3,000,000	50,000	
Bahrain	550,000	265	
Dominant Nation and % Total			
Bahraini Arabs, 68%			Semitic (Arabic) language, Shiite (60%) and Sunni (40%) Muslim
Qatar	550,000	4,400	
Dominant Nation and % Total			
Qatari Arabs, 20%			Semitic (Arabic) language, Sunni Muslim
Potential Trouble Areas and Possible Adversaries			
Hawar Islands (Bahrain)	100	9	
United Arab Emirates (U.A.E.)	2,000,000	30,000	
Dominant Nation and % Total			
Arabs from U.A.E., 30%			Semitic (Arabic) language, Sunni Muslim
Oman	1,750,000	120,000	
Dominant Nation and % Total			
Omani Arabs, 75%			Semitic (Arabic) language, Ibadi Muslim
Potential Trouble Areas and Possible Adversaries			
Dhufar (Yemen)	600,000	50,000	
Yemen	12,500,000	185,000	
Dominant Nation and % Total			
Zayadi Arabs, 47%			Semitic (Arabic) language, Shiite Muslim
Significant Regional Groups and % Total			
Shafi Arabs, 53%			Semitic (Arabic) language, Sunni Muslim

who founded the notably strict Wahhabite sect of Islam. Hejaz consisted of the Red Sea coast of the Arabian Peninsula. This area had developed a degree of affluence and cosmopolitanism from its steady contact with pilgrims to Mecca. It had been a rather vague part of the Ottoman Empire.

On the Persian Gulf to the east lay the region of Hasa. Its linkages traditionally had been to Iraq and Iran. Unlike the overwhelmingly Sunni population in western regions, it had many Shia inhabitants. A number of petty sheikhdoms had emerged along the Persian Gulf coast. Many had entered into alliances in the early nineteenth century with the United Kingdom, which was intent upon protecting the western approaches to

its Indian territory. As Ibn Saud endeavored to establish effective control over Hasa, the British rebuffed his attempts to incorporate the Persian Gulf entities.

Today, Hasa remains the principal regional problem of Saudi Arabia. In an attempt to minimize the area's identity, the Saudi regime discarded its historic name and thereafter simply called it the "Eastern Province." It treats with suspicion the Shia minority of 300,000, although they constitute between a third and a half of all Saudi petroleum-industry workers. The Shias have reason to resent the Sunnis, who, based on their strict Wahhabite doctrine of Islam, treat Shias as heretics. The Saudi government also is concerned about the large number of foreigners in Hasa, now totalling more than 2,000,000. It views the more secular and cosmopolitan Palestinians and workers from other lands as having negative influences upon Saudi traditionalism, particularly among the Shia minority.

The outer limits of Nejd and Hejaz were indeterminate frontiers, a logical consequence of Arab traditional views of the state as an association of nomadic tribes. The nomads passed through virtually empty territory and had little relevance to state functioning. However, the Saudi government soon found it necessary to establish precise boundaries under pressure from the British, who applied European border concepts to their protected territories in Transjordan, Iraq, Kuwait, and the Gulf sheikhdoms. Discovery of oil in peripheral areas gave added impetus to precise boundary location. In the northeast, disputes over territory with Iraq and Kuwait led to agreements to create two "neutral zones" to allow interior tribes pasturage and access to the coast. Petroleum discoveries caused the Saudis to negotiate elimination of the neutral zones with Iraq and Kuwait by partitioning in 1981.

A dispute over the Buraimi oasis made international headlines in 1955. This region had thriving slave markets as recently as 1950. Saudi Arabia, Abu Dhabi, and Oman each were able to press claims based upon tribal affiliations to the desert region of nine oasis villages. The area became more significant following discovery of oil. After forty years of negotiations, Saudi forces occupied one of the oases in 1952. British forces, protecting the interests of their client Abu Dhabi, ousted the Saudis in 1955. Following the British decision to end its commitments in the Persian Gulf in 1971, the contending states reached agreement on borders in 1974. Saudi Arabia gained a share of the oil fields and access to the coast. Abu Dhabi received six of the disputed villages, and Oman gained three.

Saudi Arabia continues to meet Yemen and most of Oman in indeterminate zones passing through empty areas, since there is no resource incentive to reduce the frontiers to boundary lines.

The Arab Gulf States

Persia dominated the western and southern shores of the Persian Gulf until that country's decline in the mid-eighteenth century. Small communities gained a livelihood by fishing, pearling, and piracy. Arab tribes then expanded authority over the coastal areas from bases in the interior. Their leaders became monarchs of city-states, establishing family dynasties that continue to dominate regional entities. These include the Sabah family of Kuwait and the Thani family in Qatar. To protect the western approaches to its Indian Empire, the United Kingdom entered into defense and foreign-policy agreements with the units in the period of 1820–1840. Because of the special treaty relationships with the British, the region became known as the Trucial Coast.

Most sheikhdoms benefitted from discovery of oil on their territories during the twentieth century. The Persian Gulf region became the principal provider of petroleum to Europe and Asia. Although their populations became fabulously wealthy, these tiny sheikhdoms faced severe challenges to their independence. Both Saudi Arabia and Iran raised ancient claims to these territories. An expansionist Iraq threatened to engulf the areas in 1990, and difficulties in delimiting borders based on tribal allegiances created disputes among them. Improved technologies added to these the problems of allocating petroleum-rich territories under the waters of the Persian Gulf.

One of the most serious challenges today is from the huge influx of foreign workers needed to operate equipment and provide services. Seventy percent or more of the inhabitants of these sheikhdoms are nonnatives. Although most foreign workers are Muslim, frictions exist between Arabs and non-Arabs, between traditionalists and secularists, and between haves and have-nots. A split between Sunnis and Shias also is present, but it does not assume the threatening magnitude found in adjacent Saudi Arabia. Although ruling families and natives tend to be Sunni, few subscribe to the strict Wahhabite doctrine of the Saudis. Because of the small size of the units, group tensions lack a territorial dimension to exacerbate problems (see Figure 8-7).

Bahrain

The state of Bahrain consists of thirty islands occupying a total area of 265 square miles at the northern end of the Persian Gulf. It is really a city-state of its capital Manama, located on the largest island, which has maximum dimensions of ten by thirty miles. Its population approaches a half million. Bahrain is linked to Saudia Arabia by an eighteen-mile causeway.

Although 70 percent of the population is Shia in religion, the Sunni Arab Khalifa family has dominated the territory since seizing it in the late eighteenth century. Many of Bahrain's inhabitants are of Iranian descent and the Farsi language is widely spoken. Iran long pressed irredentist claims to the territory based on history and ethnicity. However, it renounced these in 1970, following determination by a UN commission that the overwhelming majority of inhabitants wished to preserve the status quo. Iranian claims to Bahrain revived after Iran's fundamentalist revolution. An Iranian-inspired plot to mobilize Bahrain's Shias to topple the Sunni regime was foiled in 1981.

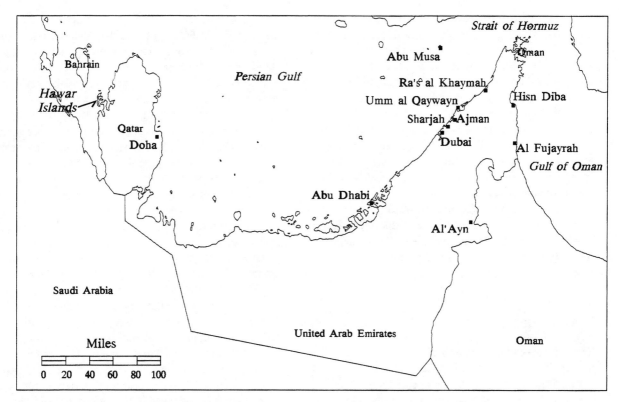

FIGURE 8-7   THE PERSIAN GULF STATES

Despite its small size, Bahrain has a lingering territorial dispute with its mainland neighbor Qatar. It involves the sixteen Hawar islands, all uninhabited and none larger than a square mile in area. Bahrain also has put forth historic claims to a small section of the Qatar Peninsula. The significance of the dispute entends beyond the territories in question, since its resolution will determine the offshore boundary between the two states. Oil has been discovered in the area under the waters of the Persian Gulf. Its exploitation awaits a border agreement, however.

Qatar

Although it occupies a desert peninsula a hundred miles long and fifty miles wide, Qatar is also best viewed as a city-state. More than 80 percent of its population is concentrated in the capital of Doha. Only a quarter of its inhabitants are native. Most foreign workers come from India and Pakistan. Qatar was the last of the Gulf sheikdoms to sign an agreement with the United Kingdom. It did so in 1916 at a time that Saudi Arabia was expanding into the eastern Hasa region from its base in Nejd.

United Arab Emirates

A 400-mile stretch of the Arabian coast between Qatar and Oman is occupied by seven sheikdoms that banded together in 1971 to form the federation of the United Arab Emirates (U.A.E.). They had enjoyed close treaty relations with the United Kingdom as so-called Trucial States until the British decided to withdraw from the Gulf in the year that the U.A.E. was founded. The emirates are Abu Dhabi, Dubai, Sharjah, Ajman, Umm al-Qaiwain, Ras al-Khaimah, and Fujairah.

The continuing unity of the federation is remarkable, given the centrifugal forces that beset it. A major difficulty is the fact that Abu Dhabi contains nearly 90 percent of the territory and 40 percent of the population. It also has the greatest share of petroleum wealth. Its chief rival in the U.A.E. is Dubai, with insignificant area but 15 percent of the population. The two ministates went to war in 1940 over a boundary dispute. The other emirates amounted to little more than fishing villages until recently. However, all have unresolved feuds with each other and with the larger states of Bahrain, Qatar, and Oman. They also have reason to fear neighboring Iran and Saudi Arabia.

The Arabian Peninsula   187

When British forces withdrew from the region in 1971, Iran sent forces to occupy three islands in the Persian Gulf that had been considered territories of the emirates. Iran claimed that they had been Iranian until the end of the nineteenth century. Their significance derived from strategic positioning at the entrance to the Gulf and to their future role in partitioning undersea oil fields. Abu Musa had only 800 inhabitants and was part of Sharjah, whose ruler reluctantly agreed to share sovereignty with Iran. The two nearly uninhabited Tumb Islands had been managed as part of Ras al-Khaimah. Iran's seizure was not contested.

Ras al-Khaimah also was involved in a territorial dispute with Oman in 1977, when discovery of oil reopened an old border disagreement. Oman claimed a ten-mile strip of the emirate and sent a naval unit to assert its rights.

Oman

The barren southeastern corner of Arabia is occupied by the Sultanate of Oman. It has an area of 100,000 square miles and a population of slightly more than a million. It consists of two contrasting parts. The 1,000 miles of coast is known as Muscat. It contains the principal towns and much of the sedentary agriculture. The interior, traditionally termed Oman, is a plateau separated from the coast by mountains reaching elevations of 10,000 feet.

Portugal dominated the state from 1507 to 1649. In the mid eighteenth century the Al-Busaid family came into power and continues to rule Oman. The dynasty also controlled Zanzibar until deposed by revolution in 1964. Coastal Muscat has long been linked to east Africa and peninsular India. For centuries Muscat maintained a enclave on the Baluchistan coast of the Indian subcontinent. It transferred the tiny unit to Pakistan in 1958. In addition to native Arabs, Muscat's port towns are notably inhabited by Iranians, Baluchis, Pakistanis, and Indians.

Interior Oman traditionally has been ruled by Ibadi Muslim imams. The Ibadi schism occurred early in the history of Islam. Persecution by orthodox Muslims led Ibadis to flee Iraq in the eighth century and settle in interior Oman. They have maintained what amounts to a theocratic state, at times challenging the authority of sultans resident in Muscat. Imams traditionally held the view that sultans merely ruled over the coastal section of the imamate, while sultans saw imams only as spiritual leaders of an interior section of their domain. After a major disorder in 1920, agreement was reached that sultans would limit their direct rule to coastal areas and Ibadi imams would have full authority in the interior region. Symbolically, the name of the state was changed to the Sultanate of Oman and Muscat. The arrangement lasted until the mid-1950s, when the interior rebelled and sought recognition as a separate state. Saudi Arabia supported the insurrection, while the United Kingdom backed the sultan. British forces suppressed the rebellion and ended the imamate.

Another rebellion began in the 1960s in the western territory of Dhufar. Its significance was more social than regional, however. Marxists led the uprising, seeking to overthrow the autocratic rule of the sultan. The leftist regime of the People's Democratic Republic of Yemen gave it both financial and logistical support. Guerrilla warfare lasted for more than a decade, until finally suppressed with the aid of British, Iranian, and Jordanian forces. A bloodless coup did depose the tyrannical sultan in 1970. His son became ruler and reestablished the single name Oman for the state to emphasize unity of coast and interior.

Oman has boundary tensions with each of its neighbors. It claims an oil-rich section of Ras al-Khaimah. It continues to harbor animosities toward Yemen for cross-border support of the Dhufar rebels. It has not been able to come to agreement with Saudi Arabia on location of their mutual frontier. Oman has gained great significance in recent decades by its control of the main shipping channels of the strategic Strait of Hormuz, through which pass tankers laden with Persian Gulf petroleum for the rest of the world.

Yemen

Several key political-geographic features of the southeastern region of the Arabian Peninsula also characterize its southwestern corner. Only fractions of these territories are effectively settled. They both occupy strategic positions controlling narrow straits, and their populations are split between Shia Muslims in the interior and Sunnis along the coast. Their central Shia tribes traditionally have been organized into xenophobic theocracies, while their coastal peoples have been outward-oriented, engaging in trade and forming migrant colonies in distant regions. Interior areas have withstood foreign domination, whereas coastal zones have been tied to outside powers. Arabian Sea sheikdoms of both territories enjoyed treaty protection by the British for much of the nineteenth and twentieth centuries.

Until the formation of a united republic in May 1990, the southwestern region, traditionally known to Arabs as the Yemen, never had been unified politically. The territory was sometimes called Arabia Felix, reflecting a favorable climate linked to the area's northern mountains, which rise to 12,000 feet. The terrain lowers to plateaus and coastal highlands in the southeast and east. Only 10 percent of the region's 200,000 square miles can be termed ecumene, however. Soils tend to be thin and poor, and dryness is characteristic, particularly in the south.

Yemenis are Arabs. However, they are profoundly divided by religion and tribe. Islam came to the Yemen in the seventh century A.D. Before that, Christianity flourished for a period. In pagan times, coastal cities had grown rich from their trading monopolies in the resins myrrh and frankinscence. The former served as a base for cosmetics. The latter was important for rituals, particularly cremation. The Christian practice of burying the dead in the ground ended that trade, particularly after the Roman Empire forbade pagan rituals in 325 A.D.

A dissident Shia band settled in the northern mountains of Yemen in 897. The group was known as the Zayadis, and their imams claimed direct descent from the Prophet Mohammed. They remained tribally organized to the present, although, in contrast to other parts of Arabia, most tribal members are sedentary rather than nomadic. Coastal peoples accepted the Sunni branch of Islam and locally became known as Shafis. The Zayadi imams of the interior dominated surrounding tribes by keeping them at odds with each other. They also exerted a degree of political authority over coastal Shafis, although a high proportion of the latter eventually came under direct control of the Turks and the British.

The Ottoman Empire extended its authority along the Red Sea coast of Arabia to Yemen in 1538. Its degree of dominion over the coastal peoples fluctuated in time, and it was never able to subdue the Zayadi tribes of the interior. In the early nineteenth century those tribes also faced pressures from Wahhabites of interior Arabia. Egyptian forces, operating independently of the Ottoman government, expelled the Wahhabites in 1818 and remained in Yemen until withdrawing in 1840. Turkish forces then reestablished Ottoman authority over coastal areas. They faced continuing resistance from the Yemenis, including a full-scale revolt in 1911.

The United Kingdom became a player in the region in 1839 when it took control of the town of Aden. Its aims were to protect the approaches to its Indian Empire and to establish a coal-bunkering port for steamships. Four decades later, this fishing village of barely 500 inhabitants had grown large, following its greater strategic significance after opening of the Suez Canal in 1869. In addition to direct control over Aden, the British signed treaties with a number of native sheikhs along the coast. At the beginning of the twentieth century they negotiated a boundary that came to be known as "the violet line," which separated British protectorates from Ottoman-claimed territory.

Ottoman rule in the region ended with the empire's defeat in World War I. Yemen became formally independent under the rule of its Zayadi imam. The United Kingdom continued to control Aden and its associated Shafi sheikdoms along the Arabian Sea, although Yemen's government refused to recognize the validity of the British presence. It began to seize bits of territory south of the violet line in the 1920s, until driven back by the Royal Air Force. At length, in 1934, it signed a border treaty with the British. The Yemenis also clashed with Saudi Arabia over claims to the adjacent Asir region. The Saudis prevailed and forced Yemen to sign a treaty demarcating a section of their mutual border.

The British took increasing interest in southwestern Arabia in the 1930s, partly in response to Italian overtures to Yemen. They made Aden a Crown colony in 1937 and also sought to establish order among tribes of the hinterland, particularly in the eastern Hadramaut area, where rivalries between Quaiti and Kashiri tribal groups had resulted in a state of anarchy dating back to the nineteenth century. In the early 1960s the United Kingdom attempted to create a federation of the two-dozen tribal entities so as to form a stable government structure to assume authority after British withdrawal from the region. The British had to contend with rival national liberation movements, however, which staged terrorist attacks against British rule. When the United Kingdom left Aden in 1967, radical Marxists seized control and declared formation of the People's Republic of South Yemen. Many refugees fled across the border to Yemen. In 1970 the young state was renamed the People's Democratic Republic of Yemen.

The imamate of Yemen had maintained a policy of isolation to minimize the influence of foreign ideas and to perpetuate its rule. However, to counter pressures from Saudi Arabia, it asked Egypt in 1958 to allow it to join the United Arab Republic. An agreement was reached for Yemen, Egypt, and Syria to form the short-lived United Arab States. Four years later, discontented Zayadi military officers deposed the imam and declared a republic. The imam escaped, however, and rallied loyal tribes. Civil war ensued for the next seven years. Because Shafis in Yemen felt excluded from power under the old regime, most supported the republican side. The Egyptian government also aided the republicans, sending more than 80,000 Egyptian troops to Yemen. Some Zayadi tribes with grievances against the imam also joined with the republicans. The royalists included most of the Zayadi tribes, however. They received material support from Saudi Arabia.

As Soviet forces subsequently discovered in Afghanistan during the 1980s, tanks and jet planes had little effectiveness against tribes defending a mountainous homeland. A stalemate ensued, until withdrawal of support by Egypt and Saudi Arabia led to a reconciliation of opposing forces, although the imam was not allowed to return to power.

The young Yemen Arab Republic continued to experience clashes along its border with the Marxist government to the south, however. Both regimes viewed themselves as rightful rulers of all of Yemen. Their rivalry was tempered by destitution after years of internal struggles. Neither enjoyed the benefit of revenues from petroleum. Although Aden had grown to a city of a quarter-million under the British, exhibiting many attributes comparable to Hong Kong's, it lost most of its income in 1967, when the Arab–Israeli war closed the Suez Canal. Although the canal eventually reopened, its vulnerability and the increasing size of oil tankers made its route obsolescent, and only a fraction of former traffic came back to Aden. For a time the revenue loss was made up by aid from the USSR and the East European states. The fall of the Communist regimes ended this support, however. In the north, Yemen lost a major source of income in 1990 when Yemeni workers in Saudi Arabia and the Persian Gulf sheikdoms were expelled following their state's support of Iraq in the Gulf War. The local economy had come to depend upon remittances to the workers' families. Unification of the two states came following Iraq's defeat.

The new united Yemeni Arab Republic faces a number of centrifugal forces. The old discontinuity between xenophobic traditionalists in the north and radical Marxists in the south has been blurred by discreditation of both past regimes. Parochial allegiances to tribe and religion remain, however. Moreover, the century-and-a-half division between former Ottoman- and British-controlled territories forged regional identities likely to persist long after government unification.

Ancient rivalries and antagonisms continue to frustrate development of a common sense of nationhood. Shia Zayadis long were accustomed to a dominating position over Sunni Shafis. The addition of the Shafi population of the people's republic means that the Zayadi situation has declined from a rough parity in Yemen to a distinctly minority status. It can be assumed that Zayadis will not easily accept political majority rule by Shafis. Urban rivalries also contribute to disunity. Aden's larger size and connectivity to the outside world make it a more logical choice for a capital city than the small and traditional Zayadi capital of Sana.

The combined regime can count on several centripetal forces to maintain its unity. These include a combination of Arabism and anticolonialism. Urbanization and the broadening of education have created a more favorable situation for ripening of a national identity based on secular considerations. Despite its sectarian split, the Islamic heritage also provides common ground. The former tribal quarrels among the petty states of Aden Protectorate were minimized by purges of the former Marxist regime. The present shared poverty and general weariness after decades of struggle

also contribute to acceptance of a government promising stability and relief. Nevertheless, tensions remain because each part of Yemen has retained its separate armed forces, which engaged in open clashes in 1994.

The Northeastern Periphery

Adjoining the Fertile Crescent states to the north and east are Iran and Turkey (Table 8-4). Despite fundamental differences in cultural attributes and historical evolution, the two states share a number of political-geographic similarities. Both states can point to a glorious past in which each had been the core of a major empire. Both long served as bridges from the Middle East to other cultural realms: Turkey to the Balkans and Caucasus; Iran to central and southern Asia. Both are dominated by non-Arab nations that have been influenced by Arab cultures and, in turn, have exerted influence upon the Arab world. Both accepted Islam. Both entered the twentieth century as declining entities under severe pressures from great powers. Both were reinvigorated by strong leaders who seized personal power. In the contemporary world both countries are multinational states facing separatist problems, particularly from their Kurdish minorities. Both have implacable foes for neighbors—the Turks with the Greeks, the Iranians with the Iraqis. Both are relatively large states, with populations several times the size of those of all other states of the Middle East except Egypt.

Although Iran and Turkey share many similarities, they also exhibit some profound differences. Turks are part of the Sunni tradition of Islam, whereas Iranians long have been the core of the Shia faith. Turkey disestablished religion, creating a secular society; Iran adopted religious fundamentalism as a state creed in 1979. Turkey has yet to discover profitable oil reserves; Iran has become one of the world's major oil producers.

Iran

The territory of Iran occupies more than 630,000 square miles, with a population approaching 60,000,000. This amounts to nearly a quarter of the total population of the Middle East and North Africa. In 1971, the ruling shah, Mohammad Reza Pahlavi, ordered lavish fetes to celebrate the 2500th anniversary of the establishment of the Iranian monarchy. Although the exact founding date of the state may be questioned, the event dramatized Iran's antiquity. Earlier, in 1935, the shah's father had ordered the name "Iran" to replace "Persia" as the country's designation. The new appellation meant "Aryan" and conjured allusions to the early peoples

TABLE 8.4   THE NORTHEASTERN PERIPHERY: IRAN AND TURKEY

The northeastern periphery of the Middle East consists of two large and rival multinational states. Their dominant nations are divided by language and religion. In addition to contesting with each other, both Iran and Turkey have sought to impose their wills upon neighboring Arab territories. Each state must contend with serious internal regional problems.

State	Total Population	Area (sq. miles)	Distinctive Features of Group
Iran	60,000,000	630,000	
Dominant Nation and % Total			
Persians, 55%			Iranian (Persian) language, Shiite Muslim
Significant Regional Groups and % Total			
Azeri Turks, 17%			Altaic (Turkish) language, Shiite Muslim
Kurds, 9%			Iranian (Kurdish) language, Sunni Muslim
Turkomans, 2%			Altaic (Turkmen) language, Sunni Muslim
Baluchis, 2%			Iranian (Baluchi) language, Sunni Muslim
Arabs, 2%			Semitic (Arab) language, Shiite Muslim
Bakhtiaris, 2%			Iranian (Bakhtiari) language, Shiite Muslim
Potential Trouble Areas and Possible Adversaries			
Azerbaijan	7,000,000	40,000	
(Azerbaijan Republic)			
Turkey	60,000,000	300,000	
Dominant Nation and % Total			
Turks, 85%			Altaic (Turkish) language, Sunni Muslim
Significant Regional Groups and % Total			
Kurds, 10%			Iranian (Kurdish) language, Sunni (67%) and Shiite (33%) Muslim
Arabs, 2%			Semitic (Arabic) language, Sunni Muslim
Potential Trouble Areas and Possible Adversaries			
Hatay (Syria)	1,000,000	10,000	
Aegean seabed (Greece)	30,000		

occupying the territory. "Persia" was a term bestowed by ancient Greeks and was a corruption of "Fars," a district centered around Shiraz in the south-central part of the state.

Much of Iran occupies a high plateau that is shared with Afghanistan to the east. Elevations range from 3,000 feet to 5,000 feet. The plateau is a region of interior drainage, culminating in two virtually empty salt desert basins in its center. The plateau in Iran is fringed by mountains to north, west, and south, save for a strip of lowlands adjacent to the Caspian Sea. Particularly notable are the Zagros Mountains, which rise to heights of 15,000 feet and higher along the western frontier. The ecumene is limited. More than 70 percent of Iran consists of uninhabited deserts, mountains, and forests. Only 10 percent is suitable for cultivation. Most farmland is concentrated in the northern section of the country, occupying hillsides and the Caspian coastal plain.

Iran's history has alternated between indigenous and foreign control. In the sixth century B.C., Cyrus the Great created an empire stretching from the southern Balkans to northeastern India. Greeks under Alexander the Great destroyed this realm. After a period of development under native rulers, Turkistan tribesmen from the east swept across Iran. In the seventh century A.D., Arabs incorporated Iran into their empire, imposing Islam upon the region. It should be noted, however, that Iranians began to play a major religious role when the Muslim caliphate was moved from Damascus to Baghdad. Later, Iran was again conquered by tribes of Turks, followed in the thirteenth century by the forces of Genghis Khan. Iranian opposition to the Mongol-Tatars led to vast destruction.

The present state usually is dated to 1499, when the Safavid family of Azerbaijan rose to power over a territory more or less coincident with Iran's present boundaries, establishing a framework of social and political organization among its disparate tribes. The Safavids adopted the Shia branch of Islam and made it the official state religion. This brought them into conflict with the Ottoman Turks, who were Sunni Muslims. Constant clashes with the Turks led to a sense of commonality among tribes in Iran, as did later struggles with the Russians and British.

Although Peter the Great had advanced the borders of Russia as far as Iran's Caspian lowlands in the early 1700s, his successors soon withdrew, believing the territory too costly to defend. Russia renewed interest in the region at the beginning of the nineteenth century and captured Georgia and northern Azerbaijan from the Iranians. In moving south, Russia ran into increasing confrontation with the United Kingdom, however, which was determined to protect approaches to India. Neither state would permit the other to acquire Iran. It became a classic buffer state with existence guaranteed by contending forces on either side. Iran thus resembled Belgium, whose separateness was maintained by Franco–German rivalry after emergence at roughly the same time in the early nineteenth century.

The growing importance of petroleum at the beginning of the twentieth century heightened interests in Iran by both Russia and the United Kingdom. Rather than contend for domination of Iran, they reached agreement in 1907 to divide Iran into respective "spheres of influence." This occurred at a time when both states were concerned about the rise of a militant Germany. The partitioning of Iran took place without involvement of the Iranians themselves, and it contributed to xenophobia and a growing sense of national identity among Persians. Such nationalism became particularly manifest after 1890, when Iran's notoriously weak ruling shah sold tobacco monopoly rights to a British company. Popular demonstrations led by religious mullahs forced the shah to rescind the act.

In 1909 growing public opposition forced the shah to abdicate in favor of his twelve-year-old son. Subsequently, World War I saw Turkish, German, Russian, and British forces active in Iranian territory. Military defeat of the Ottoman and German empires, revolution in Russia, and postwar military languor in the United Kingdom permitted Iranians to assert their sovereignty. Leadership came from the elite Iranian Cossack division, created by the Russians but no longer under their control. A colonel in the division, Reza Khan, assumed power in 1921 and had himself declared shah in 1925. He adopted the dynastic name Pahlavi and strove to make Iranians aware of their glorious past. His armed forces curtailed traditional warfare among tribal groups. He embarked upon economic modernization by building a communications infrastructure, and he also weakened the stifling power of Iran's clergy by creating a school system and establishing civil courts modelled on the French judicial system. Mosques were opened to foreign tourists. Although an admirer of Turkey's Kemal Atatürk, Reza Shah's accomplishments were limited when compared with those of the founder of modern Turkey.

The Iranian ruler was impressed by the achievements and efficiency of the German people. He utilized German assistance in his ambitious modernization schemes. After his refusal to expel the numerous Germans who resided in Iran following Germany's attack on the USSR in 1941, the Russians and British again seized control over Iran, forcing Reza Shah to abdicate in favor of his son, Mohammad Reza Pahlavi.

In the postwar period following Russian and British withdrawal from Iran, the son carried on the father's modernization program. Contending with both nationalist and religious opposition forces, Reza Pahlavi (now shah) inaugurated a program of granting land to landless peasants. This stirred the enmity of the Muslim clergy, who controlled a high proportion of the agricultural land. Mohammad Reza Shah also encouraged development of industry and fostered emancipation of women. He imposed unprecedented measures to curb corruption and to reform the civil service.

When the Iranian economy took a downturn at the end of the 1970s, the shah's enemies mounted increasing opposition to his rule. Particularly important was a Shia religious leader, Ayatollah Khomeini, who agitated Iranians for fifteen years from exile in Iraq. The shah at length had to abdicate and leave Iran. Khomeini returned and proclaimed the establishment of an Iranian Muslim republic in April 1979.

The Iranian republic is ethnically diverse. Half the population identifies itself specifically as Iranian. Because several other peoples consider themselves to be part of the Iranian nation, it is useful to identify the majority group by their ancient name of Persians. They are concentrated on the central plateau and speak Farsi, an Indo-European language related to Urdu and Hindi of southern Asia. Most Persians have a feeling of racial uniqueness and believe that their society is a product of a political and cultural continuity extending over several millennia. Individuals find pleasure in the recitation of medieval poetry. Virtually all are Shia Muslim. A few significant regional divisions exist among the Persians. In the northern lowlands live the Gilani and Mazanderani, whose dialects other Persians find difficult to understand, although most also now speak standard Iranian.

Persians are surrounded territorially by a variety of tribal groups, each speaking a distinctive language and sharing a sense of common kinship. Each tribe tends to have group differences from Persians in levels of education and economic well-being. Virtually all trace their origins to ancient invaders of Iran. Most straddle Iran's international boundaries. Inhabitants of the Iranian state generally believe that they can distinguish members of groups by racial appearance, though mixing of peoples over time renders this illusory. The perception is rein-

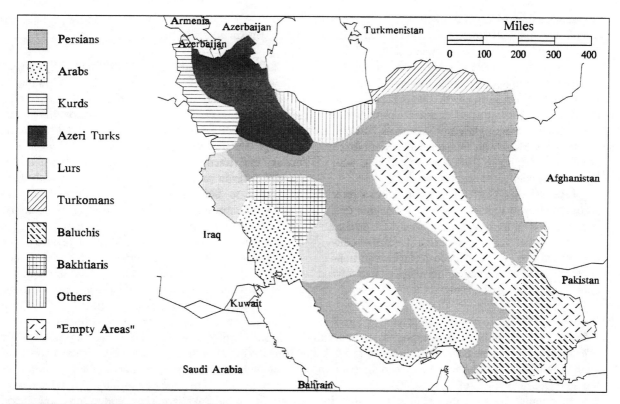

FIGURE 8-8   ETHNIC GROUPS OF IRAN

forced, however, by distinctive garments that many groups continue to wear (Figure 8-8).

Azeris. Azeri Turks constitute the largest minority in Iran, numbering some 17 percent of the total population. They live along the Caspian shores of northern Iran, adjacent to the recently proclaimed Azerbaijan Republic that formerly was part of the USSR. Their non-Indo-European Turkic language is quite different from that of the Persians, and only a small percentage have learned to speak Farsi. However, despite their linguistic similarity to the Turks of Turkey and independent Azerbaijan, Iran's Azeris have shown virtually no irredentist sentiments toward either state. Despite a conviction that they suffered discrimination under Reza Shah, they appear to share with the Persians a common sense of Iranian national identity.

The Soviet Union promoted separatism among Iran's Azeris in 1945 by encouraging the Iranian Communist Tudeh party to sponsor an autonomous Azerbaijani government in the part of Iran placed under USSR authority. Soviet troops prevented Iranian security forces from entering the territory. At that time the USSR was finding itself unsuccessful in gaining petroleum concessions for itself from Iran. When Soviet forces finally withdrew in 1946, Iranian troops entered the region and the autonomous movement collapsed.

Shared religion has led a majority of Azeris in Iran to identify with the Iranian nation, despite the fundamental difference in language. In the turmoil that accompanied the 1979 fundamentalist revolution in Iran, many observers anticipated that Iran's Azeris would seek sovereignty. There were massive public demonstrations. However, most seemed to reflect resentment at what appeared to be an Azeri loss of status under the centralized Khomeini regime. Azeris had played substantial roles in Iranian society. Many of Iran's leading writers, artists, and musicians were Azeri. Two-thirds of the military officers and a high percentage of Tehran's merchants came from Azerbaijan.

It is likely that the 1991 establishment of an independent Azerbaijan Republic in the former USSR will create uncertainties over future Iranian Azeri allegiances, however. Alternatively, Iran may well absorb the northern Azeris, who are beginning to witness their own revival of Shia Islam.

The Turkomans. Iran's northeastern corner is populated by formerly nomadic Turkoman tribes. These Turkic-speaking Sunni Muslims long were a scourge, frequently raiding Iranian settlements far into the central plateau. Iran's shahs could not contain them because their marauding bands could escape to havens in the north. Russian conquest of Central Asia in the 1860s limited the traditional Turkoman freedom of action. The Communist regime forcibly settled Russia's nomadic peoples in the 1930s as part of its collectivization program. It also imposed tight control over its borders. These measures allowed the Iranian military to establish effective authority over Turkoman within Iran, who increasingly adopted a sedentary way of life.

Like the Azeris, the Turkoman tribes can look across the border to a nation-state of their people that emerged in 1991 in former Soviet Central Asia. Turkoman irredentism is likely to become a substantial centrifugal force in Iran. They have been outsiders in Iranian society and do not share the Shia religious faith that binds Azeri Turks to the Persians.

Baluchis. Baluchi tribesmen constitute another Sunni group in Iran. They live in the southeastern deserts and overlap into substantial areas of Afghanistan and Pakistan. Their language is a bridge between the Farsi of the Persians and the Urdu of the Pakistanis. They remain divided among tribes having long-standing quarrels with each other.

Baluchi nationalism manifested itself in 1979, when the new Khomeini regime announced that it would not allow separatist activities nor grant autonomy to any groups. Some Baluchis began attacking Persians within their territory, including representatives of the fundamentalist Shia revolutionary guards. They were not able to develop a consensus on a sovereign future, however, and differences among the tribes continued to permit their control by central authorities. Iran's Baluchis exhibit little or no irredentist feelings for incorporation into either Pakistan or Afghanistan.

Arabs. Up to 2,000,000 Arabs live in Iran's coastal province of Khuzistan, which many now call Arabistan. Other tribes live in the southern Zagros Mountains. They are almost entirely Shia Muslims. They constitute two-thirds of the work force in Iran's petroleum industry. Many have grievances over discrimination and ill treatment by Persians. In the spring of 1979, Arab guerrilla forces in the Khoramshar region adjacent to Iraq were the first of Iran's minorities to challenge the authority and new policies of the Khomeini government.

The government of Iraq sought to exploit such feelings. It gave military training and support to the Iranian Arabs before attacking Iran directly in 1980. To Iraq's surprise, the Arabs in Khuzistan generally remained loyal to the Iranian regime. The Shia religion appeared be a more attractive force binding them to Iran than their common Arabic culture did to Iraq, reflecting the oppression felt by the Shia majority in Iraq to the dominantly Sunni secular regime.

The Qashqai, Lurs, and Bakhtiaris. Three tribal groups are significant in the central Zagros Mountains of western Iran. Significant numbers still practice transhumance, annually moving their herds over great distances. Each group exhibits its own sense of common kinship. They see themselves descended from legendary individuals who conquered the Persians. The groups differ in language from the Persians, but share adherence to Shia Islam. They traditionally have resisted Teheran's attempts to impose central authority.

The Turkic-speaking Qashqai live principally in Fars Province. Many exhibit Mongol features. The Bakhtiari occupy a 150-mile stretch of the Zagros. They are partitioned into a dozen bands that are grouped into two major divisions: the Hafts and the Chabars. Most speak a language closely related to Farsi, but Turkic- and Arabic-speaking Bakhtiari tribes also exist. Although Shia in religion, they are noteworthy for having no mullahs. They were virtually independent until the Reza Shah regime imposed control over them in 1924. The Lurs have a Farsi-related language similar to the Bakhtiari. They tend to look down upon the Kurds and other groups, who, in turn, consider the Lurs to be a wild, hunting people.

The tribal groups are beset by blood feuds that have origins in livestock raiding and disputes over pasturage. The Lurs and Bakhtiari can point to their own medieval states and dynasties. The Bakhtiari have played significant roles in Iranian history. In recent times their leaders have maintained homes in Teheran. The wife of the last shah was from a Bakhtiari tribe. A prominent Bakhtiar leader was one of the few Iranians who supported the Iraqi attack upon Iran. Despite anticipation that the Bakhtiaris would rise to topple the fundamentalist regime, this did not happen.

The Kurds. The 2,500,000 Kurds in Iran are concentrated along the country's northwestern Zagros Mountains. Their language is related to Persian, but they differ from the Persians in their adoption of the Sunni branch of Islam. Traditionally they have been seminomadic. Like Kurds in Iraq, Syria, and Turkey, they are tribally organized and are respected as fierce fighters.

Iranian regimes have sought to control the Kurds by forcing them to settle in villages. At times they moved large numbers to areas distant from their native Kurdistan. In the seventeenth century, an Iranian shah transferred many Kurds to northeastern Iran, both to break up their territorial concentration and to use them to control Turkoman raiders.

The Reza Shah regime early came into conflict with the Kurds of Iran. The Kurds particularly resented a 1925 decree requiring them to wear modern dress. There were five separate Kurdish rebellions in Iran beween 1925 and 1937. In addition to a policy of forced settlement in villages, the shah managed the Kurds by requiring tribal leaders to live away from their homelands in Teheran. In 1941 Kurdish tribes again rebelled in the territory between the spheres of influence in Iran established by the Russians and British.

Kurds in the Soviet sphere received active encouragement to form a Kurdish republic in late 1945. The entity gained support from many Kurds in Iraq and Turkey, but was opposed by governments in the United Kingdom and the United States. Iranian armed forces caused its collapse within a year after Soviet troops withdrew from the area. A number of Kurdish leaders were hanged, although some escaped to exile in the USSR.

Although subsequent Kurdish revolts occurred in 1946, 1950, and 1956, the Iranian regime bought a period of peace with its Kurds by giving support to Kurdish guerrillas in Iraq and providing sanctuaries for them in Iran. This ended in 1975, when Iraq granted Iran riparian rights to the Shatt-al-Arab waterway in return for ending its support for Kurdish rebels in Iraq. As a consequence, more than 35,000 Kurdish fighters and 100,000 dependents fled Iraq for Iran.

Kurds initially welcomed the 1979 fundamentalist Islamic revolution in Iran, seeing it as an opportunity to gain autonomy. However, clashes began with Iranian forces barely eleven days after the new regime had established itself. Kurds seized several towns before being suppressed once again. Subsequently, Kurds suffered greatly during the eight years of warfare between Iran and Iraq.

Turkey

Although modern Turkey occupies one of the oldest continuously inhabited parts of Eurasia and was the core of the extensive medieval Ottoman Empire, it really is one of the youngest states of Europe and Asia. It emerged only in 1923, when nationalist forces put an end to the last remnants of Ottoman authority. Before then, no precedent existed even for the term "Turkey." Turkish speakers had been but one of a multitude of pre-national ethnic groups within the Ottoman Empire, and "Turk" connoted a concept of boorishness.

The peninsula comprising the principal area of Turkish settlement was generally known as "Anatolia," a term coined by ancient Greeks and meaning "sunrise region." In the fifth century A.D., scholars identified the area as "Asia Minor" to distinguish it from the rest of "Asia," a designation derived from the Assawa tribe that dominated its eastern reaches.

By the end of World War I, the Western Allies had negotiated an agreement among themselves to form within Anatolia two new states, Armenia and Kurdistan, and to partition the remainder of the peninsula among Greece, Italy, and France. The region on either side of the strategic straits between the Black and Aegean seas was to be an international zone. Some political leaders had seriously proposed that it be constituted a League of Nations mandate administered by the United States. Earlier, before the Bolshevik Revolution, the straits area had been assigned to Russia. The rapid transformation of the Turkish-speaking population from a passive Muslim religious identity into a modern national group forestalled Anatolia's fragmentation.

The territory of modern Turkey long has been a bridge between Europe and Asia, across which a multitude of conquerers have left their imprint. Each invading group sought to impress its traditions on the local populace, but each also found itself assimilated into elements of the existing civilization. Archaeologists have found evidence of flourishing urban life in Turkey more than 8,000 years ago. Around 2500 B.C., the Hittites established a broad territorial state in Anatolia. Greeks controlled much of present Turkey after 1200 B.C., and all of the area had become part of the Roman Empire by A.D. 43. With Rome's decline and division, northwestern Turkey became the nucleus of the Byzantine Empire, which lasted for a thousand years more.

Turks were not a fixture of the region until the eleventh century A.D. Seljuk Turks captured Baghdad in 1065, expelling its Arab inhabitants and building a broad empire that contested with the Byzantines for Anatolian lands and peoples. Additional Turkish tribes entered the area about the year 1300. These Ottoman Turks derived their name from Osman, their legendary leader. They conquered much of Anatolia and the Balkan Peninsula, including Byzantium (Constantinople) itself in 1458. In accord with their adopted Muslim religion, the Turks officially tolerated other "people of the book," including large numbers of Christians settled in Constantinople and along the Aegean and Black seacoasts of Anatolia. The Ottoman "millet" system gave a degree of autonomy in religious and secular affairs to each recognized religious community. While the sultan was always a Turk, leading officials were Muslims from all groups in the empire. Many had been taken from Christian homes in the Balkans and forcibly converted to Islam.

After almost capturing Vienna in the seventeenth century, the Ottoman Empire entered a period of decline as a result of internal weakness and external enemies. Domestically, it acquired all the vices of the decadent Byzantine Empire that it supplanted. By the eighteenth century, its foreign affairs involved nearly continuous warfare with its neighbors—Russia, Persia,

Poland, and Austria. It lost control over most of its former territory in the Balkans, Caucasus, and North Africa. The Ottoman Empire's last decades of existence were supported by efforts of France, Russia, and the United Kingdom, none of which wanted the others to secure dominance over it.

The nineteenth-century wave of nationalism across Europe had shaken the Ottoman Empire. Greeks, Serbs, Romanians, and Bulgarians became nations and successfully broke away to form their own nation-states. Turks lagged behind these groups in developing national awareness, however. It was only at the beginning of the twentieth century that Turkish nationalist manifestations began. Partly this came on the eve of World War I as a result of defeats in the Balkan Wars. Turkish nationalism often is dated from activities of a group called the "Young Turks" who attempted to reform Ottoman governance in 1907.

World War I was the death knell for the Ottoman Empire, although its institutions lingered for a few more years. The empire entered the war because its leaders feared further territorial encroachment by the Russians. They admired the Germans, who had assisted in attempts to modernize the empire by a number of projects, including building a railroad "from Berlin to Baghdad" across Ottoman territory. Ottoman forces had some successes in the war, including defeat of a joint British, French, and Australian attempt to seize The Straits (between the Aegean and Black seas). However, the empire ultimately suffered defeat.

The victorious Allies imposed a humiliating peace upon the Turkish sultan. The Treaty of Sévres included the previously negotiated Allied provisions to establish nation-states for Kurds and Armenians and to partition Anatolia. Turkish nationalists forced its revision. The turning point came in 1920, under leadership of an extraordinary army officer, Mustafa Kemal, who had played a major role defending the Dardanelles. He roused the military to defeat invading Greek forces, who had penetrated a hundred miles into the interior of Anatolia from a beachhead at the city of Smyrna. The Turks then began moving against the Greeks in the European region of Thrace. Turkish successes led the French and Italians to withdraw from the region. British intervention ultimately established Turkey's western European boundary along the Maritsa River, which flowed out of Bulgaria.

The nationalists formed their own governing body in Ankara that coexisted with the lingering formal Ottoman government in Istanbul until 1923, when the office of sultan was abolished. A new Treaty of Lausanne marked an end to Allied partition plans and established Turkey essentially within its present borders. Greece received some 2,000 islands in the Aegean, but lost its claim to Greek-inhabited parts of Anatolia. A negotiated exchange of populations ensued. More than 1,500,000 Greek and Turkish Christians left for Greece in exchange for 500,000 Muslims received in Turkey. By special provision of the exchange agreement, some Greeks were allowed to remain in Istanbul and some Turks to stay in sections of eastern Thrace under Greek sovereignty. The new state of Turkey became 95 percent Muslim.

The greatest losers in the revised peace treaty were the Armenians. Instead of gaining a nation-state for themselves in eastern Anatolia, their homeland shrank to a small section of the Transcaucasus region attached to Soviet Russia. Armenians had adopted Christianity as a religion in the third century A.D., one of the first groups to do so. Their Indo-European language differed markedly from Altaic Turkish. More than 2,000,000 Armenians were living in the Ottoman Empire toward the end of the nineteenth century. They became targets of retaliation in the 1890s, following reports of Russia's mistreatment of its conquered Muslim Circassians and Turkomans. Armenians responded to oppression by demanding independence in an 1894 uprising. More than 300,000 died in hostilities ensuing over the next two years. In World War I the Ottoman Empire, fearing Armenian support of Russian forces, ordered the forced exodus of Armenians from their homeland to Mesopotamia. Between 600,000 and 1,000,000 perished in the process. Kurdish cavalry forces carried out much of the transfer. Ironically, both Kurds and Armenians lost nation states promised them by the Treaty of Sévres.

Mustafa Kemal assumed the name Kemal Atatürk, meaning "Father of the Turk." He set about creating a secular national state modelled after successful states in Western Europe. He felt strongly that a major problem plaguing the old empire had been the preeminent role played in state affairs by Muslim clergy. One of his early reforms was abolition of the Caliphate, which had become headquartered in Istanbul. He closed religious schools and suppressed religious orders. The Turkish school system was secularized. Atatürk replaced traditional religious law with a new legal code based on European secular legal traditions.

Atatürk's view of the new Turkish nation focused on the western Turks of Anatolia. He put an end to Pan-Islamic and Pan-Turkish irredentist movements that reached out to Turkish groups in Soviet Central Asia and to fellow Muslim Arabs of the Middle East and North Africa. He sought to end Arabic influences on Turkish society by a number of measures, including creation of a new Turkish literary language purified of Arabic and other foreign words and written in the Latin alphabet. The 1929 decree outlawing use of the Arabic alphabet had the effect of cutting off Turkey's new generations from their Ottoman past. Atatürk's attempt to require use of Turkish in Muslim religious services, however, resulted in such strong public protests that traditional Arabic-language prayers were permitted to resume. Atatürk also distanced Turkey from its decadent Ottoman past by such measures as moving its capital from cosmopolitan Istanbul to Ankara in the core of Anatolia and requiring Turkish forms be used to designate towns and cities. Such Greek-derived names as Angora and Smyrna became Ankara and Izmir.

Atatürk compromised his goal of a purely Turkish nation-state by demanding retention of Anatolian areas inhabited by Kurdish tribes. He refused to recognize their distinctive traditions and Indo-European language, however. In 1924 he forbade use of the Kurdish language in schools, courts, and the media. Even the name "Kurd" disappeared, as the groups officially were termed "Mountain Turks."

Although Turks constituted between 85 and 90 percent of the young state, they were divided by dialect and tradition among three major groups—Anatolians, Rumelians, and Central Asians. Indigenous Anatolian Turks constituted a majority, but they included their own eastern territorial minority of so-called Yürüks. The term "Rumelian" was derived from the word for "Rome" and was applied to Turks native to the Balkans. They tended to be more Western-oriented and better educated. The Central Asian Turks consisted primarily of Turkomans and Crimean Tatars. The former maintained ancient traditions derived from a nomadic past. Differences in dialect and outlook of the two lesser Turkish-speaking groups have not assumed major political dimensions, however, for they do not form significant regional concentrations but are dispersed throughout Turkey.

In addition to division according to traditional homelands, the country's Turkish population also is split between Sunni and Shia religious traditions. Up to 20 percent of the people are Shia, termed *Alevi* in Turkey. Turkey's Shias have some linkages to the Alawites of Syria, and their faith suffers a similar rejection by other Shia groups, particularly in Iran and Iraq. Because they have been persecuted for centuries, they have become highly secretive. They are regionally dispersed and constitute little territorial threat to the Turkish state. As recently as 1979, however, sectarian disturbances between Alevis and Sunnis resulted in more than a hundred deaths.

Kurds are dominant in the mountains of eastern Anatolia and constitute 10 percent of the total population of Turkey. Although the majority are Sunni Muslims, up to a third are Alevi. Kemal Atatürk's harsh policies to suppress their separate identity resulted in a high percentage of Kurds who are bilingual and a large number who know only modern Turkish. At the time of

Turkey's founding, Kurdish identities were tribal and religious. Kurdish tribes spearheaded a revolt against abolition of the Caliphate and shariah religious law. The Atatürk regime defeated them and introduced severe repression. Up to a half million were killed and another half million forcibly transferred to western Anatolia. Turkish forces destroyed more than 200 Kurdish villages.

Thousands more Kurds died in a 1937 revolt, and the regime deported an additional 3,000 families to western Turkey. Another short-lived Kurdish revolt occurred in 1943. During the 1970s many Kurds allied themselves with the Turkish Liberation Army, a Marxist group. The Turkish regime again engaged in harsh repression, particularly against educated Kurds. Because of their own internal divisions, the Kurds themselves have not been able to withstand Turkish domination. Outlooks tend to be intensely local. The Ankara government has sought to offer some positive inducements for Kurdish loyalty. These include investment in a huge irrigation and hydroelectric power project in the upper Euphrates valley. This has brought Turkey into conflict with neighboring Iraq and Syria, who are themselves dependent upon the Euphrates River system.

Turkey also has up to a million Arabs living in its southeastern region of Hatay around the town of Iskanderum. They became part of the state only in 1939, when the French transferred the region from their Syrian mandate. Syria maintains an irredentist view toward them. The Arabs, like the Kurds, are a minimal threat because of their internal lack of unity. They remain divided by tribes. A number of Arabs from Egypt and North Africa have migrated to Turkey in recent times.

Several lingering territorial disputes beset the Turks. The most active is Greek opposition to Turkish occupation of northern Cyprus. As noted above in the description of Greece, Turkey deployed 30,000 troops following attempted annexation of the island by Greece. One-third of the island's population of 600,000 became refugees. Another confrontation with Greece involves the bed of the Aegean Sea, where oil was discovered in 1970. Greece claims rights to most of the continental shelf because of its 2,000 islands in the region. Turkey demands that the shelf boundary be a median line between the respective Greek and Turkish mainland coasts.

Turkey also is concerned about the fate of some 900,000 Turks living in Bulgaria. Although it accepts the present international boundary, which dates from 1923, Turkey has expressed displeasure at attempts at forcible assimilation of the Bulgarian Turks that began in 1985. In the early 1950s Bulgaria expelled more than 150,000 Turks to Turkey. Thousands more fled Bulgaria when it opened its borders in 1989.

North Africa

The North African region of the Arab world is "African" by convention only. Its population differs markedly in culture and race from Africans living south of the Sahara Desert. North Africans exhibit a homogeneity in language and religion that contrasts notably with the intricate diversity of the rest of the continent. In marked dissimilarity with the prevailingly tribal organization in the south, North Africa's areas have witnessed the development and maintainance of large-scale territorial units since antiquity.

North Africans have experienced much stronger historic, cultural, and economic bonds with the Middle East and Southern Europe than they have with other parts of the African continent. The Arab invasion of the seventh century left a lasting legacy of Arabic speech and the Muslim religion, the latter requiring interaction with the Arabian Peninsula by large numbers of people. In contemporary times, North Africa has experienced the political currents rocking the adjacent Middle East, including conflicts between haves and have-nots, traditionalism and modernism, fundamentalism and secular-ism. European imperialism during the nineteenth and twentieth centuries contributed to the region's present framework of political organization and notions of national identity. Ties established in the colonial past, coupled with proximity to Europe, have resulted in continuing interactions with former mother countries, including massive flows of North Africans to Europe looking for temporary work.

Although North African states loom large on political maps, their effectively settled territories are quite small. For the most part ecumenes are confined to limited sections of the Mediterranean coast and to the narrow valley of the Nile. The vast desert regions are empty or contain only small numbers of Bedouins moving with their flocks. The few population concentrations around oases are small and generally occupied by peoples who differ markedly from those in dominant clusters (Figure 8-9).

Traditionally, Arabs have divided North Africa between *Maghreb* and *Mishriq* regions, with a boundary at the Gulf of Sidra. The Maghreb to the west includes Morocco, Algeria, Tunisia, and western Libya. It is characterized by a distinctive Berber tradition, despite more than a millennium of Arabic acculturation.

FIGURE 8-9   THE NORTH AFRICAN ECUMENE

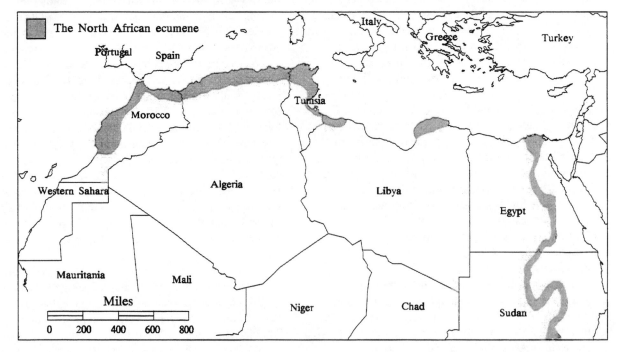

TABLE 8.5   NILE RIVER STATES

Egypt and Sudan constitute a distinctive region whose ancient traditions have survived amid substantial cultural changes resulting from centuries of outside domination by Arab, Ottoman, and British empires. Despite the large size of the two states, their populations are concentrated within a few miles astride the Nile River.

State	Total Population	Area (sq. miles)	Distinctive Features of Group
Egypt	60,000,000	386,000	
Dominant Nation and % Total			
Egyptian Arabs, 99%			Semitic (Arabic) language, Sunni Muslim (90%) and Coptic Christian (10%)
Sudan	30,000,000	967,000	
Dominant Nation and % Total			
Sudanese Arab, 50%			Semitic (Arabic) language, Sunni Muslim
Significant Regional Groups and % Total			
Dinkas			Nilotic (Dinka) language, Animist and Christian

The region has experienced close linkages with Iberia and later with France. Although much of its territory came under Ottoman suzereignty in the sixteenth century, ties tended to be more nominal than operational.

The Nile River States

Egypt and Sudan are traditionally part of the Mishriq, which also extends eastward to embrace the Arabian Peninsula. It is useful to identify Egypt and Sudan as the Nile River states because of the determining role that the Nile has played in their development and political functioning (Table 8-5). Despite a thick veneer of Arab traditions, local societies in this part of North Africa continue to reflect aspects of the civilization of ancient Egypt. The Nile River states have experienced close bonds with the Middle East, including Ottoman domination that was more direct and long-lasting than in the Maghreb.

Egypt

The most populous state of North Africa—and of the entire dry world—is Egypt, with nearly 60,000,000 inhabitants in an area of 386,000 square miles. However, 99 percent of its population is confined to less than 3 percent of the territory. Egypt's ecumene is essentially the delta and valley of the Nile River, which flows northward from tropical Africa through Sudan and across 600 miles of Egyptian territory. In many sections the ribbon of settlement is less than two miles wide. Like other parts of the dry world, Egypt has seen spectacular population growth in the twentieth century. When Napoleon invaded the area in 1798, it had fewer than 3,000,000 inhabitants.

Although conquered by outside invaders on numerous occasions, Egypt has harbored a notable continuity of culture and political organization. Its distinctive civilization has perpetuated itself through the insulating effects of the desert zones on either side of the Nile, and by the internal linking role of the easily navigated river. Aside from scattered Bedouin tribes and a group of some 100,000 Nubians, Egypt's population is remarkably homogeneous and coherent. Most professes Sunni Islam, but close examination indicates a syncretic belief system, with elements traceable to the time of the pharaohs.

Coptic Christians constitute a 10 percent minority, but they are indistinguishable from their Muslim neighbors and lack a regional concentration that would present problems for integrity of the state. They are descended from ancestors converted to Christianity in Roman times. Their name is derived from *qubt*, the Arab word for Egyptian. In the fifth century A.D., doctrinal disputes led to secession of Coptic Christians from the eastern branch of the Church.

Copts represent a steadily shrinking remnant of Pre-Arab Egyptian traditions. In addition to their Christianity, adopted during a long period of Roman control, Egypt's inhabitants spoke a distinctive language, also termed Coptic. Following the Arab conquest of A.D. 642, discrimination in taxation and other matters led most Christians to adopt Islam. Egyptians also gradually lost their ancient language after A.D. 706, when the conquerors required Arabic for all official transactions. The conquest also signalled a loss of indigenous leadership. Rebellion against Arabs in the eighth century resulted in the imposition of a succession of rulers of Circassian, Turkish, Kurdish, and even Mongol origin. Collectively, these foreign ruling classes are known as the Mamluks.

Mamluks continued to rule Egypt well into the nineteenth century, long after the Arab Caliphate gave way to the Ottoman Empire. Egyptians regarded both Ottoman officials and Mamluks as aliens, and in turn they were treated as objects of scorn by their rulers. A change in Egyptian political fortunes began during the Napoleonic occupation of 1708–1801, which initiated an interest in European culture, particularly that of France, that continues to this day. After the French legions withdrew, the Ottoman Empire installed an Albanian army officer, Mohammed Ali, as ruler of Egypt. He was welcomed for his progressive actions, including the sending of students to Europe to master contemporary ideas and technologies. He also extended Egyptian influence southward along the Nile deep into Sudan. His immediate successors created a profound change in Egypt's role in the world by permitting the French to construct the Suez Canal linking the Mediterranean Sea with the Indian Ocean.

The British government soon became involved in Egypt through purchase of the Egyptian government's 50 percent share of stock in the canal when that regime ran into fiscal difficulties. Egypt's ultimate bankruptcy, coupled with increasingly violent manifestations of national feelings, led the British to occupy Egypt in 1882 and to establish a protectorate relationship. Nominally, Egypt continued to be part of the Ottoman Empire, a status lasting until the Ottoman Empire disintegrated following World War I. The United Kingdom then permitted Egyptians to declare sovereignty in 1922 under their own king. The British retained a number of rights, however, including the stationing of troops to protect the Suez Canal. Much of Egypt's history for the next three decades revolved around attempts to reestablish control over its own fate. In 1936 a new treaty redefined the special relationship with the United Kingdom. The British used their position in Egypt during World War II to repel Italian and German forces who were moving east along the Mediterranean coast from Libya. It was not until the 1950s that the British finally terminated the last vestiges of control over Egypt.

In the subsequent period, Egypt joined with India and Yugoslavia in adopting a posture of nonalignment with either East or West. It shared the humiliating defeats of the Middle Eastern Arab states at the hands of Israel. A group of army officers in 1952 overthrew the by then discredited Egyptian monarchy. They established close ties with the Communist bloc as a source of modern military weaponry with which to confront the Western-armed Israelis. They also nationalized the Suez Canal, prompting a joint invasion by Britain, France, and Israel in 1956. Although pressure from the United States and the Soviet Union forced the British and French to retire, Israelis retained control of the Sinai Peninsula. Following America's withdrawal of an offer to build a high dam across the Nile at Aswan, Egypt accepted Soviet aid to construct the facility.

As a consequence of modernization and long struggles with the British and, later, the Israelis, the Egyptian population developed a strong sense of national identity. Like the Iraqis, their collective iconography included images of glories of an ancient past. However, many intellectuals, among them the political leadership, were oriented toward a broader Arab identity. In 1958, Syrian leaders, subscribing to a similar Pan-Arab outlook, asked for and received union with Egypt. To deemphasize popular attachments to what were deemed parochial segments of the broad Arab world, the new leadership eliminated the designations Egypt and Syria and adopted the name United Arab Republic.

The new entity did not become an Arab nation-state, however. Despite abolition of the ancient name, the combined entity functioned as a greater Egypt by virtue of the overwhelming size of the Nile Valley population. Syrian Arabs increasingly found their interests subverted by Egyptian domination. Other Arab states showed no enthusiasm for joining the UAR, with the sole exception of feudal Yemen. Problems brought about by spatial discontinuity, separate economic systems, and cultural differences led the Syrians to withdraw in 1961. Egypt retained the name United Arab Republic until the 1970s, however, when new leadership reaffirmed Egyptian national distinctiveness by officially designating the state the Arab Republic of Egypt.

Egypt broke ranks with other Arab states in 1977, when its president flew to Israel and began negotiations that led eventually to a treaty of peace. As a consequence, Egypt regained all of the Sinai Peninsula. However, Israel did not return the Gaza Strip, which Egypt had annexed following Israel's war of independence. A potential exists for Egyptian border disputes with both Sudan and Libya, but any actions taken in these essentially empty desert areas would likely reflect deeper strains between the governments involved.

Egypt's principal minority remains its 6,000,000 Copts. During the twentieth century their relative numbers have declined from 20 percent to 10 percent of the population. Nevertheless, they are still more numerous than the Kurds of the Middle East. Nearly all live in the Nile Valley south of the delta region, but they are dispersed among Muslim Egyptians. Although indistinguishable in language from their neighbors, they generally are better educated than Muslims and suffer discrimination for their faith. The development of fundamentalist Islamic religious views in contemporary Egypt has placed increasing pressures upon Coptic Christians.

Sudan

In biblical times the territory of modern Sudan was known as the Land of Cush. Greeks treated it as part of Abyssinia ("Land of Burned Faces"), and Romans termed it Nubia. Its present designation derives from the Arabic *bilad as sudan* ("Land of the Blacks"). Its name often is confused with the regional appellation "Sudan" applied to the entire belt of tropical grasslands extending from Africa's Atlantic coast to the Indian Ocean. During the first half of the twentieth century the entity was known as the Anglo-Egyptian Sudan. Its regime adopted the name "the Sudan" at independence in 1956. Two decades later the article "the" officially was dropped from the English version of its name, as was its counterpart *al* in Arabic. (In similar fashion, "the Ukraine" became "Ukraine" in 1991.)

Sudan is a bridge between northern and sub-Saharan Africa. It lies astride the Nile, which flows northward from the tropical region. Characteristics of its inhabitants are derived from both North African and sub-Saharan cultural worlds. The presence of the Nile has made Sudan an object of Egyptian interest since antiquity. For most of its history, however, the territory has not functioned as part of Egypt, owing both to the distinctive black Nilotic racial characteristics of much of its population, and to the region's traditional poverty. This is especially true of its southern reaches.

While not often a part of Egypt in a political sense, Sudan has been the steady recipient of cultural influences coming from the north. The Arab invasion of North Africa brought Arab tribesmen, the Arabic language, and the Muslim religion to Sudan via Egypt. Earlier, Coptic Christianity had penetrated southward, and pockets of Coptic believers still remain. Ottoman influence travelled south along the Nile in the sixteenth century, although its effect was tenuous and confined to the northern two-thirds of its territory.

Contemporarenously, the black African state of Funj emerged in the south. It should be stressed, however, that tribal identities remained basic allegiances for all Sudanese of that era, and continue so to the present.

The modern political unit descends directly from a territorial organization imposed by Egypt, following Mohammed Ali's conquest of the upper Nile in 1821. A major consequence of this Egyptian expansion southward was rapid growth in the slave trade. During the period immediately following the conquest, as many as 30,000 slaves were sent annually to Egypt for training. Slavery had always been a feature of this part of Africa, but never on such a scale. Large areas of the south became depopulated by enslavement or flight to avoid slavers. The present chronic rebellion of southern Sudan traces back to the trauma that followed the nineteenth century Egyptian annexation. Largely through pressures from Europeans, the Ottoman Empire finally declared an end to the slave trade in 1860.

Under a Muslim religious leader proclaiming himself the *Mahdi* ("Savior"), Sudanese expelled the Egyptians in 1885. Egypt by this time had itself become a protectorate of the United Kingdom. In 1898, joint British and Egyptian forces reimposed Egypt's authority over Sudan. In doing so, they not only reclaimed rebellious territory commanded by the Mahdi, but also thwarted French attempts to extend their empire eastward across the Sudanese grasslands from their colony in Chad. An additional two decades was required for British and Egyptian forces to subdue the last pockets of Sudanese resistance, however.

The victors organized the region into a condominium named the Anglo-Egyptian Sudan. Although the British scrupulously adhered to terms of their agreement with Egypt for joint management, the United Kingdom effectively made decisions for the area. One of the most significant of these was establishment of a "closed door" policy in regard to the black population inhabiting the southern third of Sudan. This action virtually excluded northerners from the region and permitted no proselytizing by Muslim missionaries. It also forbade use of the Arabic language. The British made provision for indirect rule by tribal chiefs in the south. A 1930 directive specified that southerners were a "distinctive people" and set a course for their eventual integration into British East Africa.

A sense of Sudanese national identity emerged among a large proportion of northerners during the period after World War I. Frictions with Egyptians holding official posts contributed to this development, as did the "closed-door" policy. The United Kingdom ended the use of Egyptian administrators in 1924. However, restrictions imposed by the Anglo-Egyptian treaty continued to pose problems for its effective governance of Sudan. Egypt wielded a veto power and maintained a claim of suzerainty over the territory. Only in 1952 did Egypt recognize a Sudanese right to self-determination. The United Kingdom then set into motion plans for a popular vote on self-government.

As a result of that referendum, the British granted Sudan's independence in 1956. By this time, however, the south was in open rebellion. Among numerous grievances was an announced plan to establish Arabic as official language of the new state. Although nearly all northerners spoke Arabic, southerners employed a variety of local tongues and used English as a second language. Southerners felt that their lack of Arabic would put them at a marked disadvantage in competing for government jobs. Their initial rebellion lasted fifteen years and took at least 500,000 lives.

The north-south division of independent Sudan remains a substantial centrifugal force. Although only 40 percent of the population is ethnically Arab, the government has embarked upon a general campaign of Arabization. Its efforts have been relatively successful among the 70 percent of the population concentrated in the northern two-thirds of the state, facilitated by the fact that virtually all practice the Sunni version of Islam. It has been less successful among Christian and animist black Sudanese in the south. Their cultures are markedly different, and they chafe against contemptuous actions directed against them by northerners, including their general designation by Arabs as *abt* ("slaves"). Guerrilla warfare by the southern Sudanese erupted again in the 1980s.

Both parts of Sudan are far from being homogeneous. Differences exist in the north, particularly between Arabs and dark-skinned Nubians, although the latter long have spoken the Arabic language. Both are further divided by tribal allegiances and adherence to differing Islamic sects. Southerners speak more than 100 different languages. Among these, Dinka, used by 40 percent, dominates. Complicating the ethnic mosaic of both regions is the presence of large numbers of refugees from Chad and Ethiopia in border areas. Sudanese also resent the many Egyptians who have migrated to their country.

As in most former colonial areas, potential disputes exist over precise delimitation of borders. Most were drawn through virtually empty territory by imperial negotiators who had broader international considerations in mind than the immediate parochial problem at hand. In 1934 the British conceded to Italian Libya the so-called Sarra Triangle that had been Sudan's northwest corner. Sudanese tensions with Ethiopia over their 1,300-mile mutual border were eased when both sides reached agreement in principle on its location. Unresolved differences continue to exist with Egypt, however. An 1899 treaty defined the Anglo-Egyptian Sudan's northern boundary as the parallel 22°N. In practice, however, jurisdiction of Sudanese administrators east of the Nile was advanced seventy miles northward to the 23rd parallel. The British adopted this *de facto* boundary to accommodate traditional grazing areas of Sudanese tribes. Since independence, however, Egypt has insisted upon maintaining the *de jure* border of 22°N, in part because it contains the temple of Abu Simnel.

The Maghreb

Following their conquest of Africa in the seventh century, Arabs came to term the cluster of settlements in the northwest as the *jazirat al maghreb* ("island of the west"), between the "sea of sand" to the south and the Mediterranean to the north. The name has remained to designate this isolated part of the Arab-Muslim world (Table 8-6). The indigenous population descends from Berber tribes who migrated from southwest Asia some 5,000 years ago. About 1100 B.C. those living along the coast became a significant part of the Phoenician trading empire based in the Levant. Beginning in 600 B.C., the city of Carthage, located in modern Tunisia, came to dominate the Mediterranean coastal strip and the scattered commercial colonies extending down the Atlantic coast.

Carthage became involved in a series of wars with the rival city-state of Rome, beginning in 264 B.C. Rome finally prevailed in 147 B.C., and the region became the granary of the Roman Empire. Romans resettled large numbers of Jews in the region, following suppression of the Jewish revolt in Palestine. The new arrivals had a significant impact on native Berber tribes, many of whom adopted Judaism. During the second century A.D. most Judaic Berbers became Christian. From this milieu emerged St. Augustine, one of the towering figures of early Christianity.

Northwest Africa remained part of the Roman and Byzantine empires for more than 500 years. As elsewhere, Romans imposed law and order and created an infrastructure encouraging economic development. They protected coastal holdings from Saharan nomads by constructing a line of forts in the interior. As Roman power declined during the fifth century A.D., Germanic Vandal tribes took over northwest Africa from a base in Iberia.

Two centuries later, Arabs conquered the region. As they had done in the Levant and elsewhere, they imposed their language, religion, and political structure upon local inhabitants. Because Arab armies moved without women, many soldiers took native wives. This facilitated Arabization of the territory, particularly of

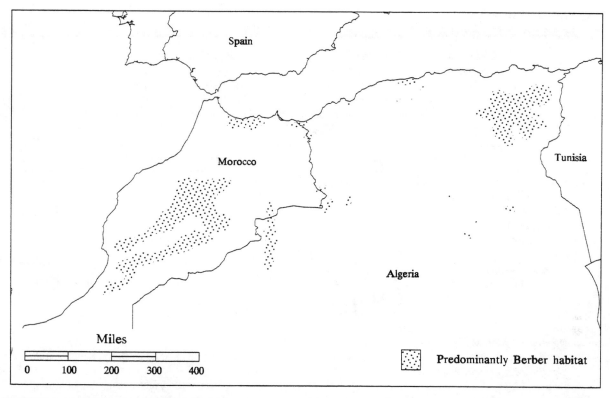

FIGURE 8-10 BERBERS OF THE MAGHREB

the coastal region. Many Berbers fled southward into the mountains, where they were able to maintain their traditional culture and tribal organization.

Islam replaced Christianity among these Berbers, however, as it did in the coastal strip. The new religion soon suffered a number of divisions. Although Arab-based Sunni Islam dominated coastal communities, unassimilated Berbers developed their own distinctive Kharidjite sect of Islam in the eighth century. The dispute between Shia and Sunni divisions revolved around which Arab group was legitimate heir to the Caliphate. In part as a protest against Arab domination of their society, Berbers who became Kharidjites rejected both divisions and proclaimed that any Muslim with appropriate credentials could be elected Caliph, whether or nor he happened to be Arab or a descendant of Mohammed. The militant Ismaili sect of Shia Islam also gained adherents in northwest Africa. Its followers eventually destroyed Kharidjite tribal kingdoms and moved eastward, eventually to seize all Egypt. Subsequently, Sunni Islam reestablished a dominating position among the Maghreb Berbers, who, in their remoteness from Arabia, had become for all practical purposes independent.

The original Arab invasion extended into the Iberian Peninsula and southern France. In the twelfh century, a Berber tribal confederation in the Maghreb expanded to dominate the flourishing Muslim states in Spain. A fusion of the two societies led to establishment of a distinctive culture known as Moorish civilization. It was a scene of remarkable learning and creativity, still reflected in its magnificent architecture. Ultimately, however, the Moors failed politically. As Muslim Berber power weakened in Spain, Christian kingdoms expanded from their northern bases. Finally, in 1492, the Moorish stronghold of Granada fell, ending seven centuries of Christian reconquest of Spain. The victors forcibly converted Spanish Jews and Muslims to Christianity or forced them to flee to the Maghreb. Many refugees subsequently rose to high positions or otherwise made significant contributions to northwestern Africa's cultural development.

Christian Spaniards established several footholds along the coast of the Maghreb in the fifteenth century. From these they threatened to expand their increasingly dynamic reconquest into North Africa. Discovery of the Americas put an end to such plans, however. The Spanish task would not have been diffi-

TABLE 8.6 THE MAGHREB

The states of northwest Africa share a common heritage of Carthagenian, Roman, Arab, Moorish, Ottoman, and French/Italian traditions. European colonialism ended after World War II, but economic and cultural linkages tend to be stronger with Western Europe than with other sections of the Middle East. Divisions exist within each state between Arabized and Europeanized Mediterranean coastal peoples and Berber-speaking nomadic peoples of the interior. Effectively settled areas constitute only a small fraction of total territories.

State	Total Population	Area (sq. miles)	Distinctive Features of Group
Morocco	27,000,000	180,000	
Dominant Nation and % Total			
Moroccan Arabs, 70%			Semitic (Arabic) language, Sunni Muslim
Significant Regional Groups and % Total			
Berbers, 30%			Semitic (Berber) language, Sunni Muslim
Algeria	27,000,000	920,000	
Dominant Nation and % Total			
Algerian Arabs, 82%			Semitic (Arabic) language, Sunni Muslim
Significant Regional Groups and % Total			
Berbers, 17%			Semitic (Berber) language, Sunni Muslim
Tunisia	8,500,000	60,000	
Dominant Nation and % Total			
Tunisian Arabs, 98%			Semitic (Arabic) language, Sunni Muslim
Significant Regional Groups and % Total			
Berbers, 1%%			Semitic (Berber) language, Sunni Muslim
Libya	4,500,000	680,000	
Dominant Nation and % Total			
Libyan Arabs, 85%			Semitic (Arabic) language, Sunni Muslim
Significant Regional Groups and % Total			
Berbers, 5%			Semitic (Berber) language, Sunni Muslim

cult, since Muslims south of the Straits of Gibraltar had become fragmented politically into territorial units roughly approximating modern Morocco, Algeria, and Tunisia. In addition, many coastal communities maintained a separate self-governing existence. Some became lairs of pirates, who most often were expellees from Spain (*Moriscos*). They saw their occupation as a profitable continuation of holy war against the infidels.

One pirate leader, nicknamed Barbarossa, or "Redbeard," by Europeans, established personal authority over the flourishing city-state of Algiers. The Spanish garrison stationed on a harbor island contested his rule, as did inhabitants of Algiers itself. Seeking outside assistance, in 1518 he concluded an agreement with the Ottoman Empire recognizing suzerainty of the sultan. Turkish troops soon arrived to assist Barbarossa in defeating the Spanish forces and consolidating power within the city. Barbarossa later expanded his region of authority to the entire coastal strip between the communities of Oran and Constantine.

Thus began three centuries of linkage of this portion of the Maghreb to Constantinople. The Turks expelled Spanish forces from their several North African footholds. Farther west, Moroccans managed to maintain a territorial state under their own sultan, eluding Ottoman ties. They drove the Portuguese from enclaves established on the Atlantic coast. Tunisia and Tripolitania to the east did succumb to Ottoman imperial control, however. In 1587, the empire divided its northwest African territory into three administrative parts, centered, respectively, on Algiers, Tunis, and Tripoli. Ottoman representatives generated hostility by treating the local population as inferiors. Turks reserved for themselves the right to be called "Algerians" and excluded the Arab-Berber population from governmental activities. Direct Ottoman control steadily weakened, however, and, by the eighteenth century, the Maghreb territories had become essentially self-governing entities.

For the next 300 years piracy was a principal occupation of the Maghreb ports. Barbary corsairs ranged widely throughout the Mediterranean and even as far as the North Sea. Many participants were renegade Europeans who had adopted Islam. Particularly profitable was the seizure of sailors and passengers for ransom. Local officials regularized the activity, making provision for keeping prisoners and establishing prices for repatriation. They sold as slaves those not ransomed. Several foreign states paid substantial tribute to local Maghreb authorities to protect shipping. Among these was the fledgling United States of America, which in a treaty of 1797 guaranteed that $10,000,000 would be paid over a twelve-year period to the Barbary states. In 1800 this amounted to 20 percent of the country's annual revenues. The tribute was deemed necessary because the British navy no longer protected American ships.

After the end of the Napoleonic Wars, European states turned their attention to suppressing piracy in the Mediterranean. In 1815 the Barbary states found themselves at war with at least a half-dozen countries. In that year the United States made a dramatic show of force. Commodore Stephen Decatur led a squadron of ten warships into Algiers to force an end to the paying of tribute. He required the local ruler sign a treaty that included freeing American prisoners without ransom, paying reparations, and ending interference with American shipping. The ruler renounced the treaty as soon as Decatur sailed out of the harbor, but a joint British and Dutch force demanded similar terms the following year and was able to exact compliance.

European colonial control came to the Maghreb early in the nineteenth century. Following decades of frictions between Algiers and France, the French government decided to seize the area in 1830. France asserted that Algiers had become a threat to other states and was unable to manage its own affairs. In contrast to the relatively well-ordered neighboring states of Morocco and Tunisia, the Algerian region lacked political integration and could not withstand the Europeans. The invasion of Algeria was not universally popular in France. In response, the regime founded the French Foreign Legion in 1831. Under its statute, it could recruit only foreign mercenaries, not Frenchmen. The Foreign Legion conveniently provided a source of employment for the many Germans, Poles, and others who had flocked to France after the July 1830 Revolution. Arab-Berber tribal groups resisted the French for many decades. It is estimated that more than 3,000,000 were killed in the period from 1830 to 1930.

Algeria became a region of overseas European settlement. The French government offered free land and other inducements to immigrants. Natives lost 40 percent of their agricultural lands. By 1950, the European community had grown to more than 1,000,000. They were known generally as *colons* or *pieds noir* ("black feet"). Although many settlers were French from Corsica and the south of France, the majority of settlers actually came from Spain and Italy. All were assimilated into the French cultural world. Not all became wealthy, but most developed attitudes of superiority toward the native population.

The French regime formally incorporated Algeria as a part of metropolitan France. It treated Arab-Berbers as equals only if they adopted a European way of life. This was impossible for devout Muslims, who viewed civil administration and the legal system as inseparable from the Islamic religion. Most Muslims thus did not attain the status of full French citizenship. They were treated as subject peoples with the inferior status of "nationals."

France expanded eastward into Tunisia a half century after its acquisition of Algeria. Tunisia had played a significant role in Europe during the Renaissance as a source of revived Greek and Roman learning. It had maintained itself as a successful state from the thirteenth to the sixteenth centuries, when it became part of the Ottoman Empire. It developed virtual independence again after 1705.

Both France and Italy cast covetous eyes on Tunisia in the second half of the nineteenth century. For Italians, it was the closest area available for colonial development. Many emigrants from the overpopulated Italian *Mezzogiorno* had acquired farming land there. In addition to seeking ever more lands for their empire, the French considered Tunisia a troublesome sanctuary for tribes raiding their settlements in Algeria. Using this as a pretext, the French invaded Tunisia and established a protectorate there in 1883. They maintained the ruling bey (native ruler) of Tunis as a nominal head of government. The new regime opened up Tunisian lands to European agricultural colonization, and a large group of *colons* (settlers) developed. They acquired a fifth of the land suitable for farming. The French eventually compensated Italian pretentions to Tunisia by allowing Italy a free hand farther east in Tripolitania and Cyrenaica.

West of French Algeria was Morocco. Its sultans had evaded Ottoman control and escaped European domination until the beginning of the twentieth century. It is interesting to note that Morocco was the first state to recognize the independence of the United States of America. Its success in resisting imperialism can be explained in part by rivalry among the European powers. Like Belgium and Switzerland, it was a kind of buffer state whose existence was perpetuated by resistance of each major state to any other country taking control of it.

Morocco's independence ended in 1904, however, when the United Kingdom tacitly allowed France to extend "influence" into Morocco in return for recognition of British domination of Egypt. France's expansion was not easy, however, because Germany immediately made known its displeasure at not being consulted in the matter. The German kaiser actually came to the city of Tangier to denounce the French move. The French bought off German objections by granting Germany 100,000 square miles of Cameroon territory in equatorial Africa.

Spain also had an interest in the fate of Morocco. France allowed Spain to establish its own zones of influence in Morocco's northern and southern extremities. The arrangement was formalized in 1912, when a French protectorate was proclaimed for the main part of Morocco and a Spanish protectorate established along the north coast and in the south adjacent to Spain's Western Sahara colony. To ease British and other concerns about free navigation through the Straits of Gibraltar, the adjacent town of Tangier was declared an international zone. Native tribes resisted the forces of both European states. France eventually settled 300,000 *colons* in its Morocco Protectorate. They acquired about 8 percent of the arable farmland. Spain pacified its territory by the mid-1920s. It was from the Spanish northern protectorate, using Moroccan troops, that Generalissimo Francisco Franco launched his successful campaign to overthrow the republican government of Spain.

Sovereignty came to French-controlled sections of the Maghreb after World War II, but only following years of struggle against French domination. Agitation against the French in the three major Maghreb areas began in 1952. Successes of anticolonial forces in the Dutch East Indies and French Indo-China buoyed those leading the campaign. The murder of a popular native labor leader in Tunisia by vigilante *colons* touched off events. Until that time, Tunisians had lacked the anti-French mood that long had smoldered in Algeria. Their violent reaction to the assassination had reverberations across North Africa. In Morocco, the reigning sultan assumed leadership of a growing nationalist movement that was not radical or anti-French, but sought an end to protectorate status. The French exiled him to the island of Madagascar for his activities and this made him a hero and a martyr to those demanding independence. A more pliant elderly relative installed on the throne could not win the allegiance of the population, however, most of whom continued to recognize the legitimacy of his predecessor as both secular and religious leader of Morocco. Only Berber tribes of the interior accepted the change, reflecting their enmity toward the Arabized coastal peoples and positive view of the French as protectors of their interests.

Overt anti-French actions were minor in Tunisia and Morocco in comparison with development of a national liberation war in Algeria lasting for eight years and ultimately resulting in loss of more than a million lives and relocation of more than a third of the native population. Initial demands of most of the Muslim population were for equality and fairness. It was still possible in 1952 for France to make concessions and develop a relationship with Algeria similar to that of the United States with Hawaii. However, diehard demands of the Algerian nationalists and intense resistance to change by the million *colons* frustrated appropriate action by the weak postwar governments of France, which were still smarting from military defeat in Indo-China.

France conceded an end to its protectorates in Tunisia and Morocco in 1956 (Spain simultaneously gave up its Moroccan protectorate also). The French did not end their struggle to hold Algeria until 1962. In that year, following signing of a peace accord with Algerian liberation forces, more than 1,000,000 *colons* emigrated to France. Among them were 140,000 Jews, who saw no future for themselves in a Muslim national state after the successful founding of Israel in the Middle East. Most emigres had known no other country than Algeria, and their absorption into metropolitan France was accompanied by many economic and political problems. As noted earlier, their arrival in Corsica generated strong local reaction affecting that island's relations with the mainland.

The three former French areas pursued quite different courses following independence. The sultan of Morocco returned from exile to maintain a conservative royalist regime. Triumphant nationalists in Algeria established a radical socialist state bolstered by a popular unity generated over the many years of struggle. Tunisia became a national republic that stressed its distinctive Cathagenian and Roman heritage. The Berber inheritance of all three states is reflected in the distance that they have maintained from trends besetting other parts of the Arab world. Although the majority of the population long has been Arabized in language and religion, its distinctive traditions continue to frustrate those who would forge a Pan-Arab national identity.

The different paths taken by these postcolonial regimes have generated some frictions among them. These are particularly reflected in disputes over inherited borders. Algeria and Morocco engaged in a border war in the early 1960s. The young states also assumed different stances in international relations. Algeria cultivated close relations with the Soviet bloc, whereas Morocco and Tunisia maintained ties with the United States and Western Europe. Within the Muslim world,

Algeria has found common cause with the radical states of Syria and Iraq, while Morocco has tended to identify with policies of Saudi Arabia.

The Maghreb states face problems of integrating Berber tribesmen who have not been Arabized. They constitute more than 40 percent of the population of Morocco and 25 percent of Algeria's inhabitants. Most are concentrated in the mountains. Their Hamitic speech is divided among three major dialects and has no written form. A majority are bilingual in Arabic, and less than 15 percent speak only Berber. Their tribes have maintained an individualism that contrasts with the more authoritarian Byzantine traditions of the Arabized population. In many ways the Berber situation parallels that of the Kurds of the Middle East. However, Berbers manifest virtually none of the separatism characteristic of Kurds in the twentieth century. Personal allegiances remain tribal, and the various tribes exhibit little sense of political cohesion. Arabic remains a language of status among them, and there is little agitation for institutionalizing the Berber language in schools and official activities.

Morocco

Contemporary Morocco continues unbroken rule by a dynasty founded in 1666. Following ending of the French and Spanish protectorates in 1956, Morocco soon acquired the internationalized city of Tangier as a result of joint agreement among the several states that had involved themselves in Tangier's affairs. Spain granted Morocco a northern strip of its Western Sahara colony in 1958, and in 1969 further conceded its colony of Ifni. Spain continues to retain its enclaves of Ceuta and Melilla, but Morocco has not ceded its claim to them.

Moroccans take pride in their resistance to incorporation into the Ottoman Empire and into the European empires that engulfed their neighbors. Many maintain views of a historic Greater Morocco stretching south to the Senegal River and incorporating substantial parts of the Sahara occupied by Algeria and Mauritania. This brings Morocco into conflict with its neighbors.

Its border with Algeria is a product of negotiations dating back to the French Algerian conquest of 1830. France recognized in vague terms Morocco's claim to North African territory not part of the Ottoman Empire. After suffering raids from Moroccan-based Berber tribes, France insisted on reducing to a border line the prevailing frontier zone existing between its Algerian holdings and Morocco. An 1845 treaty established a line for 100 miles, but noted only a division among cus-

tomary tribal territories farther south. Conflicts continued with the Moroccan tribes. In 1912, following establishment of its protectorate over Morocco, a new "Varnier Line" was established as the border between the two colonial areas. It added several hundred square miles to Algeria west of the old boundary.

Following French departure from Algeria, Morocco sent troops to the Algerian Sahara to occupy areas that it viewed as being unfairly lost. Algeria claimed that Morocco had agreed to a westward shift of the boundary, but Morocco insisted that it had not acquiesed to a fixed boundary. The existence of rich iron ore in the disputed region complicated the problem. Severe fighting ensued during 1962 and 1963. A decade later, the two states finally established a firm border, with Algeria gaining the iron deposits.

Relations between the two states have also been strained by Algerian support for rebels in the former Spanish colony of Western Sahara. Spain announced in 1975 that it was abandoning this territory of 100,000 square miles and 80,000 inhabitants. The Moroccan government initially claimed the entire region as a historic part of Greater Morocco. Recently independent Mauritania pressed similar historic claims. Negotiations between the two states resulted in a decision to allot two-thirds of the colony to Morocco and one-third to Mauritania.

Neither party consulted the local inhabitants. Militants there created the *Frente Popular para la Liberación de Saguia el Hamra y Río de Oro* (Popular Front for the Liberation of Saguia el Hamra and the Río de Oro). It became better known under its acronym Polisario. The Polisario Front declared establishment of a Sahrawi Arab Democratic Republic. Its guerrilla forces attacked Moroccan troops sent to the Western Sahara and raided deep into southern Morocco. Mauritania, beset by its own problems after independence, renounced its claims to the southern part of Western Sahara in 1979. Morocco then occupied the territory.

Algeria gave aid and sanctuary to the Polisario guerrillas. In addition to an adopted ideology of support for national liberation movements, it saw advantages in tying down forces of the rival state of Morocco. The action soured relations with the Moroccans, who closed the mutual boundary from 1975 to 1982. In a successful attempt to restrict the activities of Polisario raiders, Morocco built an extensive sand wall in 1982 around settled areas in the north of Western Sahara.

Algeria

In contrast to the long-established independence of Morocco, Algerians could not hearken to reestablishment of sovereignty in building a nation-state. Historically their territory had been fragmented and controlled by foreigners. Algeria's leaders, moreover, shared with counterparts in the Middle East a vision of broad Arab unity. They embarked on a policy termed "Arabization" that sought to eliminate French influences from the young state. They placed emphasis upon the Islamic heritage and use of the Arabic language. Strong resistance to Arabization developed among many in the educated elite, however, who saw themselves as part of a Francophone culture world.

Algeria's Berber tribes also reacted against the policy. Berbers in the Kabylia Mountains particularly resisted the enforced cultural changes. They had enjoyed an equal, if not favored, status under the French and saw themselves at a disadvantage in the process of Arabization. Their fears were shared by the Chaouia Berber tribes in the Aurès Mountains farther east. The some 10,000 Tuareg peoples of the Algerian Sahara remained unaffected by the program. Remote from the coastal ecumene, they maintained their traditional nomadic existence, wearing blue-dyed clothing and the men—not the women—donning a veil.

Tunisia

The relatively small state of Tunisia continued its precolonial traditions of separateness. In contrast to the emphasis upon Islam in Morocco and Algeria, its regime stressed a secular identity based upon the area's Carthaginian, Roman, Arab, and Southern European heritage. Tunisia's constituent assembly abolished the traditional monarchy of the bey of Tunis and established a republic. Tunisia long had disputed its French-established border with Algeria. During the Algerian war of liberation, the newly independent Tunisian republican regime negotiated a possible change in its Algerian boundary with the governments on both sides of the conflict. Its interests were heightened by awareness that oil was present in the disputed area. Tunisia dropped its claims after Algerian independence, however, since it saw little chance of winning any territory from its neighbor. It also was able to develop oil production on territory unambiguously belonging to itself.

Libya

The state of Libya represents a transition between the Maghreb and Mishriq. Twenty-five hundred years ago, long before the Arab conquest, Phoenicians and Greeks erected an altar on the Sirtica Desert adjacent to the 300-mile wide Gulf of Sidra to mark the dividing line between their respective colonies. When the south Mediterranean coast became part of the Roman Empire in 146 B.C., following Rome's defeat of Carthage, the Gulf of Sidra and the Sirtica became the boundary zone between the Roman provinces of Tripolitania and Cyrenaica. The north-south dividing line between Western and Eastern Roman Empires established in A.D. 395 similarly began in the Sirtica Desert.

Scholars and politicians in most states of the contemporary Middle East and North Africa can cite ancestral political units that in antiquity occupied the same favored ecumene and were set apart from neighboring units by empty deserts, mountains, and seas. Tunisia can look to Carthage, Iran to Persia, Iraq to Mesopotamia. Libya is a notable exception. Its political unity dates only from the mid-twentieth century. The Sahara occupies more than 90 percent of its territory. Its three widely separated areas of settlement have experienced differing historical-political processes.

Tripolitania in northwest Libya traces its origins to the pre-Christian era. Its name means "Three Cities" and derives from the three Phoenician colonies of Oea (modern Tripoli), Labdah, and Sabratah. They developed as commercial depots for the far-flung empire and were closely tied to adjacent Carthage. The coastal settlements were the termini of a major caravan route across the Sahara from tropical Africa. Their indigenous population was of Berber stock. After the Arab conquest, Tripolitanians came to speak the Maghrebi dialect of Arabic. A high proportion were sedentary farmers. Under the Ottoman Empire, Tripolitania functioned in a highly autonomous manner and was famous for its pirates.

Cyrenaica to the east was Greek territory from the seventh century B.C. The classical city-state of Cyrene amassed a distinguished history. Its territory represented the closest southern mainland to Crete, 180 miles away. Romans, in fact, incorporated Crete within Cyrenaica's provincial borders. The region's subsequent ties were much closer to Egypt than to Tripoli and the Maghreb. It became more Arabized in culture than did western areas. Its spoken dialect of Arabic tended to be much closer to that of Egypt than to the Maghrebi dialect. Much of its population remained Bedouin and tribal. During the nineteenth century, the Cyrenaican populace developed a degree of regional homogeneity and integration through adherence to the local Sanusi sect of Islam.

Fezzan's population is strung across a group of oases spread over a distance of 250 miles along the Wadi Ajal of the Sahara. Its people belong to several minority ethnic groups. Among them are a few thousand Tuaregs, thought to be direct descendants of the Garamentes, who seized the region about 1000 B.C. The Garamentes controlled the main caravan routes to tropical Africa and traded with Phoenician and Greek colonies. The Romans sent several expeditions against the oasis dwellers, and, in the first century A.D., concluded an alliance with them. Although converted from animism to Islam after the Arab conquest, the Fezzan population generally adopted the essentially anti-Arab Kharidjite doctrine.

Although the territory of modern Libya formally became part of the Ottoman Empire in the sixteenth century, imperial officials exercised only nominal control during later periods. In contrast to neighboring Egypt and Tunisia, Libyans managed to escape European domination well into the twentieth century. Their situation began to change with the unification of Italy in the 1860s.

After successful political unification of the Appenine Peninsula, Italian nationalist leaders had visions of re-creating the glories of the Roman Empire. However, formidable neighbors denied them territorial aggrandizement in Europe. They were only partially successful during the 1880s in securing a foothold on the Horn of Africa. Ottoman lands on the south shore of the Mediterranean thus presented themselves temptingly as the last territory readily available for imperial ventures.

Aside from economic avarice, there was little to justify Italian invasion of Tripolitania and Cyrenaica, however. No standard grounds for punitive actions had occurred, such as hostage-taking or massacres of missionaries. Nevertheless, the Italian government, bent upon expansion, sent an ultimatum to Constantinople in 1911 decrying supposed ills besetting the territory. Ottoman officials sent a conciliatory reply, but Italy quickly proceeded to occupy the territory. Coastal areas were taken easily enough, but the interior populace resisted Italian forces for two decades, until finally pacified in 1931. The resistant tribes received significant assistance from experienced military officers of the defunct Ottoman Empire.

At first Italy administered Tripolitania, Cyrenaica, and Fezzan separately. The first two became individual colonies and Fezzan was designated a military territory. In 1934 Italy united them into a single colony that it named Libya. The appellation dated back to the ancient Egyptians, who identified a Berber tribe threatening the Nile Valley from the west as the *Lebu*. Greeks and Romans later applied the derivative term "Libyan" to all Berbers in North Africa. In the fourth century A.D. the Roman Empire split Cyrenaica into Upper Libya and Lower Libya.

Italian impact upon the region was minor in comparison with influences of other Europeans upon colo-

nial territories. Beginning in 1938, the Mussolini regime encouraged Italian emigration to Libya from overpopulated areas as an alternative to ongoing migration to Latin America and Australia. Libya's total number of Italians reached only 120,000 by the outbreak of World War II, however. Most left at war's end.

Adoption of Italian as a second language by native Libyans was limited. Some 90 percent remained illiterate throughout the colonial period. Following wartime and postwar British occupation, English became the preferred second language for coastal settlements. France exerted similar cultural influences in Fezzan during a half dozen years of occupation. Little sentiment existed for creation of an independent Libyan state at war's end. Local allegiances were to regions and tribal groups. Fascist Italy successfully had thwarted the development of nationalist movements. Inhabitants of each region remained suspicious of groups living in the others.

Complicating the question of eventual independence was the fact that the wartime victors harbored desires to dominate sections of Libyan territory. The British pressed to control Cyrenaica, and the French wanted the Fezzan oases. The Soviet Union sought its own role in the Mediterranean by administering a United Nations trusteeship over Tripolitania. The British, French, and Americans considered this unacceptable, however. After prolonged wrangling, all agreed to a compromise that established a Libyan state independent of any foreign tutelage. This occurred in 1951.

The new state experienced troubles from the onset. Inhabitants of Cyrenaica and Fezzan were wary of domination by Tripolitanians, who constituted two-thirds of the total population. Tripolitanians were unhappy with selection of a Cyrenaican to be the area's king, despite his record of heroic resistance against the Italians. The inhabitants of Fezzan lived more than 800 miles from coastal areas and had virtually no means of easy communication with the population there. An overriding problem in all areas was general poverty resulting from lack of a developed resource base outside agriculture.

To resolve inherent regional difficulties, Libyans initially adopted a loose federal form of government. Each area was autonomous in local affairs. As in most federal states, the question of location of the capital city proved a major divisive force. To defuse the problem, the rival cities of Tripolitanian Tripoli and Cyrenaican Benghazi initially received the status of rotating capitals. This arrangement proved unsatisfactory, and preparations were set in motion to establish a compromise capital at Al-Bayda. However, the site was located in the eastern part of Cyrenaica, and not in a medial position between major regions comparable to such successful federal capitals as Washington, Ottawa, or Canberra. The project was soon abandoned, and Tripoli was made the sole seat of government. Paralysis stemming from regional divisiveness led to adoption of a unitary state structure in 1963. Libya's problems of pervasive poverty began to alleviate following discovery of petroleum reserves in 1959.

Continuing administrative, political, and economic difficulties prompted a group of young military officers to overthrow the monarchy in 1969. The singular idealistic vision of Islamic society by one of the conspirators, Muhammar Qadaffi, became the guiding iconography of the state. It included official elimination of reference to traditional regional divisions. The names Tripolitania, Cyrenaica, and Fezzan were replaced by the designations "Western Province," "Eastern Province," and "Southern Province."

Libya under Qadaffi developed quarrels both with its neighbors and with outside states. Soon after the coup, the government sought unsuccessfully to merge with Egypt, and, later, with Tunisia. In subsequent years, Qadaffi openly called for overthrow of governmental leaderships of the two neighbors. European and American governments accused Libya of supporting terrorist activities abroad being conducted by minority separatist and anti-Israeli groups. The United States bombed Tripoli in retaliation for one alleged Libyan-supported incident directed against American military forces in Berlin.

Independent Libya has involved itself repeatedly in the affairs of Chad, lying to the south. The two mother countries had fixed the colonial boundary between French Equatorial Africa and Italian Libya as a geometric line in 1919. Subsequently, in 1935, Italy's Fascist government successfully negotiated with France to move the border sixty miles south of the earlier limit. The area is termed the "Aouzou Strip," after the principal oasis settlement in the area. The French parliament refused to ratify the agreement, however, and World War II made the matter moot.

In 1973 Libyan armed forces seized the Aouzou Strip from Chad, which had become independent in 1960. A decade later Libyan troops moved farther south, accompanying Chadian Muslims rebelling against a regime dominated by non-Islamic black southerners. Chad's government, however, with assistance from France, drove the combined forces back to the Aouzou Strip. In 1991 Libya again gave support to Chadian Muslim rebels based in the Aouzou Strip, who this time were successful in seizing control over all Chad.

Another potential boundary problem of Libya involves the Sarra Triangle, a section of former Sudanese territory adjacent to the Aouzou Strip that the United Kingdom conceded to Italy in 1934. Libya also has a quarrel with Tunisia involving rights to exploit petroleum deposits under the Gulf of Gabès.

Bibliography

AJAMI, F., *The Arab Predicament: Arab Political Thought and Practice since 1967.* Cambridge: Cambridge University Press, 1981.

BEAUMONT, PETER, GERALD H. BLAKE, and J. MALCOLM WAGSTAFF, *The Middle East: A Geographical Study.* London: John Wiley, 1976.

CLARKE, C., D. LEY, and C. PEACH, eds., *Geography and Ethnic Pluralism.* London, Allen & Unwin, 1984.

DRYSDALE, ALASDAIR, "National Integration Problems in the Arab World," in *Nationalism, Self-Determination, and Political Geography*, eds. R.J. Johnston, David B. Knight, and Eleonore Kofman. London: Croom Helm, 1988.

DRYSDALE, ALASDAIR, and G. H. BLAKE, *The Middle East and North Africa: A Political Geography.* New York: Oxford University Press, 1985.

FARAH, T. E., ed., *Pan-Arabism and Arab Nationalism: The Continuing Debate.* Boulder, CO: Westview Press, 1986.

HELD, COLBERT C., *Middle East Patterns: Places, Peoples, and Politics.* Boulder, CO: Westview Press, 1989.

HELMS, CHRISTINE, *Arabism and Islam: Stateless Nations and Nationless States.* Washington, DC: U.S. Government, Superintendent of Documents, 1990.

HOURANI, A., *Minorities in the Arab World.* London: Oxford University Press, 1947.

HOURANI, ALBERT, *A History of the Arab Peoples.* Cambridge: Harvard University Press, 1991.

HUDSON, M., *Arab Politics: The Search for Legitimacy.* New Haven: Yale University Press, 1977.

LONGRIGG, STEPHEN H., *The Middle East: A Social Geography*, 2nd ed. London: Duckworth, 1970.

MANSFIELD, PETER, *The Middle East: A Political and Economic Survey*, 4th ed. London: Oxford University Press, 1973.

McLAUREN, R.D., *The Political Role of Minority Groups in the Middle East.* New York: Praeger, 1979.

MELAMID, A., "The Political Geography of the Gulf of Aqaba," *Annals, Association of American Geographers*, Vol. 47 (1957), pp. 231–240.

MELAMID, A. "The Shatt-al-Arab Boundary Dispute," *Middle East Journal*, Vol. 22 (1968), pp. 350–357.

MELAMID, A., "The Buraimi Oasis Dispute," *Middle East Affairs*, Vol. 7 (1956), pp. 56–63.

MELAMID, A., "Political Geography of Trucial Oman and Qatar," *Geographical Review*, Vol. 43 (1953), pp. 194–206.

REYNER, ANTHONY S., "The Case of an Indeterminate Boundary: Algeria-Morocco," in *Essays in Political Geography*, ed. Charles A. Fisher. London: Methuen, 1968, pp. 243–251.

WILKINSON, J.C., "The Oman Question: The Background to the Political Geography of South East Arabia," *Geographical Journal*, Vol. 137 (1971), pp. 361–371.

ZARTMAN, I.W., "The Politics of Boundaries in North and West Africa," *Journal of Modern African Studies*, Vol. 3 (1965), pp. 155–173.

9

Africa South of the Sahara

THE geographic designation "Africa" identifies a huge, roughly triangular, landmass lying between the Atlantic and Indian oceans and the Mediterranean Sea. It occupies an area of almost 12,000,000 square miles, making it nearly 50 percent larger than North America or the former Soviet Union. Its population, more than 500,000,000, is nearly equivalent to that of the other two realms taken together. However, as is the case with other conventional first-order partitionings of space, the notion of Africa being a "continent" is misleading. It is neither a coherent territory, nor is its population homogeneous. Rather, it embraces two quite distinctive major land units, North Africa and sub-Saharan Africa, and a case can be made for distinguishing southern Africa as at least a subcontinent.

North Africa has been examined above as part of the Middle Eastern world. The population of its six states is racially and culturally distinctive. Its historic, political, and economic linkages are far closer to Mediterranean Europe and the Arabian Peninsula than they are to those parts of Africa lying south of the great emptiness of the Sahara Desert. Although only partially set apart from the rest of sub-Saharan Africa by an empty zone, the Republic of South Africa is markedly different owing to its Europeanization over three centuries of settlement by Dutch and English colonists.

Like other world realms, the total area of sub-Saharan Africa is only partially occupied. More than half is virtually empty, with less than two persons per square mile (see Figure 9-1). It also is more diverse culturally than the collections of peoples of Europe or South Asia. More than 500 different languages are spoken. Yet sub-

TABLE 9.1 SUB-SAHARAN AFRICA

Sub-Saharan Africa is a vast area, four times the size of Europe west of the former Soviet Union. It contains approximately the same total numbers of inhabitants as Europe, reflecting the fact that substantially more than half the region consists of rainforests or deserts empty of population. The land is culturally and politically diverse. Each of the more than forty states incorporates a multitude of regionally significant groups, most bearing grievances against some or all of their neighbors. All states but Liberia and Ethiopia experienced decades of European colonialism, although few Europeans actually settled in the region. A notable exception is the Caucasian population of South Africa, who began pioneer colonization in the mid-1600s. The former dependent areas became sovereign only in the mid-twentieth century. Virtually all politically binding forces of the present states are legacies of the colonial period. These include common languages, infrastructures, and governmental institutions. Due to the inherent diversity within states, few can yet claim to have forged unified nations. A majority have witnessed establishment of military dictatorships, at least partly as a response to internal fragmentation. Although most units harbor potential border claims against adjacent states, all but Somalia have refrained from pressing them.

Subregion	Total Poplation	Area (square miles)
Francophone West Africa	65,200,000	1,800,000
Component States		
Senegal, Mauritania, Mali, Guinea, Côte d'Ivoire, Togo, Burkina Faso, Benin, Niger		
Non-Francophone West Africa	115,000,000	540,000
Component States		
Nigeria, Ghana, Liberia, Sierra Leone, Guinea-Bissau, The Gambia		
Equatorial Africa	80,000,000	2,100,000
Component States		
Cameroon, Chad, Central African Republic, Congo, Gabon, Equatorial Guinea, Zaire, Rwanda, Burundi		
Eastern Africa	130,000,000	1,460,000
Component States and Territories		
Kenya, Uganda, Tanzania, Ethiopia, Eritrea, Somalia, Djibouti		
Southern Africa	105,000,000	2,500,000
Component States		
Republic of South Africa, Namibia, Angola, Botswana, Zimbabwe, Zambia, Malawi, Mozambique, Madagascar, Comoros		
Total	495,000,000	8,400,000

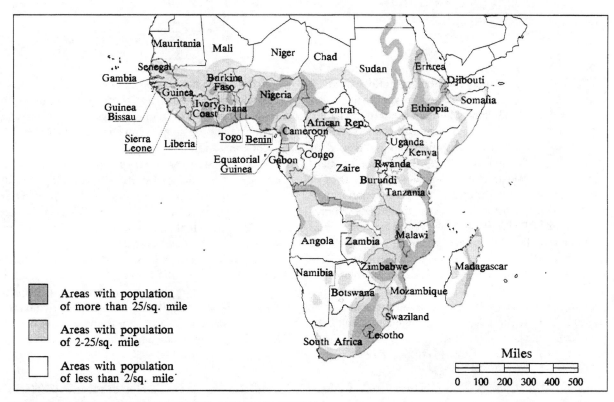

FIGURE 9-1   THE ECUMENE OF SUB-SAHARAN AFRICA

Saharan Africa exhibits a commonality that merits its consideration as a single entity. Its peoples are relatively homogeneous in race and have shared common historical experiences. Each of its forty-seven political entities exhibits similar internal and external problems. Each is beset by severe strains stemming from tribal diversity, and each lags behind counterparts in the rest of the world in economic and political development.

As in the cases of Latin America and the periphery of Asia, the basic building blocks of territorial organization reflect more the exogenous forces of European colonialism than indigenous political processes. Although several large-scale territorial entities existed for long periods on the Sahel periphery of the Sahara (Ghana, Songai, Timbuktu), in scattered parts of West Africa (Ashanti, Dahomey, Benin) and in the interior of East Africa (Buganda, Lunda, Changamir), the majority of sub-Saharan Africans traditionally lived in relatively small tribal groups whose identities generally were based upon presumed kinship rather than shared land areas. In the past, most such groups engaged in seminomadic subsistence agriculture within a prevailing tropical forest habitat, although peripheral grassland areas saw cattle raising, irrigated farming, and manu-

facturing industry, and there were remarkable large-scale iron works in Zimbabwe.

Contact with the outside world began to have a profound effect upon sub-Saharan Africa more than a millennium ago when Arabs first pushed southward along the region's east coast as far as latitude 20°S and later crossed the Sahara on camels. The Arab presence expanded markets in slaves, ivory, and other objects of trade. Arabs brought their Islamic faith, which continues to penetrate and dominate sub-Saharan Africa's northern frontier region, almost universally besting the efforts of European- and American-based Christian missionaries.

The Colonial Experience

Although European colonialism had a universal, profound effect upon the region, in most areas it was a relatively recent phenomenon. European powers bypassed sub-Saharan Africa in their initial scramble for raw materials and captive markets during the period of the "Great Discoveries." The lack of ready evidence of great accumulations of wealth, coupled with difficult and hostile access to the interior, led Iberian adventurers to dismiss sub-Saharan Africa on their way to richer rewards in India, the East Indies, and the Americas.

Soon after securing independence from the Moors in the twelfth century, the Portuguese did explore sections of the western coast of Africa. They were motivated to find both a water route to India and also the fabled source of West African gold. A papal bull granted them title to the entire region in 1441. By 1444 they had reached the mouth of the Senegal River and within a half century had rounded the Cape of Good Hope. However, after passing the desolate fringe of the Sahara the Portuguese found little of interest along the mangrove coasts of equatorial Africa or the arid Namibi Desert of the southwest. They encountered few sheltered harbors. Water level access to the interior was blocked close to the coast by rapids and cataracts formed where rivers cascaded from sub-Saharan Africa's vast tablelands, which often came to the edge of the sea. In virtually all tropical areas a dense jungle prevailed along coastlines and river banks wherever sunlight penetrated the otherwise interlocking canopy of rainforest leaves. Nevertheless, several Portuguese adventurers did penetrate the interior, exploring as far as Mali, the Congo, and Zimbabwe.

The Portuguese established a number of fortified coastal settlements, primarily for provisioning ships sailing to the east. The first was São Jorge da Mina (Elmina), founded in 1471 on the Gold Coast of West Africa. In the following century appeared Algoa ("To India") near Port Elizabeth and Delagoa ("From India") in the vicinity of the present Lourenco Marques. Comparable forts of other European powers subsequently appeared, including those of the Dutch at Table Bay in the 1500s, the English on the Island of St. Helena in 1659, and the French on Goree Island near Dakar in the eighteenth century. In addition to providing food and water to passing merchant ships, each settlement engaged in trading metals, cloth, and manufactured goods with adjacent African tribal groups for gold, ivory, and other native products. Most such European stations were on islands or protected promontories, some consisting only of ships sunk in the shallows of river mouths. Swedes, Danes, and Brandenburg Germans established later coastal enclaves.

The numbers manning these posts were very small. Unlike the extensive migration of farmers and merchants to fertile lands in the Americas, few Europeans came to the African colonies. It is estimated that fewer than a thousand were in sub-Saharan Africa in the 1850s. It was an unknown land, disease-ridden and beset by hostile threats. An exception was the temperate southern tip of the continent, which witnessed a large influx of Dutch settlers in the seventeenth century,

followed later, after the Napoleonic Wars, by British subjects. The distinctive development of southern Africa is treated at the end of this chapter.

The peripheral coastal outposts took on substantially greater significance in the sixteenth century. In 1530, the Portuguese transported the first African slaves to the New World to work on plantations. Demand grew overwhelming in the incessant quest for additional manpower in Brazil and the West Indies. Slave-taking had long been characteristic of indigenous African tribal groups. The appearance of the Arabs encouraged its transformation to a profitable commercial activity. The insatiable markets later developing in the Americas led to a devastating expansion of the slave trade. Estimates are that at least 10,000,000 tropical Africans were transported to the New World between the sixteenth and the nineteenth centuries. Europeans, Arabs, and Africans provided markets and middlemen for this horrendous traffic in human lives. In West Africa, actual enslavement was virtually all carried out by Africans themselves, although they utilized firearms obtained from the Europeans. In the east, Arabs, based on the island of Zanzibar, were much more directly involved in capturing slaves and in mounting expeditions that penetrated far into the African interior.

The human geography of sub-Saharan Africa was profoundly transformed by the epoch of slavery. Many regions became empty; dense, permanent forests succeeded lightly wooded areas that had been kept open by centuries of subsistence slash-and-burn agriculture. The new dense woodlands provided shelter for tse-tse flies harboring sleeping sickness, effectively precluding resettlement. Paradoxically, expansion of the slave trade further limited European penetration of the interior from forts on the west coast because slave-raiding engendered anarchy and African middlemen were loathe to have the Europeans involved directly in their lucrative business. The Europeans did begin to lay claim to stretches of coastline adjacent to trading settlements, however, motivated most often by desires to prevent rivals from encroaching upon monopoly markets. Later, in the nineteenth century, resettlement of freed slaves in coastal stretches of Liberia and Sierra Leone further complicated ethnographic patterns and affected the political functioning of territories.

European penetration into the interior of sub-Saharan Africa was also delayed until the nineteenth century by a continuing lack of information about its geographic characteristics. The popular term "dark continent" referred as much to the paucity of knowledge about the region as it did to racial characteristics of Africa's inhabitants. In addition, further imperial expansion was limited by a growing awareness in Europe of the high costs and low benefits of maintain-

TABLE 9.2 FRANCOPHONE WEST AFRICA

The nine Francophone states of West Africa share a common heritage of French colonialism, including the use of French as a common language and republican institutions modeled after those in France. All were contiguous administrative subdivisions of French West Africa. However, despite attempts at the time of independence to unite them into a single "Mali Federation," particularist politics saw each assume its own independent course. Tribal diversity is as great as in any other part of Africa, and each government must be alert to regional discontent. A majority of tribal groups extend across borders, the Fulani being found in significant numbers in six of the states. Potentials for irredentism are strong. The Sahel states on the fringe of the Sahara are characterized by extensive empty areas and dominance of Islam. Populations of coastal states generally adhere to Animism or Roman Catholicism. A majority of the Francophone states are cut by the fault line between Islam and Animism/Christianity and face increasing ethnic tensions. Also, within the Muslim area exist strong regional divisions between nomads and settled farmers. The most serious separatist activity has been in the Casamance River region of Senegal, which is isolated from the rest of that state by the former British territory of The Gambia.

State	Total Population	Area (sq. miles)
Senegal	7,750,000	75,000
Number of Ethnic Groups: 12		
Lingua Franca		
French and Wolof		
Dominant Regional Group and % Total		
Wolof, 43% (North Coast)		
Significant Regional Groups and % Total		
Serer, 15% (South Coast); Fulani, 24% (Interior); Diolo, 5% (Casamance River Region)		
Mauritania	2,000,000	400,000
Number of Ethnic Groups: 6		
Lingua Franca		
French		
Dominant Regional Group and % Total		
Maure (Arab-Berbers), 40%		
Significant Regional Groups and % Total		
Toucouleur Fulani, 6% (Black Ancestry)		
Mali	8,500,000	480,000
Number of Ethnic Groups: 30		
Lingua Franca		
French		
Dominant Regional Group and % Total		
Bambara, 32% (Black Ancestry)		
Significant Regional Groups and % Total		
Fulani, 14% (Black Ancestry); Tuareg, 7% (Berber Ancestry)		
Guinea	7,250,000	95,000
Number of Ethnic Groups: 24		
Lingua Franca		
French		
Dominant Regional Group and % Total		
Fulani, 39%		
Significant Regional Groups and % Total		
Malinke (Mandingo), 23%; Susu, 11%		
Côte d'Ivoire (Ivory Coast)	13,000,000	125,000
Number of Ethnic Groups: 60		
Lingua Franca		
French		
Dominant Regional Group and % Total		
Akan, 42% (Southeast)		
Significant Regional Groups and % Total		
Kru, 17% (Southwest); Malinke (Mandingo), 15% (Interior)		

State	Total Population	Area (sq. miles)
Togo	4,000,000	22,000
Number of Ethnic Groups: 37		
Lingua Franca		
French		
Dominant Regional Group and % Total		
Tem-Kabre, 27% (North)		
Significant Regional Groups and % Total		
Ewe, 43%		
Burkina Faso (Upper Volta)	9,500,000	105,000
Number of Ethnic Groups: 50		
Lingua Franca		
French, Mossi		
Dominant Regional Group and % Total		
Mossi, 48%		
Significant Regional Groups and % Total		
Mande, 9%; Fulani, 8%; Tuareg, 3%		
Benin (Dahomey)	5,000,000	45,000
Number of Ethnic Groups: 42		
Lingua Franca		
French		
Dominant Regional Group and % Total		
Fon, 40%		
Significant Regional Groups and % Total		
Yoruba, 12%; Bariba, 9%		
Niger	8,200,000	460,000
Number of Ethnic Groups: 10		
Lingua Franca		
French, Hausa, Songhai		
Dominant Regional Group and % Total		
Hausa, 53%		
Significant Regional Groups and % Total		
Songhai, 21%; Tuareg, 11%; Fulani, 10%		

ing colonial empires. Early in the century Britain and Spain had suffered huge expenditures in futile attempts to resist independence movements in the Americas. Antislavery sentiments had grown in Europe, culminating in the British decision to suppress the slave trade worldwide in the 1830s. Most existing African colonies then lost prospects of profitability. Several European states decided to leave Africa altogether, the Danes selling their Gold Coast fort to the United Kingdom in 1850. (Its buildings later became a visitors' residency when the British Gold Coast colony emerged as the independent state of Ghana.)

The situation changed during the 1870s. Unification movements in Europe among Italians and Germans in that period had trumpeted the advantages of having unitary states strong enough to secure the assumed economic benefits of colonial possessions that long had been enjoyed by the centralized states of the French,

Dutch, and English. When statehood was achieved, the new Italian and German governments immediately set out to gain "their share" of overseas possessions. By that time, however, few regions of the world had avoided the impress of European colonialism. Chief among these were Africa's more desolate coastlines and its unknown interior.

Italians directed their interests to the desert areas of Libya and along the "horn" of East Africa. Although they were able to establish control over the arid coasts of Eritrea and Somalia, the Italians found their passage inland repulsed by the Ethiopians. Germans acquired a strip of East African coast from the Arab ruler of Zanzibar and also planted several colonial footholds on the western coast. The latter included the Togoland colony, situated where a wedge of Saharan dryness came down to the coast; the Cameroons, whose mountains abruptly rose from the sea; and South-West Africa, an excep-

TABLE 9.3   NON-FRANCOPHONE WEST AFRICA

Four of the non-Francophone states of West Africa (Nigeria, Ghana, The Gambia, and Sierra Leone) were widely separated colonial areas of the British Empire. Liberia was established by freed American slaves and Guinea-Bissau was a colony of Portugal. All use English as a *lingua franca* (except Portuguese in Guinea-Bissau). Like the Francophone states, they encompass large numbers of ethnic groups with a multiplicity of local languages. Most face internal tensions between Muslims and Christians/Animists. A serious regional secessionist movement occurred in Nigeria, where Ibos attempted to create an independent state of Biafra in the 1960s.

State	*Total Population*	*Area (sq. miles)*
Nigeria	90,000,000	360,000
Number of Ethnic Groups: 300		
Lingua Franca		
English		
Dominant Regional Group and % Total		
Hausa, 22% (North)		
Significant Regional Groups and % Total		
Fulani, 11% (North); Yoruba, 21% (Southwest); Ibo, 18% (Southeast)		
Ghana	15,000,000	92,000
Number of Ethnic Groups: 100		
Lingua Franca		
English		
Dominant Regional Group and % Total		
Akan, 52% (South)		
Significant Regional Groups and % Total		
Moshi-Dagomba, 16% (North); Ewe, 12% (South)		
The Gambia	950,000	4,000
Number of Ethnic Groups: 38		
Lingua Franca		
English		
Dominant Regional Group and % Total		
Malinke (Mandingo), 40% (Coast)		
Significant Regional Groups and % Total		
Fulani, 19% (Interior)		
Sierra Leone	4,500,000	28,000
Number of Ethnic Groups: 18		
Lingua Franca		
English		
Dominant Regional Group and % Total		
Creoles, 2% (descendents of freed slaves) (West)		
Significant Regional Groups and % Total		
Mendes, 34% (South); Temnes, 32% (Northwest)		
Liberia	2,750,000	38,000
Number of Ethnic Groups: 28		
Lingua Franca		
English		
Dominant Regional Group and % Total		
Krahns, 9% (Central Coast)		
Significant Regional Groups and % Total		
American-Liberians, 3% (descendents of freed American slaves) (coast); Krus, 7% (Southeast); Kpelles, 19% (Center); Lomas, 10% (North)		
Guinea-Bissau	1,000,000	14,000
Number of Ethnic Groups: 20		
Lingua Franca		
Portuguese (Criulo)		

State	Total Population	Area (sq. miles)

Dominant Regional Group and % Total
Balanta Brassa, 27% (Coast)
Significant Regional Groups and % Total
Fulani, 23% (Interior)

tionally arid desert zone. Other colonial powers had bypassed these territories in the past as unlikely to have any commercial significance.

The British and French governments grew alarmed when the Germans sent expeditions into the African interior with an eye to linking their new eastern and western coastal footholds. The regimes also were concerned about the involvement of Leopold, king of the Belgians, in establishment of his "free state" in the Congo Basin. They were loathe to see upstart neighbors make economic gains by moving into unclaimed territories. This set into motion a scramble for tropical African territory that put virtually all of the continent under European control within three decades.

The nineteenth century preceding the German and Italian political advance into the interior had witnessed an increasing uncovering of the riddles of sub-Saharan Africa. Beginning with Mungo Park's exploration of the Niger River in 1796, a series of nineteenth-century expeditions began to lay out the realm's topography. Sources of the Nile and other rivers were found. Christian missionaries, pressing into the interior from their country's coastal footholds, brought back information on political realms and tribal groups.

Imperial penetration generally was accomplished non-violently, with little actual military conquest. Most colonial territory was gained by governmental expeditions establishing political relations with tribes adjacent to lands already acquired. Negotiators used combinations of carrot and stick to win signatures of tribal chiefs to agreements for political association, alternately promising material rewards and threatening punitive actions.

Although the act of signing a treaty on paper was a novelty to local leaders, most had fairly sophisticated political views of the situations they faced, based upon their own experiences with rival tribes. Many resigned themselves to making the best of bad situations. A number sought out Europeans for treaties in order to gain commercial advantages or protection from traditional enemies. European governments also found that missionaries and explorers frequently presented them with territorial *faits accompli*, as venturers into the interior brought back agreements with local chiefs.

Europeans were generally motivated to gain a maximum of territory, although the British notably tended to be selective in lands they sought. Several governments developed grand policy schemes for territorial acquisition. German desires to tie South-West Africa to its coastal possessions in East Africa were matched by Portuguese aims for overland linkages between its long-held opposing seaboard colonies of Angola and Mozambique. The French saw advantages in pressing across the grassland margins of the Sahara from Dakar to the Red Sea. The grandest scheme of all was Cecil Rhodes's vision of building a railroad on British-controlled territory from the Cape of Good Hope to Cairo.

All states attached great importance to securing formal agreements with native leaders. This not only met perceived needs for diplomatic legitimacy in territorial acquisition, but also afforded a stronger bargaining position in negotiations with other European states in which the given area might be a concession for a territorial gain elsewhere. Governments also considered that a treaty with an indigenous ruler conferred rights in all territory for which the ruler claimed control, thus preempting pretensions by rival states.

The Treaty of Berlin

Such contrasting aims were bound to create frictions and possibly even to generate wars in Europe itself. To ward off the possibility of such colonial conflicts, the major powers acceded to the invitation of the Germans to meet in Berlin to regulate the acquisition of African territories. Negotiators worked during 1884 and 1885 to establish procedures for carving up the African continent. Among agreements was the concord that a claim to land required establishment of a physical presence in an area. Participants often made decisions with only slight knowledge of regions that they were addressing. They expressed little or no concern for native cultural characteristics. With impunity they traded territories and the fates of inhabitants.

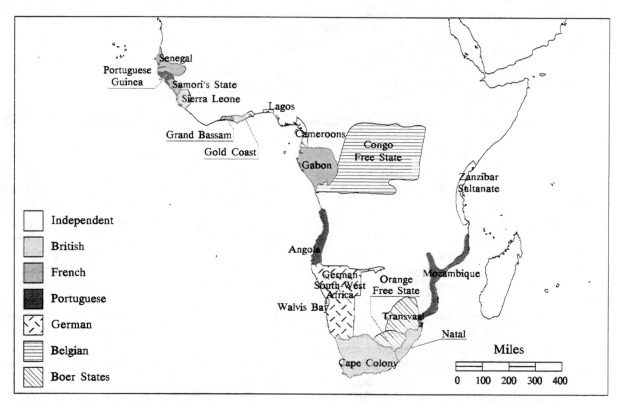

FIGURE 9-2   SUB-SAHARAN AFRICA IN 1880

Representatives had divided up less than a quarter of sub-Saharan Africa before the conference ended (Figure 9-2). However, the procedures to which they agreed for establishing authority led to the swift partitioning of remaining unclaimed territory. By 1914 only Liberia and Ethiopia (Abyssinia) lay outside European control (Figure 9-3).

In the general absence of topographic and ethnographic surveys, negotiators resorted to quickly conceivable lines to delimit colonial boundaries. They frequently utilized rivers, despite the multitude of problems that riverine boundaries generate. The Germans, mindful of the linking roles played in their own realm by the Rhine, Elbe, and Danube waterways, particularly sought access to interior river basins. One result was the odd-shaped piece of land known as "Caprivi's Finger," named for the German foreign minister who, in 1890, successfully achieved an access corridor of formerly British territory to the Zambezi River from German Southwest Africa. In 1911 the Germans had gained a corridor to the Congo River from part of the French Middle Congo colony. Lake shores and watersheds also were employed as borders. A high proportion of the new boundaries were geometric lines.

Substantial changes in the political map of sub-Saharan Africa followed World War I. Germany was stripped of all its colonial territories, which were made "mandates" to be prepared for eventual independence under League of Nations supervision. Germany's African possessions variously were assigned to the French, British, Belgian, and South African governments. The former German Togoland and Cameroons were each partitioned between separate French and British mandates.

The Impact of Colonialism

Europeans generally are castigated for their imperial ventures into Africa and for the "artificial" boundaries that they established. However reprehensible colonialism may have been, it would seem part of an inevitable historical process, given the mutual economic comple-

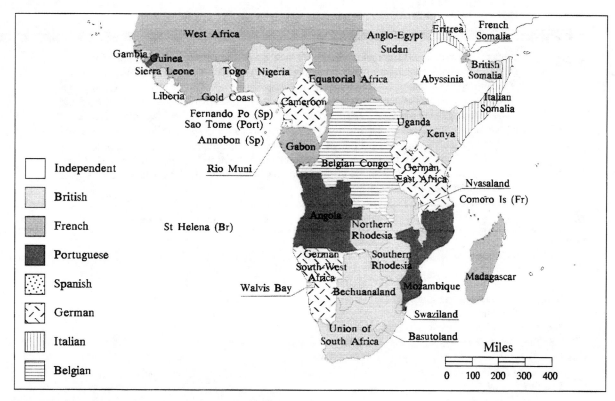

FIGURE 9-3 AFRICA ON THE EVE OF WORLD WAR I

mentarities between Europe and sub-Saharan Africa. Although some local African leaders opposed the Europeans, many others eagerly sought relations with them. Benefits from such ties were not restricted solely to the European powers. Colonial governments can be credited for establishing law and order in areas of perpetual conflict, for extending the length and quality of life of indigenous peoples by public health measures and introduction of education and labor-saving technologies, and for creating an economic infrastructure upon which modern commercial economies must rest. The Europeans forged integrated territories, homogeneous institutions, and a common second language; rail and road lines linked various regions to coastal seaports and to each other. For their efforts, Europeans found that costs of maintaining security and developing productive facilities in colonial areas in virtually all cases exceeded the profits accruing to mother countries from controlled sources of raw materials and captive markets.

The fact that the innate heterogeneity within each colony created a legacy of problems for the subsequent independent state is undeniable. However, it is doubtful that any more appropriate pattern of large-scale ter-

ritorial units could have emerged. Nineteenth-century sub-Saharan Africa had not developed the broad areas of uniform culture that characterized other parts of the world such as Southest Asia. Moreover, the international community lacked any more appropriate accepted criterion for partitioning territory.

It is true that the borders adopted by the Europeans were "artificial," but, in fact, all international boundaries are "artificial" in the sense of being determined and implemented by human negotiators. Most of the so-called natural boundaries (in the sense of following topographic features) that were established in Africa probably did as much or more violence to indigenous political or tribal organization than did adopted geometric lines. This is particularly true of riverine boundaries, since streams serve as arteries for the areas through which they pass, linking inhabitants on either side together rather than separating them. Actually, the process of carving up Africa into colonial units was quite comparable to the partitioning of territory in Europe itself, particularly following the end of World War I. There, as in Africa, boundaries were established by outsiders at international conferences with little input from the local peoples.

TABLE 9.4   EQUATORIAL AFRICA

Equatorial Africa is divided among nine states. French is a *lingua franca* throughout most of the region, although local languages fulfil a similar function in five countries: Sango in the Central African Republic, Lingala in Congo, Fang in Equatorial Guinea, Kinyarwanda in Rwanda, and Kirundi in Burundi. The northern states were formerly administrative subdivisions of French Equatorial Africa, and Zaire, Rwanda, and Burundi were controlled by Belgium. Equatorial Guinea was a Spanish colony. Frictions between Muslims and Christians/Animists characterize northern states, but Islam has only a minor foothold in the south. Following Belgium's granting of independence to Zaire in 1959, the huge territory was beset by regional rebellions in Katanga, Kasai, and the Orientale Province. Military intervention by outside forces reunited the territory, which since has been governed by a one-party dictatorship.

State	Total Poplation	Area (square miles)
Cameroon	13,000,000	180,000
Number of Ethnic Groups: 200		
Lingua Franca		
French and English		
Dominant Regional Group and % Total		
Fulani, 10% (North)		
Significant Regional Groups and % Total		
Bamiliki, 19% (Western Highlands); Pahouins, 19% (South Coast)		
Chad	6,000,000	500,000
Number of Ethnic Groups: 200		
Lingua Franca		
French		
Dominant Regional Group and % Total		
Sudanic Arabs, 26% (North)		
Significant Regional Groups and % Total		
Saras, 30% (South)		
Central African Republic	3,000,000	240,000
Number of Ethnic Groups: 80		
Lingua Franca		
Sango, French		
Dominant Regional Group and % Total		
Mbaka, 4%		
Significant Regional Groups and % Total		
Banda, 29%; Baya (Gbaya), 25%		
Congo	2,750,000	130,000
Number of Ethnic Groups: 75		
Lingua Franca		
French, Lingala		
Dominant Regional Group and % Total		
Mboshi (Boubangui), 12%		
Significant Regional Groups and % Total		
Kongo, 52%; Sangha, 20% (Northeast); Teke, 17% (South)		
Gabon	1,250,000	100,000
Number of Ethnic Groups: 46		
Lingua Franca		
French		
Dominant Regional Group and % Total		
Fang, 35% (North)		
Significant Regional Groups and % Total		
Mpongwe, 15% (Coast); Mbete, 14% (South); Punu, 12% (East)		
Equatorial Guinea	400,000	11,000
Number of Ethnic Groups: 8		
Lingua Franca		
Fang, Spanish		

State	Total Population	Area (sq. miles)
Dominant Regional Group and % Total		
Fang, 82% (Rio Muni Mainland)		
Significant Regional Groups and % Total		
Bubi, 10% (Island of Bioko— formerly Fernando Po)		
Zaire	41,000,000	900,000
Number of Ethnic Groups: 200		
Lingua Franca		
French		
Dominant Regional Group and % Total		
Kongo, 16% (West)		
Significant Regional Groups and % Total		
Lulua (Luba-Kasai), 18% (South); Mongo, 14% (North); Rwanda, 10% (East)		
Rwanda	7,500,000	10,000
Number of Ethnic Groups: 3		
Lingua Franca		
Kinyarwanda		
Dominant Regional Group and % Total		
Hutsi, 90%		
Significant Regional Groups and % Total		
Tutsi, 9%		
Burundi	5,750,000	11,000
Number of Ethnic Groups: 3		
Lingua Franca		
Kirundi (similar to Kinyarwanda)		
Dominant Regional Group and % Total		
Tutsi, 14%		
Significant Regional Groups and % Total		
Hutu (Hutsi), 82%		

Although all sub-Saharan Africa, save Liberia and Ethiopia, came under European domination, relatively few Europeans ever migrated there. In contrast to French colonization in Algeria and British and Dutch settlement in South Africa, the tropical regions witnessed mere handfuls of colonial administrators living chiefly in district towns. Only in a few favored areas, chiefly the highlands of Kenya and Rhodesia and the long-held Portuguese coastal strip of Angola, did Europeans establish a significant presence. A very small fraction of nineteenth-century Africans even saw Europeans, since most colonial powers administered their possessions indirectly through native chiefs advised by solitary residents. The need of hard-pressed European administrations to minimize administrative costs was a principal reason for such policies.

This is not to say that Europeans had only a minor impact upon sub-Saharan Africa. The partitioning of tribal groups by colonial boundaries has been cited above. Although most colonial borders remained theoretical lines across the landscape, they did become political, economic, and cultural divides. Tribal groups found members on one side of an international line subjected to differing second languages, laws, and standard operating procedures from those on the other. During World War I they were forced to become involved in struggles between Germans and the Western Allies.

Europeans often created further divisiveness within their colonial realms. For effectiveness in administration, the French subdivided their sprawling territories of western and equatorial Africa into separate colonies (see Table 9-4). In the British possessions of Sierra Leone, the Gold Coast, Nigeria, and elsewhere, the government made formal distinctions between directly managed "colonies" along the coasts and native-run "protectorates" in the interior. Generally such internal subdivision was not the result of negotiations with native chiefs, unlike the process of partitioning territory among the different European colonial powers. Internal borders were set in arbitrary fashion, often being based upon patterns of rail and river transportation.

Imperial policies frequently exacerbated diversity within colonial realms and subdivisions. Mother countries on occasion resorted to policies of "divide and rule" to maintain authority. To suppress unrest in a region they would employ native militias recruited from distant tribal groups. Investment in economic development tended to be spotty. Quite commonly, coastal zones became commercialized, with higher living standards and opportunities for greater education. Adjacent interior regions remained at the subsistence level, resulting in creation of significant economic gulfs between peoples within a colony.

The End of Colonialism

The termination of European colonialism in sub-Saharan Africa occurred in even a shorter period than its establishment. In contrast to the violent stuggle for independence north of the Sahara in Algeria, the process of sub-Saharan African decolonization was for the most part bloodless. Indeed, Europeans are blamed for abandoning colonies such as the Belgian Congo too soon—before native elites had been educated to assume authority.

As colonization appeared to be an inevitable process, so too eventual decolonization seemed inescapable. Europeans, particularly the British, had congratulated themselves that they had assumed a "white man's burden" to prepare "uncivilized" Africans for eventual self-government. However, few saw such an achievement coming as early as the mid-twentieth century. Most anticipated that decades of education and economic development would be required for any proper independent functioning.

A combination of circumstances forced European withdrawal from sub-Saharan Africa in the immediate decades following World War II. One was the economic prostration of the major European states following more than five years of warfare and occupation. The conflict had destroyed productive facilities and infrastructure in the mother countries. Their populations gave foremost priority for limited funds to domestic reconstruction. Moreover, most suffered a mood of disillusionment concerning imperial glories and responsibilities. There was a growing perception, at least among politicians, of the costliness of maintaining the flag in other climes.

On the African side, an elite core of potential leaders had emerged, well-educated in mother countries and imbued by liberal colleagues with goals of having their subjects enjoy the same freedoms and relative well-being observable among the masses in Europe. They also were aware of dramatic events in insular Southeast Asia, where the Dutch had been frustrated in resuming control over their East Indies colony by a local leadership prepared by the Japanese in the closing months of the war to assume governmental control from occupation forces. African contemplations of anticolonial rebellion long had been discouraged by a myth of European invincibility, not unlike the similar myth of permanence of Communist control once it had been established, which prolonged the lifespan of manifestly inefficient authoritarian regimes in Eastern Europe and elsewhere.

The struggle for independence in sub-Saharan Africa began in Kenya, where the presence of privileged British settlers in the temperate highlands compounded general problems associated with colonial rule. The so-called Mau Mau uprising in the early 1950s gave heart to Africans in other colonies and led Europeans to reevaluate colonial policies. The British took the lead in decisions to forsake African possessions. They earlier had granted the Gold Coast formal independence in 1948 as the new state of Ghana. After disastrous wars in Algeria and Vietnam, France under the leadership of Charles de Gaulle finally determined the wisdom of ending its colonial domain in Africa in 1958. By 1963, only the so-called front line colonies facing South Africa remained dependencies of European states. The British maintained control over Southern Rhodesia and the Portuguese retained Angola and Mozambique. Eventually these areas, too, became independent. In 1975 Portugal became the last European power to depart from Africa, paradoxically after being the first to establish a presence there four centuries earlier.

Virtually all the new states appeared within boundaries framed by Europeans in the 1884/85 Berlin Conference or by subsequent colonial border alterations. Not only did each European colonial area see a separate state, but independence also came to virtually all first-order colonial subdivisions of such realms. The only major exceptions were the combination of the British and Italian (but not French) Somali colonies on the "horn" of Africa into the new state of Somalia, the joining together again of the French and British parts of Togo and the Cameroons, and the linkage of Britain's trust territory of Tanganyika and its protectorate of Zanzibar into a unified state to be known as "Tanzania."

Statesmen charged with preparing colonial areas for independence were averse to the balkanization of sub-Saharan Africa into numerous small and separate entities. The French sought consolidation of most of their vast West African empire into a large "Mali Federation" and their equatorial domain into a "Central

African Federation." The British had developed close associations among their dependencies of Kenya, Uganda, and Tanganyika, and laid the groundwork for an anticipated East African Community. They also created elaborate plans for the formation of a federal union of Northern and Southern Rhodesia and their Nyasaland protectorate. None of these proposed larger units materialized, however.

As was the case more than a century earlier in Latin America, groups of people who had enjoyed separate identities in the colonial era were loathe to forfeit them to broader agglomerations when European departure came. Rivalries had developed in the colonial period that could not be forgotten. Local leaders saw greater opportunities for their own careers within future sovereign states than in mere provincial subdivisions. The pre-European historical enmities between groups also played a role in discouraging possible mergers. Finally, differences in second languages and standard operating procedures between adjacent areas controlled by different European states all but precluded the possibility of merger. In the combined states of Somalia and the Cameroons severe internal strains plagued the successor governments.

The Independent Sub-Saharan African States

Virtually all European colonies thus emerged intact as independent states. The new entities suffered the inherited structural problems of their colonial predecessors. As can be seen from Figure 9-4, virtually all international borders cut across tribal territories. Also, nearly all boundaries circumscribed heterogeneous collections of peoples having different tribal affiliations, speaking different languages, and, frequently, professing different religions. It is ironic that the binding forces that the new states enjoyed were almost entirely legacies of the colonial period. These included the implanting of a common European language for transactions and a common set of governmental and economic institutions, as well as the creation of communication and transportation networks to facilitate coherence.

The fact that the form and very identity of their new states was a consequence of European colonialism was troubling to sub-Saharan Africa's initial leaders. To assert further their independence from mother coun-

FIGURE 9-4 TRIBAL BOUNDARIES IN SUB-SAHARAN AFRICA

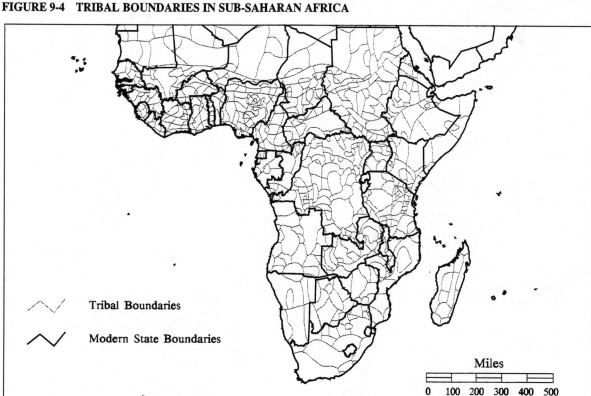

Tribal Boundaries

Modern State Boundaries

Miles

0   100   200   300   400   500

TABLE 9.5   EASTERN AFRICA

Eastern Africa falls into two contrasting parts: a western section composed of former British colonial areas and an eastern section of past predominantly Italian influence. The western states of Kenya, Uganda, and Tanganyika are mainly Bantu- and Nilotic-speaking and the eastern countries are dominated by Cushitic and Semitic languages. English and Swahili are *lingua franca* in the western states and Somali and Arabic in the east. The western states are mainly Roman Catholic, Protestant, or Animist and the eastern regions are principally Muslim or Ethiopian Orthodox. Most states are rather large but have extensive sparsely inhabited rainforest or desert territories. All are divided among regional groups whose members extend across international borders.

State	Total Poplation	Area (sq. miles)
Kenya	27,000,000	225,000

Number of Ethnic Groups: 35
Lingua Franca
English, Swahili
Dominant Regional Group and % Total
Kikuyu, 21% (Central Highlands)
Significant Regional Groups and % Total
Luhya, 14% (Lake Victoria Basin); Luo, 13% (Lake Victoria Basin); Kamba, 11% (Central Highlands); Kalenjin, 11% (Western Plateau); Somali, 4% (Eastern Nomads); Masai, 2% (Southern Nomads)

Uganda	17,000,000	93,000

Number of Ethnic Groups: 45
Lingua Franca
English, Swahili
Dominant Regional Group and % Total
Ganda, 18%
Significant Regional Groups and % Total
Luo, 15% (Northwest); Teso, 9% (Northeast); Soga, 8% (Southeast)

Tanzania	26,000,000	365,000

Number of Ethnic Groups: 120
Lingua Franca
English, Swahili
Dominant Regional Group and % Total
(No group appears to dominate)
Significant Regional Groups and % Total
Sukuma, 13% (North); Nyamwezi, 4% (West); Zanzibarians, 2% (Zanzibar and Pemba Islands); Chaga, 4% (Slope of Kilimanjaro); Hehet and Bena, 7% (Southeast); Maconde, 6% (Southeast); Haya, 6% (Northwest)

Ethiopia	50,000,000	485,000

Number of Ethnic Groups: 100
Lingua Franca
Amharic
Dominant Regional Group and % Total
Amhara, 38% (Northwest)
Significant Regional Groups and % Total
Galla, 35% (West); Tigre, 9% (North); Somali, 8% (Southeast)
Potential Trouble Areas and Possible Adversaries

Ogaden Desert (Somalia)	1,000,000	70,000
Eritrea	3,500,000	36,000

Number of Ethnic Groups: 1
Lingua Franca
Tigre, Arabic
Dominant Regional Group and % Total
Eritreans, 80%

Somalia	8,000,000	246,000

Number of Ethnic Groups: 10
Lingua Franca
Somali

State	Total Population	Area (sq. miles)

Dominant Regional Group and % Total
Somalis, 98% (including all clans)
Significant Regional Clan Groups
Rahanwayn and Digel (Sab) (South); Daarood (Northeast); Hawiye (South Central Coast); Isaaq (North); Dir (South); Tunni (South Coast); Digel (South Interior)
Potential Trouble Areas and Possible Adversaries

"Somaliland Republic"	1,000,000	68,000

(Former British Somaliland adjacent to Djibouti, dominated by Isaaq Clan.)

Djibouti	600,000	9,000

Number of Ethnic Groups: 6
Lingua Franca
Somali, Arabic, French
Dominant Regional Group and % Total
Issas, 34% (South)
Significant Regional Groups and % Total
Afars (Danikils), 20% (North)
Potential Trouble Areas and Possible Adversaries
The entire state faces pressures for incorporation by Somalia for irredentist motivations and by Ethiopia for strategic/economic concerns about its function as Ethiopia's major port.

tries and to garner a degree of historical legitimacy, the new regimes frequently adopted native names for their young states. The Gold Coast led the way by immediately becoming "Ghana," derived from the name of an early kingdom in West Africa. The French Sudan appropriated the appellation "Mali," another historic kingdom, after collapse of the ambitious French plan for a broader West African "Mali Federation."

For a period, sub-Saharan Africa witnessed two separate "Congo" states with the similar names of "Congo People's Republic" (the former French Middle Congo) and "Congo Democratic Republic" (the former Belgian Congo). They were most often distinguished from each other by reference to their capital cities of Brazzaville and Leopoldville, respectively. Confusion ended in 1971, when the latter state adopted the sobriquet "Zaïre" and changed the name of its capital to "Kinshasa." Movements for independence in the southern African territories of Southern Rhodesia and South-West Africa adopted the appellations "Zimbabwe" and "Namibia," respectively, for their homelands. When colonial powers were forced to withdraw, there was no question but that these would become the new names of the young states.

As a result of inherited diversity and border problems, the potential for conflict in sub-Saharan Africa has remained high. Irredentist pressures exist among several states. Thus, the former French colony of the Congo has set forth claims to the Ogooué region of Gabon. Similarly, formerly British Ghana has pressed

for the Sanwi area of the previously French Ivory Coast. The most irredentist state has been Somalia. Although divided into tribal clans, its population is notably more homogeneous in language, religion, and culture than other sub-Saharan African states. Large numbers of Somali-speaking peoples live in adjacent Kenya and Ethiopia. Beginning in 1948, Somalia instigated disturbances in both areas. Those in Kenya were effectively suppressed by both British and subsequent independent Kenyan governments. The dispute with Ethiopia over the Somali-inhabited Ogaden Desert lingered, however, and became a major issue when Somalia invaded the region in 1977. It was forced to withdraw a few months later, following strong support of Ethiopia by the USSR and Cuba.

Some antagonisms relate to expediencies of border delimitation between the colonial powers. The British had established the boundary between their former Nyasaland Protectorate and their Mandated Territory of Tanganyika as the Tanganyika shore of Lake Nyasa. Tanzania, the successor to Tanganyika, has demanded revision of its border with Malawi, the successor state to Nyasaland, to allow Tanzanians free access and use of the lake. In like fashion, Liberia has pressed for adjustment of its Cavally River boundary with the Ivory Coast—from the banks of the river imposed by a questionable treaty with the French to a more equitable sharing of the stream.

Other problems reflect unhappiness of groups at continuing incorporation within broader regions considered hostile to their development and well-being. In 1960 the peoples of mineral-rich Katanga (Shaba) Province unsuccessfully rebelled from the successor government to the former Belgian Congo because of tribal antagonism and a desire to preserve a privileged economic situation. For similar reasons, the Ibo people of southeastern Nigeria attempted to establish a secessionist state of Biafra in 1967, but were crushed by the Nigerian army in 1970. Even the smallest states are riven by tribal dischord. Djibouti occupies less than 9,000 square miles. However, the Afars group, constituting 20 percent of the state's population of some 500,000, mounted a guerrilla war in 1991 with the Somali tribe of the Issas, who had a near-majority of 30 percent of the total population.

A number of secessionist movements exist that have yet to resort to overt rebellion. The Lozi (Barotse) people of western Zambia (formerly Northern Rhodesia) have sought separation from that territory ever since the colonial period because of tribal antagonisms and economic concerns. Inhabitants of the old Buganda Kingdom within Uganda resisted loss of traditional autonomy and dominant status within the former protectorate by pressing for separation from Uganda in 1966. In 1991, the peoples of the Casamance region of southern Senegal, long isolated from the main part of the state by the intervening former British colony of Gambia, agitated for their own state.

Such secessionist pressures reflect the inability of virtually all sub-Saharan African regimes to secure for themselves a sense of legitimacy by all inhabitants within their states. In part this derives from a sorry record of corruption and incompetence characterizing a majority of governments in the postcolonial period. Beyond such discreditation, the lack of general support for regimes has been due to an absence of a common sense of national identity within each state. In contrast to Europe and other major world realms, the peoples of sub-Saharan Africa have lacked the common historic associations over broad areas that breed cultural homogeneity and, beginning in the nineteenth century, a sense of nation. African political associations over broad area's have tended to be localized and based upon tribal inheritance. Each state consists of a multitude of tribal groups (Figure 9-3), usually speaking languages or dialects distinctive from those of their neighbors. Most have preserved awareness of conflicts with adjacent groups that date back to the era of slavery and before.

Complicating tribal enmities and disunity is the gulf between religious groups. Long-colonized coastal areas frequently were Christianized, setting their inhabitants apart from the native animists of the interior. In the frontier zone with North Africa even greater chasms separate Muslim from non-Muslim groups. Fundamental differences in outlook in such matters as proper forms of government, education, and attitudes toward women have made common political cause difficult between Muslims and their neighbors. Proclivities of Muslims toward domination have resulted in serious tensions, if not open conflicts, from Senegal to the Red Sea. These are seen in the short-lived attempt of the Nigerian Ibos to establish their separate state of Biafra and the long-simmering guerrilla war of black tribal groups against Arabs in the southern Sudan. Muslims have sought control even in states where they are a small minority, as witness the assumption of power by Idi Amin in Uganda, using his role in the Ugandan armed forces to oust the elected regime.

Military coups have been a common phenomenon throughout sub-Saharan Africa. Although Amin's seizure of power appeared mainly to pursue his own ambition, military leaders have frequently assumed authority in reaction to blatant corruption and general ineffectiveness of established governments. Armed forces are often the only institutions within a state that are committed to the preservation and well being of the state as a whole. However, military regimes generally have not proven themselves more able or less prone to corruption than the civilian governments that they have overthrown.

The Republic of South Africa

The southern tip of Africa is distinctive in history, politics, and economics from the rest of Africa south of the Sahara. It is an area of extensive settlement by Europeans, with a history preoccupied by the question of relationships among its differing racial, linguistic, and tribal groups. It is the most developed part of the continent, providing higher living standards for virtually all citizens than enjoyed by ethnic counterparts elsewhere in Africa.

Before the first Dutch colony was established at the Cape of Good Hope in 1652, southern Africa was a relatively empty area. Its inhabitants were primarily Khoi peoples (pejoratively termed Hottentots by the Dutch). Their racial ancestry is closer to the dark-skinned groups living around the Indian Ocean (Indian Dravidians and Australian Aborigenes) than to African inhabitants of the tropical zone. For the most part hunters and gatherers, the Khoi had not created for themselves political organizations beyond clan and tribe that were comparable, say, to the old tropical kingdoms of Benin and Buganda. Large numbers of Khoi perished from smallpox and other diseases brought to their homeland by Europeans. This also occurred to native peoples in many parts of the Americas, Australia, and elsewhere.

Two-thirds of southern Africa was arid. The better-watered area to the south and east was divided between a Mediterranean-type climate with dry summers and moderate winters in the Cape of Good Hope region, and a humid subtropical environment to the east that featured a maximum summer rainfall similar to that of Florida.

Continental Europeans began settlement of southern Africa at about the same time that the English were colonizing the eastern seaboard of North America. Like New Englanders, the settlers in southern Africa were largely Protestant in religion. The largest group came from the Netherlands, but there were also French Huguenots and immigrants from Germany. Their prevailing Calvinist religious beliefs, instituted through the Dutch Reformed Church, gave justification for enslavement and domination of the indigenous inhabitants.

For the most part, the Europeans were hard working farmers—"Boers" in Afrikaans, the version of the Dutch language that evolved in southern Africa over the ensuing three-and-a-half centuries. They early sought to force indigenous Khoi peoples to toil in their fields, and when this forced labor proved insufficient, they imported slaves from elsewhere in Africa. Their farms provided basic food needs and also the basis for a brisk trade in provisions of grain and meat for European ship crews that were engaged in commerce with the Orient.

In accord with Germanic traditions derived from their Dutch origins, the Boers granted existing farms to their eldest sons, requiring younger sons continuously to move farther inland to establish farmsteads of their own. As the latter pushed eastward and northward in the late eighteenth century, they came increasingly into contact with Bantu peoples, whose numbers were rapidly growing through migrants from tropical Africa. Caught between advancing Europeans on one side and migrating Bantus on the other, the native Khoi peoples all but disappeared as a significant group. Some found refuge in the more inhospitable dry margins of the region. Others simply became submerged in the cultures of the dominant Bantus.

After 150 years of colonization under a Dutch flag, the European inhabitants of southern Africa found themselves British subjects at the end of the eighteenth century. When Napoleon's forces overran the Netherlands in 1795, British troops occupied the Cape of Good Hope. As an aftermath of the Napoleonic Wars, the United Kingdom formally annexed the southern tip of Africa in 1812. Immigration from the British Isles began to flow there in 1820.

The establishment of British authority did not sit well with the Boers. The new government insisted upon conducting its affairs in English, and it imposed a system of laws and procedures that were foreign to Dutch colonial traditions. It also appeared insensitive to perceived needs of the Boers, particularly by refusing to annex new lands on the frontier. The British decision in 1834 to outlaw slavery dealt a severe economic blow to the Afrikaaners, as early settlers came to be known. At the same time, the demonstrated ability of small groups of raiders (commandos) to terrorize and dominate native Africans increased the attraction of settlement on the frontier.

Many settlers resolved to move to territories unclaimed by Europeans north of the Orange River, which had become depopulated by tribal wars. The Great Trek that began in 1836 involved more than 10,000 pioneers in a movement somewhat comparable to migration along the Oregon Trail in the western United States that occurred at roughly the same time. Afrikaaners established two independent republics, the Orange Free State and the Transvaal. They faced continuing problems with the British government, which initially claimed their territories but at length recognized the independence of the two states in 1853. This did not prevent subsequent temporary British annexation of the Transvaal in 1873 and its complete subjugation at the end of the nineteenth century.

Many British South Africans during the same period moved eastward from the Cape of Good Hope across the Great Fish River, which earlier had been unilaterally established by the British as the eastern limits of their colonial activities. This advance into the Natal region was a circumstance not originally anticipated by the British government, but colonial administrators could not stop it. The newly settled territory became the separate Crown Colony of Natal in 1844. Unlike the Boers, the descendants of British settlers tended not to remain for generations on pioneer farms but drifted into the region's rapidly growing towns and cities. The spatial separation of the two European streams heightened the cultural division, which persists to the present.

Both European groups came into increasing contact with Bantu peoples during the course of the nineteenth century. The Bantus grew dominant in the eastern reaches of southern Africa, although few established themselves in the western two-thirds of the present South African state. Much of their influx was the result of domineering activities by the Zulu tribe after 1800. Members of other tribal groups found themselves compelled to flee to the relatively empty lands in Natal, where they came to predominate in many areas. Following their prolonged warfare with the Zulus, refugees tended to abandon their traditional authoritarian tribal organizations. They fragmented into small groups, which collectively formed the basis for the subsequent establishment of native reserves in southern Africa.

TABLE 9.6   SOUTHERN AFRICA

Southern Africa's political geography revolves around the Republic of South Africa and nine so-called "Frontline" Black African states on its margins. For convenience, Madagascar and the Comoros Islands also are included in this section, but their populations see themselves properly as parts of South Asia and the Middle East, respectively. All states contain numerous ethnic groups, although increasingly individuals are identifying with broader linguistic groupings. Most Black Africans speak one of the Bantu languages and are either Christian or Animist. The languages of the former colonial power (English, Portuguese, French) constitute an imported unifying element in each state. During the second half of the twentieth century the *apartheid* regional segregation policy of the dominating White minority of South Africa was successfully challenged by the hitherto powerless Black majority. South African Blacks, however, have a major division between Zulus (with related tribes) and remaining groups.

State	Total Population	Area (sq. miles)
Republic of South Africa	32,000,000	430,000

Number of Ethnic Groups: 200
Lingua Franca
English, Afrikaans
Dominant Regional Groups and % Total
Afrikaans-speaking Whites, 9%
English-speaking Whites, 6%
Significant Regional Groups and % Total
Zulus, 25% (East); Sotho-Tswana, 25% (Highveld); Khosa, 10% (Southeast); Tsonga, 5% (Eastern Transvaal); Swazi, 4% (East); Venda, 2% (Northern Transvaal)

Namibia (Southwest Africa)	1,500,000	320,000

Number of Ethnic Groups: 30
Lingua Franca
English
Dominant Regional Group and % Total
Ovambo, 50%
Significant Regional Groups and % Total
Kavango, 9%; Herero, 8%; Damara, 7%

Angola	11,000,000	480,000

Number of Ethnic Groups: 100
Lingua Franca
Portuguese
Dominant Regional Group and % Total
Mbundu, 22% (South-Central)
Significant Regional Groups and % Total
Ovimbundu, 37%; Kongo, 13% (North); Lunda-Chokwe, 11% (Northeast); Luimbe-Nganguela, 7% (Southeast); Nyaneka-Humbe, 5% (Southwest); Yombe, <1% (Inhabit Cabinda)

Botswana (Bechuanaland)	1,400,000	225,000

Number of Ethnic Groups: 20
Lingua Franca
English
Dominant Regional Group and % Total
Tswana, 75%
Significant Regional Groups and % Total
Shona, 12%; Bushmen, 5%

Zimbabwe	10,000,000	150,000

Number of Ethnic Groups: 30
Lingua Franca
English
Dominant Regional Group and % Total
Mashona, 70%
Significant Regional Groups and % Total
Matebele, 16%

State	Total Population	Area (sq. miles)
Zambia	8,500,000	290,000

Number of Ethnic Groups: 73
Lingua Franca
English
Dominant Regional Group and % Total
Maravi (Njanja), 18%
Significant Regional Groups and % Total
Bemba, 36%; Tonga, 15%; Barotze, 8%

State	Total Population	Area (sq. miles)
Malawi	9,500,000	45,000

Number of Ethnic Groups: 10
Lingua Franca
Chichewa, English
Dominant Regional Group and % Total
Chewa, 6%
Significant Regional Groups and % Total
Nyanja, 50%; Tumbuka, 9%; Tonga, 2%; Ngoni, 7%; Yao, 13%

State	Total Population	Area (sq. miles)
Mozambique	15,000,000	315,000

Number of Ethnic Groups: 28
Lingua Franca
Portuguese
Dominant Regional Group and % Total
Tsonga, 23%
Significant Regional Groups and % Total
Makua, 47%; Maravi, 12%; Shona, 11%; Yao, 4%

State	Total Population	Area (sq. miles)
Madagascar (Malagasy)	13,000,000	225,000

Number of Ethnic Groups: 20
Lingua Franca
French
Dominant Regional Group and % Total
Merina, 27% (Central Highlands)
Significant Regional Groups and % Total
Betsimisaraka, 15% (East Coast); Betsilco, 12% (Southern Highlands); Tsimihety, 7% (Northern Highlands); Sakalava, 6% (West Coast)

State	Total Population	Area (sq. miles)
Comoros (with Mayote)	585,000	863

Number of Ethnic Groups: 4
Lingua Franca
Comorian (Swahili), Arabic, French
Significant Regional Groups and % Total
Mohairais, 30% (Mayotte); Anjouanese, (Anjouan); Grand Comorians, (Grand Comoro); Mohélians (Mohéli)

State	Total Population	Area (sq. miles)
Lesotho (Basutoland)	1,850,000	11,700

Number of Ethnic Groups: 1
Lingua Franca
Sesotho
Dominant Regional Group and % Total
Basotho, 90%
Significant Regional Groups and % Total
Zulu, 10%

State	Total Population	Area (sq. miles)
Swaziland	850,000	6,700

Number of Ethnic Groups: 70 (clans)
Lingua Franca
SiSwati, English
Dominant Regional Group and % Total
Swazi, 84%
Significant Regional Groups and % Total
Zulus, 11%

Natal saw another migrant stream in the 1860s when British entrepreneurs established sugar plantations. Unable to attract sufficient native workers, they recruited indentured servants from Malaya and India. The offspring of these South Asians tended to leave agriculture, frequently becoming petty traders in the countryside or migrating to the cities. Today, more than half the population of the city of Durban is of Indian ancestry.

Patterns of population continued to change during the nineteenth century. The 1867 discovery of diamonds in Kimberley and the 1886 gold strikes in the Rand drew hordes of British miners and adventurers into the northern republics. They soon outnumbered the Afrikaaner population, leading to frictions and eventually the Boer War of 1899–1902. The subjugation of the Orange Free State and the Transvaal was followed by their amalgamation with the Cape of Good Hope and Natal into a Union of South Africa in 1910. Like Australia, New Zealand, and Australia, the Union of South Africa was cast as a self-governing "dominion" under the British Crown. It was organized on a federal basis, with its legislature meeting in Cape Town, its central government offices operating in Pretoria, and its Supreme Court sitting in Bloemfontein.

South Africa's Racial Amalgam

The Republic of South Africa embraces a total area of 472,000 square miles, or roughly one-seventh the area of the United States of America. Its population numbers just over 35,000,000, of whom 74 percent are black, 15 percent white, 9 percent "coloured" (of mixed racial ancestry), and 2 percent Asian. Each of these groups is further fragmented by language, ethnicity, and/or religion. The largest share of the population lives within a hundred miles of the coast.

South African blacks are divided into four primary linguistic groups. About half speak languages of the Nguni family, which includes Ndbele, Swazi, Khosa, and Zulu. Nguni-speakers live principally in the eastern coastal regions. The high veld region of the interior is home to the Sotho-Tswana linguistic family that includes the Sotho, Pedi, and Tswana peoples. The Tsong-speaking peoples occupy the eastern Transvaal region, and Venda speakers live in northern Transvaal.

Tribally, about 60 percent of South African blacks identify themselves as Zulus or members of tribes related to a degree to Zulus. The remainder generally

FIGURE 9-5 SOUTH AFRICAN PROVINCES AND NATIVE HOMELANDS UNDER APARTHEID

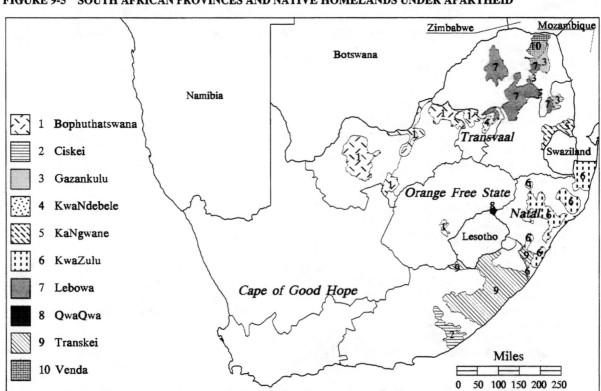

1	Bophuthatswana
2	Ciskei
3	Gazankulu
4	KwaNdebele
5	KaNgwane
6	KwaZulu
7	Lebowa
8	QwaQwa
9	Transkei
10	Venda

maintain an anti-Zulu attitude. About half the blacks live in tribal reserves (including the former so-called self-governing states) and the other half live in the vicinity of towns and cities (Figure 9-5). Many of the latter are men whose families remain in tribal reserves often great distances away. A number of blacks residing in South Africa are from other African states; they work temporarily in mines and factories for the higher wages afforded.

The white population remains spatially divided between Afrikaaners, who predominate in rural areas and the eastern interior, and those of English heritage living in urban areas and the Cape of Good Hope. About two-thirds of white South Africans speak Afrikaans and one-third English. The coloured population of mixed racial ancestry generally speaks the Afrikaaner language. Most live in Cape of Good Hope province, with more than half residing within 200 miles of Cape Town. They outnumber the white population in this area by a ratio of 2:1. The Asian population remains concentrated in KwaZulu-Natal province. Generally referred to as "Indian," they include Hindus, Muslims, and Christians and speak Tamil, Hindi, Telugu, Gujarati, Urdu, and other languages.

South Africa's Apartheid Policy

South Africa received universal condemnation during the second half of the twentieth century for establishing an official policy of segregation based upon race. Through internal political agitation and external economic pressures the domination by European groups formally ended in 1994 with the establishment of equality for all inhabitants.

As noted above, slavery was an acceptable institution in South Africa well into the nineteenth century. Following the ending of slavery by the British, racial discrimination and segregation continued throughout the region as a fact of life. To alleviate some of the worst injustices against the black population, the British government in 1913 established a number of territorial reserves for native groups. A program to expand areas of native reserves was promulgated in 1936.

In 1948 the Afrikaaner-based National Party came to power in South Africa, partly in reaction to perceived pressures to adopt English as a universal language. Its leadership was determined to preserve the way of life and prerogatives of the white population. It justified its announced policy of *apartheid* (literally "apartness" in

FIGURE 9-6   SOUTH AFRICAN PROVINCES UNDER 1994 CONSTITUTION

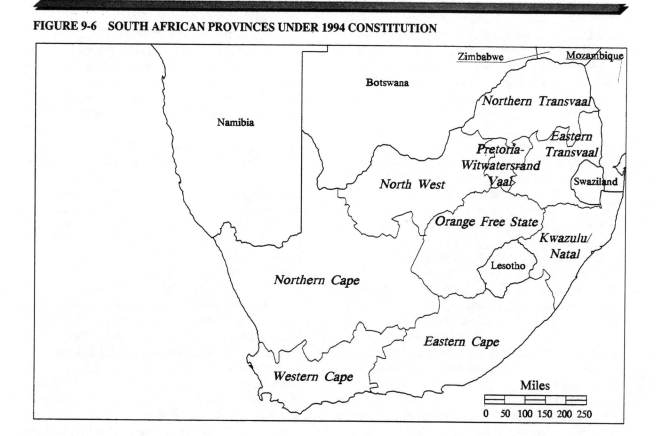

Afrikaans) on grounds that cultural diversity made impossible the existence of a single South African nation. Rather, the new regime maintained, the state should recognize that it consisted of a collection of quite different national groups whose futures were best assured by separate self-development.

In 1950 the new government pushed a Population Registration Act through the South African parliament. The act required that all inhabitants go through a process of official classification as "White," "Coloured," "Indian," or "Bantu." Thousands of personal tragedies occurred, as a member of a mixed-race family might be able to secure status in the privileged "White" category, but with the consequence of forsaking ties to other family members.

In 1951 the Bantu Authorities Act strengthened the positions of traditional chiefs within tribal groups. This had the effect of weakening linkages of the black population to the broader society. The act also somewhat consolidated and enlarged native reserves, which came to be called "Bantustans." Other regulations required separate schools and public facilities for each race. Many occupational categories were reserved solely for whites. Strict laws forbade sexual intercourse and marriage between members of different racial groups.

Later legislation designated some 1,700 residential areas in South Africa as exclusive for one race. In 1983 alone the regime ejected more than 3,500,000 blacks from towns and white-designated rural areas, often from lands long occupied by their families. To accommodate blacks whose labor was required in adjacent cities, the government designated a number of so-called Black Spots in suburban areas. One of these, Soweto, outside Johannesburg, became a major city of its own with 1,500,000 inhabitants.

Governmental affairs became an exclusively white enterprise. Coloureds and blacks who earlier had achieved the right to vote found that they had lost their franchise. The blatant racialist policies of the South African regime led to universal condemnation. In reaction to increasing pressures from the United Kingdom and other members of the Commonwealth of Nations to change its course, South Africa severed all ties with the British Crown in 1961 and declared itself a republic.

A key political-geographic feature of apartheid was the creation of a number of ostensibly autonomous territories for the black African population. Four of these were termed self-administered states—Transkei, Bophuthatswana, Venda, and Ciskei. Collectively they occupied an area of 40,000 square miles and had a combined population of 7,000,000. Although declared independent entities by the South African government, no foreign government recognized them as such. They exercised a number of self-governing functions, however, including education, public health, law enforcement,

and road maintenance. All were dependent upon financial aid from the South African government. A curious feature was their territorial fragmentation. The four units consisted of more than 200 widely scattered enclaves. South Africa recognized an additional six lower-ranking "national states" that were not "self-administered": Gazankulu, KaNgwane, KwaNdelbele, and Lebowa in Transvaal; KwaZulu in Natal; and Qwaqwa in the Orange Free State.

South Africa's openly racial policies generated repugnance throughout the world. Early in the 1980s most governments under United Nations leadership cut off trade with the republic and imposed other sanctions that had ruinous effects on the South African economy. Political problems increased within the country. The native homelands did not function as intended by their creators. Leadership was corrupt and their chief export to the rest of the state continued to be laborers for white areas.

The regime under new leadership in the 1980s began to relax many aspects of apartheid. In 1991 it repealed the Population Registration Act along with other restrictive laws. It freed from prison Nelson Mandela and entered into negotiations with him on South Africa's future. Mandela was a long-time leader of the African National Congress, one of the two major black African political organizations. South Africa's progress in racial relations led to most states ending their sanctions against it by the end of 1993.

Deep divisions remain to be resolved in South Africa, however. These include the basic conflict between a prosperous white population and a poverty-stricken black majority. Long-standing frictions between Afrikaaners and English-speakers, suppressed during decades of confrontation by blacks, are slowly reemerging. Some Afrikaaner leaders in the northern Transvaal province have reportedly negotiated with black representatives for establishment of a separate white Afrikaaner homeland in their region. The threat of black majority rule has led many whites to contemplate leaving, particularly individuals from the English-speaking community. Up to 40,000 Europeans moved to South Africa annually through the 1970s, but since the mid-1980s those leaving the country have far exceeded new immigrants coming in.

More deeply divided are South Africa's blacks. Almost daily reports of murderous incidents, particularly in Black Spot settlements, cast doubts about a stable future. Adherents to the dominant African National Congress (ANC) have been challenged by the Inkatha political movement. The latter is essentially a Zulu organization, whereas the ANC is composed mainly of non-Zulus. More than 10,000 have died in clashes during the 1990s.

Although the establishment of the so-called independent homelands was condemned from the beginning by the outside world, they functioned for several years, and their governments gained a degree of allegiance from their inhabitants. This includes particularly the Zulu entity of KwaZulu. It appears that future governments of South Africa will have to accommodate their reality. Conflicts over rival claims to territory could well occur. It is noteworthy that constitutional revision of South Africa's provinces in 1994 resulted in renaming Natal Province as KwaZulu-Natal. (See Figure 9.5)

Bibliography

ASIWAJU, A.I., ed., *Partitioned Africa: Ethnic Relations across Africa's International Boundaries, 1884–1984*. London: Hurst, 1985.

BOATENG, E.A., *A Political Geography of Africa*. Cambridge: Cambridge University Press, 1978.

BROWNLIE, I., and I.R. BURNS, *African Boundaries: A Legal and Diplomatic Encyclopedia*. London: Hurst, 1979.

COBBAH, J.A.M., "Toward a Geography of Peace in Africa: Redefining sub-State Self-Determination Rights," in *Nationalism, Self-Determination and Political Geography,* eds. R.J. Johnston, David B. Knight, and E. Kofman. London: Croom Helm, 1988, pp. 70–86.

CROWDER, M., and J.F. AJAYI, eds., *A History of West Africa*. Harlow, UK: Longmans, 1987.

GIBBS, J.L., *Peoples of Africa*. New York: Holt, Reinhart & Winston, 1978.

GOODY, J., *Technology, Tradition and the State in Africa*. Cambridge: Cambridge University Press, 1980.

GROVE, A.T., *The Changing Geography of Africa*. Oxford: Oxford University Press, 1989.

HARRISON-CHURCH, R.J., "African Boundaries," in *The Changing World: Studies in Political Geography,* eds. W.G. East and A.E. Moodie. Yonkers, NY: World Book Company, 1956.

LEMON, ANTHONY, "Imposed Separation: The Case of South Africa," in *Shared Space: Divided Space: Essays on Conflict and Territorial Organization,* eds. Michael Chisholm and David M. Smith. London: Unwin Hyman, 1990, pp. 194–216.

OLIVER, R., and J.D. FAGE, *A Short History of Africa*. London: Penguin, 1988.

PACKENHAM, THOMAS, *The Scramble for Africa, 1876–1912*. New York: Random House, 1991.

ROTHCHILD, D., and VICTOR A. OLORUNSOLA, eds., *State Versus Ethnic Claims: African Policy Dilemmas*. Boulder, CO: Westview Press, 1983.

TOUVAL, SAADIA, *The Boundary Politics of Independent Africa*. Cambridge, MA: Harvard University Press, 1972.

TOUVAL, SAADIA, "Treaties, Borders, and the Partition of Africa," *Journal of African History,* Vol. 7 (1966), pp. 279–292.

10

South Asia

ALTHOUGH it is most often termed a "subcontinent," from many points of view South Asia fully merits consideration as a continent as much as does Europe. The Indian Peninsula and its associated areas (the Himalayan kingdoms, Afghanistan, and Sri Lanka) have a total area exceeding 2,000,000 square miles, which is roughly equivalent to the area of Europe west of the former USSR border. They have a combined population nearly triple that of Europe, and their diverse peoples share numerous cultural traits in common, much as Europeans share a "Western civilization." Moreover, South Asia's empty zones of high mountains, rainforests, and tropical deserts make it far more isolated from the main body of Eurasia than is Europe, which grades imperceptibly eastward across the East European Plain into Russia, Siberia, and Central Asia (Table 10-1).

The Diversity of South Asia

While one may thus identify a South Asian culture world that can be compared to European civilization, it is by no means a homogeneous entity. South Asia is fragmented culturally and politically in very much the same way as is Europe. These differences include contrasts in religion, language, and racial composition. An important distinguishing quality of South Asia's diversity, however, is the coexistence of contrasting traits within limited areas. Strict family rules of marriage have minimized the mixing and homogenization that tended to occur within local areas in Europe. In most places South Asian society consists of associations of different cultures. Regional differences in the mix of people do emerge when one takes a broader perspective, however. Its great diversities notwithstanding, South Asia's present political fragmentation is much less than Europe's —it is divided among only seven states, as opposed to Europe's twenty-four. However, it has had its past periods of extreme disunity, and there currently are separatist pressures in each of its larger states.

Religion remains the principal divisive factor in South Asia. Roughly 60 percent of the population is Hindu, 25 percent is Muslim, and the remaining 15 percent is apportioned among Buddhists, Sikhs, Christians, and other faiths. Although a small but significant share of the population has adopted European-style national identities, group enmities based upon religious tradition lie behind most of the region's internal conflicts. As in Northern Ireland, religion's principal political role lies in group isolation and categorization, rather than in actions based upon theological differences. However, this is not to say that the all-too-frequent Muslim defacing of Hindu idols or Hindu running of pigs through mosques does not serve to provoke massive retaliation.

The dominant faith of the mainland is Hinduism, which is practiced by nearly 800,000,000 adherents. It is polytheistic and rests on a belief in reincarnation based upon deeds in a previous life. It assumes a basic inequality among humankind. Associated with this outlook is the social organization of "caste" based upon inheritance. The caste that a person is born into determines one's status in society, the range of potential mates available, and the trade that one can pursue.

Although the once-rigid occupational structure associated with caste has begun to break down in the cities, it remains a significant element in rural areas. There are some 3,000 distinctive castes among the Hindus, differing regionally as well as hierarchically. They are subdivisions of four principal stations: Brahmins, who are the priests and scholars; Kshatriyas, who are the warriors and secular rulers; Vaisyas, who are the merchants; and Sudras, who are the laborers. About 20 percent of the Hindu-identified population are classed as "untouchables," those without a caste. Gandhi coined the term "Harijans," or "Children of God," to designate them. This group has traditionally suffered social disabilities, and it has provided recruits for alternative religious beliefs, including converts to Islam and Christianity.

Hinduism has been challenged by at least three major reform movements that developed within it. An early one was Jainism, which probably arose in opposition to the caste domination of the Brahmins. Its asceticism is legendary, including even the renunciation of clothes. It has an exaggerated reverence for animal life. Ancient Greeks reported that the members of this sect wore cloths over their mouths to avoid accidentally swallowing insects. Most of the 2,500,000 Jains live in the western Indian provinces of Rajasthan and Gujarat.

A second Hindu reform movement was the rise of Buddhism in the third century B.C. Buddhism gained adherents throughout all of South Asia. However, Hinduism came to prevail once again in peninsular India,

TABLE 10.1 SOUTH ASIA

The people of South Asia share a distinctive cultural heritage that is one of the most ancient on earth. Their territory is home to the Hindu religion and its reform movement Buddhism. Physical isolation of the ecumene by empty deserts and mountains has contributed to the region's distinctiveness. Despite the subcontinent's many elements of homogeneity, it long has been characterized by cultural diversity. Political unity has been the result of outside forces, most recently the British. Currently, the region is divided among two large states and several smaller ones. Each is beset by internal regional pressures.

State	Total Population	Area (sq. miles)	Distinctive Features of Group
India	900,000,000	1,225,000	
Dominant Nation and % Total			
Northern Indians, 45%			Indoaryan (Hindi) language, Hindu
Significant Regional Groups and % Total			
Dravidians, 25%			Dravidian (Telegu, Tamil, et al.) languages, Hindu
Sikhs, 2%			Indoaryan (Punjabi) language, Sikh Religion
Assamese, 1%			Mon-Khmer and Tibeto-Burman languages, Buddhist and Animist
Kashmiris, <1%			Indoaryan (Kashmiri) language, Sunni Muslim
Potential Trouble Areas and Possible Adversaries			
Kashmir (Pakistan)	8,000,000	40,000	
Northern Assam (China)	1,000,000	36,000	
Pakistan	130,000,000	300,000	
Dominant Nation and % Total			
Punjabis, 48%			Indoaryan (Punjabi) language, Sunni Muslim
Significant Regional Groups and % Total			
Pathans, 13%			Iranian (Pathan) language, Sunni Muslim
Sindhis, 12%			Indoaryan (Sindhi) language, Sunni Muslim
Baluchis, 2%			Iranian (Baluchi) language, Sunni and Zakri Muslim
Potential Trouble Areas and Possible Adversaries			
Pakhtunistan (Afghanistan)	15,000,000	30,000	
Bangladesh	110,000,000	55,000	
Dominant Nation and % Total			
Bengalis, 98%			Indoaryan (Bengali) language, Sunni Muslim
Significant Regional Groups and % Total			
Tribal Groups, 1%			Sino-Tibetan (Chakma et al.) languages, Animist or Buddhist
Sri Lanka	18,000,000	25,000	
Dominant Nation and % Total			
Sinhalese, 74%			Indoaryan (Sinhalese) language, Theravada Buddhist
Significant Regional Groups and % Total			
Tamils, 18%			Dravidian (Tamil) language, Hindu
Moors, 7%			Dravidian (Tamil) language, Sunni Muslim
Afghanistan	18,000,000	250,000	
Dominant Nation and % Total			
Pathans, 52%			Iranian (Pathan) language, Sunni Muslim
Significant Regional Groups and % Total			
Tajiks, 20%			Iranian (Tajik) language, Izmaili and Sunni Muslim
Uzbeks, 9%			Altaic (Uzbek) language, Sunni Muslim
Hazaras, 9%			Iranian (Hazara) language, Shia, Izmaili, and Sunni Muslim
Turkomans, 2%			Altaic (Uzbek) language, Sunni Muslim
Nuristanis, <1%			Iranian (Dari) language, Sunni Muslim
Potential Trouble Areas and Possible Adversaries			
Northern Afghanistan (Uzbekistan, Tajikistan)	4,000,000	80,000	

State	Total Population	Area (sq. miles)	Distinctive Features of Group
Nepal	20,000,000	57,000	
Dominant Nation and % Total			
Nepalis, 58%			Indoaryan (Nepali) language, Hindu
Bhutan	1,500,000	18,000	
Dominant Nation and % Total			
Bhutanese, 62%			Tibetan-Burmese (Bhutia) language, Lamaistic Buddhist
Significant Regional Groups and % Total			
Nepalese, 18%			Indoaryan (Nepali) language, Hindu

and Buddhism was relegated to the periphery—to the island of Sri Lanka, to the northeastern, so-called tribal areas, and to the Himalayan territories of Bhutan, Sikkim, and Ladakh. It also became the established religion of most of Southeast Asia, Tibet, and Mongolia, and came to play a significant role in China, Korea, and Japan. In India there are now perhaps 4,000,000 Buddhists.

The third and most recent reform movement is Sikhism, concentrated in the Punjab region of northern peninsular India. It was founded at the end of the fifteenth century by the Guru Nanak, who drew elements of his new faith from both Hinduism and Islam. Although believing in one deity, like the Muslims, the Sikhs worship in the same type of temples as Hindus. Indeed, there often is intermarriage between Sikhs and Hindus. Sikhs reject caste ideologically, but in fact up to half the Sikh population is landless and has a status akin to Hindu untouchables. Persecution by Muslims in the seventeenth century led to a Sikh militancy and assertiveness for which they became famous. The Sikh state of Punjab was the last South Asian country to be conquered by the British, who defeated the Sikhs in 1857. South Asia now has nearly 15,000,000 Sikhs.

Mention should also be made of the so-called tribal peoples of South Asia who are concentrated in the northeastern hill country and in the jungles of central India. Like other Asian shifting cultivators, their religious views should be classed as animist. There is a steady assimilation of these peoples into the lowest level of Hinduism.

Religious challenges also have come from outside the region. Christianity arrived in the early sixteenth century with the Portuguese, taking hold particularly in southern peninsular India and Sri Lanka. There are now some 21,000,000 Christians, 75 percent of whom are Roman Catholic.

Islam also penetrated South Asian civilization, moving overland from the Middle East as a legacy of conquest by the Moguls from Central Asia. Its impact waned gradually southeastward. The proportion of adherents drops from near 100 percent on the frontiers of Afghanistan to under 10 percent at the tip of the peninsula. Islam, however, did gain large numbers of converts in the eastern outlying Bengal region that now forms the state of Bangladesh.

The main part of South Asia is divided linguistically by Sanskrit-derived Indo-European languages in the north and the quite different Dravidian family of languages in the south. This division roughly correlates with a racial division between fairer-skinned Aryans in northern South Asia and darker-skinned Dravidians in the southern parts. Within these broad families are numerous separate regional languages comparable to the linguistic diversity of Europe. India has fourteen major languages, and Pakistan has four. There are at least 500 other languages, and nearly that many more local dialects. Several languages have distinctive writing systems. In addition to the two major language families, peoples on the northern and eastern periphery of South Asia often speak languages belonging to the Tibetan family. Most often they represent a third racial stock, the Mongoloid peoples.

However, it is possible to exaggerate the significance of linguistic diversity. About two-thirds of South Asia's people speak one of six principal tongues. The language most widely spoken is Hindi, an Indo-European language of the Ganges Plain. Perhaps 40 percent of the population of the Republic of India speaks it. Adjacent languages, including Punjabi and Bengali, share many aspects of vocabulary and grammar with Hindi and permit at least rudimentary communication. In this context it should also be noted that a significant number of people with middle and higher educations from all linguistic groups understand and speak English as a second language.

Despite the homogeneity and coherence of much of South Asia, political unity has largely eluded it over the centuries. On four occasions before the arrival of the Europeans, relatively short-lived states emerged embracing much of the Indian Peninsula. All had their political and economic bases in the fertile Ganges Plain of the north. None were able to incorporate all of the South Asian Deccan Plateau, particularly its southernmost peninsular tip. Each disintegrated internally, rather than being destroyed by external forces. In periods between the supremacy of these empires, the region fell apart into hundreds of locally self-governing states.

In the third century B.C., the legendary figure Aśoka welded much of South Asia into a single territorial unit, proclaiming recently evolved Buddhism as the official religion. Like the personal empire forged by Charlemagne, Aśoka's empire did not last long after its founder, nor did its state religion. Five centuries later, beginning in the third century A.D., the Hindu-based Gupta Empire dominated much of the northern regions for nearly 200 years. After another long period of localized political authority, Muslim invaders from the northwest established the Sultanate of Delhi in the twelfth century A.D. It embraced most of the north and lasted until about 1400. Following another period of territorial fragmentation, the Mogul Empire was established in the north at the beginning of the sixteenth century. This was coincident with the appearance of the first Europeans, the Portuguese, who established coastal trading communities in the politically fragmented southern reaches of the area. Dutch traders soon followed.

British Influence In South Asia

The British East India Company was formed in 1600. It operated much as a governmental entity in its dealings with South Asians, signing treaties, maintaining an administrative organization, and deploying a police force. It early forced rival Portuguese and Dutch traders to depart South Asia. The French proved more formidable competitors, however. In the decay of the Mogul Empire, the East India Company and French trading interests used local princes to fight what amounted to a proxy war. By 1760 the British had triumphed, reducing French holdings to a few southern coastal villages. In the process the East India Company had acquired control over a substantial part of the northeastern province of Bengal, and this served as a platform for

eventual accretion of most of the rest of South Asia. The company experienced severe difficulties in governing the huge territory, however, and after the Sepoy Rebellion of 1857, the British government assumed direct responsibility for administration.

The British used different forms of governance over their vast domain. They directly ruled substantial territories around their main bases in Calcutta, Bombay, and Madras. However, they concluded treaties with more than 700 of the princely states that had emerged as locally self-governing units in the waning Mogul Empire. These ranged from mini-states of only a few acres to Hyderabad, which occupied 82,000 square miles in the central Deccan Plateau. Collectively, the native states constituted 40 percent of the territory of the British Indian Empire and about 25 percent of its inhabitants.

After nearly two centuries of domination of South Asia, the British departure in 1947 left a legacy that on the whole favored broad territorial unity. The British have often been accused of implementing a "divide and rule" policy, but political and religious divisions existed long before their arrival, and they have continued to plague the successor states after the British departure.

Among the contributions of the British to future unity was the implanting of a degree of homogeneity throughout much of South Asia in language and institutions. English became a common denominator of an intelligentsia trained in British-style schools and universities. A system of secular law was established that could administer justice to people of all religions. Perhaps most important was the dissemination of European ideals of democracy and individual freedom.

The British also laid the groundwork for political-geographic coherence by developing an infrastructure of transportation and communication. Railroads linked virtually all parts of the South Asian core region. Postal service, the telegraph, and telephones made distant territories readily accessible to each other. A universal monetary system encouraged the beginnings of commercial production and facilitated exchange relations.

Independence and Partition

Although the British genuinely wanted to see their Indian Empire remain an intact unit after their eventual departure, the regionally centrifugal forces of the area precluded this. Particularly crucial were Muslim fears of political and economic domination by the Hindu majority. In 1940 a group of Muslim political leaders called for the establishment of a separate Muslim state, to be known as Pakistan, in the Indus Valley, where a majority of the population was Islamic. The Muslims feared that their generally less educated and less economically advanced population would fall prey to Hindu commercial exploitation following departure of the British. The Indian Congress party, the leading force for Independence, initially was implacable in rejection of territorial partition. Following a British offer of independence during World War II, representatives of the Muslims and the Congress party eventually did hammer out an agreement that resulted in a partitioned India. It was implemented in 1947.

Under terms of the agreement, separate Hindu and Muslim states were created out of the British Indian Empire. The Muslim state was named Pakistan. It included not only the Indus Valley territory that had been sought originally, but also the Muslim-dominated eastern portion of Bengal, which lay 1,000 miles eastward across territory awarded to India. The new Indian Union would contain more than 1,100,000 square miles and a population in excess of 300,000,000. Western Pakistan would have an area of some 300,000 square miles and a population of 28,000,000; Eastern Pakistan would have barely 54,000 square miles, but it would contain a much larger population, numbering 42,000,000.

Provincial territories administered directly by the British were assigned on the basis of the religion of the majority of the population. Three were divided, however, reflecting long-standing cultural divisions within them. As noted above, the Muslim-dominated western part of Bengal went to Eastern Pakistan; the remainder became part of India. The adjacent province of Assam was also partitioned, its Sylhet District of 4,600 square miles, densely populated by Muslims, going to Eastern Pakistan, and the remaining 58,000 square miles, populated primarily by Hindus and tribal peoples, becoming part of India. Similarly, the western Muslim-majority section of Punjab was awarded to Pakistan, and its eastern zone was given to India. The result, however, divided the province's significant Sikh population into two parts.

Rulers of the native states controlled indirectly by Britain were given a choice of acceding to either Pakistan or India. Most chose India, with the exception of four western entities with Muslim majorities, whose leaders elected to join Pakistan. The Muslim ruler of Junagadh also sought to join Pakistan, even though he headed an overwhelmingly Hindu state. Indian military forces occupied the territory, however, and a subsequent plebiscite showed overwhelming sentiment to join India.

Two other states, Hyderabad and Kashmir, sought to remain independent of both India and Pakistan. Hyderabad, situated in the southern Deccan region, was larger than many European states and had a population of more than 16,000,000. Although overwhelmingly Hindu, it had a Muslim ruler who traced his ancestry back to viceroys of the Mogul Empire. Indian forces invaded the region in September 1948, and it was incorporated into India.

Kashmir, which is more properly known as Jammu and Kashmir, is located in the western Himalayas and is renowned as a resort region. Its territory is about the same size as that of Hyderabad, but its population in 1947 was only 4,500,000. Its situation was the reverse of Hyderabad—it had a Muslim majority under a Hindu maharajah. Muslims predominate in the northern upland Vale of Kashmir, where the capital Srinagar is located. Hindus are a majority in the lowland territory of Jammu. Originally, the ruler sought to be separate from both new states. Kashmir Muslims, however, revolted against the maharajah soon after the implementation of partition, and they were immediately joined in fighting by Muslim Pathan tribesmen from territory that had become part of Pakistan. The maharajah appealed to the Indian government for aid, agreeing in the process to attach Kashmir to India. The appearance of Indian troops led to regular Pakistani forces also entering the territory, and warfare continued until a cease-fire line was established in January 1949 under auspices of the United Nations. The Kashmir situation has remained a problem for relations between the two states ever since.

Consequences of partition. The immediate effects of partitioning the British Indian Empire into independent Hindu and Muslim states were felt by individuals caught on the wrong side of the border. At least 50,000,000 of peninsular India's 400,000,000 inhabitants found themselves in this position. The situation was particularly acute near the new international boundaries. The traditional Indian intermixture of peoples in local areas made it impossible for any border to be drawn that could completely separate religious groups. It is estimated that between 12,000,000 and 16,000,000 individuals felt impelled to leave the new state to which they had been assigned. Up to a million of such refugees died in horrible atrocities that were perpetrated by both sides. Even after the mass flight, substantial numbers of people were left on the "wrong" side of the border. At least 75,000,000 Muslims live among India's 750,000,000 people. Perhaps 2,000,000 Hindus still remain within Pakistan. These minorities periodically create problems for the respective states in which they find themselves.

Division on the basis of religion also disrupted economic functioning. Indian road, rail, and telegraph connections with its northeastern province of Assam now had to cross foreign Pakistani territory. Traditional long-distance linkages between complementary companies were sundered by goods having to cross unaccustomed international borders and by protectionist policies adopted by the newly independent states. The delta of the Ganges had long been the world's principal producers of jute. Partition placed the jute fields in Eastern Pakistan, while their traditional processing plants were across the border in India. To complicate the situation further, the Pakistan government placed an export tax on jute, and India banned all jute imports. In the northwest, irrigation projects allotted to Pakistan found the sources of their water on the Indian side of the border. After troubles erupted in Kashmir, India diverted this water, blackening Pakistani fields. Currencies of the two states could no longer be exchanged for the other.

The Portuguese and French Territories

Although the British had defeated their European rivals for supremacy in India, both the Portuguese and the French were able to retain coastal footholds of Indian territory up to the period of independence. All of these territories bordered the new state of India. The territory of Goa had functioned as a Portuguese colony since 1510. With two other exclaves, it occupied 1,500 miles and had a population in excess of 600,000. Its people played a disproportionate role in the trade of the lands fronting along the Arabian Sea. The French had held on to Pondichéry and four other south Indian villages with a total area of 196 square miles and a population of more than 300,000.

The new Indian government almost immediately demanded that the Portuguese and French depart from South Asia as the British had done. After negotiations, the French ceded their territories to India in 1954. They had found little reason to continue control over insignificant and costly coastal exclaves, and the local, predominantly Hindu, populations were in favor of union with India.

The Portuguese defied the Indians, however, citing the fact that, under their constitution, Goa and associated territories were integral parts of Portugal. Moreover, nearly half the local populations were Roman Catholics who feared the consequences of being merged into an overwhelmingly Hindu state. They also enjoyed a notably higher living standard than did the adjacent parts of India (although much of this could be accounted for by profitable smuggling activities). Unable to acquire the territories by negotiation, the Indian army abruptly took over Goa in late 1961, ending 450 years of Portuguese sovereignty. The Goans and their territory have retained a distinctive identity within India, however, and they periodically pose problems to government officials.

Areas of Instability

After more than four decades of independence, both Pakistan and India continue to confront both internal and external political-geographic problems. Each has faced separatist movements among their contrasting populations, and each also has had to deal with a legacy of unsettled borders with one another and with surrounding neighbors.

Bangladesh

Internal centrifugal strains eventually took their toll on Pakistan. It was a textbook example of an "impossible" state. Pakistan lacked the elements of homogeneity and coherence essential for maintaining modern statehood. Because it was divided between Eastern and Western Pakistan, its only unifying features were a predominant Muslim religion and a fear of domination by the Hindus of India. But even the Muslim religion differed significantly between Western Pakistan and Eastern Pakistan. The population of Western Pakistan tended to practice a conservative, orthodox form of Islam, which saw all Muslims as brothers; in contrast, in Eastern Pakistan (a thousand miles distant) the Muslim Bengalis had continued to maintain such Hindu customs as caste relationships.

The principal language of Western Pakistan was Urdu. Its Sanskrit base was heavily influenced by Persian, and it was written in the Arabic alphabet. The Bengali of Eastern Pakistan was much closer to Sanskrit, and it utilized its own distinctive script. The Pakistan government's declaration of Urdu as the new official language for the entire state led to riots in 1951 by Easterners against West Pakistan. Economically, the less overcrowded west actually raised living standards following independence, whereas the thickly packed east saw economic stagnation or decline. Because of enmity between India and Pakistan, overland communication between Western and Eastern Pakistan was impossible. Linkage was by sea and by air around India.

Perhaps the greatest problem besetting the young state was the attitude of West Pakistanis toward the Bengalis in the east. Originally, it had been the western Muslims based in the Punjab who had pressed for separation of the state. The eastern Muslims had joined only during later stages of the negotiations with the British and Indian Congress Party. Yet the east had a majority

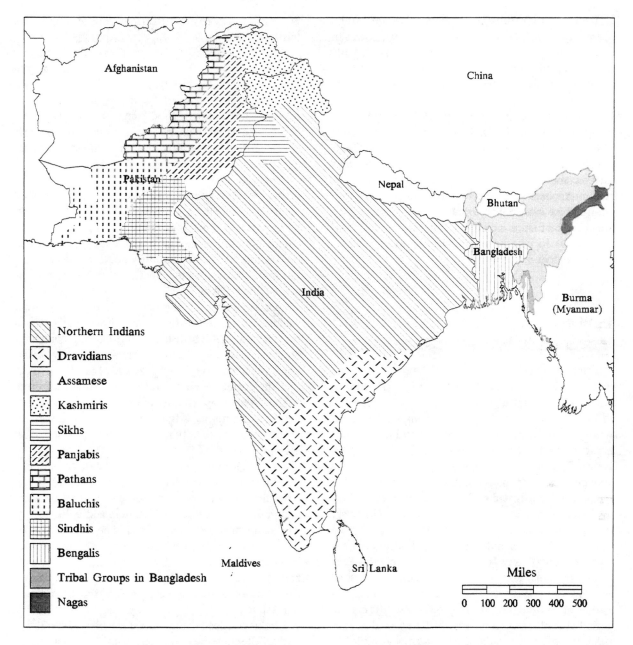

FIGURE 10-1 ETHNIC GROUPS OF PAKISTAN, INDIA, AND BANGLADESH

Legend:

- Northern Indians
- Dravidians
- Assamese
- Kashmiris
- Sikhs
- Panjabis
- Pathans
- Baluchis
- Sindhis
- Bengalis
- Tribal Groups in Bangladesh
- Nagas

Miles
0 100 200 300 400 500

of the total population, and its numbers, under a democratic government, could dictate policies for the state as a whole. Particularly concerned was the army, whose officer corps came primarily from the Punjab.

A 1971 attempt to rewrite the constitution to assure western primacy was followed by rebellion in Eastern Pakistan. The army brutally suppressed the uprising, massacring eastern intellectuals and also Hindus who had remained in the territory. This led to mass flight of refugees to India, which itself entered the fray and defeated the Pakistani army. The Indian government then supported the establishment of a new state for the Muslims of East Bengal, which was named Bangladesh.

Bangladesh inherited relatively few political-geographic problems. Although up to 15 percent of its population is Hindu, this minority is not regionally concentrated, but coexists with the Muslim majority throughout the state. It can pose no secessionist threat.

In the Chittagong Hills of Bangladesh's southeastern extremity the local population is distinctive, however. Thirteen minority groups live there and are tribally organized and animist or Buddhist in religion (Figure 10-1). The Buddhist Chakma people particularly have rebelled against the loss of their fertile agricultural lands to in-migrating Muslim Bangladeshis from East Bengal. Among the 1,000,000 people of the Chittagong Hills, more than 400,000 are now Bengali. The Chakmas seek a halt to further Muslim intrusion into the area and an autonomous status within Bangladesh. The rebellion appears to have received financial support from India for more than a decade. Parts of the region are claimed by Burma, although Burmese control is tenuous at best in its adjacent Arakanese area, which Bangladesh does not contest.

Pakistan

The Indian-assisted secession of Bangladesh by no means relieved all the political-geographic strains within the Muslim-dominated region of South Asia. Problem areas of ethnic conflict continued to exist within each successor state. Both also had tensions along their international borders.

In Pakistan the dominant Punjabi group numbers about two-thirds of the population. It is concentrated in the productive irrigated region of the upper Indus Valley, which constitutes the state's ecumene. The lower valley is dominated by the Sindhi people, numbering 6,000,000. Another million Sindhis live in adjacent parts of India (Figure 10-1). The region contains Pakistan's principal port of Karachi, which had been an outlying dependency of Bombay and had a Hindu and Parsee majority before these peoples fled during the period of partition. Karachi was the first capital of Pakistan. In 1960 a new capital, Islamabad, was built 700 miles to the north, near Rawalpindi, within the territory of the dominant Punjabis.

The Sindhi people have a strong sense of national identity and hold group grievances against other Pakistanis. Particular animosities have risen against the Mohajirs, a term used for the mostly Urdu-speaking Muslim refugees from India who settled in Sindhi cities in the aftermath of partition. The Sindhis also resent an influx of Punjabi farmers and recent migrants from the Pathan-dominated Northwest Frontier Province. Currently, less than 10 percent of the population of the city of Karachi is Sindhi, and they make up barely 52 percent of the total population of the province. One of the key demands of Sindhi politicians is the right to keep other Pakistanis out of their native territory.

In the deserts to the west are the 1,300,000 Baluchis, who have 500,000 additional kinsmen in Iran and 100,000 others in Afghanistan. Their Indo-European language belongs to the Iranian linguistic group, in contrast to Sanskrit-based Punjabi and Sindhi. Baluchis have developed an increasing group consciousness that has proved troubling to each of the states where they are found.

A more significant and nettlesome minority for Pakistan is the Pashtu (or Pathan) people, who inhabit Pakistan's western border area with Afghanistan. They total more than 8,000,000, or roughly 8 percent of Pakistan's population, and they are identical in culture to the 16,000,000 Pathan majority of Afghanistan itself. For many years after the creation of Pakistan, an irredentist "Free Paktunistan" or "Free Pastunistan" movement existed among Pakistan's Pathans, with apparent encouragement from Afghanistan. However, the Soviet involvement in Afghanistan and the haven provided for Pathan refugees by Pakistan minimized political agitation by this movement in the decade of the 1980s. Now that the former Soviet forces have withdrawn from Afghanistan, the possibility of renewed agaitation from the post-Communist Afghan regime is strong, particularly as a means to rally its divergent peoples and tribal groups.

The continuing dispute over the fate of Kashmir and Jammu remains a serious trouble spot with India. After the initial fighting and subsequent establishment of a divisive cease-fire line, Pakistan and India went to war again over the area in 1965. The territory under Pakistani control is divided among three nominally independent units—Azad (Free) Kashmir and the outlying "agencies" of Gilgit and Baltistan. All are administered by a Pakistani Secretary to the Ministry of Kashmir Affairs.

Pakistan also faces potential troubles with militant Sikhs. Although the main body of the Sikh population was concentrated in East Punjab, which was awarded to India, Pakistan received a significant number, plus the important Sikh religious city of Lahore. It has not had notably overt difficulties with its Sikhs as has India, in part because it has served as a refuge for anti-Indian Sikh militants.

The boundary across the sparsely inhabited Rann of Kutch also has been a flashpoint in Pakistan's relations with India. It is a region of saline mud flats that are flooded annually by the monsoon rains. Although of no economic value, the region long was disputed between the native states of Sindh and Kutch. The British drew an administrative boundary in 1923 between the states along the edge of the mainland Thar

Desert, in effect favoring Kutch. It was never demarcated, however, and it became an international boundary when Kutch went to India and Sindh went to Pakistan. Pakistan, as the successor state to Sindh, has never given up its claim to the territory.

India

It is a tribute to the Republic of India that it has survived more than four decades of independence without suffering major losses of territory to regional nationalist forces. Certainly pressures have been there. The diversity of languages has been the root of numerous movements for the creation of new provincial political units to recognize distinctive groups. The diversity of religions has also played a centrifugal role, particularly among the Sikhs and the Buddhist and animist tribal groups of the northeast.

A major fissure is the strong sense of separate identity felt by the Dravidian racial/linguistic population of the south, who constitute a quarter of the population. This population has been angered on occasion by attempts of the Aryan-dominated government to replace English with Hindi as the official language of the state. Dravidian representatives argue that adopting Hindi would give inherent advantages to the Aryans, half of whom speak it as natives, with most of the remainder finding it relatively easy to learn because of the linguistic family similarities. They contend that individuals seeking to enter the civil service from the very different Dravidian language areas would suffer significant handicaps in their attempts to master an entirely foreign vocabulary, grammar, and writing system. They feel that the existing system that requires all to learn English as a second language for administration is a fairer situation.

The complexity of regional languages has posed other problems for India. The 534 native states that had entered India represented accidents of history, as did the provinces delimited by the British in the areas they ruled directly. They had been created as a result of temporary local circumstances, including the weakening of Mogul power in a region, or deals struck by ambitious negotiators. The territories amassed in the larger entities often exhibited sharp regional contrasts in languages, and also religions. The smaller units fragmented essentially homogeneous regions, often in a hopeless fashion. Thus, the state of Baroda had a total area of only 8,100 square miles, but it was split among five larger pieces of territory and more than thirty smaller ones.

Pressures for a reorganized internal pattern of provincial regions confronted the young Indian government immediately. Some of these strains were a legacy of pre-independence campaigns for revision of the system of states by the Congress party to gain local support and to embarrass the British raj. There was resistance in independent India to new, linguistic-based provinces because it was feared that such units would reinforce regionalisms and lead to a weakening of an all-Indian sense of national identity. This in fact did happen. However, in 1953 the Indian government bowed to demands from Telegu-speakers pressing for administrative separation from the Tamils of Madras. A new Telegu state of Andhra Pradesh was created from the northern districts of Madras province. It later also acquired Telegu-speaking parts of the former Hyderabad state.

The creation of Andhra Pradesh was followed by claims from other groups that led to a rather complete reorganization of internal boundaries along linguistic lines. By the end of 1956 the number of state-level units had been reduced to fourteen. The number subsequently rose to twenty-two as a result of further concessions to militant groups, plus an additional nine so-called union territories ruled directly from the Indian capital in New Delhi.

The Punjab

One such division occurred in the Punjab in 1966 in response to pressures from the Sikh community. As early as 1949, Sikh leaders had called for the establishment of a "Punjabi Suba," or a Punjab with boundaries redrawn to embrace only those who spoke the Punjabi language. Ostensibly the argument for Punjabi Suba was a linguistic one and in accord with a provision in the Indian constitution for creating new states based on language. However, most people in the Punjab in fact spoke the Punjabi language, although the Sikhs generally employed the Gurmukhi script to write it, whereas adherents to the Hindu religion used the Devangari alphabet utilized generally to write Hindi. The two languages are very closely related Indo-European tongues.

The real motivations appear to have been to make members of the Sikh religion the majority in Punjab state by partitioning off a substantial part of that region's existing Hindu population. Although Sikhs had made up only 12 percent of the total population of the pre-independence Punjab, some 90 percent of South Asia's Sikh population was concentrated there. It should be noted that the Sikh role in the Punjab had been augmented by an influx of Sikh refugees from Pakistan and by the merger with the Punjab of a number of Sikh-inhabited princely states. The Sikh leaders were assisted in their goal of a Sikh state by the perhaps misguided policies of the Punjabi Hindu leadership that pressed its community to declare the Hindi language as its mother tongue to frustrate the Sikh pressures for the establishment of a Punjabi-speaking state.

The goal of Punjabi Suba was attained in 1966 when the Indian government of Indira Gandhi carved out of the Punjab a new state of Hariana for Hindi-speakers in the old province. The remaining Punjab state then had an approximately 55 percent Sikh majority. In part, this appears to have been a reward to the Sikhs for their valor in the India-Pakistan war of 1965. In an unusual political-geographic twist, the city of Chandigarh remained the capital of both states.

The creation of a Sikh-majority state did not significantly ensure the implementation of the aspirations of the Sikh militants. Although increasingly a nation on a European model, the Sikhs remained divided by class and political interests. Subsequently, radical Sikhs pressed for complete separation of the Punjab from India. Their lists of grievances included both religious and economic complaints. The radicals used terrorist tactics to achieve their political aims, their most notorious being the assassination of the Indian Prime Minister Indira Gandhi herself. Mrs. Gandhi in 1984 had ordered an Indian army assault on the Sikh Golden Temple complex in Amritsar. Her command was a response to a breakdown in law and order sparked by Sikh activists. In the course of the attack a major leader of the Sikhs, Jarnail Singh Bhindranwale, was among the activists killed in the temple. Subsequently, all Indian attempts to pacify the Punjab have failed.

Assam

India's northeastern extremity of Assam has been the scene of difficulties between the Indian government and the region's assortment of tribal peoples. Indeed, insurrection by the Naga peoples has existed rather continuously since Indian independence in 1947. A Mongoloid, Buddhist group, the Nagas number a half million in a territory of 6,000 square miles. India granted them a state of Nagaland in 1961, but this has scarcely dampened their separatist demands. Similar insurgencies by the Mizos, Tripuris, and other tribal groups led to a partitioning of Assam state into five new units in 1971.

The political problems of Assam were compounded by a flood of 10,000,000 Muslim and Hindu refugees from Bangladesh in 1971, many of whom appropriated traditional tribal lands. These refugees fled Pakistani atrocities in the former Eastern Pakistan on the eve of Bangladesh independence. Militant Bodos tribesmen responded to the new migrants by inaugurating a guerrilla war. In 1983 alone, more than 4,000 refugees were slain. The goal of the Bodos is a homeland for themselves, although intermixture with other groups is such that at best the Bodos would number only 40 percent of the population of the area to which they have staked a claim. Bodos make up only 10 percent of Assam's 23,000,000 people. The rebellion has greater implications for India, however, since its zone of activity is located in the narrow neck of land connecting Assam with the rest of the state by railroad, road, and pipeline.

Compounding the problems of Assam are unresolved Chinese claims to much of its northern fringe. In the 1870s the British had set the northern limits of its claims east of Bhutan at the foot of the Himalaya Mountains. Tibet had set its southern border at the Himalaya crest. Between them was extremely difficult territory occupied by militant tribes.

In 1910 China undertook the military occupation of Tibet. Its troops began to move across the Himalayas into the tribal buffer strip. The British reacted immediately. They decided to move their claimed boundary to include the Himalayan south slopes. After Chinese power in Tibet collapsed during the Chinese Revolution of 1911, the British negotiated a 1914 treaty with the Tibetans that established their mutual boundary at the crest. This Line came to be known as the McMahon Line, after the British representative Sir Henry McMahon. The Chinese government never recognized the validity of this treaty, however.

The Communist government of China reestablished control over Tibet in 1951. The Communists began moving troops south of the McMahon Line, and their official maps showed all the southern mountain slopes as Chinese territory. This totaled 36,000 square miles of Indian lands. A number of incidents occurred between Chinese and Indian troops, culminating in a full-scale Chinese military offensive in 1962. Although hostilities ceased, Chinese forces remained in a number of strategic positions. The lack of a boundary treaty between the two states makes this area a potential future zone of hostilities.

Kashmir

India also faces problems in its northwestern corner. The situation in Kashmir has been an irritant to all Indian governments ever since independence. None has been able to concede that the predominantly Muslim population has the right to self-determination, either to join Pakistan or to have an independent state of its own.

In addition to unrest among the Muslims of Indian-occupied Kashmir, the Himalayan borderland of Ladakh has seen the development of an unaccustomed militancy among that mountainous area's predominantly Buddhist population. The actions of the Ladakhis were precipitated by the growing insurgency among Kashmir's Muslims. They feared the possibility of being joined to Pakistan. The northwestern segment of their historic territory had already come under Pakistani control as part of the struggle for Kashmir, and the northeastern segment had been incorporated into China. The Ladakhis have also claimed discriminatory actions against them by the Indian-supported Muslim government of Kashmir. They seek the political status of a "Union Territory" within India, which would be administered directly by New Delhi. It has been reported that Ladakhi militants have put strong pressures upon Muslims living in Ladakh to convert to Buddhism. Should the Ladakhis receive a special status, it is likely that the predominantly Hindu population of Jammu would also seek separation from Kashmir, leaving that state with an overwhelmingly Muslim population.

Sri Lanka

The island state of Sri Lanka (formerly Ceylon) lies off the southern tip of India. It has an area of 25,000 square miles and a population of 17,000,000. Although the Palk Strait separating it from India is only twenty miles wide, it has served to reduce the intensity of cultural influences that have swept the Indian Peninsula throughout time. In many ways Sri Lanka's situation is like that of the United Kingdom's relationship to Europe, although Sri Lanka's area and population are only one-quarter that of Britain. Thus, Buddhism came from India, but it did not succumb to the revival of Hinduism that occurred on the Indian subcontinent.

The Sinhalese constitute the predominant population of the island. Their language is Aryan Indo-European, suggesting that they came by sea from northern India, rather than by simply migrating across the Palk Strait. Other groups have also come to the island by sea, leaving a legacy in the contemporary makeup of society. These include Arab traders, whose Muslim descendants, termed "Moors," constitute 7 percent of the population. The Moors remain concentrated in Sri Lanka's coastal areas. The Portuguese arrived at the beginning of the sixteenth century, implanting the Roman Catholic religion. Many inhabitants of Sri Lanka retain Portuguese family names. The Portuguese later were supplanted by the Dutch, who established a Roman-based system of law that still prevails. The British took over from the Dutch in 1795 and have left their mark in governmental and commercial institutions and in the English language, which is understood by at least 10 percent of the population.

The other major group that came to Sri Lanka was the Dravidian-speaking Tamil population from the adjacent tip of India. There are indications of Tamil settlement in ancient times. A Tamil colony has continuously occupied the northern Jaffna Peninsula since the medieval period, and newer migrants arrived during the past century to work on the island's tea and rubber plantations. The relative emptiness of the so-called Dry Zone lying south of the Jaffna Peninsula has long served to insulate the transplanted Tamil culture from the native Sinhalese (Figure 10-2).

While Arabs and Europeans dominated the inhabitants of the coastal lowlands for three centuries, the hilly interior remained an independent Sinhalese kingdom until the British established control over the entire island in 1815. The different histories of alien rule have had a minor effect upon the Sinhalese population. Under the British plantation system, agriculture was developed, together with urbanization.

The British gave Ceylon a degree of self-government in 1931. In 1947 it received independent dominion status within the British Commonwealth, with its

FIGURE 10-2   ETHNIC GROUPS OF SRI LANKA

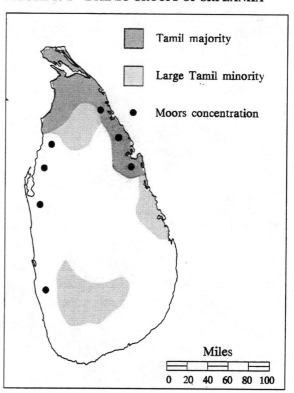

own constitution. Ceylon became the Democratic Socialist Republic of Sri Lanka in 1972.

Independence led to increasing conflicts of the Sinhalese majority with the Tamils, who were concentrated on the northern Jaffna Peninsula, but were also to be found as laborers and merchants throughout the island. In 1956 and 1958 severe riots erupted between the two groups. Tamils rebelled against attempts to make Sinhalese the sole official language of the island.

Over the past decade, many Tamils have concluded that the only solution to what they perceive as a situation of discrimination is a full independence of their area from Sri Lanka. Militant groups began a guerrilla war against the Sinhalese-dominated government in 1983. The most notable has been the Tamil Tigers, who in recent years have also directed their violent activities against other Tamil groups in order to gain dominance in the community. Many Tamils have fled in small boats across the Palk Strait to seek refuge in the Indian state of Tamil Nadu, which is home to 60,000,000 Tamils. The Tamil Tigers have also massacred villages of Muslim Moors on the grounds that they have not supported Tamil independence.

The situation became so severe in 1987 that Sri Lanka invited the Indian government to send a peacekeeping force to the island. Some 70,000 Indian troops attempted to maintain order, but were withdrawn in 1990 after suffering losses of 1,500 killed and at least 3,000 wounded.

The Himalayan Territories

On India's Himalayan Mountain fringe, between Ladakh on the west and Assam in the east, lie four distinctive political-geographic entities. They are the Indian states of Sikkim and Himachal Pradesh, and the independent kingdoms of Nepal and Bhutan. As often happens, these upland peoples exhibit a number of traits that differ from general characteristics of those living in the hills and plains of the main part of the Indian Peninsula. The entities constitute a frontier between Indian and Tibetan civilizations. Their political interests often are at odds with those of the governments of India and China, and frequently also collide with each other.

FIGURE 10-3   OCCUPIED AND CLAIMED AREAS IN SOUTH ASIA

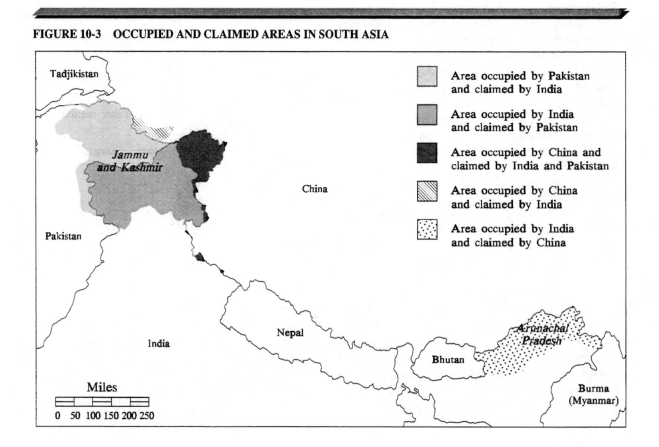

Himachal Pradesh

The westernmost territory is Himachal Pradesh, which emerged in 1948 as a conglomerate territory of former self-governing so-called hill states. It was enlarged in 1954 and again in 1966, when it received parts of Punjab state. In 1971 Himachal Pradesh became India's eighteenth state. It occupies an area of 21,500 square miles, with a population of 4,300,000. Its population is mainly tribal and Hindu, early isolated from the main Hindu area by the advance of Islam into India from the west. On its northern fringe are found Buddhist clans. As elsewhere in their mutual frontier zone, India and China have conflicting territorial claims. However, the Chinese have elected not to press for any border changes in this region.

Nepal

The Kingdom of Nepal dates to the mid-eighteenth century, when a strong leader from the community of Gurkha welded together a broad territorial entity centered on the Katmandu Valley. Subsequently, fighting men from Nepal have been identified as Gurkhas.

Nepalese society is diverse, reflecting the state's frontier situation. The majority of tribal groups are racially Mongol. Originally they were Buddhist, but now more than 90 percent of the population is Hindu. In large part this is because the ruling element for the past two centuries has been Aryan and Hindu. The two religions interpenetrate each other, as do many other aspects of Nepali culture, including borrowed Indian and Tibetan styles of architecture.

Nepal was able to avoid direct incorporation into either China or British India, despite wars with both empires. A Chinese army repulsed a late eighteenth-century Gurkha invasion of Tibet and forced the Nepalese to accept a tributary status and to send a mission to Peking every five years. They continued this relationship until 1911, when the revolution in China led to Chinese loss of control over Tibet, and thus also Nepal. Earlier, a war with Britain ended in 1816 with the cession of some territory and the establishment of a British residency in the capital city. However, the Nepalese successfully isolated their country from further penetration, keeping out even British travelers until 1947.

The reestablishment of Chinese domination of Tibet in the post–World War II period raised again the question of Nepal's sovereignty. Both the Kuomintang and Communist regimes in China had never forgotten Nepal's past dependency upon Manchu China. At the same time, Indian politicians considered Nepal's independence an anomaly, particularly as they perceived an increasing threat from China. The Nepalese were able to resist pressures from both sides, however. A palace revolution in 1950 overthrew the governing Rana family, which was Hindu and sympathetic to India, and restored to power the largely ceremonial monarchy. A decade later, the Nepalese king signed a border agreement with China that treated Nepal as an equal, fully sovereign state.

Nepal's position has remained perilous, however. Forty percent of Nepal's foreign trade is with India, which also is its principal access to the outside world and major source of aid. When Nepal decided to buy arms from China in 1988, the Indian government closed the border for more than a year, creating substantial hardships and emphasizing Nepal's dependence upon India. The Nepalese regime is also concerned about increasing difficulties experienced by Nepalese living in adjacent regions, including Sikkim and Bhutan.

Sikkim

Sikkim is a small territory of only 2,800 square miles. Although it is now an integral part of India, in the past it was much more closely associated with Tibet than was either Nepal or Bhutan. It is essentially an enclosed basin with mountains rising nearly five miles above its northern side. Its original population, the Lepcha, are a mixed Mongol and Aryan racial group who are Buddhist in religion. The British East India Company seized the southern district of Darjeeling in 1835 and began the planting of tea there. Nepalis and Indians were brought in to work the plantations. The country has become largely Hindu as a result of in-migration of plantation workers, with no more than 10 percent of the present population of 350,000 identifying itself as Lepcha.

All of Sikkim became part of the British Empire in 1886. Its status was that of a protectorate, and this form of relationship continued with India for several years after India's independence. It became a full state within India in 1975.

The border of Sikkim with Tibet, established in 1890, has the distinction of being the only portion of the long Chinese–Indian frontier that has been defined by a treaty signed by the Chinese. Although no government of China has raised formal claims to Sikkim, both Kuomintang and Communist regimes have regarded it as territory lost in a period of unequal treaties. However, Tibetans have always considered Sikkim as a forcibly alienated part of their homeland. In 1894 they removed boundary stones being laid by a Sino–British border commission. In 1948, before Tibetan subjugation by the Chinese Communists, the Dalai Lama's government asked India when it planned to return to it Sikkim, Darjeeling, and other former Tibetan territories. As part of its pressure upon India in the early 1960s, the Chinese claimed that the Indians had encroached some distance on its side of the still unde-marcated border.

India thus faces possible future irredentist claims to Sikkim by a Tibet that either remains a part of China or becomes independent. It may well feel similar pressures from a Nepal concerned about the situation of the large number of Nepalis who live in Sikkim. It is possible for a separatist movement to develop in the area itself. Agitation in Darjeeling in the 1980s forced the Indian government to give a greater degree of autonomy to that region.

Bhutan

Bhutan, like Nepal, has managed to avoid absorption by its huge neighbors to the north and south. It occupies some 18,000 square miles of mountainous territory. Its Buddhist population is closely related by race and culture to the Tibetans. It was Tibetans who established the present state in the sixteenth century. Ensuing rulers recognized a dependency upon Tibet and, to a degree, China.

The British came into contact with the Bhutanese in the late eighteenth century. They allowed Bhutan to survive as an independent buffer state in anticipation that it could be used as an intermediatary in dealing with China. The British did acquire a substantial tract along Bhutan's southern border in 1775, however. The Duars Strip consisted of eighteen connected areas where the swift-flowing rivers of Bhutan enter upon the plains of Bengal and Assam. The Bhutanese traditionally had moved into these lands during the cold season and allowed tributary plainsmen to use them at other seasons. In 1865 the British established a protectorate status for Bhutan. Independant India continued this relationship in a 1949 treaty with Bhutan, which included return of a thirty-two-square-mile territory taken by the British in 1865. India is mindful of Chinese pretentions to suzerainty over Bhutan and also of vague direct claims to Bhutanese territory.

The Duars Strip remaining within India is some 20 miles wide and 220 miles long and has become a major tea-producing region within India. As in Sikkim, the development of tea plantations has led to the influx of large numbers of Indians and Nepalis, many of whom were tempted to move from the Duars into vacant lands of Bhutan. Presently some 25 percent of Bhutan's 1,800,000 population consists of Hindus of Nepalese origin.

In the early 1990s fighting erupted between these settlers, who are concentrated on Bhutan's southern fringe, and the Drukpa tribe, which dominates the state. More than 300 Nepalese demonstrators were reported killed. They had been reacting to a 1989 Bhutanese attempt to disfranchise many of their numbers by declaring as illegal migrants those individuals who had entered Bhutan after 1958. They also strongly resented royal decrees forbidding the use of the Nepali language in schools and requiring everyone to wear traditional Drukpa clothing and even to wear their hair in Drukpa style. Nepalese insurgents against Drukpa authority have the advantage of sanctuary in the predominantly Nepalese villages that lie on the Indian side of the border. Although the Indian government has a policy against the use of its soil for overt political activity against another state, it has a difficult time in policing this remote territory.

The problems occurring on India's Himalayan fringe reflect the general dislocations that ensue when a frontier zone is reduced to a boundary line. Indian and Chinese troops now face each other directly in an area that traditionally has been one of transition from one civilization to another. The intermediate buffer states of Nepal, Bhutan, and Tibet in the past had insulated conflicting imperial aims from each other. Increasingly they have been required to be part of one side or the other.

Afghanistan

The Republic of Afghanistan is here considered with the states of South Asia principally because of its population's close ties forged with Pakistan during more than fourteen years of civil war that began in 1978. Afghanistan as well could be grouped with the Middle Eastern countries because of its long ties to Iran. In similar fashion, it could also be considered with the post-Soviet states due to its historic linkages with the Central Asian territories and the Soviet involvement in its long civil war.

This ambiguity of association represents a continuation of the traditional buffer role that Afghanistan has played throughout history. At various times it has found itself between the empire of Genghis Khan and South Asia, between the Mogul Empire of India and the Savavi Empire of Iran, and between Tsarist Russian and British empires. Although Afghanistan has offered little of critical value to its neighbors, all have considered its possession by a rival power to be unacceptable.

Afghanistan is a landlocked territory embracing 250,000 square miles. More than 85 percent consists of deserts and mountains, all virtually empty aside from passing nomadic tribes and their flocks. The Hindu

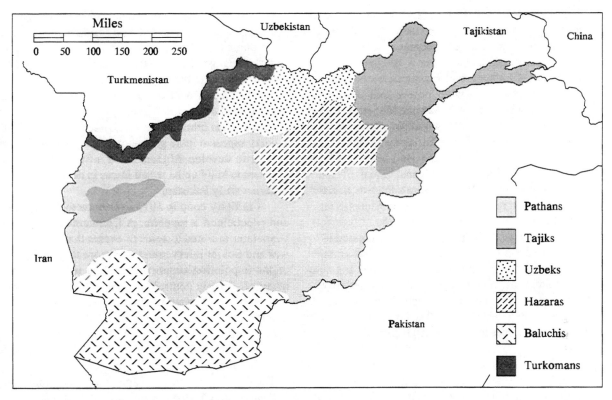

FIGURE 10-4   ETHNIC GROUPS OF AFGHANISTAN

Legend:
- Pathans
- Tajiks
- Uzbeks
- Hazaras
- Baluchis
- Turkomans

Kush ("Hindu Killer") Mountains form the state's central backbone, rising to an altitude of 22,000 feet above sea level. The population is concentrated in a handful of cities and in valleys where irrigation is feasible. The largest block of farmland lies in the fertile floodplain of the Amu Darya River, sometimes called the Oxus, which marks Afghanistan's northern boundary with former Soviet Central Asia.

Afghanistan contains a diversity of inhabitants, reflecting a multitude of invasions and migrations. Numerous languages are spoken, with many inhabitants being bilingual. Virtually all are Muslim. Numerous divisions of Islam are represented, including Sunnis, Sufis, Twelver (Imami) Shias, and Izmailis. A local Sunni dynasty withstood a Shiite Iranian invasion in the tenth century, assuring the dominance thereafter of Sunni Islam in both Afghanistan and India. Currently, 75 percent of the inhabitants of Afghanistan are Sunni.

The term "Afghan" is properly applied to Pashtu (Pushtu, Pathan)-speakers, who constitute roughly half the population. They consider themselves to be superior to all other groups in Afghanistan and generally are acknowledged as such by those groups. Afghan-

istan's rulers have all been Pashtus, aside from a brief period when a Tajik was head of state. Although Pashtu-speakers dominate the southeastern region, they are found in all parts of the country, due mainly to a past policy of planned resettlement of Pashtus among minority groups. Nearly all Pashtus are Sunni Muslims.

Tajiks number about a quarter of the population and are located along Afghanistan's northern fringe, including a concentration around the ancient fortress city of Herat. Like the Tajiks of Tajikistan, they speak Dari, a Persian language similar to Farsi. Although all Tajiks are Muslim, they are divided between Sunni and Ismaili traditions.

Up to 10 percent of the population identifies itself as Uzbek. Their language is Turkic, and they are Sunni Muslims. Many are descended from refugees who fled from the Soviet Union during its consolidation of power in Central Asia.

Hazaras constitute another 10 percent of Afghanistan's populace. They are concentrated in the central mountain region. Although they speak the Dari language of Iran, their physical features suggest that they are descendants of the Mongols. A majority of Hazaras are

Shia Muslims, but other Islamic sects including Sunnis and Izmailis also are present among them. Traditionally, other groups in Afghanistan rank Hazaras very low.

The country contains a number of other minorities, among whom Baluchis and Turkomans are notable. A significant number of Kyrgyz once tended herds in the mountains of the narrow Wakhan corridor extending to China, but it appears that few remain after years of warfare in the region. They are Turkic-speaking Sunni Muslims. Adjacent to them on the south are the Dari-speakers of Nuristan, which means "Land of the Light." Formerly the Nuristanis were known as Kafirs ("Infidels"), but received a change in names after forcible conversion to Sunni Islam in 1895.

The diversity of ethnic groups is compounded by the adherence of most to tribal identities. Thus, Pashtu-speakers are divided into numerous groupings, among whom Durranis and Ghizays are the most prominent. Clan rivalries can be strong, hampering cooperation against invaders. This was evident during the resistance to the Soviet forces involved in Afghanistan's long civil war.

Afghanistan's statehood dates from 1747, when a local leader expelled the Persians and proclaimed establishment of an Afghan Empire. In the following century the state had to contend with increasing British pressure to shore up their northwest frontier of India, beset by border troubles with Afghan tribes. During their Afghan wars of 1839–1842 and 1879–1881, the British found themselves unable to conquer Afghanistan, but the country consented to establishment of a British protectorate in the 1880s. This strengthened the Afghan response to Russian pressures from the north after the latter's conquest of Turkistan. The Amu Darya became Afghanistan's border with the Russian Empire in 1886.

Afghanistan's border with India was established in 1893. It came to be termed the Durrand Line after the chief British negotiator, and it followed territorial divisions between tribes loyal to the Afghan capital of Kabul and those tied to British-held Peshawar. It placed about half the Pashtu-speakers of the region in India, a matter of contention with the British and their Pakistani successors ever since. In 1907 Russia formally recognized the British role in Afghanistan in exchange for receiving a free hand for itself in northern Iran.

After a brief war with the United Kingdom, Afghanistan became completely independent in 1919. Over ensuing decades it functioned largely in isolation from its neighbors, although it received numerous Turkoman, Uzbek, Tajik, and Kyrgyz refugees fleeing Communist collectivization in Soviet Central Asia.

Following partition of British India in 1947, Afghanistan sought revision of its border with the successor state of Pakistan that would incorporate all Pashtu-speakers within its territory. Pakistan rejected its claims. As frictions developed between the two states, Pakistan closed the border, severing Afghanistan's outlet to the sea through the port of Karachi.

During the cold war between the Soviet Union and the United States, the Afghan regime played each country against the other and received aid from both. The Soviets appeared more generous, since America, while willing to develop Afghanistan's infrastructure, was reluctant to build up its armed forces in deference to the America's ally Pakistan.

A military coup in 1973 overthrew the monarchy and proclaimed a republic. A Communist coup five years later initiated a series of events that led to civil war and Soviet intervention. No more than 5 percent of the population supported the new regime, which never effectively controlled more than 20 percent of the territory. The new ruling party suffered from severe internal divisions between its Khalq ("Masses") and Parcham ("Banner") factions. The former was supported principally by Ghilzi Pashtun-speakers who felt excluded from power by the rival Durrani tribal group. The Parchams had a broader representation among Pashtu- and Dari-speakers, but its supporters were drawn mainly from the Kabul area. Opposing both groups were Hazara and Tajik Communists, who organized Maoist movements that reflected their resentments both of the Soviet Union and the dominant Pashtus. The overwhelming bulk of the Afghan population remained devout Muslims and resisted the avowedly atheist regime. They were particularly incensed by the government's new iconography—it had adopted a red flag with a gold emblem that omitted the traditional Islamic green color featured in the former black, red, and green banner.

The Soviet Union entered the conflict in 1979, motivated perhaps by worries over the loyalties of its own Central Asian Muslims. Beginning in Nuristan, an anti-Soviet Muslim resistance movement grew, assisted by Arab, Iranian, and American interests. Soviet forces responded with full-scale warfare. The ensuing fighting and destruction led more than a third of the population to flee abroad. Three million went to Pakistan and another 2,000,000 crossed into Iran.

Faced with an impossible military situation, the USSR began withdrawing its forces in 1988, but the civil war continued until the Communist regime was toppled in 1992. Despite the popular victory over the Communists, the new regime has found great difficulty in consolidating power. It faces a particular challenge from the Shiite Muslims, who claim 35 percent of the Afghan population. The low-status Hazaras are a backbone to the resistance movement.

Bibliography

CHAPMAN, GRAHAM, "Religious vs. Regional Determinism: India, Pakistan and Bangladesh as Inheritors of Empire," in *Shared Space: Divided Space: Essays on Conflict and Territorial Organization*, eds. Michael Chisholm and David M. Smith. London: Unwin Hyman, 1990.

EAST, W. GORDON, and O.H.K. Spate, *The Changing Map of Asia: A Political Geography*, 4th ed., London: Methuen, 1961.

LAMB, ALASTAIR, *Asian Frontiers: Studies in a Continuing Problem*. New York: Praeger, 1961.

MCLEOD, W. H., *The Sikhs: History, Religion, and Society*. New York: Columbia University Press, 1989.

NAYARA, BALDEV RAJ, *Minority Politics in the Punjab*. Princeton, NJ: Princeton University Press, 1966.

NYROP, RICHARD F., ed., *Pakistan: A Country Study* (Area Handbook Series). Washington, DC: Superintendent of Documents, U.S. Government Printing Office, 1984.

SPATE, O.H.K., *India and Pakistan: A General and Regional Geography*, 3rd ed., London: Methuen, 1967.

11

Southeast Asia

OUTHEAST Asia is a territory whose parts exhibit little in common with each other, aside from mutual proximity. Its political-geographic characteristics resemble those of Southeastern Europe: a frontier zone of contending influences from powerful adjacent civilizations, within which a diversity of distinctive peoples coexist in isolated ecumenes. Despite its compactness and limited size, Southeast Asia has never functioned as a single entity (see Table 11-1).

Its physical geography has not been conducive to homogeneity and coherence. The mainland portion consists of four roughly parallel river valleys and associated deltas, separated by nearly empty mountains and plateaus. Three-quarters of its inhabitants live concentrated on the irrigated delta lands of the Irrawaddy, Menam, Mekong, and Songhai (Red) rivers. The remaining population ekes out a living from the limited resources of the intervening uplands. The insular portion of Southeast Asia consists of more than 18,000 islands (Figure 11-1).

FIGURE 11-1   MAINLAND SOUTHEAST ASIA: ECUMENE

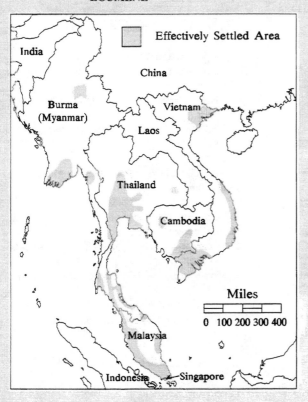

The isolated ethnic groups of Southeast Asia exhibit great diversity (Figure 11-2). They are the products of migrations from interior Asia occurring at different times from different source regions. As in Transcaucasia and the Balkans, new arrivals displaced earlier settlers into adjacent, less favorable zones. Differences in gaining a living between lowlanders and hill peoples compounded original ethnic contrasts.

External influences further differentiated populations. Foreigners from Buddhist, Hindu, Muslim, and Christian civilizations found ready access by river and sea to population concentrations in Southeast Asia. Their strongly organized homelands exerted contending political and cultural influences that led indigenous groups further apart from each other. Chinese early made the northern areas of Southeast Asia tributary to their state. On the islands of Indonesia, Indians created a Hindu empire, and later a Muslim one. Beginning in the Straits of Malacca in the sixteenth century, Europeans came to dominate extensive territories, putting their own differential stamps upon local populations.

Within each population concentration a distinctive civilization developed, acculturating new arrivals. Awareness of the need for harmony to maintain irrigation works promoted social homogeneity and coherence. Relations with neighboring concentrations generally were hostile. Groups were rival and competitive with each other, not complementary. Even in the modern era, faced with a common threat from an aggressive North Vietnamese Communist state, mainland Southeast Asian entities found cooperation difficult, despite prompting from supporting powers in Europe and America.

The boundaries of contemporary states were set during the era of colonialism. Unlike the situation in colonial Africa, European colonies in Southeast Asia tended to mirror indigenous political realities. Each colony had a major population concentration at its core, with tributary groups occupying sparsely settled peripheral areas. As Europeans drew boundary lines across the landscape, the traditional frontier character of hill peoples changed. Tribal groups of Thais, Shans, Cambodians, and Malays, otherwise sharing common languages and religious beliefs, found themselves increasingly torn away from kin across borders and oriented to interests of lowland societies that were dominated by differing foreign powers.

In addition to dividing peripheral peoples, European colonialism affected Southeast Asia's political geography by encouraging settlement of migrants from outside the region. Chinese came to dominate much of

TABLE 11.1   MAINLAND SOUTHEAST ASIA

The peninsula of Southeast Asia holds five states with ancient traditions. Although its populations speak similar languages and maintain Buddhist traditions, they are divided by historic enmities and physical separation of their limited ecumenes. Each consists of a fertile core area in an irrigated river valley surrounded by hills and mountains sparsely inhabited by distinctly different hill peoples. Traditionally, the peninsula has served as a frontier or buffer between stronger outside powers. In ancient times it was a zone of competition between India and China. During the nineteenth and early twentieth centuries, the outside rivalry was between the British and the French, who subjected all but Thailand to colonization. In contrast to the arbitrarily created units of tropical Africa, Southeast Asian colonial territories were based upon historic precedents and cultural differences. These dependent areas gained full independence in the postwar era and face common problems of managing internal diversities and contending with their neighbors.

State	Total Population	Area (sq. miles)	Distinctive Features of Group
Burma (Myanmar)	44,000,000	260,000	
Dominant Nation and % Total			
Burman, 70%			Tibeto-Burman (Burmese) language, Theravada Buddhist
Significant Regional Groups and % Total			
Shans, 9%			Thai (Shan) language, Theravada Buddhist
Karens, 6%			Tibeto-Burmese (Karen) language, Christian and Buddhist
Arakanese (Rakhines), 6%			Tibeto-Burman (Burmese) language, Theravada Buddhist
Mons, 2%			Mon-Khmer (Mon) language, Theravada Buddhist
Chins, 2%			Tibeto-Burmese (Chin) language, Animist and Christian
Kachins, 2%			Tibeto-Burmese (Kachin) language, Indigenous Kachin Religion
Thailand	57,000,000	200,000	
Dominant Nation and % Total			
Thais (including Lao-Thais), 85%			Thai language, Theravada Buddhist
Significant Regional Groups and % Total			
Malay, 3%			Indonesia (Malay) language, Muslim
Khmer (Cambodian)			Mon-Khmer (Cambodian) language, Theravada Buddhist
Karens, <1%			Tibeto-Burmese (Karen) language, Christian and Buddhist
Shans			Thai (Shan) language, Theravada Buddhist
Vietnam	70,000,000	130,000	
Dominant Nation and % Total			
Northern Vietnamese, 45%			Sino-Tibetan (Vietnamese) language, Mahayana Buddhist
Significant Regional Groups and % Total			
Southern Vietnamese, 42%			Sino-Tibetan (Vietnamese), Theravada Buddhist and Roman Catholic
Tais, 2%			Sino-Tibetan (Tai) language, Theravada Buddhist and Animist
Cambodians (Khmers), 2%			Mon-Khmer (Cambodian) language, Theravada Buddhist
Muongs, 2%			Sino-Tibetan (Muong) language, Animist
Nungs, 1%			Tibeto-Burman (Nung) language, Animist
Laos	4,500,000	92,000	
Dominant Nation and % Total			
Laotians, 67%			Sino-Tibetan (Thai) language, Theravada Buddhist

State	Total Population	Area (sq. miles)	Distinctive Features of Group
Significant Regional Groups and % Total			
Lao-Theungs, 16%			Mon-Khmer languages, Animist
Hmongs (Miaos, Lao-Soungs), 5%			Sino-Tibetan (Hmong) language, Animist
Cambodia (Kampuchea)	9,000,000	70,000	
Dominant Nation and % Total			
Cambodians (Khmers), 94%			Mon-Khmer (Cambodian) language, Theravada Buddhist

the region's commerce and industry. They were descendants of individuals responding to labor opportunities provided in European-developed mines and plantations. In the postcolonial era most Chinese now feel some degree of discrimination. A high proportion of "boat people" fleeing Communist Vietnam have been Chinese. Large numbers of Chinese in Indonesia have suffered imprisonment or death in anti-Communist excesses. Singapore remained outside the boundaries of the state of Malaysia because of Malay fears of its large Chinese ethnic component. Hindus and Muslims of Indian origin also have suffered from prejudice. Burma expelled its large Indian middle class immediately upon independence. Malaysia created disabilities for Indians similar to those endured by its Chinese.

European colonialism ended after World War II. Postcolonial regimes have experienced great difficulties in exerting effective control over inherited territories, however. Burma has engaged in a continuing civil war with its non-Burmese peoples ever since independence was won in 1948. Thailand has been unable to control peoples in the "Golden Triangle" of opium poppy cultivation along the Burmese border. Governments of Vietnam and Laos have faced continuing challenge from their *Montagnards* (hill peoples). The Philippines' regime has been unable to control large areas of insurgency by Muslims and Marxist Hukbalahops, and Indonesia maintains authority over only a tiny portion of West Irian (Western New Guinea).

Pirates long have been a scourge throughout the region, and modern regimes have proven as powerless as their predecessors to control them. The original motivation for European control of such areas as Malacca, Dindings, and Labuan was to establish bases to counter piracy. Improved technology in transportation and weaponry has given piracy a renewed momentum in recent decades.

In contrast to the tribally divided states of Africa, peoples living in the population cores of Southeast Asia express increasingly strong senses of national identity. Homogeneity and distinctiveness of lowland cultures, long-standing animosities toward neighboring agglomerations, and contact with modern European political views have provided fertile ground for development of sentiments for political unity. One feature of the postcolonial era has been nationalist rejection of colonial designations of territory in favor of more indigenous appellations. The xenophobic government of semicolonial Siam adopted the name "Thailand" on the eve of World War II. The postindependence regime of the Dutch East Indies assumed the designation "Indonesia." Communist and non-Communist governments, each claiming authority over the combined French colonies of Tonkin, Annam, and Cochin China, called their territory "Vietnam." In more recent times, Cambodia became "Kampuchea" and Burma "Myanmar."

Peripheral peoples within each state also honed distinguishing identities. Differences from core peoples in languages, religions, and traditions led to separatist activities. Among such national movements are those of the Shans and Karens in Burma, Malays in Thailand, Muslims in the Philippines, and South Moluccans and East Timorans in Indonesia.

Historical Evolution

Although the river valley and delta civilizations of Southeast Asia have enjoyed a remarkable continuity through time, many of their distinguishing characteristics derive from influences outside the region. Contact with seafarers from India early led to implantation of the subcontinent's cultural traditions. Hindu temples on Indonesian Bali reflect ancient linkage. India's Buddhist reformation also spread to mainland Southeast Asia, which managed to resist the continent's later Hindu resurgence. Islam also came to the region by way of India. It supplanted Hinduism in most of Indonesia and Malaysia and took hold in southern parts of the Philippines. However, it had only minor impact upon mainland areas.

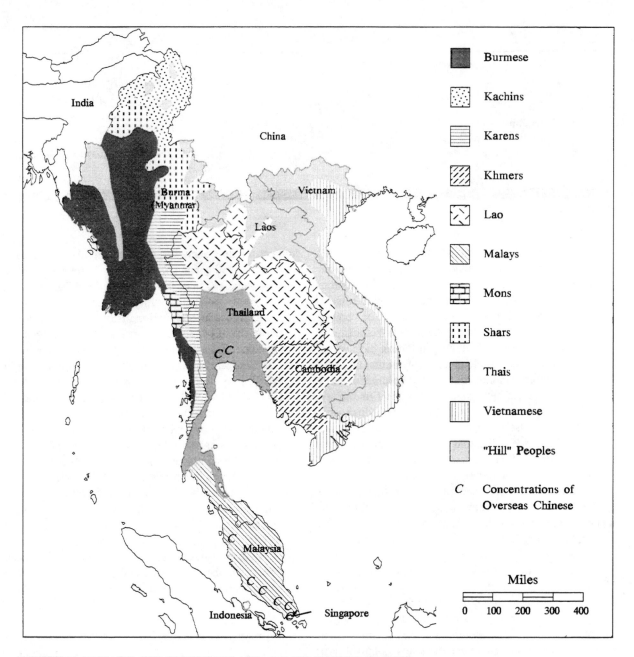

FIGURE 11-2   MAINLAND SOUTHEAST ASIA: MAJOR ETHNIC GROUPS

Legend:
- Burmese
- Kachins
- Karens
- Khmers
- Lao
- Malays
- Mons
- Shars
- Thais
- Vietnamese
- "Hill" Peoples
- *C*   Concentrations of Overseas Chinese

China conquered the Red River basin of northern Vietnam and held it as an integral part of China from 11 B.C. to A.D. 939. The area subsequently was a Chinese vassal on numerous occasions. The result was a degree of Sinification that continues to distinguish northern Vietnamese from other Southeast Asian peoples, including Vietnam's own southern inhabitants.

For a time in the fifteenth century, China expanded its realm of influence southward. It identified coastal regions and islands of Southeast Asia as "Nanyang" ("Southern Seas") and sent naval expeditions to that realm for three decades, beginning in 1403. A consequence is China's current claim to the Spratly Islands in the South China Sea, a title contested by both Vietnam and the Philippines. Subsequent Chinese influence in the region came from overseas migrants, encouraged by opportunities presented by European colonial regimes in the nineteenth century.

European Colonialism

The first Europeans to appear in Southeast Asia were the Portuguese, who arrived in Malaysia in 1511. The Spanish established dominion over the Philippines in 1565. Later, the Dutch supplanted the Portuguese in Malaysia and the Indonesian islands in 1641 as a consequence of Portugal's "sixty years' captivity" by the Spanish. Both Portuguese and Dutch governments confined early colonial ventures to the establishment of trading posts that exchanged European wares for spices and other tropical goods. Until the end of the eighteenth century, control by the Netherlands was through the chartered Dutch East India Company. The Dutch government assumed direct control in 1798, welding a network of island footholds into a coherent empire. Spain maintained its hold over the Philippines for 350 years, until yielding the colony to the United States in 1898.

In contrast to their colonial activity in the islands, Europeans ignored mainland Southeast Asia until the nineteenth century. Struggle for control of India had served to limit British and French involvement elsewhere in the Orient up to that time. After the United Kingdom prevailed in the subcontinent in 1797, it sought to protect eastern approaches to its new empire through control of coastal Burma and Malaya. France turned its attention to China. It saw opportunies for penetrating China's fabled markets by establishing a commercial base in the Red River delta region of Tonkin. Both the British and French developed renewed interests in Southeast Asia after opening of the Suez Canal in 1869.

In the process of extending their presence inland from their respective coastal bases on the Bay of Bengal and South China Sea, the United Kingdom and France faced potential confrontations with each other in Siam. To minimize the possibility of conflict, they agreed to recognize nominal Siamese sovereignty, but divided that country into respective spheres of influence. They formalized this arrangement by a convention signed in 1896. Siam thus became an independent buffer state, maintained by rival powers comparable to Belgium. However, it functioned with few differences from its colonial neighbors. It lacked a European administrative bureaucracy, but it endured the same flood of entrepreneurs from China managing trade with European powers.

The legacy of European colonialism to Southeast Asia includes both positive and negative features. As in Africa, Europeans minimized conflicts between groups. The French linked Vietnamese, Cambodians, and Laotians under a single imperial regime for the first time in history. The Dutch similarly imposed peace within a single governmental entity upon Javans, Sumatrans, and Borneans. All European powers created modern infrastructures of ports, railroads, and communications. They brought isolated peoples into contact with modern technology. Their advances in public health reduced the incidence of malaria and other age-old scourges and extended the average length of life. They opened up new areas for intensive settlement, including the rich but disease-infested deltas of the Mekong and Irrawaddy rivers. Europeans established linkages to the outside world through creation of ports at Batavia, Rangoon, Singapore, Saigon, and elsewhere.

On the negative side, Europeans subverted and supplanted indigenous institutions and traditions. They treated harshly any signs of dissidence. They fundamentally altered demographic characteristics through encouragement of Chinese and Indian in-migration. They also wreaked destruction by violent resistance to national liberation movements developing during the mid-twentieth century.

The catalyst for the end of colonialism in Southeast Asia was occupation by Japan during World War II. This marked the first time in history that the entirety of Southeast Asia was under control of one power. A principal consequence of Japan's rapid seizure of the region was destruction of the myth of European invincibility. The harshness of Japanese control belied propaganda embodied in its proclaimed Greater East Asia Co-Prosperity Sphere. Nevertheless, the Japanese prepared the way for postwar anticolonial movements. Japan declared independence for Burma and the Philippines in 1943 and did the same for Indonesia and French Indochina in 1945. In the latter, it linked Tonkin, Annam, and Cochin-China into a single entity that henceforth was known as Vietnam, while granting separate sovereignty to Cambodia and Laos.

Southeast Asia became the first colonial region to achieve independence after World War II. In doing so, it provided inspiration and a model to colonial peoples in the Middle East, Africa, and the Caribbean. The United States began the process by granting independence to the Philippines on July 4, 1946, as promised before World War II. When Dutch forces returned to their East Indies colony after the war, they found entrenched native nationalists contesting Dutch right to rule. The French experienced similar resistance in Indochina. Both European powers ultimately suffered military defeats in their colonies. In 1947 the Netherlands conceded Indonesian independence, and in 1954, after severe military defeat, France recognized insurgent areas of northern Vietnam as a sovereign entity, separate from southern Vietnam, Cambodia, and Laos, which remained under French control.

The British faced similar opposition in Burma and Malaya. They entered into negotiations with the Burmese and granted them independence in 1948. Opposition to British return to Malaya principally was from a jungle guerrilla band of leftist Chinese, who had joined together earlier to resist Japanese occupation. Before the war, the United Kingdom had ruled much of the peninsula indirectly through leaders of Malay "native states." The British reestablished this relationship, while resolutely combatting the Chinese insurgency. They ultimately vanquished the guerrillas and subsequently granted independence to their holdings in Malaya and Borneo in 1967 as a federated state named Malaysia. Paradoxically, the last colonial power to leave the region was also the first to enter it. The Portuguese held the eastern half of the small island of Timor from the early 1500s to 1973, when Indonesian forces seized the colony.

Independence did not mean an end to strife. Resistance to central authority developed in most states. In some cases it was ideological. Communist insurgency developed in the Philippines, Indonesia, Thailand, Cambodia, Laos, and South Vienam. The majority of opposition to the new governments was ethnic in character, however. Shans and Karens fought the new Burmese regime, Malays in the Kra Isthmus waged war on Thailand, and rebels in Sumatra and Celebes rose up against Indonesia.

Burma

The territory of Burma contains 260,000 square miles, with a population of about 44,000,000. In comparison with adjacent Bangladesh and China, it is relatively underpopulated. During the first half of the twentieth century it was noted for its surpluses of rice production that found ready markets in neighboring states.

Burma consists of three distinctive parts: a core region of dense population in the middle Irrawaddy Valley, a delta flanked by the Arakan coast to the north and Tenasserim coast to the south, and a complex of hills insulating settled areas from Bangladesh, India, China, Laos, and Thailand. For only a limited number of historical occasions have all three parts been linked into a single state: in the eleventh, sixteenth, and eighteenth centuries, and in the modern period, beginning with British colonial rule in 1886. Although the middle Irrawaddy Burman population has predominated through time, other groups indigenous to Burma have had their own states in the past, including the Mons and Shans.

The British East India Company initiated trade relations with the Burmese coast in the early eighteenth

century. A strong native government became a perceived threat to British interests in Bengal a century later, as it expanded westward to engulf the Chin and Naga hill tribes. The United Kingdom responded by seizing the Arakan and Tenasserim coasts of Burma in 1824. Following renewed fighting in 1852, the British moved into the Irrawaddy Delta region. In 1886 the United Kingdom acquired the Burmese central core area, and two years later joined the Shan states to its possessions.

The Burmese economy grew rapidly under British rule. Railroads were built from the coast to the interior, and the lightly populated delta was transformed into a major surplus rice-production region. The British governed Burma as a province of India, despite the Mongol racial characteristics and predominantly Buddhist religion of its population. Many Indians migrated to Burma, holding more than half of all government jobs by the 1930s. Chinese also came. In fact, Burmans constituted barely a third of the population of the coastal city of Rangoon, which under British administration replaced interior Mandalay as the capital.

In 1937 the United Kingdom made Burma a colony separate from India. At this time anti-British nationalists found encouragement from the Japanese, who secretly offered training to a select group on the occupied Chinese island of Hainan. In 1942, when Japanese forces added Burma to their Southeast Asian conquests, this group returned to form a local government. At the end of the war, the British negotiated independence with nationalist leaders, much as they were doing in India. Unlike other former British colonial possessions, Burmese leaders rejected continuing association with the United Kingdom through membership in the Commonwealth of Nations. Burma became a sovereign state in 1948.

Approximately 70 percent of the Burmese population is Burman. The Burmans have evolved a civilization that propagates a strong sense of historical identity. They utilize a distinctive alphabet for their Tibetan-related language. Virtually all Burmans are Theravada Buddhists. Their cultural-religious heritage impinges upon most aspects of daily life, and also upon the structure and functioning of government. Among the Burmese-speaking population are the coastal Arakanese, who maintain a distinctive cultural tradition separate from that of the Burmans in the Irrawaddy Valley and Delta.

Surrounding the Burmans are a variety of peoples with indigenous languages, religions, and customs. The Burmese government officially recognizes sixty-seven "racial groups." Among these are the Mons, who speak a Mon-Khmer language related to Cambodian. They were a dominant civilization along the south coast until conquered by Burmans in the eighteenth century.

Astride the Thailand border to the east are the Karens, whose ancestors migrated from China in the seventh century A.D. Missionary activity during the nineteenth and early twentieth centuries resulted in a high proportion of these people becoming Christian. Their western ties led to the evolution of a modern national identity, with a strong political movement developing in the 1880s. The British favored the Karens in recruiting for the armed forces, causing resentment toward Karens by other peoples in the colony.

North of the Karens, along the Thai, Laotian, and Chinese borders, are the Shans. Their language is similar to Thai, and the people call themselves "Tai." They are well aware that their forebears once ruled Burma. In later history, they deferred to Burman rulers, but maintained their own self-governing states.

Kachin tribesmen dominate Burma's northern hills. They have a well-earned reputation as fighters, successfully resisting British, Japanese, and Burman attempts to control their region. They have a strong indigenous religion that sets them apart from their Buddhist neighbors. Attempts by the Burmese armed forces in 1992 to extend government authority into the Kachin area were met by strong resistance and a stream of Kachin refugees into adjacent parts of India.

On the western border are a number of hill tribes. Among them are Nagas, who also inhabit the hills of northeastern India. In the mountains adjacent to Bangladesh are Chins, speaking a language related to Burmese. However, unlike the Burmans, they are not Buddhist, a quarter or more identifying themselves as Christian and the remainder practicing an animist faith.

Under the Burmese kings, outlying peoples were essentially self-governing but were required to pay tribute. The British did not interfere with this relationship until they granted Burma separate colonial status in 1937. At that time, they made special constitutional provisions to protect the interests of minority groups, a concession resented by most Burmans.

The leaders of independent Burma in 1948 modelled the organization of their new state after the Communist Yugoslav federation. They saw the Union of Burma as a republic composed of separate Burman, Shan, Kachin, and Karen states. Eventually they divided Burma into fourteen units, seven of which were identified as Burman administrative areas and the remaining seven as ethnic states, although the latter generally also contained large numbers of nontitular minorities and Burmans. The fourteen encircling stars of the Burmese flag symbolize these administrative divisions. The Burmans had little toleration for Hindu Indians, however. More than 400,000 fled to Assam when the Japanese pushed into Burma, and the postwar independent Burmese government did not allow them to return. Virtually all Indians remaining in Burma at the end of the war found strong encouragement to leave.

Although Burmans also resented Chinese immigrants, the latter had relatively small numbers and were allowed to remain in postcolonial Burma. Most lived in tin mining areas. In 1949, some 12,000 Chinese Nationalist soldiers crossed into eastern Burma, following Communist victory in China. They became a major outlaw force, involving themselves with the Shan minority in the notorious development of opium production in a region that came to be known as the Golden Triangle.

The Burmese government has been unable to assert effective control over all its territory since gaining independence, facing continuing guerrilla warfare in most non-Burman areas. Much of the time its armed forces have controlled less than two-thirds of its nominal area. The greatest opposition has come from Shans and Karens, the latter joined at times also by Mons. In the 1970s, the regime generated strong opposition in its predominantly Muslim western coastal region when it sought to expel illegal migrants from Bangladesh. More than 200,000 Burmese Muslims fled to that state in 1978, following repressive measures. A similar mass migration to Bangladesh occurred in March 1992.

In 1988, the Burmese armed forces seized control of the state and ordered that it be renamed "Myanmar." Although the name change ostensibly was to defuse ethnic conflict, it had little effect upon the restive minorities, who particularly resented the new regime's selling of economic concessions in their homelands to business interests in Thailand, South Korea, Hong Kong, and Singapore.

Thailand

With an area of approximately 200,000 square miles, Thailand is four-fifths the size of Burma. Its population of 57,000,000 is 20 percent larger than Burma's, however. The name "Thailand" (*Muang Thai* or "Land of the Free") was adopted on the eve of World War II. Before that the state was universally known as Siam.

More than 80 percent of the people of Thailand can be classed as Thai, based on language and culture. They are descended from the Tai peoples, whose cultural hearth was in Yunnan province of southern China. The Shans and Laotians also are descended from this group. In 1253, Kublai Khan, the Mongol ruler of China, caused the Tai to stream southward into Southeast Asia.

Four major linguistic and cultural divisions exist among the dominant Thai group in Thailand. The language of one region differs from that of the others in vocabulary, grammar, and pronunciation, and it can be understood in distant areas only with difficulty. Central

Thai enjoys the highest status, and is the standard language taught in schools throughout the country. It is native to about one-third of the population. Central Thai is written in an alphabet adopted in the fourteenth century, borrowing from writing systems in Cambodia and India.

Some 30 percent of the population speaks a variant Thai language that often is termed "Thai-Lao." It is essentially the same as the Laotian spoken in Laos, and is extant in the dry Korat plateau region of northeastern Thailand adjacent to Laos. To the north and northwest is the Northern Thai linguistic region, containing 17 percent of Thailand's inhabitants. In the peninsular area to the south is the Southern Thai region, with about 5 percent of the population.

Virtually all Thais are Theravada Buddhists. Their ancestors adopted the religion in the fourteenth century. Buddhist scriptures of the Thais are in an ancient Indian written language known as Pali that is comparable in usage to Latin or Classical Greek. Modern religious works increasingly are written in Central Thai.

The largest minority in Thailand is the Chinese, numbering 6,000,000, or 12 percent of the population. Unlike most minority groups in the world, Thailand's Chinese do not form a majority in any one region. Rather, they live scattered throughout the state, serving as middlemen in economic transactions. A high proportion is concentrated in the Bangkok region, however.

Thailand's Chinese tend to be more assimilated into local society than is the case with other overseas Chinese groups. More than 90 percent have acquired Thai citizenship, and a high proportion are bilingual in the Thai language. In part, this is because new arrivals have been limited since the 1950s, when severely restrictive immigration laws were passed. The Chinese community tends to differentiate itself into groups based upon original regions of emigration from China.

The Malay population of the southern margins of the state numbers about 3 percent of the total. Their language is greatly different from Thai and is written in Arabic script. Most Malays are Muslims. A large proportion feels oppressed, and the region has seen a rather constant insurgency throughout the twentieth century.

A long-standing minority that swelled substantially during the 1970s is the Khmer, or Cambodian, population. Up to 600,000 joined fellow nationals in eastern Thailand, fleeing their homeland to escape fighting and atrocities in the aftermath of victory by Khmer Rouge Communist forces in Cambodia. The establishment of a peace accord among contending Cambodian political factions led to slow repatriation, beginning in April 1992.

Various tribal groups occupy the hills on Thailand's margins, although their combined total population is less than 800,000. Most numerous are the Karens, living along the border with Burma. A substantial number of hill people are recent immigrants, fleeing fighting in Laos and Burma. Most hill people have a strong sense of separate identity, but tend to associate themselves with Thailand as their state. Many, like the Shans, speak the Thai language, yet they maintain strong group feelings of distinctiveness.

The Thais have had a succession of governmental organizations over time. They have engaged in continuous struggles with their Burman and Cambodian neighbors. At times, Thai governments have controlled all of Cambodia, Malaya, Laos, and the Tenasserim coast of Burma. In other periods they have been completely vanquished, most recently by Burma in 1767.

It was following this traumatic event that the modern Thai state emerged at the end of the eighteenth century. It was officially called "Siam," a name derived from *syam* ("dark brown"—referring to people) that has been noted on a twelfth-century inscription at Angkor Wat in Cambodia.

Although its population had been in contact with European traders ever since the early sixteenth century, Siam managed to evade direct European colonial domination. It did establish diplomatic relations with European governments and used advisers to build a modern state bureaucracy. Technological and organizational modernization permitted its kings to exert greater authority over peripheral areas, particularly to the north and northeast.

As noted in the introduction to this chapter, Siam avoided the colonial fate of its neighbors in the nineteenth century by playing British and French interests against each other. Nevertheless, it ultimately suffered similar foreign control of its economy and an influx of large numbers of Chinese who became middlemen in transactions. It lost extensive lands to the Europeans, including Laos and Cambodia. Further nibbling of Siamese territory occurred during the early twentieth centure. France added the province of Battambang to Cambodia in 1907, and the United Kingdom took four Malay states in 1909.

The population of Siam developed a strong sense of national identity, symbolized by the name change to "Thailand" in 1939. Political leaders long have preached a doctrine of a Greater Thailand, which appears to be defined as any territory to which ethnic or historical claims can be made. This chauvinism has generated substantial distrust and antipathy in adjacent areas.

During World War II, the Thai government collaborated with the Japanese, although its forces never engaged Western Allied forces in battle. As a result of acquiescence to Japanese authority, the Thais gained back territories earlier lost to France in Laos and Cambodia, and to the United Kingdom in Burma and the Malay Peninsula. At the close of the war, it forfeited these areas.

During the postwar period Thailand escaped the insurrections and civil wars that beset its neighbors. Its only overt ethnic rebellion has been in the Malay provinces of the extreme south. Popular discontent against military domination of civil affairs erupted into major demonstrations and fighting in mid-1992, however. Thai regimes have not been able to establish effective control over opium-poppy-growing areas along the western border with Burma. Thailand has also had minor disputes with Laos and Cambodia over exact locations of boundaries.

Vietnam

The eastern margin of peninsular Southeast Asia is occupied by Vietnam. This state has an area of 125,000 square miles and a population of 70,000,000. Like Burma and Thailand, its inhabitants are primarily descendants of migrants from southern China, fleeing pressures from the Han Chinese. They long have called themselves the "Viet," although Chinese traditionally referred to them as the "Yue." Their appearance in Southeast Asia began in the years following 333 B.C., when Chinese imperial forces conquered their ancient state in southern China. Viets remaining in southern China were rapidly assimilated into Chinese culture.

Those who moved southward created a new state in the delta of the Song Hai (Red River). They named it "Nam Viet," or "Southern Viet State." Their capital was at the site of modern Hanoi. Vietnamese thus justifiably have a sense of historical continuity in their homeland comparable to that of Greeks, Italians, and other European national groups.

However, China subsequently conquered Nam Viet in 111 B.C., making the territory a Chinese province in A.D. 43. The Vietnamese remained under Chinese domination for more than a thousand years, gaining independence only in the tenth century, when the ruling dynasty of China fell. During this period, the Vietnamese upper class adopted Chinese social institutions, including Confucianism, Mahayana Buddhism, and the Chinese system of writing. However, pre-Chinese traditions continued among the rural population.

China sought to reimpose control over the Vietnamese on a number of occasions during ensuing centuries. Armies of Kublai Khan invaded in 1257, 1284, and 1287, but were repulsed. The Vietnamese maintained independence, but remained part of the East Asian culture world, in contrast to the India-influenced societies in the remainder of Southeast Asia.

The territory of Vietnam often is likened to "two bags of rice hanging from a yoke." The "bags" are deltas of the Red (Song Hai) and Mekong rivers, connected by a narrow coastal plain, some 600 miles long. Nearly 90 percent of the population lives within these lowland areas. The plains are backed by forest-covered hills and mountains occupying three-fourths of the state's territory.

From their core in the Red River Delta, Vietnamese began moving southward along the coast of the South China Sea in the eleventh century. The area at that time belonged to the Chams, a Buddhist Malay group related to the Khmers of Cambodia. In 1309 Vietnamese reached the Cham coastal center of Hué, and they completed conquest of the Cham kingdom in the 1400s. During the seventeenth century, they expanded farther southward, reaching the margins of the Mekong Delta.

Vietnamese migrants to the south broke away from northern control, creating a separate kingdom with the capital at Hué. They were able to defend themselves from the northern state by establishing a fortified line across the narrow coastal strip. This defensive strip was located in the vicinity of the 17°N parallel, which became the division line between northern and southern Vietnam after World War II.

Although the Mekong Delta had once been the site of an indigenous Malay kingdom, it had fallen under domination of the Khmers in the sixteenth century. By the 1600s, that empire had gone into decline and eventually was vanquished by Siam. Vietnamese in the eighteenth century thus moved into Mekong Delta lands that were politically unorganized. Migrants settled among the relatively few Khmers and other natives still living there.

An internal rebellion in the southern Vietnamese kingdom gained momentum in the 1780s and expanded to the north, at that time known as Dai Viet. Attempted intervention by a Chinese army of 200,000 to preserve Dai Viet resulted in victory by a Vietnamese force half that number. Vietnamese were once again united within a single state. They built an imperial capital near Hué in a form closely patterned after Beijing (Peking), including even a "Forbidden City." Separate governors were appointed to administer the major delta regions to the north and south.

The new rulers initially revived "Nam Viet" as the name of their country. This was troubling to the Chinese, however, because it recalled hostilities that China had endured from the predecessor state. At China's insistence, the newly unified entity adopted the name "Viet Nam" in 1802, the first time that designation had been used.

Differences between north and south in Vietnam had grown wide during two centuries of separation. In contrast to the Sinicized north, southern rulers had been less inclined to mirror traditions of China. The stable, overcrowded demographic conditions of the Red River Delta were markedly different from pioneer conditions along the mouths of the Mekong, where inhabitants lived in a dynamically expanding frontier situation. Southerners also had greater contact with Europeans. Portuguese and French adventurers, merchants, and missionaries had been coming to central and southern coastal ports ever since the sixteenth century. Nearly a half million southern Vietnamese were converted to Roman Catholicism by the early 1800s.

Catholic missionaries created a phonetic script for the Vietnamese in the seventeenth century. Intended for prayer books, it was based on the Latin alphabet but employed a large number of diacritical marks to indicate tonal subtleties of the spoken language. This *quoc ngu* system became standard among educated Vietnamese during the nineteenth century, replacing the Chinese ideographs, *chu nam*, that traditionally were employed by the elite. The simplifed writing system permitted a higher proportion of Vietnamese to become literate.

The French

France turned attention to the Vietnamese coast after losing out in India to the United Kingdom at the end of the eighteenth century. The French saw Southeast Asia as a gateway to markets and products of China. The French government, moreover, was pressed by its Roman Catholic clergy to do something about the increasing persecutions of Christians in Vietnam that had begun in the 1830s. The French also were concerned that if they did not take steps to extend control over the region, the British would.

The French sent an expedition to the Vietnamese coast, which captured the towns of Tourane (Da Nang) and Gia Dinh (Saigon) in 1858. They expected support for their actions by local Christians, but were disappointed when this did not occur. Vietnamese resistance led to France's reinforcement of its seized holdings and expansion of the zone of occupation to surrounding territories. In 1862, France forced the Vietnamese emperor in Hué to cede three provinces in the south. The French then formed these into a French colony, which was named Cochin China.

The French originally envisioned using the Mekong River as a water route into southern China. To achieve this end, their forces pushed upstream, annexing three additional Vietnamese delta provinces to Cochin China. France also established a protectorate over the rump of the Cambodian Empire, then in the process of being partitioned between Vietnam and Siam. The latter country gave approval to the French action in return for receipt of two Cambodian provinces as compensation.

As awareness grew of the lack of feasibility of navigation on the Mekong to reach China, France turned attention to more northerly parts of Vietnam. Its forces invaded the Red River Delta in 1872, holding for a time the principal city of Hanoi. However, attempts to capture the entire delta region were thwarted by native troops, who were joined by Chinese mercenaries. The French renewed hostilities in 1882 and captured Hanoi a second time. They then took the central coast capital of Hué in the following year, forcing the emperor to accept French suzerainty over all his empire. The central coastal strip became the protectorate of Annam and the Red River Delta the protectorate of Tonkin. In 1887, France amalgamated Cochin China, Cambodia, Annam, and Tonkin into an entity it called the Indochinese union. The French joined Laos to the union as a protectorate in 1893.

French colonial rule was exploitative. Direct European development occurred mainly in the Mekong Delta region, where large tracts of empty land had been available. The French established massive rubber plantations there. Many Catholic Vietnamese in the south, long oppressed by their native regime, collaborated with the French. Sinicized elites of the north, in contrast, refused any cooperation with the invaders of their homeland, necessitating France's use of large numbers of Frenchmen as colonial administrators.

Increasing opportunities for land and employment in the Mekong Delta drew many northern Vietnamese to Cochin China. Large numbers of Chinese also came. Most of the latter became middlemen in commercial transactions and generated resentment by the local population, as occurred in Siam and elsewhere. The Chinese constructed their own city, Cholon, adjacent to Saigon.

Vietnamese in the south lost much of their lingering East Asian cultural heritage during the twentieth century, becoming significantly Europeanized. A high proportion became pro-French. Many from Confucian and Buddhist backgrounds converted to Roman Catholicism. New religions also appeared. Up to 2,000,000 adopted the Cao-Dai faith, founded in 1926. It has been described as a "blend of Buddhism, Confucianism, Taoism, Roman Catholicism, and free masonry." The Hoa Hao sect similarly emerged in this period with a million members as a modernized, militant form of Theravada Buddhism, which had major appeal to the poor and oppressed.

Northern Vietnamese maintained traditional antipathy to the European presence. They saw their culture as equal or superior to that of the French. The traditional ties of Tonkin elites to Chinese civilization were reflected in general admiration of the role played by Sun

Yat-sen in China. Northerners developed a tradition of national rebellion against French control. A number studied in France, where many were attracted to Marxist ideas then in currency. Their anticolonial endeavors came to little significance, however, because, as a class, educated northerners were estranged from the peasantry that made up the overwhelming bulk of the population.

World War II was a catalyst for change in Indochina. Although the Vichy government of defeated France retained nominal control of its Southeast Asian territory throughout the war, it could project no power there. Japan required the French administration to cease sending supplies to unoccupied China in 1940. It soon signed an agreement with France recognizing continuing French sovereignty in return for the right to station troops and move them freely throughout Indochina. The Japanese allowed French adminstrators to function throughout the war without imposing excessive demands. In effect, French Indochina became a Japanese protectorate.

As the war neared its end, Japan changed policy. In March 1945, it deposed the French governor and declared an independent united Vietnam state composed of Cochin China, Annam, and Tonkin. It also declared Cambodia and Laos as separately independent. Aware of impending defeat, the Japanese wanted to make French return as difficult as possible. In this they were successful.

Vietnamese independence. Under agreement by the Allied powers at a postwar conference in Potsdam, Germany, Chinese Nationalist troops were allowed to occupy Tonkin following Japanese surrender. For administering the region, the Kuomintang government of Chiang Kai-shek favored the Viet Minh political group based in Kunming. This body of Vietnamese exiles had already developed an underground network in Japanese-occupied Indochina. The Chinese believed them to be a native nationalist group that would further China's interests in weakening French influence in the north. They were unaware that its leader, Ho Chi Minh, was a devout Communist intent upon socialist revolution as much as Vietnamese independence. To the unhappiness of the French, the Chinese organized elections in the Red River Delta region, which the Viet Minh easily won. Ho Chi Minh became the legitimate head of government in the north.

To the south, British forces accepted Japanese surrender in Cochin China and Annam. They facilitated a quick return of French authority, against which, as in the north, strong opposition had developed. It required several months for French troops to pacify the Mekong Delta countryside.

To minimize opposition to its rule, France proposed to reorganize its Southeast Asian possessions into a self-governing Indochina Federation within the broader French Community. Ho Chi Minh accepted formation of the federal unit in return for France's provisional recognition of his authority in the north. His government had to acknowledge French reassertion of direct control over Cochin China, however.

Little cooperation ensued between the French administration and Viet Minh authorities, and hostilities broke out between them at the end of 1946. The French were able to establish authority over towns in the north, but the Viet Minh successfully denied them the countryside, using political techniques developed by the Chinese Communists to convert the peasantry under Mao Tse-tung. The Viet Minh gathered strength during 1949, following Communist victory in China. Ho Chi Minh proclaimed his Democratic Republic of Vietnam (DRV) as the only true government of the country. The DRV was soon recognized by China, the USSR, and other Communist states. The Viet Minh began receiving substantial quantities of weapons and other aid from the Communist bloc.

France wearied under burdens of the struggle. The costs in funds and manpower to maintain its presence in Southeast Asia placed severe limitations on its own recovery after World War II. It turned to America for assistance. The United States had adopted a world strategy of containment of communism, and this had already brought it into war in Korea. France was able successfully to portray its war to maintain colonial authority as a struggle of the Vietnamese people against the export of communism from China. To accomplish this, it reached agreement with the figurehead emperor of Vietnam for creation of Vietnam as an "associated state" with France, having nominal independence. America recognized the arrangement in 1950.

The Viet Minh conducted guerrilla warfare throughout Vietnam for several more years. In 1954, contending sides in Korea and Vietnam agreed to participate in a peace conference in Geneva. On the eve of the talks, the Viet Minh achieved a brilliant encirclement of the strategic Vietnamese town of Dien Bien Phu, defended by 15,000 French troops. Surrender of the French garrison occurred on the day that talks in Geneva began.

Two months later, as a result of the negotiations, a cease-fire was declared. Although the French and Viet Minh governments signed the accord, the local government in southern Viet Nam and the government of the United States did not, citing strong reservations about terms in the agreement. The accord established a provisional military demarcation line in the vicinity of the 17°N parallel. The resultant Viet Minh area covered 77,000 square miles and had a population of 12,000,000. French-supported Vietnam retained an area of 50,000 square miles and contained a population of 10,000,000.

The French and Viet Minh agreed to pull back forces from the line and to permit free movement of people across it for 300 days. During that period more than 800,000 Vietnamese moved from the north to the south. Most were Roman Catholics. An additional 10,000 ethnic Chinese also journeyed southward. In the reverse direction, some 90,000 Viet Minh supporters trekked to northern Viet Nam.

Although the cease-fire terms were announced as a temporary measure in preparation for statewide democratic elections, both sides immediately proceeded to consolidate their territories into separate states. The north established a socialist economic and political system modelled after the USSR and China. In the south, the government suppressed not only Communists but also the Cao-Dai and Hoa Hao religious groups, which had organized their own militias. The south Vietnamese broke formal ties to France, ending "associated state" linkages with the French Community. They deposed the traditional emperor and declared establishment of an independent Republic of Viet Nam. The United States supported the new government by sending aid and military advisers to create and train a modern army.

Guerrilla fighting resumed by Communist insurgents in the south in 1959 and continued for more than a decade. The United States became increasingly involved, eventually sending massive amounts of materiél and troops. It engaged in massive bombing of the north in an unsuccessful attempt to reduce the flow of troops and supplies to southern insurgent areas. The long period of fighting created severe domestic problems for all protagonists. At length, protracted peace negotiations in Paris led to an accord in 1973 in which the United States agreed to remove its troops and the Communists conceded recognition of the legitimacy of the southern regime.

Skirmishes continued in the south, however. In 1975 a renewed offensive from the north resulted in rapid conquest of southern provinces. Within four months, Saigon had fallen. The war finally ended and the Viet Minh goal of a united Vietnamese state was achieved, though at a cost of thirty years of continuous fighting and the loss of millions of lives.

Fighting did not end in 1975, however. Successful Communist insurgents in Cambodia, citing long-standing territorial claims, invaded Viet Nam. The superior Vietnamese forces soon defeated the Cambodians, but continual guerrilla attacks resulted in Vietnam's decision to occupy all of Cambodia. China expressed its displeasure at the subjugation of a Cambodian force it had long supported by attacking border areas in northern Viet Nam. The Vietnamese responded with a surprising victory. Although fighting ended, tensions between the two Communist states remained for many years. In Cambodia, the Vietnamese found it necessary to maintain a presence for many more years, during which time they faced constant skirmishes with rebel guerrillas.

Regional difficulties remain within Vietnam. Despite imposition of a uniform set of socialist institutions, differences between northern and southern Vietnamese continue to generate frictions, aggravated by bitter memories on both sides of atrocities during the long war and harsh Viet Minh settling of debts at war's end. The Communist economic system imposed by the north did not bring a better life to the south. Increasing contact of southerners with family members who found haven in the United States and other countries has exacerbated unhappiness with the system.

Ethnic Chinese concentrated in the south have felt particularly aggrieved. The subjects of vilification and discrimination because of their past traditional role as middlemen and collaborators with the French, large numbers fled the state after the Communist victory. It is estimated that 170,000 emigrated to China in the wake of border strife following Viet Nam's invasion of Cambodia. Another 80,000 or more left southern coastal harbors by rickety ships in which they were subject to natural disasters and attacks by Southeast Asian pirates. Many sailed north to Hong Kong, where British authorities interned them permanently in dismal, isolated camps. As a consequence of Chinese flight, their numbers in Vietnam dropped to under 2 percent of the population.

In addition to north/south sectionalism and disaffection of the Chinese minority, the Vietnamese government, like its counterparts elsewhere in Southeast Asia, faces discontent from tribal groups living in the hills and mountains above the delta lands and coastal strip. A variety of peoples eke out subsistence livings in the marginal conditions of the upland forests. They are collectively known to the West by their French designation *Montagnards* ("mountaineers"). Vietnamese generally term them *moi* ("savages").

They tend to differ racially from Vietnamese, generally having darker skins. The ancestors of most hill peoples migrated from southern China over the past 600 years. Others are of Malay origin, including the Chams and Khmers. Their forebears formerly occupied fertile delta lands, but were driven into the uplands by migrating Vietnamese. Most groups have animist religious beliefs, although many were converted to Protestant faiths by missionaries from America and Europe. Antipathy toward the dominating Vietnamese is long-standing. During the protracted war in Vietnam, many hill tribes actively assisted American forces in gathering intelligence and attacking Viet Minh supply routes. Tribal peoples particularly resent the recent movement of more than a million Vietnamese into their hillside homelands.

Vietnam has minor border disputes with its neighbors. At least one of these has potential for a major escalation. Between Vietnam and Borneo lie the Spratly Islands, a collection of 105 reefs and atolls claimed by several Southeast Asian states. Their significance lies in supposed quantities of undersea petroleum and natural-gas reserves. Vietnam considers them a part of its continental shelf. The People's Republic of China claims the islands as a result of Chinese assertions of authority dating to the fourteenth century. In 1992 it signed a contract with an American firm to explore underseas resources in the archipelago. The Republic of China government on Taiwan, using the same argument, placed its own troops on one of the Spratlys. Malaysia similarly has a presence on three of the islands, and the Philippines has outposts on eight. Brunei also maintains that several of the islands belong to it. In 1988 Vietnam fought a mainland Chinese naval contingent putting troops ashore on six of the islands, resulting in a number of lost lives.

Laos

To the northwest of Vietnam is the People's Democratic Republic of Laos, with an area of 91,000 square miles and a population of 4,000,000. Its inhabitants are rather evenly divided between the titular people, the Lao, and approximately seventy tribal groups concentrated in uplands of the country. Indeed, a generally recognized altitudinal zonation of peoples exists. River valleys of the Mekong River and its tributaries are mainly inhabited by Lao. On slopes up to heights of 3,500 feet elevation are the so-called Mountainside Laotians, accounting for about half the hill people. They speak a variety of Mon-Khmer languages related to Cambodian and are considered descendants of early inhabitants who had been driven into the mountains by migration of the Lao from southern China in the thirteenth century. Above the 3,500-foot contour line are the Meo, who are recent arrivals from China. They began to appear after 1840 and found available lands only in the higher elevations.

The Lao had created an ancient kingdom for themselves in the Yunnan region of China. Kublai Khan, China's Mongol emperor, conquered it in 1253, and a large proportion of its population fled southward along the Mekong River. They are a prominent part of the Tai peoples who presently can be found in a band stretching from Burma to Hainan Island off China. Ethnically, they are identical to the population of northeastern Thailand, who exceed the numbers of Lao in Laos itself. Unlike the similar Vietnamese, the culture of the Lao developed an orientation to South Asia, rather than to China. Through contact with native Mons and Khmers they accepted Theravada Buddhism and the Indian style of writing.

In the mid-fourteenth century, the Lao founded a kingdom that lasted until the end of the seventeenth century, when it broke up into three separate states. A smaller Laotian kingdom also formed in an adjacent hill region. These four entities came under competing influences from Siam and Vietnam, and at times paid nominal tribute to both. Siam conquered one of the kingdoms in the early nineteenth century, and expanded into two others in the 1880s. Vietnam annexed the fourth kingdom in 1885. Only the northern Lao kingdom of Luang Prabang remained independent by the end of the century, and Siam had seized most of its former territory.

Siam's announced rationale for its nineteenth-century conquests was to suppress Chinese bandits operating in the area. Its motivations, however, clearly were to counter French territorial expansion from bases established in the Mekong and Red River deltas. France recognized Siamese suzerainty in the Laotian territories conquered by Siam. However, in 1893 the French sent diplomatic representatives to Luang Prabang. These emissaries successfully urged its king to request establishment of a French protectorate. From its newly gained foothold in northern Laos, France successfully pressed Siam to withdraw to its old Mekong River boundary with the Laotian states. The French allowed Siam to annex substantial Lao-inhabited areas west of the Mekong River, however.

France proceeded to unite the territories of the former Laotian kingdoms into a single governmental unit. It designated its new protectorate as Laos, the first time that name had been used. France ruled Laos indirectly, maintaining the traditional authority of local elite groups. Only seventy French administrators lived throughout Laos at the turn of the twentieth century. Often France used Vietnamese administrators to direct local Lao officials. The only major colonial problem of the French in Laos before World War II was suppression of an uprising by the Meo people, rebelling against France's termination of their traditional slave trade.

Laos, like other parts of French Indochina, fell under Japanese control in World War II. When Japan withdrew in 1945, Laotian nationalists declared formation of an independent state. French forces soon returned and forced leaders of the independence movement to flee to Thailand. In 1947, France made Laos a constitutional monarchy under the royal family of Luang Prabang, and two years later it recognized Laotian independence within the French Community. France and Laos signed a treaty in 1953 recognizing the full independence of Laos.

However, Laos immediately found itself involved in the struggles wracking the rest of former French

Indochina. Dissident Laotians formed a "Pathet Lao" ("Lao State") rebel movement based in Vietnam. They were able to seize up to half the territory and a quarter of the population of Laos in the eastern hills and mountains. Across this area the Viet Minh supplied insurgents in South Vietnam by a route from North Vietnam that came to be known as the Ho Chi Minh trail.

Communist, anticommunist, and neutralist forces contended for power in Laos in a complex series of civil disturbances. The Pathet Lao was supported by men and materiél from North Vietnam, while the royalist government was aided by mercenaries from Thailand and by bombing attacks of the United States Air Force. At length, in 1973, fighting ceased, with an agreement to form a coalition government representing all sides. However, two years later, following Communist victories in Vietnam and Cambodia, the Pathet Lao took control of the state and proclaimed it the People's Democratic Republic of Laos.

Cambodia

Vietnam, Laos, and Thailand border on the troubled state of Cambodia. Its regime officially styled itself the Republic of Kampuchea until 1989, when it adopted "State of Cambodia" as its official designation. Both names are derived from local pronounciation of "Kambuja," a Sanskrit name of a northern Indian kingdom long ago embraced by regimes of Khmer peoples in the lower Mekong region. The term reflects the long-standing cultural ties of this and other parts of Southeast Asia with Indian civilization, although the peninsula has never been conquered and made a part of a South Asian state.

Cambodia occupies an area of 70,000 square miles, with about 9,000,000 inhabitants. Some 94 percent of these are Khmers, a name used interchangeably with Cambodians. Among the remainder, half are ethnic Chinese. They are descendants of immigrants who dominated local commerce long before establishment of French colonial control. Other minorities include a variety of hill people in the northeastern uplands. They are known collectively as the Khmer Leou, although most share neither the language nor the Theravada Buddhist religion of the dominant Khmers. Another group are the Chams, a formerly Buddhist people who fled to Cambodia in the fifteenth century, following destruction of their own kingdom along the South China Sea by advancing Vietnamese. Chams in Cambodia adopted Islam as a faith. Before establishment of the harsh Khmer Rouge regime of the 1970s, Chams lived scattered in separate communities of their own in many parts of Cambodia.

The Chinese recorded a Khmer state in the delta of the Mekong River as early as the second century A.D. It gave way in the fifth century to a more dynamic Khmer political entity centered around the Tonle Sap ("Great Lake") in the lower Mekong Valley. The new state projected its political authority well into territories of modern Thailand, Laos, and Vietnam. Khmers absorbed a number of South Asian cultural characteristics through contact with Indian merchants, political emissaries, and religious figures. These included governmental institutions and the use of Sanskrit as a written language, using an alphabet based on models from India. Khmers also became Hinayana Buddhists.

Like other indigenous peoples of Southeast Asia, Khmers felt pressures, beginning in the thirteenth century, from migrants from southern China fleeing devastation wrought by the troops of Kublai Khan. Into northern and western parts of the Khmer realm came the Tai peoples, ancestors of modern Laotians and Thais. On the northeastern flank moved the Viets. Tais captured and sacked the Khmer capital of Angkor in 1431. Thereafter, Cambodia never regained its greatness. Over ensuing centuries it lost most of its territory to Siam and Vietnam, leaving only a rump kingdom in the vicinity of Phnom Penh. Thai rulers viewed Cambodians as unnecessarily troublesome fellow Buddhist subjects, whereas the Sinicized Viets tended to look upon Cambodians as barbarians.

By the mid-nineteenth century, the last remnant of the Cambodian kingdom was on the verge of being partitioned between Siam and Vietnam. It was saved by France, which forcibly made it a protectorate in 1863. The French action was motivated by a desire for access up the Mekong River to China and by pressures to come to the rescue of Cambodian converts to Roman Catholicism, who were subject to increasing persecution by the local Cambodian king.

France made Cambodia a part of its Indochina Union in 1887. To a great extent, the French utilized Vietnamese to administer Cambodia. They also allowed Chinese merchants to continue to dominate commerce in the protectorate. In 1907, France forced Siam to return the Khmer-inhabited provinces of Battambang and Siemreab to Cambodia. Under French colonial rule, Cambodia saw construction of a modern infrastructure, including modernization of the region's Mekong River irrigation system. It became a major surplus rice-producing region. Members of elite families also grew familiar with the world outside Cambodia. Many of their offspring studied in France, where they were exposed to political trends current in Europe.

German defeat of France in 1940 weakened the mother country's power throughout the empire. Emboldened by the situation, Siam, which had renamed itself Thailand, invaded Cambodia in early 1941. It sought return of the provinces relinquished at the turn of the century. French colonial forces initially were able to repulse Siamese forces and to inflict defeat on the Thai navy. However, French Indochina had come under Japanese military domination, and Japan decided to force the French to cede the disputed lands to Thailand.

As in Vietnam and Laos, the last stages of the war saw Japan deposing the French administrators and encouraging young Cambodian King Sihanouk to proclaim independence in 1945. Following Japanese surrender, British forces moved in and facilitated French resumption of control. The French faced continuing guerrilla opposition to their return, however. In an attempt to defuse anticolonial feelings, France, in 1946, granted Cambodia a new self-governing constitution that allowed political parties to operate for the first time. The French also secured return of Cambodia's lost provinces from Thailand. As France became immersed in deeper troubles with insurgency in adjacent Vietnam, Sihanouk put increasing pressures upon the French that resulted in complete Cambodian independence in 1953.

Economic and political problems multiplied in Cambodia during the ensuing decade. A strong underground Communist movement developed, and rebellions broke out among rice farmers in the provinces regained from Thailand and among tribal groups in the northeastern uplands. Heavy taxation fueled the farmers' revolt. Minorities rebelled against policies of forced labor, assimilation, and resettlement. Their lands provided a safe haven for the Communists, who became known as the Khmer Rouge.

After a decade of announced nonalignment with either Western or Eastern powers, Sihanouk's regime began to seek accommodation with China and North Vietnam. This provoked a political reaction that resulted in Sihanouk's deposition in 1970. The new regime encouraged latent Cambodian anti-Vietnamese feelings, which culminated in major massacres of immigrants and refugees from Vietnam. The regime also set about to drive Viet Minh insurgent forces out of Cambodia, although its own military proved no match for the battle-tested Vietnamese. American and South Vietnamese troops at this time invaded Cambodia to eliminate insurgent sanctuaries. The Viet Minh responded by giving modern military training to Khmer Rouge guerrillas, who soon were able to dominate as much as half the area of Cambodia.

This set in motion the worst period in Cambodia's history. The withdrawal of a defeated America from Southeast Asia in 1975 and the internal weakness and corruption of the Cambodian regime permitted the Khmer Rouge to seize power quickly. Embracing a primitive Communist ideology, it set about to "purify" Cambodian society of foreign influences. The new regime deported the entire urban population of Cambodia to hastily established collective farms, where a high proportion died under the privations. Teachers, doctors, and others with Western educations were executed. The Khmer Rouge waged a merciless attack on religions. It defrocked the large number of Buddhist monks and sent them to forced labor brigades. It defaced and dumped statues of the Buddha and burned to the ground temples, pagodas, mosques, and churches.

Despite past assistance from the Viet Minh, the Khmer Rouge adopted an anti-Vietnamese stance even stronger than its predecessor regime. It murdered or drove out any Vietnamese settlers who had remained in Cambodia. It also persecuted the Thai and Cham minorities, requiring them to speak only the Khmer language. At least 40,000 Chams were killed. It appears that the Khmer Rouge did not inflict similar atrocities upon the northeast hill peoples that earlier had given them sanctuary. Indeed, it had become a badge of honor for Communist leaders to take members of Khmer Leou tribes as wives.

The Khmer Rouge stayed in power for forty-four months. During this time the population of Cambodia dropped from 7,000,000 to 4,000,000 inhabitants. An invasion by now-Communist Vietnam at the end of 1978 ended Khmer Rouge control. The Vietnamese regime had become increasingly antagonized by Cambodian actions, including massacres of Vietnamese and border incursions into the Mekong Delta region. The Cambodian capital fell after seventeen days of fighting. Victorious Vietnamese installed a puppet regime and set about bringing order to the now devastated country.

Peace did not come to Cambodia for many years, however. Although the Vietnamese had driven the Khmer Rouge from power, it had not destroyed their forces. For the next fifteen years the Communists maintained a power base in remote parts of the state and engaged in continuous guerrilla activity. Two other anti-Vietnamese insurgent forces also developed in Cambodia, both also anti-Khmer Rouge. One rallied around Sihanouk, while the other saw Sihanouk as a leading cause of Cambodia's problem. The Khmer Rouge received weapons and support from China, which saw this force as useful harassment against an increasingly hostile Vietnamese regime. European and American governments gave aid to the other insurgent groups.

As the situation among world powers changed during the 1980s, the four groups contending for control of Cambodia found themselves receiving substantially less support from their benefactors. The USSR, weakened economically and politically, reduced its aid to Vietnam, which, in turn, found its venture in Cambodia increasingly costly of scarce resources. China grew less concerned that Vietnam and its puppet regime in Cambodia had become Soviet client states intended to encircle and weaken China. It accordingly reduced its support for the Khmer Rouge. America and its allies came to view Vietnam as far less of a threat to their interests in Southeast Asia and urged their proxy forces to find some means of accommodation with other contending groups.

The result was negotiation that led to convening of an international conference on Cambodia in Paris during 1989. The conference was attended by representatives of nineteen states and the four rival Cambodian factions. Although that event foundered, the factions eventually hammered out an agreement that took effect in the spring of 1992. Fighting halted, and large numbers of refugees began returning from camps established across the Thai border. The participation of Khmer Rouge representatives in the new coalition government cast a pall among most Cambodians, however. Despite that group's renunciation of Communism, the Khmer Rouge continues to be seen as the unrepentant cause of the greatest disaster ever to befall the Khmer people.

The Malay Realm

In comparison with the five peninsular states of Southeast Asia, its five island states—Malaysia, Singapore, Indonesia, Brunei, and the Philippines—have witnessed far more control of their destinies by outside powers (Table 11-2). All three early were recipients of cultural influences from the civilizations of China and India. All three also fell under domination of European empires earlier and more thoroughly than did Southeast Asia's continental entities.

As in archipelagos and adjacent mainland areas elsewhere, the sea served much more as a linking than a dividing force in insular Southeast Asia. Merchants, missionaries, warriors, and refugees could all easily move across shared seas. A common Malay culture disseminated throughout the region, comparable to the Greek civilization dispersed across eastern Mediterranean islands and shorelines and the English-speaking black societies of the Caribbean.

While contact among islanders was frequent, it was not constant. An originally common Malay language evolved into hundreds of local tongues, as vast empty zones of water or tropical rain forest insulated areas of settlement from each other. Enough linguistic similarities remained, however, for traders and administrators to communicate with most peoples through simplified pidgin vernaculars. In modern times, the regime of Indonesia has experienced little difficulty in establishing a new, Malay-based common language among its otherwise diverse inhabitants.

Cultural innovations easily diffused throughout the region. More efficient types of domesticated animals and crops spread to even remote islands. Contacts with India brought Hinduism, and then Islam, to a majority of settled zones. Political power travelled effortlessly across water. A grand Hindu empire, Madjapahit, evolved in the thirteenth century, embracing much of the insular realm. It was succeeded by lesser Muslim sultanates, many of which controlled a number of islands.

European colonialism is responsible for the present political organization of territory. As occurred in the twentieth-century Middle East, foreign powers partitioned among themselves a generally homogeneous and coherent region. For more than three centuries, competing empires introduced and propagated separate cultures and institutions in their respective areas. Random events determined colonial boundaries, which bore virtually no relation to any indigenous discontinuities in culture and economy. Past Dutch, British, Spanish, and American imperial domination shaped contemporary native perceptions and outlooks. Even the minor but long-lasting Portuguese role in East Timor resulted in a local society at odds with all its neighbors.

Each empire impressed its own second language, form of administration, and standard operating procedures upon dependent territories. The Muslim faith, which barely preceded European entry into the islands, did prove resistant to inroads by European Christianity, as it had in North Africa. However, the Spanish succeeded in converting predominantly animist peoples in the Philippines to Roman Catholicism, aside from Moros of the Sulu Archipelago, who already had been reached by Islamic missionaries.

Despite discussions by nationalist leaders near the end of the imperial epoch concerning possible polical confederation of Malaysian, Indonesian, and Philippine territories, each of the former colonial realms elected to have its own separate independence. Earlier, Japanese occupation forces had found it virtually impossible to unite Dutch Sumatra with British Malaya, despite a common Malay language, Muslim religion, and history of association. On a more positive note, each of the collections of insular territories was able to remain intact as a state, in contrast to the the breakup of French West Africa and the ill-fated British planned Federation of the Rhodesias and Nyasaland.

Malaysia and Singapore

The state of Malaysia has an area of 125,000 square miles, of which 51,000 consists of the Malay Peninsula.

TABLE 11.2 INSULAR SOUTHEAST ASIA

Like the peninsular states of Southeast Asia, the region's island realm also has served as a frontier among Indian and Chinese civilizations and as a zone of competition among European powers. Because of ease of connection by sea, the region did not develop into several isolated, particularist states as did the mainland. However, European colonialism superimposed differences that have frustrated modern attempts at unity. The three larger states suffer threats of regional separation.

State	Total Population	Area (sq. miles)	Distinctive Features of Group
Malaysia	19,000,000	125,000	
Dominant Nation and % Total			
Malays, 47%			Malay-Polynesian (Malay) language, Sunni Muslim
Significant Regional Groups and % Total			
Paleo-Malays, 9%			Malay-Polynesian (Kadazan et al.) languages, Animist
Chinese (30%) and East Indians (8%) constitute significant minorities, but are not segregated regionally			
Potential Trouble Areas and Possible Adversaries			
Sabah	1,500,000	28,000	
(Philippines, Indonesia)			
Sarawak (Indonesia)	1,700,000	48,000	
Singapore	2,800,000	225	
Dominant Nation and % Total			
Chinese, 78%			Sino-Tibetan (Mandarin, Hakka, Cantonese, et al.) languages
Brunei	275,000	2,200	
Dominant Nation and % Total			
Brunei Malays, 68%			Malay-Polynesian (Malay) language, Shafeite Muslim
Indonesia	185,000,000	780,000	
Dominant Nation and % Total			
Javanese, 40%			Malay-Polynesian (Javanese) language, Sunni Muslim
Significant Regional Groups and % Total			
Sundanese, 15%			Malay-Polynesian (Sundanese) language, Sunni Muslim
Madurese, 5%			Malay-Polynesian (Madurese) language, Sunni Muslim
Balinese, 1%			Malay-Polynesian (Balinese) language, Hindu
South Moluccans, <1%			Malay-Polynesian (Ambonese) language, Protestant and Sunni Muslim
Eastern Timorese, <1%			Malay-Polynesian (Tetun) language, Roman Catholic
Papuans, <1%			Papuan languages, Animist
Philippines	64,000,000	115,000	
Dominant Nation and % Total			
Filipinos, 84%			Malay-Polynesian (Tagalog, Visayan, et al.) languages, Roman Catholic
Significant Regional Groups and % Total			
Moros, 4%			Malay-Polynesian (Maranao, Sulu Samal et al.) languages, Sunni Muslim

Its remaining territory of East Malaysia (Sarawak and Sabah) is situated on the large island of Kalimantan (Borneo). Four-fifths of its population of 18,000,000 is concentrated in the so-called Straits Settlements region of the southeastern peninsula. The Malaysian population is of mixed heritage. Some 47 percent are Malays in language and culture. An additional 9 percent, mainly in East Malaysia, speak related languages and are identified as Paleo-Malays. More than 30 percent are Chinese, and 8 percent are East Indians. Singapore is a small island of

225 square miles adjacent to the Malay Peninsula's south coast. Three quarters of its 2,800,000 inhabitants are Chinese, 15 are Malays, and 6 percent are Indian.

The location of the Malay Peninsula adjacent to the Strait of Malacca led to early contacts with seafarers from both India and China. Indian merchants are reported to have been there in the fourth century A.D. They particularly sought the tin found in Malaya's river gravels, which Indians used for making religious artifacts.

Commerce with India was accompanied by cultural influences from the subcontinent. Traders intermarried with local ruling families. Their families adopted the Hindu religion and, later, its reformed faith of Buddhism. The community of Palembang became reknowned as a religious studies center. Still later, Islam came to Malaya from India.

Wealth from Indian trade contributed to the development of strong native states. The earliest local powers were centered to the south of Malaya, on the island of Sumatra. By the fifteenth century, the state of Malacca on the peninsula had come to dominate the entire Straits region. Chinese began to take interest in the region in the twelfth century and negotiated a protectorate over Malacca in 1405. They established a regularized system of tribute collection. Their naval expeditions ventured far beyond the Straits, ultimately reaching the coast of Africa.

Portuguese ships appeared early in the sixteenth century. Naval superiority allowed Portugal to break the Muslim monopoly of the sea lanes. In 1511 the Portuguese captured Malacca itself, supported by their Indian base at Goa, which had been established just the year before. Portugal was motivated by desires both for trade and for Christianization of the local population. Malacca continued to flourish under Portuguese control, but commercial rivals appeared, with a Muslim state at Johore on the eastern part of the Peninsula and a new kingdom on Sumatra.

The Dutch appeared in the region in the following century, having broken away from Spanish control in 1579. Their superior ships defeated the Portuguese naval units, whose effectiveness had been weakened when Portugal became part of Spain. Dutch merchants began trading in Malayan ports in 1595. In 1602 they formed the Dutch East India Company and soon drove the Portuguese out of their islands trading posts, capturing Malacca in 1641.

Toward the end of the eighteenth century the British, through the British East India Company, began challenging the Dutch trading monopoly in the Straits and Indonesia. In 1786 they founded their own commercial base on the island of Penang, adjacent to the peninsula. It soon eclipsed Malacca in size and volume of trade. The British also established plantations that raised pepper and spices.

Following Napoleon's occupation of the Netherlands, the Dutch, in 1795, consented to British occupation of their East Indian possessions, including Malacca. The Dutch government resumed control over the Indonesian possessions after Napoleon's defeat, but the United Kingdom retained Malacca. In 1819 a British presence in Singapore was established by Thomas Stamford Raffles to protect British India from the east. It immediately became a major commercial center, paying for costs of its development within a year. The British also extended authority over the rest of Malaya by signing treaties with native sultans.

British separation of the peninsula from Dutch control created a schism within what had been a homogeneous Muslim Malay culture world. Despite similarities in language and religion, the two colonial successor states, Malaysia and Indonesia, developed too many cultural and institutional differences to come together in the postimperial era.

One of the major differences between the two realms was the greater influx of Chinese and Indians into British Malaya. Chinese laborers began arriving on the peninsula at the end of the eighteenth century to work as tin miners. More came after 1900 to labor in the new rubber plantations, which had been established after the smuggling of *Heavea braziliensis* seeds from Brazil. The British recruited Chinese, and also South Indians, after native Malays showed little interest in regimented plantation life.

Most Malays continued a traditional agricultural subsistence existence. Nearly all were Muslim. Under the British policy of indirect rule, most continued to live under the traditional authority of native sultans. However, the introduction of secular education by the British led to an increasing Malay sense of national identity during the twentieth century.

The British administrative system was quite complex and contributed to subsequent Malaysian problems of unity after independence. The British East India Company administered Penang and Singapore following their founding. They remained under British Indian authority until 1867, when they were constituted into the Crown colony of the Straits Settlements. That unit also included a strip of coast named Province Wellesley and the island of Labuan off the coast of Borneo. By the twentieth century, the Straits Settlements population predominantly consisted of immigrant Chinese and Indians, with native Malays a minority.

Mixed populations also increasingly characterized the native Malayan sultanates. In 1896 the British organized nine of them into a unit termed the Federated Malay States. Siam ceded four states to the United

Kingdom in 1909—Kedah, Perlis, Kelantan, and Trengganu. They, together with Johore, which had resisted incorporation in the 1896 federation, officially were designated Non-Federated States, and had more direct control of local affairs.

The British also developed a presence in Borneo during the nineteenth century. The sultan of Brunei in 1841 rewarded an English adventurer, James Brooke, with the gift of the territory of Sarawak for suppressing a rebellion in his realm by Dyak tribesmen. Five years later, the sultan ceded the island of Labuan off the coast to the United Kingdom, which used it as a base to clear the Borneo coast of pirates. In 1865, a private syndicate received authority from the Brunei sultan to develop the region now known as Sabah. Sarawak and Brunei, like the native states on the Malay Peninsula, became British protectorates in 1888.

British possessions in Malaya and Borneo were profoundly affected by Japanese occupation during World War II. Particularly damaging to future communal relations was Japanese encouragement of Malay antagonisms toward the Chinese. The Japanese treated Malaya's Chinese population harshly. Many young Chinese fled to the jungles, where they formed a resistance movement they called the Malayan People's Anti-Japanese Army. The Japanese used Malay police to attack the Chinese guerrillas. The Indian community in Malaya at first received cautious treatment. Later, it had to bear the brunt of Japanese forced labor, and their numbers dwindled.

Unlike other European colonies in Southeast Asia, Japanese-occupied Malaya did not receive a grant of "independence" in the closing months of the war. Nevertheless, the Japanese treated the peninsula as the rightful homeland of the Malays, and this contributed to a general mood of Malay nationalism and anticolonialism when the British returned in 1945.

The newly installed Labour government of the United Kingdom proposed a revamping of the hodgepodge of colonial areas that had emerged in Malaya over the preceding century. In 1946 it presented a plan for a Malayan Union that would end the sovereignty of each sultanate and give citizenship to members of the Chinese community. The proposed union received little support from Malays, who protested against loss of their sultans' powers and any concessions to the Chinese. The British dropped the plan. However, they did make Singapore a Crown colony separate from the other Straits Settlements. In that same year they also made Crown colonies of Sarawak and British North Borneo, renaming the latter simply North Borneo. It was renamed Sabah in 1963.

The United Kingdom implemented a new reorganization plan in 1948, creating a Federation of Malaya consisting of nine component states and two "settlements." It also increased powers of the Muslim sultans and permitted Chinese and Indians to acquire citizenship, but less than one-third could qualify. In 1957 the Federation of Malaya became self-governing.

During the immediate postwar years Malaya was continuously subjected to terrorist activities by the Malayan Races Liberation Army. The MRLA was, in fact, 99 percent Chinese and represented a continuation of the Chinese guerrilla organization that had gone to the jungle to harass the Japanese. The terrorists had adopted Marxism as an ideology and committed themselves to end the British colonial presence in Malaya. The British military resolutely tracked down the guerrillas, whose strength ebbed by 1954. The government announced an end to the state of emergency in 1960.

Although the United Kingdom was able to end the insurrection, it was sensitive to its position as the last colonial power in Southeast Asia. It also was quite aware of potentials for ethnic conflict that would face an independent Malaya. In 1963 the British set about creating a viable political entity for the region. Because barely a quarter of the population of its Borneo territories was Chinese, the United Kingdom saw inclusion of Sabah and Sarawak in a broad Malaysian Federation as a means of diluting the Chinese majority that had emerged on the peninsula. Oil-rich Brunei opted for separate independence and unsuccessfully pressed the British to attach Sabah and Sarawak to itself.

The British independence plan drew immediate objections from the neighboring Philippine Islands and Indonesia. Both earlier had been involved in inconclusive discussions with Malay leaders toward possible creation of a "Maphilindo" confederation of the three territories.

The government of the Philippines was mainly concerned about the future of Sabah, which it claimed as its own territory by being heir to the Sultanate of Sulu. The dispute dates to the end of the seventeenth century, when a contender in a civil war in Brunei promised Sabah to the sultan in return for aid. It is not clear whether the sultan actually received the land as a grant or simply seized it. Sabah remained nominally under control of the sultanate of Sulu until 1878, when the British acquired it by treaty. The Philippines government maintains that the sultan only leased it to the British and did not sell it.

Indonesia denounced the entire independence proposal as a "neocolonialist plot" intended to permit continuing British control of the region. Its position probably reflected growing problems within Indonesia itself. The centripetal "glue" of anti-Dutch colonialism, which had held the disparate islands together in the immediate postwar years, no longer was a strong binding force.

This was particularly true after Indonesia finally gained the Netherlands' last East Indian possession of western New Guinea (West Irian) in 1962. Economic and political problems beset Indonesia, including full-scale rebellions in outer islands. Many interpret Indonesia's "massive confrontation" against the neocolonialism of Malaysia as a cynical ploy ordered by its president to divert attention from misrule.

However, Indonesia did make a number of military moves, particularly along the borders of Sarawak and Sabah. The British easily suppressed all overt actions, however, and the net effect of the confrontation was to strengthen ties of northern Borneo regions with Malaya. Indonesia's stance lasted until 1966, when a military coup toppled its president.

One lasting consequence of Indonesia's actions was the fanning of ethnic tensions by the incessant anti-Chinese propaganda broadcasts to the Malays. Increasing frictions between the two groups resulted in the 1965 decision to exclude overwhelmingly Chinese Singapore as a component of the Malaysian Federation. This action did not put an end to ethnic hostility, however. Large numbers of Chinese remained in the Malay sultanates, dominating most commercial activities. Frictions led to anti-Chinese riots, most notably in Kuala Lumpur in 1969. Malays similarly gave little sympathy or support to the "boat people" refugees from Vietnam, the majority of whom were of Chinese heritage.

Malaysia and Singapore have prospered since independence. Ethnic frictions remain a perennial problem, however. In addition to tainting relations between the two states, communal tensions beset each of Malaysia's component parts. Despite the vital role they play in the economy, the Chinese feel institutionalized discrimination throughout the state. Another group resentful of the dominant Malays are Paleo-Malay tribesmen of East Malaysia. Their grievances date back to experiences under the sultanate of Brunei. The disparity in living standards between East and West Malaysia is particularly grating.

Brunei

The Sultanate of Brunei stayed out of the Malaysian Federation, becoming completely independent at the end of 1983 under terms of a treaty with the British government. The entity contains 2200 square miles and consists of two segments situated along the Borneo coast and divided and backed by Sarawak territory. Two-thirds of Brunei's population of 275,000 is Malay and one-fifth is Chinese. The remainder is classified as belonging to Paleo-Malay tribal groups. Most Malays

are Muslim and most Chinese are Buddhist. About 10 percent of the population is Christian.

Adventurers from the Malay Peninsula early established a presence on Borneo. They eventually created a kingdom that by the sixteenth century became a major power in the region, but then quickly went into decline. Although Brunei had been in contact with the Chinese since the fourteenth century, cultural influences, as in most of Southeast Asia, came mainly from India. Initially Brunei was part of the Hindu culture world, and then it became Buddhist. Islam arrived by way of Malacca to become, eventually, the dominant cultural-religious force.

After the Portuguese seized Malacca in the early sixteenth century, many Muslim merchants transfered their bases of operations to Brunei, and it became a major trading center. The British government first negotiated ties with the territory in 1751. By the mid-nineteenth century its formerly extensive lands in northern Borneo had been reduced to but a fraction of their former size. Brunei accepted British protectorate status in 1888. Subsequently, its relations to the United Kingdom were much the same as those of the Muslim sultanates in Malaya.

Geologists discovered petroleum in Brunei in 1927. Although now past its peak in output, oil has brought substantial wealth to the country. Its government has purchased a cattle station in northern Australia that is larger than Brunei itself. The oil wealth led its sultan to press the British for complete sovereignty, rather than amalgamation into Malaysia. Although small, Brunei does suffer frictions between its dominant Malays and the minority Chinese and Paleo-Malay communities.

Indonesia

The Republic of Indonesia embraces more than 6,000 islands between mainland Southeast Asia and Australia. They contain a land area of 780,000 square miles and an oceanic expanse larger than the territory of the United States of America. Four of the islands—Java, Sumatra, Borneo, and Celebes—can be classed as large, fifteen others as medium-sized, and the remainder as small. All have a tropical climate (Figure 11-3).

Indonesia's rapidly growing population approaches 185,000,000. Although 90 percent may be classed as Malay, they speak more than 250 different languages. Among these, Javanese is dominant, being native to 40 percent of the inhabitants. Sundanese, spoken by 15 percent, ranks second. The distribution of population is quite uneven. Two-thirds of Indonesia's inhabitants are concentrated on the exceptionally fertile volcanic soils

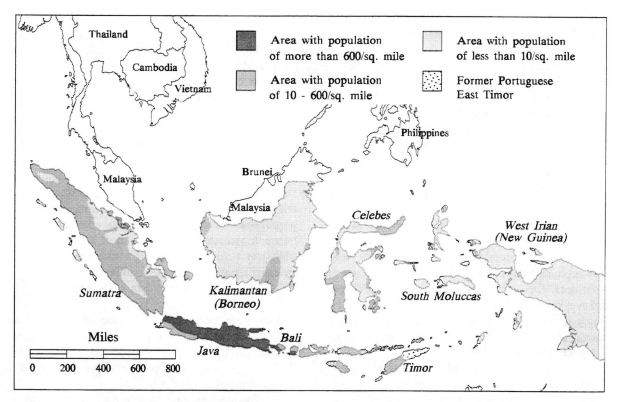

FIGURE 11-3   INDONESIA: EFFECTIVELY SETTLED REGIONS

and urban agglomerations of the island of Java, which constitutes only 10 percent of the land area. Substantial parts of the outer islands remain nonecumene.

According to census figures, 87 percent of the population is Muslim. Christians comprise 9 percent, and are dominant particularly in the South Molucca islands and Timor. Hindus number 3,500,000. Two-thirds are concentrated on the island of Bali. Chinese make up 2 percent of the population and for the most part are Buddhist.

Although most of Indonesia's early history involved struggles of tribal groups for power on individual islands, a precedent for the modern state existed in the Hindu-based empire of Madjapahit, which flourished from 1292 to 1500 and controlled a majority of Indonesia's islands. Like the contemporary state, Madjapahit's core was on Java. It disintegrated under pressures from Muslim groups and the Portuguese.

As elsewhere in both South Asia and Southeast Asia, the Dutch soon supplanted Portuguese interests. They established authority over Java in 1619 and made it the center of an extensive network of trading posts. For the next three centuries the Netherlands controlled the archipelago as one of the world's most profitable colonies. The Dutch always saw their involvement in

Indonesia as a business venture. Administration of the islands was vested in the chartered Dutch East India Company until 1798, when Napoleon's occupation of the Netherlands cut ties to the mother country. In return for British support, Dutch administrators conceded interests north of the Straits of Malacca to the United Kingdom. Following Napoleon's defeat, the Dutch transformed their remaining far-flung trading posts into a more integrated, government-administered colony.

To further Dutch interests in developing a stable, profitable plantation-based economy, they enforced peace between traditionally hostile groups. They also substantially weakened or eliminated powers of the Malay sultans within their territory and ruthlessly suppressed native rebellions against their rule. Particularly notable were uprisings in 1839, 1849, and 1888. Essentially, the Dutch pursued a divide-and-rule policy. They certainly did little to promote a sense of unity among inhabitants of the different islands.

The Dutch East Indies, like the rest of Southeast Asia, came under Japanese occupation during World War II. Japan administered the islands under differing authorities. The Japanese navy controlled Borneo and the eastern islands, while the army managed Java. Sumatra was detached from the other islands and joined with the Malay Peninsula under army control. Propaganda constantly stressed commonalities between the two populations. In doing this, the Japanese clearly were pandering to native Sumatran resentment of Java's dominance of the East Indies economy. However, the attempt to link the former British and Dutch areas proved counterproductive to Japanese interests, and separate administrations evntually were established.

As in mainland Southeast Asia, the Japanese fostered an East Indies independence movement when they saw defeat approaching. They encouraged nationalists in 1945 to establish a Republic of Indonesia that claimed inclusion of all of Borneo and the Malay Peninsula. British forces initially taking over from the Japanese did little to suppress the anticolonial movement.

When Dutch troops relieved the British, they faced well-organized supporters of independence throughout the islands. The self-proclaimed government held control over substantial parts of Java and Sumatra. At first Dutch and native representatives conducted negotiations concerning the colony's future, but widespread fighting broke out in 1947.

The government of the Netherlands at length recognized the futility of attempts to reimpose political control over the islands. The United Nations brokered a cease-fire and arranged for transfer of sovereignty at the end of 1949. The Dutch, however, insisted upon retaining possession of western New Guinea, pending some future agreement on its fate. The young state initially was established as a federated "United States of Indonesia" consisting of sixteen parts. Within a year, however, it had become a centralized, unitary state.

The preservation and maintenance of Indonesia as an intact entity over the following half century represents a major accomplishment. Like the postcolonial states of tropical Africa, the new country was an agglomeration of different peoples living in groups isolated from each other. They spoke a multitude of languages, had contrasts in religion, and exhibited substantial disparities in economic well-being. Like the islands of the Caribbean, group distinctiveness was reinforced by a mentality derived from the finite character of island existence.

Indonesia's regimes benefitted from inherited centripetal forces, and they created new ones of their own. Despite linguistic diversity, the bulk of the population shared a degree of cultural homogeneity. Most were Muslim and spoke languages belonging to a common Malay linguistic family. Their history included precedents for association. The bulk of the islands had been part of the medieval Madjapahit state. Its successor, the Dutch East Indies, had bound them together for more than three centuries, providing, among other elements of homogeneity and coherence, a common second language, uniform institutions, and a system of interisland commercial and administrative linkages.

The leadership of the young Indonesian state was assisted by general public desires to throw off colonialism. For many years it was able to keep alive the momentum of this negative commonality by constant reference to Dutch retention of western New Guinea. This binding force was lost when the Netherlands finally ceded the territory to Indonesia in 1962. Indonesian regimes, meanwhile, had adopted a "nonaligned" stance in world politics that included harsh attacks upon supposed imperialist threats from America and the United Kingdom. Beginning in 1962, it propagated, for a time, a threatening image of British "neocolonialism" in the creation of an independent Malaysia. Later, in 1965, it shifted the portrayal of an external menace to the communism of the People's Republic of China, playing upon long-standing domestic antipathies toward the Chinese community which dominated business activities throughout the islands. As a consequence of this policy, at least 80,000 mostly Chinese "Communists" were killed and hundreds of thousands more were incarcerated in camps, following an attempted coup.

The Indonesian regime introduced several more positive elements to promote popular unity. It fostered the use of an artificially created written and spoken language named "Bahasa Indonesia" ("Indonesian Language"). The new vernacular was successful largely because it was derived from the Malay linguistic family, to which most of Indonesia's languages belong. Through the schools, the government propagated an iconography celebrating common history and culture. As a national symbol the regime adopted the mythical garuda bird that was utilized on ancient Madjapahit artistic motifs. To combat parochial outlooks extant on the islands, it replaced the originally adopted sixteen ethnically based federal units by ten new provinces which notably ignored indigenous linguistic and historic regions. It also should be noted that the Indonesian regime established highly centralized institutions to maintain control over the islands, including a governmental bureaucracy, a single party, and a strong military.

Despite its many inherited and crafted binding forces, Indonesia has experienced a number of challenges to continuing territorial unity. Centrifugal forces were manifest immediately upon independence. The South Moluccan islands proclaimed separate independence in 1950. Their population was largely Christian and differed significantly in race and language from the Malay Indonesians. Many had supported Dutch forces against rebel insurgents. The South Moluccans quickly suffered defeat, and up to 40,000 refugees found their way to the Netherlands, where they remain an unassimilated minority. This group periodically has pressed the Dutch government to intervene in Indonesia to force recognition of a separate South Moluccan state. Sometimes South Moluccan pressure has taken a violent, terrorist turn. Seizures of a school and a passenger train made world headlines in the 1960s. South Moluccans in the islands did begin an armed insurrection against Indonesian forces in 1956 that was not suppressed until 1961.

Several other areas harbor bitter antagonisms toward the Indonesian government. Many inhabitants feel that Dutch colonialism simply was replaced by Javanese imperialism. They particularly resent the regime's resettlement within their home territories of millions of people from overcrowded Java. Among the disaffected are strong Islamic fundamentalist groups in the Achin area of western Sumatra, the southern portion of the island of Celebes, and the Sundanese-inhabited territory of Pasundan in western Java. Also posing a perennial problem to Indonesian regimes because of a distinctive heritage and outlook is the Hindu population concentrated on the islands of Bali and Lombok.

A long-lasting struggle that has gained international attention is Indonesia's contest with insurgents in the eastern part of the island of Timor. When Portugal lost its colonial holdings in the East Indies to the Netherlands in the seventeenth century, it retained control of a 5,600-square-mile territory located in the eastern third of Timor, maintaining it as a colony for the next three centuries. In 1974 Portugal suffered an internal revolution. Its new regime decided to terminate an empire whose costs of maintenance had become overwhelming, particularly as it vainly sought to suppress rebellion in its African territories. A struggle immediately began within Portuguese Timor between pro-Indonesian and pro-independence forces. As in the former Portuguese Indian colony of Goa, a high proportion of the population had adopted the Roman Catholic faith and saw no future as part of a Muslim state.

Indonesian forces moved into East Timor in 1975, suppressing supporters of the pro-independence Fretilin movement. The brutality of their actions galvanized East Timorans, who have maintained an active guerrilla resistance movement ever since. The fighting and accompanying famine and disease reduced the territory's population from 700,000 at the time of Indonesian annexation to a total of less than 600,000 now.

Another area in which the Indonesian regime has experienced problems in exerting effective governmental control is in West Irian (western New Guinea). Its Papuan population differs in race and culture from the Malay Indonesians. For the most part it is animist in religion, and tribal groups are known for the continuing practice of head-hunting.

In explaining their resistance to ceding western New Guinea to the Indonesians, Dutch negotiators cited the fact that the area had always been treated separately from the Dutch East Indies colony. They pointed out that the Netherlands had maintained only tenuous ties to the region, managing it indirectly through the sultan of Tidore until assuming direct control in 1872. The Dutch government had no permanent presence in western New Guinea until 1878. Dutch representatives also pointed to the low technological level of the inhabitants and their need for developmental guidance. However, it appears that a significant motivating factor on the Dutch side was a desire to provide continuing employment for the large numbers of mixed Malay-Dutch inhabitants of the East Indies, who traditionally had served in colonial administrative posts. Otherwise, most could be expected to seek haven and support in the Netherlands, which itself was still in the process of recuperating from German occupation in the period following World War II.

Although the Indonesian government continually protested Dutch retention of western New Guinea, the situation had benefitted that regime by providing a common political cause for all Indonesians during a time of severe internal difficulties. At length, however, Indonesia decided to force the issue, and it invaded western New Guinea in 1962. The Netherlands found itself without support from its allies, including the United States, and at length agreed to terminate its rule. The United Nations provided a transitional administration for a few months until Indonesia assumed control in 1963.

Under the negotiated agreement, the 800,000 inhabitants of the territory, renamed Irian Jaya (West Irian), were to be given the opportunity by 1969 to express whether or not they wanted Indonesian rule. When that year arrived, a number of disturbances occurred that were suppressed by the Indonesian military. Large numbers of local inhabitants fled to Papua New Guinea, the independent state on the eastern half of the island. Indonesia did manage to present a show of native support, but most outside observers considered it dubious. The regime has had continuing troubles throughout the area.

The Philippines

The 7,100 islands of the Republic of the Philippines are spread over approximately a half million square miles of the southwest Pacific, a region roughly equivalent to the area of Alaska. Their land area amounts to only 115,000 square miles, however, and the two main islands of Luzon and Mindanao constitute two-thirds of this total.

The islands exhibit notable demographic differences. Half the Philippine population of 64,000,000 lives on Luzon, and great inequalities in densities exist. Lowlands of central Luzon hold more than 600 inhabitants per square mile, whereas much of its outer hill country has fewer than 10. Only 850 other islands are inhabited (Figure 11-4).

Some eighty different languages are spoken on the islands. Most belong to the Malay linguistic family. The official language, Pilipino (or Tagalog), is spoken by only a quarter of the population, mostly in central Luzon. Another quarter speaks Cebuano on Cebu and adjacent islands. As in mainland Southeast Asia, hill peoples on the periphery of Luzon generally speak languages quite different from the Malay-derived languages of the dominant groups, and probably represent descendants of refugees displaced to the uplands by the arrival of immigrants.

Political organization of the islands was largely local and tribal in character until the advent of the Muslims and Spanish in the sixteenth century. Many inhabitants earlier had come into contact with traders from Indonesia, India, China, and possibly Arabia. Islam appears to have arrived in the Sulu Archipelago about 1500. The Spanish explorer Ferdinand Magellan landed in Cebu in 1521 and claimed the archipelago for Spain. A month later he was killed by a local chief.

Spain exerted control over the islands from a base in Mexico. Its first settlement was on the island of Cebu in 1565. The name Philippines is derived from Philip II, who ruled Spain from 1556 to 1598. Except in Muslim-converted areas in the south, Spaniards encountered little native resistance to their acquisition of territory. They moved their center of operations to the better-protected harbor of Manila in 1571. The colony proved of little profit to Spain, however, and it served mainly as a commercial intermediary between Mexico and China, trading Latin American silver for Chinese handicrafts.

By another measure, the Philippines proved highly successful to Spain, however. In addition to developing trade, Spaniards were motivated to acquire the islands to propagate their faith to native peoples. Through a network of missions operated by clergy known collectively as the *friars*, virtually all Filipinos became Roman Catholic. Resistance came only from the Muslim inhabitants of the Sulu Islands and Mindanao, whose descendants make up the present 4 percent Muslim minority among Filipinos. Although the friars Hispanicized the local population, for the most part they refused to teach the Spanish language to island inhabitants and otherwise treated them as inferior.

It should be noted that Spain exerted effective control over only a limited area of the Philippines. It was not able to defeat the sultans of Sulu until 1878. Much

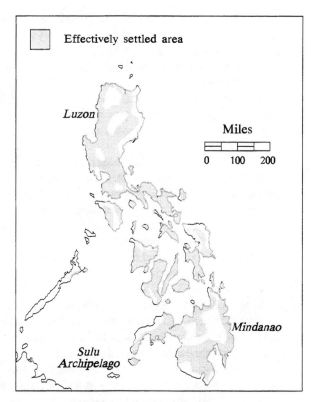

FIGURE 11-4   THE PHILIPPINE ISLANDS: ECUMENE

of the mountainous interior of islands inhabited by Igorots and other non-Malay tribes remained outside zones of activities of Spanish administrators and friars. After an uprising on the island of Bohol in 1744, a local regime was able to resist Spanish attempts at reconquest until 1829.

Over time, many Chinese came to the Philippines, at length outnumbering the Spanish inhabitants. As elsewhere in Southeast Asia, Chinese played an important middleman role in commerce. Many intermarried with local women, creating a distinctive group of Chinese mestizos who became a significant part of Philippine society. Unlike persons of mixed racial ancestry in mainland Southeast Asia, they generally were accepted by indigenous Filipinos, and most became strong Roman Catholics. Among their numbers was the famous Filipino patriot José Rizal.

Filipino intellectuals began developing a sense of national identity during the nineteenth century, led by individuals who had direct experience with political currents circulating in Europe. They grew resentful of Spain's overlordship, including Spanish contempt toward Filipinos reflected in their systematic exclusion from administrative posts and the ranks of the clergy. Another source of disaffection was the antiquated Hispanic system of land tenure. Most land came to be in large estates, comparable to the haciendas of Iberia. Ownership was vested in the friars or in a favored few Hispanicized families, while labor was performed by landless tenants.

Several ill-fated revolts against Spanish authority occurred during the nineteenth century. Particularly noteworthy was an uprising in central Luzon in 1841. Although soon suppressed, its supporters established a base in the hills around Mount San Cristobal and propagated throughout the islands an underground anti-Spanish native folk religion. Although this faith projected a vision of return to a world existing before the Spanish conquest, it did not embody the zealous political quest for self-determination characteristic of modern nationalist movements. It did provide fertile ground for Filipino nationalists returning from study in Europe. A rebellion in 1872 was precipitated by the execution of three Filipino priests. That uprising was based upon popular resentment of the domination of the Roman Catholic clergy by natives of Spain.

The United States became involved in the Philippines as a conseqence of its support of Cuban revolutionaries against Spain. In May 1898, Admiral George Dewey was instructed to destroy the Spanish fleet in Manila harbor, which he proceded to do. Filipino leaders then declared independence and prepared a constitution modelled on those of several Latin American and European states. However, under provisions of the Treaty of Paris of December 1898, the Philippines became a possession of the United States, together with Guam and Puerto Rico, while Cuba did receive its independence.

Hostilities between Filipino nationalists and American troops broke out two months later. Resistance to U.S. rule was particularly strong in the Tagalog-speaking areas of central Luzon. Fighting lasted for several years, and an estimated 200,000 peasants died from the resultant hunger and disease.

American leaders always visualized involvement in the Philippines as a preparation for independence of the islands. This was embodied in the Jones Act of 1916, which explicitly promised independence for the Philippines when a stable government had been established. Many military officers and businessmen, however, expressed attitudes toward the territory identical to those that their counterparts in Europe held toward colonies. American firms made substantial investments in developing mines and plantations in the Philippines.

An immediate consequence of American control was reinvigoration of the Roman Catholic church. It had lost popular support during the nineteenth century for its refusal to appoint Filipino priests. Under the Americans, the church was separated from the government. Subsequently, a Philippine Independent Church

appeared that had no ties to the Vatican. Between a quarter and a half of the Catholics in the Philippines flocked to the new church. The resultant pressure on the Catholic clergy caused it to undergo a counterreformation that ultimately made the church a stronger institution that won back a majority of its adherents.

Muslims in the southern Philippines posed a special problem to American authorities. Missionaries from Indonesia had brought Islam to the Sulu Archipelago, southern Palawan, and the western and southern margins of Mindanao before Spain had claimed the islands. The Spanish considered converts to Islam to be a variant of the Moors with whom their ancestors had struggled for centuries in Iberia, and they termed the Muslims "Moros." Christian and animist Filipinos feared the Muslims for their slave-raiding activities. Moros sent captured slaves to toil in forests of northern Borneo, collecting products that were traded with the Chinese.

Muslims were divided among ten different linguistic groups, each with traditional animosities toward others. Over time, three Moro sultanates emerged, comparable to those of co-religionists in Indonesia and the Malay Peninsula. The most prominent was the Sultanate of Sulu. Spain was unable to conquer the Moorish entities until late in the nineteenth century.

After America assumed Spain's mantle in the Philippines, Muslims at first remained neutral in the uprising in central Luzon that followed. However, the new regime challenged their society by insisting upon providing secular education, installing a legal system to replace the traditional Muslim shariah, and outlawing slavery. Moros soon embarked upon a guerrilla war against the Americans that was only suppressed in 1914. After the Jones Act announced America's intentions to prepare the Philippine Islands for sovereignty, Moro leaders unsuccessfully pressed for a separate independence. Subsequent American policy sought to break down further the traditional autonomy of the Muslims. There was no legal recognition of Muslim customs, and Christians from overpopulated parts of Luzon and other islands were encouraged without much success to settle in Mindanao.

After suppression of Christian and Muslim revolts against its authority, the U.S. government proceeded with a policy of economic development and political preparation of the Philippines for independence. Resistance movements continued, but they were mainly directed against perpetuation of a rural land tenure system favoring a rich ownership class that had emerged in Spanish times. In 1935 the United States granted the islands a self-governing "commonwealth" status, with an announced ten-year transition period to sovereignty.

Japan invaded the Philippines in December 1941, and it occupied Manila within a month. The last American troops surrendered on the Manila Bay island of Corregidor the following May. Japan managed the islands through a government composed of Filipino collaborators. In 1943 it declared the Philippines an independent republic. The new state had little popular support, however.

An extensive guerrilla movement developed against the Japanese, with an estimated 250,000 participants. By the end of the war, Japan controlled only a dozen of forty-eight provinces in the islands. In central Luzon the resistance was led by the People's Anti-Japanese Army, known as the Hukbalahap, or Huks after its name in Tagalog, *Hukbong Bayan Laban sa Hapon*. Its leader was a prewar Filipino Communist.

American troops landed in the Philippines in 1944, and fighting continued until Japan's capitulation in August 1945. Japanese determination to retain Manila resulted in its becoming one of the most extensively war-damaged cities in the world. An estimated million Filipinos died as a consequence of the war.

Despite the wartime disruption of the Philippine economy and political process, American leaders decided to honor the date set for independence in the 1935 act that had created the commonwealth. Accordingly, the Republic of the Philippines was proclaimed July 4, 1946. The United States government later negotiated ninety-nine-year leases to maintain twenty-six American naval and air bases on the islands, which were operated until 1991.

The young Philippine regime faced threats from insurgency, however. Chief among these was resistance of Hukbalahap veterans toward restoration of rural control by traditional landowners, most of whom bore the stigma of having collaborated with the Japanese during the war. The Communist leadership of the Huks saw an opportunity to establish a popular base for their party, whose prewar support had come only from the cities. They formed a new guerrilla organization, named the People's Liberation Army (*Hukbong Mapagpalaya ng Bayan*). Up to 15,000 armed Huks battled the Philippine military, mainly in the plains of central Luzon. The Huks alienated potential supporters by their actions. This included mistreatment of the Negrito minority, who in turn denied them sanctuary in the mountains. Huk training was less effective than that received by government forces from American instructors. Some Huks degenerated into banditry, and most suffered fatigue from being constantly on the run. The major threat to the regime posed by the Huk uprising had waned by 1954, but sporadic attacks continued for several years.

A renewed Communist attempt to seize power occurred in 1968 with the founding of an organization named the New People's Army. In contrast to their pro-Soviet predecessors, its leaders were pro-Chinese, who designated their organization as the Communist Party of the Philippines—Marxist-Leninist. The New People's Army was able to put adherents into half of the country's provinces. Its operations were mostly in remote areas, however, including southeastern and northern Luzon, eastern Mindanao, and the island of Samar. The movement withered after the Philippine government's proclamation of martial law in 1972.

Muslims in the southern Philippines continued to pose problems for the republic's leadership, as they had done for the Americans and Spanish (Figure 11-5). The Moros particularly resented the continuing flow of Christian settlers into Mindanao. In 1968 a Moro National Liberation Front was founded, with a membership that grew to more than 60,000 guerrillas by 1974. Fighting the Philippine military resulted in some 50,000 deaths and more than 100,000 Muslim refugees fleeing to Sabah. The movement received financial support from Malaysia and several Middle Eastern states, most notably Libya. Its activities weakened when assistance was reduced. The Moros gained some results from their actions when the Philippine government decided in 1976 to grant greater cultural autonomy to Muslims in an attempt to settle the growing disturbances. Periodic acts of terror continued, however.

In addition to the Moro insurgency and peasant resistance movements on Luzon, the Philippine government has had to find accommodation with the hundred or more tribal groups living in the mountains of Luzon and Mindanao in isolation from the main body of Filipinos. These tribal groups exhibit a wide range of cultural characteristics. Some have created an advanced agricultural society, responsible for impressive terracing of the hills of northern Luzon. Others, like the recently discovered Tasaday, remain in an extremely primitive stage of development.

In central Luzon the tribal peoples include ten groups who collectively are known as "Igorots" ("Mountaineers"). Their counterparts on Mindanao are known as the "Mangyan." Recent government policy has been to preserve their distinctive cultures through establishment of special areas comparable to Indian reservations in the United States. Although, like the Moros, the tribal groups do not identify with the emerging Filipino national identity, they do not pose a threat to the territorial integrity of the Philippines state, as do the Muslims.

Chinese continue to be a significant minority in the Philippines, although, as elsewhere in Southeast Asia, they are dispersed, rather than being concentrated in a distinctive territory. Most of the 700,000 Chinese on the islands have done well economically. Most Filipinos resent their success, however, which includes control of a significant share of business, newspapers, and radio and television stations on the islands. Their main-

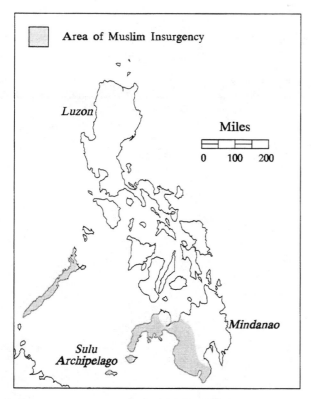

Area of Muslim Insurgency

Luzon

Miles

0 100 200

Mindanao

Sulu
Archipelago

**FIGURE 11-5 THE PHILIPPINE ISLANDS:
THE MORO REBELLION**

tenance of 120 Chinese language schools for their children also has led to charges of exclusivity and disparagement of Filipino culture. In contrast, persons of mixed Filipino-Chinese marriages who have accepted the local language and have become Roman Catholic find virtually no discrimination.

As in Malaysia and Indonesia, a distinctive nation is developing in the Philippines, one that embraces a majority of its inhabitants. It is based on the uniformities in religion and other aspects of culture that emerged during three centuries of Spanish control and a half century of American tutelage, despite the population's multilingual character. Government attempts to reinforce national identity by propagating Pilipino as a common language comparable to Bahasa Indonesia

have met with inconclusive success. A 1974 plan to replace English as a second language by Pilipino was strongly attacked.

The growth of a Filipino nation provides reinforcement for the continued functioning of a Philippine state, but also acts against any possible Pan-Malay merger with the other two island countries of Southeast Asia. Neighbors see the Filipinos as different from themselves—too American in outlook, with overtones of a Latin heritage rather than an Asian civilization.

Bibliography

BROEK, JAN O. M., "Diversity and Unity in Southeast Asia," *Geographical Review*, Vol. 34 (1944), pp. 175–195.

DUTT, ASHOK K., ed., *Southeast Asia: Realm of Contrasts*, 3rd ed. Boulder, CO: Westview Press, 1985.

FISHER, CHARLES A., *South-East Asia: A Social, Economic and Political Geography*. London: Methuen, 1964.

FISHER, CHARLES A., "Malaysia: A Study in the Political Geography of Decolonization," *Essays in Political Geography*, ed. Charles A. Fisher. London: Methuen, 1968.

HILL, RONALD, *Southeast Asia: A Systematic Geography*. Oxford: Oxford University Press, 1979.

KOLB, ALBER, *East Asia: China, Japan, Korea, Vietnam: Geography of a Cultural Region*, Trans. C.A.M. Sym. London: Methuen, 1971, pp. 391–405.

LIJPHART, AREND, *The Trauma of Decolonization: The Dutch and West New Guinea*. New Haven: Yale University Press, 1966.

SARDESAI, D. R., *Southeast Asia: Past and Present*, 2nd ed. Boulder, CO: Westview Press, 1989.

TATE, D.J.M., *The Making of Modern South-East Asia* Vol. 1. Kuala Lumpur, Malaysia: Oxford University Press, 1971.

TATE, D.J.M., *The Making of Modern South-East Asia* Vol. 2, Kuala Lumpur, Malaysia: Oxford University Press, 1979.

ULACK, RICHARD and GYULA PAUER, *Atlas of Southeast Asia*. New York: Macmillan, 1988.

12

East Asia

EAST ASIA, like South Asia, is a continental entity in its own right, despite territorial contiguity with other portions of the Eurasian landmass. The region contains three times the area and the population of Europe. It is set apart from neighboring realms by vast and empty insulating zones of mountains, deserts, and seas. Despite fragmentation into a half dozen separate states, it displays remarkable cultural unity, the product of two millennia of dominance by Chinese civilization.

The principal political divisions of East Asia are the People's Republic of China, the Republic of China (Taiwan), the Mongolian People's Republic, the People's Democratic Republic of Korea (North Korea), the Republic of Korea (South Korea), and Japan (Table 12-1). Each exhibits a greater degree of internal unity than do most states of Europe. Extended periods of statehood under highly centralized, authoritarian rule have led to notably homogeneous populations. Each state has witnessed assimilation of formerly disparate groups into peoples who share common languages, religions, and other aspects of culture. These uniformities have been the basis for the emergence of a strong sense of national identity during the nineteenth and twentieth centuries.

The states of East Asia exhibit a number of common political-geographic features. Each is set off from the others by zones of emptiness. Nearly all have limited ecumenes, their inhabitants effectively occupying but a third or less of total territories. Social and political features have been shaped by early dependence upon irrigated agriculture. Each has endured revolutionary cultural and economic change as a result of contact with Europeans and Americans. The current fragmentation of the Chinese and the Koreans reflects a continuing role in the region by external powers.

Although Chinese culture has been at the core of East Asian civilization, the region's political organization has alternated between ascendancies of Chinese and emergence to power of peripheral peoples. Mongols dominated much of East Asia in the thirteenth and fourteenth centuries by gaining control of the Chinese state. Manchus similarly became preeminent in the seventeenth century. Like German tribes that conquered Gaul, both groups eventually found themselves conquered and absorbed by the society they ruled. During the twentieth century, the offshore Japanese became paramount in the region by adjusting to Western pressures at a time when the Chinese proved unable to maintain political and economic integrity. Under its most recent, Communist, dynasty, China has begun to reassert its traditional role.

China

The People's Republic of China, with 3,700,000 square miles and more than 1,200,000,000 inhabitants, embraces a territory and population twice that of Europe west of Russia and Ukraine (Figures 12-1 and 12-2). It is focused on the watersheds of the Hwang Ho (Yellow River) and Yangtse River, but extends northeastward to the mountains of Manchuria, northward to the Inner Asian deserts, westward across the high plateau of Tibet to the Pamir and Tyan Shan ranges, and southward to the Himalayas and their eastern extensions to the sea.

China is huge in size, but only its eastern third is fully occupied, incorporating some 90 percent of the state's total inhabitants. The western half of the country, including Tibet, Sinkiang, and Inner Mongolia, contains less than 5 percent of the population, and most of these do not consider themselves to be Han, as the Chinese identify themselves.

The political organization of broad areas in China into a unified state dates from at least 1500 B.C. By then, Chinese society already had evolved a unique writing system whose characters still can be read. Centered east of the present city of Sian, this early political unit embraced the fertile soils of the middle Hwang Ho valley. Many scholars believe that the need to develop and maintain a network of irrigation canals to support a constantly growing population led to general acceptance of a strongly centralized and authoritarian government. Over ensuing centuries, strong leaders expanded the state eastward to embrace the whole of the lower Hwang Ho and southward to the middle Yangtse River region. They organized their territory into a feudal system based around distinctive walled towns.

Eventually, in the fifth century B.C., the territory fell apart into fourteen "warring states." It remained divided for more than 200 years, although this period saw the emergence of Confucius, whose philosophy remains an ethical underpinning of modern Chinese society. In 256 B.C. a new leadership reimposed strong central authority and expanded the outer margins of the state. It built the Great Wall of China to defend the northern border of its territory against nomadic tribes who ranged the grasslands of Mongolia. Although it was breeched on numerous occasions by barbarian

TABLE 12. 1   EAST ASIA

East Asia is a huge territory—three times the size of Europe west of the frontiers of the former Soviet Union. The entire region reflects a dominating impress of Chinese civilization over several millennia. Each of its component units is remarkably homogeneous, although they are divided from each other by language. Only the People's Republic of China itself has significant regional separatist problems. It is the last of the great empires of the world. Substantial portions of each state remain essentially unpopulated owing to rough terrain or desert conditions.

State	Total Population	Area (sq. miles)	Distinctive Features of Group
People's Republic of China	1,200,000,000	3,700,000	
Dominant Nation and % Total			
Chinese (Han), 92%			Sino-Tibetan (Mandarin, Cantonese, et. al.) languages
			Chinese folk religion and Buddhist
Significant Regional Groups and % Total			
Tibetans, <1%			Sino-Tibetan (Tibetan) language, Lamaistic Buddhist
Mongols, <1%			Altaic (Mongol) language
			Lamaistic Buddhist
Uighurs, <1%			Altaic Turkic (Uighur) language, Sunni Muslim
Potential Trouble Areas and Possible Adversaries			
Inner Mongolia	22,000,000	450,000	
(Mongolian People's Republic)			
Tibet	2,200,000	470,000	
Manchuria	35,000,000	180,000	
Mongolian People's Republic	2,200,000	600,000	
Dominant Nation and % Total			
Khalka Mongols, 78%			Altaic (Mongol) language, Lamaistic Buddhist
Republic of China (Taiwan)	21,000,000	14,000	
Dominant Nation and % Total			
Chinese (Han), 98%			Sino-Tibetan (Fukienese, Mandarin, et. al.) languages
			Chinese Folk Religion and Buddhist
Hong Kong (British Possession)	6,000,000	415	
Dominant Nation and % Total			
Chinese (Han), 95%			Sino-Tibetan (Cantonese, et. al.) languages
			Chinese folk religion and Buddhist
Macao (Portuguese possession)	370,000	6	
Dominant Nation and % Total			
Chinese (Han), 68%			Sino-Tibetan (Cantonese, et al.) languages
			Chinese folk religion and Buddhist
Republic of Korea (South Korea)	44,000,000	38,000	
Dominant Nation and % Total			
Korean, 99%			Korean language
			Korean folk religion and Buddhism
People's Democratic Republic of Korea (North Korea)	22,000,000	47,000	
Dominant Nation and % Total			
Korean, 99%			Korean Language, Korean Folk Religion and Buddhism
Japan	125,000,000	146,000	
Dominant Nation and % Total			
Japanese, 99%			Japanese language
			Eclectic Shinto/Buddhist

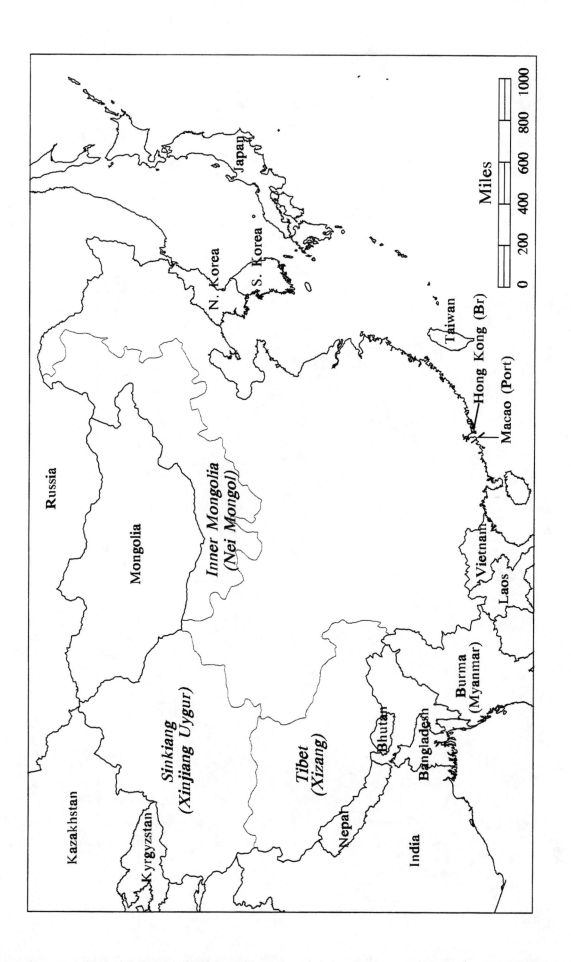

FIGURE 12-1 CHINA: AUTONOMOUS PROVINCES AND ADJACENT TERRITORIES

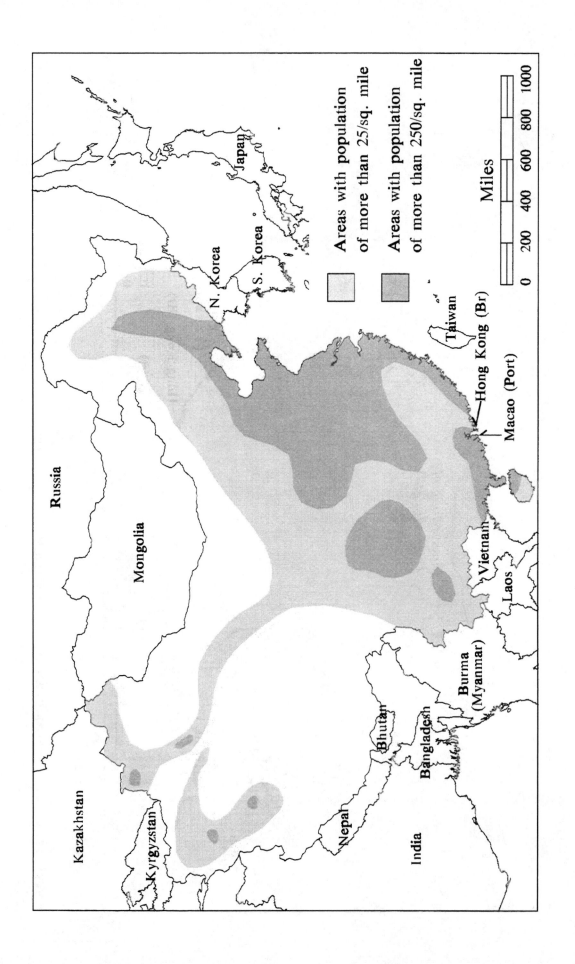

Areas with population
of more than 25/sq. mile

Areas with population
of more than 250/sq. mile

Miles

0   200   400   600   800   1000

FIGURE 12-2   CHINA: EFFECTIVELY SETTLED TERRITORY

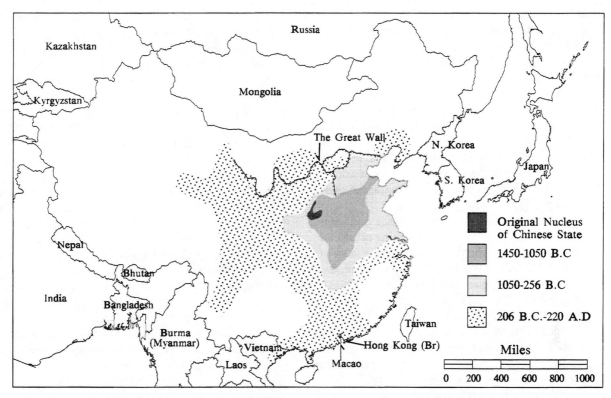

FIGURE 12-3   GROWTH OF THE CHINESE EMPIRE

raiders, the wall, like the Roman *limes*, served clearly to mark the outer edges of claimed territory (see Figure 12-3).

Over ensuing centuries China expanded its boundaries, reaching a maximum extent of territory in the late 1700s. During those centuries, central authority occasionally weakened and political power devolved, usually to China's eighteen historic provinces. Subsequently, a new dynasty would recentralize control. In 1279, Mongols seized control of the state and held it for nearly a century. After return to rule by a Chinese dynasty over the next 300 years, tribesmen from Manchuria in 1644 established the Manchu dynasty, which lasted until the Chinese Republic was declared by Sun Yat-sen in 1911. Disorder marked China during the last years of the Manchus and the early decades of the republic. In 1949, Communist forces triumphed under the leadership of Mao Tse-tung and proceeded to reestablish strong central authority.

Most educated Chinese see China particularly as a continuity of the state ruled by the Ming dynasty during the period from 1368 to the Manchu ascendancy in 1644. The elite of the Ming period shared a concept of China being the Middle Kingdom (*Chung Kuo*) whose

emperor was rightful ruler of everything under Heaven. It was his duty to bring peace to the whole of humanity and to civilize encircling barbarians.

The Chinese state expanded from its core in the Hwang Ho plain southward, mainly by migration of peasants and soldier-settlers, who infiltrated and assimilated indigenous peoples whom they encountered. Among major groups absorbed were the Yao, who formerly dominated the Shantung Peninsula and Shanghai delta region; the Miao in the province of Kweichow; and the Lolo (or Yi) of Yunnan province. Remnants of these peoples remain in the predominantly hilly region of southern China. In absorbing peoples to the south, Chinese culture itself was enriched with new ideas and values. Thus, tea consumption spread to the core region following acquisition of tea-producing areas.

During the process of outward expansion, China became increasingly an empire in which non-Chinese groups found their fortunes controlled and shaped by a remote and foreign authority. The Han expanded their state to incorporate numerous groups who resisted complete assimilation into Chinese culture, including Tibetans, Mongols, Turks, and peoples of the southern hills. In their quest to civilize barbarian peoples, Chinese regimes imposed tributary relations upon rulers of the adjacent political units of Koreans, Vietnamese, Laotians, Burmans, and others.

Chinese domination of East Asia weakened in modern times as a result of internal problems and the arrival of Europeans in the region. The Portuguese appeared on the southern China coast in 1517. The Chinese government allowed them to establish a trading post in 1557 in Macao, outside Canton. The regime, with its rigid Confucian ethic, proved unable to withstand the problems posed by the Europeans. Particularly subverting were new views of the nature of society propagated by Christian missionaries.

By the mid-nineteenth century China had been reduced to semicolonial status. The turning point was the "Opium War," fought with the United Kingdom in 1839–1841. As a consequence of China's defeat, the British received a long-term lease to Hong Kong and the opening of five "treaty ports" to foreign commerce. In these ports foreigners enjoyed special "extraterritorial" rights. This was not a completely novel situation in China. Such rights had been extended to foreigners for a thousand years, beginning with privileges granted Arab merchants in Canton in the ninth century.

The number of treaty ports had grown to fifty-six by the 1920s. Additionally, the Chinese government had opened eight ports under its own administration and sixteen frontier caravan stations. It also maintained twenty-five ports of call in which foreigners were not permitted to live. Each of the treaty ports had a "concession" or "tract" where foreigners administered themselves in the equivalent of free republics, including their own judicial systems.

Different parts of coastal China functioned as semicolonies of foreign powers. Russians controlled Manchuria and Port Arthur. Germans and Americans dominated the Shantung Peninsula aside from the British leased port of Weihaiwei. France established itself on the island of Hainan and the coastal port of Kwangchowan. The mighty Yangtse River was declared an international waterway and patrolled by European and American gunboats. China also lost its traditional influence in Vietnam and Korea.

The Chinese saw substantial areas break away during the modern era. Japan acquired Formosa (Taiwan) and Korea as colonies, following war in 1895. Outer Mongolia and Tibet functioned as independent entities after China was further weakened by internal revolution in 1911. Japan seized Manchuria in 1930. Sinkiang came under Soviet domination in the 1930s. Even in Han areas, so-called warlords established control over entire provinces, and members of the Chinese Communist party created their own territorial unit embracing a substantial portion of northern China, following their "Long March" from Shanghai.

Beginning in 1937 with an "incident" at the Marco Polo Bridge outside Peiking (modern-day Beijing), Japan invaded China. Over the ensuing eight years it established control over nearly all the coast and pushed deep into the interior. The Chinese Nationalist regime found it necessary to flee from its capital in Nanking to the remote city of Chungking in the Szechuan basin located in the west. Although the USSR supplied Chinese forces overland through the northwestern Dzhungarian basin, China's main contact with the outside world depended upon the circuitous "Burma Road" to Southeast Asia, and even that was lost when Japan occupied British Burma. Later linkages to its allies were confined to military air flights from India over the "hump" of the Himalaya Mountains.

At war's end, the Chinese regained most of their traditional lands, except for Outer Mongolia, which had opted for independence under a Soviet-controlled plebiscite. Foreigners gave up prewar extraterritorial rights. France exited from Kwangchowan in 1945. Only the colonies of Hong Kong and Macao remained as remnants of European imperialism. However, the Nationalist regime's civil war with the Communists resumed with fury. By 1949, the Communists were triumphant and the republican government fled to Taiwan just as officials of the Ming dynasty had done three centuries earlier, in 1644.

The victorious Communists in effect established a new dynasty. Attacking the Confucian belief system, which they perceived had rendered China unable to adjust to pressures from the modern world, they propagated throughout the country a new secular ideology framed by Marx and Engels and modified by Soviet experience. Moreover, Chinese leaders made their own contributions to Marxist doctrine, basing the new system on the peasant class, rather than the industrial workers favored by European Communists.

The new regime asserted control over all parts of the country. In 1951 it successfully invaded Tibet. It created a one-party state comparable to the USSR. The Chinese Communist party established a central regime presence in every village, something that no predecessor dynasties had been able to accomplish. It tackled problems in China's infrastructure by building railroads connecting north with south, east with west. It addressed the question of non-Han minority groups by establishing autonomous areas comparable to those in the Soviet Union.

In restructuring China into a modern state, the Communists could build upon the remarkable cultural homogeneity of the Han. Although forty languages are extant in China, two-thirds of the people speak Mandarin, albeit with dialectical differences. Non-Mandarin speakers are concentrated in the south and southwest. Even they share a common written language with the

Mandarin group. Chinese ideographs, or picture writing, emerged in ancient China. More than 50,000 characters evolved, although only 2,000 to 4,000 are essential for literacy.

Beginning in 1956, the Communist regime made attempts to simplify the written language. A phonetic alphabet comparable to those adopted by the Koreans and Japanese was rejected, however, because of widespread differences in vocabulary and pronunciation. However, modifications of the writing system were made, including adoption of a convention to read and write characters horizontally from left to right, rather than vertically.

The uniform writing system long has facilitated linkages among all Han (and many non-Han groups). Educated Chinese tend to see the ideographs as the paramount language and the variety of different spoken Han languages simply as dialects. This perception is erroneous linguistically, but does play a significant role in Chinese political and cultural unity. The common written language also has minimized the possible development of regional consciousness derived from local literature. In contrast to writings in dialect that have played a significant role within European national groups, it is impossible for Chinese authors to represent local speech patterns in their works.

In addition to a single written language, Chinese share a number of other common cultural features. These include a value system and institutions adopted also by Koreans, Japanese, northern Vietnamese, and other neighbors of China. The Chinese additionally have a common syncretic religion, blending elements of Confucianism, Buddhism, and Taoism. Although Christianity and Islam also entered the Han lands of China, the demands of those religions for exclusiveness have found less fertile ground for proselytization than in other realms. Han Muslims are principally in the northwest, a result of contact with Islamic missionaries following the "Silk Route" from Samarkand after A.D. 751. Han Muslims are known as Dungans. Christians are to be found mainly in the cosmopolitan coastal cities.

The most recent regime in China can also count upon a societal coherence that dates from antiquity. The need for cooperation to maintain irrigation projects was the reason for existence of the earliest Han states. A rigid bureaucracy emerged that provided a significant centripetal force perpetuating central rule. Economic interdependence reinforced unity, particularly after the annexation of the southern regions. Tea produced there became a commodity throughout China, as did porcelain wares.

China early utilized an infrastructure linking together its far-flung parts. The Hwang Ho and Yangtse rivers provided connections over vast areas. Their basins were first tied together in the sixth century A.D., and the Mongol dynasty began construction of a Grand Canal between the rivers at the end of the thirteenth century. In the nineteenth and twentieth centuries, raillines and modern roads brought China's regions closer together, although a majority of villages remained more than twenty miles from the nearest economic artery.

The ability of the central regime to project its power traditionally has been inversely proportional to distance from the capital. Chinese dynasties almost never were able to govern remote Tibet, despite that territory's inclusion within China's boundaries on maps. In times of central governmental weakness, China has fallen apart into quarreling segments, usually according to the patterns of its historic eighteen provinces.

The traditional unity of the Han does not mean that regional differences do not exist among the principal Chinese group. A rather pronounced split is observable between northerners and southerners. Differences in spoken language have been noted above. While virtually all northerners speak Mandarin, its usage hardly reaches beyond the outer margins of the Yangtse River basin. Han people in the southeast speak several distinctive languages, including Cantonese, Fukienese, Hakka, and Wu. Southerners also tend to be more open and less seriously Confucian than their northern counterparts. Buddhism plays a more important role in their lives, and generally they are less authoritarian in outlook. They also have less Mongoloid features and tend to be shorter in stature than Chinese inhabiting the northern plains.

Northern Chinese traditionally have distrusted those in the south. They view the latter as having had too much contact with foreigners, including Southeast Asians, Indians, and Europeans. South China was the source area for migrants to the Southeast Asian realm, and their descendants have maintained continuous ties with the homeland. The contrasts between cosmopolitan Shanghai and austere Beijing reflect age-long differences.

Twentieth century regimes in China have increasingly appealed to national concerns as a binding force among the Han people. Both the Kuomintang (Nationalists) and the Communists have stressed the harm done to Chinese by the unequal treaties imposed during the nineteenth century. Both have pressed for recovery of lost territories. The Communist quest for Taiwan and insistence upon British departure from Hong Kong are continuing aspects of this trend. The European-based notion of government resting upon a contract with its people contrasts with traditional Confucian views that saw all peoples as rightful subjects of a divine emperor.

Non-Han minorities make up barely 7 percent of the Chinese population. Yet given China's huge population, this still amounts to more than 70,000,000 peo-

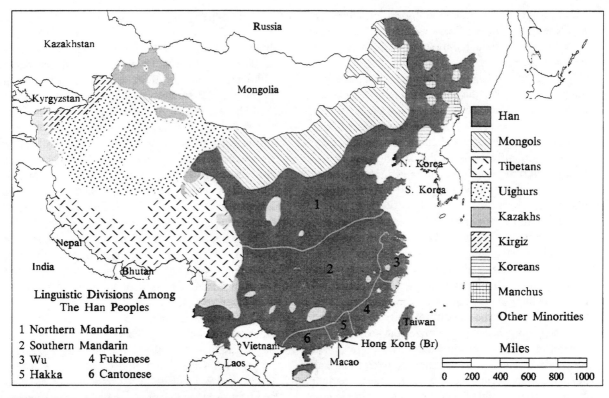

FIGURE 12-4 PEOPLES OF CHINA

Legend:
- Han
- Mongols
- Tibetans
- Uighurs
- Kazakhs
- Kirgiz
- Koreans
- Manchus
- Other Minorities

Linguistic Divisions Among
The Han Peoples

1 Northern Mandarin
2 Southern Mandarin
3 Wu   4 Fukienese
5 Hakka   6 Cantonese

ple. Moreover, they constitute the dominant groups that reside in over 60 percent of Chinese territory. The regime officially recognizes fifty-five different minority nationalities (see Figure 12-4).

In most outer areas the indigenous population constitutes a majority. Some 95 percent of the population of Tibet is Tibetan. In Sinkiang, 60 percent is Turkic, despite recent great immigration by Han settlers. In other territories, non-Han groups make up but a fraction of the total inhabitants. Inner Mongolia's Mongol population now constitutes barely 37 percent of the total. Yi and related groups are less than a third of Yunnan's population. Although Manchuria was placed off-limits to Han settlement during most of the Manchu dynasty period, native Manchus have been overwhelmed and assimilated by Han immigrants ever since the end of the nineteenth century. The same is true for Inner Mongolia. The continuing dilution of minorities by Han immigrants is a source of friction throughout non-Han areas. It has been the source of recent major disturbances in Tibet, Sinkiang, and Inner Mongolia.

Several minority groups spill across China's boundaries and constitute potential irredentist problems. Most notable are the Mongols of Inner Mongolia, who increasingly look to their counterparts in the Mongolian

People's Republic. A number of Koreans live on the Chinese side of the border with the Korean People's Democratic Republic. The fragmentation of the former Soviet Union into fifteen sovereign states has implications for the Kazakh minority in Sinkiang. Some Chinese minority groups also are minorities in adjacent states. These include Shans (in Burma), Yaos (in Thailand), and Uighurs (in Kazakhstan).

The Chinese Communist regime has pursued conflicting policies toward non-Han minorities. It early adopted the Soviet approach to nationalities, creating fifteen major minority linguistic regions, mostly in the northwest and southwest. Although specifically identified in China's constitution, the regions lack the guaranteed right of secession that were built into constitutions of the USSR. The regime's adopted flag symbolizes China's five major "races," a large star representing the Han people and four smaller stars marking Mongols, Manchus, Tibetans, and Muslims.

Communist China declared itself a "unified multinational state" in 1954. However, party emphasis upon centralized control early came into conflict with minority pressures for autonomy. The regime utilized politically reliable cadres to administer all areas, including those of the minorities. For the most part, local officials were members of the Han group, who could hardly conceal their contempt for minority peoples. China's ultra-leftist Cultural Revolution of the 1960s generated particularly strong resentments from national minorities. The Cultural Revolution denigrated all aspects of their cultural heritage, including local languages. Thus, attacks upon the Buddhist religion in Tibet resulted in destruction of numerous ancient prayer wheels and other venerated objects.

Tibet

The region giving greatest concern to the Chinese regime is Tibet. Like Mongolia, it conventionally is divided by Chinese into outer and inner zones. Outer Tibet contains nearly 500,000 square miles and is perched on a high plateau. Among its 2,000,000 inhabitants are only 75,000 Han. Inner Tibet, closer to Han regions, is a jumbled land where the Yangtse, Mekong, Hwang Ho, and Salween rivers have their origins. It is an area of substantial Han settlement.

Tibetans have evolved a distinctive language and culture. Their writing system is based on the Gupta script of India. Ancient Tibetan religious beliefs incorporated magic and demonology. These merged with Buddhist teachings from India in the eighth century to become the Tibetan form of Lamaistic Buddhism. Tibet long has been a theocracy, with spiritual leaders also serving as secular heads of state. Traditionally, the primate religious leader and ruler is the current incarnation of the Dalai Lama. Of somewhat lesser rank is the Panchen Lama.

A Tibetan tribal confederation is recorded as early as the first century A.D. Heavily influenced by Mongol-Tatars from the north, its center was in the Yalung valley. This Tibetan state expanded southward and westward, embracing at one time approaches to the Bay of Bengal and substantial parts of eastern Turkestan. It reached a maximum size in the eighth century, and had moved its capital to its present site in Lhasa.

Early Chinese contacts with Tibetans were confined mainly to Tibetan nomads, who constituted perhaps one-sixth of Tibet's population. Usually Mongols served as intermediaries in trade between the two peoples. Tibetan political ties with China developed only in the eighteenth century, when Tibet asked for Chinese assistance to resist invasion by Dzhungarian Mongols on its northern margins. A Chinese army arrived in 1751 to help repel the Central Asian invaders, but remained to establish a protectorate over Tibet. Although Tibet subsequently was depicted on maps of China, it functioned as a completely separate entity during most of the nineteenth and twentieth centuries.

The United Kingdom took an interest in Tibet at the turn of the twentieth century, capturing Lhasa in 1904. The weak Manchu regime in China could do nothing but observe the British presence. All lingering ties between Tibet and China ended with the Chinese Revolution of 1911. In 1914, Britain recognized Tibet as an independent entity ultimately under Chinese suzerainty. Although the Chinese republican regime refused to recognize the validity of the British action, it accepted the situation, in effect, by agreeing that it would establish no further Han settlements in Tibet.

Over ensuing decades Tibet functioned independently from China. Commerce grew with British India, and communications improved, including establishment of a postal system. Russians also interested themselves in Tibetan affairs. In the 1920s Tibet's spiritual and temporal leader, the Dalai Lama, died, and, according to tradition, a young boy was sought out and declared to be his reincarnation. The Nationalist Chinese government, beset with problems of provincial warlords and pressures from the Japanese, could do little to alter the status quo of Tibetan self-rule.

The situation changed in 1950. Fresh from its triumph over the Nationalists, the new Chinese Communist regime sent forces into Tibet that effectively incorporated the entire region into China. This occurred at the same time that China was sending large numbers of "volunteers" to assist the North Koreans in their struggle with UN forces under American command.

The Chinese respected Tibetan traditions to the extent that they announced establishment of an autonomous government for Tibet under nominal joint leadership of the Dalai Lama and Panchen Lama. However, the occupying forces engendered strong resentment from the local population. Among causes for unhappiness were the closing of Buddhist monasteries and the transfer of much of eastern Tibet to Szechuan province. Rebellion broke out in 1958 and was ruthlessly suppressed. Tens of thousands of Tibetans, led by the Dalai Lama, subsequently streamed across the border into India. The Panchen Lama remained in Tibet and served as head of government until removed from office in 1964. In the following year the Chinese formally declared Tibet to be an Autonomous Region of China.

Angered by the haven that India had given the Dalai Lama and his followers, the Chinese pressed claims to territory that in the past had been tributary to Tibet, including Bhutan, Nepal, and Sikkim. In 1962 it fought a border war with India over Aksai Chin, a 40,000-square-mile area located in northeastern Jammu and Kashmir.

Although the Tibetan heritage suffered greatly from the ravages of China's Cultural Revolution, the population of Tibet benefitted from Chinese investment in industry and infrastructure. Scores of factories appeared, and more than 13,000 miles of highways linked together the region's disparate parts. The 1980s signalled greater toleration for Tibet's traditions. Tibetan was reinstated as the region's "major official language." More than 180 monasteries were allowed to reopen after 1980, and a seminary began functioning in 1984. Such concessions have not notably reduced the strong Tibetan sentiments to become independent, however.

Sinkiang

North of Tibet lies another broad region of China whose inhabitants have resisted the Han assimilation pressures so successful in the east. Sinkiang occupies an area of 650,000 square miles in northwestern China. It long has been a zone of competition among Chinese, Turkic Muslim, Indian, Tibetan, and Mongol civilizations.

It consists of two broad basins, the Dzhungarian and Tarim, separated by an eastward extension of the Tyan Shan Mountains. It is surrounded by high mountain ranges, although it opens eastward to the Gobi Desert. Sinkiang is farther from the sea than any other part of the globe, but it has sufficient precipitation to support a grassland vegetation that has drawn nomadic herders to it since prehistoric times. Its mountain rim also collects sufficient snow and rain to provide an abundant source of irrigation for a string of oases stretching from Turkistan to China's ecumene.

Three-quarters of Sinkiang's population is concentrated in the southern Tarim basin. The majority are Uighurs, a Muslim people speaking a Turkic language and employing a distinctive writing system. Other Turkic speakers also are present, including Kazakhs, Kirgiz, Uzbeks, and Tatars. In contrast to the farming Uighurs, most are nomads. Kazakhs are most numerous. Although the various Turkic groups have struggled with each other through history to control the region's marginal resources, they have grown united in recent decades as they have faced a great in-migration of Han settlers.

Sinkiang also has been an object of outside interest since antiquity. Tibetans, Mongols, and Indians have sought to control the territory in addition to the Chinese, who established suzerainty only in the eighteenth century. During the nineteenth century, the Russian Empire became involved in Sinkiang and actively intervened in Chinese struggles with Kalmyks and Kazakhs. British India also long manifested interest in Sinkiang, reflecting the traditional role of Kashmiri Muslim traders throughout the region. As many as 8,000 Kashmiris lived in Sinkiang before World War II. After the Bolshevik Revolution, many Russians fled into the region. Later, during collectivization in the USSR, large numbers of Kazakhs and Kirgiz entered Sinkiang to escape the Soviet policy of

turning nomads into ranchers by forced settlement in permanent villages.

Chinese rule in Sinkiang has been marked by frequent rebellion. Uighurs have never accepted the Chinese presence. In contrast to aboriginal groups in southern China and Manchuria, their civilization was already at an advanced level when the Chinese arrived. Also, the influx of Chinese consisted almost entirely of officials, merchants, and artisans, notably lacking the peasant settlers who played such an important role in acculturation by the Han civilization elsewhere. Sinkiang's land tenure system made acquisition of farmland all but impossible for Chinese farmers. In contrast to traditional Chinese division of inherited family lands equally among sons, the Central Asian Uighurs preserved their farms intact, awarding them to eldest sons. The result was establishment of large estates that Chinese peasants could not purchase.

Chinese regimes traditionally treated Sinkiang as a colony. All government posts were held by Han officials, most of whom never learned Uighur or other Turkic languages. Local peoples, in turn, did not learn Chinese, requiring interpreters for all transactions. In towns, each ethnic group maintained its separate quarter.

After the revolution in Russia, the new Bolshevik government showed increasing interest in Sinkiang, particularly since its inhabitants were related to Turkic peoples within the Soviet Central Asian realm. The building of the Turkistan-Siberia railroad line in eastern Turkistan made Russian markets accessible to Sinkiang producers. The Soviet regime opened several trading posts in Sinkiang towns, and Indian merchants increasingly found it difficult to compete. Soviet forces occupied much of Sinkiang in 1937, following the Japanese invasion of China.

When the Communists assumed power in China they modified the traditional Chinese manner of dealing with inhabitants of Sinkiang, borrowing from successful techniques employed by the Soviet regime in Central Asia. They made Uighur an official language in the region and appointed Uighurs and other minorities as local officials. They granted a degree of cultural autonomy and even made some concessions to Islamic law in the judicial system. In 1955 they created the Sinkiang Uighur Autonomous Region, within which they established autonomous districts for other minority groups, mostly in the area north of the Tyan Shan Mountains.

The new regime, however, also facilitated Chinese settlement in the region by terminating the traditional land tenure system. It expanded the amount of irrigated land and formed new state-managed farms worked mainly by peasants brought in from eastern China. The Chinese People's Army played a major role in this development. Agricultural production came to be focused on cotton-raising, as in Soviet Central Asia. The Chinese also improved the territory's infrastructure, building modern roads connecting Sinkiang with Tibet and the rest of China. The old Silk Route became a "cotton highway." The Communist regime constructed a pipeline to bring newly found oil from Sinkiang to the rest of China.

The influx of Chinese farmers reduced the proportion of native peoples in Sinkiang from some 90 percent in the 1940s to barely 60 percent today. Of a total population approaching 15,000,000, only 7,000,000 are Uighurs and only 1,000,000 are Kazakhs. As elsewhere in China's peripheral areas, the newcomers have generated frictions with the native peoples. A number of local revolts have occurred. In 1962 a rebellion by Kazakhs resulted in 60,000 fleeing to the USSR.

Since the mid-1980s, the Chinese regime has pursued a policy more accommodating to the native peoples. A high proportion of officials are now Uighurs and Kazakhs. Local government revenues no longer are transferred to the Chinese treasury, but are retained to meet local needs.

Manchuria

China formally incorporated its northeastern provinces only after the turn of the twentieth century, and it functionally integrated them into the rest of the state only in the Communist era. During much of Chinese history the northeast was a frontier zone inhabited by three contending groups: Tungus hunting tribes lived in forests of its north and east; sheep-raising Manchus dwelled in the natural grasslands of the center; and Chinese settlers occupied the south coastal area, forming a bridge to Korea.

Although this territory of 300,000 square miles is conventionally known in the West as Manchuria, "Land of the Manchus," Chinese have never employed that term. Currently, the area is known simply as the "Northeast" or is designated by the principal province, Heilungkiang. It consists essentially of the drainage basins of the Sungari and Liao rivers, surrounded by uplands. The region's continental climate sets it apart from other Chinese territories. It has a long, cold winter comparable to that of adjacent Siberia. It also is relatively dry.

Ancient China considered Manchuria's native inhabitants to be, like the Mongols, a threat. The fear was realistic, since attacks from the region were frequent, and on at least three occasions northeastern invaders established control over much of China. Tungus tribes of the Manchurian forest zone established the Liao dynasty in 916 A.D A similar group founded the

Jin dynasty in northern China in 1115. After a century of Mongol domination beginning in 1279, followed by nearly three centuries of the Chinese Ming dynasty, Manchus became rulers of China in 1644, perpetuating their authority until the Chinese Republican Revolution of 1911.

The Manchu dynasty showed little interest in its homeland, although it prohibited colonization there by Chinese. It early constructed a 600-mile "Willow Palisade" across southern Manchuria to the border with Korea. This line connected with the Great Wall to the west and marked the northern limit of permitted Chinese settlement. Although Tungus and Manchu tribal groups lived outside territory claimed by China, the imperial regime exerted control over them. Many Chinese moved into southern Manchuria, and by the end of the seventeenth century their numbers were greater than those of native Tunguses and Manchus in the north.

Russians had moved across Siberia since conquest of the Mongol-Tatar state of Kazan in 1552. By the end of the seventeenth century, Russian Cossack forces reached the Amur River. The Chinese became alarmed at their presence and confronted them with a huge army. As a consequence, Russia signed the 1689 Treaty of Nerchinsk by which it agreed to stay north of the Argun River and the Stanovoi Range. This was China's first treaty with a European power.

Concerned by the appearance of the Russians, China sent soldier/settlers into Manchuria. Many Chinese from the coastal section also illegally moved northward into the open and fertile grasslands of the central region, despite continuing prohibitions of such migration. The regime eventually eased restrictions, but it was not until 1878 that Chinese women officially were allowed to live in Manchuria.

Russians became a threat again in the 1850s, after China's disastrous loss of the 1839–1841 Opium War with the United Kingdom. Cossacks pushed down the Amur River in 1853, the same year that Commodore Matthew Perry arrived in Japan to force that state to open itself to the outside world. China saw the Russians as lesser evils than other Europeans confronting it, and agreed to cede to Russia all territories north of the Amur and east of the Ussuri rivers.

A large-scale Chinese immigration into Manchuria began in the 1870s and continued into the mid-twentieth century. By 1900 the region's inhabitants numbered more than 6,000,000. The total doubled by 1910, and migrants grew to more than 600,000 annually after the overthrow of the Manchu dynasty. Currently, Manchuria's total population is nearly 100,000,000. Most immigrants have come from northern China, and more than 95 percent of total inhabitants now are Han.

Russia and Japan both expanded commercial interests into Manchuria at the end of the nineteenth century.

Russians invested heavily throughout the territory, which technically lay outside China although it recognized Chinese suzerainty. Russia gained a concession in 1896 to extend the Trans-Siberian railroad for 1,500 miles across Manchuria to connect to the Pacific coast port at Vladivostok. This South Manchurian railroad included extraterritorial privileges extending a half dozen miles on either side of the line.

Russian economic interests in Manchuria came into conflict with similar Japanese aspirations, as they did also in Korea. The ensuing Russo-Japanese War of 1905 resulted in a division of spheres of interest of the two powers in the region along the watershed between the Sungari and Liao rivers. Japan took over all Russian investments in the south and began developing the territory as an area of heavy industry. It allowed nominal authority to remain with China, which formally annexed Manchuria in 1907.

Following collapse of China's Manchu dynasty in 1911 and the proclamation of a republic, Chinese authority in Manchuria came into the hands of a local Han strongman who operated independently of Beijing. Many Russians later moved into the territory, following the revolution and civil war. The young Soviet government early renounced Russian extraterritorial rights in Manchuria, the first European regime to do so in China. Although Kuomintang nationalists reasserted Chinese authority in the 1920s, Japan forced them out in 1931 and a year later proclaimed establishment of the puppet state of Manchukuo. The Japanese selected the heir to the Manchu dynasty as its head of state. In 1935 Japan bought the South Manchurian railroad from the USSR.

The Soviet Union reentered Manchuria in 1945 in the closing days of World War II. It reclaimed its naval base at Port Arthur and shipped to its own industrial centers a number of Japanese-built factories. It also reached accord with China's Nationalist regime. Following the triumph of the Chinese Communists in 1949, the USSR renounced all privileges in the area, and in 1955 it returned Port Arthur to China.

Manchuria remains a distinctive area of China, although its non-Han population is but a tiny proportion of the total. The Manchu language has completely disappeared. The region continues to be distinguished by heavy industrialization based upon local resources and past investment by foreigners.

Inner Mongolia

The nineteenth-century migration of Chinese into Manchuria was accompanied by similar pioneer settlement into Mongolia to the west. This broad, subhumid realm north of the Great Wall consists of three distinc-tive latitudinal regions: a northern zone of mountains that decrease in elevation from west to east, a central desert zone occupying a broad lowland depression, and a southeastern zone with sufficient precipitation to support grassland vegetation. All areas are characterized by a harsh winter climate.

Indigenous to the region are the Mongol people, who now total some 6,000,000. They speak an Altaic language that is related to the Turkic languages and, distantly, to Korean. Although dialects exist, all tend to be readily understood, a result of constant intermingling of this traditionally nomadic people. Mongols are Lamaistic Buddhists as a conquence of conversion of their rulers following a raid on Tibet in 1586. Previously, most had been shamanistic like other groups in northeastern Asia. Some western Mongol tribes were converted to Islam by Central Asian Turks in the thirteenth century.

Mongols constructed the largest empire the world has ever known. Under the leadership of Genghis Khan ("Supreme Leader"), who directed huge armies of conquered peoples, Mongols in the thirteenth century expanded their realm to include all of Russia, much of southeastern Europe, a large part of the Middle East, the Korean Peninsula, sections of Burma and Vietnam, and all of China. To manage their empire they crafted a sophisticated administrative organization staffed by Chinese, Russians, Persians, and other peoples.

The Mongol Empire played a major role in history by bringing Asians and Europeans into overland contact with each other. Kublai Khan, Genghis Khan's grandson, became ruler of the empire and moved his capital from Karakorum to Beijing. It was to his court that the Venetian adventurer Marco Polo came. Marco Polo's subsequent return to Europe provided inhabitants there with the first popular account of the splendors of the Middle Kingdom.

It is a paradox that the Mongols who once united Europe and Asia now find themselves divided among three states. The Mongolian People's Republic has only 2,000,000 inhabitants, embracing barely a third of the Mongols. More than 3,500,000 live in the People's Republic of China, and another 500,000 are in Russia.

The present political map is a consequence of the inability of the Mongols to maintain their empire. Overextended lines of control soon caused them to withdraw from their western conquests, although they maintained a presence in Russia for four subsequent centuries. They ruled China for less than ninety years following their conquest in A.D. 1280, restive Chinese driving them from power in 1368. They lost control over their homeland itself in 1691 when troops of the new Manchu dynasty of China conquered them. Previously, the Chinese had been able to assert authority over Mongolia only for one brief period between A.D.

630 and 679. Mongols also witnessed Russian encroachment upon their northern frontiers. Tsarist forces incorporated the Buriat Mongols in 1652 during their rapid march across Siberia. Many historians attribute Mongol weakness to the role of Lamaistic Buddhism, whose monasteries held 40 percent or more of the able-bodied male population.

Although Mongol tribes formally enjoyed a semi-autonomous status within China, Chinese administration after the mid-seventeenth century distinguished between Mongols living in the hills and mountains north of the Gobi Desert and those in the south. It tended to ignore the former, but asserted increasingly firm control over the southerners.

As in neighboring Manchuria, large numbers of Chinese peasants began entering Mongolia in the mid-nineteenth century. Unlike the restrictive land tenure system that effectively kept them out of Sinkiang, Chinese farmers found opportunities to acquire lands by leasing plots from Buddhist monasteries, which then owned 20 percent or more of the territory's pastures.

Increasing Chinese encroachment upon what were their best grazing lands prompted Mongols to revolt and assert independence in 1911, as the Manchu dynasty collapsed and China fell into anarchy. Mongol leaders asserted that their tribal oaths of allegiance had been to the Manchus, not to China. The tsarist government of Russia supported rebellion by the northern Mongol tribes, but was constrained from intervention south of the Gobi Desert by terms of a secret treaty signed earlier with Japan. Chinese forces quelled the uprising of the southerners, but northerners achieved independence with Russia's help and established a theocratic monarchy similar to that of Tibet. Mongolians had long cherished their own living Buddha, whose incarnations were ranked third among Lamaistic Buddhists after the Dalai and Panchen lamas of Tibet.

China, weakened by internal disorder and foreign pressures, found it necessary to recognize the status quo. In 1915 it signed a treaty with Russian and Mongol emissaries that acknowledged northern Mongolia to be an autonomous territory, although it was to remain under formal Chinese sovereignty. The treaty marked the first time that the terms "Inner" and "Outer" Mongolia officially were employed.

Subsequently, Outer Mongolia became a scene of turmoil. As Russia disintegrated under its own revolution and civil war, a Chinese warlord army entered and seized control. Siberian troops supporting the tsar drove out the Chinese in 1921, only to be driven out in turn by the Red Army. Soviet Russia permitted Outer Mongolia again to proclaim its independence. In 1924 it changed its name to the Mongolian People's Republic.

Inner Mongolia during this period remained an integral part of China with a semiautonomous status. Chinese peasants continued to flock to the region, particularly after the opening of a railroad connection with northern China in 1923. Mongols became a diminishing minority within their own homeland. In 1928 China annulled what autonomy the Mongols had retained. Subsequently, inhabitants of Inner Mongolia suffered the fate of the rest of China, with Japanese troops advancing into the region in 1933.

At the end of World War II, the Soviet Union reached agreement with the Chinese Nationalist government of Chiang Kai-shek to permit Mongols to hold a plebiscite on independence. However, the two powers limited the territory that could vote to Outer Mongolia. Enraged at their exclusion from the plebiscite by the Chinese Nationalists, southeastern Mongols gave full support during China's burgeoning civil war to the Communist side, which had championed autonomy for Inner Mongolia. They were rewarded by the victorious Communists with establishment of an Inner Mongolia Autonomous Region in 1949, to which were added sections of Manchuria and Jehol province inhabited by Mongols.

Inner Mongolia thus received an area of 280,000 square miles. In 1969 its size was reduced by a third, but this territory was restored in 1979. Inner Mongolia's population grew to 21,000,000 by 1986. However, only 3,300,000 of these were Mongols, the rest being Han immigrants and their descendants. An additional 200,000 Mongols lived in other parts of China. Still, China contained 70 percent of Asia's Mongolian population.

The loss of grazing lands has meant that most Inner Mongols have become farmers or urban dwellers. Fewer than 350,000 remain herdsmen. Mongols have resisted assimilation into Chinese civilization, however. The Chinese Communists encouraged the preservation of Mongol culture. Mongols have been permitted since 1954 to celebrate the achievements of Genghis Khan, who remains anathema to the Chinese. Ever since the ravages of China's Cultural Revolution, Buddhist temples have been allowed to reopen. The regime has once again permitted use of the ancient Mongol script. As in Tibet and Sinkiang, however, separatism has remained a political force. China's Inner Mongols have been drawn to dramatic events that have taken place in the Mongolian People's Republic in recent times.

Mongolian People's Republic

After more than a decade of independence as a protectorate of Russia, Outer Mongolia became, in effect, but another Soviet republic during the Stalin era. In 1928 it underwent a social revolution paralleling that taking place in the USSR. A frontal attack on religion resulted in closing its more than 600 monasteries and distribution of their lands to newly formed herding cooperatives, to which most of their large numbers of monks were assigned. During Russia's period of internal purges in 1937–1938, Mongolia executed more than 2,000 higher monks and abbots as enemies of the people.

A rail link that was extended in the 1930s from the Trans-Siberian railroad to their capital of Ulaanbataar strengthened Mongol linkages with the USSR. The Soviet Union's interest in Mongolia stemmed in part from worry over threats posed to Siberia by Japan. The latter's takeover of Manchuria and subsequent invasion of northern China caused the USSR to deploy large numbers of troops in Mongolia to bolster its eastern flank. Mongols themselves were alarmed at Japanese suggestions of creating a Mongol Mengkukuo paralleling their Manchurian puppet state of Manchukuo. A probing Japanese thrust at Khalkin Gol in mid-1939 resulted in a major battle with Soviet and Mongol forces in which up to 80,000 Japanese lost their lives. Although Mongolia did not enter into war with Japan until the end of World War II, it maintained a formidable standing army throughout the war years.

The postwar period saw Mongolia pursuing an increasingly independent course, playing off the Soviet Union against China. The 1945 referendum on independence, confirmed by both Chinese Nationalists and Communists, provided legitimacy for its efforts. Initially, it maintained its close ties with the USSR, even adopting the Russian Cyrillic alphabet in 1946. It benefitted by the 1956 completion of a rail link from China to Siberia across Mongolia.

The Mongolian People's Republic has an area of slightly more than 600,000 square miles and a population exceeding 2,000,000. Ninety percent of these are Mongols, four-fifths belonging to the Khalka ("Shield") group. Eight other Mongol groups also are represented. The largest non-Mongol minority are the Kazakhs of its extreme west, who make up 5 percent of the total population. Small numbers of Russians, Chinese, and Tuvinians also are present.

Strong manifestations of Mongol nationalism have taken place since Soviet domination began to weaken in the mid-1980s. These include a resurgence of interest in the feats of Genghis Khan. Greater use of traditional Mongol script has occurred, and words borrowed from the Russian language are being replaced by equivalents based upon Mongol roots. Communist party control ended in 1991, replaced by a parliamentary democracy. Mongolia developed stronger relations with China, including signing a border treaty, and it also established ties with non-communist South Korea.

About half the Mongols remain herdsmen, wandering with their flocks from 10 to 100 miles per year, staying temporarily in up to forty different places. Although herding cooperatives were formed in the 1920s, complete collectivization of herdsmen was not completed until 1960. Following the demise of Communist rule, herding by extended families again is becoming standard.

The Republic of China

The island of Taiwan lies 100 miles off the coast of mainland China. Its dimensions are 250 miles from north to south and 80 miles from west to east, yielding an area of 14,000 square miles. This is three-quarters the size of the Japanese island of Kyushu and roughly equal to the island of Hainan off the south coast of the People's Republic of China. Since 1949, Taiwan has functioned as a territorial base for the Kuomintang government of the Republic of China, which was driven from the mainland by Communist forces.

The name "Taiwan" in Mandarin means "Terrace Land," reflecting the fact that three-quarters of the island consists of mountains, the lower slopes of which aboriginal peoples made suitable for farming by laborious terracing, much like the northern part of the Philippine island of Luzon, 200 miles to the south. The forest-covered mountains remain home to 300,000 aborigines, who share many traits in common with Filipinos and Malaysians. Portuguese sailors in the 1540s gave Taiwan the name Ilha Formosa ("Beautiful Island"), and most European languages use "Formosa" to designate it.

Taiwan has a population of 21,000,000. Although this is but a fraction of the billion people who live in mainland China, it is larger than the populations of eighteen of the more than two dozen states of Europe. Taiwan has ten times the number of inhabitants of the Mongolian People's Republic. More than 90 percent of the Taiwanese live on the 3,500 square miles of plains along the west coast. Despite the island's small population and extremely limited ecumene, it exports a third more goods than does the entire People's Republic of China, and it enjoys a gross national product per capita nearly ten times that of its mainland neighbor.

Taiwan did not become a part of China until late in the seventeenth century. Troops, merchants, and Missionaries from Portugal, the Netherlands, and Spain had come to the island long before China established a presence there. From 1624 to 1661 the Netherlands maintained a fortress named Zeelandia in the southwestern corner. Its ruins still stand. Dutch merchants found great demand for Taiwan deerskins, exporting more than 60,000 annually to Japan and other countries.

Although the Chinese had known about the island as early as the twelfth century, Taiwan never was considered an integral part of China. It lacked even the status of a tributary state comparable to Korea or northern Vietnam. A few fishermen had left Fukien province to reside there, but after 1332 the Ming government forbade its subjects to travel by sea. Chinese refugees from Luzon landed in Taiwan in 1639, after Spaniards had massacred 23,000 of their countrymen.

The enterprising Dutch on Taiwan encouraged settlement by mainland Chinese, and more than 50,000 lived on the island in 1644, when members of the Ming dynasty ruling class of China fled to Taiwan following the triumph of the Manchus. In a strange parallel to the 1949 flight to Taiwan by the Kuomintang regime, Ming officials maintained their own separate government on the island for four decades.

The Manchu regime itself invaded and occupied Taiwan in 1683, thereafter administering it as a special military district of Fukien province. At that time its Chinese population was probably 100,000. The Manchus officially prohibited further Chinese emigration, but numbers had grown to 2,000,000 in an 1811 census. The Manchu regime also kept foreigners out of the island.

Taiwan's aborigines fiercely resisted movement of Chinese settlers onto their lands. Such attacks notably

FIGURE 12-5 TAIWAN

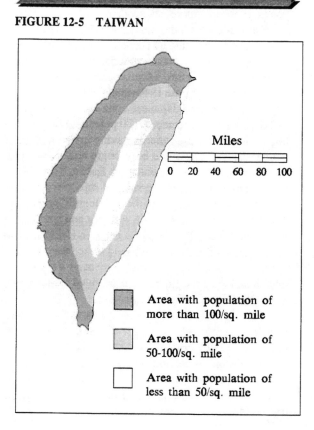

Miles

0 20 40 60 80 100

Area with population of more than 100/sq. mile

Area with population of 50-100/sq. mile

Area with population of less than 50/sq. mile

diminished after a boundary was established in 1739 at the edge of the western lowlands, east of which Chinese were prohibited from settling.

In 1860 China found itself forced to open Taiwan to foreign commerce, and it established three treaty ports. Russians, British, Americans, and the French became interested in the island at the time. To forestall Taiwan's possible seizure by westerners similar to what had occurred in Annam, the Chinese government made the island a province in 1887. It then belatedly began a process of modernization, constructing a road network and rail line.

Chinese rule ended in 1895, when Japan acquired Taiwan as its first colony in the aftermath of its successful war with China. The change in sovereignty was not well received by the local population, which manifested strong Chinese racist feelings against domination by the "dwarf people." Taiwanese unsuccessfully attempted to declare their own separate republic, and then conducted guerrilla warfare for a decade. During the first two years of its occupation, Japan allowed inhabitants to leave for China, and more than 250,000 took advantage of the opportunity. Most of those departing had arrived only during the preceding two decades.

The Japanese introduced an effective system of social control, enabling them to break up the clan relationships and secret societies that long had given rise to rebellions in China. They introduced a school system on the Japanese model to replace classical Chinese education. This reform, together with the introduction of Japanese law to replace the Manchu legal system, had the effect of weakening traditional loyalties of the Chinese on Taiwan to China.

Japan modernized the island's infrastructure, improving roads and extending the railroad system. It introduced public health measures that ended the island's age-old scourges of bubonic plague and cholera. It opened up new farming areas, including establishment of agricultural colonies for the first time along the east coast. It also built dams that generated electricity and expanded irrigation opportunities. In the process, Japan transformed the island from its status as a backwater of the Chinese Empire to a land less onerous and more prosperous than China itself, then being ruled by a Kuomintang dictatorship.

Japan had particular difficulties with Taiwan's aboriginal tribes. It established fortified lines to protect Chinese farmers and expanded them more than once. In the 1920s it decided to create aborigine reservations. It ruthlessly suppressed a revolt by tribal groups in 1930. Later, it resettled more than 50,000 on Taiwan's eastern coast.

Japanese administration was efficient and progressive, but it could not be termed benevolent. Policies were designed to enhance the economy and prestige of Japan, and all opposition was ruthlessly repressed. Japan formally annexed the island in 1942. Only in the closing months of World War II did the Japanese make any concessions to the desire by Taiwan's Chinese inhabitants for home rule.

Relatively few Japanese came to Taiwan, aside from administrators and businessmen. Farmers particularly found that they could not compete with native Chinese. When Japan suffered defeat in 1945 and was forced to relinquish the island, only 300,000 Japanese were repatriated to the mother country.

Taiwan became the 35th province of Nationalist China in 1945. Although it had suffered little wartime damage, in contrast to the extensive destruction in both China and Japan, the island had lost the key personnel who had managed its economy. Kuomintang officials from the mainland took over these positions and immediately gained a reputation for being dishonest, dirty, and technologically backward. They seized entire factories built by the Japanese and shipped them to the mainland.

The Kuomintang considered native Taiwan Chinese to be traitors, for many had served in the Japanese armed forces or at the least had not actively opposed the Japanese. They also despised local inhabitants for their lack of proper Chinese language and culture. The Taiwan Chinese, in turn, saw mainlanders as carpetbaggers and eventually launched an uprising in 1947. The Kuomintang responded by a harsh repression that resulted in the slaughter of 20,000 local inhabitants. Evidence suggests that members of the traditional Taiwan Chinese elite were specifically hunted down and killed.

Subsequently, the civil war in China turned against the Nationalist forces. Kuomintang supporters began streaming to Taiwan in 1948. More than 2,000,000 had arrived by the end of 1949 following the Communist triumph. Some 600,000 of them were soldiers. They brought with them a vast amount of China's cultural treasures from Beijing and elsewhere. Communist forces on the mainland were unable to pursue Kuomintang forces to Taiwan because the Nationalists had commandeered all naval and merchant vessels.

The Kuomintang regime of Chiang Kai-shek later was able to maintain its control over Taiwan through support from the United States. The outbreak of the Korean War led America to send its Seventh Fleet to Taiwan Strait to protect the island from invasion. The purpose of the United States was to preserve Taiwan as a support base for the American armed forces. Under American prodding, the Kuomintang regime reformed itself, becoming more honest and efficient.

American protection extended also to the Pescadore and Tachen islands. The Pescadores lie thirty miles west of Taiwan. They consist of seventy-seven islands with a total area of seventy-eight square miles and have a population of 80,000. The Tachens stretch 300 miles off the immediate coast of the mainland. The Republic of China abandoned most of the Tachens in 1955 but retained the two larger islands of Quemoy and Matsu. Quemoy lies only five miles offshore from Amoy, and Matsu could control Foochow harbor.

Kuomintang officials maintained that they constituted the only legitimate government of China. Their parliament, accordingly, continued to be based upon representation from each of China's thirty-five provinces. The regime grouped voters into electoral bodies according to provincial origins. These bodies elected representatives in proportion to province populations. Chinese natives of Taiwan thus had very limited representation. This created particularly deep resentments among them, for it institutionalized management of their country by a minority of mainlanders who did not speak their language nor have sensitivity to their needs.

Lavish American aid fostered rapid economic development. By the mid-1950s the island had become more prosperous than it had been under the Japanese. A modern industrial machine emerged that brought living standards to a level in Asia second only to Japan. The regime achieved this in part by introducing major social changes. It weakened the traditional role of the extended Chinese family, which was seen as an impediment to acceptance of new ideas, and it encouraged the young to become more independent.

Taiwan's population remains divided. Native Taiwan Chinese constitute 67 percent of the island's population. They speak a form of Fukienese that mainland refugees refuse to learn. Most are resentful of the refugee families of the late 1940s and display some nostalgia for the period of Japanese control. Mainlanders and their descendants comprise 20 percent of the total population. Most use Mandarin, having given up their native dialects. They tend to be strongly anti-Japanese in sentiments. Some 10 percent speak Hakka. These are descendants of a onetime persecuted minority group who migrated to Taiwan in the nineteenth century. Their homeland is in northern Kwantung and southern Fukien provinces. Frictions persist between Hakkas and the majority Fukienese. Hakkas tend to be less hostile toward mainlanders. Less than 2 percent of Taiwan's inhabitants are aborigines. They are divided into seven tribes, three of which predominate.

Taiwan's groups tend to be spatially and occupationally segregated. Farmers of Fukien origin are mainly on valley bottoms, whereas Hakkas work terraced lands on the margins of foothills and mountains. Mainlanders are particularly concentrated in and around the northern capital city of Taipei. Aborigines remain in the eastern mountains.

Although the majority Fukienese are to be found in all occupations, Hakkas are noted for running the railroads and staffing local police departments. They also engage in commercial fishing and small businesses. Mainlanders formerly dominated the society by having leading roles in government, education, and the armed forces. Over time, government salaries have not kept pace with those in the private sector, and they no longer constitute an elite class.

Although distinctions between groups remain a principal fact in Taiwanese politics, they are beginning to blur among the younger generation. Despite the degree of spatial segregation, there appears little threat of separatism. They share a common culture and are interdependent in a very small space. Resentments of the Taiwanese majority against mainlanders began to soften in 1987, when martial law was lifted after being in force since 1949.

The Republic of China and the People's Republic of China officially continue to maintain that each is the sole legitimate government over both Taiwan and the mainland. Both reject the notion that Taiwan is an entity separate from the rest of China. Because of these irreconcilable policies, the Republic of China suffered a major setback to its prestige. For a variety of reasons, the United States elected to end its four decades of

diplomatic isolation from the People's Republic of China. The Beijing regime's price for establishing relations with the United States was the severing of official American ties with the government of Taiwan. The United States broke off formal relations with the Republic of China in January 1979, and permitted the government of the People's Republic to assume the China seat in the United Nations Security Council. Subsequently, the United States created an "American Institute" on Taiwan and accorded it diplomatic status in 1980.

The People's Republic of China informally has offered the Taiwanese a special status within China if they would accept a federal relationship with the mainland. It would permit the island to maintain its own armed forces, local self-government, accumulated wealth, economic system, laws on private property, and ties to foreign states.

Inhabitants of Taiwan, however, see little benefit to themselves from unification with the mainland. They appreciate the much higher living standards their society has achieved. Since tensions between the two Chinese political units became relaxed at the end of the 1980s, up to 5 percent of Taiwanese have visited the mainland, seeing disparities in development at firsthand. Despite the official implacability of the two governments, a modus vivendi has emerged that permits

FIGURE 12-6 HONG KONG AND MACAO

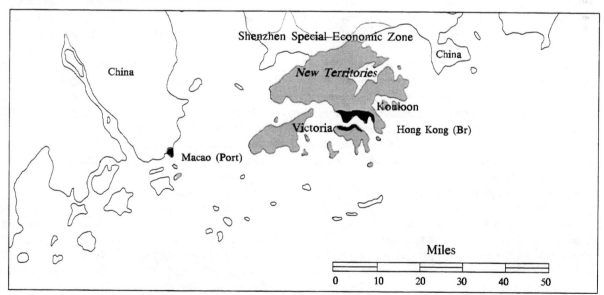

increasing interchange between the two units. Taiwanese increasingly have invested funds in modernizing mainland enterprises.

In addition to the continuing threat of engulfment by the mainland, Taiwan has potential territorial disputes with its other neighbors. These involve historic claims to small islands that hold promise of undersea petroleum reserves offshore. The Spratly Islands are subject to rival claims by the Philippines and Viet Nam, and islands at the southern end of the Ryukyu chain are contested with Japan.

Hong Kong

The British Crown Colony of Hong Kong (Figure 12-6) lies on the south coast of China, ninety miles from Canton (Guangzhou). Its 415 square miles include the island of Hong Kong, which has a third of the area, some 200 other islands, and a strip of leased mainland known as the "New Territories." For a century and a half Hong Kong has served as a link between China and the rest of the world. Its status is in the process of changing, following agreement between the People's Republic of China and the United Kingdom for reversion of sovereignty to China in 1997.

Currently, Hong Kong functions as an interface between two contrasting civilizations and economic systems. Its 6,000,000 inhabitants fret about the future change. More than 98 percent are of Chinese origin, but under decades of British administration they have developed attitudes and skills that set them apart from the main body of Chinese.

For centuries before the establishment of the British presence, the region was a rather desolate lair of pirates and smugglers. It had seen settlement by waves of differing linguistic groups wandering from the interior of southern China to the coast. The area was rather completely depopulated in the period 1662–1669, when the young Manchu dynasty ordered complete evacuation of its coastal areas.

Hong Kong became a British territory in 1842. English merchants had been active in commerce with China for a century previously. However, they had used Portuguese Macao as a trading base until 1771, when they established their own commercial mission in Canton, the city where Chinese foreign traders were concentrated. Representatives of the British East India Company's opium monopoly had particular success in selling that commodity until 1821, when the Chinese government forbade further importation of the drug into China.

The British pressed their government to force the Chinese to rescind the edict, and the British utilized coastal harbors in the vicinity of Hong Kong to smuggle opium into the country. Chinese attempts to suppress this smuggling compelled British interests to flee Canton for Macao in 1839, and open warfare soon began.

In entering into hostilities with China, the United Kingdom was motivated by more than selling opium. Accumulated frustrations in dealing with the Chinese led the British to seek to demonstrate to the Manchu regime that China was not the center of civilization nor the strongest power on earth. A further goal was to open up the vast Chinese market to international trade.

Superior British military equipment and organization prevailed in the struggle. At length, in 1842, the two sides signed the Treaty of Nanking, which granted the United Kingdom sovereignty over thirty-one square mile Hong Kong island and opened five other "treaty ports" to international trade. The British considered establishing a primary commercial base farther north near the mouth of the Yangtze River, but chose Hong Kong because of its proximity to Canton and its protected harbor, open in two directions.

A second war between the United Kingdom and China in 1860 resulted in cession to the British of four square miles of mainland territory adjacent to the small Chinese walled city of Kowloon, opposite Hong Kong Island. The area had become a lawless community of pirates and bandits threatening communications with Canton. At that time the Manchu regime was weakened by the Taiping rebellion and had lost control over much of southern China. Kowloon city initially remained part of China, but later the British unilaterally seized it. Its section of land currently has an ill-defined status within the Crown colony.

A second addition of territory to Hong Kong occurred in 1898, when the United Kingdom leased for ninety-nine years a substantial mainland area that came to be known as the "New Territories." The British wanted to provide expanded land to support Hong Kong with food and a water supply. They also sought to strengthen their position on the China coast in the face of a perceived threat from a recent alliance between France and Russia.

Hong Kong's population grew steadily by inmigration of Chinese; this was because the border of the New Territories with China was an open frontier. By the 1860s Hong Kong had 100,000 inhabitants, 3,000 of whom were not Chinese in origin. Numbers increased to 250,000 in the 1890s, 10,000 being non-Chinese. A flood of refugees entered the colony following the 1937 Japanese invasion of China. Hong Kong's total population reached 1,800,000 in 1940. It then dwindled to 600,000 during World War II, when the island and adjacent mainland were seized by Japan. Refugees again swelled the population in the postwar era, particularly following triumph of Communist forces in China in 1949. The Hong Kong government instituted severe restrictions on immigration in 1953.

Approximately one-third of Hong Kong's present population lives on Hong Kong Island. Chinese constitute 98 percent of the total, most speaking Cantonese. Although virtually all know English, less than 1 percent use it regularly. Sixty percent of the inhabitants were born in Hong Kong.

Although the United Kingdom, like other Western powers in the postwar period, had renounced extraterritorial rights in China, it resumed control of Hong Kong despite efforts of the Kuomintang government to prevent return. The subsequent communist regime applied its own pressures for the British to leave, maintaining that treaties between the United Kingdom and China had no validity because they had been coerced at a time of Chinese weakness.

The Communists could have easily dislodged the British by force, but elected not to do so. Although initially severing the colony from trade with the mainland, they gradually allowed its entrepôt role to resume. For one thing, Hong Kong proved a convenient means of circumventing trade embargoes imposed upon the People's Republic of China by the United States and other countries. The initial loss of trade with China had lasting effects upon the island, however, for it forced the colony to develop industry as an alternative means of supporting its population. Thus, Hong Kong became a major manufacturing center, utilizing its vast reservoir of low-wage labor.

As the strict socialism of the mainland gave way to market-force reforms, Hong Kong played an increasingly useful role for China itself. It served as a conduit for mutually beneficial trade between the mainland and Taiwan, despite implacable hostility between their regimes. The People's Republic encouraged Hong Kong industrialists and other overseas Chinese entrepreneurs to assist it in developing manufacturing in fourteen "special economic zones" created along the coast.

The most significant of these is the Shenzhen zone created in 1980 along the border with the New Territories. Its 125 square miles enjoy a high degree of local autonomy. Low land costs, abundant labor at low wages, and special tax inducements have attracted substantial investment, mostly from Hong Kong. It became exceptionally successful. In addition to immediate profits from enterprises, the Chinese government sees long-term benefits in improvements in infrastructure and the introduction of new technology.

Hong Kong is on the brink of reabsorption into China. The ninety-nine-year British lease on the New Territories ends June 30, 1997. The United Kingdom has acknowledged that it has no moral claim to that area

after the lease expires. Although the British insist that they retain sovereignty over Hong Kong itself, the island could not function without interconnections on the mainland side. Indeed, the entire colony is increasingly dependent upon the Shenzhen area of China for its drinking water, food, energy, and land for such essentials as cemeteries, hospitals, and waste disposal.

Britain entered into negotiations with the People's Republic of China in the 1980s to establish a future course for Hong Kong. The British position was that they had a moral obligation to the inhabitants of the colony (although this perceived responsibility did not prevent them from revoking in 1981 previously held rights of the population to emigrate to the United Kingdom). The Beijing government rejected any notion of British representation for Hong Kong's Chinese inhabitants, but nevertheless entered into talks.

It was clear that Beijing would not permit independence for Hong Kong, even though its population was larger than that of Denmark, Finland, Ireland, Norway, and many other states. It could not allow a precedent to be set that would interfere with its long-term goal of absorption of Taiwan. On the other hand, it saw benefits to itself from allowing the area to enjoy a special status. No city in China was in a position to assume Hong Kong's special bridge role between East and West. A separate identity and socioeconomic system for Hong Kong could also serve as an inducement for Taiwan at last to become associated with the People's Republic.

An agreement signed in 1984 provided for Hong Kong to become a special administrative zone under Chinese sovereignty upon expiration of the New Territories' lease. It guarantees special privileges to Hong Kong for the ensuing fifty years. These include a high degree of local autonomy within a separate administrative system, and continuation of existing legal and economic institutions. The territory can retain its own currency and establish its own financial policies. It will remain a free port. Individuals will continue to enjoy their present rights.

The situation is termed by the Chinese "one country, two systems." Hong Kong in effect will enjoy a greater degree of autonomy than is to be found in existing federal systems. China cannot annul local laws. The territory even is allowed some diplomatic powers.

Hong Kong's population is uneasy over the future, however. It realizes that a future Chinese regime unilaterally can abrogate the agreement at any time it chooses. Policies displeasing to China can result in retaliation, ranging from having the water supply shut off to possible military intervention. Present inhabitants also know that their economic success is due in part to their association with multinational corporations that could easily abandon them.

They also are mindful that their distinctive economic and political attitudes are resented by China's elite. They are very aware of the fate of Shanghai after the Communist victory in 1949. It, too, was cosmopolitan, trade oriented, and shaped by Europeans. As one of the original treaty ports, Shanghai long had operated independently from the Chinese bureaucracy and had served as a link with the West. Its people suffered grievously after its status changed and its entrepreneurial class fled abroad, mainly to Hong Kong.

Complicating implementation of the agreement are increasing pressures by Hong Kong inhabitants to have a democratic system of government. Until now, the British governor of Hong Kong has run the colony without parliamentary restriction. He is advised by an appointed executive council. A legislative council exists for the colony, but only twenty-six of its fifty-six members are elected. (At the local level, there are nineteen districts, each managed by elected boards.) In consequence, most Hong Kong citizens have been apathetic. The popular mood has changed with the impending political changes. China has reacted vigorously to British government proposals to appease such demands. It has threatened to block badly needed expansion of Hong Kong's airport, built during World War II by prisoners of war of Japan, if the United Kingdom does institute a democratic system.

Dismayed by threatened loss of a privileged position, many of the island's elite already have begun to establish family bases in Canada, Europe, and elsewhere. However, despite such doubts, investment in Hong Kong enterprises continues at a brisk pace.

Macao

Since 1557 Portugal has controlled the tiny territory of Macao. This six-square-mile area consists of a small peninsula and two islands linked to it by a bridge and a causeway. It lies at the mouth of the Pearl River, seventy-five miles south of Canton and forty miles west of Hong Kong. Its population of 370,000 is 68 percent Chinese and 29 percent Portuguese.

Its former importance as a commercial port ended with the appearance of great draft ships and the silting of its harbor. Its separate status has been preserved for more than four centuries because it has been a convenience both to China and to Portugal. Macao has become a rather quaint museum of Europe in China and

FIGURE 12-7 THE TWO KOREAS

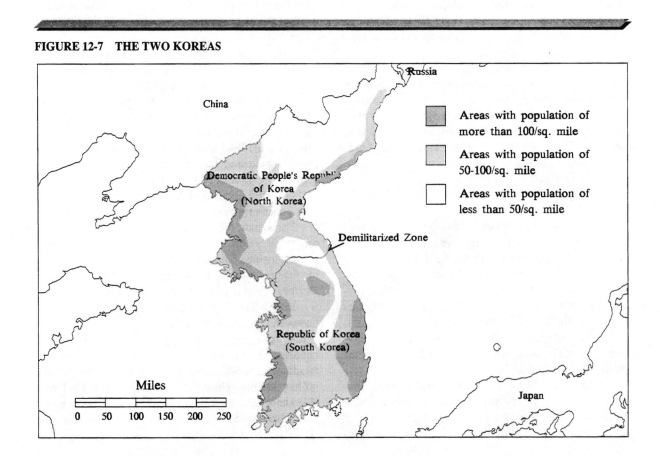

subsists particularly in catering to tourists and gamblers on excursion from Hong Kong; those visitors number more than 4,000,000 annually.

The formal relationship of Macao to Portugal has changed in recent decades. In 1961 it was declared to be an overseas province of Portugal, comparable to the Azores, and no longer a colony. After Portugal's revolution in 1974, the new regime decided to withdraw its role, as it did in Timor in Indonesia. However, the Chinese government dissuaded the Portuguese. Macao then was defined as a Chinese territory under Portuguese administration. In 1976 a formal statute declared its full autonomy in adminstration and economic affairs under Portuguese constitutional law. An agreement signed by Portugal and the People's Republic of China provides for its becoming a part of China in 1999.

The Koreas

The Korean Peninsula (Figure 12-7), like the Appenine Peninsula of Italy, would seem to offer an ideal basis for a state. It is a compact physical unit, 600 miles long and 130 to 200 miles wide. Bodies of water insulate it from neighbors on three sides, and relatively empty mountains mark its borders with the People's Republic of the China and the Russian Federation. Japan lies 120 miles from its southeastern coast, and the Shantung Peninsula of China is 120 miles to the southwest.

Its population is homogeneous and distinctive in race and culture. The peninsula was first unified politically more than two millennia ago. A Korean imperial dynasty lasted from 1392 until 1910. Mineral wealth and industrial development in the north and subtropical farmlands in the south constitute an economic complementarity that would strengthen the coherence of a single state.

However, two hostile states currently occupy the Korean Peninsula. Each triumphed over extreme hardships at the end of World War II to become a successful political entity. Similar fragmentations have alternated with periods of unity in the peninsula throughout history, refuting a widely held notion that configurations of land and sea ultimately dictate the form and nature of political organization.

The Korean Peninsula resembles the Japanese main island of Honshu in size and terrain. Although the total area of the two Koreas is approximately 80,000 square miles, four-fifths of their territory consists of sparsely inhabited hills and mountains. Effectively settled areas are a string of small river floodplains concentrated mainly along the west coast of the peninsula. The Republic of Korea occupies the southern 45 percent of the land, and the Democratic People's Republic of Korea embraces the remainder, including a substantial portion of mainland Asia adjoining the People's Republic of China.

The present division reflects the traditional intermediary position of the peninsula between strong states to the east and west. Korea has served for centuries as a bridge between China and Japan. Since the mid-nineteenth century, Russia's expansion to its northern doorstep has added another dimension to Korea's long-standing role. Although neither Korean state sees itself subordinate to its neighbors, their patterns of development and dynamics reflect influences that have emanated from across their borders. North Korea is but the most recent manifestation of China's perennial involvement in Korean affairs, whereas South Korea personifies the role Japan has played on the peninsula for centuries.

Koreans have long asserted that a Korean state was founded in the lower Taedong River region of the northeast in the year 2333 B.C. under the leadership of an individual named Tan'gun. The North Korean regime has branded this legend as a fairy tale, but the South Korean government has enshrined it in its official iconography. Chinese chronicles refer to a native state existing on the peninsula as early as 1123 B.C. By the fourth century B.C. a collection of tribal groups in the northeast of the peninsula had developed a state known as "Choson," meaning "Serenity of the Morning." The name is a poetic allusion to the peninsula's location east of the Chinese Empire, where it was bathed by the light of the "Land of the Rising Sun," namely Japan. Choson later fell into several feuding parts, one of which, Lolang, became a colony of China in 108 B.C. Lolang was centered on the site of modern Pyongyang, capital of North Korea. It served as a transmission belt for Chinese culture and technology to all tribes on the peninsula.

In A.D. 313 Lolang was conquered by the native state of Koguryo, which had developed in the Yalu River basin about 50 B.C. Koguryo maintained itself until the mid-seventh century A.D. In 612 its army of 300,000 is reported to have defeated invading Chinese forces numbering more than a million, leaving, according to legend, only 2,700 Chinese survivors. Koguryo contended with two other Korean kingdoms that also had emerged on the peninsula: Paekche to the south and Silla to the southeast.

Each of the states initially consisted of several tribes speaking differing languages. Strong central authority in each kingdom led to a homogenization of its population, abetted by the heavy influence of Chinese culture that pervaded the peninsula. Buddhism and Confucianism arrived in A.D. 372, and scholars from Paekche transmitted scriptures eastward to Japan. Still, cultural differences remained on the peninsula. Chinese scholars who visited Korea at the time commented on the significant cultural differences they observed between northerners and southerners.

In addition to struggles with each other and with the Chinese Empire, the three kingdoms also suffered intervention by the Japanese, who were interested in keeping open a valuable conduit to China. By A.D. 672 Silla had conquered the other two states and had driven Chinese forces north of the Taedong River. Thereafter, China recognized Silla as a tributary state, but with self-government.

The Silla state borrowed heavily from Chinese culture and added innovations of its own. It created several provinces on the Chinese model of administrative organization and adopted the Chinese system of selecting bureaucrats through examinations. It created a center of learning where a native Korean literature emerged in the seventh century using *idu*, a new phonetic script based on Chinese characters. Centuries later *idu* became the basis for Korea's distinctive alphabet.

In addition to cultural and economic ties with China and Japan, the Korean kingdom had contacts as far away as India. By the eighth century it had become known to Arab geographers. The state suffered from internal economic and political difficulties, however. Peasant rebellions and banditry became common features in the tenth century. In 935 a military general overthrew the regime and established a new dynasty, the Koryo, a shortened version of Koguryo. The Chinese and Japanese adopted modified forms of this name (*Kaokiuli, Korai, Kaoli*) to designate the peninsular state, and from them the English term "Korea" is derived.

Beginning with the weakening of the central government in China in the eleventh century, Koryo found itself increasingly contending with powerful Mongol and Manchu tribes on its northern border. In 1259 it was forced to become part of Mongol-dominated China. Subsequently, Koryo suffered dearly from the ill-fated Mongol attempts to invade Japan in 1274 and 1281. It regained its status as a self-governing Chinese vassal in 1368, when the Chinese-based Ming dynasty supplanted the Mongols in ruling China.

In 1392 the Yi dynasty established itself in Korea and remained nominally in power for five centuries, until finally dissolved by the Japanese in 1910. The regime adopted "Choson" as name of the state, hearkening back to Korea's beginnings. It also established Seoul as the capital. Confucianism became the state doctrine and engendered a rigidly stratified social system. Formerly dominant Buddhism assumed a lesser role. Indeed, Buddhist monks were forbidden to enter the capital city between the years 1456 and 1895.

Over ensuing centuries Korea found itself subject to continuing pressures from its neighbors. Japan twice sought to conquer the peninsula in the sixteenth century. Manchu tribes invaded in 1627 and 1637, as the ability of China's Ming dynasty to defend its protectorate weakened. Following the Manchu triumph over China in 1644, Korea became a vassal to the Manchu dynasty. However, no Chinese were allowed to settle within it, and its regime continued to be self-governing. It changed little internally until the end of the nineteenth century, remaining medieval in outlook and riddled by corruption.

In contrast to South and Southeast Asia, Korea did not suffer the impact of European colonialism. Very little was known about it, and maps by Mercator, Ortelius, and Sanson represented it as an island. In the early seventeenth century Korea did witness the introduction of Roman Catholicism by way of Japan, and it is from Catholic missionaries that the first European accounts of Korea are derived. The Western religion found acceptance principally among lowborn persons and a few scholars. It is estimated that up to 100,000 Koreans were converted. The regime banned the faith in 1786 and thereafter ruthlessly persecuted its adherents. China's defeat by the British in the 1840 Opium War led to Korea's adopting a policy of seclusion, and it became known as the "Hermit Kingdom." Fearing penetration of Western ideas, it suppressed Christianity even more ruthlessly, executing 13,000 Roman Catholics in 1866 alone.

Korea had more to fear from a rapidly developing, Westernized Japan, however. Its protector, China, no longer could defend it. After Korea renounced its seclusion policy in 1873, it found itself forced to sign a treaty three years later that opened three ports to Japanese traders. As a counterweight, it entered into a commercial arrangement with the United States in 1882 and also adopted a policy of tolerating Christian mission. Later, it reached agreements for trade with the United Kingdom, Germany, Italy, Russia, and France. The Japanese dominated Korea's foreign trade, however, receiving 91 percent of its exports and forwarding half of its imports.

Japan completely supplanted China's role in Korea as a consequence of its victory in the Sino-Japanese war of 1894–1895. Fighting between the two powers was confined entirely to the Korean Peninsula. Japan used its new authority to force a number of Westernizing reforms upon Korea, and it also set about countering a threat to its position from Russia, which had gained timber concessions in Korea in the 1890s. A war between Russia and Japan in 1904–1905 resulted in Japanese victory and imposition of a Japanese protectorate over Korea in 1905. Japan annexed the peninsula in 1910, terminating the Yi dynasty.

Japan was ruthless in suppressing any threats to its rule. It had to contend with the beginnings of a national identity that had emerged as a consequence of the education afforded by a number of schools opened by Protestant missionaries in the 1880s. The foreign religious emissaries met less resistance than in other Asian states, and their impact is still felt in the large Christian community in Korea. Their influence included a wide dissemination of literacy, as they emphasized the use of the *han'gul* phonetic alphabet. Previously, the educated elite had preferred Chinese ideographs as a loftier form of writing that made available the ancient classics and permitted communications with the Chinese and Japanese. The missionaries also contributed to an improved status of women in Korean society.

To counteract growing Korean national feelings, Japan obliged the population to rename themselves in a Japanese form. It closed private schools, and its new schools omitted all discussions of Korean history and culture. Running the colony was placed in the hands of throngs of migrants from Japan.

Although its administration of Korea was dedicated to enhancing Japanese interests, Japan played a major role in modernizing the Koreans. It introduced Western technology and ideas. It created an efficient infrastructure and modern industrial plant. Cities took on a new appearance, with wide streets and modern buildings. Electricity and telephones became available. Public health measures lowered the mortality rate. Development occurred particularly after Japan began its war with China in 1937. Northern Korea became an important mining and industrial base for the Japanese war effort. Many Koreans went to Japan, at first as wage earners in menial jobs and later as conscripts to replace workers who had entered the military as World War II expanded.

Rural Korea remained relatively unchanged, however. Its villages maintained traditional organization and outlooks. Farmers lacked incentives to produce because of the onerous terms of their tenant status. The Japanese did introduce improved seeds and production techniques, and they promoted increased production of rice, most of which was exported to Japan. The Koreans subsisted upon millet, much of it coming from Japanese-occupied Manchuria after 1931.

Soviet and American forces entered Korea when the war with Japan ended. The wartime Allies had agreed to divide their occupation zones by the parallel of 38°N. Earlier, a declaration in Cairo had called for the establishment of an independent Korean state. The young United Nations sponsored elections for a Korean government in 1948, but the USSR refused to permit electoral activities within its zone. The American-controlled south then formed the Republic of Korea, upon which event the north cut off the flow of electricity. The north also established the Korean People's Democratic Republic with its capital in Pyongyang. For the first time in 1,300 years, the Korean Peninsula was divided into more than one state.

In 1949 the United States withdrew its troops from the Republic of Korea. A year later, in June 1950, North Korea invaded South Korea, and within three months had occupied almost all the peninsula. Under United States leadership, the United Nations condemned the attack and marshalled forces to repel the North Koreans. A brilliant amphibious landing west of Seoul cut the North Korean supply lines, leading to destruction of the invading army.

The UN forces, which were principally American but included troops from fifteen other states, drove northward, capturing Pyongyang and approaching the Yalu River border with the People's Republic of China. Chinese "volunteers" then intervened on behalf of the North Koreans, driving the UN troops southward. By the middle of 1951, battle lines had become stabilized more-or-less along the 38° parallel. After two years of negotiations, the UN Command, North Korea, and China signed an armistice. It provided for creation of a demilitarized zone that followed the existing troop positions. The government of South Korea refused to sign the agreement.

Under the Japanese, the south, which contained 75 percent of the rice paddies, had specialized in surplus food production. North Korea, which had 70 percent of the peninsula's coal, most of its iron ore, and its principal power-generation facilities, became the colony's industrial base. The postwar division into two states sundered this complementarity. South Korea, with American support, began to develop its own manufacturing enterprises, whereas North Korea notably expanded food production in what was generally marginal farmland. The relative success of each state illustrates the ability of modern societies to adjust to changed conditions and to develop.

The Korean states are perhaps the most ethnically homogeneous in the world. In 1945 some 900,000 Japanese lived on the peninsula, but virtually all were repatriated. The largest minority now are the 25,000 Chinese who live in South Korea, most of them in business. The principal differences among Koreans are religious in nature, and these are significant only in the south, where the Mahayana, or Chinese, version of Buddhism is accepted by about half the population. A quarter identify with Confucianism, and another quarter are Christians, of whom 75 percent belong to Protestant faiths. North Korea has suppressed traditional religions ever since its founding. Marxism-Leninism is accorded the status of a secular religion expressing "all progressive ideas of mankind." Since the 1960s, the regime has promoted the doctrine of *chuch'e* ("national self-reliance") as enunciated by its leader, Kim Il-Sung. In many ways, *chuch'e* parallels traditional Confucian ideals of filial piety and respect for superiors. North Korea also has appropriated to itself the mythical Korean "flying horse" (*chumilla*) symbol of strength and speed. In both Koreas traditional shamanistic beliefs remain imbedded among the peasantry.

Not all Koreans live in the two states. More than a million are settled in northeast China, although 300,000 were repatriated between 1945 and 1950. Large numbers also once lived in Vladivostok and the Ussuri valley of Russia. These were all deported to Soviet Central Asia in 1937 out of fear that many were spies for Japan. Many have drifted back to the Russian Far East in recent years. More than 700,000 Koreans live in Japan, where they suffer a number of disabilities. Many Koreans have emigrated to the United States.

North Korea

The People's Democratic Republic of Korea occupies 45,000 square miles and has a population of 40,000,000. Two-thirds of these inhabitants are concentrated in the western plains, which constitute less than 20 percent of the territory. Its regime sees itself as the legitimate government of all Korea and the south as an area of American occupation supporting an administration of flunkies. For most of the postwar era it pursued a policy of seclusion similar to that of the Hermit Kingdom era. Like other Communist states, North Korea relies on a disciplined, hierarchial political party to bind its society together.

Despite its professed policy of self-reliance, North Korea became very dependent upon favorable trade terms and other forms of financial support from the USSR and the People's Republic of China. Its own economic achievements were substantially more modest than in South Korea. When the Soviet Union disintegrated in 1991, the north found itself in difficult economic straits. It also suffered humiliation from the decision of the Russians to establish diplomatic ties with the Republic of Korea. After years of isolation and hostility, it began making its own overtures to South Korea and to other non-Communist states. The possibilities of political unification of the Korean Peninsula appeared brighter in the decade of the 1990s than previously in the postwar era.

Aside from its preoccupation with the south, North Korea has few problems with its neighbors. Korea's traditional border with China had been along a mountain ridge well into southeastern Manchuria. To avoid fric-

tions, both states prohibited settlement within a 5,600-square-mile "neutral zone." China's present Korean minority is a legacy of that period. The two states agreed to recognize the Yalu River as their mutual boundary in 1875, and in 1909 they settled upon the Tumen River as the eastern border. An unresolved question over the precise boundary location on Mt. Paektu was settled in 1963. Frictions do arise occasionally with Japan and other states concerning the use of offshore waters for fishing.

South Korea

The Republic of Korea suffered grievously from the Korean War. It earlier had absorbed more than 4,000,000 refugees from North Korea, Manchuria, and Japan. Its cities grew rapidly in the immediate postwar era, in part because the refugees could not be settled in existing rural villages, whose societies were organized on a kinship basis. South Korea lacked the industrial development of the north, and also suffered from repatriation to Japan of economic managers and other skilled individuals who had run the society.

It adopted a democratic governmental organization that exhibited a number of authoritarian tendencies. Its postwar regimes were notably successful in mobilizing the population into a modern industrial society, borrowing much from the experience of the Japanese.

Japan

Despite its possession of a host of features that have frustrated political unity in other lands, Japan is one of the world's most successful states. It is small and fragmented. It has half the population of the United States, confined to a physical territory of 146,000 square miles, equivalent to the state of Montana. Its population is split among four major islands and a number of smaller ones (Figure 12-8). Settlements lie on small, separated river floodplains and deltas, the largest of which, the Kanto Plain, occupies barely 5,000-square-miles. Four-fifths of the land area is covered by virtually empty mountains. Japan also is devoid of most of the natural resources that constitute the basic necessities of modern industry.

Japan's success derives from a notable homogeneity and coherence. Despite an insular nature and fragmented ecumene, its people share a common culture that sets them apart from neighbors. They have developed a strong sense of nationhood. The surrounding sea has facilitated, rather than frustrated, mutual associa-

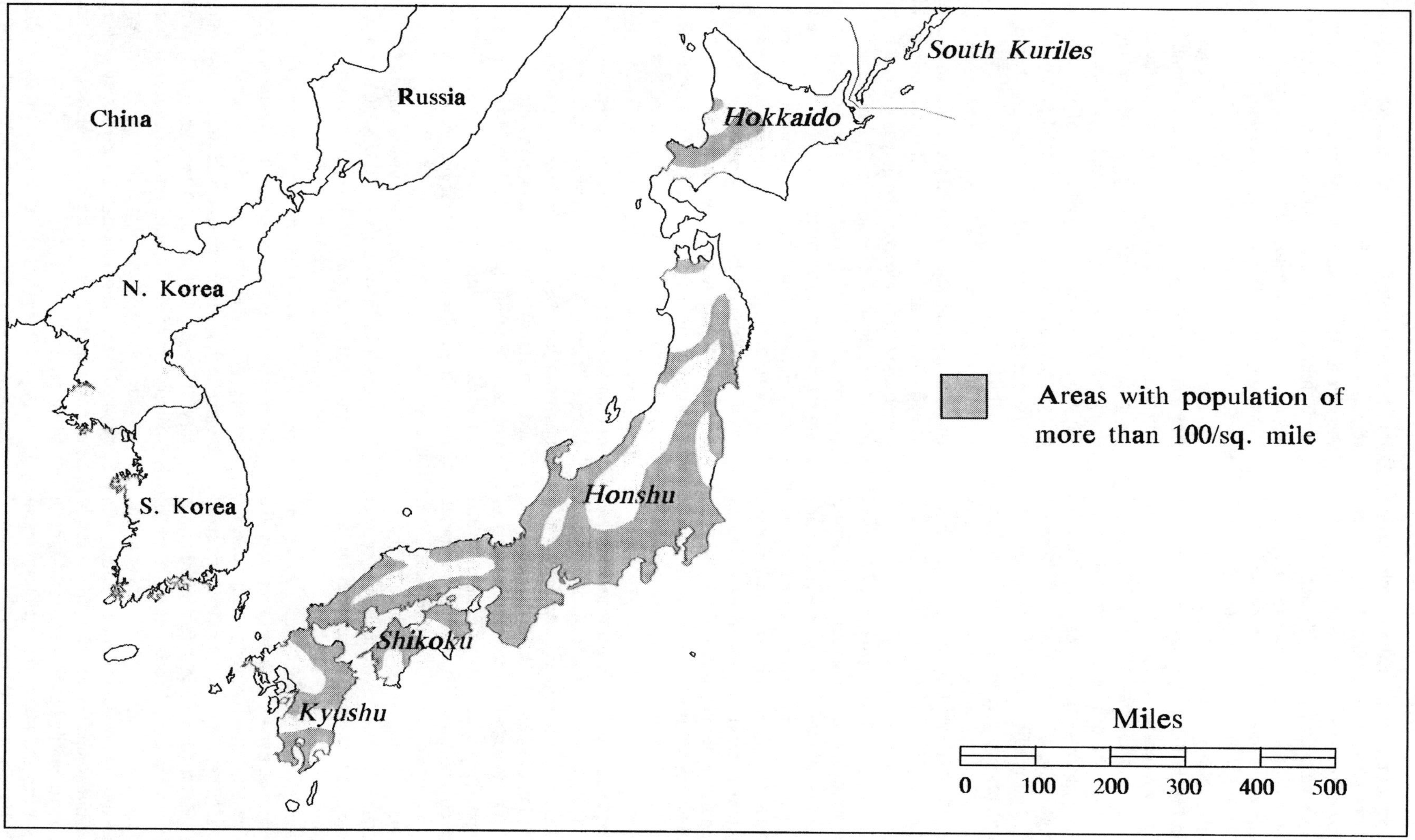

FIGURE 12-8 THE JAPANESE ISLANDS

tion of all of Japan's components. Like the population of the Mediterranean region, virtually all inhabitants live near coastlines. The greatest distance of any section of Japan from the sea is sixty-five miles. The Japanese have communicated easily with each other by water throughout history. Japan's success also is traceable to continuity as a social unit for more than 1,500 years. Its ability to marshal its people to defend the homeland enabled it to resist the Chinese forces of Kublai Khan in the thirteenth century and European imperialism in more recent times.

The Japanese call their state "Nippon" ("Land of the Rising Sun"), a term originally bestowed by the Chinese to signify Japan's offshore location from the Middle Kingdom. The Chinese form is "Nit-Pön" ("Sun-Origin"). During the period of Mongol ascendancy, the Mandarin language underwent some phonetic modification. The "n" consonant became a *j*, and Nit-Pön became "Ji-Pen" or "Ji-pön-kweh," transmitted by Marco Polo as "Zipangu" and becoming "Japan" in English.

The position of Japan on the periphery of China is often compared to the United Kingdom's relationship with Europe. In classical times both states were considered barbarian lands at the end of cultural transmission belts. Both evolved distinctive societies in isolation from trends dominant on mainlands. Both countries adapted to changing external relationships and took advantage of new opportunities that were afforded. Finally, both were able to defend themselves through control of the sea.

Although Japan is 50 percent larger than the United Kingdom, the effectively settled area of its islands is less than half that of Great Britain. It extends over a greater range of latitude, stretching 1,300 miles from the southern Ryukyu Islands to the northern tip of Hokkaido. It approximates the latitudes of northern and central China, but enjoys a very different climate because of its maritime location. Its climatic zones range from a humid subtropical south, whose mild winters permit the raising of three crops of rice per year, to a more continental north resembling the upper Midwest of the United States.

The principal island is Honshu, "Chief Land," with an area comprising 60 percent of Japan's territory. To the south is Kyushu, "Nine Districts," and Shikoku, "Four Provinces." They ring the 250-mile-long Inland Sea from Osaka Bay to Shimonoseki. In the far north is Hokkaido, whose older name, "Yeso," meant "Land of the Barbarians." The smaller islands include the Ryukyu chain extending toward China and the Bonin and Volcano island groups leading away to the southeast. The islands are marked by vulcanism. Mountain ranges are always in sight, with peaks on Honshu reaching elevations in excess of 10,000 feet.

Ancestors of the Japanese people came both from the continental mainland and from the Polynesian region. Establishing a foothold around the Inland Sea, they pressed northward on Honshu and Hokkaido into lands dominated by the primitive Ainu, a people sharing many characteristics with aboriginal peoples of the Russian Far East. The Ainu now constitute a tiny group, confined mainly to Hokkaido.

Japan's two other minorities are its Koreans and Burakamin, or Eta. The former are descendants of migrants and forced laborers coming to the islands when Korea was a Japanese colony. The latter are a distinctive lower caste in Japanese society. They traditionally have performed such culturally abhorent occupations to the dominant society as butchering and tanning. Both minorities are relatively small, scattered, and acculturated.

The historic nucleus of Japan was located on the island of Kyushu. An organized society flourished there as early as the third century B.C. It was in contact with Korea and China, receiving numerous cultural innovations from those civilizations, including horses, carts, and tools. Japan early adopted aspects of the customs and religions of its continental neighbors. Chinese visitors to Japan in this period recorded the existence of more than 100 little states in the Inland Sea region.

Centralized political organization dates from approximately A.D. 350, when a loose federation emerged at the north end of the Inland Sea. It was termed the Yamato state. In 391 it attacked Korea, motivated to preserve a conduit to China. It subsequently maintained a foothold on the southeast coast of the Korean Peninsula. Japan also began a long process of northward expansion against the Ainu, who had continued to maintain a hunting and gathering economy on northern Honshu and Hokkaido. Many historians attribute the development of Japan's martial spirit and feudal political order to the requirements of the frontier struggle with the Ainu.

Chinese influences continued strong in the Yamato state. Buddhism arrived by way of Korea in the fourth century. From the seventh to ninth centuries, Japan sent officials, priests, and students to its dominant western neighbor to ascertain and transfer to Japanese society the secrets of the Middle Kingdom's success. These efforts resulted in establishment of a centralized government in Japan in the seventh century. Its capital at Nara in 710 was modeled after the spatial form of the Chinese imperial capital in Sian, as was the successor capital at Kyoto in 794. The regime adopted the Chinese rectangular land survey system for farming plots. Even the dress of nobles aped Chinese fashions.

As the power of the Chinese dynasty declined, Japan proceeded to develop its own distinctive cultural forms and political organization. It preserved its ancient Shinto religious tradition and modified imported Buddhism into the belief system known as Zen. It did not accept Chinese Confucianism, which called for a highly centralized social order. Japanese leaders found it unsuited to conditions and needs of the fragmented ecumene. The Japanese emperor had a largely ceremonial role in what amounted to a federal system.

After 1192, the powers of the emperor were further curtailed when governing functions came into the hands of strong warlords known as *shoguns*. The domain of the shoguns was divided into as many as 1,500 separately governed territories. Gradually a stronger feudal system emerged in which local military lords, the *daimyos,* consolidated adjacent units in the small delta farming regions into strong political entities.

Europeans appeared in Japan in the sixteenth century. The Portuguese made contact in 1542, and Spaniards arrived in 1584. They initially were welcomed for their trade, and Roman Catholic missionaries had some success in converting the local population, particularly on the island of Kyushu. Dutch ships arrived in 1600 and supplanted Portuguese interests. The British established relations in 1613. However, the Japanese were able to resist the imposition of colonial relations that had occurred in India and the Americas.

Late in the sixteenth century a member of the Tokugawa family became shogun and succeeded in welding the 260 daimyo units into a centralized state. He moved the capital to the northern frontier on the Kanto plain. The small settlement of Edo became the new capital city of Tokyo. To keep the feudal nobility in line, he forced each daimyo ruler to maintain his family in Edo, a technique also used by kings of France. The Tokugawa shogunate revised the taxing system and introduced currency. It established a uniform system of weights and measures. It exerted pressures to expand and improve agriculture, doubling the arable acreage within a century. The shogunate also expanded and improved the system of roads to facilitate transportation and communication and further control the daimyos.

The new regime, alarmed at the social changes that were accompanying contact with Europeans, adopted a policy of isolating Japan from the rest of the world, severing all connections with Europeans in 1639. Only Dutch and Chinese merchants were allowed to barter goods, and only on a small island in the Inland Sea off Nagasaki. The shogunate banned all foreign travel by Japanese, including merchants, even limiting the size of ships that could be built. By such measures it was able to resist encroachment by European imperialism and to preserve its independence.

Japan's self-imposed isolation ended in 1853, when a fleet of American naval ships arrived in Uraga Bay, commanded by Commodore Matthew Perry. Bowing to what appeared inevitable, Japan entered into treaty relations with the United States and soon to other European powers. Within a short time it embarked upon a new process of centralization and modernization. In 1867 a rebellion ended the Tokugawa shogunate and vested power in the emperor Meiji.

In contrast to hidebound Confucian China, the Japanese, with their Shinto ethic, proved much readier to accept the reforms necessary to withstand Western pressures. The new regime engaged foreign advisers and sent delegations and students to study in Europe and America. It borrowed ideas from many sources.

Among early changes was the 1871 abolition of the daimyo feudal units and their replacement by an orderly system of thirty-nine administrative prefectures. This had the effect of weakening centrifugal regionalism and was comparable to the département reform in revolutionary France. The new regime, however, remained sensitive to the needs of the elite class that traditionally had ruled the society. Local daimyo families and their samurai retainers lost their governing roles, but received compensation through the opportunity to assume leadership posts within Japan's greatly expanding industry, armed forces, and government bureaucracy.

The new regime strengthened the unity of the state by embarking upon major improvements of infrastructure. It built railroads throughout the islands and improved the existing networks of roads. It established an efficient postal service that utilized 35,000 miles of routes. It completed its first telegraph line in 1869 and by 1880 had erected 7,900 miles of wire. It also developed its harbors into modern ports and imported whole factory complexes from Europe and America.

The Japanese also adopted the prevailing Western zest for imperial expansion. For the next three-quarters of a century they expanded their state's territory. Alarmed by Russian moves into the Ussuri valley, Japan sent soldier-farmers to settle the virtually empty island of Hokkaido in the 1870s. It laid claim to the Bonin and Volcano islands in 1875 and to the Ryukyus and Kuril islands four years later. It went to war with China, and as a result acquired Taiwan (Formosa) and Korea in 1895.

Japan became the first non-European state to defeat a European power (1905), when it humiliated Russia. As a consequence, it received southern Sakhalin Island, which it renamed Karafuto, and the Liaotung Peninsula and other parts of southern Manchuria. It also ended a developing Russian involvement in Korea, making the peninsula a protectorate. In 1910 Japan annexed Korea and treated it as a food-producing colony for the next three-and-one-half decades.

In 1931 Japan seized Manchuria from China, enlarging it a year later and making it the puppet state of Manchukuo. Beginning with an "incident" at the Marco Polo bridge outside Beijing in 1937, Japan launched an invasion of China that resulted in control of most of its productive territory. In late 1941 it felt strong enough to attack American, British, and Dutch possessions in the western Pacific. Its announced purpose was to create a "Greater East Asian Co-Prosperity Sphere."

After initial successes that extended its control of most of East and Southeast Asia to the margins of Australia and India, Japan ultimately suffered complete defeat in mid-1945. It was shorn of virtually all the lands it had acquired since the Meiji restoration. Particularly grating to this day has been the loss of two small islands in the southern Kuril chain off Hokkaido that traditionally had been considered to be part of Japan's home territory. Japan also suffered several years of occupation by American forces. A peace treaty signed in San Francisco in 1951 by Japan with forty-eight countries (except the Soviet Union) provided for continued stationing of American troops until the Japanese could provide for their own defense.

During the cold war period between the Soviet Union and the combined states of Western Europe and North America following World War II, Japan recovered its dynamism. The United States returned the northern Ryukyu Islands to Japan in 1953, and the Bonin and Volcano islands in 1968. In 1972 it transferred the southern Ryukyus, including the island of Okinawa, where America had established a major military base.

Japan suffers from fewer regional political problems than virtually any other state. Differences among its inhabitants exist, but they are minor. Virtually no secessionist movements have been recorded. The most disaffected territory is in the southern Ryukyu Islands. The archipelago extends for 500 miles southwest of Japan, and contains 1,300 square miles with a population of 1,500,000. Although the local language is related to Japanese, the islands traditionally have gravitated toward Chinese civilization. Native music and popular arts retain a definite Chinese stamp. Their local king was dethroned in 1874, when Japan annexed them. When they have occasion to travel to the main Japanese islands, inhabitants find themselves dismissed as second-class citizens owing to their dialect.

Japanese from northern Honshu and Hokkaido also feel discrimination. For the majority of Japanese, living in the subtropical climates from Tokyo southward, northerners inhabit a non-Japanese territory that has many connotations of a frontier. Settlement of Tohoku, as northern Honshu is termed, occurred mainly in the seventeenth and eighteenth centuries. Migrants came to Hokkaido only in the mid-nineteenth century. Both areas remain sparsely settled by Japanese standards. They are seen as lacking the long-standing cultural traditions of the Inland Sea region. Northerners resent the condescension accorded them and have formed organizations to prevent discrimination.

The Japanese have adjusted well to their loss of colonial empire. Only continued Russian occupation of the southern Kurils remains a subject of unhappiness. In many ways, what was lost politically was regained economically. Japan has become the dominant force in Eastern Asia, leading a modernized version of the "Co-Prosperity Sphere." Korea, China, Taiwan, the Philippines, Indonesia, and mainland Southeast Asia look to Japan as a major market and source of capital for development.

Devoid of its own major raw materials, Japan has mobilized its gifted society to process products garnered from all parts of the world into quality wares that enjoy international reputations. By the 1970s it had overtaken the vast USSR in industrial production, despite having less than half its population and a tiny fraction of its area. Although limited in spatial aspects, Japan's living standards are among the highest in the world.

As Japan has resumed a position of world leadership economically, pressures have mounted at home to develop a stronger military. The Japanese are well aware of the vulnerability of their vital linkages to other lands for raw materials and markets. Middle East crises have affected their petroleum supply and demonstrated their precarious situation. Their neighbors, all of whom have felt the past impress of Japanese imperialism, worry about the effects of a rearmed Japan.

The Kuril Islands dispute with Russia has plagued relations between the two powers since the end of World War II. The Kurils extend in a 700-mile arc from northeastern Hokkaido to the Kamchatka Peninsula and have a combined area of 4,000 square miles. The present population is about 20,000. Nearly all live in the southern islands off Hokkaido. Japan acquired the island chain at the beginning of the nineteenth century. In 1875 Russia recognized Japanese sovereignty in return for recognition of its own claims to Sakhalin Island.

The Soviet Union seized the Kurils in 1945 as compensation for its entry into the Pacific war. All inhabitants were expelled to Japan. Neither Japan nor the United States subsequently recognized Soviet sovereignty over the islands. The USSR returned nearby Shikotan Island and the Habomai Islands to Japan in 1965, but steadfastly refused to give up its control of the other islands. It maintained that the islands were essential for its defense by protecting its outlets from the Sea of Okhotsk.

The Japanese particularly desire the larger southern islands of Kunashiri and Etorofu. They contend that these should not be considered as part of the Kuril chain, but rather they are part of the Japanese home islands. Kunashiri lies only ten miles from Hokkaido.

Japan has made the islands an issue in dealing with the USSR and its Russian successor state. It has limited its assistance, investment, and commerce, pending their return. The decline and disintegration of the Soviet Union has lessened the strategic significance of the islands, but their retention continues to strike an emotional chord among many Russians.

Bibliography

COPPER, JOHN F., *Taiwan: Nation-State or Province?* Boulder, CO: Westview Press, 1990.

GINSBERG, NORTON, "China's Changing Political Geography," *Geographical Review*, Vol. 42 (1952), pp. 102–117.

GINSBERG, NORTON and BERNARD LALOR, eds., *China: The 80's Era,* Boulder, CO: Westview Press, 1984.

KOLB, ALBER, *East Asia: China Japan, Korea, Vietnam: Geography of a Cultural Region.* London: Methuen, 1971.

LONG, SIMON, *Taiwan: China's Last Frontier.* New York: St. Martin's Press, 1991.

KNAPP, RONALD G., ed., *China's Island Frontier: Studies in the Historical Geography of Taiwan.* Honolulu: University Press of Hawaii, 1980.

KORNHAUSER, DAVID, *Japan: Geographical Background to Urban-Industrial Development,* 2nd ed., "The World's Landscapes." London: Longman, 1981.

McCUNE, SHANNON, *Korea's Heritage: A Regional and Social Geography.* New York: Tuttle, 1964.

PANNELL, CLIFTON W., ed., *East Asia: Geographical and Historical Approaches to Foreign Area Studies.* Dubuque, IA: Kendall-Hunt, 1983.

SMITH, C.J., *China: People and Places in the Land of One Billion.* Boulder, CO: Westview Press, 1991.

TREGEAR, T.R., *China: A Geographical Survey.* New York: John Wiley, 1980.

TREWARTHA, GLENN, *Japan: A Geography.* Madison: University of Wisconsin Press, 1965.

13

Australasia and Oceania

THE decision in 1788 to use Australia as a region of exile for British convicts signaled the beginnings of modern European encroachment upon Australasia and Oceania. Colonial control of the region came late in comparison with acquisitions in India and Southeast Asia, in part because of the location of most islands away from early sailing routes across the Pacific (Figure 13-1). Even after discovery of the islands by Dutch and British explorers in the seventeenth and eighteenth centuries, their evident limited resources provided little inducement for any greater European involvement. Only Australia and New Zealand had received attention during the first half of the nineteenth century. An active quest for colonies in mid-century by an expansionist France and a unified Germany spurred the United Kingdom and the United States to stake claims in the region. Improvements in oceanic transportation also played a role. Following World War I, the League of Nations assigned Germany's Pacific territories to Japan, Australia, and New Zealand as so-called mandates. At the conclusion of World War II, Japan's Pacific island empire came under control by the United States as trusteeships of the United Nations (Table 13-1).

Australia

The continent of Australia, with 3,000,000 square miles, is more than six times larger than the combined total area of all other islands in the region, and is, in fact, the sixth largest state in the world. However, like most of the other islands, it is sparsely populated. Its latitudinal position extends from the tropic zone to the subtropics, and it is dominated by a huge interior desert. The bulk of its population is concentrated along its southern and eastern coasts in regions of Mediterranean-type climate. These inhabited areas of Australia are comparable to the locations of the ecumenes of South Africa and the southern "cone" of Latin America. Empty areas of desert insulate major population clusters from each other, and the state of Tasmania is set apart by the sea.

Most of Australia is dry, 85 percent of the land receiving less than 30 inches of precipitation per year. Only 6 percent of the total area is in cultivation. In most regions rains come during the cool season of the year. Forests grow mainly in the southeastern highlands and cover barely 120,000 miles. Of particular significance

for the maintenance of the few isolated population clusters in the dry areas is a vast artesian basin that permits tapping of stored underground water.

Australian Aborigines have lived in Australia for more than 40,000 years. They now number about 300,000 individuals, a high proportion being of mixed racial ancestry. They are a remnant of a formerly broad zone around the Indian Ocean inhabited by similar dark-skinned peoples, remaining exemplars of which are the Bushmen of Africa, the Dravidians of India, the Negritos of the Philippines, and the peoples of New Guinea. Unlike the natives of New Guinea, who developed a thriving agriculture, the Australian Aborigines remained hunters and gatherers until the advent of the Europeans. A quarter or more now live in Australia's cities and towns. They speak more than 200 different languages and group themselves into some 500 "tribes," although identity tends to be locally oriented to extended families.

Although it seems inevitable that Pacific Islanders knew about Australia, and more than likely also Chinese voyagers, the barren qualities of most Australian coastal areas likely discouraged migration and settlement. The Dutch were the first Europeans to take note of the huge body of land following several voyages in the early seventeenth center. Their most significant exploration was by Abel Tasman, who in 1642 sailed completely around Australia. However, the Dutch saw "New Holland" to be of little potential for colonial development.

In the 1680s British ships began charting much of the area's coastline. Particularly significant were three voyages of Captain James Cook to the region in the 1760s and 1770s. Subsequently, the British decided to exile convicts to Australia in order to relieve the increasing population pressures besetting English prisons. Formerly, the British had sent convicts to the North American colonies, but these had become independent. In May 1787, eleven ships sailed for Australia carrying 570 male convicts, 162 female prisoners, and 250 free persons. They landed in January 1788, at what grew into the metropolis of Sydney. A second fleet of ships arrived in 1790. The British brought more than 160,000 convicts to Australia before the practice ended in 1868. Large numbers of free settlers started arriving in Australia in the early nineteenth century. They became the basis for the colony of South Australia, whose distinctive qualities today are traced by many to the fact that it received no convicts.

The Aboriginal population living in the southeast resisted the invaders of their homeland but proved no match for the firepower and superior organizational

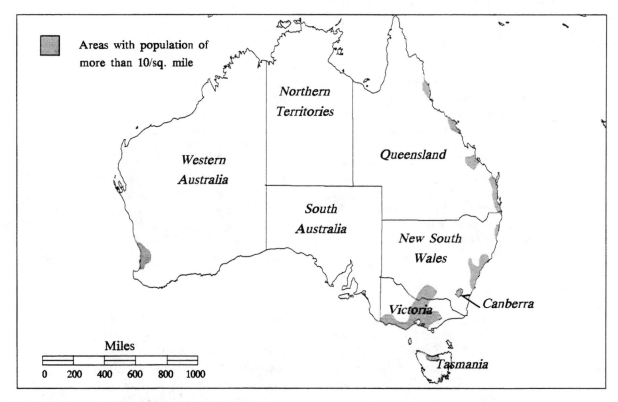

FIGURE 13-1   AUSTRALIA ECUMENE

capabilities of the settlers. In addition to large numbers killed in clashes, many perished from European-borne diseases against which they had no immune defenses. The last of the Tasmanian Aborigines died in 1879.

The area of initial settlement British settlement in Australia became the colony of New South Wales. Expansion to other sections of coast began soon thereafter. The offshore island of Tasmania saw its first Europeans in the early 1800s and gained formal political separation from New South Wales in 1825. The southwestern corner of Australia around the harbor of Perth became the colony of Western Australia in 1829. South Australia received recognition as a separate entity in 1826 and a decade later assumed control over Australia's virtually empty Northern Territory. Victoria broke away from New South Wales in 1851. The colony of Queensland appeared along the tropical east coast in 1859.

It has been suggested that the British, mindful of the earlier united revolt by the American colonies, intentionally encouraged separate development of its colonies in Australia. Whether true or not, the intrusion of Germany into the southwestern Pacific after 1871 generated British concern to protect its interests in the region. To shore up Australia's northern defenses, the United Kingdom declared eastern New Guinea to be a British protectorate in

1884. It also pressed for greater cooperation among the widely spaced units of Australian colonial settlement. A federal council of the Australian colonies appeared in 1885, and, following a popular referendum, the colonies were merged in 1901 into a new self-governing dominion of the British Empire. An Australian Capital Territory comparable to the American District of Columbia was established on a neutral site on the border between New South Wales and Victoria.

Unification was aided by the growth of a distinctive sense of Australian national identity in the second half of the nineteenth century. By the 1880s, two-thirds of Australia's 3,000,000 inhabitants were native-born. Their isolation from the United Kingdom and their concerns about French and German annexations in the southwest Pacific contributed to this sense of nationhood, as did a perceived growing threat from the Japanese. Another facilitating factor was the universal provision of mandatory secular education.

In subsequent decades Australia assumed greater independence of action from British policies. The 1931 British Statute of Westminster recognized the right of dominions to function as separate states, although not as foreign countries in relations among themselves or with the United Kingdom. Australia began to conclude separate treaties and trade agreements with a number of

European states. During World War II it assumed major responsibilities for its defense, at times at odds with British strategy. After the war, in 1951, it signed the Pacific Security Treaty (ANZUS Pact) with New Zealand and the United States.

Like Canada, Australia now functions as a completely independent country, although the British monarch remains formal head of state. Many political leaders, particularly from the Australian Labour Party, have been pressing for the country to sever all ties with the United Kingdom and to become a republic. Among their proposals is replacement of the country's flag featuring the British Union Jack with a more Australian emblem that would be comparable to Canada's mid-twentieth century flag change to the Maple Leaf banner.

Although Australia has sought a continuous increase in its population by immigration from abroad ever since the early days of convict settlement, the Australian population is remarkably homogeneous. This is due to an immigration stream coming almost entirely from the United Kingdom during the nineteenth century and to a policy announced in 1912 to exclude settlers from Asia. That racist course was derived from resentment against Chinese miners by Australians during the gold rush of the 1850s; Australians feared that their prevailing rather high standards of living would fall. Prejudice was reinvigorated in the 1880s when Chinese laborers began appearing on sugar plantations in Queensland. A strong Australian labor movement emerged at this time. The Asian exclusion policy has been relaxed in recent decades, and now 4 percent of Australians are of Asian origin.

Still, Europeans remain favored in government programs that encourage continued immigration to the continent. Currently more than 40 percent of the population either was born overseas or had a parent born overseas. Although more than half the immigrants continue to come from the British Isles, large numbers arrived from Southern and Eastern Europe after World War II, particularly from Italy and Greece. Australia also absorbed refugees from other world trouble spots. These include migrants from Hungary and Czechoslovakia after unsuccessful popular revolts against Soviet domination of those states in 1956 and 1968, respectively. Others came from troubled Lebanon and Chile during the 1970s, followed in the subsequent decade by refugees from Vietnam, Cambodia, and China. Most recently the country has seen many migrants arrive from Croatia, Bosnia, and Macedonia. A majority of the "New Australians" have settled in ethnic enclaves, particularly in Melbourne and Sydney, where they support ethnic clubs, churches, and restaurants. They often have brought prejudices and enmities from home. The Australian government recently found it necessary to ban sports clubs from using ethnic names because of the violence that such appellations have triggered.

Australia's 300,000 Aborigines have regained the total numbers estimated to have existed when European settlers first arrived. The Aborigines fall into two principal subdivisions: socially and economically marginalized groups of mixed racial ancestry living in small communities in the southeast, and "full bloods" dwelling in the Great Sandy Desert and northern regions. The establishment of native reserves in the 1920s and 1939s preserved the distinctiveness of the Aborigines, including perpetuation of their native languages. They were permitted freely to leave reserves only after the mid-1950s, and now only a third remain within reservations.

A "Land Rights" movement in the 1960s sought to grant Aborigines title to lands upon which they lived, and to cede to them traditional lands under Crown ownership. Advocates also pressed for establishment of special Aboriginal neighborhoods in cities, including separate schools. In an earlier era Aborigines had resisted such segregation, which then was imposed by the European majority.

Individual states of Australia led the way in adopting policies of reparations to Aborigines. The Aboriginal Land Rights Act of Northern Territory, among numerous provisions, granted to Aborigines ownership of the continent's most notable physical feature, Ayers Rock, although under the condition that it be leased back to the government as a park open to all visitors. In 1966 South Australia gave Aboriginal groups title to forty-three separate areas and established a central desert reserve. Aboriginal groups now have adopted a "Land Rights" flag as an emblem of distinctiveness. Their small numbers and widely dispersed settlements pose little threat to the territorial unity of the Australian state, however.

Of greater concern to Australian unity are continuing antagonisms among the separate states. Popular loyalties in Australia tend to be greater to individual states than to the Australian Commonwealth as a whole. In part this reflects the widely spaced areas of concentrated settlement and rivalries that date from the period of original settlement. More than 60 percent of Australians live in the capital cities of their states. The inhabitants of each tend to view other population clusters as competitive rather than complementary. In addition to government activities, a principal function of each capital is to process grain, wool, and meat for overseas shipment. Concern over directing the products of sparsely populated colonial hinterlands to their own facilities early led to adoption of different railroad gauges by each colony to prevent "siphoning off" of wheat and sheep to rival ports. Although it is now possible to travel on rails of unified width from Western Australia to Queensland, local railroad systems still remain incompatible with each other.

Secession by individual Australian states has been threatened more than once. This is particularly true of

TABLE 13.1 AUSTRALASIA AND THE SOUTHWEST PACIFIC

State	Total Population	Area (sq. miles)	Distinctive Features of Group
Australia	17,500,000	3,000,000	
Dominant Regional Group and % Total			
Australians, 95%			Mixed Romance/Germanic (English) language, Protestant and Roman Catholic
Significant Regional Groups and % Total			
Aborigines, 1.5%			
New Zealand	3,500,000	105,000	
Dominant Regional Group and % Total			
New Zealanders, 75%			Mixed Romance/Germanic (English) language, Protestant and Roman Catholic
Significant Regional Groups and % Total			
Maoris, 10%			
Fiji	750,000	7,000	
Dominant Regional Group and % Total			
Fijians, 50%			Mixed Romance/Germanic (English) language, Protestant and Roman Catholic
Significant Regional Groups and % Total			
(East Indians make up 47% of the population and suffer civil disabilities, but are not regionally segregated)			
Kiribati	75,000	800	
Dominant Regional Group and % Total			
I-Kiribati, 98% (including residents of all islands)			Mixed Romance/Germanic (English) language, Roman Catholic (55%) and Protestant
Significant Regional Groups and % Total			
21 inhabited islands, each with local identities			
Marshall Islands	45,000	70	
Dominant Regional Group and % Total			
Marshallese, 97% (including residents of all islands)			Kajin-Majol (Marshallese), Mixed Romance/ Germanic (English) languages, Roman Catholic (55%) and Protestant
Significant Regional Groups and % Total			
26 inhabited islands, each with local identities			
Federated States of Micronesia	110,000	270	
Component States			
Chuuk (Truk); Kozrae; Pohnpei; Yap			
Dominant Regional Group and % Total			
Trukese, 42%			
Significant Regional Groups and % Total			
Pohpeians, 25% Yapese, 6%			
Mortlockese, 9% Pingelapese, 1%			
Kosraean, 7%			

Western Australia, whose inhabitants were notably reluctant to join the Australian Commonwealth in 1901, and, like British Columbia in Canada, successfully made completion of a transcontinental rail line a condition for entrance. Western Australia has had a maverick history in relation to its neighbors. After New South Wales ended convict settlement in 1840, and other colonies followed in the ensuing decade, Western Australia, in 1850, elected to become a penal colony for the first time. The territory did not acquire responsible self-government until 1890. During the twentieth century Western Australia has rather continuously nourished a separatist movement. In the world economic crisis in 1933 more than two-thirds of Western Australians voted to secede from the Commonwealth, although their desires were not implemented.

To assuage concerns of the separate colonies, the Australian Commonwealth at its inception adopted a federal form of government similar to Canada's. Unlike the federalism of the United States, the colonies dele-

TABLE 13.1 AUSTRALASIA AND THE SOUTHWEST PACIFIC (continued)

State	Total Population	Area (sq. miles)	Distinctive Features of Group
New Caledonia	180,000	7000	
(French Overseas Territory)			
Dominant Regional Group and % Total			
Melanesians, 45%			Romance (French) language, Roman Catholic (60%), Protestant
Papua New Guinea	3,800,000	180,000	
Dominant Regional Group and % Total			
New Guinea Papuans, 85%			Mixed Romance/Germanic (English) language, Protestant (60%) and Roman Catholic
Significant Regional Groups and % Total			
New Guinea Melanesians, 15%			Mixed Romance/Germanic (English) language, Protestant and Roman Catholic
Solomon Islands	328,000	11,000	
Dominant Regional Group and % Total			
Melanesian, 95%			Mixed Romance/Germanic (English) language, Protestant (80%) and Roman Catholic
Tonga	95,000	300	
Dominant Regional Group and % Total			
Tongans, 95% (including residents of all islands)			(Tongan), Mixed Romance/Germanic (English) language, Protestant
Significant Regional Groups and % Total			
(23 inhabited islands, each with its local identity)			
Tuvalu	10,000	9	
Dominant Regional Group and % Total			
Tuvaluan, 90% (including residents of all islands)			Mixed Romance/Germanic (English) language, Protestant
Significant Regional Groups and % Total			
(9 inhabited islands, each with its local identity)			
Vanuatu	170,000	4,700	
Dominant Regional Group and % Total			
Ni-Vanuatus, 98%			(Bislama), Romance (French), and Mixed Romance/Germanic (English) languages, Protestant (80%) and Roman Catholic
Western Samoa	160,000	1,100	
Dominant Regional Group and % Total			
Samoans, 88%			(Samoan) and Mixed Romance/Germanic (English) languages, Protestant (70%) and Roman Catholic

gated only a limited range of powers to the central government, retaining to themselves all other governmental functions. Theoretically, the central government would be concerned primarily with foreign policy and other external matters. In practice, however, the federal government has gained dominance through control of funds from taxation. Its most widespread function is the provision of health care.

In addition to the rivalry among Australian states, there are at least two endemic "New States" movements seeking to break away territories to form separate new units. One of these is in Northern Queensland, whose inhabitants repeatedly have sought to divide the former colony into two or three parts. The other is the "New England" movement in northeastern New South Wales around the town of Newcastle. That region's predominantly rural and small-town inhabitants long have evinced concern about "socialist domination" by the capital city of Sydney. More than 70 percent voiced support in a 1954 poll for creation of a separate New England state embracing 64,000 square miles. Although these sentiments appear to remain, no such entity has been created.

Australia has had several colonial dependencies. These include Norfolk Island, which was attached politically to New South Wales in 1788 as a place for convicts too unruly for Australia itself. In the 1850s Norfolk Island became home to descendants of mutineers from H.M.S. *Bounty* emigrating from Pitcairn Island. After World War I, Australia received responsibility for administering the League of Nations mandates of German New Guinea, the northern Solomon Islands, and Nauru (in association with the United Kingdom and New Zealand). These mandates all became independent states during the second half of the twentieth century. Among other islands politically attached to Australia are the Coral Sea Islands, Ashmore and Cartier Islands, Heard and McDonald Islands, the Cocos (Keeling) Islands, and Christmas Island. Australia also asserts ownership of a share of Antarctica, the claims to which were transferred to it by the United Kingdom in the 1930s.

New Zealand

A thousand miles southeast of Australia lie the two principal islands of New Zealand. They embrace an area of slightly more than 100,000 square miles, roughly the size of the island of Great Britain. Their population of 3,500,000 represents a transplanted British culture comparable to Australia's. Three quarters of the inhabitants live on North Island. Both New Zealand islands are characterized by mountainous terrain, many peaks on South Island reaching more than 10,000 feet elevation. Less than two-thirds of the territory is deemed economically useful. The ecumene is concentrated on the northern and southern lowlands of North Island and on the eastern plain of South Island.

Although Abel Tasman visited New Zealand in 1642, the first Europeans settled there only in 1820. They met an indigenous Polynesian population, the Maoris, who had arrived eight centuries earlier. Large numbers of convicts who had served their time streamed to New Zealand from Australia, together with free settlers from Australia and the United Kingdom. The latter formally annexed New Zealand in 1840 and made the islands a Crown colony the following year. Settlers achieved self-government in 1856.

In the early decades strong localisms characterized New Zealand. It began functioning as a loose union of six autonomous provinces somewhat comparable to the separate colonies of Australia. The provinces had grown to ten when they were abolished in 1875 and replaced by sixty-three counties and thirty-six independent boroughs. This occurred as an aftermath of a bitter

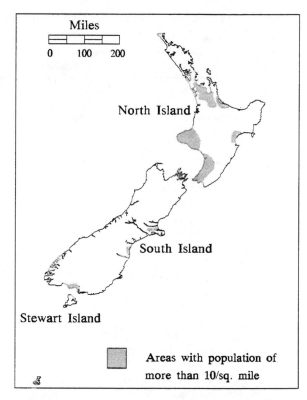

FIGURE 13-2   NEW ZEALAND ECUMENE

war with the Maoris in the 1860s. Subsequently, the number of New Zealand counties grew to 129 and the number of boroughs tripled. Like Australia, New Zealand received dominion status from the United Kingdom, its near-sovereignty verified by admission to the League of Nations in 1919.

New Zealand's population remains mainly of British and Australian descent, although numerous Central Europeans settled in New Zealand after World War I and many Dutch immigrated after World War II, both from the Netherlands and from the former Dutch East Indies. Maoris constitute about 10 percent of the population. Before arrival of the British they had evolved a structure of tribes that frequently were at war with one another. Guns made available by nineteenth century settlers notably increased the severity of strife. Like the Australian Aborigines, large numbers of Maoris were decimated by imported European diseases. They also suffered greatly during the 1860s war. By 1896, only 42,000 Maoris remained, compared to 770,000 European settlers. Maori numbers have increased by a factor of twelve since then.

The British government early attempted to place a priority upon Maori equality. Their ownership of land and other legal rights were respected, although much Maori land was alienated in questionable transactions with British settlers. Maori settlements have remained principally in rural areas of North Island, including northern parts of the Auckland Peninsula and the region fronting Poverty Bay. Many Maoris have migrated in recent times to New Zealand's cities.

In the course of time most Maoris adopted the English language, although a minority remains able to speak the Polynesian Maori tongue, now taught in a number of schools. The present government maintains a Department of Maori Affairs to safeguard traditions of marriage, inheritance, and land ownership. Increasing criticisms are voiced about this agency, which is viewed by many as a hindrance to the development of a single New Zealand community. Like the Australian Aborigines, the small numbers and dispersed locations of New Zealand's Maoris pose little threat to the territorial unity of the state.

New Zealand has a small population, and its government's policies deliberately have sought to keep it small. For more than a century after its founding, New Zealand's sheep-raising economy remained tied principally to the British Isles. New Zealand lost much of what had become a privileged position with the United Kingdom when Britain decided to become a member of the economic market of the European Community. New Zealand remains dependent economically upon Britain, although, since the advent of World War II, it has relied increasingly upon the United States for its security. In 1951 New Zealand signed the Pacific Security Treaty (ANZUS Pact) with Australia and the United States to provide mutual aid in the event of aggression. Subsequently, its relations with the United States soured over New Zealand's refusal to allow American warships carrying nuclear weapons to sail into its ports.

Like Australia, New Zealand exerts influence over several islands in the Southwest Pacific. The Cook Islands and the separately administered island of Niue hold the status of self-governing states in free association with New Zealand. The former German colony of Western Samoa and the phosphate-rich island of Nauru formerly were New Zealand trusteeships under the United Nations, but both became independent in the 1960s. The Tokelau Islands near Western Samoa still remain New Zealand dependencies. Many islanders come to New Zealand for seasonal and year-round employment.

The Pacific Islands

To the north and east of Australia and New Zealand lie more than 25,000 islands dispersed over 35,000,000 square miles, an area ten times the size of the United States of America. Most are very small. Convention-ally, they are divided into three sections: Melanesia, Micronesia, and Polynesia.

Melanesia, the "black islands," lie south of the Equator and west of the International Date Line. Europeans bestowed the regional name because of the dominant dark skin pigment (melanin) of their inhabitants. Melanesia includes a number of larger islands, including New Guinea, the Solomon Islands, New Caledonia, Vanuatu (New Hebrides), and Fiji. Micronesia—the "little islands"—consists of more than 2,000 separate islands, mostly atolls, which predominantly lie north of Melanesia. Among them are the Carolines, the Marianas, the Marshalls, the Gilberts, and Nauru. Polynesia, which means "many islands," embraces the largest area, although the number of islands is far less. It occupies a triangle extending from New Zealand to Hawaii to Easter Island in the Southeast Pacific.

Virtually every inhabited island speaks a distinctive language. More than 1,200 tongues have been identified. Most languages belong to the broad linguistic family known as Austronesian and tend to be easily learned by other islanders. In Melanesia a number of tongues are present whose mutual relationships are difficult to discern. For convenience, linguists group them together as "Papuan" languages. Over the past two centuries a lingua franca has emerged for communication between groups in Melanesia known as "Pidgin English." It has several variations and increasingly provides a basis for common Melanesian identity.

Ancestors of the present inhabitants of Micronesia and Polynesia originated in insular Southeast Asia and Melanesia. Most of the outer islands were settled comparatively recently. The first Polynesians arrived in Hawaii only about A.D. 800 Although Europeans and Americans tend to imagine life on the "South Sea" islands to have been idyllic, warfare seems to have been a constant element throughout the region.

European voyagers first encountered islands of the Southwest Pacific during the sixteenth century. Explorers from Spain, Portugal, the Netherlands, England, and France had described virtually all islands by the end of the eighteenth century. The most noteworthy among these explorers was Captain James Cook. Few islands were claimed as formal colonies until the end of the nineteenth century, however, and the area was the last world region to be divided into colonial territories by Europeans and Americans.

The lack of formal political subjugation did not mean that native peoples saw no foreigners after the initial contacts with explorers. A variety of adventurers and traders came to the islands and generally debased the population. More than 700 whaling ships were active in the Pacific during the mid-nineteenth century. Their crews introduced to the region alcohol, which continues to generate social problems for peoples who had had no

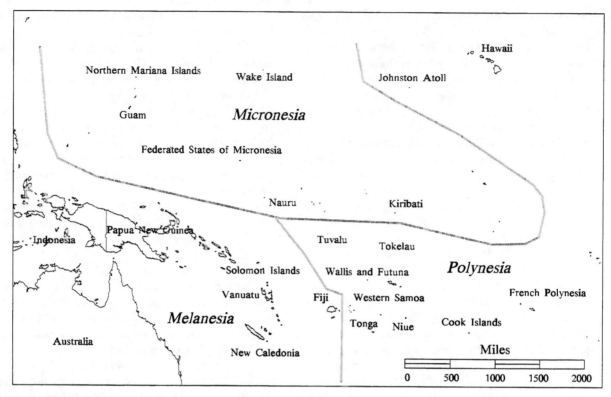

FIGURE 13-3   ISLAND STATES OF THE SOUTHWEST PACIFIC

previous experience with it. Many sailors jumped ship and chose to stay rather than return home, often creating mischief and bringing new diseases. A German enterprise virtually created a commercial economy on many islands in the mid-nineteenth century by offering to purchase copra, the dried meat of the easily grown coconut palm. This they processed into coconut oil in Western Samoa. Later, the development of sugar plantations had profound effects upon natives. Sugar companies imported foreign laborers whose descendants remain as distinctive population groups. Particularly significant are Hindus in Fiji and Japanese and Filipinos in Hawaii.

Well-meaning missionaries also created problems. Spanish authorities from the Philippines attacked the Chamarro people of the Marianas Islands in the 1680s after several Catholic missionaries were killed. The Spaniards reduced the native population from 100,000 to less than 5,000, most of whom were then resettled in Guam. After the turn of the nineteenth century, rivalries between Protestant- and Catholic-converted groups sometimes led to open conflict.

Spaniards controlled the island of Guam and claimed all of Micronesia to be Spanish territory after 1688. However, aside from the Marianas Islands, the Spanish did not actively pursue colonial control. The Dutch established trading communities along the western coast of the large Melanesian island of New Guinea,

but evinced little interest in expansion, relying instead upon working through the sultan of Tidore, who claimed title to the island. During the first half of the nineteenth century the Americans and British showed little interest in colonial expansion into the Pacific, although Australians and New Zealanders pressed the United Kingdom to annex every island possible.

It was the French who began European acquisition of territory in the nineteenth century, declaring sovereignty over the Marquesas Islands and a protectorate over Tahiti in 1842. A decade later France claimed New Caledonia, which it made into a penal colony. In the 1880s the French annexed several other islands. The United Kingdom's first venture beyond its Australian and New Zealand holdings occurred in 1874 when it reluctantly acquired the Fiji Islands in order to end local feuding and to placate its demanding Australian subjects.

Germany began claiming island groups as colonies in the decade following its achievement of political unity in 1871. It joined with the Americans and British in establishing control over Samoa in order to suppress a civil war among native clans. In 1884 Germany annexed northeastern New Guinea and the Bismarck Archipelago, alarming the British who responded by claiming southeastern New Guinea. Germany then declared a protectorate over the Marshall Islands in 1885 and, three years later, added Nauru, where German traders had been operating for more than two decades.

The British then began expanding their own holdings substantially. The United Kingdom proclaimed a protectorate over the Solomon Islands in 1883 and in 1892 took over the Cook, Phoenix, Tokelau, and Gilbert and Ellice Islands. The United States also entered actively into the Pacific at the end of the nineteenth century. In 1893 it engineered a revolt against native authority in Hawaii, and later, in 1899, annexed the islands. It also acquired Guam following the Spanish-American War of 1898, although it allowed Germany to acquire other Spanish island holdings in Micronesia. France and the United Kingdom resolved rival interests in the New Hebrides by created a joint Franco-British condominium in 1906.

The pattern of European colonies in the South Pacific changed dramatically after World War I when Germany was stripped of its possessions. All its island groups were declared to be "Class C" mandates of the League of Nations, which meant that they were judged not yet capable of self-government. The German holdings in Micronesia went to Japan. Australians received authority to administer German New Guinea, and New Zealanders acquired Western Samoa. The United Kingdom, Australia, and New Zealand jointly agreed to manage the island of Nauru, although Australia assumed day-to-day administration. The new pattern of holdings thus saw Japan and the United States controlling islands north of the Equator and France and the United Kingdom (with Australia and New Zealand) dominating the south. The Dutch remained in control of western New Guinea and the Americans maintained a position in Samoa.

Japanese forces invaded a large number of Micronesian and Melanesian islands during the course of World War II, although most of Polynesia remained under control of the Europeans and Americans. In a series of bloody engagements, Japan was forced to relinquish its island empire. Its prewar holdings in Micronesia became the American-administered Trust Territory of the Pacific Islands under authority of the new United Nations Organization.

The last four decades of the twentieth century saw substantial political-geographic changes in the Southwest Pacific. Hawaii became the fiftieth state of the United States in 1959, and the Dutch ceded western New Guinea to Indonesia in 1962. A majority of island groups achieved formal independence, although most remained economically dependent upon their former colonial powers. Western Samoa became sovereign in 1962. Subsequently, other new states appeared: Nauru (1968), Fiji (1970), Tonga (1970), Papua New Guinea (1975), the Solomon Islands (1978), Tuvalu (1978), Kiribati (1979), and Vanuatu (1980). The Trust Terri-

tory of the Pacific was terminated in 1986 to be replaced by the Republic of the Marshall Islands, the Republic of Palau, and the Commonwealth of the Northern Marianas. The remaining 2,000 islands of the former trust territory became the Federated States of Micronesia. All four of the newly independent units remained in "free association" with the United States, defined as full internal self-government but with American responsibility for defense. The island of Guam continued as an organized unincorporated territory of the United States.

A number of colonial dependencies remain in the Pacific region. In addition to Guam, the United States retains American Samoa as an unincorporated territory. The French maintain French Polynesia, Wallace and Futuna Islands, and New Caledonia as overseas territories of France, with varying degrees of autonomy. France faces active opposition in New Caledonia from the Melanesian-based Kana Liberation Front, which opposes land ownership rights and other privileges by the 37 percent of the population that is of European descent.

The independent islands face many problems in addition to economic dependence upon former colonial powers. Their governments must address a general tendency for the population of each island to have its own degree of self-awareness, leading to rivalries if not open conflict. Most notable was a 1980 revolt on the Vanuatu island of Espiritu Santo that was suppressed only with the aid of troops from Australia and Papua New Guinea.

Bibliography

CAMPBELL, EILA M. J., "New Zealand and Its Dependencies," in *The Changing World: Studies in Political Geography*, eds. W. Gordon East and A.E. Moodie. Yonkers, NY: World Book Company, 1956, pp. 831–859.

CUMBERLAND, KENNETH B., *Southwest Pacific: A Geography of Australia, New Zealand, and the Pacific Islands Neighbors*. New York: Praeger, 1968.

FREEMAN, OTIS, ed., *Geography of the Pacific*. New York: John Wiley, 1951.

GALE, FAY, "Aboriginal Australia: Survival by Separation," in *Shared Space, Divided Space: Essays on Conflict and Territorial Organization*, eds. Michael Chisholm and David M. Smith. London: Unwin Hyman, 1990, pp. 217–234.

OLIVER, DOUGLAS, *The Pacific Islands*, rev. ed., Garden City, NY: Anchor Books, 1961.

SPATE, O.H.K., "Australia and Its Dependencies," in *The Changing World: Studies in Political Geography*, eds. W. Gordon East and A.E. Moodie. Yonkers, NY: World Book Company, 1956, pp. 803–830

14

Latin America

AMERICANS hold fast to two major myths about territories that lie south of the United States. One is that there is a continental division in Panama between a "North America" and a "South America,"and the other is that these lands are part of a "Western Hemisphere" that is an American territorial preserve. Both myths lack grounding in reality.

Although separation of the New World into two continents at the Isthmus of Panama has been conventional since the sixteenth century, such conceptualization lacks cultural and political meaningfulness. Far more useful is a division of the Americas between an Anglo-America embracing the United States and Canada, and a Latin America consisting primarily of states that emerged from the Spanish and Portuguese empires. Discontinuities in languages, religions, economies, and political attitudes are far more observable at the Rio Grande than at the Panama Canal. The collection of small islands and coastal footholds in the Caribbean area with British, French, or Dutch heritages constitutes an anomalous area between Latin American and Anglo-American civilizations.

The American public has tended to view the Latin American realm in a paternalistic manner ever since the United States enunciated the famous Monroe Doctrine in 1823. That speech to Congress by President James Monroe stated that the United States would look unfavorably upon any interference by European powers in the then newly independent states of Latin America. Its thrust stemmed from a sense of commonality in throwing off European domination, even though the anticolonial process was markedly different in the two areas. The notion of inherent north/south linkage was also bolstered over ensuing decades by conventional Mercator maps of the world produced in the United States that generally centered on the Americas and exaggerated the oceanic separation of Anglo-America from Europe. The northeastern seaboard, the dominant population concentration of the United States, in fact lies much closer to Western Europe than to any of the major Latin American population clusters, aside from central Mexico. Anglo-American economic and cultural linkages are far greater with Europe and the Far East than with Latin America. Moreover, few inhabitants of Latin America share any perception of a naturally given right for the "Colossus of the North" to involve itself in southern affairs.

Overview

Latin America embraces an area of 8,215,000 square miles, making it approximately 20 percent larger than Anglo-America (Table 14-1). Its rapidly growing population exceeds 450,000,000, however, or roughly 40 percent more than Anglo-America's. Like the United States and Canada, Latin America has a population much more homogeneous than counterparts in Eurasia and Africa. The greatest numbers of its peoples speak either Spanish or Portuguese and are Roman Catholic in religion. However, in contrast to the two monolithic states of Anglo-America, Spanish and Portuguese Latin America lies fragmented among nineteen states, with an additional fourteen independent English-, French-, and Dutch-speaking countries on islands and coastal margins of the Caribbean Sea. Moreover, sixteen colonial areas remain in the Caribbean realm as dependencies of the United Kingdom, France, the Netherlands, and the United States.

Conquest and settlement by Europeans began early in the sixteenth century and soon engaged virtually all of the region. Spain and Portugal held their Latin American possessions for more than 300 years, until most colonies broke away during the European Napoleonic Wars of the early nineteenth century. Cuba became self-governing at the turn of the twentieth century, and many remaining European Caribbean territories gained sovereignty in the 1970s and 1980s. Distinctive national identities developed in each of the states throughout the region. In contrast to Anglo-America, however, in most cases they emerged as a consequence of the establishment of statehood, rather than as a factor preceding it.

Although the multitude of states and their associated nations exceeds the total to be found in all Europe, Latin America suffers far fewer international tensions. Each state contains but a single nation within its boundaries. Irredentism is virtually nonexistent. Border disputes involve conflicting historical claims to what are mostly uninhabited territories. A few regionalisms are present, but shared commonalities in culture have tended to keep them from developing into separate national identities. However, it should be noted that a substantial portion of the population of most Latin American states has maintained a self-subsistent Indian culture that tends to lack any national identity.

TABLE 14.1   LATIN AMERICA

The Latin American realm is a huge, remarkably homogeneous territory extending from the southern border of the United States nearly to Antarctica. Four-fifths of the land consists of virtually uninhabited deserts, tropical lowlands, and mountains. The relatively small population clusters tend to be widely separated from each other and to form the cores of the modern political units. Most inhabitants speak Spanish or Portuguese, aside from the Caribbean region, where the English language dominates in the small islands. Most people are Roman Catholic, although Protestant evangelists have made significant inroads. Centuries of assimilation and racial mixing since the Spanish conquest have resulted in a largely Mestizo population. However, persons of African descent are characteristic of the islands and periphery of the Caribbean, and individuals of direct European stock are notable in states of the Southern Cone. Unassimilated Indians constitute about 20 percent of the total and are found mainly in the Andes Mountains and northern Central America. Independence from Spain or Portugal came during the first half of the nineteenth century, and from the European Caribbean empires in the second half of the twentieth century. A distinctive nation has emerged in each of the political entities, with few significant regional challenges. Although territorial disputes have occurred, they mostly involve claims to uninhabited territories.

Subregion	Total Population	Area (sq. miles)
Central America	115,000,000	950,000
Component States		
Mexico, Guatemala, Belize, El Salvador, Honduras, Nicaragua, Costa Rica, Panama		
The Caribbean States	35,000,000	265,000 (including 180,000 in the three sparsely populated Guianas on the mainland)
Component States and Dependent Areas		
Haiti, Dominican Republic, Cuba, Puerto Rico, Jamaica, Trinidad and Tobago, British Antilles, Netherlands Antilles, French Antilles, American Virgin Islands, French Guiana, Suriname, Guyana		
The Northern Andes	88,000,000	1,800,000
Component States		
Colombia, Venezuela, Ecuador, Peru		
The Southern Cone	62,500,000	2,000,000
Component States		
Chile, Argentina, Uruguay, Paraguay, Bolivia		
Brazil	151,000,000	3,200,000
Total	451,000,000	8,215,000

The Land

About 80 percent of Latin America is virtually empty of population. This non-ecumene consists mainly of infertile tropical rain forests, extensive deserts, and high mountains. Settlement is concentrated principally in mid-latitude coastal plains and tropical and subtropical upland basins. Clusters of dense population are the most widely separated of any part of the globe.

The terrain is dominated by a vast continental plate, centered on Brazil and occupying about half the area. This stable section of the earth's crust disengaged itself from Africa and has long pressed toward the Pacific Ocean floor, resulting in wrinkling up a western Latin American margin that rises to heights of 10,000 feet or more. The Andes are truly a magnificent mountain range, stretching from Tierra del Fuego to Colombia and Venezuela. A related range extends through Central America to Mexico, and then northward as the North American Rocky Mountains.

For the most part the Andes consist of three or more parallel ridge crests, with upland basins between. In tropical latitudes these flat highlands (*altiplano*) have tended to be where populations have clustered, since their elevation provides respite from the high heat, humidity, and precipitation of lowland areas. Daily temperatures at mountain crests are 35°F or more cooler than at their bases. Vegetation changes vertically on their slopes in a fashion comparable to latitudinal biotic change between equator and poles. Local societies recognize a variety of climatic/vegetation belts, from the lowland *tierra caliente* to the mid-slope *tierra templada* to the highland *tierra fria* and tundra-like *paramos*.

Although they contain a number of spectacular volcanoes, the Andes for the most part are faulted and folded mountains rather than eruptive ones. Strains on the ancient rocks of the continental plate, however, did lead to surface outpourings of lava to the east of the mountains, covering much of southern Brazil, Uruguay, and Paraguay. Mountain building still continues in the Andes. Stiff earthquake jolts are felt every year, and occasionally there are eruptions of volcanic ash that settles on fields and towns.

Because of the small proportion of its land in polar and subpolar latitudes, Latin America did not suffer extensive continental glaciation. However, the height of the Andes Mountains caused them to develop glaciers during the last ice age. Natural dams created by loose rock deposited at former outer edges of the ice altered patterns of stream drainage in the crest areas. This legacy created a particular problem in defining the border between Argentina and Chile, which will be detailed below.

The mountains effectively separate the climates of the continent, particularly in the Chile-Argentina area. Catching the prevailing westerly winds of the southern mid-latitudes, the Andes collect moisture in the form of snow and leave Patagonia to the east a dry zone.

A second mountain range with some peaks rising to 10,000 feet lies a thousand miles east of the northern Andes. Its spectacular qualities are muted, however, by the fact that most of it is drowned by the Caribbean Sea. The range forms the basis for of the Greater and Lesser Antilles. It is the visible backbone of the mountainous islands, but it also undergirds most low-lying ones, whose surface was formed by generations of corals that built platforms to the surface from the higher submerged peaks. As in the Andes, the highest peaks of the submerged range are the result of volcanic activity. In 1902 an eruption of Mt. Pelée on Martinique killed 30,000 inhabitants of the island. Away from the main underwater mountain chain are several other Caribbean islands that reflect other upheavals of the earth's crust. They include Barbados, Tobago, and the Dutch islands off the Venezuelan coast.

Climate and Vegetation

The variety of climates of Latin America derives from the region's 6,000-mile latitudinal range from 55°S to 32°N. The greatest mass of land is in the tropics, where trade winds bring warm moisture onshore throughout the year from adjacent Atlantic and Caribbean waters. Here a tropical rain forest prevails upon soils generally leached of nutrients by incessant precipitation. On the eastern flanks of the tropical zone a dry winter season causes changes in vegetation, but temperatures remain high. Margins of the tropics on the west coast are notably dry, reflecting stable cells of high atmospheric pressure over the eastern Pacific in those latitudes and

trade winds that blow out to sea, away from the land. The tropical deserts of the Atacama in Chile and the Sonora in Mexico lie under the clear skies of high pressure cells throughout the year and are among the driest regions on earth.

Because of the narrowing of the land mass south of Brazil and Peru, comparatively little of Latin America extends into the mid-latitudes. It is this zone that supports the greatest concentrations of population, however. In the lowland areas the presence of a cool season means an end to tropical rain forests. Natural grasslands, with their associated fertile soils, prevail in much of Argentina and Uruguay. Farther south, the slim plateau of Patagonia is the only area comparable to the vast interior continental zones of Eurasia and Anglo-America, with their sharp contrasts in seasonal temperatures. Its dryness has already been commented upon.

Population

The differing patterns of opportunities and limitations for agricultural settlement led aboriginal peoples in Latin America to concentrate within a limited number of favored areas, although small bands ranged throughout the territory. Population clusters perpetuated themselves and expanded under Iberian domination, and they have remained to the present (see Figure 14-1). Only a few areas of new agricultural colonization subsequently appeared, chiefly in coastal Brazil and in the Rio de la Plata area of Argentina and Uruguay.

Indian population concentrations formed cores of Spanish colonial administrative regions, all of which tended to evolve into independent countries. In most states there is great discrepancy between total land area and effectively occupied ecumene. Chile, for instance, is habitually viewed as a "shoestring" country because of a long latitudinal expanse from Tierra del Fuego to the Atacama Desert and a limited longitudinal span between the crest of the Andes and the Pacific. However, its northern third is desert and its southern half consists of fjorded mountains comparable to the panhandle of Alaska. Some 90 percent of its population is concentrated in its central Vale of Chile, which occupies no more than 15 percent of its territory. In many ways Chile is best viewed as a compact unit rather comparable to Uruguay. Similarly, Brazil, despite its vast Amazonian region, is realistically conceptualized as only a 500 mile-wide belt stretching for 2,000 miles along its Atlantic coast. Uruguay and El Salvador are the only Latin American states that utilize virtually all their territory. A key to the political geography of Latin America is the fact that so very few of its international boundaries actually cut across a populated area.

FIGURE 14-1   THE SOUTH AMERICAN ECUMENE

Cultural Patterns

Language. Latin Americans mainly speak languages derived from Latin: Spanish, 210,000,000; Portuguese, 145,000,000; and French, 7,000,000. Another 9,000,000 in the Caribbean region use English. Despite acculturation pressures, many inhabitants have retained native American languages. They include 4,000,000 Aztec and Maya speakers in Mexico, 18,000,000 Quechua speakers in Peru, Ecuador and Bolivia, and 4,000,000 Guarani speakers in Paraguay and northern Argentina.

Race. Most inhabitants of Latin America are acutely conscious of the variety of racial groups that are present. Approximately 25 percent are white. They predominate in Argentina, Uruguay, Costa Rica, and Puerto Rico. In other areas whites are minorities, but almost always dominate local affairs. Mestizos of mixed Indian/white heritage are the largest single group, numbering about a third of the population. They are the dominant element in many states, particularly Chile and Mexico. Native Indians make up about 20 percent of the total. They form local majorities in states along the Pacific seaboard and are the principal groups in Paraguay and Bolivia. Blacks also number 20 percent. They are concentrated around the Caribbean and in Brazil.

Persons of mixed black and Indian origin are termed "Zambos." They are relatively few in number, since African slaves were generally not brought by the European colonizers to areas where there were concentrations of Indians sufficient to form adequate labor supplies. East Indians constitute a distinctive racial group in the Caribbean area. Most are descendants of indentured servants brought by the British from India to work in sugar plantations after the abolition of slavery. Also noteworthy are small concentrations of Japanese, particularly in Brazil, Paraguay, and Peru. They are descendants of early twentieth century agricultural colonization schemes. In 1990 a person of Japanese descent was elected president of Peru.

A number of internal problems derive from racial group politics, including troubles between blacks and East Indians in Guyana and Trinidad. Long-standing enmities between nation-states often include a racial dimension. Among these are problems between Mestizo Dominicans and black Haitians and between Indian Paraguayans and white Argentines.

Religion. Latin Americans are overwhelmingly Roman Catholic. This is the result of three centuries of missionary work during the period of Iberian domination. In some areas Catholic religious practices preserve pre-Columbian traditions. A variety of religions in the Caribbean area reflects the mixed heritage of the population. On Trinidad, for instance, one finds East Indian Hindu temples and Islamic mosques. Native African traditions are preserved in the black state of Haiti. Various Protestant churches operate in areas of British and Dutch domination. A phenomenon of recent decades is the rise of evangelical Protestant churches on the Latin American mainland that challenge not only traditional Roman Catholicism, but also the nonegalitarian social order, which, to many individuals, Catholicism appears to legitimize.

Economic inequality. No overview of Latin America is complete without reference to the contrasts between wealth and poverty that characterize most of the region. In many states two societies coexist. One is traditional and predominantly Indian or black and engaged primarily in self-subsistent agriculture. Its affairs are under the control of the other society, which is more modern, involves principally whites and Mestizos, and has production and consumption linkages to other areas and parts of the world. Political tensions and pressures for

change are gathering momentum through the diffusion of ideas and awareness in the traditional societies by enhanced opportunities for education and direct experience in the developed societies. Evangelical missionaries and the technological advance of the transistor radio have served as catalysts for change.

The Evolution of Latin America

The first human inhabitants of Latin America appeared about 20,000 years ago. Although some scientists have asserted that migration came across the mid-Pacific, the prevailing view is movement over a "land bridge" from Siberia when sealevel was 300 feet lower as a result of lockage of water in the continental ice sheets. In any event, settlement began before the postglacial colonization of Europe. Early societies consisted of roving bands of hunters and gatherers. The oldest known villages appeared several millennia later, about 3000 B.C.

Prior to the Iberian arrival at the end of the fifteenth century, four sophisticated civilizations had developed: the Aztec centered in what is now Mexico; the Maya in Guatemala and the Yucatan Peninsula, the Chibcha in Colombia; and the Inca in Peru. They incorporated perhaps three-quarters of the total population of the Americas. All were based upon the intensive production of corn (maize) as food in areas with favorable soil and climate. Other peoples engaged in so-called slash-and-burn agriculture that mined the meager nutrients of forested areas or else they were hunters and gatherers. The Mayan and Chibcha civilizations were long past their prime when Columbus discovered the New World in 1492. The Aztec and Inca societies had reached a peak and had problems of internal disarray.

The European Conquerors

Many of the characteristics of contemporary Latin America can be traced to the nature of fifteenth-century Spanish and Portuguese societies. They were Christian communities living in a peripheral frontier zone of Europe dominated by a Muslim presence. North African Moors had ruled the greater part of the Iberian Peninsula for centuries, and trade was largely in the hands of Muslim and Jewish merchants. On the northern fringe of Iberia a half-dozen Christian feudal units had resisted Moorish expansion and steadily pressed southward to reclaim their patrimony. Christian outlooks were still medieval, in contrast to the Renaissance that had occurred in much of the rest of Europe. Faith was in God more than in human potential. Christians were preoccupied with reclaiming Iberia from the infidels.

The Portuguese succeeded in driving out the Moors from the west coast of Iberia in 1249. They then proceeded to establish colonial footholds in Africa and the offshore islands. In the process they gained a degree of experience in governance. The Spaniards, in contrast, did not defeat the last of the Moorish kingdoms until two-and-a-half centuries later, in 1492, the very year that Columbus set sail for the New World. Although the Spanish had much experience in fighting, they had little in governing. They compounded problems of government and economy in the newly established state of Spain by physically expelling Moors and Jews in that same year. Those groups were made welcome by the Ottoman Empire, the so-called Sephardic Jews becoming a significant economic element in the Balkan Peninsula, Turkey, and North Africa.

The discovery of the New World by Columbus signaled a new phase of the Spanish process of *reconquista* ("reconquest"). The liberation of Spain would be extended to the conquest and salvation of the New World. The Portuguese remained as rivals, however. To minimize colonial conflict between his Christian subjects, the Pope in 1493 allocated potential conquests of the rest of the world between Portugal and Spain. His line of demarcation ran north-south about 500 miles west of the Portuguese-held Cape Verde Islands. However, subsequent negotiations between Portugal and Spain led a year later to the Treaty of Tordesillas that established the meridian of 50° west as the dividing line.

This extended the Portuguese share another 800 miles westward, giving them the eastern bulge of Latin America in addition to all of Africa and Asia. The Spanish received the rest of the Americas and islands to the west for half a world. Reasons for the revision are unknown. Some historians have suggested that Portuguese mariners may well have earlier discovered the Brazilian coast as part of explorations down the coast of Africa. Spanish negotiators believed that their share of the world would include the Moluccan Spice Islands, but unfortunately for their anticipations, they were operating with faulty information.

After gaining a foothold in the Caribbean, the Spanish lost little time in establishing control over Central and South America. Hernando Cortez seized Mexico from its Aztec rulers in 1519, and Francisco Pizarro, with 170 men, defeated the Incas in Peru in the 1530s. The Portuguese were initially more circumspect. For the first three decades after receiving "title" to what became Brazil, they were content to establish trading relations with coastal Indian groups similar to their dealings in Africa. They also initiated in the northeast area closest to Africa commercial agricultural production on the model of the profitable sugar plantations they had established in the Azores in the mid-fifteenth century. Troubles with Brazilian Indians led to a decision to eliminate them. To

supplant what had proved to be an unreliable work force, they brought blacks from their African colonies to work the plantations, beginning in 1505. Thus started the sorry history of slavery in the New World.

The Spanish had also created sugar plantations in their Canary Islands colony. They utilized their experience to establish similar enterprises on Hispaniola and other islands, beginning in 1515. Although a million Carib and Arawak Indians were living on Hispaniola in 1492, virtually all died off from disease and oppression within fifty years of contact with the Spanish. Spain also imported African slaves to replace Indian labor in the cane fields.

Beginning in the seventeenth century, other European states developed interests in the Americas. Dutch merchants had initially allied themselves with the Portuguese, providing capital to import slaves and to buy machinery. They also purchased and refined Portuguese sugar and sold it in European markets. Later, in 1630, as part of Dutch dogging of the Portuguese in southern Africa, India, and elsewhere, they seized northeastern Brazil and occupied it for twenty-five years. During their tenure they developed an understanding of the requirements of sugar production and processing, which they applied to the establishment of their own plantations on the Guiana mainland and on Caribbean islands that had been bypassed by the Spanish and Portuguese.

The appearance of the Dutch in the Caribbean region was part of a complex interplay of European powers in a region that generated huge profits from the production of sugar cane. Columbus himself had discovered most of the islands during his voyages, establishing a Spanish claim to the entire region. However, Spanish development was confined mainly to Hispaniola and Cuba. The other powers did not began seriously to encroach upon the region until a full century after the Spanish had begun their plantations. A number of ownership changes occurred over the ensuing two centuries, usually reflecting relative powers of the mother countries in Europe.

The French appeared in 1615, when they landed on the island of St. Christopher (St. Kitts). Twenty years later they claimed Guadeloupe and Martinique. They established their presence on St. Lucia and Grenada in 1650, and on the Guiana mainland in 1660. At the end of the century they occupied the western end of Hispaniola. Although the French subsequently lost or traded this empire, except for the islands of Martinique and Guadeloupe, they left a legacy of their language in the Caribbean. Creole is spoken by descendants of African slaves in Haiti and a number of smaller islands. Some 80 percent of its vocabulary is French, but it has West African morphology, syntax, and rhetoric.

A British role in the New World also began in the seventeenth century. The British contested French and

Spanish claims to a number of islands in the Lesser Antilles. They also fought fierce Carib Indians. A group of adventurers unsuccessfully sought to establish a colony in Grenada in 1607. In 1627 Barbados was established as a colony. The British seized Jamaica from Spain in 1655. Title to much of the British West Indies came only in the peace settlement following the Napoleonic Wars.

The Danes also established themselves in the Caribbean for more than two centuries. They succeeded French and Dutch influences in the Virgin Islands about 1700. In 1917 Denmark sold its colony to the United States.

American involvement in the region began with the purchase of Louisiana in 1803 and the acquisition of Florida in 1819. A war with Spain in 1898 resulted in control of Cuba and Puerto Rico. The former soon became sovereign, but the latter remains an American dependency as a "commonwealth." The United States purchased the Virgin Islands from Denmark in 1917 for $25,000,000. During the twentieth century the United States has exercised a paternalistic involvement in Caribbean affairs. It maintained military control for a time over both Haiti and the Dominican Republic. It also has military bases, most notably one at Guantanamo Bay in Cuba. It invaded Grenada in 1983 to quell a Communist takeover of the island.

The Spanish Territories

Although Spain was forced to find accommodation with other European powers in the Caribbean, it dominated the mainland virtually unchallenged for three centuries. In contrast to the British policy of maintaining separate direct relations with each colony in the New World, Spain treated its American empire as a monolith. It established a colonial hierarchy of territory. Originally there were two centers of power. The viceroyalties of New Spain and Peru were headquartered in Mexico City and Lima. To these were attached, respectively, a captaincy-general of Guatemala and a captaincy-general of Chile. Two new vice-royalties were broken off from Peru in the eighteenth century: New Granada, centered on what is now Colombia, appeared in 1717, and La Plata, in present-day Argentina and Uruguay, appeared in 1776. Remote concentrations of population were established as lower ranked presidencies. Most Indian settlements in areas intervening between Spanish and Portuguese territories were under control of the Roman Catholic Jesuit order until the order was expelled from Latin America in 1767.

Local officials communicated with the government in Spain through a cumbersome chain-of-command that passed through headquarters of higher-ranking captaincies-general and vice-royalties. In each community there were tensions between officials, who were generally drawn from Spain, and locally born whites, the *criollos*, who found themselves generally excluded from high administrative posts, although they formed a middle class that conducted local commerce. Mestizos constituted a still lower-ranking caste, but one that ranked socially above the Indians.

It was oligarchies of *criollos* in each settlement cluster who engineered separation from Spain in the period 1810–1825. Intellectuals among them were well aware of revolutionary currents in France and other parts of Europe. In contrast to the European situation, the grievances of the *criollos* were more personal than national. They were principally concerned with assuming complete power over local affairs. The success of the American and French revolutions were inspirations. The inability of Spain to project power to the Americas during the Napoleonic Wars provided the opportunity.

The revolutions of the Spanish-American states were essentially a string of coups by local *criollos*. The old social structures remained. Despite some visions of a federation of states, each separate Spanish colony gained its own independence. Efforts to bind the northern Andean region into a Confederation of Gran Colombia in 1821 fell apart in less than a decade. After Central America initially was joined to Mexico in 1821, a Confederation of Central America seceded in 1823 and lasted until 1839, when it fragmented into five separate states. Resentments by local elites were directed as much to seats of Spanish-American vice-royalties and captaincies-general as to Madrid itself. Rivalries among competing communities soon led to separation.

Eventually the whites and Mestizos of each state developed a national identity, although Indians as a group were generally excluded. Iconographies revolved around myths of revolution and enmity toward neighbors, particularly if the latter exhibited differing racial traits or had been adversaries.

The Portuguese Experience

The Portuguese experience in the Americas followed a different course from the Spanish process of colonization. The Portuguese were much more concerned with viable commercial development. Their experience in Africa had yielded a hard-headedness about economics. Even the name they gave to their new area, Brazil, derived from their first trading venture, the export to Portugal of a dyewood termed Brazilwood by the natives. The Portuguese early decimated the native Indians and came to rely upon African slaves. The fragmented Portuguese colonies along the Atlantic coast did not separate at independence in 1822, but remained together to form the largest state in Latin America.

The first Portuguese to reach the coast of Brazil actually had set sail originally for the East Indies. Initial contacts were desultory. Occasional trading ships dealt with native Indians who were encountered along the coast of the Papal-granted territory. Most Indians spoke languages related to the Guarani of present-day Paraguay. However, the interest of other European powers in the lands of the New World led the Portuguese to establish permanent colonial bases. Pressures particularly came from the French and the Spanish. The initial coastal foothold was at a fine harbor on the south coast, near the present port of Santos. Later the Portuguese established permanent settlements in the northeastern bulge of the country at San Salvador and Recife.

In contrast to the Spanish policy of royal conquest to Christianize the Indians and loot their accumulated wealth, the Portuguese were most concerned with developing viable tropical commercial enterprises. The king made proprietary land grants to individuals to organize settlements in a policy similar to colonial grants of the British in Anglo-America. Territories were very large, consisting usually of 150 miles of coastline that extended inland to the Tordesillas line of demarcation. Although subsequent events modified these patterns, many of the original boundaries can still be traced in the present outlines of Brazilian states.

The initial crop raised on the northeastern plantations was tobacco, but sugarcane soon became the principal product. A sufficient labor force was a major problem. It proved difficult to induce or coerce Indians to work in the fields. They were relatively few in numbers and these were reduced by exposure to European diseases. The Portuguese responded to Indian attacks upon settlements by wiping out entire native villages, killing their inhabitants or driving them into the interior. Without Indians to provide labor, the Portuguese began mass importation of African slaves in the sixteenth century. They had established coastal footholds in Africa to provision ships sailing to the East Indies. Sugarcane plantations proved unsuitable there, however, but the seemingly inexhaustible supply of slaves available from African chiefs provided a labor supply needed in Brazil.

Discovery of gold in Minas Gerais ("General Mines") in 1698 and diamonds in Tiuco in 1729 led to exploration and expansion into the interior of Brazil. The advance was principally by the Paulistas, named for their base in São Paulo to the south. Mainland Portuguese also played a major role, as did adventurers from the northeast. In searching for new mineral wealth, the Portuguese ignored the Tordesillas demarcation line, pushing far into the interior of the Amazonian Basin. Dense tropical rain forests served as a buffer between Paulista exploration and Spanish expansion

eastward. The two groups came into direct contact only in the south, along the Rio de la Plata.

The Portuguese did not coordinate their separate colonies as the Spanish did to the west. Each coastal settlement pursued its own course of development and had tenuous links with neighboring colonies. Like the Spanish, the Portuguese did prohibit other Europeans from entering their holdings. They also limited trade and forbade manufacturing.

In 1808 the Emperor of Portugal and his entire court fled to Brazil following Napoleon's takeover of that kingdom. The far-flung Portuguese Empire continued to function, with Rio de Janeiro as its center. The Portuguese emperor remained in Brazil until 1822. When he returned to Lisbon that year, he left his son in control of the American holdings. It was his son who declared Brazil's independence of Portugal.

A royal continuity thus existed in the Portuguese colonies in America at a time when Spanish colonial ties to the monarchy in Spain were interrupted. Historians consider this continuity a significant circumstance in the subsequent maintenance of unity in Brazil, particularly in combination with the peaceful transition to sovereignty. Brazilian settlements, after all, were just as isolated from each other by empty lands as were the Spanish colonies. Sentiments for independence were confined to the same types of small, educated groups born in America as in Spanish territories.

General Characteristics of Latin American States

In examining the political geography of the states of Latin America, one can observe a number of common features, despite the obvious unique qualities of each political unit.

Stability. The most obvious feature is the stability of states and boundaries over more than 150 years of independence. In contrast to fundamental changes in European states during the same period, the Latin American realm has seen few alterations of political-geographic patterns established in the first decades after gaining sovereignty. This rests in large part on acceptance of the legal doctrine of *uti possedetis* ("use possession"), enunciated in 1810. It essentially stated that each successor state to the Spanish Empire in America was entitled to territories that were allocated to its antecedent colony. Territorial problems developed over interpretations of vague Spanish descriptions of colonial boundaries, but they were far less than border conflicts, say, in East-Central and Southeastern Europe.

Dominance of cores. Another common pattern is the contrast between center and periphery. An ecumene of effective settlement surrounds each capital city. It contrasts with an outer zone of few, if any, people. Within the core of settlement the capital city is dominant, both in absolute numbers of people and in centrality of decision making. Commercial and governmental affairs are virtually all concentrated in the capitals. No states except Brazil and Ecuador have second-ranking cities with populations that number as many as half that of their capital cities.

Peripheral zones are often outside of effective governmental control. Dedicated leftist groups based in the outer forests of Colombia have been able to wage guerrilla warfare against their government for decades. Despite often massive assistance from the United States, Bolivia has been unable to control the production of cocaine in its frontier regions.

Distinctive nations. Within each state a national identity evolved during the nineteenth century that made virtually impossible any subsequent amalgamation into a larger unit, despite the commonality of cultural heritage. Administrative boundaries established in areas of rough terrain and low population in the colonial era became political discontinuities, despite great improvements in transportation and communication technology that subsequently could bind the separated population clusters into national unities, as occurred in Canada and the United States.

The majority of people in each state share a sense of homeland and a spatial integration of activities. Virtually no separatist movements exist. However, Indians tend to be excluded from national visions. Blacks also are treated as outsiders except in Belize and Haiti, where they dominate. Race discrimination plagues Latin American societies, but seldom does it threaten state unity. As in Anglo-America, the lack of spatial segregation of racial groups within most states is a principal factor in the maintenance of territorial wholeness. On the other hand, differences in racial composition between adjacent states contribute to international frictions.

Dominance by elites. Political power in most states continues to reside in an oligarchy that is mostly white. This is particularly true in the former Spanish colonies, where Hispanic cultural traditions persist. Inherited land ownership is a traditional source of influence. A limited number of families exert control, particularly through members who are officers in the military.

Foreign influence. Another general characteristic of Latin American states is their susceptibility to foreign influences. The nineteenth century exclusion of the Spanish and Portuguese in the process of independence led initially to a primary role for the British, who invested heavily in economic enterprises and infrastructure. Their role was steadily supplanted by the Americans, a situation accelerating after World War II. At the turn of the twentieth century, American arms drove Spain from its last holdings in Cuba and Puerto Rico. Later, the United States took direct action in the region to safeguard what it perceived were its vital interests. Internal troubles in the Dominican Republic in 1905 led to direct American management of its finances. Later, in 1916, Dominican disorders resulted in occupation by U.S. marines that lasted until 1924. Adjacent Haiti was controlled for similar reasons from 1915 to 1934. The United States also occupied Nicaragua from 1912 to 1925, and again from 1926 to 1933. More recently, the United States landed troops in Granada in 1983 and in Panama in 1989.

Boundary disputes. The borders of Latin American states are subject to far less tensions than occur in Europe, Africa, or Asia. They generally were established *antecedent* to settlement. Most were delimited in the eighteenth century or earlier as convenient administrative division lines between scattered population clusters of the Spanish Empire. They were sited in empty zones, generally following natural features. Even today, only a few actually cut across continuously populated areas. Adoption of the *uti possedetis* doctrine in the initial years of independence legitimized their positions.

The longevity, remoteness, and legitimacy of Latin American boundaries does not mean that border disputes are absent in the region. On the contrary, a number of conflicts have arisen over the past two centuries. Some developed as a consequence of aggressive economic penetration of frontier zones. Brazil's troubles with its neighbors are principally a result of its push into interior regions. Many have been generated by politicians in core areas seeking to mobilize popular support for personal ambitions.

Contending claims often reflect the vagueness and casualness in Spanish definitions of administrative lines. Unless a mountain ridge held silver or gold mines, it was simply an empty belt between areas of development. There was no need for precision in determining on the ground a line between separately run colonies, even if it was brightly emblazoned on maps. Similar ambiguities developed when streams were specified as divisions between colonies, such as the Uruguay and Pilcomayo rivers. Uninhabited riverine islands beyond the edge of settlement had little significance to colonial administrators. Likewise, the shifting of stream beds had little functional significance for imperial subdivisions, however important this might become in an age of sovereignty.

Arcane disputes over the demarcation of boundaries too often resulted in fighting, with losing sides never

TABLE 14.2   CENTRAL AMERICA

In comparison with the United States, the eight states of Central America collectively have an area and population approximately one-third as large. Mexico overwhelms the other units, with more than three times their combined populations and nearly four times their total area. Its influence among the others is far less than that of the United States, however. Most of the region bears the impress of Spain's past authority through dominance of the Spanish language and Roman Catholicism. However, the Caribbean coastal area, including nearly all of Belize, reflects long-standing British influence by the presence of the English language and Protestant Christianity (although Protestantism is making inroads throughout the region). Its black population contrasts with the region's predominantly European/Indian (Mestizo) mixture. Unassimilated Indians are significant minorities everywhere, although only in Guatemala do they exceed a quarter of the population. Each state has evolved a distinctive nation. Boundary quarrels with neighbors are minor, but civil wars have plagued Guatemala, El Salvador, and Nicaragua.

State	Total Population	Area (sq. miles)	Distinctive Features of Group
Mexico	85,000,000	750,000	
Dominant Nation and % Total			
Mexican, 75%			Romance (Spanish) language, Roman Catholic
Significant Regional Groups and % Total			
Central Plateau Indians, 10%			Uto-Aztecan languages, Roman Catholic
Gulf Coast Indians, 5%			Mayan languages, Roman Catholic
Southern Pacific Coast Indians, 10%			Oto-Manguean languages, Roman Catholic
Guatemala	9,500,000	42,000	
Dominant Nation and % Total			
Guatemalan, 45%			Romance (Spanish) language, Roman Catholic and Protestant
Significant Regional Groups and % Total			
Indian, 45%			Mayan languages, Roman Catholic and Protestant
Belize	200,000	9,000	
Dominant Nation and % Total			
Belizeans, 40%			Mixed Germanic/Romance (English) language, Roman Catholic and Protestant
Significant Regional Groups and % Total			
Garifunas (Black Caribs), 8%			Mixed Germanic/Romance (English) Language, Protestant

completely forgetting their losses. Most Latin American conflicts are best seen as colonial wars, conducted in outlying Indian territories by whites and Mestizos from the cores of states. As in other parts of the world, once such disputes arise, they seem never to be forgotten, waiting only for a new generation of leaders to make demagogic appeals to national honor and dignity.

Political-Geographic Regions of Latin America

Although commonalities of development permit consideration of Latin America as an entity, its political geography is best perceived by viewing it in parts that have similar characteristics. Five regions may be iden-

tified with notably shared qualities: Central America, the Caribbean islands, the Northern Andean States, the Southern "Cone" of states, and Brazil. Each has its own distinctive features of internal and external territorial tensions. They meet in frontiers that exhibit qualities of both realms. Thus, the Atlantic fringe of Central America tends to be black and English-speaking in common with the prevailing characteristics of the Caribbean islands.

Regional Characteristics of Central America

The narrow waist of the Americas has given rise to eight separate states: Mexico, Guatemala, Belize, El Salvador, Honduras, Nicaragua, Costa Rica, and Panama (Table 14-2). With the exception of Mexico,

TABLE 14.2   CENTRAL AMERICA (continued)

State	Total Population	Area (sq. miles)	Distinctive Features of Group
El Salvador	5,500,000	8,000	
Dominant Nation and % Total			
Salvadorans, 99%			Romance (Spanish) language, Roman Catholic
Honduras	5,000,000	43,000	
Dominant Nation and % Total			
Hondurans, 90%			Romance (Spanish) language, Roman Catholic
Significant Regional Groups and % Total			
Indians, 5%			South Aztec (Pipel, Lenka) languages, Roman Catholic
Meskito Indians, 2%			Mixed Germanic/Romance (English) language, Moravian Protestant
Nicaragua	4,200,000	50,000	
Dominant Nation and % Total			
Nicaraguans, 87%			Romance (Spanish) language, Roman Catholic
Significant Regional Groups and % Total			
Costeños (including Miskito Indians), 8%			Mixed Germanic/Romance (English) Language, Moravian Protestant
Costa Rica	3,200,000	20,000	
Dominant Nation and % Total			
Costa Ricans, 99%			Romance (Spanish) language, Roman Catholic and Protestant
Panama	2,500,000	30,000	
Dominant Nation and % Total			
Panamanians, 90%			Romance (Spanish) language, Roman Catholic and Protestant
Significant Regional Groups and % Total			
Indians, 6%			Chibcha (Terraba et al.) languages, Roman Catholic

each is small, both in effectively settled ecumene and in gross area. Each has some territorial grievances against its neighbors (Figure 14-2). Within each the population includes Mestizo, white, black, and Indian components. However, mixes vary. Belize is predominantly black. Nicaragua, Honduras, El Salvador, Panama, and Mexico are largely Mestizo. Costa Rica has a high proportion of whites, and more than half of Guatemala's population is Indian. Population on Caribbean coastal lands tends to be black and to speak English. Because of proximity to the United States, each has endured a high degree of American political and economic involvement.

Mexico. The United States of Mexico embraces more than 750,000 square miles of territory on the northern periphery of Latin America. Its ecumene is only one-eighth of this gross area, however, being confined to the approximately 85,000 square miles where water is adequate. Mexico's population of 85,000,000 is the largest of the Hispanic American states. In ancestry, 55 percent is Mestizo, 30 percent Indian, and 10 percent unmixed

European. One percent of the population is black and lives principally in the Yucatan region. As elsewhere in the Spanish New World, very few Europeans migrated to Mexico from Spain. Only 300,000 families and individuals were registered as immigrants during the three centuries of Spanish control. Linguistically, however, 92 percent speak Spanish, with the remainder using sixty different Indian dialects among five language groups.

When it was conquered by Spain, Mexico had a large, sedentary population organized into the broad Aztec Empire. Spain constituted this core of population into a vice-royalty that controlled all of Central America and also the Philippine Islands. Mexicans fought for their independence in a protracted struggle from 1810 to 1821. The young state had great difficulties in maintaining communication and control over its extensive territory. In 1836, English-speaking immigrants who had been given lands in the north revolted, creating theTexas Republic. In 1845 Texas joined the United States.

Although the border between Texas and the rest of Mexico had always been the Nueces River, the United

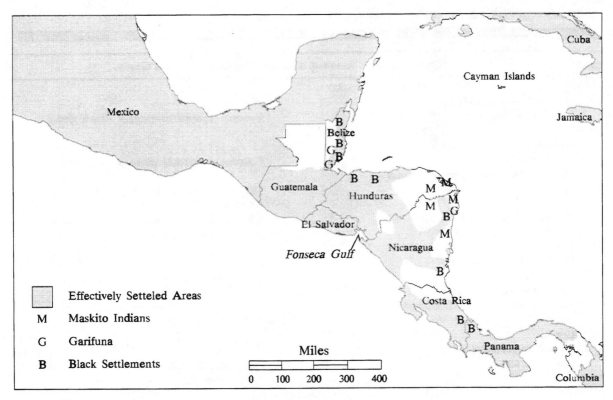

FIGURE 14-2 THE CENTRAL AMERICAN ECUMENE

States claimed territory farther south to the Rio Grande. When Mexico refused to discuss the issue, the U.S. government sent troops to the region. They soon clashed with Mexican forces. Subsequently, American troops easily occupied New Mexico and California, and ultimately captured Mexico City in 1847. A peace treaty was signed the following year, which recognized the Rio Grande as the border between the two states, with an irregular westward extension along the Gila River and across the Colorado River to the Pacific coast. Later, to raise funds for his army, the Mexican dictator in 1853 sold territory south of the Gila River to the United States for $10,000,000. The affected region of the United States is termed the Gadsden Purchase.

As a result of American expansion, Mexico lost 53 percent of its total area in the mid-nineteenth century. The adoption of the Rio Grande as a border laid the groundwork for political-geographic problems for both states in the future. The Rio Grande valley was an attractive area for rural settlement, and Spanish-speakers seeking land and a better life were drawn northward across the border. The river also changed its course after floods, leading to problems of sovereignty and ownership of areas suddenly separated from formerly contiguous lands. A celebrated instance of river course change involved the Chamizal district of the City of El

Paso, whose position changed from the south side of the river to the north in 1864. The United States returned the area to Mexico in 1967.

Mexico endured foreign invasion again in 1862 when Spain, the United Kingdom, and France organized a punitive expedition after Mexico suspended payments on huge debts it had amassed. Forces of the French emperor, Napoleon III, captured Mexico City and declared Mexico to be an empire headed by a member of the Austrian Habsburg family. The French incursion was not challenged by the United States, despite its enunciation of the Monroe Doctrine forbidding such European involvement in the Americas, since the ongoing Civil War had tied American hands. Fighting between Mexican imperial troops and guerrillas loyal to the Mexican republican leadership continued until 1867, when the republicans won victory and executed the European-installed emperor.

A high proportion of the population of Mexico has coalesced to form a national unity that is stronger than in most Latin American states. The Mexican nation shares a common language, culture, and religious heritage. Its unity dates particularly from the struggle that followed the Mexican Revolution of 1910, which ousted a president who had been dictator for thirty-five years. The popular goals of the revolution, including civil liberties, democracy, and separation of church from state, were institutionalized in a constitution of 1917. Its provisions have become a key part of the iconography of the Mexican nation ever since. However, the 8 percent of Mexico's population that does not speak Spanish has remained outside the Mexican nation. In general, these Indian groups have been quiescent, despite suffering poverty, lack of land, and various kinds of discrimination. The long period of inertness ended early in 1994 when well-organized Mayan Indian guerrillas seized several towns in Mexico's southernmost state of Chiapas. The central government quickly reestablished control of the region, but a high degree of local support for the guerrillas remains.

Mexican migrants have continued to cross the international border, particularly causing changes in local political relationships on the American side. Such out-migration has characterized the Mexican population since early in the colonial period. (A substantial proportion of the Philippine population is of Mexican origin.) It is doubtful that irredentist demands will be pressed against the United States for lost northern territories. Mexico has no active territorial claims against its neighbors, although it has in the past asserted rights to Belize. It does have its own problem, however, of large numbers of refugees from Guatemala, El Salvador, and Nicaragua settling its southern regions.

Guatemala. Guatemala is a troubled state. Its ecumene is concentrated in its southern third. Three-fourths of its 9,500,000 population live in the vicinity of the capital, Guatemala City. Only 1 percent inhabits the forested northern province of Petén, which contains a third of the state territory.

Slightly over half the Guatemalan population is Indian, mostly descended from the Mayas. They live mainly in the western highlands. Mestizos constitute somewhat more than 40 percent, and 5 percent are of direct Spanish origin. These latter two groups join with those Indians who choose to live a Latin way of life to form the *Ladinos*, who essentially can be called the Guatemalan nation. Sharp social inequalities have led reform-minded groups to attempt to mobilize the Indians to press for change. Indians have had another grievance over a government policy to uproot many from highland villages for resettlement in sparsely populated Petén. Many so displaced joined guerrilla bands, making up more than a quarter of the rebel contingents. The Guatemalan army responded by retaliations that forced many Indians to flee across the border into Mexico and Belize.

Guatemala has at times sought changes in the borders with its neighbors. In 1936 it formally agreed with Honduras and El Salvador to accept Mt. Montecristo as a common division point. It continues to harbor some pretensions to Mexico's Yucatan Peninsula on the grounds of its Mayan heritage. However, its major quarrel is over its eastern neighbor, Belize, whose right to separate independence it severely contests.

Belize. The Caribbean coast to the northeast of Guatemala was settled early in the seventeenth century by British loggers seeking tropical dyewoods. They at times also were pirates. The area became the sovereign state of Belize in 1981. Up to that time the region had been known as British Honduras. It is reported that the very appellation Belize is derived from native pronunciation of the name Peter Wallace, a notorious buccaneer whose base was there. The English settlers received certain rights from the Spanish government at the end of the eighteenth century, but Spain consistently maintained that it had sovereignty over the area. In 1780 the British government appointed an official supervisor for their settlements, but it also acknowledged Spanish sovereignty. The population of the region increased during the nineteenth century by immigrants from Mexico and former Confederate soldiers from the United States.

The Guatemalans began pressing claims to the region in 1820, soon after gaining their independence. In 1859 they signed a treaty with the United Kingdom that recognized the region as British territory. The British in turn pledged to assist in building a road through the region to permit Petén province an access to the Caribbean. This was not actually done until the mid-twentieth century. In 1862 the British declared the area to be a formal colony, subordinate to the administration of Jamaica. Two decades later, in 1884, it was made an independent colony. It received colonial self-government in 1964.

Over this time the Guatemalan government claimed sovereignty over the area on the grounds of its colonial heritage and the failure of the British to live up to terms of the treaty of 1859. It proved a convenient cause to divert attention from governmental shortcomings in other areas. It exerted particularly strong pressures in 1933, in the early 1950s, and in 1972. When the British finally built the long promised highway through Belize to the coast, Guatemala refused to build a connecting link on the grounds that the road had been too delayed, and that the United Kingdom had forfeited any rights to the territory. The British government found it necessary to maintain a military force in independent Belize because of perceived threats from Guatemala.

The population of Belize is markedly different from that of Guatemala. The majority of the people speak English. Only one-third is Spanish-speaking and Mestizo, although this proportion has been increasing by the settlement of refugees from troubled areas of Guatemala, El Salvador, Nicaragua, and elsewhere. Forty percent of the population is of mixed African-

English origin. About 15 percent are known as the "Black Caribs," or *Garifuna*. They are descendants of a mixed race African-Carib Indian group expelled to British Honduras from St. Vincent after an uprising against the English administration of that island.

In a break with its colonial past, the capital of Belize no longer is the town of Belize. After a hurricane devastated the latter in 1961, the capital was moved fifty miles inland to the planned administrative center of Belmopan.

El Salvador. In contrast to nearly all other countries of Latin America, virtually all of El Salvador's territory is effectively settled. Indeed, its rural population is very dense, and there is a land shortage that has internal and international repercussions. Its Indian population has not remained isolated from development, but has been homogenized into a common Ladino culture with El Salvador's dominant Mestizo group.

It does have severe political problems, but they are of a "vertical" social nature, rather than a "horizontal" territorial one, and they derive particularly from the land shortage. El Salvador has long had the dubious distinction of exhibiting the greatest contrasts in Latin America between wealth and poverty. Land ownership has been concentrated since colonial days in the hands of *los catorce* ("the fourteen"), a group of families dominating politics and the economy, who in large part have controlled affairs through dominance of family members in the military establishment. Suppression of disturbances by the landless have been a regular occurrence. In one particularly notable event in 1932, the army responded to a major political demonstration by surrounding the 30,000 peasants involved and killing them, an event known as *la matanza*, "the slaughter."As a consequence, more than 30,000 peasants fled to neighboring Honduras. Escape to sparsely populated Honduras continued for the ensuing decades. Many found work in the banana plantations of the east coast. By 1951 more than 300,000 Salvadorans lived in Honduras.

An active insurgency has characterized El Salvador for more than a decade. It dates from a 1972 army overthrow of an elected president, achieving major dimensions by 1979. The United States grew alarmed at its Communist political orientation and began massive aid to government forces. Insurgents were supported by covert supplies of military equipment from Nicaragua and Cuba. Continuous fighting in rural areas led to the flight of many individuals to other parts of Central America and the United States.

The shrinking amount of farmland per capita has been a stimulus for exodus to other areas. During the decade of the 1960s Salvadorans began moving in large numbers across the poorly defined international border with sparsely populated Honduras, leading to strong popular reaction in that country. Events reached a climax in 1969, when Honduran soccer fans clashed with Salvadorans in Mexico City following a heated international football match there between teams from the two states. An ensuing two-week "soccer war" resulted in Honduran expulsion of settlers from El Salvador. The war also caused the breakup of an incipient Central American Common Market. The dispute was not formally ended until a peace treaty was signed by the two states in Lima in 1980.

Honduras. Much of Honduras is in steep slope or poorly drained coastal lowlands. Per capita income is the lowest in Latin America outside of Haiti. Concentrations of settlement have developed in two rival regions. One is located in the coffee-producing highlands around the capital city of Tegucigalpa, which has the distinction of being the only Latin American capital city that is not near a railroad line. It is a typical Mestizo area. The other settlement is focused around the Caribbean coastal city of San Pedro Sula. It has a more Caribbean personality, with a number of West Indian blacks brought in to work in the region's banana plantations. A notable population component of its towns are Syrians, Lebanese, and Palestinian immigrants, who dominate commercial activities. Peripheral regions are principally the abodes of Indians. The Pipil and Lenca Indians of the highlands have given up native languages. Along the coast are the Miskito Indians, long oriented to the British. The northeastern region is essentially empty of population.

National consciousness developed late in Honduras, and largely as a result of territorial challenges from neighboring peoples. Nicaragua long claimed a wedge of Honduran territory inhabited principally by Miskito Indians and stretching 150 miles along the coast and 175 miles inland. The matter was submitted in 1906 to the king of Spain for arbitration. He found in favor of Honduras, but Nicaragua refused to accept that decision. Finally, in 1958, at the behest of the Organization of American States, rival claims were submitted to the International Court of Justice. The court again favored Honduras, and Nicaragua accepted the decision.

The region gained prominence in recent years as a haven for refugees and "Contra" rebel contingents from Nicaragua. Nearly a quarter-million individuals moved into Honduras as a result of civil disturbances in its neighbor to the south. Although many refugees subsequently returned after an agreement calling for a ceasefire and free elections was reached by the contending Nicaraguan Contra and Sandanista forces, many people remained in Honduras.

El Salvador has contested the ownership of a halfdozen pockets of territory along its land border with

Honduras, as well as the ownership of some islands in the gulf of Fonseca. The Gulf is Honduras's only opening to the Pacific, and it has long sought sovereign access through it. El Salvador has particularly pressed for recognition of its ownership of Meanguera Island, which dominates entrance to the gulf. The waterway gained importance in the 1970s as a route for covert Nicaraguan supply of El Salvadoran rebels. A now-defunct Central American Court of Justice in 1917 rendered an opinion that the Gulf of Fonseca was co-owned by Honduras, El Salvador, and Nicaragua, and any development required agreement by all three states. The dispute was submitted to the International Court of Justice in 1986.

Sections of the border with Guatemala also have been contested. Since 1921 Honduras has claimed ownership of the tiny and virtually uninhabited Swan Islands in the Caribbean. They remain occupied only by an American military contingent conducting meteorological and other scientific observations.

Nicaragua. Like Honduras, more than 80 percent of the total territory of Nicaragua lacks effective settlement. It has the largest area and least population density of the Central American states between Mexico and Colombia. Nearly 8 percent of its territory is occupied by Lake Nicaragua and Lake Managua.

Its core of settlement is situated on the western lowland. A traditional rivalry exists there between the old colonial settlements of León near the Pacific coast and Granada on the shores of Lake Nicaragua. León's citizens have long had a reputation for liberalism, whereas Granada has been well known for its reactionary perspective. The capital at Managua was established in 1858 as a neutral alternative located midway between two towns. The population of the core region is principally Mestizo, with significant minorities of Indians and white Europeans. Most are Roman Catholic in religion.

The province of Zelaya to the east has a notably different history and cultural tradition. Its inhabitants, the *costeños* ("coastal people"), are principally Indian and black, with a notably smaller proportion of Mestizos and whites. Some 75 percent of the Zelayan inhabitants are affiliated with the Protestant Moravian church. The English language is widely spoken. They resent a prevailing attitude of condescension toward them as second-class citizens by the Hispanic population of the west.

As elsewhere on the Central American Caribbean coast, Zelaya has a long history of association with the British. The latter established a protectorate for the Miskito Indians in 1678. In the following century they established colonies of blacks from Jamaica, with principal centers developing at Bluefields and Greytown

(which is now named San Juan del Norte). In Nicaragua such blacks are known as *Creoles*. The British also settled Black Carib *Garifuna* from the island of St. Vincent.

Although the British eventually recognized Spanish sovereignty over the region, they maintained close ties with the Caribbean coast for many decades after Nicaragua became independent in 1838. They supported a separate "Miskito Kingdom" until 1860, and it was 1893 before Nicaragua was able to exert full control over the region.

The 60,000 Miskito Indians have continued to present a major problem to governments of Nicaragua. The Sandanista regime, which seized power in 1979, found it necessary in 1982 to forcibly resettle 12,000 Miskitos away from the Honduran border. Another 21,000 fled across that boundary for sanctuary. A high proportion subsequently joined the Contra opposition guerrilla movement. Two years later the Sandanistas changed policy and returned 1,000 Meskitos to their former border-zone villages. With an eruption of fighting again in 1986, another 8,000 fled to Honduras.

In 1986 Nicaragua reopened a long-standing territorial dispute involving San Andres and Providencia islands, which lie 125 miles off its Caribbean coast. They have been occupied by Colombia since the mid-nineteenth century, after British recognition of Colombian authority. Their population of 25,000 is principally black, English-speaking, and Protestant, with Jamaican origins. San Andres is a duty-free port and tourist resort. Its principal export is coconuts.

The Nicaraguan government first raised a claim to the islands in 1909 on the grounds that the British recognition of Colombia's rights to the islands was for defense of its territory, but that United Kingdom action had not formerly established an international boundary. In 1928, however, Nicaragua signed an agreement with Colombia that recognized the latter's full sovereignty over the islands.

The Sandanista regime repudiated this agreement in 1980, stressing that the 1928 Nicaraguan government had been coerced into signing away the islands because the state was occupied by American marines. America had been involved in Nicaragua during the period 1912 to 1925, and again from 1926 to 1933 in a vain attempt to quell fighting that sprang from rivalries between Granada and León. At the onset of its intervention the United States was likely motivated by contemplations for building a water-level canal across Nicaragua.

Nicaragua's motivation for attacking Colombia's rights to the islands is unclear. As so often is the case involving territorial disputes, it probably reflected an attempt by an increasingly unpopular regime to rally inhabitants for a nationalist cause. Because the island inhabitants share much in common with the black population of Zelaya, the action may well have been addressed specifically to aspirations of that disaffected group. The Colombians dismissed Nicaragua's pretensions, and no overt actions occurred.

Costa Rica. An anomaly among the Latin American countries is Costa Rica. The population of 3,200,000 is mostly of European ancestry, although 15,000 West Indian blacks live along its Caribbean coast. Indians are negligible. More than four-fifths of its citizens are literate and participate in an exemplary democracy. The army was abolished in 1948. However, a Civil Guard of 6,000 is responsible for maintaining public order.

Costa Rica was part of the independent United Provinces of Central America that broke away from Mexico in 1823. It acquired its northwestern province of Guanacaste from Nicaragua during this period. In 1838 it became fully independent, although its population was barely 60,000.

As elsewhere, the lack of precision in Spain's identification of colonial borders created problems for Costa Rica as a successor state. A dispute over its boundary with Colombia continued into the twentieth century with newly independent Panama. Hostilities on a small scale commenced in 1921, but ended under American pressure.

Costa Rica has long been characterized as a land of farmers who own their own land, but it is now beginning to suffer some of the same problems of land hunger that characterize its neighbors. Two-thirds of its people live in its core area around the capital city of San Jose. It has had a rich tradition of steady expansion of a pioneer settlement frontier into its empty areas.

Although Costa Rica has continued to maintain its democratic traditions at a time of troubles among its neighbors, it has not been completely isolated. It harbors nearly 25,000 refugees, principally from Nicaragua.

Panama. The vast majority of Panama's territory also lies outside effective settlement. More than a third of its population is concentrated in the cities of Colon and Panama City at opposite ends of the Panama Canal. About 70 percent is Mestizo. Blacks make up about 14 percent and whites constitute 10 percent. Only 6 percent is Indian. Although most of the population speaks Spanish, blacks generally use English, reflecting origins in Jamaica and Barbados.

Panama's identity revolves around its isthmian character. Its narrow forty-mile width between the oceans was first discovered by the Spanish in 1513. The city of Panama was founded a half-dozen years later, and the king of Spain soon ordered exploration of a canal route. Although the canal was not built for another 350 years, Panama's subsequent fate reflected its role as a place of transit between the two oceans.

The isthmus served as a funneling point for virtually all goods and peoples passing between Spain and its Vice-Royalty of Peru. Panama City became one of the most active settlements in the Spanish Empire. In addition to its transit trade, it became a base for conquering the Pacific coast of Central America.

Panama became part of Colombia following collapse of Spain's empire in the Americas. Like other isolated settlements, its local oligarchy had chafed at external control by Bogota as much as at ultimate direction by Madrid. Following its independence, Colombia had continuing troubles with one of its most valuable territories. A Panamanian declaration of independence and revolt was suppressed by Colombia in 1841 and was but the most notable of many such disturbances during the nineteenth century.

The 1849 discovery of gold in California, which America had acquired the year before from Mexico, brought international attention to the Panamanian Isthmus, as it did to all narrow interoceanic passageways in Central America. Would-be miners and entrepreneurs streamed across on horseback and in stage coaches. Much of what they spent was siphoned off by the Colombian government, leading to more disturbances and a major revolt in 1853 that Colombia again was able to suppress.

The perception of opportunities from the deluge of people and goods in transit through Panama induced foreign investors to build the first "transcontinental" railroad in the Americas across the isthmus in 1855. Also, long entertained visions of a canal linking Atlantic with Pacific gained new currency. Its feasibility received support from the successful completion of the Suez Canal in 1869. The French were particularly interested, and a company headed by Ferdinand de Lesseps, the builder of Suez, acquired capital and Colombian approval to construct a canal. Work began in 1880. Nine years later the project failed, a victim of tropical diseases and poor management.

The United States also nourished ambitions of building a canal across Central America. A military need was dramatized at the end of the nineteenth century when the battleship *Oregon* and other naval vessels in the Pacific had to sail around the southern tip of South America in order to participate in the Caribbean phase of the Spanish-American War. Particular considerations were given to passageways through Nicaragua and Panama. Supporters of a Panamanian route gained support for their cause by distributing to members of the U.S. Congress copies of a Nicaraguan postage stamp showing a volcano adjacent to the route proposed there.

In 1903, during American negotiations with the Colombian government for rights to build a canal, there was yet another revolt in Panama, where it was feared the Colombians would refuse the American offer. The insurgents proclaimed their independence and the United States immediately recognized their *de facto* government; American naval forces prevented Colombian troops from putting down the rebellion. In return for its intervention and the promise of payment of $10,000,000 plus an annual rent of $250,000, the young government of Panama granted the United States the right to build a canal and to control "in perpetuity" a strip five miles on either side of the canal, except for the cities of Colón and Panama City at its termini. (These boundaries were subsequently modified in detail, particularly in the vicinity of Gatun Lake.) The United States also paid $40,000,000 to the French company for its rights and properties.

Work began on the canal in 1904 and was completed a decade later. In 1921 America implicitly recognized its meddling in the Panamanian revolt by paying Colombia $25,000,000 and granting it special privileges in transiting the canal. Three years later Colombia formally recognized Panama's independence. The annuity to Panama increased to $430,000 in 1936, and to nearly $2,000,000 in 1955.

The United States treated the Canal Zone as part of its own soil. The Canal Zone occupied a total area of 650 square miles and had a population of 50,000, of whom 85 percent were American citizens. They enjoyed their own schools, police force, fire protection, hospitals, and postal service. Living standards were much higher than in the rest of Panama. Because of constant challenges to their presence and privileged position, the residents of the Canal Zone tended to reflect a noticeably stronger nationalism than was characteristic of most of the American nation.

In 1977 the United States signed two new treaties with Panama concerning the canal. By their provisions, areas of the former Canal Zone not needed for military defense reverted in 1979 to Panama. The United States retained operational control of the canal itself and its associated military installations until 1999.

On several occasions during the early twentieth century American forces have intervened in Panamanian internal affairs. These activities were justified on ground of needs to protect the canal. Intervention as a policy was renounced in 1934, although the United States continued to play an influential role in Panamanian domestic politics. In 1989 it mounted an armed invasion of Panama and seized the Panamanian leader, claiming his involvement in narcotics trafficking in the United States. The United States subsequently promised payment for damage done by its invasion and continued in force its 1977 treaties.

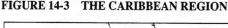

FIGURE 14-3   THE CARIBBEAN REGION

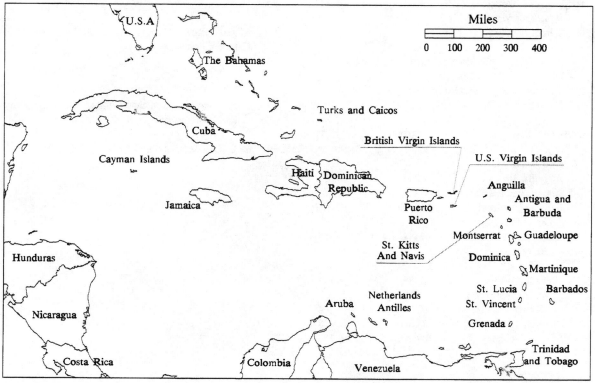

TABLE 14.3   THE CARIBBEAN STATES

The Caribbean region is one of the most densely populated on earth. Its 36,000,000 inhabitants are divided among more than 30 states and dependencies, although five-sixths live on the four large islands of Cuba, Hispaniola (Haiti and the Dominican Republic), Puerto Rico, and Jamaica. The smaller islands are nearly all English-speaking, but the French language is dominant on Guadeloupe and Martinique. Haiti also is French-speaking. Cuba, Puerto Rico, and the Dominican Republic employ Spanish. The populations of Haiti, the smaller islands, and the Guianas are mainly descended from African slaves brought by French, English, and Dutch entrepreneurs to labor in the region's sugar plantations. Following abolition of the slave trade in the early nineteenth century, significant numbers of East Indians came to the region as replacement labor, particularly to Trinidad and the Guianas. Formerly large numbers of indigenous Indians virtually disappeared except in the forests of the Guianas. Despite the region's high degree of homogeneity in race and language, each island and mainland entity has evolved its own sense of national identity. Few territorial frictions exist.

State	Total Population	Area (sq. miles)	Distinctive Features of Group
Haiti	7,000,000	11,000	
Dominant Nation and % Total			
Haitians, 100%			Romance (French) language, Roman Catholic, black
Dominican Republic	7,500,000	19,000	
Dominant Nation and % Total			
Dominicans, 98%			Romance (Spanish) language, Roman Catholic, Mestizo
Cuba	11,000,000	43,000	
Dominant Nation and % Total			
Cubans, 100%			Romance (Spanish) language, Roman Catholic
Puerto Rico (U.S. Possession)	3,600,000	3,500	
Dominant Nation and % Total			
Puerto Ricans, 95%			Romance (Spanish) language, Roman Catholic
Jamaica	2,500,000	4,250	
Dominant Nation and % Total			
Jamaicans, 98%			Mixed Germanic/Romance (English) language, Protestant
Trinidad and Tobago	1,300,000	2,000	
Dominant Nation and % Total			
Trinidadian, 93%			Mixed Germanic/Romance (English) language, Roman Catholic, Protestant
(East Indians [36%] live among the Trinidadians but retain a separate identity)			
Significant Regional Groups and % Total			
Tobagonians, 4%			Mixed Germanic/Romance (English) language, Roman Catholic, Protestant
British Antilles	1,000,000	1,037	
(All but Anguilla, Bahamas, British Virgin Islands, and Montserrat are independent but remain members of the British Commonwealth)			
Anguilla (Br. colony)	7,500	35	
Antigua and Barbuda	64,000	170	
Bahama Islands (Br. colony)	264,000	5,382	
British Virgin Islands (Br. colony)	13,000	59	
Barbados	260,000	166	
Grenada	91,000	134	
Montserrat (Br. colony)	12.000	40	
St. Kitts and Nevis	43,000	104	
St. Lucia	135,000	238	
St. Vincent and the Grenadines	109.000	150	

TABLE 14.3 THE CARIBBEAN STATES (continued)

State	Total Population	Area (sq. miles)	Distinctive Features of Group
British Antilles (continued)			

National Identity

Each island's population constitutes a separate nation. Despite a common language (English), religious background (mainly Protestant), and history of British rule, there is little sense among the populations of being "West Indian."

State	Total Population	Area (sq. miles)	Distinctive Features of Group
Netherlands Antilles (Totals)	256,000	656	

(All but Aruba are formally within the autonomous territory of the Netherlands Antilles)

Curaçao	143,000	444	
Aruba	65,000	75	

(Separate autonomous territory within the Netherlands equal to the Netherlands Antilles)

Bonaire	11,000	111	
St. Martin (south)	34,000	13	
St. Eustatius	1,800	8	
Saba	1,200	5	

National Identity

Each island's population constitutes a separate nation. Despite a common language (English), religious background (mainly Protestant), and history of association with the Netherlands, there is little sense among the populations of being "Dutch West Indian."

State	Total Population	Area (sq. miles)	Distinctive Features of Group
French Antilles	749,000	703	

(They are treated formally as parts of Metropolitan France)

Martinique	370,000	46	
Guadeloupe	345,000	629	
St. Martin (north)	29,000	20	
St. Barthélemy	5,000	8	

National Identity

Each island's population constitutes a separate nation. Despite a common language (French), religious background (Roman Catholic), and history of association with France, there is little sense among the populations of being "French West Indian."

State	Total Population	Area (sq. miles)	Distinctive Features of Group
Virgin Islands of the United States	110,000	136	

Dominant Nation and % Total

Virgin Islanders			Mixed Germanic/Romance (English) language, Protestant

State	Total Population	Area (sq. miles)	Distinctive Features of Group
French Guiana	120,000	32,000	

Dominant Nation and % Total

French Guianese, 97%			Romance (French) language, Roman Catholic

Significant Regional Groups and % Total

Indians, 3%			Tupi-Guarani languages, Animist

Potential Trouble Areas and Possible Adversaries

Headwaters of Litani River (Suriname)	2,000	300	

State	Total Population	Area (sq. miles)	Distinctive Features of Group
Suriname	400,000	65,000	

Dominant Nation and % Total

Surinamers, 33%			Romance (Dutch) and Mixed (Sranan Tongo) laguages, Roman Catholic and Protestant

(East Indians [37%] and Javanese [14%] live among the Surinamers but retain separate identities)

Significant Regional Groups and % Total

Bush Negroes, 5%			Mixed (Taki-Taki) language, Indigenous folk religion

State	Total Population	Area (sq. miles)	Distinctive Features of Group
Guyana (formerly British Guiana)	750,000	83,000	

Dominant Nation and % Total

African Guyanans, 43%			Mixed Germanic/Romance (English) language, Protestant and Roman Catholic

Significant Regional Groups and % Total

East Indian Guyanans, 51%			Mixed Germanic/Romance (English) language, Hindu (80%) and Muslim (20%)

Continued

TABLE 14.3   THE CARIBBEAN STATES (continued)

State	Total Population	Area (sq. miles)	Distinctive Features of Group
Guyana (continued)			
Bush Negroes, 8%			Mixed (Taki-Taki) language, Indigenous folk religion
Potential Trouble Areas and Possible Adversaries			
New River Triangle (Suriname)	2,000	9,000	
Essiquibo Territory (Venezuela)	2,000	50,000	

The Caribbean Region

The islands of the Caribbean Sea and Gulf of Mexico constitute a major part of Latin America (Figure 14-3). Their combined population of 30,000,000 is exceeded in the Americas only by the United States, Brazil, and Mexico. The region embraces 1,350,000 square miles, which is half the area of the United States or Brazil. However, only 90,000 square miles lie above sealevel, making the island region one of the most densely populated on earth (Table 14-3).

Considering the small amount of available land, it is also the most politically diverse part of the world. It is currently divided into twenty-four states and dependencies. Four of its political entities are comparable in size and population to the states of Central America: Cuba, Haiti, the Dominican Republic, and Puerto Rico. They incorporate five-sixths of the population and are either Spanish- or French-speaking. The other one-sixth speaks mainly English, but is spread among eight small independent island states and eleven European and American dependencies. Sixteen of these each have fewer than 700 square miles of area, and populations of under 350,000. Tiny Grenada occupies only 133 square miles, and the Turks and Caicos Islands have barely 11,000 inhabitants.

The three Guianas on the South American mainland—Guyana, Suriname, and French Guiana—should properly be considered with the island states of the Caribbean. They share common population characteristics and historical experiences with the island units. Indeed, they also exhibit very insular qualities themselves. More than 90 percent of their populations are located along their coastlines, with virtually no connections to their interior regions. Their numbers are small. Only 1,350,000 inhabitants occupy their total combined area of 180,000 square miles. Their commonalities with their neighbors are recognized within the region, and they routinely are included in Caribbean organizations. Belize, already discussed in the Central American section of this chapter, is also more properly seen as part of the Caribbean world.

Virtually all the peoples of the region are descendants of African slaves. Their ancestors suffered incredible hardships when brought to the Americas. Records indicate that field hands, after being brought to the Caribbean, lasted only seven years on the average. Although it is known that more than 300,000 Africans were landed in Dutch Guiana, only 60,000 blacks were living there when it became the independent state of Suriname.

Most inhabitants also have some European ancestry. Color consciousness is ingrained everywhere. Individuals with pronounced European features are classed as "white"and tend to have far greater opportunities for social and economic mobility. (In contrast, people in the United States exhibiting even slight traces of African ancestry are invariably classed as "black.")

The dense native Indian populations disappeared within a half century of European colonization from imported diseases and oppression. The region does contain significant numbers of people of Asian origin as a legacy of contract labor brought to its plantations following the abolition of slavery. These include a half million East Indians and 100,000 Chinese who came to British colonies in the period 1850–1917. A substantial number of Javanese were also brought to work in Dutch Guiana.

High population densities on many islands have prompted extensive out-migration. Many people have gone to other islands that have employment opportunities. Cuba received many after gaining its independence. Trinidad also has been a major destination. The entire Caribbean rim of the mainland has attracted large numbers, particularly Venezuela for its petroleum industry opportunities, and Panama, when the canal was built. In recent times the United States has been a major recipient of West Indian migrants. The 1980 American census identified 50,000 from Barbados, 150,000 from Trinidad, and 500,000 from Jamaica. Increasing restrictions on movement into the United States has resulted in large numbers now going to Canada and Europe. It is estimated that there are

300,000 West Indians in the United Kingdom, 150,000 in France, and 20,000 in the Netherlands.

The involvement of several different European states in the region has contributed to the cultural diversity among its inhabitants. Those living in the larger Spanish colonies of Cuba, Puerto Rico, and the Dominican Republic have retained their Hispanic language and Roman Catholic religion. Haitians speak a French *patois* and are also Catholics, and the same can be said for the inhabitants of Guadeloupe and Martinique. Most of the populations on the small islands speak English and are Protestant, even if their past colonial relations happened to be with the Netherlands, Denmark, or France. An exception is found on the Dutch islands off Venezuela, where Papiamento is spoken. This language developed in the eighteenth century as a conglomerate with elements of English, Spanish, Dutch, Portuguese, Carib, and African tongues.

Compounding the diversities of differing historical and cultural influences has been the development of separate island identities that have tended in most instances to evolve into true nationhoods. Even the British colonies of the Lesser Antilles have not been able to develop a sense of commonality, despite their homogeneity in language, religion, and historical experience. Indeed, long-standing associations have broken off. Anguilla dissolved its bonds with St. Kitts-Nevis, and Tobago contains a separatist movement directed against Trinidad, despite their joint association since 1888. On the other hand, only two islands are politically fragmented. The large island of Hispaniola saw separate Spanish and French colonial developments on its eastern and western extremities that led to the evolution of the separate states of the Dominican Republic and Haiti, and tiny St. Martin retains a curious division between a French northern half and a Dutch southern one.

A common feature of the Caribbean entities is their continuing economic and political dependency upon European States and America. Most do not produce enough food to feed themselves. Agriculture is oriented to tropical crops for export to the mid-latitudes. They also depend upon European and American tourists to generate substantial portions of income. Drug trafficking with foreigners is also important, as are remittances sent home by overseas migrants.

Aid from present or former mother countries is also substantial. Most of the small states have continued to receive various forms of subsidy. New supporters have also been found. After Cuba severed its economic dependency upon the United States, it developed substantially greater reliance upon aid from the Soviet Union. Estimates of its magnitude have ranged as high as $8,000,000 to $10,000,000 per day before the Soviet Union's own economic problems forced a curtailment.

The United States has exercised a substantial role in the Caribbean. In addition to direct aid and investment, it has been the source area of a high proportion of the region's tourists and a major market for produce. It also has involved itself directly in local affairs, justifying its actions by citing the need to protect its borders and the approaches to the Panama Canal. It established a major naval base on Cuba's Guantanamo Bay after assisting Cuba's independence from Spain. It created a colonial relationship with Puerto Rico and purchased the Virgin Islands from Denmark. The United States intervened several times to quell unrest in Haiti and the Dominican Republic, and it invaded Grenada in 1983 on ideological and military grounds. During World War II it arranged with the United Kingdom to establish a number of military bases on the islands in trade for naval vessels badly needed by Britain.

For all of its political fragmentation, the region holds few actual territorial disputes. Although the Caribbean seabed is completely parceled out among the island states and those on the mainland shores, some conflicting claims are likely to occur, should undersea resources be found. A political movement on the Dutch island of Aruba, which successfully gained separation from the rest of the Netherlands Antilles in 1981, has raised questions over its seafloor boundary with Venezuela. That country also has its ownership of the tiny island of Aves contested by Guadeloupe, which lies only seventy-five miles to the east of it. The disputes between Colombia and Nicaragua over Providencia and San Andrés islands and between Honduras and the United States over the Swan Islands have been noted above.

Haiti. The island of Santo Domingo covers 30,000 square miles, and its western third is occupied by the Republic of Haiti, whose name means "Mountain Land" in the Carib language. It developed in the early seventeenth century when French buccaneers established a settlement. France declared it to be the colony of Saint Domingue in 1655, and four decades later the Spanish, who controlled the rest of the island, recognized its legitimacy.

The French developed sugarcane plantations based upon African slave labor. The slaves constituted 90 percent of the colony's 500,000 population when they rebelled in 1791. They killed all French colonists who could not escape and broke up the plantations into peasant farms. France recognized their independence in 1804. Haitians thus became the first Latin Americans to separate from European control.

In subsequent decades Haiti became the most impoverished part of the Americas. Its growing population took up virtually all land that could be farmed. The society retained aspects of both its African heritage and its colonial French culture. Virtually all inhabitants are black. Although Roman Catholicism and the French language remain strong, spiritual practices derived from West Africa play an important role among the populace.

The Dominican Republic. In contrast to Haiti's dense population, the Spanish colony of Santo Domingo had barely 100,000 people at the beginning of the nineteenth century. It had seen the settlement of many more Europeans, and only a third of its population consisted of slaves. In 1821 it became one of the last Spanish colonies to declare independence. The Haitians to the west immediately invaded and began a reign of terror against the white population.

It was only in 1844 when the Dominicans could again assert their independence. However, continuing troubles with the Haitians led them to accede to Spain again in 1861 for protection. They declared independence a third time in 1865. A subsequent attempt to join the United States of America was rebuffed, but American capital put new life into its sugar plantation economy. Its commercial agriculture contrasts with the peasant plots of Haiti.

The present population of the Dominican Republic numbers 7,500,000 and is concentrated in the eastern and northern parts of the territory. In contrast to Haiti, much of the land remains empty. The Dominicans share a strong sense of nationhood, with an iconography of pride in their Spanish heritage and antipathy toward Haitians.

Although the border with Haiti was long disputed, the Dominican dictator Rafael Trujillo reached agreement with Haiti to accept the *de facto* boundary between them as permanent. He then proceeded to evict Haitian squatters on Dominican lands east of the line at a cost of at least 17,000 lives. Pressures from Haitian migrants seeking farm plots have continued to the present, however.

Cuba. The largest Caribbean island is Cuba. It did not gain independence from Spain at the beginning of the nineteenth century with the other Spanish American colonies, but separated only in 1898 as a result of American intervention. As part of its treaty arrangements with the United States, it accepted the so-called Platt Amendment of 1901, which, among other provisions, allowed the United States to maintain military bases and to intervene in local Cuban affairs. The United States exercised the latter right in 1906, 1912, and in the period from 1917 to 1922. It also established a naval base at Guantanamo Bay that it still retains, despite America's renunciation of the Platt Amendment in 1934.

Cuba's present population is classed as 11 percent black, 51 percent Mulatto, 37 percent white, and 1 per-

cent Chinese. As in other Caribbean states, the meaningfulness of definitions can be questioned. The different groups are not regionally segregated, and all share a strong sense of Cuban national identity. Much of the Cuban iconography involves negative images of American interference in Cuban affairs. Recent additions include an abortive American-supported invasion by exiles at the Bay of Pigs in 1961 and a naval blockade against the importation of Soviet Missiles in 1962. The United States has maintained a trade embargo against Cuba ever since its dictator, Fidel Castro, confiscated American properties following his seizure of power in 1959.

Puerto Rico. The 3,500-square-mile island of Puerto Rico, like Cuba, separated from Spain in 1898 through American intervention. It did not share the early nineteenth century passions of the mainland colonies for independence. As a consequence, it continued to receive Spanish immigrants, as well as many Spanish loyalists who left Latin American colonies that had broken away. The result was a far smaller proportion of blacks in its population than was the case on other Caribbean islands. Presently 99 percent of Puerto Ricans are classified as being of European ancestry.

After its separation from Spain, Puerto Rico did not gain independence as Cuba did, and popular sentiments even now do not press for it. Its people received American citizenship in 1917, and the island was declared a commonwealth in 1948. Puerto Ricans share a strong sense of insular identity that includes pride in their Hispanic heritage. At the same time, they value ties that permit free movement to the United States and participation by local entrepreneurs in its huge market. The United States also provides a "safety valve" for rapid population growth. The city of New York now has more Puerto Rican inhabitants than Puerto Rico's capital of San Juan.

Remaining a dependency of the United States has not led to an absorption into the American nation. Among the island population of 3,500,000, only 500,000 speak English, and they are bilingual. The remainder speak only Spanish. The Puerto Rican nation may be unique in its current lack of a quest for sovereignty.

Jamaica. The island of Jamaica covers 4,400 square miles. It was under Spanish control for 150 years before the British seized it in 1655. Three-quarters of its population of 2,300,000 are black, and another 21 percent are of mixed racial ancestry. Only 3 percent of Jamaicans are European. Its black population has retained far less of its African cultural heritage than is the case of the Haitians. Many Jamaicans have migrated to other islands, to the Caribbean mainland, and overseas to the United States, Canada, and the United Kingdom.

Jamaica gained colonial self-government in 1942 and full independence within the British Commonwealth in 1962, following collapse of the planned Federation of the West Indies.

Trinidad and Tobago. The large island of Trinidad off the Venezuelan coast had a history of three centuries of Spanish rule before becoming a British colony in 1797. In that period many Frenchmen established plantations that utilized African slave labor. When slavery was abolished during the nineteenth century, the planters contracted with laborers from India. Trinidad long has had a reputation of underpopulation, and many West Indians have migrated to it from densely populated islands.

Trinidad's present population of 1,200,000 reflects these past events. Blacks and East Indians are equal in numbers, and they make up slightly more than 80 percent of the total. Persons of mixed ancestry constitute another 16 percent, with small numbers of Europeans and Chinese. All groups speak English.

In contrast to other islands, the blacks and East Indians tend to live in segregated areas. Most of the latter are concentrated in sugar plantation areas of the western plains. Trinidad's politics have revolved around the two principal ethnic groups. Since independence, the island has been dominated by its black and mixed-race groups. Flagrant gerrymandering reduced the representation of the rural East Indian minority, which makes up 40 percent of the country's population, to less than a third of the seats in parliament. Only in 1976 did a racially pluralistic political party develop. It was based upon a union of black oil workers and East Indian sugar workers. It has not been able to gain political power over the entrenched black party, however.

The island of Tobago lies twenty miles northeast of Trinidad. At one time it had five times as many inhabitants as Trinidad, but it now counts only 45,000 people. Its history is much more checkered than its neighbor's. By 1800 it had changed hands thirty-one times. There is a significant island consciousness that one day may lead to separation. Tobago now enjoys a high degree of internal self-government.

Trinidad's only territorial dispute involves a conflict with Venezuela over jurisdiction of the seven miles of water separating them. Venezuela frequently seizes Trinidad fishermen, despite a treaty signed between the United Kingdom and Venezuela in 1942 and signed again by Trinidad and Venezuela in 1977.

The British Lesser Antilles. The majority of the small islands in the Caribbean had come under British control by the beginning of the nineteenth century. All had witnessed a common history of seventeenth-century European involvement followed by a dying off of native Indian peoples, the introduction of African slaves to work in the sugarcane fields, eighteenth-century island prosperity, emancipation of slaves in the

nineteenth century, and twentieth-century economic decline. Among consequences of British colonial rule was the development of a variety of common political, economic, and cultural institutions. Most colonies had local democratically elected assemblies, used the British monetary system, and worshipped in Protestant churches. There were also various kinds of interisland linkages, including the prestigious West Indian College of Tropical Agriculture and the highly successful West Indian cricket team. The smaller islands had been joined administratively since the late nineteenth century into the Leeward and the Windward island federations. The populations of all islands were predominantly black and English-speaking and had developed a degree of anticolonialist feeling. Individually, however, most were small in area and population, and they were far from being economically self-sufficient.

As the British recognized the need to dismantle their far-flung empire, they developed a plan to create a West Indies Federation that would be sufficiently large and viable to be able to sustain itself. It would be based upon existing British West Indian politically centripetal forces of homogeneity and coherence as cited above. The proposed unit would include Jamaica, Trinidad, Tobago, Antigua, Barbados, Grenada, Montserrat, St. Kitts-Nevis-Anguilla, St. Lucia, and St. Vincent. The unit would have 3,000,000 inhabitants and an area of 8,000 square miles. It should be noted that several British colonies did not participate in the planning, including the British Virgin Islands, the Bahamas, British Honduras (present-day Belize), and British Guiana.

Organizational work began in 1956, but by 1962 the project had failed. In the end, a variety of centrifugal forces overcame the centripetal ones. They may be summarized as follows:

- *Distance.* A thousand miles lay between Jamaica and Antigua, and another 500 were between Antigua and Trinidad.
- *Communication Difficulties.* Sea communications were poor and uncertain, and many islands lacked adequate airfields.
- *Lack of Contiguity.* The components of the federation were not only isolated islands, but between them were intervening French, Dutch, and American possessions, as well as the independent states of Haiti and the Dominican Republic.
- *Contrasts in Size.* Jamaica would have half the area and population of the proposed new unit, whereas many of the components would be less than thirty square miles in size.
- *Lack of Economic Complementarity.* Most islands produced the same types of crops and were in competition with each other for foreign markets, rather

than having a basis for meeting each other's needs.

- *Religious Differences.* Although the overwhelming majority of island inhabitants were Protestant, four islands had Roman Catholic majorities, including Trinidad, which also had two-fifths of its population Hindu or Muslim.
- *Racial Differences.* Although most island dwellers had black ancestors, degrees of racial mixture varied from island to island, and 40 percent of Trinidad was East Indian; Barbados was denigrated by the others as a "white" island because 5 percent of its population was of unmixed British ancestry.
- *Linguistic Differences.* Although all educated persons spoke English, dialects varied greatly, with Trinidadians having great difficulties understanding Jamaicans; on four islands a French-based *Creole* language was utilized.
- *Particularist Feelings.* The most critical centrifugal force was the lack of a sense of being "West Indian"; individuals identified with their own islands and shared generally negative stereotyped views of the inhabitants of other ones; there was also a concern by more favored islands of being swamped by immigrants from less affluent units.

The ultimate cause of failure of the proposed federation was the inability to agree upon which of the islands would gain the benefits of having the federal capital complex. When a commission ultimately selected Trinidad in 1961, its rival Jamaica reacted by holding a referendum on withdrawal from the planned federation. A 54 percent majority voted to withdraw and seek separate independence, which the British granted in 1962. This caused the entire project to collapse. Trinidad and Tobago also successfully gained their own independence in 1962. The remaining islands made an attempt at a smaller federation in 1964, but they had an area of only 1,500 square miles and a population of 750,000. Moreover, the major centrifugal forces remained, and that project also failed. Half became independent, although they, like the remaining British dependencies, continued to maintain close ties with the United Kingdom.

Sovereignty has not meant an end to political geographic problems, however. Smaller islands have sought separation from the dominant ones. Thus, the 1,500 inhabitants of Barbuda have tried to leave Antigua. In 1967 British paratroops were called upon to prevent an armed rebellion in Anguilla against St. Kitts and Nevis, but two years later, with British intervention, the sixty-square-mile island and its 7,000 inhabitants became a separate dependency of the United Kingdom.

The Netherlands Antilles. Dutch involvement with islands in the Caribbean began in 1632 when the Netherlands acquired Saba and Sint Eustatius. Two years later it gained Aruba, Curaçao, and Bonaire, and in 1648 it divided the island of St. Martin with France. The six islands were constituted into the colony of the Dutch West Indies in 1828, renamed the Netherlands Antilles in 1845.

Curaçao, Aruba, and Bonaire lie from twenty to fifty miles off the Venezuelan coast, and are grouped into the Dutch Leeward Islands. The other three are 500 miles away in the Lesser Antilles south of Puerto Rico, and are designated the Dutch Windward Islands. Their combined area is only 300 square miles, and their population is 250,000. Despite the long association with the Netherlands, islanders do not speak Dutch. English is the language of the Windward group, and the mixed language Papiamento is the Leeward vernacular.

In 1954 the Netherlands Antilles were constituted into a state constitutionally equal to the Kingdom of the Netherlands and sharing the same sovereign. Rivalries with the other islands led Aruba to seek a disconnected status in 1977. The government of the Netherlands made Aruba constitutionally separate from the Netherlands Antilles in 1986, with a promise of full independence in 1996.

The French Antilles. Although the French controlled nearly all the Lesser Antilles at one time or another before the nineteenth century, their holdings have been reduced to Martinique and Guadeloupe, with nearby small islands and the northern part of St. Martin. Their combined area is less than 1,000 miles with a population of 700,000.

In 1946 both main islands with their dependencies were declared to be "overseas departments" of France, with a legal status comparable to that of Hawaii to the United States. Their populations enjoy all of the benefits of French citizens, including welfare services. Most speak Creole, a dialect derived from French.

French Guiana. The French established a permanent foothold in South America in creating their colony of Cayenne in 1604. They expanded inland in 1817. The colony of French Guiana became notorious after 1852 for its penal colony on Devil's Island, although it in fact was more favored by its climate than several other convict camps established in the interior. The penal colonies were closed in 1945.

The territory has an area of 32,000 square miles, although 90 percent is uninhabited. The population speaks Creole. It is predominantly black or mulatto, but 15 percent of the people are Chinese and 8 percent are East Indian. French Guiana shelters a number of refugees, including 7,000 from Haiti and another 10,000 who have fled Suriname since 1986.

Like Martinique and Guadeloupe, French Guiana was made an overseas French department in 1946. Its population appears content with its status, and there has been no move for independence. It does have a dispute with Suriname, which claims 300 square miles of its territory. The argument involves the location of the tributary river specified as a border between the two states.

Suriname. The former colony of Dutch Guiana was a region of contest between the English and French in the early seventeenth century before the former traded it to the Dutch in exchange for the colony of New Netherlands, which became New York. It went through the common history of the Caribbean of sugar plantations and slavery. One departure was the development of interior self-governing colonies of "Bush Negroes" who managed to flee the coastal plantations. The colony also saw large numbers of East Indians and Javanese replace emancipated slaves. Suriname became independent of Dutch rule in 1975.

The present population reflects the past. East Indians (termed "Hindustanis") make up 37 percent of the total. Coastal blacks and mulattos constitute 31 percent, and Bush Negroes add 10 percent more. Muslim Javanese are 15 percent of the total, and there are small groups of Chinese, Indians, and Europeans. The various groups have preserved their native languages, but a *lingua franca* termed "Sranan Tongo" or "Taki-Taki" has emerged as a means of intergroup communication. The official languages are English and Dutch, but in 1976 it was announced that Spanish would become the principal working language.

Suriname has an active territorial claim against neighboring Guyana. The "New River Triangle" controversy is a legacy of a long-standing dispute between the Dutch and British over which branch of the Courantyne River was the agreed upon boundary between the two former colonies. About 9,000 square miles are involved. Some fighting over the region actually took place in 1969.

Guyana. In their dealings with the Dutch over their Guiana holdings following the Napoleonic Wars, the British retained the western region, which they renamed British Guiana in 1814. Like Dutch Guiana, its population changed during the nineteenth century as East Indians, Azoreans, and Chinese were brought in to replace emancipated slaves. In 1966 the region received its independence from the United Kingdom and renamed itself Guyana.

Its present population of 850,000 is divided between 51 percent who are of East Indian origin and 43 percent of black and mulatto ancestry. In addition, 4 percent are Indian and there are a scattering of Europeans and Chinese. Guyana has yet to develop a sense of national unity. The East Indians identify themselves by their religions, 80 percent being Hindu and 20 per-

cent Muslim. They tend to live in areas segregated from the black population.

In addition to its internal stresses, Guyana has to contend with pressures on its territory from neighbors to the east and west. Suriname's dispute has been noted above, and the claims of Venezuela are discussed below.

The Northern Andes Region

The Hispanic states of northwestern South America during the colonial period were part of the Spanish Vice-Royalties of New Granada and Peru. When it gained independence from Spain in 1819, New Granada became the state of Gran Colombia. Difficulties among the scattered developed areas led Colombia, Venezuela, and Ecuador to achieve separate independence in 1830. Since that time each has developed a distinctive national identity (Table 14-4).

Colombia. Colombia is a large state, embracing 440,000 square miles with a population of 34,000,000. However, only the western third of Colombia is effectively occupied, and this ecumene is subdivided among a half-dozen principal concentrations by the intervening three north-south trending ranges of the Andes and other topographic features. Much of this area is outside the effective control of the Colombian government. The empty eastern two-thirds of Colombia lies in the lowlands of the Orinoco and Amazon rivers. Scattered groups of Chibcha Indians compete with a limited number of Mestizos for the region's meager resources.

The Spaniards, penetrating up the Cauca and other north-flowing rivers from the Caribbean coast, found clusters of Chibcha settlements to be located mainly in mountain basins above 6,500 feet elevation. The Chibchas were settled agriculturalists who had once been organized into a large realm, but at the time of conquest lived in separate chiefdoms. They were beyond control of the Peruvian Incas.

A much higher proportion of the Chibcha population amalgamated with the Europeans to form a Mestizo civilization than was the case of Indians in Peru. Several lower valley areas empty of Indians were later colonized, creating particularly the settlement clusters of Santander and Antioquia. On the tropical slopes facing the Pacific the Spaniards imported large numbers of black slaves, who came to outnumber persons of European ancestry.

During the colonial period Colombia initially was part of the Vice-Royalty of Peru. Reforms by the Bourbon kings in Spain at the end of the eighteenth century led to the creation of a Vice-Royalty of New Granada embracing the territories of present-day Colombia, Ecuador, Venezuela, and Panama. Simon Bolivar, the

TABLE 14.4 THE NORTHERN ANDES

Although Colombia, Venezuela, Ecuador, and Peru form a massive region of Latin American territory, they share a surprising amount in common with the narrow string of Central American states. The total populations of the two regions roughly are comparable, as are the areas, numbers, and degrees of isolation of effectively settled territories. More than half the Northern Andes lies in the Amazon lowlands, which essentially are as empty as the Caribbean seabed off Central America. The Northern Andes peoples share general Latin American characteristics of mixed racial ancestry, Spanish language, and Roman Catholicism. However, a high proportion of the populations of Peru and Ecuador are unassimilated Quechuan-speaking Indians. Each of the states harbors territorial grievances against its neighbors that have erupted into serious strife, despite a notable lack of population and resources in the affected territories.

State	Total Population	Area (sq. miles)	Distinctive Features of Group
Colombia	34,000,000	440,000	
Dominant Nation and % Total			
Bogotá Colombians, 20%			Romance (Spanish) language, Roman Catholic, predominantly Mestizo
Significant Regional Groups and % Total			
Antioqueños, 13%			Romance (Spanish) language, Roman Catholic, predominantly European
Indians, 3%			Chibchan and Arawakan languages, Roman Catholic or Animist
Venezuela	20,000,000	350,000	
Dominant Nation and % Total			
Venezuelans, 90%			Romance (Spanish) language, Roman Catholic
Significant Regional Groups and % Total			
Caribbean Blacks, 9%			Romance (Spanish) language, Roman Catholic
Indians, 2%			Cariban and Arawakan languages, Roman Catholic or Animist
Potential Trouble Areas and Possible Adversaries			
Monjes Archipelago (Colombia)	2,000	50	
Ecuador	10,500,000	109,000	
Dominant Nation and % Total			
Ecuadoran, 55%			Romance (Spanish) language, Roman Catholic
Significant Regional Groups and % Total			
Indians, 36%			Quechuan languages, Roman Catholic
Peru	23,000,000	500,000	
Dominant Nation and % Total			
Peruvians, 44%			Romance (Spanish) language, Roman Catholic and Protestant
Significant Regional Groups and % Total			
Indians, 54%			Quechua and other languages, Roman Catholic and Animist
Potential Trouble Areas and Possible Adversaries			
Amazon Triangle (Ecuador)	10,000	80,000	

liberator of the Northern Andes states, attempted to hold New Granada together in the State of "Gran Colombia" when independence was achieved in 1819. In 1830, however, Gran Colombia split into Venezuela, Ecuador, and New Granada, which was renamed the "United States of Colombia" in 1863.

Each of the nine major population clusters in Colombia was the focus of a state that operated rather independently. In 1886 a Republic of Colombia was formed, centralized around the Bogotá basin. Each of the former states became a "department," although it retained ancient rights, including management of its own finances.

The subsequent history of Colombia has revolved around maintaining the unity among the separate and distinctive regions. This it has managed to do in contrast to the separated Central American states, whose total combined territory from Guatemala to Panama is roughly comparable to that of Colombia. Only the population cluster around Panama City eventually broke away, and the circumstances involved outside interference, as noted above.

Although unity has been maintained, regional rivalries continue to plague Colombia. Political parties tend to be regional in scope. Particularly strong antagonisms have existed between Antioquia, noted for very conservative traditions, and Bogotá, which has a liberal reputation. Tensions between the two were a contributing cause to *La Violencia*, the period between 1948 and 1962 when struggles between right and left resulted in more than 200,000 Colombians being killed. More recently, bitter rivalry developed between drug cartels based in the settlement clusters of Cali and Medellin over the lucrative production and international distribution of cocaine.

The Guajira Peninsula dispute. Colombia has two notable territorial disputes with its neighbors. Its contest with Nicaragua over the islands of Providencia and San Andres has been noted above. Its other active controversy is with Venezuela over the location of their northern boundary in the Guajira Peninsula and its extension into the Caribbean.

The peninsula attracted little development during the colonial period. It was empty enough to be designated as a frontier between the colonial Captaincy General of Venezuela and the rest of New Granada. With independence, the specific location of a boundary became important. For more than a century Colombia and Venezuela disputed their mutual border. In 1941 they signed a treaty establishing the present line. Venezuelans were not happy at the outcome, however, believing that their government had been overly generous to the Colombians.

The unhappiness of the Venezuelans reflected several persistent worries: a concern to protect their extensive oil reserves, upon which their economy rests; a general perception that the state has lost too much territory to greedy neighbors; and an image of Colombians as "aloof, cold, austere, effete, and snobbish." The iconography of the Colombians, in return, pictures Venezuelans as a "rather boorish, crude, undisciplined, and loud group who are more Caribbean than Andean...uncultured nouveau riche" (Child, 1985, p. 153).

After a long series of talks and border incidents between the two states during the 1970s, the Venezuelans in 1981 declared a nullification of the 1941 treaty. The particular bone of contention was conflicting inter-pretation of the seaward boundary from the peninsula. Venezuela argued that the east-northeast trending boundary adopted within the northern peninsula itself should be extended directly seaward north of the oil-rich Gulf of Venezuela, with territorial waters then divided by a perpendicular north-northwest line that placed the Los Monjes Archipelago under Venezuelan jurisdiction. Colombians countered equally forcefully that the seaward extension should be due eastward, perpendicular to the coast of the peninsula, with a right angle Caribbean extension that put the islands on the Colombian side. The significance of the islands lay in their possible future role in establishing claims to underseas petroleum resources.

Negotiators worked out a compromise treaty in 1980 that would divide equally between the two states any oil that might be found. The Venezuelan military made its objections to this solution known, and the new draft of the treaty was not ratified. Nullification of the old ·treaty then was approved by the Venezuelan Supreme Court.

·Border incidents have continued. The problem is exacerbated from the Venezuelan point of view by the immigration through the porous boundary of more than 1,500,000 undocumented Colombians, prompted by higher living standards and far less political unrest. The Colombians find it easy to assimilate into Venezuelan society. Another problem involves the active smuggling of narcotics and other goods across the border.

Venezuela. The name "Venezuela" means "Little Venice" and was applied by Spanish explorers who found Indian stilt villages on the shores of Lake Maracaibo. Like neighboring Colombia, only one-third of the territory of Venezuela is effectively settled, mostly on the east-trending extension of the Andes that parallels the Caribbean. The southern two-thirds of the state territory lie in the tropical grassland plains of the Orinoco River or in the hard rock Guiana Highlands to the east.

A compact and more-or-less contiguous ecumene has meant that Venezuela has not evolved the type of rivalry between population clusters that has occurred in Colombia. Some regional differences exist. Ten percent of the population is black and concentrated primarily along the Caribbean coast. About two-thirds is Mestizo and 20 percent is of unmixed European origins. They are concentrated in the narrow belt of northern highlands paralleling the Caribbean. As in Colombia, most Spaniards in the colonies took Indian wives. The 2 percent of the population that remains unmixed Indian is found only in remote areas of the periphery.

Resentment at distant control by the elite of Bogotá caused Venezuela to break away from Gran Colombia in 1830. It suffered many internal problems stemming from personal rather than regional rivalries. During the

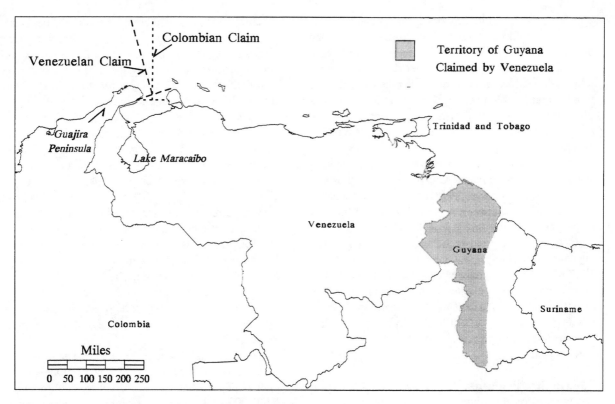

FIGURE 14-4   VENEZUELA'S TERRITORIAL DISPUTES

nineteenth century there were forty revolutions and more than 125 lesser uprisings. Economic development based upon its rich petroleum reserves has stabilized the state since 1917.

The dispute with Guyana. In addition to its boundary quarrel with Colombia, Venezuela also has continuously pressed a claim to more than 50,000 square miles of territory that presently lies within its eastern neighbor Guyana (Figure 14-4).

Its case rests upon a colonial treaty between Spain and the Netherlands that established the Essequibo River as their boundary. In 1796 the British captured Guyana from the Dutch, gaining full title in 1814. During the nineteenth century prospectors pressed westward through the unpopulated frontier zone looking for gold. A Prussian naturalist named Schomburgk explored the area in 1835 and published a map showing the Essequibo as the border. However, he later produced new maps showing the border to be progressively farther west. Venezuelans claim that the British pressed the naturalist to alter his cartography in their favor. They also note that Venezuela was disorganized at that time and in no position to defend itself against British incursions.

In 1897 the two countries sought outside arbitration of their dispute. Two years later most of the disputed territory was awarded by an international tribunal to the United Kingdom. A disappointed Venezuela reluctantly accepted the decision, and helped mark the border along the Essequibo in 1905. It did receive all of the Orinoco valley, part of which had been claimed by the British.

After six decades, Venezuela reopened the dispute, as British Guiana began its transition to becoming the independent state of Guyana. In 1962 it declared that the old decision had been reached by a secret deal between a Russian arbitrator and the British and demanded the recovery of its lost territory. It further protested against the granting of independence to Guyana in 1966, and successfully kept it out of the Organization of American States (OAS).

To avoid conflict, the Venezuelans, British, and Guyanans agreed to form a joint border commission to examine the respective claims. The commission set a deadline for itself to reach a decision by 1970, but no agreement could be established. A subsequent agreement instituted a twelve-year period for "cooling off." When this expired in 1982, Venezuela again pressed its claim. Border incursions heightened tensions, as did Guyana's appeal for assistance from Communist Cuba. Venezuela proclaimed the dispute comparable to the Falkland Islands controversy between Argentina and the United Kingdom. It supported the Argentines when conflict erupted in April 1982.

Although Guyana continues in possession of the area and has taken steps toward development of a major hydroelectric project, the problem continues. For Venezuela, the dispute reflects a national preoccupation with past domination by outside powers and loss of territory. It is also a convenient diversion by politicians from uncomfortable domestic realities. For newly independent Guyana, it is a question of 60 percent of its state territory and major resource potential.

Ecuador. Gran Colombia saw the peaceful secession of its southwestern corner, the Presidency of Quito, in 1830. The young republic adopted the name "Ecuador" to commemorate its brief glory as the site of an eighteenth-century French expedition that came to measure the land distance of an arc of 1° on the equator. Its boundary with Colombia was one of only three in Latin America that cut across a populated area, reflecting its drawing at a time when Quito was having internal difficulties and the Colombian capital at Bogotá was momentarily strong.

Quito was the center of a string of Indian settlements in an upland valley between two ranges of the Andes. When the Spanish arrived in 1554, they found an area that only recently had been made part of the Inca Empire. The Inca king had begun to live there for part of the year, and the Quechua language had made inroads among the local inhabitants.

Spain established an Audiencia of Quito in 1563. To it was attached the coastal community of Guayaquil, which it had founded in 1538. In addition to its administrative role, Quito also served as a base for missionary activities among the Indians to the east. For most of the Spanish period the lowland Indians in the Oriente remained fierce headhunters, and virtually no economic development occurred there.

Ecuador currently occupies an area of 109,000 square miles and has a population of 10,500,000. Its inhabitants are rather evenly divided between the coastal communities around Guayaquil and the settlements in the upland valley. Less than 3 percent live east of the Andes.

The two settlement clusters have a pronounced rivalry. Guayaquil is a seaport oriented to the rest of the world. Its dynamic economy focuses upon international trade. Quito remains a traditional regional center that benefits particularly from its governmental role. More than two-thirds of its population is Indian or Mestizo, and the remainder is of unmixed European ancestry. In contrast, barely a third of the coastal peoples are Mestizo or Indian. More than 40 percent are black or mulatto, with a quarter or more unmixed European. Despite a growing majority of population along the coast, its leaders perceive that the government in Quito ignores their region's needs and is oriented solely to the country's interior.

FIGURE 14-5 ECUADOR-PERU TERRITORIAL DISPUTE

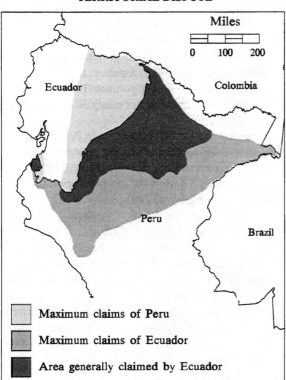

Maximum claims of Peru

Maximum claims of Ecuador

Area generally claimed by Ecuador

FIGURE 14-6 BOLIVIA-PARAGUAY TERRITORIAL DISPUTE

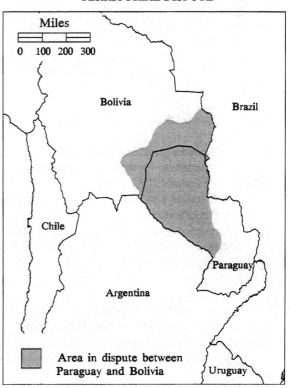

Area in dispute between Paraguay and Bolivia

Political-Geographic Regions of Latin America 351

The Amazon Triangle Dispute. The Oriente of Ecuador is only a fraction of that state's territory claimed at independence. Nearly 80,000 square miles were lost in a 1941 short war with Peru in a dispute that had its origins while Ecuador was still part of Colombia. The disputed lands are in the form of a triangle marked by the eastern front of the Andes, the southern border of Colombia, and the Marañon River (see Figure 14-5).

Evidence of jurisdiction during the Spanish period is ambiguous and contradictory. Although some documents indicate that the Quito Audiencia had authority over the eastern slope to the Amazon, it never was able to exert any control over the Amazonian Indians. The few settlements that did develop, such as the river port of Iquitos, founded in 1863 during the Amazonian rubber boom, were established by Peruvians who had bypassed the Indians by crossing the Andes farther south and working their way northward through the lowlands.

Ecuador earned the enmity of Peru during the nineteenth century by giving large grants of land in the disputed Oriente to settle its foreign debts, even though the territory was clearly not theirs to give. Chile also sent forces to occupy a section of the area during the period when Peru lay exhausted by its overwhelming defeat in the War of the Pacific with Chile.

Border skirmishes between the two states became common during the 1930s. The Peruvian army was still burdened by the Chilean defeat, and saw victory in the Amazon as redemption. In 1941 it moved northward, not only into the Oriente, but also toward Guayaquil. Ecuador quickly agreed to a truce. Early in 1942 the foreign ministers of the Western Hemispheric states met in Rio de Janeiro to discuss the impact of Japan's attack upon Pearl Harbor. In the interest of minimizing threats to unity, the ministers prevailed upon Ecuador to sign a protocol with Peru that accepted Peru's Amazonian claims in exchange for withdrawal from the coastal area.

In 1960 Ecuador declared that protocol null and void on the grounds that it contained erroneous descriptions of surface features. The motivation for its actions reflected an obsession with access to the Amazon comparable to Bolivia's unceasing quest for access to the Pacific. The supposed benefits were just as illusory. Possibilities for development of the leached rain forest soils were extremely limited. Only a tiny population was able to support itself in the section of the Oriente retained by Ecuador. There were no bases for trade in the Amazon basin, and linkages to the Atlantic were incomparably easier from Guayaquil through Panama than down 2,500 miles of river. The possibility of discovering oil was a lure, and in 1967 small deposits were discovered near the existing eastern border. Oil has also been found in the Peruvian Amazon.

Skirmishing between forces of the two states have continued. In 1981 more than 200 died in fighting over a fifty-mile border segment that had never been marked on the ground. There is some evidence that the government of Ecuador believes it benefits from the continuing tension because it unifies its rival regions and advertises its national loss to the rest of the world. Peruvians believe that their country is threatened by secret agreements that Ecuador has signed with its old enemies Brazil and Chile.

Peru. When Pizarro captured the Inca capital of Cuzco in 1533, he acquired for Spain a territorial unit that extended from central Chile to northern Ecuador along the Andean highlands. Resistance to the Spanish invaders continued for four decades. During this period the population of what is now Peru declined from 23,000,000 to 8,000,000, and when independence came in 1824, it was only 1,300,000. Peru now has 23,000,000 inhabitants. A quarter of these live in Lima, which was founded by Pizarro as a colonial capital because of its protected location close to the sea.

The population is principally confined to about 30,000 square miles of the state's 500,000. No other Latin American country has such a high proportion of uninhabited land. Sixty percent is in tropical rain forest in the eastern regions, and much of the rest consists of arid desert and high mountains.

Unlike Latin America's ABC countries—Argentina, Brazil, Chile—Peru saw no subsequent huge influx of European immigrants. Nearly half its population remains pure Indian, and another 35 percent are Mestizo. Most of the remaining 15 percent are of unmixed European heritage, although Japanese and other oriental colonists make up about 1 percent. Two-thirds of its population knows Spanish, but nearly 30 percent speaks only Quechua.

Two separate cultures coexist in Peru. The Mestizo- and white-dominated coastal region is the politically active part of Peru. It contrasts with a highland interior where 70 percent of the population is Indian pursuing a traditional subsistence way of life.

Beginning in the late 1960s, the *Sendero Luminoso* ("Shining Path") political movement has sought to mobilize the highland Indians. Since 1980, this Maoist organization, founded by radical university students from Peru's middle classes, has waged in earnest a guerrilla campaign of terror. It has been responsible for killing perhaps 10,000 persons. It has found it difficult to enlist the active support of the Indian masses, however, and has resorted to coercion of local populations in its struggle with the regime.

Its actions have not been able to mobilize a regional separatist movement comparable to the ultimately unsuccessful Indian-Mestizo rebellion led by Tupac Amaru against the Spanish in 1780–1781. Concern for this possibility has led the Peruvian authorities to give greater concerns to the Indians than has been the case in the past. In 1975 it recognized Quechua as the second official language of the state, and Tupac Amaru has been raised to the status of national hero in the officially propagated iconography.

Territorial disputes with Brazil and Colombia. Peru has had disputes with all of its neighbors over the locations of boundaries. The principle of *uti possedetis* proved to be fine in theory but difficult in implementation. The ambiguity of Spanish documents and the imperfect knowledge of physical geography of empty frontier zones have left a legacy of bitterness. Peru's dispute with Ecuador has been discussed above. Its border troubles with Chile and Bolivia are noted in subsequent sections.

In the twentieth century it almost went to war with Colombia and Brazil over boundaries in the Amazon region. Spain and Portugal had signed a treaty in 1777 that set the border along the Amazon River and its tributaries, the Marañon and Javary. Prior to that time the frontier region had been under the jurisdiction of the Jesuit Order. When Peru became independent, it asserted claims far to the east of the Javary. The significance was largely cartographical until the rubber boom made the region economically valuable at the end of the nineteenth century.

After decades of argumentation, a border was at length negotiated in 1909 between the two states. Of the 170,000 square miles at issue, Peru received 15,000. However, Colombia protested that the division of lands between Peru and Brazil included territory Colombia had inherited from the Vice-Royalty of New Granada. To placate Colombia, Peru ceded to it in 1922 a trapezium of territory that gave it a strip along the Amazon, including the river port of Leticia with 300 inhabitants. The region's total area of 4,500 square miles had a population of 1,500 Indians and 500 Mestizos and Europeans.

The agreement was implemented in 1930, but it immediately generated opposition by local Peruvians. Particularly strong complaints came from an entrepreneur who had earlier received a large Peruvian concession to gather rubber. The dissidents were supported by local army detachments. Disorders led Colombia to protect its new territory by sending a shipload of troops up the Amazon. Cooler heads prevailed, however. The Peruvian government clamped down on the activists, and the area has ceased to be a region of contention.

The Southern Cone

The southern margins of mainland Latin America contain its most densely populated and developed areas. Because of the triangular narrowing of South America toward the South Pole, it has become conventional to designate this region as "the southern cone," although the term seems awkward, and perhaps meaningless, to many (Table 14-5).

Argentina, Chile, and Uruguay were on the outer fringe of the Spanish Empire and had the most tenuous linkages to the mother country. The southern lands exhibited limited possibilities for mining precious metals. Indian population concentrations were minor. Most Indians in Argentina and Uruguay were decimated in the settlement of the Pampas, the broad grasslands that have formed an agricultural base for the raising of cattle and wheat. Their fate paralleled that of the Plains Indians of Anglo-America.

Unlike the northern Andean states, large numbers of Europeans came to the southern cone countries after independence. At first the majority came from Italy and Spain as temporary agricultural laborers, although many settled. Later, significant numbers of Germans, Jews, and Central Europeans added to the mix of populations. Virtually all were assimilated into an Hispanic civilization comparable to the Americanization of the United States.

Chile. Hispanic development in Chile began in 1541 when the settlement of Santiago was established in an isolated region of Araucanian farming Indians. It had been an outer frontier of the Inca Empire, which could not subdue the Araucanians in the forests farther south. Indeed, the forest Indians held out against the Spanish and successor Chileans for another three centuries until finally pacified in the 1880s.

The colony became a captaincy-general of Peru, with territory defined as extending 100 leagues east of the Pacific shore. This would include most of Patagonia. It also embraced irrigated settlements across the Andes to the northeast known as Cuyo. These were assigned to the new Vice-Royalty of the Plata in 1776, however. Chileans were never able to assert effective control over Patagonia because of the hostility of its Indians. They allowed it to be absorbed by Argentina in 1881, which finally did defeat the native inhabitants. Chile began its drive for independence in 1810, and was successful in 1818.

In contrast to primarily Indian Bolivia and Peru to the north and European Argentina to the east, the Chilean nation is principally Mestizo. Two-thirds of its population are of Spanish-Indian parentage. An additional 25 percent is of unmixed European origin, with a

TABLE 14.5   SOUTH AMERICA'S "SOUTHERN CONE"

The Southern Cone states are located in the narrowing triangle of southern Latin America. Despite the frontage of Chile and Argentina on the sea, Spain required overland communication and trade of the region with its southern colonial core area of Peru. The Spanish found few concentrations of Indians in the south, aside from Quechuan speakers in the highlands of Bolivia, Guarani speakers in Paraguay, and Auracanians in central Chile. It remained a sparsely populated territory until large-scale immigration of Italians, Spaniards, and Germans during the nineteenth century. Chile, Argentina, and Uruguay remain distinguished from the rest of Latin America by the high proportions of their populations of direct European descent. Despite large size, the states have relatively small effectively settled territories. Their sparsely inhabited marginal holdings have seen tensions and active colonial wars since independence, including the Atacama Desert, the Patagonian Desert, the Andes Crest, and the tropical lowland Chaco.

State	Total Population	Area (sq. miles)	Distinctive Features of Group
Chile	14,000,000	292,000	
Dominant Nation and % Total			
Chileans, 92%			Romance (Spanish) language, Roman Catholic (80%) and Protestant, Mestizo and European ancestry
Significant Regional Groups and % Total			
Araucanian Indians, 7%			Araucanian language, Roman Catholic
Potential Trouble Areas and Possible Adversaries			
Atacama Desert	1,300,000	65,000	
(Bolivia, Peru)			
Argentina	33,000,000	1,000,000	
Dominant Nation and % Total			
Argentinians, 91%			Romance (Spanish) language, Roman Catholic (90%) and Protestant, European ancestry
Potential Trouble Areas and Possible Adversaries			
Patagonia	500,000	180,000	
(Chile)			
Andes Crest	2,000	36,000	
Beagle Channel Islands (uninhabited)			
(Chile)			
Falkland Islands	1,900	6,400	
(United Kingdom)			
Uruguay	3,000,000	68,000	
Dominant Nation and % Total			
Uruguayans, 99%			Romance (Spanish) language, Roman Catholic, European ancestry
Paraguay	4,500,000	157,000	
Dominant Nation and % Total			
Paraguayans, 55%			Romance (Spanish) and Guarani languages, Roman Catholic, Indian ancestry
Significant Regional Groups and % Total			
Indians, 40%			Guarani languages, Roman Catholic
Potential Trouble Areas and Possible Adversaries			
Gran Chaco (Bolivia)	140,000	190,000	
Bolivia	8,000,000	425,000	
Dominant Nation and % Total			
Bolivians, 45%			Romance (Spanish) and Guarani languages, Roman Catholic, Indian ancestry
Significant Regional Groups and % Total			
Quechuan Indians, 25%			Quechuan languages, Roman Catholic
Aymara Indians, 17%			Aymaran Languages, Roman Catholic

notably high percentage of Spanish Basque ancestry. Some historians have asserted that their cultural progressiveness helps to account for Chile's early economic successes. There are a half million Indians, constituting about 5 percent of the total population.

Despite its 2,500 miles of latitudinal extent along the Pacific shore, Chile's area of effective settlement is relatively small and compact. More than 90 percent of the total population is concentrated in the Central Vale of Chile. This ecumene has an area approximating 30,000 square miles out of Chile's total of 292,000. Its climate and landscape resemble Southern California. To the north is the Atacama Desert and to the south a fjorded coastline extending into the high southern latitudes.

Non-Spanish Europeans have settled much of this forested southern frontier region. Germans established communities south of the Bío-bío River. They were long isolated from the Central Vale by a coastal zone where fierce Indians held out against the authorities until 1883. On the large southern island of Tierra del Fuego is a settlement of Yugoslav Dalmatians and other Europeans living in a setting not unlike coastal communities of Alaska. Fairly large numbers of Chileans have migrated across the Andes into Argentina, particularly into northern Patagonia.

Disputes with Peru and Bolivia. Chile has had its share of boundary disputes arising from the vagueness of Spanish colonial delimitations of administrative boundaries. Its potentially most threatening controversy, however, is the result of its direct aggression against Bolivia and Peru during the War of the Pacific, which lasted from 1879 to 1883.

The region of controversy is the Atacama Desert, one of the driest regions in the world. In the mid-nineteenth century a worldwide demand arose for sodium nitrate, a commodity with applications as a fertilizer and also as a raw material for smokeless powder. The Atacama abounded in nitrates, and Chilean miners aggressively exploited them. Much lay in sections of the desert allocated in colonial times to Bolivia, which had an outlet to the sea at Antofagasta. It should be noted that under the doctrine of *uti possidetis*, Bolivia was entitled to territory as far poleward as 26°20'S, but in 1866 it had conceded to Chile a 150-mile strip of territory to the parallel of 24°S, which lay just south of its port of Antofagasta.

Bolivia lacked the ability to develop its share of the resource and watched helplessly as Chilean miners encroached upon its territory. To strengthen its hand in dealing with the Chileans, it signed a secret treaty with Peru. It then set about to tax Chilean mining enterprises. Chile responded by seizing Antofagasta in 1879. When Peru refused to declare neutrality in the conflict, Chile also declared war upon it. There is reason to believe that the United Kingdom may have had a role in development of hostilities, for the British had major interests in nitrate development.

Chile was far better organized and equipped for a war than were its opponents. Its navy boasted battleships that soon destroyed the small ships of the Peruvians. In 1881 Chile actually occupied the Peruvian capital of Lima, maintaining a force there until 1884. It had done the same thing sixty years before, when it forced Spain to recognize its independence in return for evacuating Lima. Chile soundly defeated its neighbors and gained all of the Atacama Desert including the particularly nitrate-rich Tarapacá province that had been part of Peru. Peru and Bolivia never forgot the humiliation. Bolivia became particularly obsessed with the need to regain access to the sea.

The 1883 Treaty of Ancón that marked an end to hostilities made special provisions for the Tacna-Arica section of the Peruvian province of Tarapacá, whose 38,000 inhabitants were clearly Peruvian. It specified that a plebiscite would be held to determine ultimate possession. The Chileans, however, never held a vote. The nitrate resources were too valuable in the nineteenth century. Moreover, they permitted persecution of the Peruvian inhabitants, causing many to flee across the border. Chile expelled all Peruvian priests in 1910 and closed their churches. In 1919 Chilean mobs forced the closure of Peruvian shops and drove many more inhabitants to Peru.

War seemed imminent in 1922, when the United States agreed to arbitrate the dispute. It determined that persecution and exiling of Peruvians had made a plebiscite meaningless. In 1929 it awarded the northern Tacna area to Peru and the Arica region to Chile. It also provided that Chile could not award any former territory of Peru to a third party, which could only be Bolivia. A free port at Arica was given the Bolivians. By this time, it should be noted, the value of Atacama nitrates had substantially dwindled.

Chile subsequently sought to assist Bolivia by giving it Arica as an access to the sea. It would not yield the old Bolivian port of Antofagasta on the grounds that this would separate its Arica holdings from the main part of the republic. However, Peru exercised its right to veto the handover of its former Arica territory to the Bolivians.

In ensuing decades the dispute lay dormant. Peru was preoccupied with its territorial dispute with Ecuador, and Bolivia was involved in a contest with Paraguay for the Chaco region. The accession of nationalist parties to power in Bolivia in 1952 and in Peru after 1968 led to a renewal of acrimony.

Calling attention to the loss of territory during the War of the Pacific had always been a useful diversion of the public from government failures in other spheres.

Bolivian school children learned almost immediately of their country's loss of access to the sea. In both countries popular slogans stated that "not a hundred years would pass" before the loss would be avenged. Sentiments became particularly strong in 1973, as the centennial of the War of the Pacific approached. Peru's military government purchased guns, tanks, and planes from the Soviet Union in the early 1970s, heightening tensions. They softened, however, as the hundredth anniversary passed in 1983 without overt hostilities.

Argentina. Although a Spaniard discovered the mouth of the Rio de la Plata (termed "River Plate" by the British) in 1515 and the city "Puerto de Santa Maria del Buen Aire" (Buenos Aires) was founded in 1536, for three centuries Argentina was a remote part of the Spanish Empire in the Americas. For most of its colonial history its northwestern territory was part of the Charcas Audiencia attached to the Peruvian Vice-Royalty. Cujo, the western Argentine region of irrigated settlements, was part of the Captaincy General of Chile, and actually served as its administrative center. It was only in 1776 that both regions were attached to Buenos Aires in the creation of a new Rio de la Plata Vice-Royalty. Patagonia in the south and the Chaco region of the northeast were sparsely inhabited Indian regions with virtually no Spanish presence.

In contrast to northern Spanish colonies established amid concentrations of Indians, Buenos Aires was founded in the humid pampas where very few Indians lived. Colonization was by European families who expanded a true frontier of settlement over a period of three centuries in the face of hostile Indian resistance. However, unlike settlement of the American Midwest and Great Plains, colonists found no free public lands, since the territory early had been parceled out by the Spanish king to ranchers in large *estancias*. The emphasis was not upon raising grain crops, but upon slaughtering free-roaming cattle for their hides. Despite the colony's access to the Atlantic, the Spanish insisted that all products be sent overland to the Pacific shore and then to Peru for further disposition.

The fetters of the trade monopoly was one of the major elements in local unhappiness with Spain. Rebellion began in 1810, and independence was proclaimed in 1816. As in Colombia and elsewhere, outlying communities had resentments as much against the oligarchy of Buenos Aires as against the Spanish regime in Europe. They consented to join initially only as parts of a federation of equals. Most of the Charcas Audiencia successfully broke away in 1825 to form the new state of Bolivia. For more than four decades the young country of Argentina was wracked by civil wars. Eventually it became a centralized state, dominated by the capital city of Buenos Aires.

Argentina had to contest territorial claims by neighboring secessionist states. Although subscribing to the 1810 Latin American doctrine of *uti possidetis*, the vagueness of Spanish administrative documents allowed wide latitudes in interpretations. A serious dispute arose with Chile, which claimed all of Patagonia. However, that territory was inhabited by the fierce Araucanian Indians and was outside effective control of both states. Several incidents and clashes ensued, particularly in 1873.

Because Chile was preparing for the War of the Pacific, it decided to come to a formal boundary agreement with Argentina and conceded Patagonia to it. The 1881 treaty signed by the two states stated that their north/south boundary extended along the crest of the Andes, specifying that it was "to run by the most lofty peaks of the Andes which divide the waters and to pass between the slopes which incline to one side and the other." The southernmost boundary was set along the Beagle Channel, with "all the islands to the south of Beagle Channel to Cape Horn and those west of Tierra del Fuego to belong to Chile."

Although the description of the mutual boundary would seem clear-cut, it contained contradictions and ambiguities that subsequently became serious threats to the peace between the two countries. In the Andes the "highest peaks" lay as much as 100 miles west of the water divides, since in four areas ancient mountain glaciers had deposited natural dams ("moraines") that diverted streams westward into the Pacific. More than 36,000 square miles of territory was involved. When joint teams marking the boundary became aware of the problem, the Argentines claimed that the border ran along the highest peaks, while the Chileans insisted that it followed the water divides. A long series of negotiations followed. In 1902 a compromise line drawn by an arbitrator pleased neither side, but was accepted. To mark the peaceful settlement of a troubling dispute, a statue of Jesus Christ was erected at Uspallata Pass, the main commercial route between the two states. It is rarely seen, however, since the present railroad and highway pass through tunnels beneath it.

The Beagle Channel dispute. The 1881 treaty had never defined the exact location of the Beagle Channel, which lay south of Tierra del Fuego. The Chileans asserted that Picton, Nueva, and Lennox islands at its easterly entrance lay south of the passage, and thus were Chilean territory. The Argentines claimed that the islands were adjacent to their section of Tierra del Fuego, and the channel was positioned south of them (Figure 14-7). In 1967, arguments over ownership of the islands became heated.

The windswept small islands have little intrinsic value. However, their possession has implications for

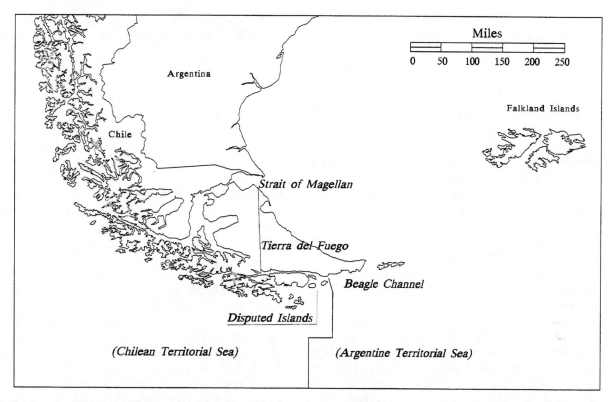

FIGURE 14-7 THE FALKLAND ISLANDS AND BEAGLE CHANNEL

claims by both countries to the offshore continental shelf, with its possible oil reserves, and to sectors of Antarctica. To assert their ownership, Chile in the early 1970s placed five settlers and 300 sheep on the islands. The Argentines responded by asking for outside arbitration. Under terms of the 1881 treaty, the British monarch was specified as the arbitrator. However, the Argentines considered the United Kingdom predisposed toward Chile and demanded that arbitration be done by members of the International Court of Justice in The Hague, with the British queen either approving or rejecting that decision. The Chileans agreed to this.

In 1978 the Court of Justice found in favor of Chile. The Argentines then repudiated the arbitration award and sent warships to the region, including an aircraft carrier. Part of their reaction was due to the appearance of maps in Chile showing its territory extending 200 miles into the Atlantic Ocean. In all previous treaties it had been agreed that Argentina had claim to the Atlantic shore, Chile to the Pacific. The dispute also reflected other long-standing tensions between the two states. The Chileans have come to believe that they were cheated out of a legitimate claim to Patagonia. The Argentines have grown alarmed at increasing Chilean migration into northern Patagonia and other parts of Argentina. To complicate the matter, the Peruvians, who have never

forgotten the loss of territory to Chile in the War of the Pacific, were reported to be sending troops to Peru's southern border with Chile.

Through mediation by the Vatican, strife was averted and a settlement announced in 1984. The papal award gave the islands to Chile, but denied any eastward shift of Chilean borders through the continental shelf or in Antarctica.

The Falklands/Malvinas dispute. Three hundred miles east of the Patagonian coast lies an island group with a total area of 6,400 square miles. There are two main islands and more than 200 smaller ones. Some 1,900 people inhabit them, mostly of British ancestry. Half live in the town of Port Stanley; the others are dispersed throughout the archipelago, raising sheep. The United Kingdom has controlled the territory continuously for 150 years and terms it the Falkland Islands. Argentina has protested the British occupation for the past century and a half and identifies the islands as the Malvinas, a name bestowed by a French explorer after the town of St. Malo in France. In 1982 an Argentine amphibious force temporarily seized the region.

As in most territorial disputes, there is no clear-cut evidence to assign the islands to one or another of the contenders. Argentina claims that Ferdinand Magellan discovered the islands in his world voyage of 1502. The United Kingdom asserts that it was a British ship captain who made the first sighting in 1596. The fact is that whalers, sealers, and explorers from many lands lived on the islands during the seventeenth and early eighteenth century. The British established a permanent settlement on West Falkland Island in 1764. The French did the same on East Falkland in 1765, but they sold their settlement to Spain a year later. Spain drove the British from West Falkland in 1770, nearly creating a war. They returned the settlement to the British a year later, but the British left in 1774 because of the high cost of maintaining control.

Spain did not assign the islands to Argentina when the latter declared independence in 1806. It maintained control until 1811, but then withdrew. In 1820 Argentine representatives landed and took possession of the islands. Following complaints of harassment of American sealers by island inhabitants, a United States naval vessel landed and destroyed the Argentine settlement in 1832. A year later the British drove out remaining Argentines, making the islands a Crown colony. Argentina never accepted the British presence as legitimate, however. The dispute remained dormant until revived in the 1940s by the Argentine president, Juan Peron. In 1976 a naval incident occurred.

This renewed interest in the islands reflected general Argentine perceptions of negative past involvements of the British in Argentina. These included British presence in the Rio de la Plata at the time of independence and the role of British capital investment during the nineteenth century, which was seen as "keeping Argentina from its greatness." Concern for the Falklands/Malvinas also related to Argentine territorial claims to the Antarctic and to South Georgia and the South Sandwich islands and to underseas deposits of petroleum.

The military regime in Argentina was also well aware of its faltering domestic economic and political position. It had concerns about the negative image it had earned by mass executions of leftist radicals during a period known as "the dirty war." It saw that prestige could be regained by catering to popular sentiments whipped up by the approaching 150th anniversary of loss of the Falklands/Malvinas to the British. It miscalculated British ability and resolve to defend their island possessions, however.

The April 1982 Argentine invasion of the Falklands directly touched upon elements of the British iconography, including injured national pride and concern for principles. A successful counterinvasion and repulse of the Argentines in June of that year had the effect of boosting the political prestige of the British prime minister, Margaret Thatcher. In Argentina it led to the end of the military regime. It also severed the *de*

facto economic integration of the Falklands into Argentina, which had been progressing for many years.

Uruguay. Wedged between Argentina and Brazil is Uruguay, a state intentionally created by its neighbors to serve as a buffer between their interests. It is the smallest of the South American states, although its total area of 68,000 square miles is larger than many European countries. Ninety percent of its population of more than 3,000,000 is of European ancestry, 5 percent are black, and 5 percent Mestizo. More than two-fifths live within the metropolitan region of its capital city, Montevideo. However, in contrast to most other Latin American states, all of its rolling plains territory is effectively settled.

Uruguay was populated by fierce hunting Indians when Jesuits established missions in the 1620s. The Spanish had termed the region the Banda Oriental, referring to its location on the east side of the Rio de la Plata, a 200 mile-long combined estuary of the Parana and Uruguay rivers whose width varies from 25 miles at the tributary river confluence to 135 miles at the mouth. The Portuguese expanded into Uruguay's present territory in the 1680s to stake a claim to the Pampas region. Their base was at Colonia do Sacramento, across from Buenos Aires. Spain dislodged the Portuguese more than once from their foothold, but each time they were able to reestablish themselves. In 1726 the Spanish founded their own permanent settlement east of the Rio de la Plata at Montevideo. The interior was a true frontier region, occupied by the *gauchos*, who were bands of army deserters, criminals, and vagabonds gaining a living by slaughtering the wild-running Pampas cattle for their hides. In many ways they were comparable to the Cossacks, their contemporaries in the Ukrainian steppes of Russia.

The elite of Montevideo sought their own independence from Spain at the same time as did their counterparts in Buenos Aires to the west. They had to contend not only with Argentine claims to their settlement, but also those of Brazil, which had gained independence in 1822 and claimed all of Uruguay as its inheritance. With help from the Argentines, Uruguayan forces defeated troops from Brazil in 1827. The British played their own role in the Rio de la Plata, occupying both Buenos Aires and Montevideo for a time.

In 1828 Argentina and Brazil, with British encouragement, agreed to recognize Uruguay as an independent and neutral buffer state between their respective interests. Subsequently, Uruguay developed into a prosperous and democratic state. It attracted many European settlers, particularly from France and Italy.

Without a vaguely defined outer frontier zone, Uruguay has not experienced the boundary problems of other Latin American states. Its one minor spot of contention is a historical claim against Argentina for the small island of Mártin García, which occupies a strategic location in the Rio de la Plata at the confluence of the Parana and Uruguay rivers.

Paraguay. Paraguay is an impoverished, predominantly Indian state, whose fate has been to serve as a buffer between Argentina and Brazil. Spaniards from Buenos Aires first settled the area in the early sixteenth century. They founded Asuncion in 1537. It was in the center of a dense Indian settlement. Intermixing was so complete that 95 percent of the present population still speaks the native Guarani language, 40 percent exclusively.

The Jesuit Order played an important early role in Paraguay. Jesuits first arrived in 1608, and eventually established thirty-two missions among the Indians. Their development of the Indian economy brought them into conflict with the Hispanic landowners. In 1767, as elsewhere in Latin America, they were expelled.

Paraguay was a peripheral part of the Plata Vice-Royalty centered on Buenos Aires. When Spanish power crumbled, Paraguay asserted its independence in 1811, although it was claimed by Buenos Aires. Its subsequent history has revolved around two disastrous wars: the War of the Triple Alliance of 1865–1870, and the Chaco War of 1932–1935.

The War of the Triple Alliance saw Paraguay simultaneously get into conflict with Brazil, Argentina, and Bolivia. It began when Paraguay sought to gain an independent access to the sea across territory claimed by Brazil. Its poorly equipped forces were no match for its opponents. As a consequence, it lost 80 percent of its male population and 50,000 square miles of territory.

The 1930s Chaco War with Bolivia involved the first Latin American fighting in half a century. It started over control of 150,000 square miles of virtually useless land. Both sides had contested the Chaco region west of the Paraguay River since 1878. There had been some actual conflict in 1928.

Both sides could produce legal evidence from Spanish archives to bolster their claims. Bolivia argued that it had long had frontier settlements of its citizens in the region. It also was motivated to secure title to the Chaco to provide an outlet to the Atlantic Ocean via the Parana and Plata rivers. Redemption of national honor after being shut out from the Pacific by Chile likewise was a factor. Paraguay could cite colonial documents assigning the territory to Asuncion. It also sought redemption from its horrendous losses in the War of the Triple Alliance. Both sides were also mindful of the possibility of petroleum reserves in the region.

Despite pressures from its neighbors and the League of Nations, the conflict lasted for four years. More than 100,000 were killed and another 150,000 wounded. Finally, a truce was established, and ultimately the new international boundary followed the truce line. Paraguay received 80 percent of the territory. The victory was pyrrhic, however. No oil was ever found, and its area supports less than 3 percent of Paraguay's population. The region still sees armed troops facing each other across the line.

The Chaco remains outside the ecumene of Paraguay. Its inhabitants include some 20,000 Indians and 13,000 Mennonite colonists from Canada and Russia. The latter arrived in three waves in 1927, 1930, and 1947. The earlier ones were among precipitating elements of the Chaco War, since the Paraguayans gave them land in nominally Bolivian territory. They have established more than 100 villages.

Virtually all the remaining Paraguayan population lives east of the Parana River in the region known as the Oriental. It has also seen rural colonization by foreigners. These include some 7,000 Japanese who arrived in 1935 and again after World War II. A 1966 agreement with South Korea has resulted in the immigration of 20,000 Koreans. The largest group of foreign immigrants, however, comes from Brazil. The eastern fringe of the country has been purchased by Brazilian land companies anticipating an expansion of coffee production into the region. This did not materialize, but many small settler colonies have been planted. Numerous other Brazilians came to the area to build the world's largest hydroelectric dam at Itaipu. Paraguay faces similar pressures from Argentina to the south as it has set about building another large hydroelectric plant on the Parana River.

Bolivia. Paraguay's antagonist in the Chaco, Bolivia, has had major problems in maintaining control of its colonial patrimony and developing a modern national identity. Its predominantly Indian population has had great difficulties in competing with aggressive neighbors. Bolivian governments have lost formal control of access to the Pacific Ocean and otherwise have seen half of their originally claimed territory go to other states.

The Spanish found the Altoplano region south of Lake Titicaca between the two eastern ranges of the Andes to be densely populated by Aymará Indians. The Quechua-speaking Incas had conquered them and planted Quechua colonies in outer regions to maintain their control. In 1559 the Spanish made the distinctive region into a separate Audiencia of Charcas. Two major settlement nodes emerged at opposite ends of the Altiplano, La Paz in the northwest and Chuquisaca to the southeast. The Jesuits appeared a century later, in 1668, to minister to the Indians in eastern areas descending into the Amazon and Parana valleys.

Spain transferred Charcas to the Vice-Royalty of the Plata in 1778. Its local *criollos* developed intense dislikes for both Lima and Buenos Aires. Although Buenos Aires forces fought the Spanish for independence particularly in Charcas, the imperial forces held out for many years. Bolivia declared its independence from both its neighbors in 1825. However, the 810,000 square miles it claimed at independence has shrunk to 424,000. Its coastline was taken by Chile, and its eastern and northern extremities have gone to Paraguay, Argentina, Brazil, and Peru.

Its weakness has come in large part from a lack of political unity. Settlement clusters are widely scattered across the high plateau and lowland landscapes. A substantial portion of the territory lies outside effective settlement, insulating clusters from each other. A high percentage of the population remains outside the political process, continuing a communal Indian way of life. A quarter are Aymará Indians, most of whom do not know Spanish. Another third are Quechua-speakers like their neighbors in Peru. Barely a third are Mestizo, and less than 10 percent are of unmixed European ancestry.

Compounding the problem of national unity is the existence of strong rivalry between the politically participating populations of La Paz and Sucre (formerly Chuquisaca). Sucre became the formal capital in 1825, but La Paz became the *de facto* capital in 1898.

The loss of the Pacific Coast has been detailed in the discussion of Chile. The problem for Bolivian economic development engendered by being landlocked is more apparent than real, however. Three different railroads connect Bolivia with the coast at Antofagasta, Arica, and Mollendo, although trains must transit Lake Titicaca on barges in order to utilize the last-named. The chief consequence of loss of sovereignty over the Atacama has been to provide one of the few internal binding forces among the population. All Bolivian school children at an early age learn the slogan *salida al mar* ("access to the sea").

The basis for its Chaco War with Paraguay has also been discussed above. Here, too, its main losses were illusions and hopes, although expenditures of blood and treasure were real enough.

Acre Territory. Boliva's lands lost to Brazil fall into much the same category. Bolivia's nineteenth century governments had little ability to project power into frontier areas. The relatively empty Acre Territory was claimed by both Bolivia and Brazil on the basis of antecedent actions by the Spanish and Portuguese, although a third force, the Jesuits, were the principal early European actors in the region. The territory gained sudden significance in the 1890s as Brazil underwent its "rubber boom." The region had some of the best stands of *Hevea brasiliensis* in the Amazon Basin. Between 15,000 and 30,000 Brazilian rubber gatherers began working the area.

In reaction to Bolivian attempts to control them, they proclaimed an "Independent State of Acre" in 1899. Although Bolivia regained authority in 1901, the rubber gatherers took up arms again in 1903. Brazil acceded to Bolivia's request to suppress the rebellion and negotiated to purchase the territory. At length it arranged acquisition of the extensive area for a payment of £2,000,000 and a promise to build a railroad into Bolivia. It also transferred an 890-square-mile parcel of land to Bolivia and accepted responsibility for dealing with Peru, which had historic claims to the region.

Madre de Dios. Bolivia's territorial troubles with Peru dated back to the early years of independence. Its dictator actually seized Peru and declared a Peru-Bolivia Federation in 1836 that lasted for three years. The antagonisms that were created at that time have lingered ever since. They contributed to a clash over boundaries on the eastern slope of the Andes. Both claimed the valley of the Madre de Dios River. Under the doctrine of *uti possidetis*, its fate hinged upon whether it was part of the Vice-Royalty of Peru or the Audiencia of Charcas. As part of the complexities created by Bolivia's sale of the Acre Territory, both Bolivia and Peru agreed to submit the ownership of the Madre de Dios area to arbitration by Argentina.

In 1909 a decision was rendered. The arbitrator could find no legitimate evidence for claims by either side. He concluded that the region had been unexplored and undivided up to 1810. His decision was to split the area, giving 22,000 square miles to Bolivia and 33,000 to Peru. Both sides were unhappy with the decision and found the new line to be unsatisfactory. They then negotiated a new border, preserving the essence of the arbitration.

Although Bolivia has acknowledged its territorial losses by signing treaties with its neighbors, the politically involved segment of its population can never forget them. The temptation remains for enterprising future politicians to seize upon the losses in order to rally the population behind their cause, particularly if their neighbors should be weakened by internal disorder. To accomplish this, however, politicians will have to raise the political consciousness of a far higher proportion of the population than now exists.

Brazil

The last of the major regions of Latin America to be discussed is Brazil (Table 14-6). It also has the fewest political geographic problems. Its separate colonies on the Atlantic held together in the transition to sovereignty. A true sense of nationhood evolved as a binding force. Although it has had disputes over territory with all of its neighbors, it managed to settle all but one peacefully.

TABLE 14.6 BRAZIL

Although but a single state, Brazil merits consideration as a separate Latin American region by virtue of its huge size and population and its distinctive Portuguese language. It does share much in common with other Latin American states, including limited and isolated ecumenes and large empty areas dominated by a native Indian population. Unlike the Spanish Empire in the Americas, the holdings of Portugal remained together after independence, due largely to the peaceful nature of the change of authority. Brazil's diverse population of primarily European and African origins has melded into a single nation, although the Paulistas of the central coastal region continue to maintain a strong regional identity. Brazil has contested for territory with its neighbors in the past, but it has found ways to settle its disputes amicably.

State	Total Population	Area (sq. miles)	Distinctive Features of Group
Brazil	151,000,000	3,200,000	
Dominant Nation and % Total			
Brazilians, 99% (Including Paulistas)			Romance (Portuguese) language, Roman Catholic
Significant Regional Groups and % Total			
Paulistas of Saõ Paulo, 20%			Romance (Portuguese) language, Roman Catholic
Potential Trouble Areas and Possible Adversaries			
Acre Territory (Bolivia)	450,000	60,000	

Brazil is by far the largest state of Latin America. Its area of 3,200,000 square miles is about 300,000 less than the total area of the United States of America. It exceeds the area of the contiguous forty-eight American states. The bulk of the population, however, is concentrated on about 15 percent of the territory. Forty percent of the land lying outside the ecumene is in tropical rain forest, with the remainder in other types of forest or in tropical savanna grasslands.

Its population of 151,000,000 is 60 percent that of the United States, but one-third of the total population of Latin America. In 1700, during the early colonial period, 70 percent of the population was concentrated in early settlement nodes in the northeast. By 1800, on the eve of independence, there was an even balance between the northeast and the central coastal region. Presently, 40,000,000 people live in the northeastern states and twice as many—81,000,000—in the central and southern ones. Only 17,000,000 are in the Amazon Basin and other parts of the western interior.

The population overwhelmingly speaks Portuguese, although its ancestry is from a variety of European, African, and Asian areas. The early period saw many colonists from Portugal as well as African slaves brought to work the sugar plantations, particularly in the northeast. Many newcomers arrived in Brazil during the nineteenth and twentieth centuries, although recent restrictions have substantially diminished the flow of immigrants. Only 30 percent were from Portugal itself. More than a third were from Italy, 12 percent from Spain, and 3 percent from Germany. Poles and other Slavic peoples also were important. Brazil has more than 750,000 inhabitants of Japanese ancestry, four-fifths of whom were born in Brazil. Their families came particularly during the period around World War I when there was a labor shortage in the coffee plantations. The Indian population numbers 200,000, barely one-fourth of the total occupying the region when Europeans first appeared. Ninety percent of the Brazilian population is Roman Catholic in religion. Protestants number another 7 percent. One and one-half million identify their religion as "spiritualism."

The Portuguese established several colonies on the Atlantic Coast of Latin America within the area allocated to them by the Treaty of Tordesillas. Most originated as grants of land from the king of Portugal. Development took place independently, without the hierarchy of administration that characterized the Spanish Empire. The northeastern colonies developed plantation economies not unlike the southern states of the United States. For a time an independent state existed based on runaway African slaves. The southern colonies around Saõ Paulo were engaged more in cattle and mining activities. The area was noted for its *Bandeirantes*, bands who roamed into the interior, searching for gold and enslaving Indians.

The separate colonies were constituted into a united kingdom when the Portuguese king sought refuge in the Americas during the Napoleonic Wars. After his return to Europe following Napoleon's defeat and exile, his son in 1822 proclaimed Brazil to be an independent empire. The empire was overthrown in 1889, and Brazil was then declared a republic.

As in the Spanish colonies, nationhood developed after statehood. It was based on the Portuguese language and Roman Catholic religion, and it embraced all of the population, whatever its antecedents. Its iconography included stereotyped images of other groups, including the French, Dutch, and British who had involved themselves in its affairs. It also featured a particularly strong sense of rivalry with the Argentines.

One notable contrast with the outlooks of the Hispanic states was a preoccupation with commerce. While peoples of the successor states to the Spanish Empire continued to place traditional Hispanic values upon ownership of land and military glory, the Brazilians shared a quest to make money. In contrast with the slow pace of economic innovation and development of its neighbors, Brazil's history has been one of continuous feverish speculation in the commercial production of a series of products, including sugar, gold, cotton, rubber, and coffee.

The development of a unified national identity did not put an end to regional distinctiveness and rivalry, however. Four main regions have developed distinctive features and consciousness comparable to sectionalism in the United States. The oldest region, the northeast, has a sense of having been left behind in the development of other areas. The *Sertão*, as it is termed, is one of the poorest regions of Latin America. Its population retains a primarily Portuguese and African heritage.

The central region developed around the rival cities of Rio de Janeiro and Saõ Paulo. This was the source area of Brazilian adventurers. It now contains nearly 70 percent of Brazil's productive capacity. Its ascendancy during the eighteenth century was symbolized by the 1763 transfer of the center of administration from the northeastern city of Bahia, which had been the capital for two centuries, to Rio de Janeiro.

The southern coastal regions saw development mainly during the nineteenth century. Groups of Europeans established small farms on the frontier of settlement. Germans began the colonization, but were later joined by many Italians and Slavs. This area has seen more dynamic regional development than other Brazilian regions in recent years. A distinctive regional consciousness has evolved, based upon its distinctive ethnicity and frontier characteristics.

Although it lies to the west of the old established regions, the Amazon Basin and adjacent interior regions are conventionally called "the North" in Brazil. Its settlement has been likened to the westward movement in the United States. Part of the Brazilian iconography is the notion of *Marcha para o Oeste* ("March to the West"), not unlike the German notion of *Drang nach Osten*. The bursting of the rubber boom by World War I caused a temporary cessation of movement, but it revived after World War II. However, the region suffers from a lack of infrastructure.

Despite their diversity of ancestry and patterns of historical development, the sections of Brazil have not developed the regional feelings promoting separation that led to fragmentation of the Spanish Empire. The Portuguese colonies did exhibit characteristics similar to their Hispanic counterparts: developed cores of settlement around administrative centers; empty zones between settlement concentrations; and locally born elites chafing at administrators from the mother country. However, the ease of transition to a joint independence from Portugal contrasted markedly with the decade or more of struggles with troops loyal to Spain in the Hispanic colonies.

A single nation of Brazilians emerged within the single state of Brazil. Regional differences are recognized by a federal system that permits each state to have its own constitution and laws, as long as they are in conformity with the federal constitution. Flexibility to meet new circumstances also is present. In 1975 the states of Rio de Janeiro and Guanabara were consolidated into a single state of Rio de Janeiro; in 1979 the state of Mato Grosso was divided into the new states of Mato Grosso and Mato Grosso do Sul. Currently, Brazil consists of twenty-three states, three federal territories (intended particularly to preserve Indian rights), and the federal district of Brasilia.

The establishment of a neutral capital in Brasilia has dampened the rivalry between Saõ Paulo and Rio de Janeiro, which was perhaps the greatest centrifugal force in Brazil. Its creation as a modern city of more than 400,000 inhabitants in a wilderness area demonstrates the triumph of an abstract idea over matters of practicality. The notion of a capital located near the geometric center of the state was suggested in 1822. All subsequent constitutions provided authorization for its creation. Finally, in the late 1950s, it was implemented. It is, of course, not central to a Brazil defined by its areas of development. It lies eccentric to the ecumene, with great difficulties of access. Nevertheless, Brasilia now functions as an effective capital and has served as an encouragement for the national *Marcha para o Oeste*.

External problems. Brazil has been faced with the same problems of reducing frontier zones to boundary lines that characterize the Hispanic states. To its credit, it has resolved all but one by peaceful negotiations. Only in its contest with Argentina over Uruguay in the Banda Oriental War of 1825–1828 did it resort to arms.

Incidentally, some lingering border questions have affected its internal states. Territories of about 1,000 square miles each are disputed between Amazonas and Pará, and between Piauí and Ceará.

Although contrasting territorial claims are not an issue, Brazil does face a continuing strong rivalry with Argentina. The quest is for influence in the buffer states of Uruguay, Paraguay, and Bolivia that lie between them. It appears to be a modern manifestation of the old competition in the Americas between Spain and Portugal. Some scholars have identified it as a quest for "sub-paramountcy" over Latin America, recognizing that the United States has achieved the dominating role in the area. Earlier, it was the British who were the external power involved in affairs throughout the realm, and they in turn had supplanted the paramountcy of the Portuguese and Spanish after independence came.

It is the Argentines who pay most direct attention to the rivalry. Their iconography views the matter as containment of traditional Portuguese expansionism westward of the Tordesillas line. Their concern is reinforced by a perception of their own relative decline in relation to Brazil as a product of Brazil's rather close relations with the United States during World War II.

The Brazilians feel much more secure. They view the Argentines as wanting to create a new Vice-Royalty of the Plata. Part of their attempts to project political and economic influence into the buffer states is to forestall Argentine penetration. Much of the colonialism of the nineteenth century throughout the world stemmed from such motivations.

Bibliography

ANDERSON, THOMAS A., *Geopolitics of the Caribbean: Ministates in a Wider World.* New York: Praeger, 1984.

BLAKEMORE, HAROLD and CLIFFORD SMITH, eds., *Latin America: Geographical Perspectives.* London: Methuen, 1971.

BLUME, HELMUT, *The Caribbean Islands*, trans. Johannes Maczewski and Ann Norton. London: Longman, 1974.

BRAVEBOY-WAGNER, J.A., *The Venezuela-Guyana Border Dispute: Britain's Colonial Legacy in Latin America.* Boulder, CO: Westview Press, 1984.

CHILD, JACK, *Geopolitics and Conflict in South America: Quarrels Among Neighbors.* New York: Praeger, 1985.

CLARKE, COLIN G., "Insularity and Identity in the Caribbean," *Geography*, Vol. 61 (1) (January 1976), pp. 8–16.

GREBENDORFF, WOLF, "Interstate Conflict Behavior and Regional Potential for Conflict in Latin America," *Journal of Inter-American Studies and World Affairs.* Vol. 24 (August 1982), pp. 267–294.

HODGSON, ROBER D. and ROBERT W. SMITH, "Boundary Issues Created by Extended National Maritime Claims," *Geographical Review*, Vol. 69 (1979), pp. 424–433.

IRELAND, GORDON, *Boundaries, Possessions and Conflicts in Central and North America and the Caribbean.* Cambridge, MA: Harvard University Press, 1941.

IRELAND, GORDON, *Boundaries, Possessions, and Conflicts in South America*, Cambridge, MA: Harvard University Press, 1938.

JAMES, PRESTON E. and C.W. MINKEL, *Latin America.* 5th ed. New York: John Wiley, 1986.

JAMES, PRESTON E., "Latin America: State Patterns and Boundary Problems," in *The Changing World: Studies in Political Geography.* eds. W. Gordon East and A.E. Moodie. Yonkers, NY: World Book Company, 1956, pp. 881–897.

LEONOV, N.S. "Ethnic Aspects of the El Salvador-Honduras Conflict," *Rasy i Narody: Sovremennye Etnicheskiye i Rasovye Problemy.* Moscow: Institute of Ethnography, 1971, pp. 203–220.

LOWENTHAL, DAVID, "The Range and Variation of Caribbean Societies," reprinted in *Readings in Cultural Geography*, eds. Philip L. Wagner and Marvin W. Mikesell. Chicago: University of Chicago Press, 1962, pp. 186–194.

MACPHERSON, JOHN, *Caribbean Lands: A Geography of the West Indies*, 4th ed. Trinidad: Longman, 1980.

MENON, P.K., "The Anglo-Guatemalan Dispute over the Colony of Belize (British Honduras)," *The Journal of Latin American Studies*, Vol. 11, Pt. 2 (1979), pp. 343–371.

MORRIS, ARTHUR, *South America*, 3rd ed., Totowa, NJ: Barnes & Noble, 1987.

PEARCY, G. ETZEL, *The West Indian Scene.* Princeton, NJ: Van Nostrand, 1965.

PLATT, ROBERT S., "Conflicting Territorial Claims in the Upper Amazon," in *Geographic Aspects of International Relations*, ed. C.C. Colby. Chicago: Lectures of the Harris Foundation, 1938.

WEST, ROBERT C. and JOHN P. AUGELLI, *Middle America: Its Lands and Peoples*, 2nd ed. Englewood Cliffs, NJ: Prentice Hall, 1971.

WOOD, BRYCE, *Aggression and History: The Case of Ecuador and Peru.* New York: Columbia University, Institute of Latin American Studies, 1978.

15

Anglo-America

CANADA and the United States occupy the Western Hemisphere lands north of Latin America. Although conventionally identified as parts of North America, that designation has little political geographic meaning, since a substantial portion of the continent's southern area is properly considered with the South American states as a component of Latin America. For want of a better term, geographers often employ "Anglo-America" (Figure 15-1) to designate the north (Table 15-1).

The name reflects the fact that British culture permeates the broad region in a manner comparable to Hispanic civilization in Latin America. Other traditions also are present, including a compact area of French-derived culture in Canada's St. Lawrence valley and extensive aboriginal areas functioning much like the colonial peripheries of Latin American states. France retains a tiny relic of its once vast New World holdings in the islands of St. Pierre and Miquelon off

the coast of Labrador. Chapter 3 described Denmark's role in the huge, but sparsely populated, island of Greenland.

In contrast to the border wars characterizing Latin American development, the boundary between the United States and Canada is a peaceful one. Despite the evolution of quite separate national identities, the two states have not engaged in hostilities with each other since the early nineteenth century. The 4,000-mile border line is unfortified. Much of its success can be traced to the fact that it was established antecedent to settlement. The United States also shares a 1,900-mile land border with Mexico that currently is not in dispute.

Anglo-America occupies more than 7,500,000 square miles, making it larger than Russia and, indeed, than most other political-geographic realms considered in this book. Like other regions, a significant portion remains with little or no human settlement. About half of Anglo-America is nonecumene. Empty lands include

FIGURE 15-1   THE ANGLO-AMERICAN ECUMENE

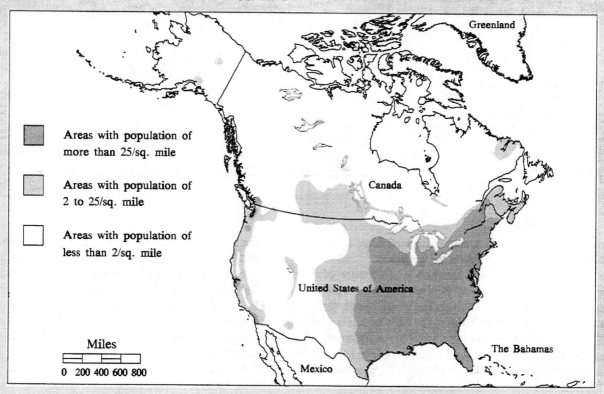

Areas with population of more than 25/sq. mile

Areas with population of 2 to 25/sq. mile

Areas with population of less than 2/sq. mile

Miles

0   200 400 600 800

TABLE 15.1   ANGLO-AMERICA

Anglo-America consists of just two states (and the French possession of St. Pierre et Miquelon). Both are predominantly English-speaking, a reflection of their heritage of British settlement. Although roughly equal in territory, Canada's population is only one-ninth that of the United States. This is due to the virtually uninhabited character of 80 percent of its territory. Its ecumene for the most lies within 100 miles of its southern border. More than 30 percent of the United States also is empty, yet its effectively settled territory is the largest of any state in the world. Despite their huge territories and large populations, the Anglo-American states are notably less complex politically than a majority of states. Although both witness sectional differences, only Canada faces a significant threat of regional secession in French-speaking Quebéc. Adoption of a federal system allowing a high degree of local control of affairs has minimized regional grievances within each country. Strong senses of national identity characterize both states, although Canada has seen two nations emerge divided along linguistic lines. A further contribution to their coherence is the fact that each state has evolved a regionally complementary economy based upon a well-developed infrastructure. Although tensions and conflicts have marked relations between the two states in the past, they have lived in harmony for more than a century. Their 4,000-mile mutual unfortified border is a model for the rest of the world.

State	Total Population	Area (sq. miles)	Distinctive Features of Group
United States of America	255,000,000	3,680,000	
Dominant Nation and % Total			
American, 98% (Including Hispanic Americans and African Americans)			Mixed Germanic/Romance (English) language, Protestant and Roman Catholic
Significant Regional Groups and % Total			
Hispanic Americans, 9%			Romance (Spanish) language, Roman Catholic
Native Americans (Indians), <1%			Indigenous languages, Roman Catholic, Protestant, and Animist
(African Americans, 12%, are territorially dispersed throughout the United States and do not constitute a regional group)			
Canada	28,000,000	3,850,000	
Dominant Nation and % Total			
English-speaking Canadians, 60%			Mixed Germanic/Romance (English) language, Protestant and Roman Catholic
Significant Regional Groups and % Total			
French Canadians, 26%			Romance (French) language, Roman Catholic
Inuits (Eskimos), <1%			Inuit language, Animist and Christian
Potential Trouble Areas			
Quebéc	7,000,000	600,000	
St. Pierre et Miquelon (France)	6,200	83	
Dominant Nation and % Total			
French, 100%			Romance (French) language, Roman Catholic

substantial areas of short, cool summer climates in the north and a broad, arid zone in the southwest.

The terrain of Anglo-America is a sequence of north-south trending features. Beginning with the western shore, these include (1) coastal mountain ranges, (2) a line of lowlands and valleys, (3) the Cascade and Sierra Nevada mountains, (4) a broad basin-and-range country, (5) the Rocky Mountains, (6) the Great Plains along the Rockies' eastern margins, (7) the interior plains (or Midwest), (8) the Appalachian ranges, and (9) the Atlantic coastal plain. A substantial zone of ancient crystalline rock known as the "Canadian Shield" occupies much of the northeast.

It is remarkable that the main segment of the international border between Canada and the United States cuts perpendicularly across all these terrain features. Although it is the antithesis of a "natural boundary," it certainly is one of the world's most successful borders.

The stability of boundaries is a product of their degree of acceptance by populations on either side, not of their "naturalness."

The first inhabitants of Anglo-America probably arrived about 20,000 years ago from eastern Eurasia. They most likely came across a temporary "land bridge" spanning the Bering Strait when sea level was much lower due to the substantial quantities of water locked up in the great continental glaciers. Many common traits can yet be observed between aboriginal peoples of northeastern Siberia and northwestern America.

Europeans did not establish a permanent settlement in Anglo-America until the end of the sixteenth century, when Spain founded the community of St. Augustine, Florida, to defend the northern reaches of its sea lanes leading from Latin America to Europe. Evidence exists of Norse, Irish, and, possibly, Basque and other visitors in earlier periods, including coins, trade goods, and remains of dwellings. A number of European fishing fleets began utilizing the rich banks off Newfoundland in the early 1500s. John Cabot in 1498 claimed for England the Atlantic Coast of the continent as far south as the parallel of 34°N, and the explorer Jacques Cartier declared the Gaspé Peninsula for France in 1534.

Europeans did not find large-scale indigenous empires in Anglo-America comparable to those encountered by the Spanish in Latin America. Archeological investigations indicate that natives in earlier eras had created impressive civilizations, particularly the so-called mound builders of the Midwest. By the time of European penetration, however, native political cultures were at a tribal level. At most, tribes of related peoples, such as that of the Iroquois, might form confederations. It is estimated that about sixty major groupings of Indians existed in Anglo-America, with a total population of no more than 3,000,000 when Europeans first arrived. Warfare between tribes was a frequent occurrence.

The French and English founded settlements on the margins of Labrador and Newfoundland in the first decade of the seventeenth century to support their fishing fleets. France later created farming communities along the St. Lawrence River to provide a base for extensive fur-trading activities with the natives. The English inaugurated a colony at Jamestown on Chesapeake Bay in 1607 as a commercial venture to raise tobacco. English religious dissenters came to New England in 1620 to create what amounted to a theocratic community. Other settlements of farmers soon followed, including Dutch colonists in the Hudson River valley and Swedes and Finns in Delaware. Native Americans showed little interest in laboring on the plantations founded along the southern Atlantic seaboard, and, as in the Caribbean and Brazil, entrepreneurs imported Africans as slaves, beginning with a shipment in 1619.

Although settlers eventually came to Anglo-America from a number of areas, the French in the north and the English in the south remained predominant. Immigrants from other lands found it expedient to adopt the prevailing language of the area in which they settled. Succeeding generations absorbed other elements of culture from the dominant group, including social and political institutions and attitudes. French areas were colonized at a time when France still had a feudal form of organization and the Roman Catholic church played a powerful role in society. English areas developed while England itself was undergoing a democratic transformation. Their colonists shared a view of political change by evolutionary means, in contrast, say, to the revolutionary tradition of the Latin Americans.

Struggles between the French and British in Europe were reflected in their American colonies. Eventually, in 1763, the United Kingdom forced France to yield all holdings in Anglo-America, except for fishing bases on the small islands of St. Pierre and Miquelon. Although French colonists received guarantees for preserving their traditions, empty areas of what had been New France, such as the Ontario Peninsula, became open to English-speaking settlement.

The English-held territory became an area of cultural homogeneity larger than any comparable social-linguistic region in Western Europe. It also developed a significant degree of coherence through trade and other types of association. Although England remained the home country for most inhabitants, it was remote, requiring an arduous six-week sea journey to visit. Moreover, frictions developed between American colonists and representatives of the English Crown.

This was a time of emerging new ideas. Urbanization and industrialization in Europe were spawning changed social conditions. Political philosophers were proposing new views on relationships between governments and the governed. The role of traditional religion as a force for conservatism was weakening. These currents affected colonial leaders, who constantly were in contact with counterparts in London.

The process of change from feudal and monarchial tradition culminated in the development of a sense of national identity embracing an ever-increasing proportion of the people. For many in the American colonies, group self-awareness involved a notion of significant difference from the evolving British nation. As a distinctive American national identity evolved, it pressed for political control of its own fortunes. In 1776, the Revolutionary War broke out, resulting in formation of the United States of America as the world's first large nation-state. The three northern English-speaking colonies of Newfoundland, Nova Scotia, and Prince Edward Island were unable to break away with the other thirteen, despite sharing the same sentiments for separation. French-speaking Quebéc stayed aloof from the struggle.

The differing situations among the three groups of breakaway British colonies, retained British colonies, and French settlements gave birth to three distinctive and often competing nations: American, Canadian, and Canadienne (French Canadian). The American Civil War in the 1860s might have resulted in solidifying a fourth, American Southern, nation, but successful suppression of the Confederate States of America ultimately resulted in a stronger, unified American national identity. English- and French-speaking Canadians were unable to meld their linguistic diversity into a common identity, however, and they remain today two nations struggling within a single state.

Canada

The largest of the two states in Anglo-America is Canada, with 3,850,000 square miles. Its size is misleading, however. Despite a latitudinal expanse extending 2,800 miles north of the boundary with the United States, more than half the population of Canada is concentrated within 100 miles of the American border, and most of the rest live within 200 miles. The Canadian ecumene is only 20 percent of the total area. Empty regions include the northern two-thirds of the state, which has short, cool summers comparable to Siberia's, and the massive hard rock area of the Canadian Shield dominating the east, which lost most of its soils to the scraping actions of the continental ice sheets (see Figure 15-2).

The Canadian population of 28,000,000 is about the same as that of California, North Korea, or Taiwan. Roughly one-third is of direct British descent, one-third of French ancestry, and one-third of other European or of mixed heritage. Less than a half million inhabitants are of aboriginal lineage, but they are the dominant group in a disproportionate segment of Canada's territory.

The French planted a settlement colony at the site of Quebéc on the St. Lawrence River in 1608. Later, French settlers founded the colonies of Acadia and Ile St. Jean on the shores of Nova Scotia and Prince Edward Island, respectively. These *habitants*, as they were called, perpetuated the feudal social system still prevalent in France and rendered service to the royal favorites who had brought them to the New World to work the *seigneuries*, which were grants of land received from the French king.

France had several motivations for establishing a New France in America. It quested for the glories of a broad empire; it sought a westward passage to the elusive Orient; it wanted an assured supply of North American furs; and it aspired to convert natives to Christianity. Its merchants and voyagers forged an alliance with the Algonquin Indians and expanded the French presence westward through the Great Lakes and southward into the Mississippi Valley.

The English established their first settlement in Canada on the southeastern coast of Newfoundland in 1610. Its purpose was to safeguard the property of English fishermen. England, too, became interested in further imperial expansion and the acquisition of furs from Indians. In 1670, King Charles II of England granted a charter for exclusive trading rights within the entire watershed draining into Hudson's Bay to the Hudson's Bay Company, which was headed by Charles's cousin, Prince Rupert. The area came to be known as "Rupert's Land." The royal grant overlapped claims of France over a wide zone. The English allied themselves with the Iroquois Indians, enemies of both the Algonquins and their French allies, whose expansion of settlements threatened them.

Struggles between the two colonial areas mirrored European wars between England and France that occurred between 1689 and 1763. In 1713 the English forced the French to relinquish the colony of Acadia and to recognize British claims to Newfoundland. French colonists evacuated Acadia and resettled in Louisiana, where their descendants remain the distinctive French-speaking "Cajun" community. Scots, escaping what they viewed as English oppression in their homeland, acquired the former French farms through a lottery process. The territory was renamed Nova Scotia. Migrants also came to Acadia from English colonies farther south on the Atlantic seaboard.

Renewed fighting between the two European powers resulted in British capture of Quebéc City in 1759 and Montreal a year later. In 1763, France conceded all its North American claims to England, except for offshore fishing bases on the tiny islands of St. Pierre and Miquelon in the St. Lawrence estuary. The French colonists, numbering 70,000, stayed, although those on Ile St. Jean departed for the mainland, following that island's annexation to the English colony of Nova Scotia. It subsequently was renamed Prince Edward Island.

The French found themselves subject to English laws and governed by a council whose members were required to take anti-Catholic oaths. Subsequent unrest led the United Kingdom in 1774 to proclaim the Quebéc Act, which guaranteed French Canadian rights to

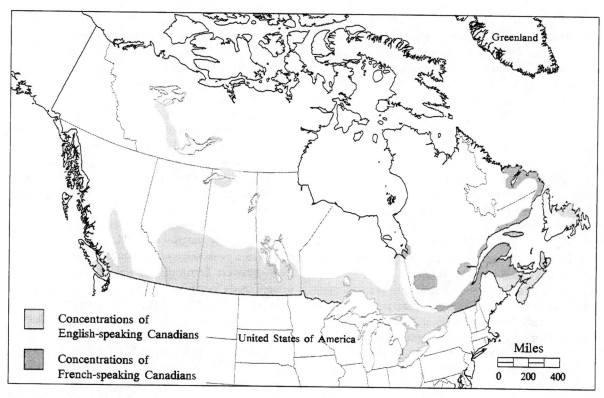

FIGURE 15-2   CANADA

practice Roman Catholicism and to be governed by French civil law.

Algonquin and other Indian allies of the French grew restive after the British victory cut off their flow of trade goods. They also were concerned about encroachment upon hunting and trapping grounds. To avoid an Indian war, Britain declared in 1763 that all lands west of the former French settlement colony were to be reserved for the natives. Although calming the Indian population, the act enraged the English inhabitants of the Atlantic colonies, whose numbers had grown to more than 2,000,000, and who cast covetous eyes upon the empty lands in the former French territory. Their anger was one of the causes fueling the American Revolutionary War.

When that war began in 1776, sentiments for separation were as strong in Newfoundland, Nova Scotia and Prince Edward Island as they were in the thirteen colonies to the south. Indeed, half their populations had migrated from other American colonies. However, remoteness from the others and the strong British presence in the Halifax naval base assured English maintenance of control. The French-speaking population of Quebéc evinced little interest in the struggle.

Under terms of the subsequent treaty of peace signed in 1783, the United Kingdom retained Quebéc, Newfoundland, Nova Scotia, and Prince Edward Island (which had been made a colony separate from Nova Scotia in 1769 because of problems of communication). More than 40,000 Americans loyal to the British Crown migrated northward. English authorities encouraged many to settle in the empty lands between Nova Scotia and the United States. They would provide a significant buffer to dampen influences from the south upon inhabitants of the other northern colonies. In 1784 the British government formed the newcomers into a separate colony named New Brunswick. Farther west, many loyalists settled south of the St. Lawrence River in the so-called Eastern Townships of Quebéc. They were joined after 1789 by additional migrants from the United States, when the English offered free lands to settlers in the Ontario Peninsula.

Following defeat of the French in 1763, the United Kingdom initially had reduced the area of the colony of Quebéc to a small segment of land around the St. Lawrence River. It granted the coast of Labrador to the colony of Newfoundland, and it reserved Quebéc's western and northern lands for their Indian inhabitants.

To placate French-speakers and their Indian allies, the Quebéc Act of 1774 restored these territories to Quebéc, but a substantial portion was lost by the peace treaty of 1783, which granted the areas of Quebéc south of the Great Lakes to the United States.

The influx of American loyalists after the Revolutionary War led the British to truncate Quebéc once again, dividing it into separate colonies of Lower Canada and Upper Canada. Lower Canada embraced the French settlements along the St. Lawrence, which continued to enjoy traditional French laws and social organization. Upper Canada consisted essentially of the Ontario Peninsula. Its inhabitants predominantly were of English heritage and had no sympathy for the feudal traditions and Catholic religion of the French. Like the northeastern maritime colonies, Upper Canada was governed by English common law.

Citizens of the two units increasingly found themselves at odds with the London parliament and with each other. Both sought control over their own finances and pressed for truly representative government. Upper Canadians chafed at Lower Canada's customs control of goods coming into their territory. Rebellions erupted in both colonies in 1837, but were suppressed. They did lead to the merger of the two units into a new Province of Canada three years later, however. The British had hoped the new union would lead to assimilation of the troublesome French Canadians, who were characterized as "an old and stationary society in a new and progressive world" in a famous report prepared in 1839 by Lord Durham. They were disappointed.

Financial difficulties and other problems plagued the British colonies in Anglo-America. To remedy the situation, the British North America Act in 1867 merged the Province of Canada with the colonies of Nova Scotia and New Brunswick into a Confederation of the Dominion of Canada. The act also provided for eventual admission into the new unit of Prince Edward Island, Newfoundland, British Columbia, and the extensive northern and western territories of Rupert's Land and the North-Western Territory, both of which continued to be controlled by the Hudson's Bay Company. The Province of Canada was divided along its former boundary to become the separate provinces of Ontario (Upper Canada) and Quebéc (Lower Canada).

The United Kingdom created British Columbia in 1866 to unite three colonies earlier established on the Pacific coast. After the 1848 resolution of the contest for the Oregon Territory with the United States, the British had constituted their settlements on Vancouver Island into a Crown colony. They formed a separate colony of British Columbia in 1858 composed of mainland communities north of the parallel of 49°N, the agreed upon boundary with the United States. Addition-

ally, they organized lands adjacent to the "panhandle" of Alaska into a Stikeen (Stikine) Territory. After its 1866 consolidation, British Columbia joined Canada in 1871, following the dominion's promise to link it by rail with the eastern provinces. Prince Edward Island entered Canada in 1873.

In 1870, the Hudson's Bay Company sold its holdings to the government of Canada, resulting in a vastly expanded size of the dominion. From these lands the confederation separated a new Province of Manitoba in 1870. As settlement expanded westward, it created the additional provinces of Alberta and Saskatchewan in 1905 from former Hudson's Bay Company lands. The northern boundaries of the three provinces were established along the parallel of 60°N. Poleward, the area remained a possession of the confederation known as the Northwest Territories. It was expanded in 1880, when Canada formally claimed the entire Arctic Archipelago to the North Pole. Until 1930, Norway challenged this annexation, however, on grounds of discovery of the islands by the Norwegian explorer Otto Sverdrup. In 1898, during a gold rush, the western portion of the Northwest Territories was detached to form the separate Yukon Territory. A referendum in the Northwest Territories in 1982 resulted in division of the broad (1,300,000 square miles) region into two entities. The eastern one became an Inuit (Eskimo) self-governing region in 1992.

Newfoundland, with Labrador, remained a separate British colony outside the Canadian confederation for many decades, although its precise boundary with Quebéc was indefinite. It received the right to self-government as a dominion in 1927, but had great difficulty in supporting itself financially. In 1935 it reverted to the lesser status of a colony. Following a referendum in 1948, it joined Canada as its tenth province.

Canada progressively became self-governing, although it continues to share a common sovereign with the United Kingdom. Delegates to the Versailles Peace Conference after World War I accepted it as an independent state during their deliberations. The United Kingdom officially recognized Canada as an equal entity in 1926, and the 1931 Statute of Westminster removed the last legal impediments to autonomy. Subsequently, Canada dropped the title "Dominion" from its name. In 1981 it replaced the British North America Act by a new constitution. A number of sentimental ties remain with the United Kingdom, however, at least among the English-speaking population.

Canada thus emerged by stages from a collection of small and separate British colonies to a unified state playing a role in international affairs disproportionate to its population size. Its continued success in the face of internal difficulties may be ascribed to the emergence of a strong national identity among its English-speaking population and notable concessions to its principal minority, the French-speaking Québécois. Quebéc and the other Canadian provinces have greater freedom of local action than do states in the United States. In contrast to America, where the federal government holds all prerogatives not specifically delegated to the individual states, the Canadian provinces retain all rights not expressly yielded to the federal government.

A major unifying force in Canada also has been concern by both of its internal nations (see section below) over economic and possibly political domination by its southern neighbor, the United States, which has more than ten times its population and economic strength. Centrifugal forces remain within Canada, however. In addition to the increasing militancy of its French-speaking minority, Canada suffers difficulties with its Indian inhabitants and has sectional problems, including separatist sentiments in its western Prairie Provinces and in the Maritime Provinces along the Atlantic seaboard.

The English-Speaking Canadian Nation

The emergence of Canadian identity paralleled evolution of the Canadian state. However, two differing nations developed within Canada, reflecting its long-standing and territorially based cultural differences. The English-speaking population of Canada came to see itself as a distinctive group, not British, not American, and also not French-Canadian.

Although the population of the Maritime colonies mirrored sentiments of the thirteen colonies to the south at the time of the American Revolution, attitudes changed in the decades that followed. The influx of embittered loyalists set a tone for Canadian outlooks. Many Canadians participated in the United Empire Loyalists organization, which paralleled the similar Sons and Daughters of the American Revolution in the United States. Anti-American attitudes hardened during the American–British War of 1812.

Over the course of the nineteenth century, British Canadians constantly feared being overwhelmed by the aggressively expanding United States of America. British Canadians had particular worries at the time of the American Civil War. The British Empire's support for the Confederacy had generated open American hostility. French Canadians also feared greater pressures for assimilation into English-speaking culture if they were to become incorporated within the United States, and this provided impetus for Quebéc to agree to confederation with the other Canadian colonies in 1867.

Three-quarters of the Canadian population could trace its ancestry to England by the end of the nineteenth century. However, they no longer were Englishmen. The lack of day-to-day contact took its toll in sentiments, as it did in Australia, New Zealand, Natal, and other overseas British settlements. All saw themselves as part of a glorious empire and they valiantly fought its wars in South Africa and Europe. But they also saw that the British did not perceive them as part of the British nation, and they grew frustrated at their lack of influence in British decision making that had profound impacts upon their lives.

British Canadian fear of economic submission to the United States replaced that of American political expansion by the mid-twentieth century. American corporations grew to hold substantial control of Canadian resources and industries. Resentment against economic domination by the "Colossus to the South" was a major component of British Canadian iconography. It is paradoxical that a principal reason for such great American economic involvement was that Canadians themselves were reluctant to invest in their own country, preferring to entrust their funds in investments south of the border.

The principal problem confronting English-speaking Canadians is that posed by their French-speaking co-inhabitants. The majority group traditionally has viewed French Canadians as a troublesome minority—priest-ridden, ill-educated, and close to treasonous. They feel that they have done more than most nations in making concessions to placate the unreasonable sensitivities of the inhabitants of Quebéc. As the end of the twentieth century approaches, separation of Quebéc from the rest of Canada looms as an increasing possiblity.

The Québécois

Until the mid-twentieth century, Canada's Francophone (French-speaking) population was one of the most rapidly growing groups in the world. Numbers increased from 70,000 in 1763 to more than 6,000,000 by the 1970s. Although most live in the province of Quebéc, Francophones now constitute more than a third of the population of New Brunswick and are found scattered throughout the other Canadian provinces.

The Quebéc Act of 1774 guaranteed their rights to the French language, the traditional French legal system, and the Roman Catholic religion. In contrast to the strict separation of church and state in English-speaking provinces, the Roman Catholic clergy came to play a dominant role in Quebéc politics during the nineteenth century. It had enjoyed a much lesser role earlier in New France, when fewer than 200 priests served the entire territory and population.

The unusually strong position of Roman Catholicism in Quebéc can be explained by several factors. Its clergy retained the traditional attitudes, prerogatives, and wealth that the church enjoyed in eighteenth century France, and which subsequently were destroyed there as part of the French Revolution (1789). The church controlled Quebéc's educational system, including the public schools and the province's two universities. It groomed the best students for service to itself, and was not averse to using its power to discourage dissident currents of thought.

Schools played a major role in the development of national consciousness throughout the world during the nineteenth century. The church schools of Quebéc guided generations of students into a view of their people as a beleaguered but righteous minority oppressed by heretics. The clergy was aided by their constituents' reactions to attitudes of English-speaking Canadians, among many of whom anti-Catholicism was strong, as were fears about the rapid natural increase of the Francophones.

Numerous contrasts in public attitudes existed between the two linguistic groups. A major one involved military service. Whereas most English-speakers tended to feel stirrings of patriotism when called to the colors, French-speakers evinced little desire to "fight Britain's wars." During the Boer War in South Africa, most French Canadians had strong sympathies for the Dutch farmers fighting the British. They also strongly resisted conscription in both world wars.

While church education played a major role in the development of the Québécois national identity, it did not prepare students to compete effectively with their English-speaking counterparts. The classical teaching in Quebéc's schools contrasted with the applied curricula adopted by other provinces. Few of its graduates were able to climb to the top of the social and economic ladder, even in the province's principal city of Montreal, whose power structure long remained a British Canadian stronghold. Most Québécois lived in rural villages and perpetuated habits of thought dating back to the old French *seigneuries*.

A church-based national iconography continued to characterize Francophones during the first half of the twentieth century. Indeed, in Quebéc the church assumed an active, paternalistic role in activities that were the preserve of secular governments elsewhere. Each urban and rural parish managed social welfare services for the poor and even operated such normally commercial ventures as loan agencies.

The position of the church in Quebéc waned during the second half of the century. Beginning in the 1950s, the province underwent a "quiet revolution" that saw modernization of its social and economic institutions. A well-educated group of leaders assumed positions of power. They secularized schools and celebrated the French cultural heritage more than they did religious traditions. They founded a national theater, art center, and museum. In the process, the church itself became notably more liberal.

An upswing in Francophone national feelings accompanied these developments. In contrast to parochial separatist views of the past, the new mood of the Québécois focused upon securing equal partnership in running the state. They required Canada to recognize French as a language equal to English in all public affairs. They pressed English-speaking Canadians to acknowledge the "distinct society" of the French Canadians as part of a dualist national identity.

While seeking broader equality within Canada, French Canadians manifested less tolerance for diversity within their own province. The government of Quebéc passed laws compelling children of immigrants to attend French-language schools, although most parents saw English-language education as preferable. The provincial regime also declared French to be the only official language in Quebéc, requiring use of French in all public transactions, including advertising. The severity of Quebéc's language laws led many Canadian corporations to leave the province and resettle in Ontario or other English-speaking provinces.

An impetus for French Canadian ascendency came from France. Although that country previously had not interfered in its lost colony's politics, during a visit in 1967 the French president, Charles DeGaulle, shouted from the balcony of the Montreal City Hall "*Vive le Quebéc Libre!*" ("Long live a free Quebéc!"). (As Jane Jacobs has noted, he never had been recorded as shouting "Long live a free Brittany" or "Long live a free Provence.")

An extremist group, the *Front Libération de Quebéc*, engaged in terrorist acts, beginning in 1963. These included more than eighty bombings, two dozen armed robberies, and the 1970 kidnapping of the British Trade Commissioner in Montreal and the murder of the Labor Minister of Quebéc. Although Canadian authorities eventually suppressed the terrorism, a strongly nationalistic political party came to power in the province in 1976. The new regime generated great insecurity among Quebéc's English-speakers, numbering 20 percent of the total population.

The Quebéc government prepared a referendum in 1977 on sovereignty for the province. Under its proposal, Quebéc would have exclusive rights to make its own laws, levy its own taxes, and establish its own relations abroad. At the same time, it would maintain an economic association with Canada, including a common currency. Although strong support for separation manifested itself initially, the measure failed by a ratio of 60:40. Only 54 percent of Francophones ultimate supported the measure, whereas 80 percent of Anglophones opposed it.

The Québécois believed that they had institutionalized their aspirations in 1987, when the premiers of the Canadian provinces, meeting in the community of Meech Lake, agreed to a set of principles that included formal recognition of French Canadians as a "distinct society." However, irritation at Quebec's internal language policy and other matters led some provincial governments to refuse to ratify the accord. The result was a turning away by French Canadians from nationalist dualism to a revived separatism.

An independent French-speaking state is an increasing possibility. The "Quiet Revolution" has resulted in economic development that makes independence more feasible, particularly if Quebéc could become part of an Anglo-American common market agreement. In size and population, Quebéc is larger than a number of successful European states.

Should Quebéc secede, a major question would revolve around the location of its northern border. When it entered the Canadian confederation, its limits were considered to follow the watershed between Hudson's Bay and the St. Lawrence River. To its north lay Rupert's land. Ontario had the same situation. However, following Canadian acquisition of Rupert's land, Ontario in 1889 successfully pressed claims to territory as far north as the Albany River within the Hudson's Bay watershed. Quebéc argued that, in fairness, it too should receive a comparable part of Rupert's Land. The federal government eventually endorsed this demand in 1898. Quebéc additionally received from Rupert's Land in 1912 the Ungava Peninsula northeast of Hudson's Bay. Many legal scholars in Canada argue that if the province should secede, it should be within the boundaries with which it entered the confederation in 1867.

Additionally, arguments could arise over Quebéc's boundary with Labrador. In 1809 the British Parliament transferred "the coast of Labrador" from Quebéc to Newfoundland to permit easier regulation of fishing there, particularly by Americans coming north. Later, in 1825, it returned much of Labrador's southern coast to Quebéc to accommodate demands of French-speaking fishermen settled there.

When Labrador's interior became more accessible for development, the question of precise location of the provincial boundary became significant. Quebéc argued that the "coast" implied that Newfoundland's claim extended no more than a mile from the Atlantic. Newfoundland asserted that "coast" should embody the watersheds of all streams entering the ocean, and the British Privy Council agreed with that position in 1927. As part of Newfoundland's entry into Canada in 1949, the 127,000-square-mile area was confirmed in the Terms of Union, which became part of the Canadian constitution. An independent Quebéc could well contest that claim.

Sectionalism. Canada faces several regional political problems in addition to Francophone separatism. Western provinces resent domination by the large population concentrations in the Ontario Peninsula and St. Lawrence valley. The citizens of Alberta particularly take offense at restrictive regulation of their resource development by federal authorities. Their representatives to the Canadian parliament tend to band together in voting with those from the other "Prairie Provinces" of Manitoba and Saskatchewan, which are rather misnamed, since less than 20 percent of their areas constitute grassland landscapes.

A similar sectionalism exists in the "Maritime Provinces" among Nova Scotia, New Brunswick, Prince Edward Island, and Newfoundland. They have generally weak economies and, like the Prairie Provinces, resent domination of Canada by Ontario. The population of Newfoundland evinces perhaps a greater degree of alienation because the province entered the confederation late. It also is offended by the prevalent depiction in Canadian popular humor of Newfoundlanders ("Newfies") as naive and unsophisticated.

Aboriginal groups. Native peoples have become an increasingly significant centrifugal force in Canada out of proportion to their relatively small numbers. French Canadians have encountered unanticipated problems with native peoples in their own resource development. Cree Indians in northern Quebéc forced recognition of their claims to land. More recently, they imposed major obstacles for the province's expanded Great Whale hydroelectric power project on James Bay. Other native groups similarly have pressed for recognition of special rights to land, including the Naskapi tribe.

The 30,000 Inuits (Eskimos) were able to negotiate separate self-government in 1992 for the eastern two-thirds of the Northwest Territories. Their Nunavit ("Our Land") Territory covers 770,000 square miles. The Canadian government guaranteed them $1,400,000,000 over a period of fourteen years. It also granted the Inuit people outright title to 135,000 square miles within Nunavit. The remainder of Northwest Territories is set aside for its predominantly Indian population.

The unchallenged character of Canada's international boundaries has been noted above. It has only one land neighbor, and the United States harbors no pretentions to Canadian territory. Border frictions between the two states have existed in the past, however, and flare up from time to time. In recent decades they involve the management and exploitation of offshore resources.

In 1898, a dispute erupted involving the precise extent of the "panhandle" of Alaska. A treaty between Russia and the United Kingdom had specified that their mutual boundary followed the crests of the coastal mountains. No mention was made of the coastal inlets that drained streams originating east of the mountains. The issue developed at a time of great interest in the region owing to the discovery of gold in Yukon Territory. Americans, as successors to the Russians, took the position that the boundary properly followed the water divide; the Canadians asserted that it consisted of a line connecting the coastal mountain peaks. By the latter reckoning, the Alaskan city of Skagway lay within Canada. The dispute was strikingly similar to the positions of Chile and Argentina over their mutual border in the Andes Mountains. However, both Canada and the United States accepted a compromise in 1903, which followed mountain crests, but included indentations of American territory around tidal inlets.

The two states also have disputed the location of seaward extensions of their land boundaries as they affect fishing and mining rights. Arguments have arisen along both Atlantic and Pacific coasts. The Point Roberts Peninsula south of the Canadian city of Vancouver has been one source of irritation. It consists of a few square miles cut off from mainland British Columbia by the parallel of 49°N, which serves as the boundary between the two states in the west. The peninsula is a nuisance to both governments. Its population is insufficient to support a school system, and its children must travel twenty miles by bus through Canadian territory to attend American schools in the Washington State town of Blaine. Border posts have to be maintained. Canada has proposed eliminating the friction by exchanging the peninsula for an addition of territory in Alaska. The United States has refused the offer, however, primarily because possession of Point Roberts permits American fishermen to harvest the rich salmon resources in adjacent waters.

The two states have developed a remarkable degree of collaboration. Each is the best customer for the other's exports. In 1987 they reached agreement in principle to create a free trade zone. In 1993 they formed the North American Free Trade Association (NAFTA) together with Mexico. Earlier, in 1954, they developed an accord jointly to construct the Great Lakes Seaway, linking those water bodies with the Atlantic Ocean by a channel having a minimum depth of twenty-seven feet. Similarly, they have cooperated on a variety of projects, including regulation of the Columbia River, flowing through both countries, and mutual defense against external attack.

The United States of America

The last state in this world survey is one of the largest, yet suffers fewer political geographic problems than virtually any of its counterparts. Its inhabitants appear preoccupied with resolving minority questions, yet it is difficult to point out a land with fewer threats to national unity. Its minorities for the most part share the language and cultural traditions of the majority group, and their grievances center around lack of acceptance as coequal members of the prevailing nation.

Only the peoples of Puerto Rico and the Virgin Islands pose threats of possible secession, yet separatism has not proven to be a popular cause in either area. If anything, the United States faces potential pressures from Canadian provinces to attach themselves to it, should Québec depart from Canada. The American citizenry perceives itself as being part of a young country, yet it was perhaps the first of the nation-states to evolve, and it has witnessed less institutional change over the ensuing two centuries than nearly every other country. Its international boundaries suffer fewer challenges than do most in the world.

Three states—Russia, China, and Canada—exceed the United States in size, yet the United States contains an ecumene larger than any of them. More than 60 percent of its territory is effectively settled. No other place matches its physical endowment in lands suitable for cultivation and abundant natural resources.

Although Native Americans entered the territory in the waning period of the last great ice age, they constitute less than 1 percent of the present population of the United States. The majority of America's inhabitants are descended from waves of immigrants coming from all parts of the world, and many still continue to flock to its shores. More than 80 percent have origins in Europe, and 13 percent have African antecedents. Whatever their origins, virtually all have melded into a common cultural-political entity, the American nation.

Historical Evolution

Large-scale European settlement of the territory of the United States began with colonies of English settlers planted along the Atlantic seaboard in the seventeenth century, although Spaniards several decades earlier had established a military presence in Florida. The American iconography, as exhibited in the annual Thanksgiving Day holiday, projects an image of initial colonization in 1620 by Pilgrim religious dissenters landing at Plymouth Rock in Massachusetts. However, numerous settlements had developed farther to the south during the preceding two decades, beginning with Jamestown in Virginia in 1607.

At this time England was undergoing a commercial and agricultural revolution that witnessed mass expulsion of subsistence farmers from traditional lands. Many were quite willing to trade their misery in squatter camps for indentured servitude in an unknown new world threatened by Frenchmen and savages. Dissenting religious congregations became an important element in the immigration stream after the fall of the Puritan Commonwealth in England's Civil War. England also sent many convicted criminals to exile in the American colonies.

Although several colonial ventures failed, including the initial Virginia settlement at Roanoake in the 1580s, many succeeded. Most developed representative local governments to meet pressing problems in a situation of general neglect by a British regime involved with other difficulties. Regional differences in local governance emerged, based upon distinctions in problems and group antecedents.

The dispersed commercial plantations of the subtropical southeast essentially represented transplanted English aristocratic traditions. Their rural proprietors consulted on mutual problems, but saw a wide gulf between themselves and the indentured servants and slaves who worked their fields. They organized their local governments by counties, patterned after the basic civil divisions of England itself.

The subsistence farmers in the marginal lands of New England had arrived as communal religious fellowships, led by their pastors. Most sought freedom of worship outside the established Church of England. They lived together in theocratic villages called "towns," where equality was a rule. Dissenting groups broke away to establish new communities in the wilderness. The seventeenth-century royal charters of the New England colonies granted a high degree of autonomy, reflecting toleration by England's Puritan government. The colonies subsequently suffered when a restored British monarchy abrogated these charters and sought to institute more direct colonial rule through appointed governors.

The middle colonies between the New England settlements and the southern plantations appeared a half century after the others. They particularly drew settlers from continental Europe. A group of 500 Swedes and Finns lived in the Delaware valley at the time that William Penn established his colony (Pennsylvania) there in 1681. Dutch Calvinists created a community in the lower Hudson River valley. They numbered 7,000 in 1664, when their colony of New Netherland came under British control.

In the 1720s Scots Irish began immigrating to America from the "plantation" established by the English in Ulster (Ireland) a century earlier. In America they formed a vanguard pushing westward into the long valleys of the Appalachian Mountain frontier. Germans also settled in the middle colonies, mainly in Pennsylvania and the Hudson River valley. Farther south, in Lord Baltimore's colony of Maryland, English Catholics, French Huguenots, and Jews found haven. In contrast to the theocratic village communities to the north and the aristocratic self-sufficient plantation establishments in the south, most immigrant families in the middle colonies lived widely separated from each other on farms in a pattern of dispersed settlement that continues to stamp the American countryside as distinctive from most rural areas of the world.

Although several colonies claimed bands of territory extending from their Atlantic coastlines westward across the continent, their inhabitants faced barriers to settling in western lands. A major obstacle was the terrain. No easy passages lay across the Appalachian Mountains, whose continuous ridge tops trended northeast/southwest, blocking westward movement. Even more significant was the political barrier. France asserted ownership of the entire Mississippi River drainage. To protect its profitable fur-trading relations with the Indians, it established a number of forts in the region. After the French lands fell to the United Kingdom in 1763, the British government continued to prohibit settlement there, motivated to maintain the fur trade and minimize conflict with the Indians.

Despite regional differences in origins and economies, inhabitants of the British seaboard colonies exhibited a remarkable degree of homogeneity and coherence. Most came from the British Isles and shared common institutions and traditions. They quickly assimilated foreigners into their language and culture. Trade by sailing ship along the coast was frequent and easier than interchange of individual colonies with the mother country on the other side of the Atlantic. Chesapeake Bay and the coastal plain rivers allowed connectivity with the interior. A postal service permitted relatively easy exchange of communications. Moreover, neglect of colonies by an England beset by domestic turmoil and foreign wars forced colonists to rely upon themselves to resolve pressing problems.

Within this fertile political-geographic setting, a common sense of national identity began to emerge during the mid-eighteenth century. The perceived lack of British sensitivity to growing colonial needs prompted reactions from the American shore. Deemed particularly onerous were the English "Navigation Acts," measures imposed by Parliament from the mid-seventeenth century to control and direct colonial commerce to the benefit of the mother country.

Americans also rebelled against taxes imposed by British Parliament to finance wars with the French and the Indians, although the chief beneficiaries of the struggle were the colonists themselves. The British reservation of Quebéc lands beyond the Appalachians for Indian inhabitants further angered colonial governments, several of which continued to claim strips of land extending westward across the mountains. "Committees of Correspondence" facilitated sharing of views. The issues discussed reflected conflicting currents then existing within British society between aristrocratic and egalitarian ideas.

It is significant that the ensuing Revolutionary War was fought by one army under one leader, despite the political fragmentation into separate colonies. To be sure, not all Americans endorsed the rebellion. Only a third supported the revolutionary cause, another third remained loyal to the United Kingdom, and the remainder appeared apathetic to events.

At the end of war in 1783, the independent United States of America comprised thirteen of the seventeen English colonies in Anglo-America. Newfoundland, Nova Scotia, Prince Edward Island, and Quebéc remained British. The treaty of peace also gave the new country title to Quebéc lands east of the Mississippi River and south of the Great Lakes as far as the northern boundary of Florida. (The United Kingdom had acquired the latter area from Spain in 1763, and ceded it back in 1783.) The total area of the young United States was 800,000 square miles, less than a quarter of its present size. This made it larger than any European state west of Russia, however, although its population of 4,000,000 was less than half that of the United Kingdom and barely one-seventh that of France.

The new country adopted a federal form of government to accommodate the parochial identities that had emerged among inhabitants of each colony after nearly two centuries of seperate functioning. The federal system also helped resolve substantial sectional differences that had emerged between the aristocratic plantation societies of the south and the free farmer communities of the north. A reflection of this polarity was the decision to found a new capital city, Washington, in the frontier zone between the two groupings, rather than continuing to seat government in Philadelphia or adopting as a capital the significant commercial centers of Boston or New York.

The United States more than tripled its area during the first half of the nineteenth century. In 1803 it acquired the western drainage of the Mississippi River from Napoleonic France in a transaction termed the "Louisiana Purchase." In 1818, it gained the basin of the north-flowing Red River in what is now Minnesota and North Dakota. Three years later it purchased Florida from Spain.

In 1845 Texas joined the country as a new state, following its functioning for a decade as an independent unit of American settlers in territory claimed by Mexico. The Pacific Northwest saw a stream of American immigrants enter by way of the "Oregon Trail" for several years before the United States acquired the region through agreement with the United Kingdom in 1846. Although Spanish missionaries to the Indians had maintained a network of settlements for many decades in California and other parts of what came to be called the "Southwest," that area became part of the American state in 1848. Mexico ceded additional territory in southern Arizona and southwestern New Mexico in the "Gadsden Purchase" of 1853. This marked the end of contiguous territorial expansion of the United States, although several overseas lands later were acquired. These included the purchase of Alaska from Russia in 1867 and the accession of independent Hawaii and the colonies of Puerto Rico, Guam, and the Philippine Islands from defeated Spain in 1898.

Motivations for westward expansion were several. A major impetus was the need for new farmland by a rapidly growing population, augmented by increasing numbers of immigrants from Europe. A quest for gold and silver mining sites also played a role. Group perceptions of the American identity were particularly significant. The American iconography came to embody a belief that Americans were a unique people who had the "Manifest Destiny" to expand across the continent.

Pioneer settlement quickly followed the acquisition of western lands (Figure 15-3). A land survey system based upon square-mile "sections" facilitated establishment of family "homestead" farms on the rich soils

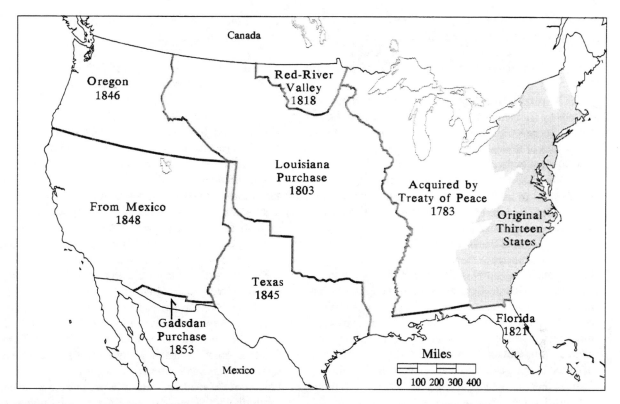

FIGURE 15-3   UNITED STATES-WESTWARD EXPANSION

west of the Appalachian Mountains. Many marginal areas of the original colonies lost population, particularly in the glaciated lands of New England. Subtropical areas in the south saw a parallel westward expansion of that region's slave-holding society.

This agricultural colonization generated conflict with aboriginal inhabitants. However, Native Americans were unable effectively to resist the hordes of settlers of European ancestry who converted traditional Indian hunting lands into plowed fields. They proved little match for the technologically superior and well-supported American armed forces sent to "pacify" territory. They also succumbed to exposure to diseases for which they had not developed immunity.

New lands posed problems of political organization from the onset of independence. Several colonies had overlapping territorial claims to the former Québec lands. An "Ordinance" of 1787 resolved the problem by agreement to organize this "Northwest Territory" into coequal new American states. Additionally acquired areas witnessed similar fashioning into state units. To accommodate sectional differences, the federal government admitted the new states in pairs, one

based upon free farming and one based upon a plantation economy.

Terrain barriers hampered integration of new lands into the coherent system that had emerged among the seaboard colonies. The territories of Tennessee and Kentucky actually threatened to withdraw from the United States because of their isolation. The federal government played a role in overcoming problems by financing improvements in infrastructure. It commissioned a "National Road" in 1806 to extend from Washington, DC, across the Appalachians to St. Louis on the Mississippi, providing funds for the project over the next four decades. Beginning in the 1850s, federal authorities encouraged railroad building through grants of land to construction companies. The extension of rails westward to the Pacific Shore particularly was the result of government subsidy.

To operate economically, railroads require the generation of freight and passenger traffic throughout their entire routes. However, the western third of the United States was an arid or mountainous region that had little prospect for continuous settlement to create such traffic. By subsidizing rail construction across empty spaces of the west through grants of real estate, the federal government prompted linkage of the isolated Pacific coast settlements to the eastern core. The first transcontinental rail line required only six years to build.

The American federal government also facilitated coherence by encouraging merger of individual railroad lines into more efficiently operated rail networks. It required use of a standardized rail gauge permitting interconnection between different company lines.

Individual state governments also contributed to improvements in infrastructure. Most notable was the 1825 completion of the Erie Canal by New York State. This allowed barges to move from surplus grain-producing areas around the Great Lakes into the Hudson River system tributary to the Atlantic. The functioning of the canal enhanced New York City, which soon overtook previously dominant Boston and Philadelphia in volume of port activity. Access to interior raw materials and attraction of immigrants from Europe also made New York the country's principal manufacturing center. Other notable improvements in transportation occurred in the upper Mississippi valley. Both Ohio and Indiana encouraged construction of canals linking streams that were tributary to the Great Lakes with the Ohio-Mississippi River system.

The midwestern states became significantly more productive than the southeastern region. Their agriculture changed from subsistence farms yielding sustenance for family producers to commercial enterprises selling virtually all production to distant areas. Farmers specialized in crops offering the greatest remuneration. Manufacturing similarly developed, combining labor and materials at optimally situated sites for distribution throughout an ever-enlarging common market.

The ascendancy of the midwestern and northeastern states upset the relative economic and political balance existing between north and south since the Revolutionary War. Southerners found themselves increasingly a minority, particularly after 1850, when, following California's admission, no additional plantation-based states appeared likely to be developed in western lands that would balance free new farmer entities.

Dissention between sections focused upon the issue of slavery. It had been a legal institution in all colonies before the revolution, but northern states abolished it soon after independence. New Englanders particularly found slavery abhorrent to the religious ideals that had fostered their original settlements. They provided the vanguard of efforts to abolish slavery throughout the United States. Formerly united Protestant religious groups split into separate northern and southern wings over the issue. European immigrants, drawn mainly to economic opportunities in northern states, had strong antipathies to slavery.

Only a third of the white population of the south owned slaves, and slavery was proving increasingly unprofitable. However, the institution was a basic element of a society evolved over the course of two centuries. Southerners viewed the increasing economic and political power of northern and midwestern states as a threat to maintenance of distinctive traditions.

The majority vote for antislavery Republican candidate Abraham Lincoln in the 1860 presidential election signaled to southerners a turning point in fortunes. Their politicians responded by declaring withdrawal of their states from the federal union. Eleven southeastern states seceded, organizing themselves into the Confederate States of America. They contained a quarter of the area of the United States and 38 percent of its population. The bitter American Civil War ensued.

If the Confederacy had been successful in separating, it is likely that a new nation would have emerged in Anglo-America that would have been as different from the American nation as Americans are from Canadians or Venezuelans from Colombians. The white population of the southern states was well aware of its cultural distinctiveness. In contrast to the increasing mixture of European immigrants with settlers of British heritage in northern states, the south remained an area of old American stock with distinctive patterns of speech. As in Latin America, prestige came from ownership of land rather than acquisition of monetary wealth.

Victory by the northern forces in the Civil War arrested the development of southern nationhood, and a unified American nation continued. The compromises and balances between northern and southern sectional interests that had characterized functioning of the United States since independence gave way to an increasingly centralized nation-state government. This was symbolized grammatically by usage of a singular verb when the "United States" was the subject of a sentence. It became standard to say "The United States *is*" rather than "The United States *are*."

Military defeat of the Confederate states did not immediately end prevailing sectional differences. Resentment against northerners long remained, fanned by postwar poverty and the many "carpetbaggers" who came from the north to exploit the chaotic situation. Slavery ended, but former slaves received no assistance to support themselves in their freeman status. They stayed in the southern states, dependent upon the white population under a new, and often more onerous, economic relationship known as "share-cropping." The white population excluded them socially by local "Jim Crow" laws that segregated schools, churches, and other public and private activities. Still, the southern states grew less parochial, as they increasingly developed their own manufacturing activities and participated in the American common market.

Foreign Immigration

Over ensuing decades the United States became increasingly homogeneous and coherent. Although more than 50,000,000 individuals freely came to America from other lands during the nineteenth and twentieth centuries, they, or at least their descendants, for the most part abandoned their distinctive heritages and became Americans. Not only did they become part of a common culture with English roots, but all enriched their adopted society with contributions from their own group's accumulated experiences and wisdom. Americans with good reason believed that their civilization was a "melting pot."

Several factors are responsible for the remarkable blending of diverse cultural streams into a common identity. They are numerated below.

- **Rejection of past heritage.** As in all migrations, there were "pulls" and "pushes" affecting personal decisions to seek a new home. America held the attractiveness of a dynamic society in which individuals could succeed by dint of hard work and application of skills. Too often this contrasted with economic stagnation and lingering feudal traditions of class and religious prejudice in home countries. America drew migrants because of its promise of achievement. A high percentage of the newcomers were leaving an unhappy situation, and most sought to shed the past and become interchangeable parts of their adopted society.
- **Remoteness from homelands.** In addition to immigrant rejection of homeland social environments, ties to places of origin suffered from their remoteness. In contrast to Chinese peasants entering Manchuria or German settlers in the Hungarian Burgenland, most migrants to the United States lived great operational and psychological distances away from their culture hearths. Like the Francophones of Quebéc, they lost contact with day-to-day transformations occurring in motherland societies, growing ever more isolated from the roots of home. The broad emptiness of the Atlantic pre-

FIGURE 15-4   MINORITY GROUPS IN THE UNITED STATES

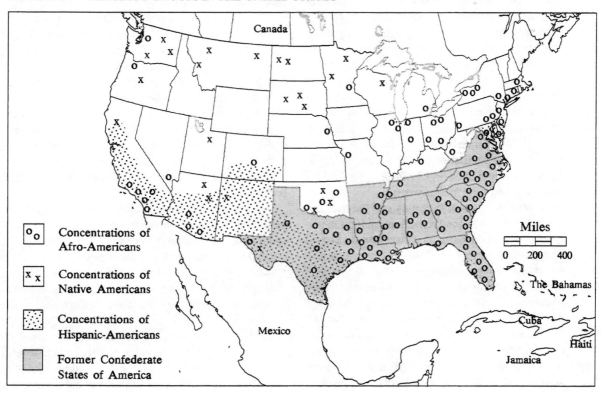

cluded the kinds of continuing ties that gave birth to irredentism elsewhere. Among only a few groups did organizations like the German-American Bund or the Irish Republican Army provide continuing linkages to mother countries.

- **The scattering of immigrants.** Although bonds of religion and language tended to link many immigrants to their heritage, numbers of a group in most areas were too small to resist surrounding influences for assimilation. This was particularly true for migrants to rural areas, in which pressures for newcomer conformity were strong. The situation was somewhat different in major cities, where ethnic enclaves developed sufficient numbers to support and perpetuate distinctive churches, schools, and other institutions

- **Mobility.** Advances in transportation and communications increasingly linked all together in what was the largest developed state area in the world. San Francisco could send immediate messages to New York after inauguration of the transcontinental telegraph in the 1860s. Trains became faster, automobiles and trucks appeared, and the airplane eventually permitted movement between opposite coasts in a handful of hours. The resultant mobility led to greater population homogenization, as developing areas saw the influxes and interactions of people from all parts of the world and all corners of the country.

- **Universal education.** A belief in the benefits of education permeated America. The federal government program regularizing acquisition of free lands made provision to assist public education by setting aside one square mile section in every thirty-six to provide support for local schools. Each city developed a public school system. State laws made school attendance obligatory. The schools assured that younger generations would master the English language and be indoctrinated in the American iconography. Few students did not learn the popular American myth of George Washington and his vandalism of his father's cherry tree.

- **Mass media.** The twentieth century saw the development of voice and sound recordings, motion pictures, radio, and television that increasingly augmented the traditional role of literature and newspapers in propagating a popular culture to be shared in common by most Americans. These advances led to standarized intonation of American English, supplanting regional pronounciations in New England, the South, and elsewhere. Associated with the mass media in homogenizing the population was the commercialization of sporting activities. Professional team rivalries projected a

sense of association and linkage with distant places.

- **Federal coercive pressures.** Although the initial success of the American state can be attributed in no little part to adoption of a federal system that permitted diversity among individual states and regions, its government grew more centralized and normative over the decades. During the nineteenth century it forced the abolition of slavery in the South and required Mormon settlers of Utah to abandon the practice of bigamy. In the mid-twentieth century it put an end to institutionalized segregation of racial groups in the southeastern states.

African-Americans. The 4,000,000 slaves of African origin at the time of the Civil War had multiplied to more than 30,000,000 descendants by the final decade of the twentieth century. Although subject to the same acculturation pressures that melded diverse European streams together, Afro-Americans, constituting some 12 percent of the population, have remained a separate body within American society. They suffer discrimination by the white majority, and as a group enjoy lower incomes and fewer opportunities for economic and educational advancement than other Americans. However, in their minority they pose a far smaller threat to the functioning of the United States than most minorities discussed in this book. (See Figure 15-4 for map showing concentrations of various minorities in the United States.)

One factor is that Afro-Americans partake of the values and traditions of the American nation. They differ little in heritage from European-Americans. They share the same language, religious background, and popular culture of other members of American society. Indeed, they have made disproportionate contributions to that emerging culture. They also have made disproportionate contributions to defense of the American nation. Their distinctive position is a result of rejection as fellow nationals by the majority group on the basis of external appearance. They are seen as different because of their race.

Unlike other groups subject to racial discrimination, such as the Dravidian population of India, they cannot pose a threat of secession from the state. They constitute a majority in only limited areas, including inner parts of cities and a few rural counties in the South. Like Americans of other origins, increasing opportunities for mobility have resulted in dispersion throughout the United States. At the conclusion of the Civil War, 90 percent of African-Americans lived in the seventeen southeastern states, mostly in rural localities. This proportion remained fairly constant for the next half century. Growing opportunities in northern industrial centers, created in part by limitations on further immigration from abroad, led large numbers to move out of the southern states. Only three-quarters remained in the southeastern states by 1940, and barely half are there now.

In addition to the promise of greater economic opportunity, most Afro-Americans were prompted to move to other areas by persistence of the system of racial segregation prevailing in the former slave states. Local laws prohibited intermarriage between members of different races, barred attendance at the same schools, or eating in the same restaurants, and even forbade use of the same restroom facilities.

National feelings increasingly grew against such discrimination, which ran counter to the egalitarian ideals of the American iconography. The strengthening of the power of the federal government led to reduction of discrimination against African-Americans by the 1950s. Civil rights laws formally voided local statutes perpetuating segregation in schools and public facilities. Later, federal adoption of a process of affirmative action succeeded in creating career opportunities by African-Americans in governmental and private sectors of the economy.

African-Americans retain strong grievances against the white majority, however. Despite the ending of formal disabilities, as a group they remain lower in educational attainments and economic well-being than other Americans. Currently their average incomes are only 63 percent that of the white population. Most find themselves continuing to live in segregated conditions, as "white flight" to suburbs has abandoned to them the older areas of cities where they can afford housing.

Hispanic Americans. The second largest minority in the United States is made up of Americans of Latin American ancestry. They number nearly 23,000,000, or approximately 9 percent of the total American population, having more than doubled their proportion since 1970. Most have roots in Mexico, but many have come in recent years from Cuba, Guatemala, El Salvador, and other Central American states. In contrast to past immigrant streams, significant numbers retain their native Spanish as a primary language.

Although Hispanic Americans live throughout the United States, 60 percent are concentrated in the Southwest along the international boundary with Mexico. They make up a third of the population of New Mexico and constitute more than 20 percent of the populations of Texas and California. Many border areas have majorities of Hispanic Americans. Three-quarters of the population of Brownsville, Texas, has a Hispanic heritage.

Because of their concentrations contiguous to Mexico, they constitute a potential irredentist problem for the United States, although their political leaders until now have expressed virtually no sentiments for secession. Despite lower incomes and educational attainments than the American majority group, the economic and social situation of most Hispanic Americans is higher than that of their counterparts in Latin America. However, successful demands for official recognition of their Spanish language in education, voting, and other affairs has contributed to greater resistance to acculturation than among other immigrants to America.

Asian Americans. Up to 3,000,000 Americans are of Asian origin. The three main groups are of Chinese, Japanese, and Filipino origin. They have approximately equal numbers. Immigrants from the Republic of Korea have become a significant fourth Asian group in recent years.

About 20 percent of Asian Americans live in the Hawaiian Islands, where they constitute approximately two-thirds of the population. The remainder are scattered across the mainland of the United States, with notable concentrations in the Pacific coast states. Although subject to discrimination by the majority because of racial background, they have fared well as a group in American society, with educational attainments and income levels higher than the average. Like their counterparts of European heritage, most identify themselves with the American nation and have few emotional ties to areas of ancestry.

Native Americans

The American Indian, Aleut, and Eskimo population numbers about 1,750,000. Half live in southwestern border areas, and most of the rest are concentrated in western states. American expansion across the continent displaced most Native Americans from traditional lands. The United States government created special "tribal reservations" for them. Often, it forcibly resettled inconveniently located Indians great distances from their customary homes. The U.S. Cavalry's transfer of members of the Cherokee tribe more than a thousand miles westward from the southeastern United States to the "Indian Territory" of modern-day Oklahoma was particularly outrageous. Indian reservations now comprise a combined territory of 80,000 square miles, equivalent to the area of Minnesota or Utah. Between half and three-quarters of Native Americans continue to live on reservations.

After decades of dependency status, Native Americans received full American citizenship rights in 1924, although those living on reservations remained under federal government supervision. Within their reservations they enjoy substantial political and economic autonomy under elected tribal councils, and their lands are subject to little state taxation or regulation. Many have adopted casino gambling as a source of income from surrounding populations, taking advantage of a distinctive political-geographic status.

The retention of tribal organization of Native Americans on federal reservations has served to keep alive ancient languages and traditions that otherwise would have fallen victim to American acculturation. However, it also has kept many Native Americans out of the mainstream of American development. As a group, they suffer greater disparities in social and economic well-being than do other American minorities. A federal government policy in the 1950s to encourage detribalization and entrance into mainstream society had few positive effects. Many disbanded tribal reservations subsequently were reconstituted, after petitioning by former members.

Alaska

The United States of America contains four major non-contiguous areas that pose problems to its coherence and homogeneity: Alaska, Hawaii, Puerto Rico, and the Virgin Islands. The last two have been discussed above in the chapter on Latin America. They remain political and economic dependencies of the United States and are comparable to other colonial areas in the world. Alaska and Hawaii, however, have the formal status of states within the United States, giving them legal coequality. Despite significant numbers of residents having non-European origins, their inhabitants overwhelmingly consider themselves part of the American nation.

The state of Alaska has nearly 600,000 square miles, making it more than twice the size of Texas, the next largest American state. However, Alaska's population of less than 500,000 is smallest among the fifty American states, save for sparsely populated Wyoming. Virtually all of Alaska is empty of population, and optimistic estimates see at best 11 percent of the land as suitable for any settlement. Only limited areas around the principal towns of Juneau, Anchorage, and Fairbanks currently are developed.

Alaska is remote from the main area of the United States. A road did not link it to the rest of the country until 1942, when the American government constructed a route across Canadian territory during World War II. Before then, its settled communities were accessible by 1,500-mile ferry connection with Seattle or by passenger airlines. Alaska's principal ties remain by air and marine travel. These provide linkages that only marginally are more costly and time-consuming than between major regional centers within the "lower forty-eight" states. It is easier to travel by air from Anchorage to Seattle than to fly from Seattle to Chicago.

However, a psychological perception of isolation magnifies operational frictions of space. The lack of territorial contiguity with the rest of the United States, as depicted on maps, gives inhabitants of small settlements in Alaska a sense of isolation from mainstream America greater than that found among counterpart communities in Montana or Idaho, which may well have even greater difficulties in external connection.

Alaska's internal cohesion depends also upon airplanes and ships. Its one major railroad only connects Anchorage with Fairbanks. Two minor rail lines have been constructed in its southeastern "panhandle." A network of roads exists, but settlements, particularly of Native Americans, lie great distances in space and travel time from each other.

Russians confined their establishments in Alaska mainly to coastal areas. Alaska's marginal climate could offer little contribution to provision of grain for Siberia. In a quest for farmlands to feed Siberian miners and fur traders, Russians pushed southward along the Pacific coast of Anglo-America nearly to San Francisco, before abandoning an operation that had become overextended. Russia left an Alaskan legacy after sale of the territory to America in 1867 for $7,200,000. Many natives have retained the Orthodox religious faith preached by hardy Russian missionaries in the wilderness country.

Many in nineteenth-century America derided the purchase of the Alaskan "icebox." They saw little promise for development of such a remote frontier area in contrast to the benefits enjoyed from acquisition of lands in the trans-Mississippi west. Attitudes changed following discovery of gold deposits during the 1890s. Later, the wealth of Alaska's fisheries and minerals substantially contributed to American economic well-being.

The federal government integrated Alaska into the rest of the country over a lengthy period. The land retained the status of purchased real estate until 1884, when it was made a distinctive "district" of the United States under a legal code borrowed from the State of Oregon. In 1912, the American government designated

Alaska a "territory." Nearly a half century later, in 1959, it was constituted as a state.

Alaska has become one of the most prosperous states per capita in the United States because of its wealth in petroleum. Its North Slope, adjacent to the Arctic Ocean, has proven to be a major oil-bearing reservoir. The federal government fostered construction of a controversial trans-Alaskan pipeline to bring crude oil to the Pacific coast port of Valdez. Its profits augment the 100,000,000 acres of vacant land that federal authorities transferred to the state to provide a tax base for public services. Alaskans pay no taxes to the state government, and instead receive annual dividends from the state's oil revenues.

The state territory retains many characteristics of a classic frontier. Its aboriginal inhabitants constitute approximately 20 percent of the population and dominate extensive areas. Alaska has long served as an American military outpost against real and perceived adversaries. During World War II, its western Aleutian Islands temporarily suffered occupation by Japanese forces. Later, it became a zone of American confrontation with the Soviet Union. Military garrisons for defense and intelligence continue to constitute a significant portion of its total population.

Alaska has again become "outer-oriented," using Ladis Kristof's terminology for frontiers. After seven decades of almost complete isolation from the Russian landscape, Alaskans again are able to reach out to Siberia. Native groups on both sides of the Bering Strait have resumed old ties forcibly sundered by the advent of the Communist system of the USSR. Inuits (Eskimos) freely travel now to the Chukchi Peninsula by a popular local air service, in addition to using traditional boats in summer and dog sleds across the frozen sea in winter. Entrepreneurs from Anchorage and Fairbanks journey frequently to Khabarovsk and Vladivostok to take part in restructuring their shattered economies.

Hawaii

Some 2,400 miles west of the Pacific coastline of the continental forty-eight states lies Hawaii. Its seven major islands, eight minor ones, and 120 islets have a combined total of 6,400 square miles, making the state larger than Rhode Island, Connecticut, and Delaware. The largest island, Hawaii, occupies nearly two-thirds of the area. The Hawaiian population of 1,200,000 is more than twice that of Alaska, and exceeds the populations of ten other American states.

A British explorer, Captain James Cook, discovered the islands in 1778. Their Polynesian population maintained an independent government through most of nineteenth century, although Americans, British, and Russians established commercial bases. Dissidents overturned the royal dynasty in 1893 and declared a republic the following year. The Hawaiian legislature petitioned the United States for annexation in 1898. The American government accepted the offer, and organized Hawaii into a "territory" of the United States in 1900. In 1959, Hawaii became America's fiftieth state.

The population of Hawaii represents a variety of racial groups. Only 6 percent are native Hawaiian. About one-quarter are Japanese, one-third of European ancestry, 14 percent Filipino, and 2 percent African-American. In contrast to the tendency toward racial exclusivity in the mainland United States, more than 40 percent of marriages in Hawaii are between individuals of different races. At least a third of the population has mixed racial ancestry. Inhabitants of all races consider themselves firmly a part of the American nation.

In recent years, Japanese business firms have shown great interest in Hawaii, investing heavily in its land and economy. It has become a major destination for Japanese tourists, as it is for mainland Americans. The islands are dependent upon sea and air links to the United States to meet basic needs. Steady improvements in the technology of transportation and communication firmly incorporate Hawaii within the American common market.

Other Possessions in the Pacific

The United States acquired several dependent areas in the Pacific basin as a consequence of victory in wars fought with Spain and Japan. These include the island of Guam, the Republic of Palau, the Republic of the Marshall Islands, the Federated States of Micronesia, and the Northern Mariana Islands. It also possesses American Samoa, Johnston Atoll, the Midway Islands, and Wake Island, which were acquired in various ways during the nineteenth and early twentieth centuries. The larger territories enjoy a high degree of local self-government under a variety of formal status arrangements.

Guam was discovered by Ferdinand Magellan in 1521. The United States acquired it from Spain in 1898. It has an area of slightly more than 200 square miles and a population of 150,000, half of whom are of native Guamanian ancestry. The natives speak the indigenous Chamorro language, but all are conversant in English. Virtually all are Roman Catholic in religion. They enjoy full U.S. citizenship under the status of a commonwealth.

Palau is held by the United States as a Trust Territory of the United Nations. Its 26 islands and 300 islets had belonged to Spain until 1899, when that country sold the Caroline Islands to the German Empire. Following Germany's defeat in World War I, Palau was made part of a League of Nations mandate administered by Japan. It became an American possession following Japan's defeat in World War II. The original UN trusteeship embraced the Caroline, Marshall, and Mariana groups of Islands. All the others, except Palau, achieved separate status in association with the United States. Palau's population differs in ethnicity from the other Caroline Islands. The island group formally received designation as a republic in 1983. Its total area is less than 200 square miles and its population is barely 15,000.

The Marshall Islands became a free republic in association with the United States in 1986. They consist of two island chains with a total land area of seventy square miles and a population of 40,000. Spaniards discovered the islands in the seventeenth century, but they did not establish a colony because the islands were so remote from Manila. British captains Gilbert and Marshall explored the islands in 1788, and Russian explorers mapped the islands early in the nineteenth century. Germany established a protectorate over the Marshall Islands in 1885 during its quest for colonies following German unification. Japan invaded the islands in 1914 and administered them as part of its League of Nations mandate until the end of World War II. They then became part of the UN trusteeship administered by the United States.

The Federated States of Micronesia is the name adopted by the former Caroline Islands in 1983 when they became an independent state under a compact of free association with the United States. They consist of 607 islands, having a total area of 270 square miles. Their population of 108,000 speaks twelve different languages and several dialects. Spanish explorers named them the Carolines in 1686 after King Charles II of Spain. Spain did not make them a colony, but avowed title to them until 1875, when pressure from the United Kingdom forced Spain to give up its claim. Germany occupied some of the islands in 1885. This led Spain to reassert authority. Increasing trouble with the natives caused Spain to cede the islands to Germany in 1899. Japan invaded in 1914 and received them as part of its Pacific Island mandate. The United States assumed responsibility for them after World War II as part of its UN Trusteeship area.

The Northern Marianas were discovered by Magellan in 1519. He called them the Ladrone ("Thief")

Islands, because natives stole some of his goods. The Spanish government renamed them after the Queen of Spain in the seventeenth century. Subsequently, Spain administered the islands as part of the Philippines until ceding them to the United States in 1898. The United States retained Guam and sold the others to Germany in the following year. Japan seized the islands in 1914, and held them under League of Nations mandate until 1944, when the islands were invaded by United States forces. There are sixteen islands with a combined area of 184 square miles and 22,000 inhabitants. In 1976, island residents voted in favor of commonwealth status in union with the United States. About half the population speaks the native Chamorro language.

American Samoa was acquired by the United States in 1899 through a treaty signed with the United Kingdom and Germany. Europeans had visited the islands in the early eighteenth century. Beginning in 1860, the three major powers had recognized the island group as an independent entity. In 1889 they established a joint trusteeship. Ten years later, the arrangement was abrogated in favor of United States possession of the ten eastern islands and German control of the western ones. American Samoa has an area of seventy-six square miles and a population of 40,000. It is officially an "unorganized unincorporated territory" administered by the U.S. Department of the Interior. Its inhabitants have the status of "American nationals" (as opposed to "citizens").

Bibliography

BROWN, RALPH, *Historical Geography of the United States*. New York: Harcourt, Brace, 1948.

JACOBS, JANE, *The Question of Separatism: Quebec and the Struggle over Sovereignty*. New York: Random House, 1980.

JANIGAN, MARY, "The Roots of the Struggle: A Turbulent Past Haunts Quebec," *Maclean's*, November 25, 1991, pp. 26–29.

MORRILL, RICHARD L., "Dilemmas of Pluralism in the United States," in *Pluralism and Political Geography: People, Territory and State*, eds. Nurit Kliot and Stanley Waterman. New York: St. Martin's Press, 1983.

NICHOLSON, NORMAN, *The Boundaries of Canada, Its Provinces and Territories*. Ottawa: Department of Mines and Technical Surveys, Geographical Branch, Memoir 2, 1954.

NICHOLSON, NORMAN, "The Confederation of Canada," in *The Changing World: Studies in Political Geog-*

raphy, W. Gordon East and A.E. Moodie. Yonkers, NY: World Book Co., 1956, pp. 312–329.

SLOWE, PETER, "Nationhood and Statehood in Canada," in *Shared Space, Divided Space: Essays on Conflict and Territorial Organization*, eds. Michael Chisholm and David M. Smith. London: Unwin Hyman, 1990.

WHITTLESEY, DERWENT, "The United States," in *The Changing World: Studies in Political Geography*, eds. W. Gordon East and A. E. Moodie. Yonkers, NY: World Book Co., 1956, pp. 239–284.

INDEX

Finnish language, 64
Finnmark, 68
Finno-Ugrian languages, 103, 144, 151
    Lapp, 69
Finns, 67
    in Sweden, 69
Fiume, 89-91, 118-20
Flanders, 19, 57
Flemings, 57, 59-60
Florida, 376
Fonseca, Gulf of, 337
Formosa, *see* Taiwan
France, 39-48, 90
    anti-clericalism, 42
    centralization, 43
    départements, 43, 45
    Langue d'oc, 46
    nation, 42
Franco, Gen. Francisco, 76
Franks, 57
Frederick the Great, 101
French Antilles, 346
French Canadians, 19, 368, 371
French Foreign Legion, 46, 205
French Guiana, 346
French Language, 42
French Revolution, 15, 42, 70
Frisians, 58, 98
Friulans, 92
Front line territories (Africa), 224
Frontier zones, 19, 23, 54
Fueros (traditional rights and laws), 75, 78
Fujairah, 187

G

Gadsden Purchase, 334, 376
Gaelic language, 30, 50, 53
Gagauz, 128, 151
Galego language, 77
Galicia (East Central Europe), 110
Galicia (Spain), 76-77
Garifuna (Black Caribs), 336-37
Gaza Strip, 172, 182-83, 200
Genghiz Khan, 294
Genoa, 45, 87
Geography
    areal functional approach, 6
    holistic field, 4
    theory, 6
Geopolitics, 4, 5, 17, 96
Georgia, 137, 143, 147, 158
German Democratic Republic, 9, 85, 94, 97-98
German Empire, 85, 103
German Federal Republic, 97
German nation, 9, 85
Germans
    Baltic States, 151, 153
    Belgium, 60
    Czechoslovakia, 107
    Romania, 126-27
    Volga, 143, 146
    Southwest Pacific, 320
Germany, 72, 85, 93-98
    colonies, 313

Ghana, 227
Gibraltar, 81
Gilbert and Ellice Islands, 321
Goa, 242
Golan Heights, 182-83
Golden Triangle, 19, 261
Gottman, Jean, 6, 14
Gran Colombia, 329, 347
Granada, 75, 203
Great Britain, 48
Great Trek, 229
Greater East Asia Co-Prosperity Sphere, 259
Greece, 86, 90, 118, 133-35
    objection to "Macedonia," 134
    regional divisiveness, 133
Greek Macedonia, 133
Greek Phanariots, 125
Greeks in Southeastern Europe, 116-17
Greenland, 13, 72-73
Grenada, 329, 343
Guajira peninsula, 349
Guam, 320-21, 376, 383
Guantánamo Bay, 343-44
Guarani language, 359
Guatemala, 335
Guernsey, 52
Guianas, 342
Gulf of Sidra, 208
Gulf States, 186-88
Gurkhas, 249
Guyana, 347, 350
Gypsies, 14, 110
    Greece, 133
    Romania, 126

H

Habsburg Empire, 61, 87, 94, 96, 103-106, 108, 117-19, 125
Hadhramaut, 189
Haiti, 343
Hakka, 289, 298
Han (Chinese), 283, 288-89
    Sinkiang, 292
Hanseatic League, 67, 152
Hartshorne, Richard, 6
Hasa, 185, 187
Haushofer, Karl, 4
Hawaii, 321, 376, 381, 383
Hawar islands, 187
Hazaras, 251
Heartland (geopolitics), 5
Hebrew language, 184
Hejaz, 166, 185
Himachal Pradesh, 248
Hinduism, 272
    Southeast Asia, 257, 275
    Indonesia, 277
Hippocrates, 3
Hispaniola (Santo Domingo), 328, 343-44
"Historic imitation" capital cities, 89
Historical determinism, 7
Hitler, Adolf, 96
Holists, 8
Holy Roman Empire, 33, 42, 60-61, 74, 87, 94, 103
Honduras, 336

Hong Kong, 288, 300-302
  reversion to China, 301
Horn (of Africa), 224
Hudson's Bay Company, 370
Hukbalahap (Huks), 280
Hungarians, 116-17, 119, 125
  Romania, 125-28
Hungary, 18, 103, 104, 106-107
Hussites, 103
Hyderabad, 241

I

Iberian Peninsula, 74-82
Ibos, 228
Iceland, 73-74
  fishing dispute, 74
Iconography, 6, 14, 16, 19
Idiographic approach, 3
Ifni, 207
Illyrian languages, 31, 131
Illyrian Provinces, 15, 118
Incas, 328, 351-52
India, 245-50
  French, 242
  linguistic states, 245
  partition, 241
  Portuguese, 242
  princely states, 245
Indian Peninsula, 237
Indians, 375
Indo-European languages, 26
Indonesia, 18, 274-77
  "neo-colonialism" in Malaysia, 273
  Chinese, 276
  Hindus, 277
  Japan, 275
  languages, 274
  Sundanese, 277
  West Irian, 321
Inner Mongolia, 290, 294-95
Intuitionists, 8
Inuits (Eskimos), 73, 370, 373, 381, 383
Ionian Islands, 133
IRA (Northern Ireland), 54
Iran, 190-95
Iraq, 161, 169, 174-77
  Baath Party, 174
  Shia Muslims, 174
Ireland, 21, 52-54
  "Plantation," 52
Irish Free State, 53
Iron Curtain, 19
Iron Gates, 113
Irredentism, 8, 19
  Albania, 132
  Germany, 111
  Hungary, 107
  Italy, 86, 89
  Southeast Europe, 118-19
Islam, 116, 149, 161, 164, 167, 239
  Afghanistan, 251
  China, 289
  Europe, 116
  Ibadi sect, 188

Ismailis, 203, 251
  Kharidjites, 203
  Pillars, 164
  Shariah, 164
  Shia tradition, 164, 184, 188, 190, 192
  Southeast Asia, 257, 275
  Sunni tradition, 144, 164, 184, 190, 203
  Wahhabite sect, 185-86, 189
  Zaydi sect, 167, 189-90
Isle of Man, 52
Israel, 165, 169, 181, 182-84, 200
Issas, 228
Istria, 89-91, 118-20
Italian Social Republic, 90
Italy, 85-93, 118
  Alpine border, 20, 91-92
Ivory Coast, 227

J

Jaffna peninsula (Sri Lanka), 248
Jamaica, 344, 346
Janissary legions, 117
Japan, 306-11
  daimyos, 309
  ecumene, 308
  environment, 308
  Southwest Pacific, 321
  Southeast Asia, 259
  United States, 309
Java, 275
  Sundanese, 277
Javanese, 274, 277
Jefferson, Mark, 8
Jersey, 52
Jesuits, 74, 77, 78, 329, 353, 358, 359
Jews, 96, 103, 109-10, 117, 126, 128, 143, 150, 152, 154, 155, 164, 169-72, 182-84, 202-203, 206, 375
  Ashkenazim, 171, 184
  Sephardim, 117, 171, 184
Jones Act, 279
Jordan, 166, 181-82
Judea and Samaria, 183
Jurassians, 63
Jutland Peninsula, 71

K

Kaliningrad Oblast (former East Prussia), 154
Kalmyks, 144
Kana Liberation Front, 321
Karelia, 69-70
Karelian resettlement program, 71
Karelo-Finnish SSR, 145
Karens, 261
Kashmir, 241, 244, 246-47, 291
Katanga, 228
Kazakhs
  former USSR, 157
  China, 292, 293, 296
Kazakhstan, 157
Kemal Atatürk, 196-97
Khmers (Cambodians), 268-70
  Thailand, 262
  Vietnam, 263

"Rimland," 5
Risorgimento, 87, 89
Ritter, Karl, 4, 17
Roman Catholic Church, 53, 57, 74, 103, 116-17, 154, 277, 327, 329, 367
    Canada, 368
    Southwest Pacific, 320
    Pacific, 383
    Korea, 304
    Philippine Islands, 279
    Quebéc, 372
Roman Empire, 32, 49, 57, 86, 113, 116, 195, 202
    division into western and eastern parts, 116
Romance languages, 144
Romania, 16, 18, 118, 125-28
    Magyar minority, 101
    Russian protection, 125
Romansch language, 63, 90
Rumelian Turks, 197
Rupert's Land, 368, 373
Russia, 137-59
    ecumene, 137
    iconography, 140
Russian Empire, 103, 140
    Alaska, 382
Russian Orthodox Church, 70, 137
Russians
    nation, 144
Ruthenia, 21, 107, 151
Ryukyu islands, 300, 309-10

S

Saarland, 20, 42, 96
Sabah, 271-74
Safavids, 191
Saint Martin, 346
Sakhalin island, 143, 309, 310
San Andres island, 337
San Marino, 86
San Stefano, Treaty of, 128
Sanjak of Novi Pazar, 118, 129
Sanskrit language, 152, 242, 268
Santo Domingo (Hispaniola), 328, 343-44
Sarawak, 271, 274
Sardinia, 87, 93
Sards, 93
Sarra Triangle, 202, 210
Saskatchewan, 370
Saudi Arabia, 17, 184-86, 188
    Shia minority, 185
Savoy, 41, 87-88
Saxons, 126
Schaefer, Fred, 6
Schleswig-Holstein, 71, 72, 96
Schwyzerdütsch, 61
Scientific method, 8
Scotland, 49-52
Sea floor boundaries, 20
Self-determination of nations, 104
Sendero Luminoso ("Shining Path"), 352
Serbia, 19, 90, 113, 117-19, 123-25
Serbs
    In Ukraine, 150

Serbs, Croatians, and Slovenes, Kingdom of, 89, 104, 118-19
Sertão, 362
Shafis, 189
Shans, 261-62, 290
Sharjah, 187
Shatt-al-Arab Waterway, 176
Shatterbelt of Eastern Europe, 34, 103, 151
Shenzhen economic zone (China), 301
Shetland Islands, 51
Shiite Muslims, 144, 158
Siam, *see* Thailand
Siberia, 20, 137, 149
Sicily, 93
Sikhs, 239, 241, 244-45
Sikkim, 249, 291
Silesia, 109
Silk Road, 293
Sinai Peninsula, 182, 200
Sindhis, 244
Singapore, 271-74
Sinhalese, 247
Sinkiang, 290, 292
Six-Day War, 172, 182
Skåne, 67, 71
Slavic languages, 103, 129, 143, 155
Slavs, 94, 116
Slovakia, 98, 107-108
    Magyar minority, 103, 108
Slovaks, 106-108
Slovenes, 106, 118-19
Slovenia, 90, 101, 113, 118, 123
Solomon Islands, 321
Somalia, 224, 227
Sorbs, 94
South Africa, 19, 228-35
    Asians, 232
    bantustans (self-administered states), 234
    blacks (Bantus), 232
    coloured (mixed race) population, 232
    environment, 229
    reserves for native groups, 233
    slave trade, 233
    Union of South Africa, 232
South America, 323, 347-63
South Asia, 237
    area, 237
    caste, 237
    Dutch, 240
    French, 240
    Islam, 239
    linguistic diversity, 239
    population, 237
    Portuguese, 240
    princely states, 240
    religions, 237
South Australia, 313
South Mollucca Islands, 275-76
South Ossetians, 158
South Tyrol, 86, 89-92
Southeast Asia, 255-81
    boat people, 274
    boundaries, 255
    Chinese, 259, 272-74, 276
    colonialism, 255, 259, 270, 276
    diversity, 255
    Dutch, 259, 272, 275